William Roulston is a native of Bready, County Tyrone, and was raised on a farm that has been in his family's possession for nearly two centuries. He joined the Ulster Historical Foundation as a researcher in 1997, becoming Research Officer in 2002 and Research Director in 2006. He was awarded a PhD in Archaeology by Queen's University Belfast in 2004. He is the author of a number of books looking at different aspects of the history of Ulster, including *Abercorn: The Hamiltons of Barons Court* (2014). Now living in rural Mid-Antrim, he is married to Heather and they are the parents of Harry and Sarah.

Dedicated to
the memory of
Dr Brian Trainor
(1928–2018)

Researching
Scots-Irish Ancestors

The essential genealogical guide
to early modern Ulster, 1600–1800

William J. Roulston

ULSTER HISTORICAL FOUNDATION

Published 2018, reprinted 2021 by
Ulster Historical Foundation
www.ancestryireland.com
www.booksireland.org.uk

This book is also published under the title of *Researching Ulster Ancestors*
(ISBN 978-1-909556-66-9)

© William J. Roulston
ISBN 978-1-909556-65-2

Front cover: Bradeshaw tombstone, Bangor Abbey, County Down (photograph by the author)
Back cover: 'A New Map of Ireland' by John Senex, 1720 (Library of the Oireachtas, Dublin)

Printed by GPS Colour Graphics Limited
Design by J. P. Morrison

CONTENTS

PREFACE AND ACKNOWLEDGEMENTS

It is now 13 years since the first edition of this book was published. Until around three years ago I had no intention of producing a new edition. Increasingly, however, I was encouraged to give some thought to it and the end result is this revised, expanded and updated second edition. There are a number of differences with the first edition, most obviously that it is a good deal bulkier. There are several reasons for this. In the first place, the new edition includes items which were omitted or simply overlooked in the first edition or which have been accessioned by archives since 2005. There is a more thorough listing of local, parish, and congregational histories and an expanded discussion of sources for particular historical episodes, such as the period of the 1798 Rebellion. New sections on business records, documents relating to fraternal organisations, publications of the eighteenth century, and surviving diaries and journals have been included. There is also a chapter on records relating to emigration from Ulster, especially to North America. Attention is also focused on material of potential interest in archives in England and Scotland.

I have incurred many debts in the course of writing both of these editions and it is only right and proper that I acknowledge at least some of these. First of all, my greatest debt is to my own family who have backed me ever since I decided to embark on a career encompassing history, archaeology and genealogy. The first edition was produced when I was still a bachelor. Since then I have had the happy addition to my family of my wife Heather, son Harry and daughter Sarah. I am grateful to my colleagues at the Ulster Historical Foundation – Fintan, Kathryn, Gillian, Conleth, Heather, Kevin and Ruaidhrí – for their interest and encouragement, and for tolerating my numerous absences from the office on research excursions. A special word of thanks is due to Jill Morrison who designed the book with her customary efficiency and patience.

This book would not have been written without the assistance of the staff of numerous archival institutions and libraries that I visited or corresponded with in the course of research for this publication. In particular, I wish to acknowledge the tremendous assistance given to me by the staff of the Public Record Office of Northern Ireland. Those who helped me to understand more about the records held there or who provided assistance in gaining access to some of the collections include Lorraine Bourke, Janet Hancock, Brett Irwin, Des McCabe, Ian Montgomery and Stephen Scarth. My thanks are also due to the many members of staff in the Search Room and Reading Room and those who retrieved documents for me from the stores. As far as other archives are concerned, I am very grateful to Valerie Adams at the Presbyterian Historical Society of Ireland, Dr Jonathan Mattison at the Museum of Orange Heritage, and Rebecca Hayes at Grand Lodge Library and Archive for assistance in tracing records of interest.

For drawing my attention to some of the lesser-known sources included in this book, or who helped me to understand something of their significance, or who encouraged me in my endeavours I am grateful to the following: the Duke of Abercorn KG, Harry Allen, Toby Barnard, Keith Beattie, Catherine Blumsom, Mary Bradley, Arthur Chapman, Kathleen Connolly, Robert Corbett, Sir Denis Desmond, John Dooher, Eull Dunlop, Bruce Durie, Terry Eakin, Simon Elliott, Paddy Fitzgerald, Bobby Forrest, Raymond Gillespie, George Gilmore, Peter Gilmore, Tom Gribben, Jonathan Hamill, Amy Harris, John Hastings, David Hayton, Gillian Hunt, Bob Hunter, Jack Johnston, Andrew Kane, James Kane, Brian Lambkin, Pamela Linden, Faye Logue, Linde Lunney, John McCabe, Trevor McCavery, Robert McClure, Finbar McCormick, Leslie McKeague, Annette McKee, David McMeekin, Alister McReynolds, Bill Macafee, Anthony Malcomson, Graham Mawhinney, Ian Maxwell, Brian Mitchell, Dave Mitchell, Grace Moloney, Sharon Oddie Brown, Chris Paton, Helen Perry, Andrew Pierce, Cliff Radcliffe, Duncan Scarlett, Brendan Scott, Helen Smiley, Mary Sullivan, Len Swindley, Mark Thompson, Brian Turner and John Turner.

I owe a huge debt of gratitude to two giants of local studies in Ulster, Bill Crawford and Brian Trainor. Over many years they encouraged my interest in the history of early modern Ulster and the sources for its study. Their pioneering work preserved many records which would otherwise have been lost and allowed countless thousands of people to pursue avenues of research that would have been closed to them. Sadly, both of them are no longer with us, though their legacy lives on. Dr Trainor passed away at the age of 90 just before the completion of this book and it is to him that I dedicate this volume as a token of my appreciation for his support for my work and for his friendship.

ABBREVIATIONS

CI	Church of Ireland
DIFHR	*Directory of Irish Family History Research*
GLI	Grand Lodge of Ireland (Freemasons)
GO	Genealogical Office
JRSAI	*Journal of the Royal Society of Antiquaries of Ireland*
LMA	London Metropolitan Archives
MOR	Moravian
NAI	National Archives of Ireland
NLI	National Library of Ireland
NRS	National Records of Scotland
NSP	Non-Subscribing Presbyterian
P	Presbyterian
PRIA	*Proceedings of the Royal Irish Academy*
PRONI	Public Record Office of Northern Ireland
RC	Roman Catholic
RCB	Representative Church Body Library
RGSU	*Records of the General Synod of Ulster, 1691–1820*
RP	Reformed Presbyterian
RSF	Religious Society of Friends (Quakers)
TNA	The National Archives (London)
TCD	Trinity College Dublin
UHF	Ulster Historical Foundation
UJA	*Ulster Journal of Archaeology*

NOTE ON SOURCES

All references to documents in this book, unless otherwise stated, are for items held at PRONI. There is no guarantee that any of these will be available to researchers at all times. Some documents are held off-site – this particularly applies to records held by NAI – and need to be ordered in advance. Occasionally documents go missing – which usually means misplaced – and at times records are closed on preservation grounds. If researchers wish to clarify that a particular document is available for inspection, it is best to contact the relevant archive in advance of a visit. Researchers should also be aware that until 1752 the new year in Ireland did not begin until 25 March and should take this into consideration when looking at sources prior to this date.

A brief history of Ulster in the seventeenth and eighteenth centuries

The Nine Years' War (1593–1603) and the passing of the Act of Union (1800) provide convenient brackets within which to study the history of Ulster. As a result of the former the entire island of Ireland was brought under the control of the British Crown. With the latter the Irish Parliament was abolished and henceforth Ireland was governed as an integral part of the United Kingdom. During the intervening two centuries immense changes to the nature of Ulster society took place, which were to have profound demographic, economic, political and religious consequences. This essay provides a brief introduction to Ulster in the seventeenth and eighteenth centuries.[1]

Prelude to plantation
In the late sixteenth century, apart from a couple of English outposts at Carrickfergus and Newry, Ulster was organised into a series of Gaelic lordships. The strongest of the ruling families were the O'Neills of Tyrone, followed by the O'Donnells of Tyrconnell (now Donegal). Other lordships in south and west Ulster included those of the Maguires, MacMahons and O'Reillys, whose territories were reflected in the counties which were created in the late sixteenth century, respectively, Fermanagh, Monaghan and Cavan. The O'Cahan lordship covered most of what became County Londonderry. In east Ulster the Clandeboye O'Neills controlled much of south County Antrim and north County Down, while the Magennises dominated west and south Down. In north Antrim the MacDonnells, Scots from the Highlands and Islands, had established a strong presence by the middle of the sixteenth century at the expense of the Irish McQuillans. As the Crown began to extend its power in Ulster it adopted a variety of strategies to bring the Gaelic lordships under its authority. Increasingly, however, English intervention in Ulster led to conflict with the northern lords. The abolition of the MacMahon lordship as the result of a land settlement of 1590–91 created considerable alarm among the other lords in Ulster and was a major factor in the outbreak of the Nine Years' War in 1593.

To begin with the war proved disastrous for the English. However, following the arrival in Ireland of Lord Mountjoy as lord deputy in 1600, the conflict was pursued with increased vigour and began to turn in the Crown's favour. Eventually the leader of the Irish, Hugh O'Neill, earl of Tyrone, was forced to surrender and in March 1603 the Treaty of Mellifont, which formally ended the war, was signed. O'Neill was pardoned and allowed to retain a large portion of his possessions in Tyrone. This was to the considerable dissatisfaction of many of the officers in the English army in Ireland and those Irish lords who had sided with the English during the recent war. Unable to adapt to changed circumstances and with many enemies in the English administration, O'Neill left Ireland in September 1607 along with the earl of Tyrconnell, Rory O'Donnell, and almost one hundred followers in what has become known as the 'Flight of the Earls'. O'Neill failed in his plan to sail to Spain and he died in Rome in 1616.

Plantation in Ulster
Following the 'Flight of the Earls', the government embarked upon a scheme of plantation whereby lands formerly in the possession of Irish lords were confiscated and parcelled out, for the most part, to new landowners of British origin. More than one-third of the area distributed went to the English and Scottish undertakers (so-called because of what they were undertaking). Servitors – usually Englishmen who had served the Crown in Ireland in a civil or military capacity – 'deserving' Irish, and institutions such as Trinity College Dublin and the Protestant Church were also beneficiaries of the scheme, which took over two years to plan and was not implemented until 1610. Six counties were to be part of the official plantation: Armagh, Cavan, Coleraine (renamed Londonderry), Donegal, Fermanagh and Tyrone (collectively known as the 'escheated counties'). Excepting Londonderry, which was granted to the livery companies of London and had its own rules, a fairly uniform plan was followed. Different obligations were placed on each of the groups with the most onerous falling on the undertakers who were the only grantees expected to colonise, being required to plant ten families or 24 men for every 1,000 acres they received.[2]

Schemes devised in London proved more difficult to implement in Ulster with the population of a particular plantation estate being determined not so much by government policy as by a combination of factors including distance from a port and the individual landlord's leasing policy and opportunity for profit. However, by about 1620 progress was being made with most of the disinterested grantees having sold out to men who were more prepared to invest in their lands. By this time British settlement was well established in the Foyle Valley (north Tyrone, east Donegal and west Londonderry). Other important areas of British settlement were in north County Londonderry and north

County Armagh. Areas with smaller concentrations of British settlers included the shores of Upper and Lower Lough Erne in County Fermanagh and south and east County Tyrone.

Under the rules of the plantation the English and Scottish undertakers were forbidden to lease land to Irish tenants. As with so much else about the scheme, the theory was very different from the practice. Though concerns were voiced on a regular basis about the presence of Irish families on the undertakers' estates, in general terms, no systematic and thorough government-conducted driving off of all of the native population from the undertakers' lands was carried out. It was observed in 1619 that 'if the Irish be put away with their Cattle, the British must either forsake their Dwellings, or endure great Distress on the suddain'. A shortage of British tenants and the willingness of the Irish to pay higher rents in order to hold on to their lands meant that significant numbers of Gaelic families continued to live on the undertakers' proportions.[3]

The official plantation scheme did not extend to counties Antrim, Down and Monaghan. Large parts of Antrim and Down remained in Irish ownership in the early seventeenth century.[4] Most of the land in the south and west of County Down was parcelled out in small freeholds to the Magennises. However, private plantations resulted in the large-scale migration of English and Scottish settlers to these counties. In the southern part of County Antrim as a result of the acquisition of estates by English landowners such as Sir Arthur Chichester, Sir Fulke Conway and Sir Hugh Clotworthy, much of the settlement was by migrants from England. In north-east County Down, two Scots, James Hamilton and Hugh Montgomery, carved out large estates from lands formerly owned by Con O'Neill. The British – overwhelmingly Scottish – settlement on the Hamilton and Montgomery estates was heavier than in any other part of Ulster.

The largest land grant made in Ulster in the early seventeenth century was the allocation of the greater part of the four northern baronies in County Antrim – Cary, Dunluce, Glenarm and Kilconway, an area of well over 300,000 acres – to Randal MacDonnell in 1603.[5] In order to develop his massive estate, MacDonnell, who became earl of Antrim in 1620, invited lowland Scots to settle on his lands and to encourage Protestants to move to a Catholic-owned estate, he contributed to the building and repair of churches.[6] Early seventeenth-century County Monaghan differed again. Here the land settlement of 1591 was confirmed in 1606. There were, however, a number of settler estates in the county in the early seventeenth century, mainly based on former ecclesiastical lands, and in 1575, the earl of Essex had been granted almost the whole of the barony of Farney in the south of the county. However, the sale and mortgaging of Irish lands to settler landowners reduced the proportion of land in County Monaghan in native hands to less than 40% in 1641.[7]

Urban and rural settlement

Prior to the seventeenth century Ulster was the least urbanised part of Ireland. However, there were a number of towns in Ulster that had existed for centuries. The two most important towns founded by the Anglo-Normans were Carrickfergus and Downpatrick. Cavan was the best established Gaelic market town in Ulster in the late sixteenth century, while other places, such as Dungannon and Omagh, were developing into important market centres. In addition, coastal towns, including Ardglass and Killybegs had well-established trading links with Britain and Continental Europe. The Ulster Plantation was the first colonising scheme in Ireland with formal urban proposals. At the apex of the hierarchy of settlement, at least in terms of status and legal privileges, though not necessarily in size, was the borough town with a written charter guaranteeing its rights and liberties. Between November 1610 and June 1613 20 places in Ulster received charters of incorporation.

The corporate towns varied considerably in size. In the officially planted counties the three largest were Derry (renamed Londonderry), Coleraine and Strabane with approximate adult male populations of, respectively, 500, 300 and 200 in 1630. The populations of most of the other corporate towns were considerably smaller than this. Below the corporate towns, in terms of status, though not necessarily scale, were the villages founded by the new landowners on their estates. The more substantial villages included Lisnaskea, Letterkenny and Ramelton, all of which had 40 houses or more by 1622, which was more than many of the corporate towns. The infrastructure of these settlements varied and while most were simply collections of houses, others possessed buildings and features of importance, including schools and market houses.

By and large, however, towns in Ulster remained fairly modest in comparison with urban centres in Britain. When Bishop William Bedell first arrived in County Cavan in the early 1630s, he found that 'the only considerable town in the whole county was Belturbet which yet was but as one of our ordinary market towns here in England'.[8] The settlement adjoining his cathedral at Kilmore was 'a mere country village'. Furthermore, most of the settlers did not live in a formal urban setting, but rather dispersedly across the countryside, either in stand-alone dwellings or in small clusters of houses.[9] This was in direct contravention of the rules of the plantation which envisaged a settlement structured around a network of villages. The sheer impracticality of having to live in a village and travel out to one's farm every day militated against nucleated settlements on plantation estates. This was due in part to the nature of the Irish townland system upon which the tenants' holdings were based.

Religion in the early 1600s

The Reformation, which had its formal beginnings in Ireland in the 1530s, made little impact in Ulster until the early seventeenth century. The final eclipse of Gaelic power in 1603, followed by the official and unofficial plantation schemes made possible the extension of Protestantism to the region. There were attempts by some of the Protestant bishops to involve Irishmen in the pastorate of the Church of Ireland, while in a number of areas there is evidence that some of the Irish conformed. On the whole, however, Protestantism failed to win the hearts and minds of the Irish population, most of whom remained adherents of Catholicism. Increasingly the Church of Ireland came to be seen as the church of the settler population with its ministers nearly all British and English-speaking. In 1622, it was found that the Protestant minister of Killelagh, County Londonderry, did not live in the parish, but visited the church occasionally 'where no man cometh at him', the parish being entirely inhabited by Irish.[10] For many of the Irish, the spread of Protestantism as a result of the plantation was a major concern. In 1636, the Catholic bishop of Raphoe wrote to Rome 'not without deep sadness of heart' at 'how thick [were] the weeds which the persistent heresy daily sows' through the influx of Protestant settlers to his diocese.[11]

The disruption to Ulster society in the late sixteenth century, culminating in the Nine Years' War, had left the Roman Catholic Church in a weakened position, in terms of its structures, personnel and physical fabric. Many places of worship, especially the friaries and other religious houses, had been used as strongholds during the war, resulting in considerable damage to them. In the early 1600s the Catholic clergy were targeted by government officials with frequent complaints of harassment and persecution by the authorities. Fines were imposed on 'recusants', i.e. those who would not attend the Church of Ireland, and some of the funds raised were used to finance the construction of Protestant churches. However, despite these difficulties, the Catholic Church continued to maintain a witness. By the late 1620s many of the northern dioceses had a resident bishop for the first time in decades, while Catholic worship was being conducted freely in many areas. For example, in Strabane, County Tyrone, Mass was openly said with the connivance of the Scottish settler population in the late 1620s. In 1631, it was noted that there were several mass-houses on the estates owned by the London companies in County Londonderry. Furthermore, there was a priest in every parish, while it was also alleged that the Londoners' representatives used the priests to secure higher rents than might otherwise have been the case.[12]

It can be reasonably assumed that most of the settlers who came to Ulster in the early seventeenth century were Protestants, even if only nominally so. The Church of Ireland was organised along episcopalian lines with a hierarchy of clergy rising to the archbishop of Armagh who was the chief Anglican cleric on the island. However, several ministers from Scotland came to Ulster in this period who dissented from this view of church government, preferring the Presbyterian system. To begin with such men were tolerated within the Church of Ireland and there was no distinct Presbyterian denomination at this time.

In the 1630s, however, the government led by the new lord deputy, Thomas Wentworth, earl of Strafford, began to take steps to bring the Church of Ireland into closer conformity with the Church of England. This meant clamping down on the activities of ministers with Presbyterian convictions. Those ministers who were not prepared to renounce their Presbyterianism were excommunicated. In 1636, some of these men, with about 140 followers, set sail in the *Eagle Wing* for America; they never reached their destination as storms drove the ship back.[13] Other Presbyterians returned to Scotland. Here Presbyterian opposition to Charles I was reaching boiling point. In 1638, the National Covenant was drawn up in Scotland which declared Presbyterianism the only true form of church government and bound the nation to the principles of the Reformation. Many in Ulster also signed the Covenant. In response Wentworth insisted that all Scots in Ulster over the age of 16 take an oath – the infamous 'Black Oath' as it became known – abjuring the Covenant. Those who refused to take the oath could be fined and imprisoned. The result was that large numbers of Scottish settlers fled to their homeland; so many left in fact that in some places there were not enough people to bring in the harvest.

The 1641 rising

Even allowing for a high degree of continuity with the past, there is no denying that early seventeenth-century Ulster was being transformed at many different levels, whether social, economic, demographic or religious. These changes were especially felt by the native Irish population. The rapid social mobility brought about by the momentous changes arising from the plantation scheme was to the advantage of some Irishmen and to the detriment of others. On the other hand, to some contemporary observers it appeared that the accommodations necessary to make society function effectively were being worked out by the various groupings. Richard Head, an Englishman who had grown up in Ireland, went so far as to write that the Irish and English 'had lived forty Years in peace with such great security and comfort that it had in a manner consolidated them into one body knit and compacted together'.[14] By the end of the 1630s, however, life for nearly everyone in Ulster had become much more difficult.

The civil and religious policies pursued by the English administration in Dublin led by Thomas Wentworth had a destabilising effect across all levels of society. Many of the Irish landowners found the transition to a market economy extremely difficult and as a result fell heavily into debt, forcing some of them to sell their estates. There was also the fear that a Puritan-dominated Parliament in London would further restrict their rights as Catholics, and they looked with alarm at the unfolding of events in Scotland. For these and other reasons several of the leading Irish landowners in Ulster, most notably Sir Phelim O'Neill, began to make plans for an uprising. Beginning on the evening of 22 October 1641, castles and towns over much of Ulster were seized. Initially bloodshed was limited with a number of the Irish leaders insisting that Scots should not be interfered with. Soon, however, the leaders of the uprising lost control and indiscriminate massacres of settlers began. The numbers killed in the rising have been a source of contention ever since the autumn of 1641. At the time, wildly exaggerated estimates were circulated, mainly in the English press to drum up support for crushing the rising. Nonetheless, thousands of settlers did die in the rising, at least as many from exposure and disease as from violence. Those who had the means of doing so fled to Dublin or across the Irish Sea to England and Scotland. Other sought refuge in the towns that had not been captured.

In north-west Ulster resistance to the insurrection was organised by two Stewarts, Sir William of Newtownstewart and Sir Robert, who recruited a force from among the settlers known as the Laggan Army. Additional support for the settlers came in the form of a Scottish army under the command of Major-General Robert Munro which landed at Carrickfergus in April 1642. In June of that year the chaplains in this army met with a number of ruling elders to form what is regarded as the inaugural Irish Presbytery meeting, from which, in a formal sense, today's Presbyterian Church in Ireland descends. Soon afterwards Owen Roe O'Neill, nephew of Hugh O'Neill, earl of Tyrone, arrived from the Continent and took control of the Irish army in Ulster. By this time the war had become an all-Ireland conflict with the Old English and Catholic Church declaring their support for the insurgents. The conflict continued for the rest of the 1640s and it was not until Cromwell arrived in Ireland with a Parliamentarian army in August 1649 that the island began to be brought under control. In Ulster most of the Scots supported the claims of Prince Charles, son of the recently beheaded king. Derry was briefly besieged by the Scots and in December 1649 an army of royalists was decisively defeated by a Parliamentarian force near Lisburn. Owen Roe O'Neill was dead by this time and by the following summer Irish resistance had been all but crushed.

The Cromwellian and Restoration periods
Under the Cromwellians, the remaining Gaelic landownership in Ulster was virtually wiped out. For a time Scottish landowners in Ulster were also in a difficult situation with the threat of confiscation and transplantation hanging over them for their support of the royalist cause. Eventually, however, their possessions were secured on payment of heavy fines. Cromwell died in 1658 and in 1660 the monarchy was restored. The new king, Charles II, was faced with the difficulty of having to find land for those Catholics who had remained loyal to the Crown during the previous 20 years. Several Scottish Catholics – the earl of Antrim and the Hamiltons in Strabane – were restored to the estates they had held prior to 1641. Because the land settlements did not overturn the existing estate system as far as the settler population was concerned, a high degree of continuity prevailed. The most significant changes occurred in those areas that had been owned by Irish lords in the early seventeenth century, which now witnessed an influx of British settlers. For example, Sir George Rawdon

acquired two significant blocks of land in the Ballynahinch and Moira areas of County Down. When these were erected into a manor by royal patent in 1682 Rawdon was commended for having 'built a considerable town' at Ballynahinch, while at Moira he had 'built a market town ... which was inhabited with conformable Protestants'.[15]

Migration to the north of Ireland in the 1650s was encouraged by low rents in the aftermath of a decade of warfare. Religious factors also contributed to the movement of individuals and families from Britain to Ulster. The Quaker Act of 1662 and the Conventicle Act of 1664 resulted in many Quakers leaving England for Ireland and significant Quaker settlements developed in the Lagan Valley and north County Armagh. Records for the Quaker meeting in Lurgan, which was established in 1653, include details of the place of origin for 21 men who moved to Ireland in the period up to 1701. With the exception of one man from the Scottish Borders, all of them were from the north of England: ten were Yorkshiremen, four were from Cumberland, two each from Lancashire and Northumberland, and one each from Durham and Westmorland.[16] In the 1670s and 1680s migration from Scotland was encouraged by the persecution of Covenanters during the 'Killing Time'.

These fresh migrations were having a noticeable impact on local demographics. Around 1670 Oliver Plunkett, the Catholic archbishop of Armagh, noted that the city of Armagh had a population of approximately 3,000 persons, 'almost all Scottish or English, with very few Irish'.[17] This contrasted with the towns and villages in County Armagh which, according to Plunkett, were mainly inhabited with Catholic leaseholders and peasants. In the town of Dungannon Plunkett believed that of 1,000 families barely 20 were not English or Scottish.[18] A description of County Donegal from April 1683 noted that it was 'plentifully planted with Protestant inhabitants, especially with great numbers out of Scotland'.[19] In areas with heavy British settlement, increased competition for land could result in the displacement of the local Catholic farming class. In 1675, Plunkett wrote: 'Sometimes it happens that a parish which one year has two hundred Catholic families will not have thirty the following year ... because the Catholics being, as a rule, leaseholders, often lose their leases, which are then given to Protestants or Presbyterians or Anabaptists or Quakers.'[20] At the same time, large areas of Ulster continued to be sparsely populated with families of British origin. In 1666, Langfield parish, County Tyrone, was described as 'full of woods, mountains, bad ways ... the congregation 5 or 6, sometimes 10 or 12 might be 100, but all Irish, except some Scotch and 1 English family'.[21]

In the second half of the seventeenth century the Presbyterian Church emerged as a distinct denomination and there were clear lines of demarcation between it and the Church of Ireland. On the whole Scottish settlers were Presbyterian, while English settlers were Anglican, although there were numerous exceptions to this rule. Captain John Hamilton of Cavan, near

Stranorlar, County Donegal, was described as a 'most zealous Catholic … a pious and liberal man and a great apologist for the faith', having previously been both an Anglican and a Presbyterian.[22] He later emigrated to Germany and in 1695 became a count in the Holy Roman Empire. In 1673, Plunkett commented that in the dioceses of Connor and Down (comprising almost all of County Antrim and north and east County Down, Presbyterians – 'whose belief is an aborted form of Protestantism' – were more numerous than Catholics and Anglicans put together.[23]

As well as immigration to Ulster, the late seventeenth century witnessed the beginnings of emigration from Ulster to America. A high proportion of these early migrants – among them Rev. Francis Makemie, the 'Father of American Presbyterianism' – were from the north-west and they departed from the port of Derry-Londonderry, which by the 1680s was part of the transatlantic trading network that connected America, Ireland and Britain. In part, this emigration was driven by the difficulties faced by Presbyterians who experienced considerable state hostility at different times, including the arrest and imprisonment of ministers. In 1684, during another difficult period for Presbyterians, ministers in County Donegal considered emigrating to America en masse to escape persecution, but in the end they did not go through with this. Many of the earliest migrants settled in the Delmarva peninsula (comprising parts of Delaware, Maryland and Virginia) and in 1692, it was noted that Somerset County on the peninsula was 'a place pestered with Scotch & Irish'.[24]

The Williamite War in Ulster and its aftermath
The accession of James II, a Catholic, to the throne in 1685 created considerable concern among Ulster's Protestants and raised hopes among the dispossessed and impoverished Catholic gentry of being restored to estates they had lost under Cromwell. The promotion of Catholics to important positions in the judiciary and in central and local government only served to heighten Protestant fears. Events in England and the Continent brought matters to a head. In 1688, the Dutch prince William of Orange arrived in England and was declared king in what was known as the 'Glorious Revolution'. James II sought refuge in France and the following year landed in Ireland with a large French army. By this time Protestant resistance in Ulster had already been mobilised. In December 1688, as a Catholic army under the command of the earl of Antrim was on its way to Derry, a group of apprentice boys shut the gates of the city, while at Enniskillen a force of mainly Fermanagh settlers known as the Inniskilling Men secured the town. The famous 105-day siege of Derry began in April 1689. As many as 30,000 settlers as well as a garrison of 7,000 men were packed into the city; it was reckoned that 15,000 of them died of fever or starvation or were killed in battle. The siege was lifted in late July and this coincided with a major defeat of the Jacobites at the hands of the Inniskilling Men at Newtownbutler, County Fermanagh. Soon afterwards a large Williamite

force landed near Bangor, County Down, and by the autumn of 1689 James's forces had been all but removed from Ulster. As the war moved south, with decisive battles fought at the Boyne on 1 July 1690 and Aughrim on 12 July 1691, the province began to recover from the consequences of the conflict.

Because the military campaign was shorter in this war than it had been in the 1640s, its effects were not as severe. Nonetheless large parts of Ulster experienced considerable devastation. William King, who became bishop of Derry in January 1691, recalled that when he first arrived in his diocese, 'I found the land almost desolate'. In the autumn of 1691 William Waring of Waringstown, County Down, wrote the following on the condition of his estate: 'I have no hopes of getting any of it planted. The Irish natives that live on it are all fled into Connaught and the British inhabitants are wasted by warfare and sickness'.[25] The aftermath of the Williamite War saw a fresh influx of Scots into the north of Ireland – perhaps as many as 50,000 – encouraged in part by harvest crises in their native land.[26] About 1700 Bishop King wrote that due to this wave of migration from Scotland, 'the dissenters measure mightily in the north'.[27]

Migration to Ulster, mainly from Scotland, continued into the early eighteenth century. This was impacting on local demographics in areas where British settlement had hitherto been fairly sparse. In 1714, Hugh McMahon, the Catholic bishop of the diocese of Clogher, wrote that 'from the neighbouring country of Scotland Calvinists are coming over here daily in large groups of families, occupying the towns and villages, seizing the farms in the richer parts of the country and expelling the natives.'[28] To take County Monaghan as an example, in 1660 British settlement was patchy and in the south of the county – aside from the town of Carrickmacross – virtually non-existent. By 1730, however, there was a British presence in every parish in the county and in some there were fairly sizeable communities.[29] Changes in settlement patterns were also discernable in parts of south County Armagh. In the 1730s a number of landowners in the parish of Creggan invited Presbyterians, many of them from County Down, to settle on their estates and as an inducement promised to provide an income for a Presbyterian minister.[30]

Commentators were able to differentiate between areas on the basis of the characteristics of the local inhabitants or the changes they had introduced to the landscape. In 1708, north Armagh was described as a 'mighty pretty English-like enclosed countrey'. In County Donegal in the late 1730s, Rev. William Henry distinguished between people of English and of Scottish descent by the way they lived and worked: 'The English planters are easily known by the neatness of their houses and pleasant plantations of trees'; the Scots, on the other hand, neglected this, but made up for it through their efforts to improve the soil.[31] Others noted the differences in speech of the province's inhabitants. Journeying through east County Antrim c. 1760 Edward Willes commented that 'all the people of this part of the world speaks the broad lowland Scotch and have all the Scotch phrases. It will be a dispute between the two kingdoms until the end of time whether Ireland was peopled from Scotland or Scotland from Ireland'.[32] On the other hand, Irish continued to be the everyday language of most of the indigenous population, though an increasing number were familiar with English.

Protestants, Catholics and Dissenters

Although the Church of Ireland was the state or Established Church in Ireland, it enjoyed the support of only around 10% of the population of Ireland as whole (in the north of Ireland this figure was around 20–25%). Its dominance, however, can be demonstrated from a list of c. 1730 of the gentlemen in Ulster believed to be worth more than £100 per annum. This list included the names of 490 members of the Church of Ireland, but only 41 Presbyterians and a mere eight Catholics.[33] Beginning in 1695, legislation known as the Penal Laws was passed in the Irish Parliament to preserve the privileged position of the Anglican elite by keeping Catholics – felt to be disloyal and untrustworthy on the basis of events in the seventeenth century – in subjection. As a result of the Penal Laws, Catholics were forbidden from, among other things, bearing arms, entering the legal profession, owning a horse worth more than £5, buying land and leasing land for more than 31 years. Finally, in 1728, Catholics were denied the vote. By conforming to the Church of Ireland Catholics could avoid these restrictions, though only a fraction did so and these were often members of the gentry anxious to hold on to their estates. One of the most prominent converts was Alexander MacDonnell, earl of Antrim, who conformed in 1734. Among the very few Ulster landowners to remain Catholic were the Whytes of Loughbrickland, County Down, who seem to have worked with local Protestant landowners in safeguarding their estate.[34]

The Penal Laws not only impacted upon Catholics as individuals, but upon the Catholic Church as an institution, with the senior clergy being targeted in particular. For example, in 1735, it was noted that the bishop of Raphoe 'lives in misery, and wanders about, unknown, like a fugitive, at the greatest risk to himself'.[35] However, the enforcement of the Penal Laws was uneven and in large parts of the country priests, and eventually bishops, were able to operate with relative impunity. Venues for Catholic worship ranged from the open air to very basic structures known as 'mass-houses'. At times, landlords used their authority to prevent the construction of a mass-house. For instance, a 1727 lease of a farm in County Fermanagh included a prohibition on erecting a mass-house or dwelling for a 'Popish Priest or any Preacher or Teacher dissenting from the Church of Ireland'.[36] However, it is also clear that many Catholic places of worship were built with the approbation of local landowners. As the century progressed, larger and more elaborate Catholic churches were built. In Derry the 'Long Tower' church was built 1784–6 at a cost of £2,800, while in 1787 a new Catholic place of worship near Lifford was described as 'built just like a large handsome church, except steeple or belfry'.[37] By this time the gradual repeal of the Penal Laws was underway and in 1793 Catholics were again allowed to vote.

Catholics were not the only religious denomination to face institutional discrimination in this period. Presbyterians also felt aggrieved at laws which restricted their rights and freedoms in certain areas. Presbyterians were particularly angered when the provisions of the Test Act were extended to Ireland in 1704. Henceforth those wishing to hold civil and military office had to produce evidence that they had taken communion in the Church of Ireland; this effectively disbarred Presbyterians from public office. Presbyterians also resented having to pay the tithes that were demanded by the Church of Ireland clergy and the manner in which these tithes were sometimes collected provoked consternation. In 1719, the Toleration Act was passed, but this simply gave Presbyterians the right to attend their own places of worship without being penalised. For many members of the establishment, Presbyterians were regarded as more of a threat than Catholics, especially because of their numerical superiority over Anglicans in much of Ulster. No less a figure than Jonathan Swift is believed to have been the author of a 1733 tract in which the writer asked 'Whether the Scottish Ulster Presbyterian Farmers, Tradesmen and Cottagers' were a 'more knavish, wicked, thievish race than even the natural Irish of the other three provinces'.[38]

In the early eighteenth century there occurred the first major dispute within Irish Presbyterianism. This was over the issue of subscription to the Westminster Confession of Faith. Those who denied the necessity of subscribing to the Confession were known as non-subscribers or 'New Light' Presbyterians. In 1725, those who took this stance were placed in the Presbytery of Antrim, which became effectively a separate denomination, a forerunner of today's Non-Subscribing Presbyterian Church. Other strands of Presbyterianism originating in Scotland were established in Ulster during the course of the eighteenth century. The Seceders – so called because they had seceded from the Church of Scotland in 1733 – established congregations and presbyteries in Ulster from the 1740s onwards. The first Irish presbytery of the Reformed Presbyterian Church was established in 1763. The origins of this denomination went back to the National Covenant of 1638 and the Solemn League and Covenant of 1643. The Reformed Presbyterians, or Covenanters, as they were also known, refused to accept that the state had any authority over the church and did not participate in parliamentary elections. These denominations provided an alternative to mainstream Presbyterianism.

The Ulster economy in the eighteenth century

In 1759, Edward Willes, the Lord Chief Baron, commented that he had never seen 'a more beautiful country for length of way' between Monaghan and Carrickfergus. It was 'extremely well cultivated and very populous and you see the spirit of industry every step you go'.[39] Many other travellers and commentators made similar statements, reflecting on the transformation of Ulster in the eighteenth century as it changed from the poorest province in Ireland in 1650 to the most prosperous in 1800. The single most important reason for the development of the north of Ireland in this period and its increasing prosperity was the rise of the domestic linen industry.[40] Linen had been part of the Ulster economy prior to 1700, but it was in the eighteenth century that it emerged as its most powerful element. Why was the linen industry so successful in Ulster? Bill Crawford has suggested that 'Whereas Irish society outside Ulster evolved along traditional lines so that local craftsmen could continue to meet the demand for textiles in Ireland, Ulster society was unstable and disorganised but enterprising and ready to experiment'.[41] Another important factor was the passing of an act in the English Parliament which allowed Irish linens to be exported directly to America from 1705 onwards. Around this time Ireland as a whole exported one million yards of cloth. By 1800 this had risen to 40 million yards, most of it from Ulster.

In 1744, Walter Harris noted that the 'staple commodity of the country is linen, a due care of which manufacture has brought great wealth among the people. The northern inhabitants already feel the benefit of it, and are freed from much of that poverty and wretchedness too visible among the lower class of people in other parts of the Kingdom, where this valuable branch of trade has not been improved to advantage'.[42] In Fermanagh, Rev. William Henry was in no doubt that the linen industry was the decisive factor in the increasing prosperity of the county.[43] By the end of the eighteenth century the rise in living standards was being felt at different levels of society. In 1790, it was said that the influence of industry and manufactures in County Monaghan was 'meliorating the condition of the peasant [and] improving the state of the husbandman'.[44] Progress, however, was not entirely in one direction and there were many fluctuations in the economy which impacted upon the livelihoods of families in Ulster. Despite the general rise in prosperity, therefore, many people continued to live close to or below the poverty line. There was also a high degree of vulnerability to the elements, such as extreme weather conditions. In 1740–41, Ireland experienced a famine that was proportionately even more devastating than the Great Famine of the 1840s.[45]

Farming varied considerably across Ulster in the eighteenth century, depending on such things as local economics and the suitability of the terrain for agricultural production. Some areas were heavily focused on the cultivation of flax and the production of linen. If food was grown on their holdings it was generally for subsistence rather than for sale. Linen production was their main, and for many, sole form of income. In other regions the emphasis was on pastoral farming. Elsewhere, however, such as the barony of Lecale in County Down, arable farming was an important part of the local economy. With the increase in Ulster's population from an estimated 600,000 in the mid 1730s to

2,000,000 by the early 1820s (when it was almost the same as the population of the whole of Scotland), there was greater competition for land. In the process the size of farms became smaller so that areas where the domestic linen industry was most concentrated, such as north County Armagh, the average size of a holding fell to less than 12 acres. This left many families vulnerable to economic downturn, especially during harvest failures. With the rise in population and the accompanying increase in the demand for land, a noticeable feature of the settlement pattern, particularly in the second half of the eighteenth century, was the expansion into previously marginal lands. Upland areas were also experiencing population increase as farming families began to settle on the mountainsides. What permitted families to survive in these areas was the potato, which could be cultivated on poorer quality ground and still produce a good crop.

Improvements in communications and urban development

Travellers through the Ulster countryside in the eighteenth century made frequent mention of the condition of the roads. Something of the variability in the quality of roads can be found in Dubliner Thomas Molyneux's account of his tour through the north of Ireland in August 1708. His journey between Shanes's Castle and Ahoghill in County Antrim – a distance of a little over 10 miles – took him 4–5 hours and was through 'a miserable, wild, Barbarous, boggy countrey'. On the other hand, he was full of praise for the new road from Coleraine to Limavady, describing it was 'all a most Excellent, new, artificially-made Cawsey in dismall, wild, boggy mountains. It runs for Some miles in an Exact Straight Line, and it makes a pretty figure to see a work so perfectly owing to Art and Industry in So wild a place.'[46]

In County Fermanagh in the late 1730s, Rev. William Henry found that 'the many fastnesses [that] made most part of the county formerly impassable' were 'now entirely removed by the indefatigable pains and public spirit which is exerted in making roads'. These roads were 'well executed by the spirit of the gentlemen and the cheerfulness wherewith the common people fulfil their statute labour'.[47] The latter remark referred to the obligation of every lessee to supply six days of free labour to mend the roads in his parish. On the other hand, Walter Harris, writing in 1744, lamented the difficulty of travellers journeying to Ballynahinch who were forced to 'hobble through the broken and narrow causeways'; he added that the existing legislation relating to roads was inadequate and that some of the local gentry felt that the routes around the town would have to be repaired at the expense of the county.[48]

In 1765, an act of parliament transferred the responsibility for major roads to the county grand jury. Grand juries were also allowed to finance road building by being able to impose a county cess. Later an act of parliament allowed parishes to raise an extra tax to maintain minor roads, while an *Act for the making of narrow roads through the mountainous unimproved parts of this kingdom* permitted grand juries to raise money for this purpose also. The result of this legislation was a dramatic increase in the number of miles of road in the province so that by 1800 Ulster had one of the densest road networks in Western Europe. This in turn stimulated trade and commerce as goods were more easily transported between the places of production, sale and export.

Intertwined with the rise of the domestic linen industry and the improvement in communications in Ulster was the development of new market towns as well as the revival of settlements originally founded in the seventeenth century. In many instances, the role of the landowner was of paramount importance in stimulating growth. In 1708, Thomas Molyneux noted that Lurgan, County Armagh, was 'the greatest mart of Linnen Manufactories in the North'. A major factor in Lurgan's development was the initiative of the town's landlord, Arthur Brownlow, who 'on his first Establishing the trade here, bought up everything that was brought to the market of Cloath and lost at first considerably; but at Length the thing fixing itself, he is now by the same methods a considerable Gainer.'[49] Other landlords promoted urban development through investing in buildings or in encouraging the settlement of manufacturers. Writing about Cootehill, County Cavan, in 1740, Rev. John Richardson noted that there was 'a great number of weavers and bleachers in this town and neighbourhood' due to the efforts of the town's landlord who had taken care to 'have this new town tenderly nursed and cherished in its infancy that many of its inhabitants soon grew rich and brought it to the perfection which it is now at.'[50]

Landowners hoped to attract suitable tenants to their towns by offering them leases on advantageous terms.[51] Other proprietors, such as those at Greyabbey, Hillsborough and Saintfield in County Down, built houses for 'the habitation of manufacturers'.[52] Public buildings, such as market houses, were constructed in increasing numbers in Ulster's towns. Often these were impressive edifices, designed to show off the munificence of a patron and his awareness of current architectural trends (and therefore his taste and civility). Many survive today as striking reminders of past glories. One of the most striking examples of urban planning from this period is Cookstown, County Tyrone, where a new main street 130 feet in width and extending in a straight line for over a mile was laid out by the landlord, William Stewart, around 1750.

Not every attempt to encourage town development was successful, however. At Church Hill in County Fermanagh Sir Gustavus Hume established a market and built an inn and a number of houses 'proper for tradesmen to live in' *c.* 1714. Five years later Hume advertised his intention to establish a linen manufactory there, build a bleachyard, and provide financial backing to anyone who was prepared to carry on the business and improve the village. However, by the end of the eighteenth century this settlement had petered out.[53] Nor was it always the case that a town was able to enjoy the patronage of a single landowner. Writing about Omagh, County Tyrone, in 1787, Daniel Beaufort commented: 'The town is frittered among a number of landlords who give no encouragement'.[54]

Emigration from Ulster to the New World

One of the historical processes most closely associated with eighteenth-century Ulster was large-scale emigration to the American colonies.[55] A discussion of publications relating to emigration can be found in Chapter 13 and here only a few general comments will be made. It has already been noted that the origins of Ulster emigration to the New World can be traced to the late 1600s. Migration to North America intensified in the late 1710s with a major exodus from the northern parts of Ulster to New England in 1718. At around the same time there was a rise in emigration to Pennsylvania, via the Delaware ports of New Castle and Philadelphia. Later on, Charleston, South Carolina, became a popular port of arrival for families from Ulster. The most important emigration ports in the north of Ireland were Belfast and Londonderry, followed by Newry, Larne and Coleraine/Portrush, though it must be acknowledged that a proportion of Ulster emigrants left from ports in other parts of Ireland and even across the Irish Sea in Britain. Depending on the weather conditions, the voyage itself lasted typically 6–10 weeks, while the cost of a passage could be £3–9. However, many emigrants went out as indentured servants and paid their passage through working for an agreed period after they arrived in America. One of the major areas of discussion has been the number of emigrants departing from Ulster to Colonial America. Estimates range from under 100,000 to over 250,000 for the period 1718–75.[56]

The factors stimulating emigration were numerous and complex and varied over time. Academic debate on the subject has focused on the economic motivation of the migrants set against the issue of religious freedom, particularly for Presbyterians. Both issues were clearly at play, though in the minds of our forebears there was probably not such an obvious separation of the two. Religious pressures and economic difficulties were bound up together; as has been observed by others, hardship and oppression went hand-in-hand.[57] The numbers of people emigrating was not constant and certain peaks can be detected, which tended to coincide with periods of major economic recession. The late 1720s, for example, witnessed several years of harvest failure and a surge in emigration. In early 1729, the Anglican archbishop of Armagh compared emigration to America to a 'humour', which 'spreads like an infectious distemper amongst people of substance and poor alike.'[58]

The payment of tithes to support the Anglican clergy was certainly a factor in emigration, combining as it did a religious grievance with economic strain. In 1719, Edmund Kaine, agent on the Barrett Lennard estate at Clones in County Monaghan, noted that one hundred families had passed through his town in the past week heading for New England, adding that those departing 'complain most the hardship of the tithes makes them all go, which is true, for the clergy is [sic] unreasonable'.[59] Rent increases were also blamed for the departure of so many individuals and families. In August 1718, at a time when large numbers were leaving the Bann Valley, Joseph Marriott commented that 'one reason they give for their going is the raising of the rent of the land to such a high rate that they cannot support their families thereon with the greatest industry'. James Willson, the lessee of the Mercers' Company estate in County Londonderry, wrote in 1735 that one of the principal reasons for emigration was the 'great oppression of landlords' which had left the tenantry in 'such a state of despair that they chose rather to leave their native country and seek their fortunes in a strange land than starve at home'.[60]

While people of all religious backgrounds emigrated to America in this era, there is no doubt that Presbyterians dominated the outflow from Ulster, at certain times even forming a majority of total numbers crossing the Atlantic from Ireland. There were various reasons for this. First of all, there were the religious factors that have been noted already. As a comparatively literate people who placed a high premium on education they had a greater awareness of the opportunities America offered through newspaper reports and letters sent back to Ulster. As James Murray informed Rev. Baptist Boyd, Presbyterian minister of Aughnacloy, County Tyrone, in 1737, 'Read this Letter, and look, and tell aw the poor Folk of your Place, that God has open'd a Door for their Deliverance'.[61] Some viewed Ulster's Presbyterians as ideal settlers for the fringes of the colonies. In the 1720s Lurgan-born James Logan was eager to settle men who 'had so bravely defended Derry & Inniskillen' on what was then the Pennsylvania frontier. In addition, the way in which the Ulster economy developed in the eighteenth century and in particular the rise of the linen industry facilitated emigration from the north of Ireland. Ships bringing flaxseed to Ulster returned to America carrying human cargoes.

Presbyterian ministers were considered to be important drivers of emigration. In 1729, Ezekiel Stewart of Fortstewart, near Ramelton, County Donegal, wrote that: 'The Presbiteirien Ministers have taken their shear of pains to seduce their poor ignorant heare[r]s by bellowing from their pulpits against ye landlords and ye clargey'. According to Stewart, these ministers has been telling their congregations 'that God had appoynted a country for them to dwell in (nameing New England) and desires them to depart thence, where they will be freed from the bondage of Egipt and go to ye land of Cannan'.[62] Notable ministers in this regard include Rev. James McGregor of Aghadowey and Rev. James Woodside of Dunboe, both in County Londonderry, who led sections of their congregations to New England in 1718. Other ministers involved in leading substantial numbers of people to America included Rev. Thomas Clark, minister of the Secession congregation of Cahans, County Monaghan, who, in 1764, led 300 people to New York. In 1772, the Reformed Presbyterian minister Rev. William Martin, whose meeting house was at Kellswater, near Ballymena led a major exodus of families, mainly from County Antrim, to South Carolina at a time when agrarian unrest was threatening the stability of the north of Ireland.

The departure of so many of families was a cause of considerable concern to the authorities. Ulster's landlords lamented the loss of their tenants and the consequences of this for the value of their estates. In 1735, the abovementioned James Willson wrote that due to emigration many estates 'are become almost entirely desolate'. There was realistically little landowners could do to prevent tenants from leaving their farms. Robert McCausland advised William Conolly in November 1718 that if there was any decree from the government forbidding people from emigrating 'it would make them the fonder to go'. He set out his own position on the matter: 'all I would have done, if it were possible, to oblige these "rougs" who goes of[f] to pay their just debts before they go, and then let all go when they please who are inclined to go'.[63] Others were concerned that emigration was draining Ulster of its Protestants and would harm the linen industry. Rev. John Wilson, Church of Ireland minister in Lettermacaward parish, County Donegal, wrote in 1766 of the 'apparent decay of the Protestant religion in this whole country' and estimated that 18 of the 72 Protestants in his parish 'will certainly go abroad, so that it is to be feared, that in a few years, there will be few or none to cultivate that religion for which our ancestors gloriously and virtuously laid down their lives'.[64] In the event, the concerns raised by clerics and landowners were not realised.

While the outbreak of the American War of Independence has often been used as a terminal point in the study of eighteenth-century emigration to America, it represented simply an interruption to the story and once peace had been signed in 1783 the migrant flow resumed once again. It must also be acknowledged that while the focus of emigration studies has tended to be on the colonies that became part of the United States, the second half of the eighteenth century witnessed the beginnings of the departure of individuals and families from Ulster to what became Canada. In fact, the first official attempt to establish an Ulster colony in Canada occurred in 1761 when Alexander McNutt advertised for 'industrious farmers and useful mechanics' to settle in Nova Scotia. The first settlers arrived later that year and began a new settlement which was given the name Londonderry.[65]

The closing years of the eighteenth century saw the departure from Ulster of many people caught up in the radical politics of the day (see below). Some left in the years before the 1798 Rebellion, especially in 1797 when the government introduced repressive measures against the United Irishmen. They included several men from the Cullybackey area of County Antrim who went on to establish the Reformed Presbyterian Church in the United States. Others left in the aftermath of the rebellion, either banished by the authorities or fleeing on their own initiative. According to Rev. Dr William Campbell, a Presbyterian minister in the city of Armagh at the time of the rebellion, 'Presbyterians went in thousands to America, and if ships had been found, thousands more would have sought a peaceful asylum in that land of liberty'.[66]

Popular protest, the 1798 Rebellion and the Act of Union

Popular protests, many emanating from agrarian and religious grievances, were a recurring feature of the latter part of eighteenth-century Ulster. In the early 1760s the Hearts of Oak (also known as the Oak Boys or Green Boys) protested against such things as local taxes levied by the grand jury, the 'small dues' paid to the Church of Ireland clergy and the requirement to provide six days of labour towards road maintenance.[67] The movement was active in much of Ulster, though it was particularly strong in the southern half of the province. While the movement was religiously mixed, its leadership was predominantly Presbyterian. In some areas there was considerable animosity towards the clergy of the Church of Ireland. In 1766, Rev. Charles Humble, rector of Killeeshil parish, County Tyrone, described those involved in recent Hearts of Oak protests in his area as 'the Spawn of Scottish Covenanters, avowed enemies to all Civil and Religious Establishments, and the most violent and furious persecutors of the Established clergy during the late troubles in the North of Ireland'.[68] The Hearts of Steel was a Protestant movement of agrarian protest that originated on the Donegall estate in County Antrim over the general re-letting of farms in 1770. The movement spread to other parts of Ulster over the following two years, with the protests concentrating on rent levels, evictions and local taxation. Frequently these protests were violent and included the burning of houses and the maiming of livestock.

Influenced by the American and French Revolutions, some began to consider more radical solutions to what they believed were Ireland's problems. The Society of United Irishmen was founded in Belfast on 18 October 1791 by a group of mainly middle-class Presbyterians led by Dr William Drennan, son of a former minister of the First Presbyterian Church in the town. Soon afterwards clubs were founded in Dublin and a number of other places. The aims of the Society were parliamentary reform and the elimination of English interference in Irish matters. Following efforts to suppress it, the Society reorganised itself as a secret organisation and began to prepare for rebellion. In the aftermath of a failed French expedition in December 1796, the repressive measures taken by the government in 1797 severely weakened the United Irishmen in Ulster.

Rebellion began in Leinster in late May 1798. On the night of 6–7 June it spread to Ulster when a party of United Irishmen advanced into Larne and forced a contingent of government troops back to their barracks. Soon afterwards Ballymena and Randalstown were taken, but at Antrim Town the rebels were defeated. In County Down, following an initial success at Saintfield, the rebels were roundly defeated at nearby Ballynahinch on 12 June and the rebellion in Ulster was all but finished. There followed a series of executions including that of Rev. James Porter of Greyabbey, the only ordained minister of the Presbyterian Church to be put to death in what was widely regarded as a serious miscarriage of justice. One of the last to be hanged was the most famous Ulster rebel of them all, Henry Joy McCracken, a member of the Third Presbyterian Church, Belfast.[69]

Even before the rebellion had been fully suppressed, the government in London sent Lord Cornwallis to Ireland, delegating to him responsibility for forcing legislation through the Irish Parliament to bring about a union between Britain and Ireland. There was considerable opposition to this from the Irish elite, but eventually, after much lobbying, the Act of Union was passed in 1800, coming into effect on 1 January 1801. It was a defining moment in Irish history, though at the time one that meant little to the majority of Ulster's people, still recovering from the effects of the rebellion.

1   For a more detailed consideration of the province in this period, see Jonathan Bardon, *A History of Ulster* (Belfast, 1992); Raymond Gillespie, *Seventeenth-century Ireland: Making Ireland Modern* (Dublin, 2006); Ian McBride, *Eighteenth-century Ireland: The Isle of Slaves* (Dublin, 2009); and Liam Kennedy and Philip Ollerenshaw (eds), *Ulster Since 1600: Politics, Economy and Society* (2013). See also the chapters by Raymond Gillespie, 'Continuity and change: Ulster in the seventeenth century' and W. H. Crawford, 'The political economy of linen: Ulster in the eighteenth century' in Ciaran Brady, Mary O'Dowd and Brian Walker (eds), *Ulster: An Illustrated History* (London, 1989).

2   For a general background to the plantation, see Philip Robinson, *The Plantation of Ulster* (Dublin and New York, 1984).

3   For more on the Irish and the Plantation, see Gerard Farrell, *The 'Mere Irish' and the Colonisation of Ulster, 1570–1641* (Cambridge, 2017).

4   Settlement in Antrim and Down is considered in Raymond Gillespie, *Colonial Ulster* (Cork, 1985).

5   Michael Perceval-Maxwell, *The Scottish Migration to Ulster in the Reign of James I* (London, 1973), p. 48.

6   *Calendar of the State Papers Relating to Ireland, 1625–32*, p. 607.

7   P. J. Duffy, 'The evolution of estate properties in south Ulster, 1600–1900' in William J. Smyth and Kevin Whelan (eds), *Common Ground. Essays on the Historical Geography of Ireland* (Cork, 1988), p. 96.

8   Quoted in Raymond Gillespie, 'Faith, family and fortune: the structures of everyday life in early modern Cavan' in Raymond Gillespie (ed.), *Cavan. Essays on the History of an Irish County* (Blackrock, 1995), p. 113.

9   Robinson, *Plantation of Ulster*, p. 158.

10 PRONI, DIO/4/23/1/1.

11 R. J. Hunter, 'Plantation in Donegal' in William Nolan, Liam Ronayne, Mairead Dunlevy (eds), *Donegal: History and Society* (Dublin, 1995), p. 318.

12 For more on this subject, see Brian Mac Cuarta, *Catholic Revival in the North of Ireland, 1603–41* (Dublin, 2007).

13 For the early Presbyterian story in Ulster, see *Presbyterian History in Ireland: Two Seventeenth-Century Narratives*, edited by Robert Armstrong, Andrew Holmes, Scott Spurlock and Patrick Walsh (Belfast, 2016).

14   [Richard Head], *The English Rogue: Described, in the Life of Meriton Latroon* (London, 1665), p. 11.
15   NAI, Lodge MSS, viii, 130–131.
16   W. H. Crawford, 'Evolution of towns in County Armagh' in A. J. Hughes and William Nolan (eds), *Armagh: History and Society* (Dublin, 2001), p. 857.
17   John Hanly (ed.), *The Letters of Saint Oliver Plunkett, 1625–1681* (Dublin, 1979), p. 74.
18   Ibid., p. 75.
19   TCD, MS 883/1.
20   Hanly, *Letters*, pp 454–5.
21   J. B. Leslie, *Derry Clergy and Parishes* (Dundalk, 1937), p. 248.
22   Hanly, *Letters*, p. 226.
23   Ibid., p. 394.
24   Rankin Sherling, *The Invisible Irish: Finding Protestants in the Nineteenth-Century Migrations to America* (Montreal and Kingston, 2016), p. 105.
25   Private possession.
26   Patrick Fitzgerald, '"Black '97": reconsidering Scottish migration to Ireland in the seventeenth century and the Scotch Irish in America' in William Kelly and John Young (eds), *Ulster and Scotland, 1600–2000: History, Language and Identity* (Dublin, 2004), pp 71–84.
27   PRONI, DIO/4/29/2/1/2, no. 10.
28   P. J. Flanagan, 'The diocese of Clogher in 1714', *Clogher Record*, 1:2 (1954), p. 40.
29   PRONI, DIO/4/24/2/1.
30   W. H. Crawford, 'The reshaping of the borderlands, 1700–1840' in Raymond Gillespie and Harold O'Sullivan (eds), *The Borderlands. Essays on the History of the Ulster-Leinster Border* (Belfast, 1989), p. 95.
31   NAI, M 2533, fol. 408.
32   James Kelly (ed.), *The Letters of Lord Chief Baron Edward Willes to the Earl of Warwick, 1757–62* (Aberystwyth, 1990), p. 36.
33   PRONI, T3446/1
34   PRONI, D2918.
35   Cathaldus Giblin, 'Catalogue of Material of Irish Interest in the Collection Nunziatura di Fiandra, Vatican Archives: Part 5, vols. 123–132', *Collectanea Hibernica*, 9, (1966), p. 47.
36   PRONI, D580/34.
37   PRONI, MIC250/1.
38   McBride, *Eighteenth-century Ireland*, p. 291.
39   Kelly, *Letters of … Edward Willes*, pp 30–31.
40   For more on the linen industry, see W. H. Crawford, *The Impact of the Domestic Linen Industry in Ulster* (Belfast, 2005).
41   Crawford, 'The political economy of linen', p. 135.
42   Walter Harris, *The Antient and Present State of the County of Down* (Dublin, 1744), p. 108.
43   PRONI, T2521/3/1.
44   E. M. Johnston-Liik, *History of the Irish Parliament* (6 vols, Belfast, 2002), vol. 2, p. 308.
45   David Dickson, *Arctic Ireland: The Extraordinary Story of the Great Frost and Forgotten Famine of 1740–41* (Dundonald, 1997).
46   R. M. Young (ed.), *Historical Notices of Old Belfast and its Vicinity* (Belfast, 1896), p. 158.
47   PRONI, T2521/3/1.
48   Harris, *Antient and Present State of the County of Down*, p. 77.
49   Young, *Historical Notices*, p. 154.
50   Armagh Robinson Library, Physico-Historical Society Papers.
51   Martin Dowling, *Tenant Right and Agrarian Society in Ulster, 1600–1870* (Dublin, 1999), p. 136.

52 Harris, *Antient and Present State of the County of Down*, pp 49, 71, 95.
53 Graeme Kirkham, '"To pay the rent and lay up riches": economic opportunity in eighteenth-century north-west Ulster', in R. Mitchison and P. Roebuck (eds), *Economy and Society in Scotland and Ireland, 1500–1939* (Edinburgh, 1988), p. 97.
54 TCD, MS 1019.
55 The best introduction to this subject remains R. J. Dickson, *Ulster Emigration to Colonial America* (London, 1966).
56 For a summary of the discussion of the numbers of emigrants, see Patrick Fitzgerald and Brian Lambkin, *Migration in Irish History, 1607–2007* (Basingstoke, 2008), pp 123.
57 Patrick Griffin, *The People with No Name: Ireland's Ulster Scots, America's Scots Irish, and the creation of a British Atlantic World, 1689–1764* (Princeton, 2001), p. 83.
58 PRONI, D4108/1/14O.
59 PRONI, MIC170/2.
60 PRONI, MIC225/2.
61 Published in the *Pennsylvania Gazette*, 27 Oct. 1737.
62 PRONI, D2092/1/3.
63 PRONI, T2825/C/27/2.
64 PRONI, T808/15266.
65 Dickson, *Ulster Emigration to Colonial America*, pp 134–152.
66 Peter Gilmore, Trevor Parkhill and William Roulston, *Exiles of '98: Ulster Presbyterians and the United States* (Belfast, 2018), p. 220.
67 Eoin Magennis, 'A "Presbyterian Insurrection": reconsidering the Hearts of Oak disturbances of July 1763', *Irish Historical Studies*, 31 (1998), pp 165–87.
68 PRONI, T808/15266.
69 The best account of the Ulster story is A. T. Q. Stewart, *The Summer Soldiers: The 1798 Rebellion in Antrim and Down* (1995).

1. Introduction

The purpose of this book is to provide a practical guide for the family historian searching for ancestors in the province of Ulster in the seventeenth and eighteenth centuries. The need for this volume is obvious. Many people who have successfully researched their family history in the nineteenth and twentieth centuries find it difficult to take that research back before 1800. There is no denying that the loss of so many records in the destruction of the Public Record Office, Dublin, in 1922 was a catastrophe as far as historical and genealogical research is concerned. However, since 1922 the work of archivists to gather records of historical importance has resulted in a vast amount of material being available for the genealogical researcher to peruse. In addition, there are other repositories in Ireland, such as the Registry of Deeds in Dublin, where the collections have survived virtually intact, as well as categories of records now available that were not in the Public Record Office in 1922 and so escaped destruction.

This book is divided into two main sections. The first deals with the sources available to researchers and provides information on their significance and where they may be found. Some of these sources will be familiar to many genealogists, though others may not. The second part includes two major appendices, one listing in summary form the sources available for each parish in Ulster and the other providing information on over 350 estate collections with relevant material from the pre-1800 period. While I have tried to be as comprehensive as possible, I cannot claim to have covered every single record of genealogical interest from these centuries. Such an undertaking would require a multi-volume set rather than a single handbook. The book is undeniably skewed towards sources in PRONI, but it is here that the great majority of records relating to Ulster can be found. Nonetheless, I have noted records in repositories elsewhere in Ireland and occasionally in Britain and North America.

1.1 Getting started with research

Those who wish to carry out research into family history in Ulster in the period before 1800 can be divided into two categories. The first category comprises those who have been carrying out research on family members in the nineteenth and twentieth centuries, and who wish to extend their research by going back further generations. For others the pre-1800 period will be the starting point for the simple reason that their ancestor left Ulster prior to the nineteenth century.

As researchers are well aware, it is important to know not only the names of one's ancestors, but also the areas in which they lived. The ideal is to know the townland in which the ancestor lived or, if this is not available, the name of the parish (see below for explanations of Irish land divisions). However, for many people searching for pre-1800 families – and this usually applies to those in the second category outlined above – the only locational information they have is that their forebear was born somewhere in Ulster, or at best they may know the name of the county. There are obvious difficulties to be overcome here – not necessarily insurmountable, but considerable nonetheless. Ulster is a province of nine counties, some 350 parishes and thousands of townlands. To have any chance of success it is vital that the place of origin of an ancestor can be narrowed down to a specific area. A major obstacle in trying to do this is the fact that there is no comprehensive index to names from the seventeenth and eighteenth centuries, notwithstanding the increasing volume of material being made available online.

If the precise area an ancestor came from is not known, the nineteenth-century Householders' Index (also known as the Index of Surnames) may be helpful. This is based on information derived from the Tithe Valuation of 1823–38 and Griffith's Valuation of 1847–64. The Tithe Valuation lists the names of those paying tithes to support the Church of Ireland clergy (tithes were paid by those occupying tithable land – mainly tenant-farmers – regardless of the religious affiliation of the occupier). Griffith's Valuation is a much more comprehensive source for it lists the names of all occupiers of rateable property in Ireland. The Householders' Index lists surnames by parish, indicating the number of occurrences of a surname in Griffith's Valuation and simply whether or not it appears in the Tithe Valuation. Using the information in the Householders Index, it may be possible to narrow down the likely area your ancestor came from. It is particularly useful if it reveals that a surname was concentrated in a small number of parishes. Copies of the Householders Index are available in PRONI, the National Archives of Ireland, the National Library of Ireland and, for Ulster counties, on the website of the Ulster Historical Foundation (www.ancestryireland.com).

The most extensive single source from the pre-1800 period is the list of names of those who applied for flaxseed premiums in 1796 (see Chapter 5). This runs to over 56,000 names, over 36,000 of which relate to parishes in Ulster. While by no means comprehensive, it can be used as a guide to the distribution of surnames in the province in the late eighteenth century. The names in this source can be accessed via the Ulster Historical Foundation's website (www.ancestryireland.com/scotsinulster). Having identified the likely or even possible area from which an ancestor came, it will then be possible to focus on the sources that relate to that area. This book identifies those sources and shows you how to go about accessing them.

1.2 Background reading
Numerous publications are available that can assist with understanding more about tracing ancestors in Ireland or with uncovering additional information on a particular subject or geographical area. Some of the more valuable published resources are highlighted below.

Genealogy guides
A major resource for those researching Ulster ancestors is the multi-volume guide to sources compiled under the editorship of Richard Hayes. *Manuscript Sources for the History of Irish Civilisation* (1965) includes four volumes on persons, two each on subjects, places and dates, and a single volume containing a list of manuscripts. Places are arranged alphabetically within counties. Estate records and maps are also listed by county. Five years later there appeared *Sources for the History of Irish Civilisation: Articles in Irish Periodicals* (1970). This included five volumes on persons, three on subjects and a single volume covering places and dates. After a further nine years the *First Supplement, 1965–75* (1979) was published in three volumes. The information in these volumes has now been captured digitally and can be searched via the Sources Catalogue on the website of the National Library of Ireland (http://sources.nli.ie).

Many books on tracing ancestors in Ireland have been written. The best general guide is John Grenham's *Tracing Your Irish Ancestors* (4th edition, 2012). Grenham discusses the principal sources available for those wishing to find out more about their family history and has a county by county listing of relevant records and publications. A recent volume that provides much practical guidance is Claire Santry's *The Family Tree Irish Genealogy Guide: How to Trace Your Ancestors in Ireland* (2017). Margaret Falley's *Irish and Scotch-Irish Ancestral Research: A Guide to the Genealogical Records, Methods and Sources in Ireland* (1962) is a remarkable publication and, though first published over half a century ago, is still worth consulting for its vast amount of detail.

Other genealogical guides deal more closely with a specific area, period or theme. For example, Ian Maxwell is the author of two county guides published by the Ulster Historical Foundation: *Researching Armagh Ancestors* (2000) and *Researching Down Ancestors* (2004). Bill Macafee has produced *Researching Derry & Londonderry Ancestors* as a CD-ROM. Flyleaf Press has published *Tracing Your Donegal Ancestors* by Godfrey F. Duffy and Helen Meehan (2015). The North of Ireland Family History Society has issued guides in booklet form for several counties, including Cavan, Londonderry, Monaghan and Tyrone.

Books on the history of Ulster
Those wishing to read about the history of Ulster will find the following selection of books very helpful.

> Ciaran Brady, Mary O'Dowd and Brian Walker (eds), *Ulster: An Illustrated History* (1989), especially the chapters on the seventeenth and eighteenth centuries by, respectively, Raymond Gillespie and W. H. Crawford
> Jonathan Bardon, *A History of Ulster* (1992)
> Raymond Gillespie, *Seventeenth-century Ireland: Making Ireland Modern* (2006)
> Ian McBride, *Eighteenth-century Ireland: The Isle of Slaves* (2009)
> Liam Kennedy and Philip Ollerenshaw (eds), *Ulster Since 1600: Politics, Economy and Society* (2013)

County histories
The History and Society series of volumes produced by Dr Willie Nolan of Geography Publications is an excellent starting place for local studies. Eight of Ulster's nine counties have been published to date.

> *Armagh*, edited by A. J. Hughes and William Nolan (2001)
> *Cavan*, edited by Jonathan Cherry and Brendan Scott (2014)
> *Derry-Londonderry*, edited by Gerard O'Brien (1999)
> *Donegal*, edited by William Nolan, Liam Ronayne and Mairead Dunleavy (1995)
> *Down*, edited by Lindsay Proudfoot (1997)
> *Fermanagh*, edited by Eileen M. Murphy and William J. Roulston (2004)
> *Monaghan*, edited by Patrick J. Duffy and Eamon Ó Ciardha (2017)
> *Tyrone*, edited by Henry Jefferies and Charles Dillon (2000)

These volumes are hefty tomes, some of them running to upwards of 1,000 pages and containing as many as 30 chapters, each looking at a different aspect of the history of the county from prehistory to present. Other county histories are listed below.

County Down
Alexander Knox, *A History of the County of Down, from the Most Remote Period to the Present Day* (1875)
John Stevenson, *Two Centuries of Life in Down, 1600–1800* (1920)

County Fermanagh
Peadar Livingstone, *The Fermanagh Story: A Documented History of the County Fermanagh from the Earliest Times to the Present Day* (1969)

County Londonderry
J. W. Kernohan, *The County of Londonderry in Three Centuries: With Notices of the Ironmongers' Estate* (1921)

County Monaghan
E. P. Shirley, *The History of the County of Monaghan* (1879)
D. C. Rushe, *History of Monaghan for Two Hundred Years, 1660–1860* (1921, reprinted 1996)
Peadar Livingstone, *The Monaghan Story: A Documented History of the County Monaghan from the earliest times to 1976* (1980)

Local histories and journals
Many histories have been written of particular localities, especially at parish level, as well as individual congregations. These books, frequently based on local knowledge gained over a lifetime, can include information of inestimable value, such as details of individual families and place-names. Many local societies produce a journal on a regular basis and these can also be exceptionally useful for researchers. Genealogical journals include *Familia: Ulster Genealogical Review*, published by the Ulster Historical Foundation, *The Irish Genealogist*, issued by the Irish Genealogical Research Society, and *North Irish Roots* by the North of Ireland Family History Society. A number of local journals can now be accessed electronically via JSTOR. Appendix 1 of this book lists local publications by parish. The Federation for Ulster Local Studies acts as an umbrella organisation for local groups across the north of Ireland. Contact details for individual societies will be found on its website (www.fuls.org.uk).

1.3 Contemporary descriptive accounts
Descriptive accounts, such as the journals kept by travellers as they passed through the Ulster countryside, may not necessarily contain very much of genealogical value – though sometimes they do – but they can provide an insight into the natural and built environment in which our ancestors lived. A selection relating to Ulster is highlighted below. For a general survey of this material, see C. J. Woods, *Travellers' Accounts as Source-Material for Irish Historians* (2009).

Down Survey maps
The Down Survey maps were prepared in 1656–8 during the period in which the Cromwellians were in power. The surviving copies are available at county, barony and parish level. Collectively, the maps form the earliest detailed land survey of any country in the world. The name of the maps derives from the fact that information was mapped *down*. Since the purpose of the maps was to facilitate the redistribution of land forfeited by Catholics (mainly), the maps are most detailed for those areas that were in Catholic ownership prior to the

1641 uprising. Accompanying 'terriers' may provide a brief description of the featured area along with information on landownership and the quality of the land. Copies of the maps are available in various libraries and archives and what survives can now be accessed online (http://downsurvey.tcd.ie/index.html).

Pitt's English Atlas

A valuable set of descriptive accounts date from the 1680s and derive from an attempt, ultimately unrealised, to produce a volume for Ireland in Moses Pitt's *English Atlas* series. William Molyneux took on the task of writing a description of Ireland and he looked for information from well-informed individuals around the country. For example, Richard Dobbs of Castle Dobbs, near Carrickfergus, provided a description of County Antrim, while William Montgomery of Rosemount compiled an account of the Ards peninsula in County Down. The surviving papers relating to this venture are in Manuscripts & Archives Research Library of Trinity College Dublin (MS 883/1–2). Published extracts include:

> County Antrim – printed in George Hill, *The MacDonnells of Antrim* (1873), pp 377–89
>
> The barony of Oneilland, County Armagh – printed in *UJA*, 2nd series, 4 (1898), pp 239–41
>
> The barony of Ards, County Down – printed in R. M. Young (ed.), *Historical Notices of Old Belfast and its Vicinity* (1896); the author, William Montgomery, later updated his description (PRONI, D552/B/4/1/3A), which was published in the 1830 edition of *The Montgomery Manuscripts*; see also David B. Quinn, 'Description of Ards peninsula by William Montgomery of Rosemount in 1683 and 1701', *The Irish Book Lover*, 20 (March–April 1932), pp 28–32

Physico-Historical Society

In the 1730s and 1740s a number of societies were formed in Ireland to encourage the study of the natural history of the island. In part, these were a response to the ways in which Ireland was being misrepresented in publications emanating from Britain. One of these initiatives has been given the title 'Hibernia', though its actual name – if indeed it had any – is not known, and it led to the creation of the Physico-Historical Society in 1744. Plans to publish county surveys had only limited success, though two works by Walter Harris for County Down did appear: *A Topographical and Chorographical Survey of the County of Down* (1740); and its better known revision, *The Antient and Present State of the County of Down* (1744).

Many of the descriptive accounts of various parts of Ireland generated by 'Hibernia' as well as some of the records of the Physico-Historical Society are in Armagh Robinson Library (formerly Armagh Public Library). One particularly active contributor was Rev. William Henry, an Anglican clergyman in Fermanagh and later Tyrone, whose topographical descriptions are part of this collection. A typescript copy is in PRONI (T2521/3) and another version is available in the National Archives of Ireland (M 2533). Part of Henry's account was edited and published by C. S. King as *Henry's Upper Lough Erne in 1739* (1892, reprinted 1987); this was derived from a manuscript now in the British Library (Add. MS 4,436). For further reading, see Eoin Magennis, 'A land of milk and honey: the Physico-Historical Society, improvement and the surveys of mid-eighteenth-century Ireland', *PRIA*, 102C (2002), pp 199–217.

Other eighteenth-century descriptive accounts
A selection of other eighteenth-century descriptive accounts is set out below.

> Thomas Molyneux, 'Journey to the North, 7th August 1708' in
> *Historical Notices of Old Belfast and its Vicinity*, edited by R. M. Young
> (1896), pp 152–60
> A manuscript history of County Fermanagh, 1718–19, by J. or T.
> Dolan: very good on the families of the county – NLI, MS 2085
> (copy in PRONI, T1875/1 and printed in *Clogher Record* over several
> issues, 1955–62)
> Isaac Butler, 'A Journey to Lough Derg [1740s]', *JRSAI*, 22 (1892),
> pp 126–36
> *Pococke's Tour in Ireland in 1752*, edited by G. T. Stokes (1891)
> *The Letters of Lord Chief Baron Edward Willes to the Earl of Warwick,*
> *1757–62*, edited by James Kelly (1990)
> Arthur Young, *A Tour in Ireland*, 2 vols (1780): very good on
> agricultural improvement
> A journal of a tour through part of Ireland by Rev. Daniel Beaufort,
> 1787–8 – MIC250/1

1.4 The Internet

Over the last two decades and more the Internet has revolutionised genealogy. A vast amount of information relating to Irish family history is now available online. Some websites focus on a particular county and contain extensive lists of digitised sources, while others contain information on a specific family. Many genealogy websites provide information for free, while access to the data hosted on others is on a pay-per-view or subscription basis. To list all websites with genealogical material relating to Ulster would be impossible and has not been attempted in this book. The websites that have been referenced tend to be those of the major archives and libraries. Likewise the online resources cited are primarily those hosted by an official institution. That is not to deny the value of details hosted elsewhere, but researchers will be well aware that websites come and go and know the frustration of broken links. Probably the best way of finding potentially relevant information on the Internet, and in particular whether a manuscript source highlighted in this book has been digitised and made available online, is to use a search engine such as Google. Researchers should also consult Chris Paton's books: *Tracing Your Irish Family History on the Internet: A Guide for Family Historians* (2013) and *Irish Family History Resources Online* (2015).

A few of the most important online providers may be mentioned briefly. RootsIreland (www.rootsireland.ie), the website of the Irish Family History Foundation, has the most extensive collection of Irish church records online. These collections include a number of churches for which pre-1800 records survive. FamilySearch (www.familysearch.org) contains a vast amount of information drawn from a wide range of records. Among its most useful assets for researchers interested in the pre-1800 period is a set of digitised scans of the transcript and index volumes of the Registry of Deeds (see Chapter 7). The FamilySearch catalogue is a very helpful tool, especially for identifying records held in the Family History Library in Salt Lake City. Ancestry (www.ancestry.com) is the best known online provider of genealogical data and its Irish materials include scans of surviving issues of the *Belfast Newsletter* from 1738 onwards (see Chapter 12), as well as records of the Freemasons in Ireland (see Chapter 16). Findmypast Ireland (www.findmypast.ie) is another online provider with a range of sources including its database of Landed Estates Court Rentals, which can give details of leases issued prior to 1800 (see Chapter 6).

1.5 Surnames

The subject of surnames is a major one in its own right and only few general observations will be made here. Below some publications on surnames are highlighted and researchers should consider examining these in more detail. The importance of keeping as open a mind as possible on surnames when carrying out research in Ulster, or anywhere for that matter, cannot be overstated. This applies both to the spelling of the surname and its possible origin.

Spelling variations
With regard to spelling, it is essential to take into consideration all possible variants of a surname, especially when researching in an era in which there was an absence of standardisation in spelling. For one thing, if you find an ancestor's name it will nearly always have been written by someone else – a clergyman or the agent for a landed estate, for example – rather than by your ancestor or a member of the family. This individual may well have had a preferred spelling for the surname in question, which may or may not have been the same as that used by the family. It might also have been the case, and this particularly applies to names of Gaelic origin, that the scribe simply wrote the name down as it sounded to him. Even if a person was writing his or her own surname they may not have been consistent in spelling it, even in the same document. Within families, the preferred spelling could easily change over several generations. The spelling of the present writer's surname evolved from

Rolleston at the beginning of the nineteenth century to Roulston by the end of that same century.

Spelling variations can range from the very slight to the rather significant. However, even minor differences can have major implications when searching through indexes or using electronic databases. Some surnames have variants that are far from obvious. Pollock, for instance, has been rendered Poak, Poag, Poge, Pogue and Polk, to give a few alternative spellings. In 1699, Thomas Pollock of Castlewarren was appointed a churchwarden in Donagheady parish, County Tyrone, though he consistently spelled his surname Poge on the ten occasions that he signed the vestry book over the period 1699–1701 (MIC1/35). From 1773 there is a surviving abstract of a document relating to a 'John Pollock alias Poag' of Ballycor, County Antrim (T687/13). Among other examples, we find that in some parts of counties Armagh and Down the names Pentland and Pentleton were used interchangeably, as were Maitland/Metland and Mettleton. Surnames were also altered after a family left Ulster, sometimes less subtly than others. Examples include Hasty to Hastings, Mooney to Moodie and Robinson to Robertson. Often names were changed slightly to remove some of the 'Irishness' about them and to allow newcomers to better assimilate into the host population.

The Gaelic prefixes O and Mac, signify descent from a particular individual or family group. In the early 1600s especially it is not unusual to find the names of Gaelic Irishmen rendered in official documents in a format that highlights their recent ancestry. For example, the first party to a deed of 1623 was 'Rosse mc Owen mc Cooleboy mc Mahon' of Dromgrony, County Monaghan (D3465/A/1/3). During the course of the seventeenth and eighteenth centuries the O and Mac were dropped in many instances so that, for example, O'Donnell became Donnell and O'Neill became Neill (this does not mean, however, that everyone called Donnell or Neill descends from an O'Donnell or an O'Neill). When it is used, the prefix 'Mac' can be found in a variety of forms, including Mc, Mack, Mck, Me and M'. Gaelic Irish names can include epithets that signify a personal characteristic, such as Roe from *ruadh*, the Irish for red (as in Owen Roe O'Neill, commander of the Irish forces in the 1640s).

Surname origins

Some caution must always be exercised in attributing a geographical origin to a name, i.e. whether it is of English, Scottish or Irish derivation. A great many names that appear to be from Britain may in fact be anglicised forms of Irish names. Some Irish surnames can be anglicised completely; for example, in some instances McShane (meaning 'son of John') became Johnson. The name Smith can be an anglicisation of McGowan (*Mac Gabhann*), which means 'son or descendant of the smith'. Other anglicised renderings of surnames have little in common with their original form, whether in pronunciation or translation. The common name Bradley, though undoubtedly of English origin in some instances, is generally an anglicisation of O'Brallaghan (*Ó Brollacháin*). Eighteenth-century documents for the Abercorn estate in north-west Ulster reveal that in this region the name Lynch is a shortened form of Lynchaghan (itself spelled in numerous ways), which derives from the Irish name *Mac Loingseacháin*.

It must also be borne in mind that the same name could have two or more entirely different and independent origins. A name like Cunningham might appear to be very obviously Scottish and many Cunninghams are known to have moved to Ulster during the 1600s. However, Cunningham might also be an anglicisation of several Irish names, including *Mac Donnagáin,* which initially became McCunigan before being rendered Cunningham. Families of French Protestant refugees known as Huguenots arrived in Ulster in some numbers in the late seventeenth century and many of them settled in and around Lisburn in County Antrim. However, there is the temptation to ascribe a Huguenot origin to even a vaguely French-sounding name when this might not be the case.

Surname distribution

The study of the distribution of surnames can assist in understanding more about the people of a locality as well as the story of how a particular surname fits into that overall picture. The seventeenth century is particularly interesting in this regard for not only did it witness the large-scale movement of families from Britain into Ulster, the disruption arising from the various wars and land settlements resulted in the displacement of many Irish families from one part of the province to another. As a result of this, surnames associated historically with a particular region ended up in an entirely different area. For instance, Rev. Hugh O'Donnell, who was parish priest of Belfast from 1770 to 1814, was not from the traditional O'Donnell homeland of County Donegal, but rather was from Glore, near Glenarm, on the east coast of County Antrim.

The concentration of names from a clearly defined area in Britain in a specific part of Ulster also tells us something of the nature of the immigration of families to the north of Ireland and can help to explain subsequent developments in the region in which they settled. One of the best examples of this is Fermanagh where, in 1963, three of the top five names – Armstrong, Elliott and Johnston – were from the the western and middle marches of England and Scotland. The historical connections between the Glens of Antrim and the Highlands and Islands of Scotland are reflected in some of the names in the former, such as McAllister and McCambridge. For less certain reasons, several names associated with the area around Loch Lomond in Scotland, such as Buchanan, Colhoun, Galbraith and McFarland, can be found in some numbers in west County Tyrone.

Publications on surnames

Books on Irish surnames include Edward MacLysaght's *The Surnames of Ireland* (1969, numerous reprints), considered to be the standard reference work on this subject, as well as his volumes, *Irish Families* (1957), *More Irish Families* (1960) and *Supplement to Irish Families* (1964). An earlier work of interest is Patrick Woulfe, *Sloinnte Gaedheal is Gall ((Irish Names and Surnames)* (1923, reprinted 2014). For the north of Ireland, see Robert Bell, *Book of Ulster Surnames* (1988, several reprints). The most comprehensive recent work is *The Oxford Dictionary of Family Names in Britain and Ireland* (4 vols, 2016), which provides details on over 45,000 names. Given the preponderance of Scottish names in Ulster, George F. Black's *Surnames of Scotland* (1946, several reprints) ought to be consulted.

Many local histories include a section on the surnames of a particular locality. The first serious studies of Ulster surnames were those carried out by Abraham Hume on counties Antrim and Down, which appeared in the *Ulster Journal of Archaeology*, first series, in 1857 and 1858. More recently, useful studies of surnames can be found in Peadar Livingstone's *Fermanagh Story* (1969) and *Monaghan Story* (1980). The many surname studies by Brian Turner are worth perusing. Some of his explorations of names in the Glens of Antrim can be read in *The Glynns*, the journal of the Glens of Antrim Historical Society. Of his other studies, his work on settler names in Fermanagh was published in *Clogher Record* (1975) and reprinted in *Familia* (1992), and is also available as a folding map, *Surname Landscape in the County of Fermanagh* (2002).

1.6 Place-names and land divisions

Visitors to this island often remark on – and are frequently mystified by – the number and great variety of place-names that they encounter. There is no doubt that our heritage of place-names is one of the most enriching legacies that have been passed down to us by earlier generations. Ireland is divided into multiple categories of land divisions, some overlapping, but others sub-divisions of larger areas. The origins of place-names derive from many sources – predominantly Gaelic Irish, but also English and Scottish, among others – and their meanings can tell us much about the character and history of a locality. What follows is a basic guide to the place-names and land divisions found in Ulster.

County

To begin with, Ulster is one of four provinces in Ireland, the others being Connacht, Leinster and Munster. It comprises nine of the 32 counties on this island: Antrim, Armagh, Cavan, Donegal, Down, Fermanagh, Londonderry, Monaghan and Tyrone. The origins of the county as a territorial unit can be traced to the period following the arrival of the Normans in Ireland in the late twelfth century. However, it was not until the early seventeenth century that the network of counties was finalised. A number of counties in Ulster can be correlated with the lordships of the leading Irish families in pre-Plantation times. For instance, the lordships of the O'Donnells, Maguires, McMahons and O'Reillys, became the basis of, respectively, the counties of Donegal, Fermanagh, Monaghan and Cavan.

The last Ulster county to be created was Londonderry, the boundaries of which were settled in 1613. This county was an amalgam of the earlier county of Coleraine, the barony of Loughinsholin, which had previously been part of County Tyrone, a portion of County Antrim adjoining the east side of the River Bann (focused on Coleraine), and a portion of County Donegal adjoining the west side of the River Foyle (focused on Derry). The county's name derived from the involvement of the London livery companies in its development under the terms of the scheme for the Ulster Plantation.

The county was an important unit in local administration, being the basis of the grand jury system (see Chapter 9). In addition, during the period covered by this book each county returned two MPs to the Irish House of Commons. Counties remain the basis of local government in the Republic of Ireland, but no longer have any administrative role in Northern Ireland, though they remain important markers of identity. Books relating to counties were noted above.

Barony

Each county was divided into a number of baronies. These were based to a large extent on earlier Gaelic land divisions. A number of baronies were subdivided to make them more manageable as units of administration. For example, Dungannon barony was divided into Upper, Middle and Lower, while the huge barony of Iveagh in County Down was divided into Upper and Lower, with these subdivisions in turn split into smaller areas (e.g. Lower Iveagh, Upper Half). Baronies no longer have any administrative function.

Diocese

The creation of a network of dioceses in Ireland was the product of the twelfth-century reforms of the Irish church. Each diocese was divided into a number of parishes (see below). The diocesesan structures created at this time continue to be used by both the Church of Ireland and Roman Catholic Church. Each diocese is headed by a bishop, though two or more dioceses have been held by the same individual simultaneously. In addition to their religious significance, it is important to note that prior to 1858 testamentary affairs were dealt with primarily at diocesan level (see Chapter 8).

Nearly all of the province of Ulster is divided between eight dioceses. They are:

Armagh – covering nearly all of County Armagh and portions of counties
  Londonderry and Tyrone

Clogher – covering all of County Monaghan, most of County Fermanagh, and portions of counties Donegal and Tyrone

Connor – covering nearly all of County Antrim, a portion of County Londonderry and a very small area in County Down

Derry – covering most of County Londonderry and portions of counties Donegal and Tyrone

Down – found almost entirely within County Down, with a tiny portion in County Antrim

Dromore – found mainly in County Down with small portions in counties Antrim and Armagh

Kilmore – covering most of County Cavan and a portion of County Fermanagh

Raphoe – found entirely within County Donegal

It should be noted that several of these dioceses extend beyond Ulster. Armagh, for example, includes nearly all of County Louth, while Kilmore takes in a large area of County Leitrim. In addition to the above dioceses, three parishes in County Cavan are in the diocese of Ardagh and another three parishes in this county are in the diocese of Meath. Appendix 1 lists the diocese for each parish in Ulster.

Several detailed diocesan histories have been published, usually written primarily from the perspective of the Catholic Church. The outstanding example of the genre is James O'Laverty, *A Historical Account of the Diocese of Down and Connor* (5 vols, 1878–95). Others include Edward Maguire, *A History of the Diocese of Raphoe* (2 vols, 1920); James E. McKenna, *Diocese of Clogher: Parochial Records* (2 vols, 1920), Phillip O'Connell, *The Diocese of Kilmore: Its History and Antiquities* (1937); Liam Kelly, *The Diocese of Kilmore, c.1100–1800* (2017); Henry A. Jefferies and Ciaran Devlin (eds), *History of the Diocese of Derry from Earliest Times* (2000); and Henry A. Jefferies (ed.), *History of the Diocese of Clogher* (2005). A very helpful book on the diocese of Clogher is Patrick J. Duffy, *Landscapes of South Ulster: A Parish Atlas of the Diocese of Clogher* (1993).

Parish
The development of the territorial division of the parish had its origins in the twelfth-century reforms of the Irish church which, as noted above, had resulted in the creation of diocesan structures across the island. The size of parishes varied quite considerably. Parishes tended to be smaller in those areas most strongly influenced by the Anglo-Normans in the medieval period and larger in regions controlled by Gaelic lords. The quality of the land also had a major influence on parish size, with mountainous parishes of greater extent than those in low-lying areas.

Following the Reformation, the Protestant Church of Ireland took over and largely retained the existing network of parishes. There was a suggestion in the early seventeenth century that each parish should correspond with a Plantation manor, which would have resulted in a major redrawing of parish boundaries, but in the end this proposal was not carried out. Some alterations to the parish network were made, however, and a number of new parishes were created out of one or more existing parishes. Occasionally a parish was increased in size by attaching to it an area from a neighbouring parish. In addition, a few parishes, such as Drumcaw in County Down, disappeared altogether as they were merged with a neighbouring parish. Appendix 1 of this book provides information on the creation of new parishes and the fate of those that ceased to exist.

During the period covered by this book, the parish also had a civil function as an arm of local government, hence the term civil parish. The parish vestry was tasked with ensuring that particular areas of responsibility, such as road maintenance, were carried out effectively (see Chapter 2). When the Catholic Church began its institutional re-emergence in the late eighteenth and early nineteenth centuries, it did not always build its parochial structures on earlier foundations. Therefore, researchers should be aware that Catholic parishes do not necessarily equate with civil/Church of Ireland parishes.

As noted already, parishes are subdivisions of dioceses. However, parishes were never designed to be subdivisions of counties and so while most parishes will be found entirely within a single county, a number will straddle a county boundary. Urney parish, for example, is divided between counties Donegal and Tyrone, while Kinawley is partly in Cavan and partly in Fermanagh. Parishes can also be divided between two or more baronies. To take Kinawley again, the Cavan portion is in the barony of Tullyhaw, while the Fermanagh portion is split between the baronies of Clanawley and Knockninny. While nearly all parishes are compact units of land, several include outlying portions. Newry parish, for example, includes several small outlying areas in counties Armagh and Down.

Townland

The townland is a land division that is unique to Ireland. The townland system has been in existence for hundreds of years and continues to be important for local identity, especially in rural areas. The first thing to note about townlands is that they do not necessarily contain urban settlements. The word has its origins in the Old English word 'tun', meaning farmstead or settlement. By the early nineteenth century 'townland' had become a general term for a number of local words for small units of land. For instance, in Cavan the term used was 'poll', while in Fermanagh and Monaghan it was 'tate', with 'ballyboe' used across much of the rest of Ulster.

Across Ireland as a whole there are over 60,000 townlands, of which some 16,000 are in Ulster. Their average size is approximately 300–350 acres, though this varies from 172 acres in County Monaghan to 457 acres in County Down. Generally speaking, the acreage of a townland depends on the quality of the land, so that in upland areas townlands will be much larger, occasionally extending to several thousand acres. Conversely, in low-lying areas townlands may be less than 100 acres. The smallest townland in Ulster is Old Church Yard in the parish of Termonmaguirk, which extends to just over half of one acre. As its name suggests, it is an old graveyard, in fact the site of the medieval parish church.

Townlands are entities in their own right and are not subdivisions of counties, baronies or parishes. Therefore, while most townlands will be found in their entirety within these larger land divisions, a proportion will be divided between two or more of them. For instance, more than half a dozen townlands in the parish of Ballymoney are split between counties Antrim and Londonderry. The townland of Dundooan in County Londonderry is divided between three parishes: Ballyaghran, Ballywillin and Coleraine.

The earliest opportunity to examine the network of townlands in several Ulster counties is provided by the maps prepared under the direction of Sir Josias Bodley in 1609. Prior to the implementation of the Plantation scheme the government was interested in finding out how much land was available for distribution. Bodley was commissioned to visit Ulster and interview knowledgeable local people. The maps were then prepared on the basis of this information. They survive for Armagh, Cavan, Fermanagh and Tyrone (which at that time included the barony of Loughinsholin, soon to be detached from it and added to the new county of Londonderry). These maps were used as the basis for allocating lands to the various categories of grantee. Though deficient in some respects, they provide a fascinating insight into the townland system over a large part of the province at the beginning of the seventeenth century.

Since the seventeenth century there have been a number of alterations to the townland system in Ulster. To begin with, many townlands were subdivided into smaller units. They perhaps simply acquired a descriptive qualifier, often based on geography – such as North and South, Upper and Lower, East and West – or the characteristics of the population – such as Scotch and Irish – though on other occasions entirely new names emerged. In addition to the creation of new townlands, some places known to have existed in the seventeenth and eighteenth centuries disappeared as they were amalgamated with or subsumed within other townlands. Others were renamed, with the new name bearing little resemblance to the original. In the parish of Donagheady, County Tyrone, Mountcastle was formerly known as Ardnegloy or Ardugboy, Ballyheather was Falnasloy, while Sandville was Altnagalloglagh.

Townlands are important for genealogists for a number of reasons. They were crucial location identifiers for individuals and families across Ulster for centuries (and still are in many rural areas, especially in the Republic of Ireland). In church registers, newspaper advertisements, and gravestone inscriptions, to name a few, the address given for a particular individual or family will usually be the townland of residence. Landed estates were composed of blocks of townlands and farms were the subdivisions of those townlands (unless the townland comprised a single farm). Some 'census substitutes' of the seventeenth and eighteenth centuries, such as the hearth money rolls of the 1660s, recorded names by townland. Many immigrants in the New World named their homesteads after their townland of origin. For some examples of mainly Donegal place-names in Colonial Maryland, see the article by John F. Polk in *DIFHR*, 40 (2017), pp 24–5.

The meanings of townland names reflect many different things, including local geography, family names, animals, plants and folklore. 'Bally' is the most frequently met with prefix for a townland name and can be translated as 'place' or even simply as 'townland'. Other popular prefixes include Derry (oak wood), Kil/Kill (church), Knock (hill), Drum (ridge) and Gort (field). A number of townlands include an attached surname. Clady (known in earlier times as Altaclady) in Ardstraw parish, County Tyrone, is a good example of this. Originally a single unit of land, it is now five townlands, each with a surname attached: Clady Blair, Clady Haliday, Clady Hood, Clady Johnston and Liscreevaghan or Clady Sproul. It seems likely that these names derived from families resident in each of these divisions of Clady.

It is also important to acknowledge that numerous 'unofficial' place-names are found within townlands. Often these subdenominational names apply to a farm or even a field and may have been acquired in the post 1600 period, though others have a medieval origin. They often include a personal name element. By way of example, the following list concerns a selection of the minor place-names found in the historic parish of Ahoghill (now also including the parishes of Craigs and Portglenone), County Antrim.

> Allanstown (in Drumramer townland)
> Burnetstown (Ballylummin)
> Dobbinstown (Ballybollen)
> Dugganstown (Killygarn)
> Finlaystown (Mullinsallagh)
> Hamillstown (Killygarn)
> Heanystown (Craignageeragh)
> Hillistown (Casheltown)
> Hiltonstown (Tullynahinnion)
> Kylestown (Garvaghy)
> McDowellstown (Carninny)
> McKeestown (Ballyminstra)

It will be clear that a study of all of the place-name evidence for a locality can be potentially of great genealogical value. A database of unofficial/ subdenominational place-names in the six counties of Northern Ireland is available on the website of the Ulster Historical Foundation.

Books and online resources on place-names
A very helpful introduction to this subject area is Patrick McKay, *A Dictionary of Ulster Place-Names* (2nd edition, 2007), which includes information on the derivation and meaning of some 1,300 places in the province. Usefully, the book includes an index of place-name elements and a bibliography. Another book worth consulting is Deirdre and Laurence Flanagan, *Irish Place Names* (1994). The Northern Ireland Place-Name Project at Queen's University Belfast was responsible for publishing a series of volumes between 1992 and 2004 providing detailed information on place-names in various parts of Northern Ireland. These were:

Vol. 1: County Down I: Newry and South-West Down
Vol. 2: County Down II: The Ards
Vol. 3: County Down III: The Mournes
Vol. 4: County Antrim I: The Baronies of Toome
Vol. 5: County Derry I: The Moyola Valley
Vol. 6: County Down IV: North-West Down/Iveagh
Vol. 7: County Antrim II: Ballycastle and North-East Antrim
Vol. 8: County Fermanagh I: Lisnaskea and District: The Parish of
    Aghalurcher

A further volume is Patrick McKay and Kay Muhr, *Lough Neagh Places: Their Names and Origins* (2007). These volumes are very helpful in that they list the variant spellings of the place-name found in a range of sources from the medieval period to the twentieth century. While townlands occupy the greater proportion of these books, attention is also given to minor place-names. These volumes can provide information of a genealogical nature. For example, Folly Hill, or Folly Brae, in the parish of Ballyscullion, County Londonderry, is noted as having been the name of a large house built by two men named Rankin around 1750, the ruins of which were cleared away about 1820.

In addition to the above published books, the information gathered by the Northern Ireland Place-Name Project can be accessed online (www.placenamesni.org). Given their importance as markers of local identity, many local histories devote at least some space to a discussion of the townlands found in their district. Mention should also be made of the the Ulster Place-Name Society and its journal, *Ainm*.

1.7 Archives and libraries on the island of Ireland
This book has collated research materials from a wide range of archives and libraries. By far the most important of these for those researching Ulster ancestors is the Public Record Office of Northern Ireland in Belfast. Other records exist in repositories elsewhere in Northern Ireland, as well as in the rest of the United Kingdom, the Republic of Ireland, and further afield. Appendix

3 includes contact information for the archives and libraries referred to in this book. A very helpful guide to institutions of interest on the island of Ireland is Robert K. O'Neill, *Irish Libraries, Archives, Museums and Genealogical Centres: A Visitors' Guide* (3rd edition, 2013), which provides a brief summary of the collections held. Up to date information on access arrangements will be found on the institutions' websites. What follows is a brief summary of the main archives and libraries on this island.

1.7.1 Northern Ireland

Public Record Office of Northern Ireland
The Public Record Office of Northern Ireland (PRONI) is one of the best regional archives in the world. One of the main features of the documentary collections is the fact that they cover both public (i.e. official) and private records Furthermore, PRONI's holdings of private records include documentation for not just Northern Ireland, but for the entire province of Ulster and further afield. Of great value for genealogists is the huge collection of church records for all of the major religious denominations in Ulster. In addition, there are thousands of documents relating to the management of the great landed estates, as well as records relating to local government and businesses, among many others. These record categories are discussed in more detail in this book.

Genealogical collections form an important element within PRONI's holdings. The papers of Tenison Groves, purchased by PRONI in 1939 and running to over 9,000 items, form the largest collection of genealogical notes in the archive (T808). The value of this collection lies in the fact that it contains a vast amount of information derived from documents in the Public Record Office of Ireland prior to its destruction in 1922. The Groves collection is, for example, the best single source in PRONI for abstracts of pre-1858 wills. In addition to wills, the Groves collection includes muster rolls, militia lists, collectors' accounts, gravestone inscriptions, numerous abstracts from the Registry of Deeds, and extracts from court cases. The genealogical material on families in the Groves collection has been arranged roughly by surname starting with the same letter. The arrangement under each letter is not strictly alphabetical and material on the same surname can appear in several volumes. The one drawback for the researcher is that Groves's handwriting is almost indecipherable in places. Fortunately, many of his notes were typed.

PRONI has catalogued genealogical material deposited by those who have commissioned or carried out research into their ancestry under reference D3000. This material includes a broad range of items, including pedigrees, transcripts of original documents and detailed family histories. For example, D3000/1/1 comprises notes from 'Francis Shaw's Bible', recording, among other things, deaths of the Shaw family of Carnmoney parish, County Antrim,

1770–1811. The antiquarian and genealogical papers of Rev. David Stewart were catalogued under reference D1759 (now microfilmed with reference MIC637). These include many transcripts of Presbyterian records, as well as extensive notes on families, with a particular focus on County Down. Other genealogical collections include those assembled by Francis Crossle and his son Philip, which have a particular focus on Newry, County Down (T618, T699, T780, T845, T1046, T1689, etc).

With regard to the referencing system used by PRONI, a record prefixed D is an original document from a private (i.e. not governmental) collection, while T is the prefix for transcriptions or copies of private documents. MIC refers to microfilms, while CR is the prefix for original church records. Various prefixes are used for official records, e.g. LA for local authority records and HOS for hospital records. For preservation reasons a number of PRONI's collections of original records have been microfilmed. For example, the Dobbs Papers, catalogued under reference D162, are now closed and researchers should use MIC533. It is important, however, to have the original reference in order to find the item of interest on the microfilm.

Many of PRONI collections have been catalogued in some detail and the information in its once voluminous paper catalogues is now available electronically via the institution's eCatalogue (www.nidirect.gov.uk/services/search-ecatalogue). The PRONI website includes a number of databases, some of which are of particular relevance for those researching ancestors in the pre-1800 period. These include the database of Freeholders' Records listing those who registered to vote (see Chapter 10), and the Name Search database, which includes, among other items, a number of eighteenth-century 'census substitutes' (see Chapter 5). The relevant sections in this book provide further information on these resources. For many of the larger collections, especially those relating to landed estates, there are detailed introductions, many of them prepared by a former Director of PRONI, Dr Anthony Malcomson, the acknowledged authority on landed families in the eighteenth century. These introductions can be downloaded from the PRONI website. Finally, mention should also be made of the *Deputy Keeper's Reports* produced by PRONI. These include much valuable information on collections deposited in the archive and are worth consulting. A set of these reports is available in the Search Room.

Presbyterian Historical Society of Ireland

The Presbyterian Historical Society of Ireland was founded in 1907 to promote public awareness of the history of the various strands of Presbyterianism in Ireland. Once described as a 'Treasure House of Ulster's History', the Library of the Presbyterian Historical Society contains some 12,000 books and pamphlets, with a large number of congregational histories. Manuscript materials include session minutes, baptisms and marriages from individual congregations. These include, for example, the session book of Aghadowey

Presbyterian Church for the period 1702–61. Other items on deposit include administrative records, such as presbytery minutes, and some diaries and notebooks kept by Presbyterian ministers. The PHSI also has a duplicate set of the microfilm copies of Presbyterian registers held by PRONI covering the vast majority of congregations in Ireland.

Libraries NI
The network of public libraries across Northern Ireland is managed by Libraries NI. Most libraries have a local studies section with significant heritage collections in the libraries in Armagh, Ballymena, Belfast, Derry, Downpatrick, Enniskillen, Newry and Omagh and in the Mellon Centre for Migration Studies at the Ulster American Folk Park, near Omagh, County Tyrone.

Mellon Centre for Migration Studies
Not only is the Mellon Centre for Migration Studies (MCMS) a library within Libraries NI, it is an important institution for the study of the processes of migration in Ireland and contains an excellent collection of publications relating to this subject. MCMS has been responsible for creating the Irish Emigration Database, which contains some 32,500 primary source documents on all aspects of Irish emigration from the early 1700s to the 1900s. The Irish Emigration Database is now available online (www.dippam.ac.uk).

Linen Hall Library
The Linen Hall Library was founded in 1788 as the Belfast Reading Society and is the oldest library in Belfast. Its genealogical collection includes a large number of published family histories. Among its manuscript holdings are the Joy Manuscripts, which contain much information about the early history of Belfast. A former president of the library, Reginald Walter Henry Blackwood, was a very keen genealogist and his collection of pedigrees, running to 94 volumes of handwritten family trees with a separate index, is on deposit. (Microfilm copies of the pedigrees are available at PRONI (MIC315).)

Other institutions
The city of Armagh is particularly well served in terms of institutions with important collections of genealogical interest. Armagh Robinson Library (fomerly Armagh Public Library) has a vast library of books as well as manuscript records, including documentation concerning the corporation of Armagh in the eighteenth century. The Cardinal Tomás Ó Fiaich Memorial Library & Archive is the official repository for the Catholic archdiocese of Armagh. The library in Armagh County Museum includes a huge collection of materials relating to County Armagh assembled by the first curator and renowned antiquarian, T. G. F. Paterson. Newry and Mourne Museum in

Bagenal's Castle, Newry, County Down, holds the Reside Collection, which includes documents dating back to the early 1700s. Another valuable genealogical collection can be found in the library in Newtownabbey maintained by the North of Ireland Family History Society.

1.7.2 Republic of Ireland

National Archives of Ireland

Established in 1988 through the amalgamation of the Public Record Office of Ireland and the State Paper Office in Dublin Castle, the National Archives of Ireland (NAI) is the official repository of governmental records relating to the Republic of Ireland. Of particular interest for those researching ancestors prior to 1800 will be the records deriving from the former State Paper Office, such as the Rebellion Papers (see Chapter 9). The National Archives also holds a large collection of privately-deposited records, including business records and the working papers of genealogists, such as Gertrude Thrift. The Thift Collection covers the period from the 1500s to the early 1900s and includes extracts from wills, parish registers and court records, many of which were lost in 1922, as well as family trees. At present there is no single comprehensive catalogue of the records held by NAI, though a catalogue relating to some collections is available on the institution's website (www.nationalarchives.ie). A number of important sets of records, several of which are of particular interest to those carrying out research on Ulster families in the seventeenth and eighteenth centuries, can be searched on its website (www.genealogy.nationalarchives.ie).

National Library of Ireland

The National Library of Ireland was created under the terms of the Dublin Science and Art Museum Act of 1877. In addition to a huge collection of books and printed materials, the National Library holds an extensive collection of manuscripts. These include papers relating to the management of landed estates in Ireland, a proportion of which are concerned with properties in Ulster. The National Library's website hosts two important catalogues: the Main Catalogue (http://catalogue.nli.ie) and the Sources Catalogue (http://sources.nli.ie), the latter of which includes information derived from the abovementioned multi-volume guide compiled under the editorship of a former director of the institution, Richard Hayes: *Manuscript Sources for the History of Irish Civilisation* (plus subsequent volumes). Detailed catalogues for many individual sets of manuscripts, among them estates papers, can also be downloaded from the National Library's website. The Newsplan database, providing information on Irish newspapers, can also be accessed through the National Library's website (see Chapter 12).

Genealogical Office
The Office of the Ulster King of Arms was established in 1552 and is the oldest office of state in Ireland. It passed to the control of the Irish government in 1943, since when it has been known as the Genealogical Office. It is now a department of the National Library of Ireland. Although, as might be expected, the landed gentry and aristocracy feature prominently, the information held by the Genealogical Office is not limited to the elite in Irish society. For an in-depth look at the Genealogical Office and its sources researchers should consult *Guide to the Genealogical Office, Dublin* (1998), published by the Irish Manuscripts Commission. This includes a listing of the manuscripts (numbered 1 to 822) and an index to some 7,500 will abstracts in the Office. Also very helpful is chapter 7 in John Grenham's *Tracing Your Irish Ancestors* (4th edition, 2012). A 'Consolidated Index to the Records of the Genealogical Office' in four volumes was prepared by Virginia Wade McAnlis and can be downloaded from the website of the National Library of Ireland. For a historical survey of the institution, see Susan Hood, *Royal Roots, Republican Inheritance: The Survival of the Office of Arms* (2002).

Registry of Deeds
The Registry of Deeds in Henrietta Street, Dublin, opened in 1708 as a repository for all kinds of documents relating to the transfer of title to land. Unlike other archives in Ireland, its records are intact. It will be of particular value for those searching for farming ancestors before 1800 and is the subject of Chapter 7 of this book.

County libraries and archives
In the Republic of Ireland the local library network is maintained by each county council. Johnston Central Library in Cavan Town has the best collection of materials for local studies in County Cavan. Central Library in Letterkenny houses the main local studies/family history collection for County Donegal. For County Monaghan the local studies collection is based in Clones Library. Many county councils in the Republic of Ireland provide an archives service. Donegal County Archives is based in Lifford and has a particularly strong collection of records relating to the grand jury going back to the mid eighteenth century. The Cavan County Archives Service is located at the abovementioned Johnston Central Library. Documentary materials for Monaghan can be found in the County Museum in Monaghan Town.

1.8 Repositories in Britain

This section does not attempt to provide an in-depth exploration of documentation in repositories in England, Scotland and Wales, but rather it seeks to draw attention to the possibilities that exist for researchers in archives in Britain. With many of these institutions now having online catalogues it is possible to carry out preliminary searches for families from Ulster before visiting the archives in person. A book worth consulting is *British Sources for Irish History, 1485–1641*, compiled and edited by Brian Donovan and David Edwards (Irish Manuscripts Commission, 1997).

1.8.1 England and Wales

The National Archives (TNA) in Kew, London, is the official archive of the United Kingdom government and of England and Wales. In addition, there are hundreds of other local authority, university, institutional, business and private archives. A major resource with which researchers should become familiar is the Discovery catalogue (http://discovery.nationalarchives.gov.uk). This vast database includes listings of archival materials from repositories across the UK and beyond, as well as records, such as wills, that can be downloaded from from TNA. The Discovery catalogue also includes details of over 2,500 repositories across the UK.

Church registers

English church registers can occasionally include references to individuals and families from Ulster. Many early parish registers in England have been published and can now be read online at Archive.org. Some entries from the registers of St Nicholas's Church, Liverpool, are noted here by way of example of the type of information that exists (see *The Earliest Registers of the Parish of Liverpool (St Nicholas's Church)* ... (Lancashire Parish Register Society, 1909)). In April 1687 the burial took place of Thomas Wright, who, according to the register, had been 'borne in Southworth neare Winwick in Lankeshire but lived in Larne in the North of Ireland'. During the Williamite War (1689–91) Liverpool was a place of refuge for families fleeing the conflict in Ireland. This is reflected in an increased number of Irish entries in the registers of this period. These include the baptism of Thomas, son of Rev. Thomas Ward, dean of Carrickfergus, in September 1689, and the burial of Margaret, wife of Alexander Tompkins of Londonderry, in January 1690. Marriages involving individuals from Ulster are also recorded. In December 1702 Thomas Hill of the 'oyle of Mackgee [Islandmagee] in the county of Anthrem in the kingdom of Ireland' married Mary Allen of Liverpool, a widow, while in January 1704, James Martland of 'Olderfleeft [Olderfleet, Larne] married Mary Hill of Moore Street, Liverpool.

Law and order

Court records in Britain can be a fruitful source of information on persons from Ulster. Records relating to the Old Bailey in London survive from the 1670s onwards. The Old Bailey Proceedings, which contain accounts of trials, begin in 1674, while the Ordinary of Newgate's Accounts exist for the period 1676–1772. A digitised set of these records is available online (www.oldbaileyonline.org). Cases involving people from Ulster regularly came before the court. The following extracts provide an indication of the type of information that can be found. The first is from *A full and true Account, of the Behaviours, Confessions, and last Dying Speeches, of the Condemn'd Criminals, that were Executed at Tyburn, on Friday the 19th of April, 1700*:

> John Larkin, alias Robert Young, Condemn'd for High-Treason, in Counterfeiting the Current Coin of the Kingdom. Being examined, said, that he was born in Antrim in Ireland, that his Parents perceiving his Genius inclin'd to Learning, kept him at School for some time, and then sent him to the University of Glascow in Scotland, where he made some proficiency in the Study of Philosophy; then he returned to Ireland, and took upon him the care of a School; which painful Office he discharg'd so well, that it gained him a general Applause. But having a roving unsettled Mind, he resolv'd to leave that Place, and visit the remotest Parts of that Kingdom, and assuming the Habit of a Minister, performed several Offices belong to that Sacred Function.

The second extract is from *THE ORDINARY of NEWGATE, His ACCOUNT of the Behaviour, Confessions, and Dying Words, OF THE MALEFACTORS, Who were EXECUTED at TYBURN, On FRIDAY the 24th of this Instant SEPTEMBER, 1731* and concerns one of those who was executed that day:

> William Tracey about 50 Years of Age, of honest Parents, but had no Education at School. When he was a Boy of seven or eight Years of Age, as he said, he was with his Father in the Seige of Londonderry, where he continu'd till the City was reliev'd. His Father was Poor and did not put him to any Trade; when of Age, he serv'd as a Soldier for several Years in Ireland, Flanders and Spain. Afterwards being weary of the Army, he came to London, married a Wife and kept House in and about Hedge-lane, for Twentyfive Years past.

Matters relating to vagrancy occupied a great deal of the courts' time and cases with an Ulster connection feature from time to time. The 'Vagrancy Examinations and Removal Orders' of Cumberland Quarter Sessions make mention of a number of persons from Ulster. For example, in 1740 a removal order was issued for William Watson and his family who were to be relocated from Petteril Crooks in the parish of Hesket to 'Coyner' (Connor) in County Antrim (Cumbria Archive Service: Carlisle, Q/11/1/199/27–28). The court issued instructions that they were to be taken directly to Whitehaven and from there shipped to Ireland. The court documents reveal that William Watson was a 46-year-old tinker, who had been born in 'Coyner'. His wife was Jane and they had two sons, George, aged about 11, and William, aged about eight.

The 'sessions roll' for the quarter sessions in Appleby, Westmorland, of Michaelmas 1759 includes the case of Mary Mullraign who was arrested for vagrancy (Cumbria Archive Service: Kendal, WQ/SR/278/35). The court records reveal that she was a 13-year-old orphan from Glenduff (possibly Clonduff), County Down, to where she was returned. A further case from Easter 1767 concerned James MacDonald who had been born in Glenarran (possibly Glenarm), County Antrim (Cumbria Archive Service: Kendal, WQ/SR/330/23–25). When he was aged five his father, mother and relatives were burned when their home was set on fire, after which he came to England and lived the life of a vagrant. In 1765, he stole an old surtout (frock) coat from the stable of a gentleman's house near Morpeth for which he was arrested and gaoled. Subsequently, he escaped through a window, but was apprehended and was now, at the direction of the quarter sessions, being sent back to Ireland.

Estate records
A number of collections of records relating to the management of landed states in Ulster are in repositories in England. This may be because the owner of the estate in Ulster also possessed property on the other side of the Irish Sea. For example, the Cumbria Archive and Local Studies Centre in Whitehaven holds the Curwen family of Workington Hall papers, which include letters and other documents concerning Thomas Pottinger's estate at Mount Pottinger, Ballymacarrett, County Down, 1744–81, while the Coventry History Centre has eighteenth-century leases and rentals for the manor of Orwell, County Donegal, owned successively by the Basil and Hewitt families. Estate collections for properties in Ulster that have been identified in archives in England are listed in Appendix 2 of this book.

Military records
Records relating to men who served in the British armed forces are discussed in Chapter 11 of this book. In addition to the documentation held in the War Office papers in The National Archives, Kew, some information may be found in local archives. For example, records that have been digitised by the Lancashire Archives include quarter sessions papers relating to the raising of men for the army in the 1790s. Among the men enrolled in Lonsdale South in 1796 was John McKary, a 24-year-old sailcloth weaver who was originally from Bushmills in County Antrim (Lancashire Archives, QDV/26/8/1).

Wills and testamentary papers
Unlike in Ireland, early testamentary papers in England were not the victims of wholesale destruction. The most important collection of wills are those deriving from the Prerogative Court of Canterbury, which are preserved in The National Archives, which have now been digitised and made available via its website. Around 250 wills can be identified that were made by Ulster testators in the seventeenth and eighteenth centuries. Local archives also have collections of testamentary records. For example, among the 'Disputed Probate Papers'

held by the Lancashire Archives is an administration bond of 1765 relating to William Stewart of Liverpool, a mariner and merchant. Those named in the documentation included Stewart's father Patrick, brother Andrew, and another brother named Archibald who was described as a tailor in Ballymena, County Antrim.

Home Office papers

Records relating to the Home Office in London begin in 1782. The original documents are in The National Archives, Kew; they can also be viewed on microfilm at PRONI (MIC224). Information relating to people from Ulster recurs regularly. A good example is the case of Alexander Henry of County Londonderry, which can be found in the Home Office files for 1791 (HO 42/18/188, fos 442–3, 42/18/199, fos 467–70). By way of background, the *Belfast Newsletter* of 8–11 February 1791 carried a news item giving an account of the 'most inhuman, barbarous and unprovoked murder' of William Ronald (spelled variously), a 17-year-old schoolmaster, in the home of James Henry, an apothecary in Dungiven, on 29 January. The alleged perpetrator of this crime was Alexander Henry the younger, who was from Derrycree [Derrychrier] and who was a deserter from the 40th Regiment.

The Home Office papers reveal that Alexander was charged with murder by Thomas Faning, a Londonderry magistrate, and soon afterwards absconded. On 31 March 1791 the North West Circuit of Ulster issued a warrant for Henry's arrest for failing to appear at his trial. Subsequently, he was arrested in the south of England and incarcerated in Portsmouth gaol. A local magistrate, Sir John Carter, heard evidence from John Boyle of Dungiven on 7 June that the man in custody had been known to him for five years as Alexander McKee whilst being known at 'Derrecreer' as Alexander Henry. A week later Carter wrote to a senior Bow Street magistrate in London seeking advice on how to return the prisoner to Ireland as this was not a situation he had had to deal with previously. Directions having been received, Henry was returned to Ireland and stood trial in Londonderry in March 1792. In the event, Henry was found not guilty. (See the *Belfast Newsletter* of 30 March–3 April 1792 for a detailed account of his trial.)

In the months before the 1798 Rebellion there were investigations into those believed to be involved in revolutionary activities. For example, on 15 April 1798 James Hughes of Whittle's Croft, Manchester, a cotton weaver, was interviewed before the Home Secretary about alleged seditious activity (HO 42/45/139, fos 533–4). The account of this interrogation recorded that Hughes was originally from Loughgall, County Armagh, and had been living in England for four years. Some very useful material contained in the Home Office papers for the summer of 1798 takes the form of lists of passengers disembarking at Liverpool from vessels that had arrived from Ireland. Their ports of embarkation included Londonderry, Newry and Strangford. For example, the following persons arrived in Liverpool from Newry on the ship *Molly* on 7 July 1798 (HO 42/44/14, fos 32–43):

Daniel Feran, Rostrevor
Augustus Frederick John Franks, tailor
Daniel McAnally, Bellyholan
Hugh O'Hare, Aughnagun
John Currin, Bellyholan
James Brice, shoemaker
Patrick Turley, Carnacally
Edward O'Hare, Clonallan
Rose Magin alias Rose Murphy
Thomas Trynor, Aughnagun
Pat Cunningham, Leesart
Owen Haughey, Castle Anagan
Edward Rice, Newry
John McManus, dealer, Aughnagun
Dandy Rony, Edinmore
Jane Ryan, Mullaghlass

Published calendars
Published calendars of records from The National Archives include the *Calendars of the State Papers relating to Ireland*, which are discussed in more detail in Chapter 4. Other calendars can include material of Ulster interest. For example, the *Calendar of State Papers Colonial, America and West Indies: Volume 18, 1700* (1910) includes a note on the examination of Derby Mullings, who had been born near Londonderry and who was for many years a servant at Jamaica. He had joined Captain Kidd at New York and had fallen sick at Madagascar, where Kidd allowed him to remain; after two years on the island he took a passage on the *Nassau* for New York. The *Calendar of Home Office Papers of the Reign of George III, Preserved in Her Majesty's Public Record Office: 1760 (25 Oct.)–1765* (1878) includes an entry from 1761 concerning an order for the the removal of James Spears, otherwise John Templeton, from prison in Clerkenwell, London, to Ireland, to stand trial for the murder of John McFaden at Coleraine.

1.8.2 Scotland
Numerous books provide guidance on researching ancestors in Scotland, among them *Tracing Your Scottish Ancestors: The Official Guide*, published by what was then the National Archives of Scotland (2011) and Bruce Durie, *Scottish Genealogy* (4th edition, 2017). Also very helpful are the works of David Dobson, including his volume *Searching for Scotch-Irish Roots in Scottish Records, 1600–1750* (2007). This focuses on counties in south-west Scotland – Ayrshire, Dumfries-shire, Kirkcudbrightshire, Wigtownshire, Renfrewshire and Lanarkshire – but provides information on sources and research methodologies

that can be applied to almost anywhere in Scotland. In addition to this book, Dr Dobson has produced through Genealogical Publishing a multi-volume series entitled *Scots-Irish Links, 1575–1725*. These volumes include listings of names found in a range of different sources, from published works to manuscripts. He has also produced in a similar style a series entitled *Scotland During the Plantation of Ulster … 1600–1699*, which includes separate volumes for Ayrshire, Dumfries and Galloway, Lanarkshire and Renfrewshire.

The principal Scottish repository is the National Records of Scotland (formerly the National Archives of Scotland and before that the Scottish Record Office), based in Edinburgh. It has a huge collection of church records, estate papers and administrative records. Researchers should refer to the National Records website (www.nrscotland.gov.uk) and also the website of Scotland's People (www.scotlandspeople.gov.uk) for guidance on what is available (bearing in mind that many records are held off-site and have to be ordered in advance), what has been digitised, and how this documentation can be accessed. The paragraphs that follow are based primarily on records held by the National Records of Scotland.

Church records

The Old Parish Registers comprise the records of births/baptisms, banns/marriages and deaths/burials kept by parishes of the Church of Scotland, which for most of its history has been a Presbyterian denomination. In addition, there are surviving records of other Protestant churches as well as the Roman Catholic Church. Some registers reflect the close links that existed across the North Channel. For instance, the marriage register of Portpatrick in Wigtownshire includes many entries where at least one party was from Ulster, for example, the union in 1770 of Alexander Milwain, a sailor in Donaghadee, County Down, and Grisal McKaig of Portpatrick. PRONI holds a typescript copy of the entries relating to Ireland in this register for the period 1720–1846 (T1005/1); see also the article in *The Irish Ancestor*, 9:2 (1977), pp 107–29.

Among the most useful of Scottish church records are those of the kirk session. These relate in many instances to disciplinary cases. For example, in 1692 James Fulton was accused by the Dumfries kirk session of having bigamously married a woman in Dumfries despite having a wife and three children in Antrim. Scottish presbytery records can also include references to individuals from Ulster. For instance, in 1716 the presbytery of Kintyre was forced to deal with the case of Agnes Bruce who was 'with child' to Henry Ker, a shoemaker in Ballymena, County Antrim, who had lived for some time in Kintyre before revealing that he was in fact married (CH2/1153/2). Other entries concern the granting of assistance to persons who had returned from Ireland to Scotland in straitened circumstances. Others were given help to make the journey from Scotland to Ireland.

Burgh records

Burgh records are concerned with the administration of towns with burgh status. The burgh records include rolls of burgesses, registers of sasines (recording the transfer of property within the burghs), court books, registers of apprentices, and craft and trade guilds. A burgess who left his burgh to live elsewhere could be removed from the burgess roll. Occasionally this happened to a burgess who settled in Ireland. For example, a merchant named Allan Cuthbert was stripped of his burgess rights in 1655 when he left Glasgow for Ireland. (One wonders whether this was the same man as the Allan Cuthbert who appears in Strabane, County Tyrone, around this time.) The registers of apprentices will occasionally include references to teenagers or young men from Ulster who were apprenticed to merchants or others in Scotland. One young apprentice was James Jardine, son of William Jardine of Coleraine, who was apprenticed to an Edinburgh merchant in 1649. The Irvine burgh writs include, from 1728, 'letters of general charge' concerning John Thomson, only son and heir of deceased Hugh Thomson, merchant and sailor in Coleraine, and heir to his deceased grandfather, Hugh Thomson, flesher, burgess of Irvine (GD1/693/22).

Court records

Court records form another vast body of documentation that include references to persons in Ulster, or who had a connection with the north of Ireland. The Register of Deeds held by the National Records of Scotland is an important category of court records. In it may be found a broad range of items, from marriage contracts to bills of exchange. For example, from 1715 there is a protest concerning an unpaid bill of exchange for £50 stg in favour of Rev. James Pearson at Killybegs, County Donegal, and endorsed in favour of Isaac 'McKertney' [McCartney], merchant of Belfast.

In Scotland divorce has been possible since the Refomation. The records of the Edinburgh Commissary Court include a process of divorce from 1693 concerning Anna Montgomery, daughter of Sir Robert Montgomery of Skeilmorlie, and Captain James Marshall, 'late merchant in Newportoun' (Ballinamallard), County Fermanagh (CC8/6/57). Among the records of the Court of Session is a ledger of an anonymous merchant, which covers the period 1707–12 and includes an index, though for B–M only (CS96/3074). The ledger reveals that the merchant, who was possibly based in Greenock, dealt in a broad range of commodities, including brandy, yarn, lintseed, iron, deals, tobacco, wool, hops, herrings, butter, cheese, almonds, and traded with, among other places, Belfast, Newry and Loughbrickland, County Down.

Testamentary records

Testamentary matters were dealt with very differently in Scotland compared with Ireland (and England for that matter). In Scotland from the Reformation of 1560 until the early nineteenth century Scots had their wills confirmed by Commissary Courts. An individual concerned to settle matters with regard to the disposal of his or her possessions would draw up a will. A testament was the name given to the legal document that was prepared following a person's death. It named the executor who was authorised to settle the affairs of the deceased and included an inventory of the person's possessions (which might be a very detailed record of these, but which could also be presented in rather general terms). A testament testamentar was prepared when someone died leaving a will, while a testament dative concerned the estate of an individual who died intestate. Researchers should also bear in mind that Scottish property law distinguished between heritable property (e.g. land and buildings), which went to the eldest son, and moveable property (e.g. household goods, farm implements), to which his widow and children were entitled.

Occasionally, Scottish testamentary records can make reference to family members in Ulster. For example, the testament of 'Jonet Archibald, spous to Johne Huid, in Kirktoun of Lairgs', confirmed on 23 March 1630, refers to Petir Barclay of 'Strangfuird' (Strangford, County Down) and Archibald Thomesoun of 'Clannybowie' (probably referring to the lands of Sir James Hamilton, Viscount Claneboye, in north-east County Down). Other records concern individuals who had possessions in both Scotland and Ireland, or who were at least resident in Ireland at the time of their decease.

Estate papers
A few collections of estate papers relating to Ulster may be found in Scottish archives. They include records of the Murrays of Broughton, Wigtownshire, and Cally, Kirkcudbrightshire, concerning the family's estate in County Donegal (GD10). These are listed in the relevant section of Appendix 2. Stray items in this collection include the minutes of a meeting in 1757 of the Farmers' Society of the County of Donegal concerning premiums for ditching and flax-growing (GD10/953).

2. Church records

If one is researching Irish ancestors prior to the introduction of civil registration of all births, deaths and marriages in 1864 (non-Catholic marriages were registered from 1845), the main sources of information on family history are the records generated by the different religious denominations. These records include registers of baptisms, marriages and burials. In addition, there are other types of documentation that may be found listed under the heading of church records. Most importantly, these include vestry minutes, which detail the business of the parish and which are dealt with in some detail below. Other materials include records relating to the various levels of administration within the local church or wider denomination (the Presbyterian denominations are particularly good in this regard). Personal items relating to individual clergy, such as diaries, also have the potential to record details of the members of their congregations.

Unfortunately, the records of most churches survive from no earlier than the nineteenth century. The loss of the registers from over 1,000 Church of Ireland parishes in 1922 created an enormous gap. Poor record-keeping and the accidental loss of other registers has further contributed to the paucity of church records from the seventeenth and eighteenth centuries. Nonetheless, pre-1800 records of one form or another exist for more than 200 churches in Ulster and these are identified in Appendix 1 of this book. The majority of surviving church records for the province of Ulster are available for consultation in the Public Record Office of Northern Ireland, though some will be found in other archives (such as the Presbyterian Historical Society of Ireland), while others remain in local custody. With the advent of the Internet, the indexing and digitisation of church records has gathered pace and much is now accessible online.

2.1 The Church of Ireland

The Church of Ireland is an episcopal church with a hierarchical system of church government and services that follow an accepted liturgical form and structure. From 1537 until 1870 the Church of Ireland was the state church in Ireland, and was therefore often referred to as the Established Church or simply the Church. Because of its close links with the Church of England, it is also known as the Anglican Church. Due to its official position, the Church of

Ireland enjoyed privileges denied to other denominations. Despite its standing, however, the Church of Ireland never enjoyed the support of more than a minority of the population of Ireland, probably no more than 10% during the eighteenth century. In Ulster it enjoyed strongest support from the general populace in those districts where the immigration of English families had been significant during the seventeenth century, including south Antrim, north Armagh and north-west Down. In other areas it was noticeably weaker, but through its legal underpinning and support from the landed classes it was able to maintain a presence as an institution across the province.

The basic administrative unit in the Church of Ireland is the parish. For the most part, the Church of Ireland continued with the existing network of medieval parishes. Occasionally parish boundaries were altered and new parishes created. Moira parish in County Down, for instance, was created in 1722 by detaching a number of townlands from Magheralin, while Clogherny parish in County Tyrone was created out of Termonmaguirk in 1732. In areas where the Anglican population was low, several parishes may have formed an ecclesiastical union. For example, at the beginning of the eighteenth century the parishes of Ballyhalbert, Ballywalter and Inishargy in County Down (overwhelmingly populated by Presbyterians) were united, with the Anglican place of worship for all three at Balliggan in Inishargy.

Parishes are grouped together to form dioceses, each of which is headed by a bishop. Again, the medieval network of dioceses was continued post Reformation. Ulster is divided between eight dioceses – Armagh, Clogher, Connor, Derry, Down, Dromore, Kilmore and Raphoe – which form part of the ecclesiastical province of Armagh headed by the archbishop of Armagh. Within the Church of Ireland the archbishop of Armagh is the most senior churchman and is known as the Primate of All Ireland.

2.1.1 Church of Ireland registers

From 1634 each Church of Ireland parish was required to keep proper records of baptisms, marriages and burials. As noted above, among the most serious casualties of the destruction of the old Public Record Office of Ireland in Dublin in 1922 was the loss of over 1,000 sets of Church of Ireland registers, many of which were for parishes in the province of Ulster. Nonetheless, a greater number of Anglican registers survive from the pre-1800 period than those of other religious denominations. For a small number of parishes there are records dating from the seventeenth century onwards. The earliest surviving records are those for St Thomas's Church (later Christ Church cathedral) in Lisburn (then called Lisnagarvey), in Blaris parish, which exist from as early as 1637. The original register has been published as *The Register of the Parish Church of St Thomas, Lisnagarvey, Co. Antrim, 1637–1646*, edited by Raymond Refaussé (1996). The next earliest registers are those of St Columb's cathedral in Derry (Templemore parish) which begin in 1642. These too have been published: *Registers of Derry*

Cathedral, 1642–1703, issued by the Parish Register Society of Dublin (1910). Not all parish registers run continuously from the earliest entry, and there are frequent and often lengthy gaps in the records. For a number of other parishes, while the original registers were destroyed, there are surviving extracts, e.g. Enniskillen, which has extracts from 1667 onwards.

If there are no early registers for a particular parish it may be that the parish was too small, either geographically or with regard to the size of the Anglican population, to sustain a separate identity within the Church of Ireland system. For example, at the southern end of the Ards peninsula, County Down, there were a number of small parishes – Ballytrustan, Slanes and Witter – that never had a Church of Ireland place of worship. Members of the Church of Ireland living in these parishes attended the Anglican church in Portaferry in the parish of Ballyphilip. Important churches drew people from a wider area than the parish in which they were situated. The registers of St Columb's cathedral in Derry include references to people from far beyond the bounds of Templemore parish. Likewise, the registers for Christ Church cathedral in Lisburn include names drawn from across the Lagan Valley.

Analysis of Church of Ireland records has shown that many people with an affiliation to another denomination appear in Anglican registers. There are various reasons for this. For instance, while there had been some provision for Presbyterian marriages in 1737, it was not until 1782 that marriages conducted by Presbyterian ministers were given the same legal standing as those performed by Anglican clergy. In fact, until 1844 Presbyterian ministers could not perform 'mixed marriages', i.e. marry a Presbyterian to a member of the Church of Ireland. For this reason many marriages of members of other denominations, especially those classed as Dissenters, are recorded in Church of Ireland registers. Marriages between Protestants and Catholics may also be found. For example, the marriage register of Donagheady parish in County Tyrone includes a record of the marriage of Alexander Sterling and Ann Kelly on 11 August 1707 with the comment that they had been 'formerly married by a popish priest, [and] remarried by the Chancellor's order'.

Information found in registers
The degree of information recorded in Anglican registers varied from parish to parish and even within parishes it could vary depending on who was keeping the register. However, baptism registers typically included the date of baptism, the name of the child and the father's name. More detailed registers included the mother's name (including sometimes her maiden name) and the family's place of residence. The father's occupation might also have been stated. On rare occasions the names of the godfathers and godmothers were recorded.

Marriage registers recorded the date of the marriage and the names of the bride and groom. Additional information might include the groom's occupation and the name of the bride's father. In their most basic form burial registers included the date of burial and the name of the deceased. More detailed burial registers could include the age, occupation and residence of the deceased. Some extra information was often provided for women and children, such as 'widow of' and 'son/daughter of'.

Occasionally, additional information of interest is recorded in a Church of Ireland register. For instance, the baptisms of abandoned children (foundlings) are recorded with some regularity. Sometimes such children are recorded under a given forename and nothing more. For example, the Glenavy register records the baptism in 1743 of a foundling left at the door of Thomas Carslaw, whose name was given simply as Charity. The register of what became St Ann's Church (now St Anne's Cathedral) in Belfast includes the baptism in 1767 of John Grims, 'so called from being found in Grim's Entry, and now taken care of by Ann McGarrell'.

The keepers of the baptismal register for Antrim in the first half of the 1700s were careful to note who was resident in the parish and who was not. In 1721 the baptism took place of John McCarter. His parents, Alexander, described as a poor man from North Britain (Scotland), and Janet, were seeking alms in the parish when John was born between the town of Antrim and Shane's Castle. James Burns, baptised in 1734, was the son of a poor woman who was travelling with her husband from Grange to Broomhedge, between Lisburn and Moira, when she gave birth in Antrim. Baptised in 1748 was John, son of Hugh McNeal from Rasharkin and his presumed wife Katharine Black; a note appended to this entry recorded that the mother was travelling from Belfast when she went into labour and gave birth at the home of Daniel O'Neill.

The point has been made already that Church of Ireland registers should be checked for information on families whose primary affiliation was to another denomination. The Antrim register includes the baptisms of several children in the years 1718–21 where the parents are specifically identified as 'Papists', i.e. Catholics. In other instances, a baptism or marriage took place in a different parish from the one in which the parties lived due to the absence of clerical provision. For example, in 1739 Archibald McIlwain and Abigail McCleland married in Antrim, though they were from Ballymena, 'where there is no minister'. Occasionally, baptisms of persons of more exotic background can be found. The Blaris register includes the baptism in 1727 of Patrick Kelly, 'from Jamaica West Indies a native' and the baptism in 1746 of John Oroonoko, noted as being a black man from Belfast.

Looking in detail at the burial register for Carrickfergus, which begins in 1740, we find a range of additional information being recorded about the deceased. The register records the burials in 1752 of four men killed when a cannon exploded. In the late eighteenth century smallpox was a recurring problem in Carrickfergus. Ten burials in the period June–August 1798 record the cause of death as principally due to smallpox. Several of the deaths were of children, but others included a burgess of Carrickfergus and an Ensign in the

Lough Tay Fencibles. A note added to the register in late 1798, following the burial entries for a number of children, states, 'the funerals of several of these children were not attended by Rev. Richard Dobbs, curate; they died for most part of the smallpox'. Other unusual entries include the burial in 1747 of John Morrison who, according to the register, was known as 'Pinky the fiddler'.

Instances of longevity can be found on a regular basis and burials of people who had lived to 100, though rare, are to be found in a number of the registers. The Blaris register included a record of the burial in 1695 of Thomas Loe who died at the age of 132, though a note of incredulity is to be found in the added comment, 'as he himself said'. The Donaghadee burial register includes the following entry from 1782 for one of its more famous sons:

> account came of the death of Captain St Lawrence Boyd, of 38th regiment who died end of last month in Falmouth, [Cornwall], three days after his arrival in England from America where he had served with reputation since the beginning of the rebellion and for some time commanded the second batallion of Light Infantry.

Margaret Travers, who died in 1798 aged 74, was, according to the Dromore (County Down) burial register, the mother of thirteen daughters, but no sons; the last four daughters were quadruplets and all of them lived to be baptised.

The burial register of Ballyphilip (Portaferry) includes victims of shipwrecks who were washed up on the coastline around the southern end of the Ards peninsula. For example, after the *Wolf* was wrecked on Kearney Point on 30 December 1748, the ship's captain, George Vachell, was buried in the churchyard in Portaferry on 2 January following. On the same day 45 of the ship's crew were buried in the nearby churchyard of Slanes and over the following days other bodies that were washed ashore were interred. In all, some 66 men were buried in Slanes. The register includes a list of the names, where known, of these seamen, along with their occupation, e.g. armourer, surgeon's mate, and 'man before the mast'.

Marriage licence bonds

Marriage licence bonds were administered by the Church of Ireland. Before a marriage licence was granted the couple intending to marry had to enter a bond at a diocesan court. These bonds included the names of the bride and groom and their ages and place of residence. This practice was popular with those who may have wanted to be married under the auspices of the Church of Ireland, but who, for whatever reason, wished to avoid the publication of banns. Most of the bonds and licences were destroyed in the Public Record Office of Ireland in 1922, though copies and abstracts can be found in many genealogical collections. Most of the indexes to marriage licence bonds have survived and these indexes contain the names of the bridegroom and bride and the date of the bond.

The National Archives of Ireland has created an online database of surviving indexes. In addition to the Prerogative Court, this covers the following Ulster dioceses:

Armagh (1727–1845)
Clogher (1709–1866)
Down, Connor and Dromore (1721–1845)
Kilmore (1697–1844)
Raphoe (1710–55, 1817–30)

The index for Derry diocese does not seem to have survived. Indexes to marriage licence bonds for Armagh, Clogher and Down, Connor and Dromore can also be viewed on microfilm at PRONI (MIC5B/1–6). For the diocese of Raphoe, see also Rosemary ffolliott, *Index to Raphoe Marriage Licence Bonds, 1710–1755 and 1817–1830* (1969, supplement to *The Irish Ancestor*). Indexes to marriage licence bonds issued by the Prerogative Court in Dublin are available in PRONI from *c.* 1625 onwards (T932).

2.1.2 Vestry minute books

The vestry was a gathering of parishioners who met together to discuss and deliberate on various matters relating to the business of the parish. It acquired its name from the room in which the meetings were held originally – the vestry where the minister's vestments were kept. Vestry meetings were organised under the auspices of the Established Church with the Anglican rector or his curate presiding. Though vestry minutes will be found with Church of Ireland records, it should not be thought that they are merely of relevance to Anglicans: people from all denominational backgrounds can be found in a vestry book.

Typically the vestry met early in the week following Easter Sunday, usually on the Monday or Tuesday, though other meetings through the year could be held if required. The matters dealt with ranged widely from the appointment of the parish schoolmaster to the care of the infirm and destitute. The names appearing in the vestry books, therefore, include many different individuals and cumulatively these names can run to a considerable number. For example, the Donagheady vestry book for the period 1697–1723 names over 220 different individuals from all denominations and various walks of life.

Names of parishioners present at vestry meetings

In theory attendance at vestry meetings was open to all those who were liable for parish taxes. However, judging from the number of signatures and marks in the surviving vestry minute books, it would appear that most meetings were attended by a small and select grouping: the rector or his curate and the leading parishioners – the landowners, if actually resident in the parish, and the principal farmers, or merchants if the parish contained a significant urban settlement. The attendees were almost exclusively male. In 1725, Catholics were prevented by law from voting at vestry meetings held for the purpose of repairing or rebuilding parish churches. Subsequent legislation further hindered the involvement of Catholics at vestry meetings, meaning that in effect the vestry became a Protestant body. An act passed in the Irish Parliament in 1774 restricted the participation of Presbyterians at vestry meetings. However, the outcry against this legislation resulted in it being repealed.

At the more important vestry meetings, particularly if a contentious issue was being discussed, attendance was much higher. For instance, more than 140 parishioners signed – or made their mark – the minutes of the vestry meeting held in Clones on 25 August 1715 (MIC1/147). Those in attendance were opposed to the plans to build a chapel of ease in the parish, arguing that the taxes paid to maintain the fabric of the parish church in Clones town were more than the parishioners could bear. Others argued that more than one chapel was needed to accommodate the people living in the remote parts of the parish. It was suggested that the application made to the archbishop 'for erecting the said chaple was done by some few of the most inconsiderable persons of the said parish, more to satisfie thire private picques and resentments than for the service of God'. Despite further opposition it seems that the chapel of ease was built.

Names of persons appointed to carry out parish business
The officers of the parish in both civil and ecclesiastical matters were the churchwardens. There were two in each parish and they were elected on an annual basis, although one man could hold the post for several years at a time. A churchwarden was not necessarily a member of the Church of Ireland and adherents of other denominations did hold this position. Those who did not wish to discharge the responsibilities of a churchwarden could appoint a deputy to act for them. To help the churchwardens many parishes appointed assistants known as sidesmen.

The churchwardens were responsible for ensuring the the money entrusted to them was spent correctly. They were expected to provide evidence for this by submitting accounts itemising expenditure. Generally, these accounts will appear in the vestry book itself, though separate churchwardens' accounts exist occasionally. Other persons undertaking parish business included the parish clerk, parish schoolmaster, masons and craftsmen employed to work on the parish church, and persons appointed to care for the elderly and infirm or abandoned children.

A major responsibility of the vestry concerned the upkeep of the road network in the parish. While a parliamentary statute of 1765 made the county grand jury the primary agent in road building and maintenance schemes, a further act of 1772 empowered vestries in Ulster parishes to levy one penny per acre to maintain minor public roads. The names of those appointed to oversee the repair of roads were recorded in vestry books. The tasks assigned to such individuals could be set out in some detail. For example, the vestry minutes of 1782 for Moira parish tabulate the names of the applotter, overseer, collector and director for eight different roads; each stretch of road is identified carefully, e.g. 'Repairing the road in Lurganaveel from John Megary's March to Widow McElroy's in Lurganaveel'.

Names of those paying the parish cess

Parish activities were financed by a levy or tax known as the parish cess. Occasionally, vestry minutes can include a lengthy list of names of those liable for the cess, arranged by townland indicating the value of the levy that each was to pay. The levy might have been based on the value of the land possessed by each householder in the parish or it could have been on the extent of his or her holding. In the second half of the eighteenth century the Clontibret vestry typically made the following distinction between householders when raising the parish cess: those in possession of 20 or more acres, those in possession of less than 20 acres, and cottiers, while individuals deemed 'very poor' were excused from paying the cess (D2365/1).

Names of parishioners receiving financial assistance

An important responsibility for the parish was looking after those in need. The names of poor parishioners in receipt of alms, together with the sum of money provided to them (or non-monetary donation), appear with some regularity in vestry books. Widows and orphans feature prominently in such lists. In the Dunboe vestry book those identified as requiring assistance were termed 'reduced housekeepers'. Those supporting the application for relief might also be recorded. It would appear that assistance was not simply provided to the Anglican poor and that support was forthcoming to people of all denominations. Several lists of the poor in Donagh parish in County Monaghan from the 1770s distinguished between Protestants and Catholics. In addition, the vestry could decide to provide financial assistance to families to help them in particular situations. These could include donations towards the cost of a funeral or to support families who had suffered the loss of personal possessions due to a fire.

Related to the provision of poor relief was the practice of issuing badges to those allowed alms or permitted to beg. Those not in possession of such badges were known as strolling beggars; such individuals could be whipped to drive them out of a parish. For the year 1774 the vestry book for Inishargy includes a list headed 'Names of the resident poor, who are considered objects of charity, therefore badged by the different inhabitants of the united parishes of Innishargie, Ballhalbert & Ballywalter, receive church alms & granted a liberty of begging throughout said union'.

Names of seat-holders in the Church of Ireland church

In this period the seating arrangements in a Church of Ireland church were carefully regulated by the parish vestry. Parishioners of high status, such as the local gentry, sat at the front of the church in large and impressive pews. The middling sort of people occupied simpler pews in the middle of the church, while the lower orders sat on benches or stood at the back of the church. In this way the elite were segregated from their social inferiors during worship in a way that imitated, at least in part, the secular divisions. Some vestry minutes include details of discussions over how areas within the church should be apportioned to particular families. On other occasions there will be a detailed listing of the families and where they sat in church. Such a list exists from 1725 for the newly-built church in Lurgan in the parish of Shankill, County Armagh. The Clones vestry book includes 'A regulation of seats made at a vestry in Clones ... [in 1735] and newly transcribed now out of that former registry ... [in 1783]', with information on the reallocation of seats between 1735 and 1783.

The churchyard

Vestry minutes can also include various matters concerning the burial ground adjoining the parish church (and sometimes other places of interment in the parish). These could relate to the construction of a fence or stone wall around the churchyard with a proper entrance gate. Not only did this help to demarcate the limits of the burial ground, it also helped to secure the site from human and animal trespassers. In 1673, the vestry of Enniskillen parish resolved to take action against 'many loose and idle people' who gathered in the churchyard to cause trouble (D1558/6). Twenty-one years later, the same vestry issued an order to 'have every beast trespassing in the churchyard impounded and the owner to pay sixpence for each trespass to the churchwardens, besides poundage'. On other occasions, rulings were made about grave-digging. For example, in 1720 the vestry of Culdaff parish issued the following instructions: 'no grave be made in any part of the church or churchyard, but what is to be made by the sexton' (D803/1). In 1760, the Killowen vestry ruled that 'the graves in the churchyard of this parish shall hereafter be made four feet deep at least' (D4164/A/23).

A number of parish vestries adjudicated at different times on the allocation of burial space within the churchyard. For example, in 1739 the Tynan vestry agreed that Edward Bond would be allowed to have 'that peice of ground on the southwest of the steeple of this church to be a bureing place for him and his ffamiley with liberty to set up gravestones or monuments'. In 1770, the vestry of Inver parish, County Antrim, issued the following directive:

> We present and approve of the burial place in the church yard of Inver formerly occupied by the Reverend Mr Thomas Hall, late a minister for the Dissentery of Inver, Rallow and Glyn, to be occupied by the Reverend Mr Hall, now Dissenting minister for the aforesaid parish, there being no objection to the same.

On several occasions in the second half of the eighteenth century, the vestry of Clontibret parish, County Monaghan, allotted burial space in the churchyard or issued rulings on who should be permitted to be interred in a particular grave. For instance, the following was agreed in 1772:

> Whereas the tomb next the gate in the church yard of Clontibret appears to have been built by Terrance Duffy, late of Monaghan, grandfather to Terry Duffy, now of Monaghan, which has appeared by several witnesses, therefore, we in a publick vestry held in our church this 20th day of April 1772 do agree that the property of said tomb is vested in the said Terry Duffy but that he, the said Terry, doth hereby for him & his heirs for ever allow the decendants of Owen Duffy, brother to the above mentiond Terrance Duffy dec^d, to be interrd in said tomb on aplication to the said Terry or his heirs.

Other lists of names

Other lists of names, some of them drawn up in response to particular situations, can be found in vestry books. In the Kilrea vestry book there is a loyal declaration by the inhabitants of Kilrea and Tamlaght O'Crilly, County Londonderry, dating from 1745–6, the time of the Jacobite rising in Scotland, which includes over 130 names. The vestry book of Magheragall parish, County Antrim, includes a declaration from 1796 in respect of the disturbed nature of the country at that time which was signed by around 150 parishioners. More unusual, is a petition in the Dunluce vestry book for 1801 advocating the discouragement of liquor consumption at funerals, which had over 40 subscribers.

Vestry minute books sometimes contain baptism, marriage and burial entries. The vestry book of Killygarvan parish, County Donegal, is one such example. The names of those who were 'confirmed' in the parish church might also be recorded. The Arboe vestry book names children to whom prayer books were given in 1773. The Raphoe vestry book lists the names of those given responsibility for planting trees in the parish in 1703.

A few parishes have what is, in effect, a census of the congregation. This may be included in the vestry book or it could be a separate document. The 'census' of Clondevaddock Church of Ireland in County Donegal of 1796 is arranged by townland and names the head of each household, indicating the relationship of others in the household to him/her (e.g. spouse, children, servants); the census concerns the Anglican population in the parish, but indicates if a member of a household was affiliated to another denomination.

The Gordon family of Donagheady

The way in which vestry minutes can cast light on individual families in this period can be demonstrated in the example of the Gordon family in the parish of Donagheady. Roger Gordon and his wife Sarah Hutcheson were the parents of several children. Their daughters Margaret and Isbell were baptised in the parish church in December 1699 and October 1702. There was at least one other child in the family, a blind son named James. In 1698, the vestry agreed to give Roger Gordon 30 shillings towards caring for James. Roger's mother died in 1704. The family was too poor to bury her and so the vestry gave £0 2s. 6d. to cover the cost of her funeral. Roger Gordon regularly received money from the poor fund. In 1727, he was given five shillings. He was still receiving money in 1729, but had evidently died by 1731 when his widow was given £0 2s. 2d. Sarah and James were still alive in 1737 when they were each given £0 1s. 1d. The experiences of the Gordon family provide a glimpse into the world of many poor families at this time.

2.1.3 Information on Anglican clergymen

A Church of Ireland clergyman with responsibility for looking after a parish or group of parishes was usually known as a rector, though occasionally the title vicar was applied. A clergyman assisting a rector or vicar was known as a curate. For those seeking information on Church of Ireland ministers, the best source is the series of *Clergy and Parishes* volumes meticulously compiled on a diocesan basis by Canon J. B. Leslie. Through years of research Leslie was able to compile brief biographical notes on nearly all ministers in the Church of Ireland from the early seventeenth century through to the early twentieth century. He gathered a vast amount of information from a broad range of sources, many of which were destroyed in 1922. In addition to information on appointments and positions held, the biographical notes can include information on the family background and education of the cleric, as well as details of his own family and descendants.

For dioceses in the north of Ireland the following volumes were published by Leslie in his lifetime: *Armagh* (1911), *Clogher* (1929), *Derry* (1937), *Down* (with H. B. Swanzy) (1936), *Dromore* (with H. B. Swanzy) (1933), *Raphoe* (1941), and *Supplement to Armagh* (1948). In these volumes, in addition to biographical data on the clergymen, Leslie also included historical notes on each of the parishes in the featured diocese. This information could include names of churchwardens, sidesmen, parish clerks, schoolmasters, etc drawn from visitation books (see below) and other sources, many of which perished in 1922.

The Ulster Historical Foundation has published *Clergy of Connor* (1993), based largely on the unpublished succession lists drawn up by Canon Leslie, and has issued reprints and updates of *Down* and *Dromore* (1996), and *Derry* and *Raphoe* (1999). A reprint and update of *Clogher* appeared in 2006, while the succession list for the diocese of Kilmore was published for the first time in 2008 (this volume also included Ardagh and Elphin).

It must not be thought that all Anglican ministers were of English background. Many Church of Ireland ministers in the seventeenth and eighteenth centuries were Scots or had Scottish ancestry. Many of these Scottish ministers were vehemently opposed to Presbyterianism and used their position to stifle nonconformity. The inscription on the memorial to John Sinclair (d. 1703), the Scottish-born rector of Camus-juxta-Mourne and Leckpatrick parishes in County Tyrone, praises him for his efforts in suppressing Dissenters. Occasionally native Irishmen served in the Church of Ireland pastorate. In Inishowen, County Donegal, in the late seventeenth century two McLaughlin brothers were ministers: one was Church of Ireland, the other Roman Catholic.

2.1.4 Tithe records

The tithe system earmarked one-tenth of the produce of the land for the maintenance of the clergy of the Church of Ireland. Until 1823 tithes could be paid in money or in kind (the Tithe Composition Act of that year stipulated that henceforth all tithes were to be paid in money). For more information on this subject, see Maurice J. Bric, 'The tithe system in eighteenth-century Ireland', *PRIA*, 86C (1986), pp 271–88. The payment of tithes was deeply resented by nonconformist Protestant denominations and by Catholics, and was a major source of contention. Disputes over the payments of tithes were common. In Donagheady parish in the 1730s, for example, when two farmers were unable to agree the value of their tithe with the rector, the latter came with a posse of 60 horsemen and rode through their farm, tearing up the fields and destroying the crops. Early tithe records are extremely rare and may be no more than a list of names by townland with perhaps the value of the tithe indicated. Those tithe records that have survived are listed under the parish to which they relate in Appendix 1.

2.1.5 Records of bishops and diocesan archives

The upper levels of the administration of the Church of Ireland created numerous records, ranging from visitation books to diocesan registers. Furthermore, the Church of Ireland was a major landowner in its own right and records relating to the management of its estates have survived.

Visitation books

Bishops regularly carried out inspections of their dioceses; the results of these investigations are contained in visitation books. The information is fairly limited for genealogists, but the names listed can include those of the churchwardens, parish clerk and parish schoolmaster. Occasionally some items of interest about individual parishioners may turn up. The main visitation for the early seventeenth century is the so-called 'Royal Visitation' of 1622. There are several copies and transcripts of it, including a late seventeenth-century manuscript copy in the Armagh diocesan registry in PRONI (DIO/4/23/1/1). This version covers the dioceses of Armagh, Clogher, Connor, Derry, Down, Kilmore and Raphoe. A copy of the 1622 visitation for the diocese of Dromore is in Marsh's Library in Dublin and has been printed in its entirety in E. D. Atkinson, *Dromore: An Ulster Diocese* (1925). A visitation book from 1679 covers the dioceses of Clogher, Connor, Derry, Down and Dromore (DIO/4/23/1/4).

The following listing by diocese is not exhaustive, but provides an idea of which visitations are available for the period 1680–1800.

Armagh
Visitation, 1693 – T505/1
Visitation, 1704 – DIO/4/29/2/1/3–4

Connor
Visitation, 1685 – printed in Charles McNeill (ed.), *The Tanner Letters*
    (1943), pp 470–77
Visitation, 1693 – DIO/4/26/2/2
State of the diocese of Connor returned to the House of Lords,
    1768 – DIO/1/24/26/8

Clogher
Visitation, 1693 – DIO/4/4/4
Visitations, 1666–1829 – D242/1–30
Visitations, 1717–1802 – D250/1–16
Visitation, 1733 – DIO/4/24/2/1

Derry
Visitation, 1686 – D683/218 (printed in T. W. Moody and J. G. Simms
    (eds), *The Bishopric of Derry and the Irish Society of London*, vol. 2
    (1983), pp 106–14)
Visitation, 1692 – D683/228 (printed in Moody and Simms, *Bishopric
    of Derry and the Irish Society of London*, vol. 2, pp 130–37)
Visitation, 1693 – DIO/3/26, T505/1, T1075/5
Visitations, 1722, 1733 – RCB, GS/2/7/3/34
Visitation, 1733 – T1075/5

Down
Visitation, 1685 – printed in McNeill, *Tanner Letters*, pp 470–77
Visitation, 1693 – DIO/4/26/2/1

Dromore
Visitation, 1694 – T552, no. 21
Visitation, 1703 – DIO/4/26/2/3A
Visitations, 1722, 1733 – RCB, GS/2/7/3/34

Kilmore
Visitation, 1733 – DIO/4/24/2/1

Raphoe
Visitation, 1692 – NLI, MS 41,575/6
Visitations, 1722, *c.* 1733 – T1075/5

Armagh diocese

The Armagh diocesan registry archive in PRONI (DIO/4) comprises a huge collection of documentation about the diocese of Armagh from the thirteenth century onwards. As well as records concerning the administration of the diocese, a significant body of material, in the form of leases, rentals, maps and surveys, relates to the the management of the extensive property belonging to the archbishopric (these are listed in some detail in Appendix 2). In addition, there are documents arising from various educational and charitable bodies with which the archbishop was associated.

Records relating to the administration of the diocese include the following items:

> Register of Michael Boyle and Narcissus Marsh, 1678–1713 –
> DIO/4/2/14
> Register of Michael Boyle, Narcissus Marsh, and Thomas Lindsay,
> 1690–1719 – DIO/4/2/15
> 'The commonplace book of his Grace, Richard, Lord Archbishop of
> Armagh', 1768 (100-page folio volume) – DIO/4/29/7/2

A very significant document is the 'View of the Archbishopric of Armagh' of 1703, which provides a detailed look at the possessions of the archbishop and the tenants and undertenants; this is examined in more detail in Chapter 5.

The most celebrated prelate of early seventeenth-century Ireland is James Ussher, who was appointed archbishop of Armagh in 1626. His letters have been published by the Irish Manuscripts Commission: *The Correspondence of James Ussher, 1600–1656*, edited by Elizabethanne Boran (3 vols, 2015). The correspondence of Hugh Boulter, archbishop 1724–44, has also been published: *The Boulter Letters*, edited by Kenneth Milne and Paddy McNally (2016).

Clogher diocese

The Clogher diocesan archive in PRONI (DIO/2) includes a range of material from the 1600s and 1700s, most of which relates to individual parishes. These include documents concerning the appointment of particular individuals as parish schoolmasters. For example, the following letter was written by Joseph Wilkins in 1715 in relation to the schoolmaster at Clogher:

> I received your letter by John Ross wherein you gave me to understand
> hath served as English Schoolmaster at Clogher since I. Walker died but is
> not well qualified for teaching to write; and that one William Murdogh
> can both write well and teach arithmetic; I depend on your [decision?]

concerning their fitness and if Thos Holmes have no licence I do hereby nominate William Murdogh to be English Schoolmaster at Clogher. Let Thos be paid his salary for the time he has served ... (DIO/2/9/209).

Other items in this diocesan archive include 'A list of Christnings maryags & buryalls in the [Parish] of Clogher this present yeare' [1666] (DIO/2/9/206). There is also a volume relating to the 'Clogher Diocesan Widow's Fund Society', beginning in 1799 (DIO/2/11/1). A separate collection comprises a bundle of *c.* 30 letters, etc relating to the administration of the diocese for the period 1798–1817 (D1208/3). With regard to material relating to individual bishops, James Spottiswood, appointed bishop of Clogher in 1620, left a fascinating autobiographical account which was eventually published as *A breefe memoriall of the lyfe and death of Doctor James Spottswood, bishop of Clogher in Ireland* (1811).

Derry diocese
The Derry diocesan archive in PRONI (DIO/3), which also covers the diocese of Raphoe, contains relatively little of interest to genealogists. Of much greater importance are the Ellis Papers in PRONI, which comprise some 400 documents covering the period 1585–*c.* 1850 (D683). These concern the administration of the bishopric of Derry and the management of the diocesan lands at the time of the Plantation of Ulster and afterwards. Many of the items in this collection were published in T. W. Moody and J. G. Simms (eds), *The Bishopric of Derry and the Irish Society of London, 1602–1705* (2 vols, 1968–83). The documents comprise rentals of the lands belonging to the bishopric of Derry, correspondence on various matters, and investigations (often referred to as inquisitions) into the property owned by the bishopric. All of these can provide names of individuals, such as witnesses and the occupiers of land, as well as those who sat on investigating panels. For example, on 22 September 1634 Rev. Oliver Mather wrote to the bishop of Derry concerning a dispute over the townland of Ballynegawnagh in the parish of Desertmartin which belonged to the bishopric and which had been in the possession of Patrick O'Doell. The letter includes the names and ages of four of O'Doell's sons (D683/56).

Volume 2 of the abovementioned work includes a considerable body of material concerning fishing rights on the River Bann and River Foyle. Numerous witness statements are included, which typically give the name, address, occupation and age of the witnesses. Those interviewed in 1683–4 are listed below (ages are 'or thereabouts'):

Henry Quigg of Castleroe, County Londonderry, yeoman, aged 78
Phelemy McIlgee of Litterloan, County Londonderry, yeoman, aged 77
Donoghy O Mullan of Bellrogh, County Londonderry, yeoman, aged 42

John Stockman of Castleroe, County Londonderry, tanner, aged 93
William Mitchell of Colerain, County Londonderry, burgess, aged 50
W'm Loftus of Castleroe, tailor, County Londonderry, aged 60
Patrick Jordan of Castleroe, gentleman, County Londonderry, aged 28
Thomas Beck of Magilligan, gentleman, County Londonderry, aged 40
John Nightingall of the city of Londonderry, gentleman, aged 30
John Henry of Newtown Lemavady, County Londonderry, gentleman,
    aged 50
Samuel Norman of the city of Londonderry, Esq., aged 45
Neal more O Carolan of Clonlee, County Donegal, fisherman, aged 77
Matthew Strong of Clonlee, County Donegal, gentleman, aged 50
Phelymy Mc Linchy of Clonlee, County Donegal, aged 30
Donell O Keralan of Clonlee, County Donegal, fisherman, aged 73
Owen O ffiny of Anagh in the Liberties of Londonderry, fisherman, aged 67
Cormuk Corran of Grange in the Liberties of Londonderry, fisherman,
    aged 69
Donogh O ffiny of Anagh in the Liberties of Londonderry, fisherman,
    aged 40
Shane Ballagh Mc Itagart of Anagh in the Liberties of Londonderry,
    yeoman, aged 80
Owin O Corran of the Grange of Anagh, County Londonderry,
    fisherman, aged 32
William Squire of the city of Londonderry, alderman, aged 38

Useful records from this collection relating to individual parishes have been
listed in Appendix 1, while documents relating to the estate of the bishopric
are found in Appendix 2.

A hugely important set of records, not just for Derry diocese, but also for
Ireland as a whole in the late seventeenth and early eighteenth centuries, is the
extensive collection of documents relating to William King. Born into an
Ulster-Scots family in humble circumstances in Antrim in 1650, King was
raised in a Presbyterian household before converting to Anglicanism. Entering
the Church of Ireland ministry, he rose to become bishop of Derry in 1691
and archbishop of Dublin in 1703, and was one of the most influential
churchmen of his day. Studies of his career include Charles Simeon King, *A
Great Archbishop of Dublin: William King, D.D. 1650–1729* (1906), Philip
O'Regan, *Archbishop William King of Dublin (1650–1729) and the Constitution
in Church and State* (2000), Robert Matteson with Gayle Barton, *A Large
Private Park: The Collection of Archbishop William King 1650–1729* (2003), and
Christopher Fauske, *A Political Biography of William King* (2011).

King's papers are on deposit in the Manuscripts & Archives Research Library
of Trinity College Dublin. These include:

Incoming letters ('Lyon's Collection') – TCD, MS 1995–2008
Outgoing letters – TCD, MS 750

Accounts – TCD, MS 751
Letterbook, 1699, 1702–03 – TCD MS 1489

The 'Lyon's Collection' concerns incoming letters to William King, as well as some later papers relating to Nicholas Forster, bishop of Raphoe, and the Spence family of Donaghmore, County Donegal; in addition, it includes over 180 letters written by King himself. The letters have been catalogued in three volumes and these are now available as downloadable PDFs from the Manuscripts & Archives Research Library website. While many of the letters are concerned with administrative matters, there is also much of interest for the family and local historian. For example, in a letter to King of 30 April 1693, Dominic Heyland enclosed a rent roll of the lands held from the bishopric of Derry by the heir of Sir John Rowley (MS 1995–2008/271). This included the names of under-tenants in townlands in the parishes of Aghadowey, Camus-juxta-Bann, Desertoghill, Errigal, Killowen and Tamlaght O'Crilly. On 22 June 1699 Rev. Robert Morgan wrote to King with the names of masters of families in the parishes of Bodoney, Cappagh and Drumragh (MS 1995–2008/140; copy in PRONI, T542).

PRONI holds microfilm copies (MIC69) of William Nicolson's diaries and accounts covering the period he was bishop of Derry (1718–27). PRONI also holds a microfilm copy of his letters to William Wake, bishop of Lincoln and subsequently archbishop of Canterbury (MIC240/1). Copies of these letters can also be found at T1910/3 and T2711/5/39. He was the subject of a study by F. G. James, *North Country Bishop: A Biography of William Nicolson* (1956).

Frederick Augustus Hervey was one of the most remarkable men to have held an Irish bishopric. He was bishop of Derry for over three decades from 1768 (from 1779 he was also the fourth earl of Bristol). Biographies include William S. Childe-Pemberton, *The Earl Bishop: The Life of Frederick Hervey, Bishop of Derry, Earl of Bristol* (2 vols, 1924) and Brian Fothergill, *The Mitred Earl* (1974). See also Peter Rankin, *Irish Building Ventures of the Earl Bishop of Derry, 1730–1803* (1972), as well as the author's working papers in PRONI (D4624). PRONI holds an extensive and well-catalogued collection of documentation relating in particular to his building endeavours at Downhill in Magilligan parish and in Ballyscullion parish, as well as some smaller caches of correspondence (D1514). These records can be summarised as follows:

Accounts, drafts and receipts, 1775–1803 – D1514/1/1
A significant portion of these records concerns payment to tradesmen and labourers working for the bishop of Derry at Downhill and Ballyscullion. For instance, from *c.* 1780 there is 'A List of Duty Work', listing the names of workmen, the places of their work, and the wages due to them (D1514/1/1/41). Other records relate to building projects in his diocese, such as spires for churches or the building of glebe houses. Miscellaneous items include, for example,

a petition of 1783 from Widow Donnelly of 'Killcronaghan' to the
bishop of Derry for charity, with a testimonial from Archdeacon
Clotworthy Soden (D1514/1/1/72).
Correspondence concerning in particular the bishop of Derry's building
projects at Downhill and Ballyscullion, 1780–1809 – D1514/1/2
Political correspondence, resolutions addresses, etc of the bishop of
Derry, 1767–1806 – D1514/1/5

Down, Connor and Dromore
The records in PRONI for these dioceses (Down and Connor were held by the
same bishop while Dromore was occasionally united to them) are fairly limited
for the pre-1800 period (DIO/1). Returns and extracts from the registers of a
number of parishes were once in this archive (DIO/1/14), though these are not
now to be found. The collection includes the antiquarian papers of the
nineteenth-century cleric William Reeves (DIO/1/24), which includes material
gleaned from a broad range of documentation, though relatively little of it is of
genealogical interest.
    A number of volumes relating to Francis Hutchinson's period as bishop of
Down and Connor (1720–39) are extant. These include:

Account and memorandum book of Bishop Hutchinson which includes
details of leases of the bishopric, etc, 1720–30 – DIO/1/22/1
Personal expenditure books of Bishop Hutchinson, 1728–34, 1734–7 –
DIO/1/22/2, /3

A further volume kept by Hutchinson covers the period *c.* 1729–*c.* 1739 and
includes rentals of his personal estate at Portglenone; it has been transferred to
PRONI from the diocesan offices in Belfast, but has not yet been added to the
catalogue. PRONI also holds a personal account book kept by a member of
the O'Hara or Hamilton family, Portglenone, possibly Charles Hamilton, a
grandson of Bishop Hutchinson, 1763–7 (DIO/1/22/4A).
    Hutchinson is well known for his patronage of the Irish language 'Rathlin
Catechism', published in Belfast in 1722. A manuscript version can be read in
PRONI (D3577/1A; MIC580/1), along with accounts and a list of persons
who received Irish catechisms. See also J. Fred Rankin, 'The account book of
an 18th century bishop', *Lisburn Historical Society Journal*, 5 (1984), pp 6–16;
Andrew Sneddon, *Witchcraft and Whigs: The Life of Bishop Francis Hutchinson,
1660–1739* (2008); and Gordon Wheeler, 'Bishop Francis Hutchinson: his
Irish publications and his library' in John Gray and Wesley McCann (eds), *An
Uncommon Bookman: Essays in Memory of J. R. R. Adams* (1996), pp 140–58.
    Some records relating to the maladministration of Down and Connor in the
late seventeenth century are available. Thomas Hackett, appointed bishop of
Down and Connor in 1672, proved one of the more ineffective holders of an
Ulster bishopric in the late 1600s. He was absent from Ireland for most of his

episcopacy, earning himself the nickname 'Bishop of Hammersmith' because of his residence there. Eventually in 1694 Hacket was deprived of his office by a royal commission for non-residence, neglect and other offences. Copies of the papers relating to his dismissal are in PRONI (T545/6, /7). The Representative Church Body Library in Dublin holds a fascinating manuscript which contains an abstract of the proceedings against Thomas Ward, the dean of Connor, in 1694 (MS 566). Ward was investigated for adultery and other offences and the evidence gathered against him reveals a significant amount of detail about east Antrim at this time. See also Eamon Darcy, *The World of Thomas Ward: Sex and Scandal in Late-17th Century Co. Antrim* (2016).

Letters written by John Ryder while bishop of Down and Connor can be found in the Harrowby Papers in PRONI (T3228/1). See *Eighteenth-Century Irish Official Papers in Great Britain. Private Collections: Volume Two* (PRONI, 1990), pp 10–33 for extracts.

Thomas Percy, the bishop of Dromore from 1782 to 1811, is celebrated for his scholarship and his patronage of poets and writers. The *Index of English Literary Manuscripts*, vol. 3, pt 4 (1998) includes a lengthy essay which provides in some detail the whereabouts of papers relating to the bishop, most of them concerned with literary matters. According to this same work, several items relating to the administration of his diocese and bishopric lands were in the recent past in the possession of a descendant (not identified), including visitations of Dromore, 1782–1804; 'Improvements made at Dromore', 1783–6; a rental of the see of Dromore, 1784; a map and survey of the former demesne of the see of Dromore, 1785, as well as leases and rent rolls (pp 268–9). The Bodleian Library, Oxford, has a booklet of printed receipt forms for rent to Percy as bishop, 1783–4 (MS Johnson.e.12) as well as some papers relating to his duties as bishop (MS Percy.c.6, ff 70–75).

Kilmore diocese

William Smyth (1638–99) was successively dean of Dromore (1673–81), bishop of Killala (1681–2), bishop of Raphoe (1682–93) and bishop of Kilmore (1693–9). There is an extensive collection of his records, including a long run of correspondence, in the Smythe of Barbavilla Papers in the National Library of Ireland. See the NLI Collection List No. 120 for a detailed catalogue of this documentation. These records include:

> Seventeenth-century accounts and papers of Bishop William Smyth, including an undated rental of the Kilmore bishopric estate – NLI, MS 41,575/1–7
>
> Cash book of Bishop William Smyth, 1674–86 [missing] – NLI, MS 41,572/1
>
> Correspondence of Bishop William Smyth, 1673–98 – NLI, MS 41,575/8–19

Extracts from his correspondence have been included in the NLI Collection List and make for interesting reading. For example, on 26 April 1694 William Hansard wrote from Belturbet to Smyth on the matter of one Magan, a Dissenter: 'He was presented by the subsheriff for ploughing nigh the church on Christmas Day, and when he was desired to go to Church impudently replied he was better employed. He ploughed two or three furrows in land not fit to be broke up, and has not ploughed in that field since' (MS 41,575/14).

Raphoe
A handful of early items are found in the diocesan archive in PRONI (DIO/3). Other material can be found in the abovementioned Smythe of Barbavilla Papers from the time of William Smyth's episcopacy. Of specific relevance to his time in Raphoe is the following item:

> List of subscribers, with their original signatures and the sums they respectively subscribed, to the cost of building a new steeple on the church at Raphoe, 1684 – MS 41,574/1

2.2 The Presbyterian Churches
The roots of Presbyterianism in Ireland can be traced to religious developments in Scotland in the mid to late sixteenth century. In the early seventeenth century, with the influx of large numbers of Scottish settlers, a number of clergymen with Presbyterian convictions arrived in Ulster from Scotland. To begin with they were accommodated within the Church of Ireland and were allowed a certain amount of freedom to organise their churches along Presbyterian lines. However, in the 1630s there were moves to bring the Church of Ireland more closely into line with the Church of England and a number of clergymen who held to Presbyterian beliefs were expelled for refusing to accept the changes.

In 1642, an army from Scotland landed at Carrickfergus to defend Scottish settlers from attacks from the Irish in the wake of the uprising that began in October of the previous year. Accompanying this army were several Presbyterian ministers acting as chaplains, and in June 1642 these ministers, along with a number of elders, established what is regarded as the inaugural Irish presbytery meeting, from which, in a formal sense, today's Presbyterian churches in Ireland descend. (See below for more information on the role and function of a presbytery). From the mid 1650s, during the period known as the Commonwealth, there was greater freedom of worship and many ministers in Ulster were Scottish Presbyterians.

Following the Restoration of 1660, ministers who refused to conform to the teachings and government of the newly reinstated Church of Ireland were dismissed. Despite periods of persecution, Presbyterians continued to form congregations and from around 1670 they began to build their own places of worship, which were known as meeting houses (reflecting the belief that the significance of the edifice lies not in and of itself, but rather in the group of people gathered there). By the end of the seventeenth century Presbyterians were numerically superior to Anglicans across much of Ulster, and this was a major source of concern for the both the government and the Established Church. For much of the eighteenth century Presbyterians were subject to the Penal Laws passed by the Irish Parliament, which affected marriages and the right to hold public office, among other things. (See the historical introduction to this volume for more on this.)

Researching Presbyterian ancestors is complicated by the fact that Presbyterians do not all belong to one single denomination. The largest denomination is today known as the Presbyterian Church in Ireland and its ruling body is the General Assembly. Prior to 1840 this ruling body was known as the General Synod of Ulster. Three other historic Presbyterian denominations, two of which still exist today, are discussed in more detail below. There is little difference in the range of documentation generated by the various Presbyterian denominations, though there may be occasional differences in emphasis. PRONI has the largest collection of congregational records, as well as copies of many administrative records deriving from the various levels of church government within the different Presbyterian denominations. In addition, the Presbyterian Historical Society of Ireland (PHSI) has a significant archive of original records as well as a large collection of publications. Another repository with a valuable collection of Presbyterian records is Union Theological College in Belfast, the training college for Presbyterian ministers.

2.2.1 The Presbyterian Church in Ireland

Information on congregations
The basic organisational unit within the Presbyterian Church is the congregation. By 1690 around 90 congregations had been established in Ireland, the great majority of which were in Ulster. Another 50 or so congregations were established in the period to 1720. Further congregations were established in the following decades, some as a result of the division within the main body of Presbyterians over the issue of subscription (see the Non-Subscribing Presbyterian Church below), or simply an internal dispute, and others because of the formation of other Presbyterian denominations (see the Seceders and Covenanters below). The opening up of new areas to Presbyterian settlement also resulted in the creation of new congregations, such as Creggan, or Freeduff, in south County Armagh, *c.* 1733. The formation of new congregations was often resisted due to concerns that it would weaken existing congregations. The congregation of Buckna, County Antrim, was founded in 1756 despite protests from Broughshane. Once formed, relatively few congregations were dissolved within the period covered by this book.

Though in the early days of organised Presbyterianism there seems to have been some attempt to use the parish as the geographical basis of a congregation, this proved impracticable to maintain. For one thing, not every parish, even large ones, had a Presbyterian congregation. Without clear lines of division, the boundaries between congregations could become a contentious issue. For instance, there was no Presbyterian congregation in the parish of Leckpatrick, County Tyrone, prior to the nineteenth century, but there was a congregation in the parish to the north, Donagheady, and another in the parish to the south, Camus-juxta-Mourne (Strabane). In 1729, it was settled that the boundary between the congregations of Donagheady and Strabane should be the burn, now known as the Glenmornan River, which flowed, roughly speaking, through the centre of Leckpatrick parish.

An indispensable guide is the *History of Congregations* published by the Presbyterian Historical Society in 1982. It provides brief sketches of each of the congregations, mainly focusing on the succession of ministers. It is particularly useful in determining when a particular congregation came into being and other names by which it may have been known. For example, the congregation of Corvally in south County Monaghan was formed around 1700, but until 1880 was known as Carrickmaclim. A *Supplement of Additions, Emendations and Corrections with an Index* was published in association with the Ulster Historical Foundation in 1996. The two volumes have been brought together in digitised form and are now available to members of the Presbyterian Historical Society as a searchable database via its website.

Information on Presbyterian ministers

Biographical information on Presbyterian ministers was published by the Presbyterian Historical Society as *Fasti of the Irish Presbyterian Church, 1613–1840*, compiled by James McConnell and revised by his son Samuel G. McConnell (1951). The biographical sketches are fairly succinct, but can include the name of the father and possibly mother of the minister, his place of birth, where he was educated, where he served as pastor, and details of his own family. Publications by the minister, if any, may also be noted, and perhaps something exceptional about his career. Information on Presbyterian ministers can also be found in a range of other sources, such as abstracts of wills and gravestone inscriptions. Most rural ministers also had a farm to supplement their income and so they may appear in estate records (see Chapter 6). A few of the more prominent ministers appear in the *Dictionary of Irish Biography*.

Calls

When the members of a Presbyterian congregation identified a man they wished to have as their minister they issued what was known as a 'call'. This was a written invitation to him which set out the reasons for the call and which was signed by the members. For example, the members of Carntall (Clogher)

Presbyterian Church met on 14 February 1773 and issued the following call to Rev. Andrew Millar, which was signed by 76 members of the congregation:

> We the Session and Congregation of Carntall being sensible of the great loss we laboaur under by the Want of a Pastor settled among us, and having a Good Account of the Piety, Learning and Ministerial Abilities of you, Mr Andrew Millar; being also fully satisfied of your virtuous Disposition and regular Conversation, and having heard you preach the Gospel to our satisfaction; do therefore unanimously invite and call you to take the pastoral Charge of this Congration: And we solemnly promise to subject ourselves to your Ministry in the Lord, and to allow you such maintenance as we hope will be satisfactory. ... We earnestly request you, therefore, to take this our Call under your consideration; and hope that from a generous Concern for our present desolate Situation, you will be disposed to declare in our favour (T2655/4/3).

Records of ministers

A number of records kept by individual ministers survive. For example, the diary of Rev. John Kennedy of Benburb, held by the Presbyterian Historical Society of Ireland, provides huge detail on the life of this minister and his congregation between 1714 and 1737. Kennedy noted, for example, pastoral visits to members of his congregation and recorded details of baptisms, marriages and funerals that he had conducted. For instance, on 20 January 1726 Kennedy visited Andrew and Widow Trimble, married Dick Tinsly and Agnes Paton, called with Jo. McGee, and finally that day baptised William Campbell's child. The value of this diary for anyone researching an ancestor who belonged to Benburb Presbyterian Church cannot be overstated for registers of baptisms and marriages of the congregation do not begin until the nineteenth century (in fact, there are no baptism registers until the 1870s). An edition of this diary is in preparation by the PHSI.

The PHSI also holds the common-place book of Rev. Samuel Barber of Rathfriland, County Down, which includes records of the marriages in his congregation from 1782 to 1811 and a list of the Rathfriland Volunteers in 1781, as well as various other jottings. Some collections of correspondence relating to individual ministers survive from the eighteenth century, though admittedly, these tend not to throw much light on the members of the pastor's congregation. Transcripts of letters written between 1707 and 1713 by Rev. Alexander McCracken, minister of First Lisburn, to Joshua Dawson, Under-Secretary at Dublin Castle, have been published (*JRSAI*, 5th series, 16 (1906), pp 51–8). These include an eyewitness account of the burning of Lisburn in April 1707. Extensive material relating to the Bruce ministers is available in PRONI (T3041), including letters from Rev. Michael Bruce of Holywood to his cousin James Traill in Killyleagh, 1717–35.

Baptisms and marriages

Presbyterian congregations kept registers of baptisms and marriages. Though comparatively few congregations have surviving records from before the nineteenth century, there are some very early Presbyterian registers, including those for Antrim (baptisms from 1677 and marriages from 1675), Drumbo (baptisms from 1692), Killyleagh (baptisms from 1693 and marriages from 1692), Lisburn (baptisms from 1692 and marriages from 1688), and Portaferry (baptisms from 1699). It is also worth looking at Church of Ireland registers for baptisms, marriages and burials involving Presbyterians, for reasons outlined above.

The information found in early Presbyterian baptismal registers is fairly basic, often being no more than the name of the child (and sometimes not even that), the name of the father and the date of the baptism, though some will name the mother and the family's place of residence. Baptisms which took place in unusual circumstances might have an explanatory note. For example, the following note was entered in the Lisburn register:

> In the month of Decr 1736 John Dixson, having come to the years of maturity & had nevr been baptised came & earnestly desired the benefit of Christian priveledge, was baptized & received as a membr of this congrega: also at the same time had his son Silas bapt. per Mr Patten.

On other occasions, the circumstances of the birth may have been recorded. On 8 November 1698 Elizabeth, daughter of John Berry, was baptised in Lisburn. The register records that 'she was born ye 6th of 9ber [November] 98, about ye eleventh hour at night, an hour before her mother died.' The Antrim register includes the following record:

> Teag Rice of 5 towns had a child baptized Elizabeth, in the meantime denyed to be Roman and confessed to be a presbiterian protastant by renoncing popry in all its Artickels befor the congregation.

Presbyterian marriage registers of this era will often be limited to the date of the ceremony and the names of the bride and groom. Sometimes the date or dates that the marriage was announced ('proclaimed') as well as the date of the marriage ceremony itself will be provided. The early register of Antrim Presbyterian Church adopts this format as the following entry from 30 April 1698 demonstrates:

> A purpose of marriage betwixt James Hood and Martha Strain of this parish were proclaimed the 1st day of May for the 1st time, the 8th day of May for the last time, were married the 18th of the same month.

The following example from the Ballykelly register shows the role of the parents in sanctioning the marriage of their offspring:

John Steel and Jean Aleson gave in there names to be proclaimed in ordeur to marriage, there parents & both the parties being content this 20th of December 1701 both of them in Ballykelly and were married ye 10th of Jenry 1701 [1702].

Session records

The session in a Presbyterian congregation was composed of the minister and elders. The elders were chosen from within the congregation. A relatively small number of session records from the seventeenth and eighteenth centuries have survived for Ulster, but where they do exist they can provide a fascinating range of information about the members of a congregation. Taking the Aghadowey session book of 1702–61 (held by the Presbyterian Historical Society of Ireland) as an example, we find that the session dealt with a range of issues, many of which related to the internal discipline of members of the congregation for a variety of misdemeanours. These extended beyond the moral conduct of the members to include such matters as disputes between farmers over the tenancy of land. Several times the session dealt with farmers using charms to cure livestock of diseases. One woman was accused of being a witch.

The Aghadowey session book also includes accounts showing the distribution of funds to those in need. Seating arrangements in the meeting house were also regulated by the session. Interestingly, a number of Gaelic Irish names appear in the session book – O'Cahan and O'Dugan, for example – indicating that the congregation was not entirely composed of families with Scottish roots. Having said that, it would seem that none of these individuals held a particularly important role in the congregation, though John O'Quig had possession of the keys of the meeting house and may have been the sexton.

Occasionally session minutes may contain actual records of baptisms and marriages. On other occasions they may provide such details indirectly through recording, for instance, disciplinary action against members who had married 'irregularly'. For example, on 8 August 1765 Andrew Davison and Elizabeth Grant appeared before the session of First Dromara Presbyterian Church 'confessing their sin and offence of irregular marriage by a popish priest'; they were rebuked before the session and again publicly before the congregation.

Session records can also include financial information relating to the congregation's income and expenditure. Sometimes these details might be recorded within the minutes, though at other times they will be listed separately. The Armagh session accounts for the early eighteenth century include payments to cover the cost of funerals (e.g. 25 July 1707: 'For burying Widow Jackson', 2s. 6d.), providing coffins, payments to cover school fees, repairs to the meeting house, and relief to those in situations of need (e.g. 5 March 1721: William Thomson 'a captive slave in Barbary', £2).

Other congregational records

A range of other records were generated by individual congregations. For instance, for First Lisburn there is a subscription list for the new meeting house, 1764–5. Pews in meeting houses were rented to particular families and records of the payments made for these seats survive in a few instances. Those for the Third Presbyterian Church in Belfast cover the period 1726–73 and 1788–96. Stray items include a record of 1749 of the sale of a pew in the Third Presbyterian Church, Belfast, which had formerly been occupied by Samuel Smith; the purchasers were John Potts and Thomas Greg who paid £11 for it (D298/16).

One very interesting early eighteenth-century document relating to the burial of Presbyterians survives among the records of First Presbyterian Church in Belfast. It is a record of the hiring out of funeral gear – palls, cloaks and hats, etc – for about 2,000 funerals which took place between 1712 and 1736. This document has been published as *Funeral Register of Rosemary Street Non-Subscribing Presbyterian Church (known as the First Presbyterian Church of Belfast), 1712–36*, edited by Jean Agnew (Ulster Historical Foundation, 1995).

Those planning to emigrate would often apply for a certificate testifying to their credentials as good Presbyterians. This would enable them to join a Presbyterian congregation in America without having to undergo a rigorous examination of their character and religious beliefs. Sometimes such requests will be found recorded in session and presbytery records, but often they will survive within family papers. (See Chapter 13 on emigration records for more on certifcates of disjunction.)

Presbytery records

Presbytery is the middle layer of government in the Presbyterian Church, above session and below synod. It was a gathering of the ministers and representative elders of the congregations affiliated to the presbytery and meetings were held on a regular basis. Researchers should be aware that presbyteries were frequently reorganised. The presbytery of Strabane, for example, was formed in 1717 and when originally constituted included the congregations of Strabane, Ardstraw, Urney, Donagheady, Ballindrait, Derg, Omagh, Badoney and Pettigo. The records of the Synod of Ulster (see below) can help to identify which presbytery a congregation was in at a particular time.

Presbytery meetings dealt with a range of issues. Frequently, matters were discussed that could not be settled at the level of session, either because there was a dispute of a nature that could not be resolved without recourse to a higher authority or because the issues related to more than one congregation. In 1707–08, the presbytery of Down was forced to intervene in a dispute over seating arrangements in the congregation of Knock (Castlereagh). A low point occurred when, during a Sunday service, some of the servants of Hugh Montgomery and David Williamson came to blows. The case dragged on for over a year without resolution. The records of the presbytery of Strabane also include references to attempts to settle disagreements over seating arrangements. For example, in 1721 the presbytery intervened in a dispute between two members of Donagheady, William Hamilton and Daniel Elliott, where the former complained that the latter sat in front of him in church even though he paid less for his seat.

Among the other matters dealt with by the presbytery of Strabane was the issue of families attending the meeting house in Strabane when they lived within the bounds of the Urney congregation. In 1726, the session of Strabane was instructed by the presbytery not to take up collections from any families living in the parish of Urney, 'otherwise they will be held disorderly'. Occasionally, matters relating to emigration were dealt with at presbytery level. In 1730, the presbytery of Strabane rebuked John Patterson and Mary Atchison for marrying without making sure that Atchison's former husband, who had emigrated to America, was definitely dead.

Original and duplicate copies of presbytery minute books and related records in PRONI are as follows:

> Antrim presbytery, 1654–8 – CR5/5E/2; D1759/1A/1 (MIC637/1);
>   this has been published as Mark S. Sweetnam (ed.), *The Minutes of the Antrim Ministers' Meeting 1654–8* (2012)
> Antrim presbytery, 1671–91 – D1759/1A/2 (MIC637/1)
> Biographical notes on ministers and reports of the meetings of the
>   Antrim presbytery, 1681 – D1759/1A/3 (MIC637/1)
> Bangor presbytery, 1707 – D1759/1D/21 (MIC637/5)
> Bangor presbytery, 1739–74 – CR5/5E/2
> Bangor presbytery, 1739–1842 – D1759/1D/15 (MIC637/4)
> Belfast Presbytery (notes from) – D1759/1D/21 (MIC637/5)
> Down presbytery, 1706–15 – CR5/5E/2
> Down presbytery, 1707–15, 1785–1800 – D1759/1D/16 (MIC637/4, /5)
> Killyleagh presbytery, 1725–32 – D1759/1D/10 (MIC637/4)
> Laggan presbytery, 1672–1700 – CR5/5E/2; D/1759/1E/1–2
>   (MIC637/6)
> Route presbytery, 1701–5 – D1759/2A/13 (MIC637/8)
> Strabane presbytery, 1717–40 – CR3/26/2/1

The Presbyterian Historical Society has copies of the following presbytery records

> Antrim meeting, 1654–58, 1671–91, 1697–1713
> Bangor presbytery, 1739–90
> Killyleagh presbytery, 1725–32
> Laggan presbytery, 1672–*c.* 1700
> Letterkenny presbytery, 1717–49 – PBY 28/A/1
> Monaghan presbytery, 1702–12, 1738–44, 1791–1809 – PBY 33/1A

Route presbytery, 1701–05/6
Tyrone presbytery, 1759–61, 1781–1809 – PBY 41/A//1–2

Union Theological College holds the minutes of the Belfast presbytery, 1774–1800, and those of the Derry presbytery, 1764–96.

Synod of Ulster records
The Synod of Ulster was the highest authority in the Presbyterian Church. It met once a year usually and was composed of representatives from every congregation in each of the presbyteries. The minutes of the meetings of the Synod of Ulster for the period 1691–1820 were published in three volumes by the Presbyterian Church in the late nineteenth century: *Records of the General Synod of Ulster* (1890–98). A typescript index to these volumes is available in PRONI. To a large extent the minutes deal with matters of procedure within the Church. Occasionally, however, information of genealogical value will be recorded as the following examples show.

Plans to form a new congregation at Coagh on the boundary between counties Londonderry and Tyrone were resisted strongly by two existing congregations in this area, but in 1709 the Synod of Ulster ruled in favour of the people of Coagh. The entry in the Synod minutes provides considerable detail on the bounds of this congregation and its founding members:

> That the new Erection at Coagh, made by the late Committee at Ballenderry, July 20th, 1708, for that People, stand & continue a distinct Congregation, bounded as follows, viz:—that Wm McMullen & Neighbours in Millinaho, Thos Bell and Neighbours in Tirkvillan, Rich: Rankin & Neigbours in Tirkvillan, John McCreigh in Drumady, Wm Vans & Hugh Fleck in Achavan, Richd McGau in Ballynargan, Jas Dun & his Neighbours in Inniskillin, Thos McCord & Moses Redman in Edruna, Alexr Mitchell in Liscasy, James McCord in the Moor, Claud Rolan in Ballynahone, James Johnston & Andw Ferguson in Drummullan, at the little Bridge, James McKee & Wm Hamilton in Ballydally, Jas Hogg and John McKee in Ballygurch, Wm Aikin & John Barnet in Ballycogly, & from that to the Logh by Ballyronan, and all these People, and all these within those Bounds, be the new Erection of Coagh, and apply to the Meeting of Tyrone to plant them (vol. 1, p. 176).

At the Synod of 1738 a petition was presented from a section of the Drummaul (Randalstown) congregation that wished to be disannexed from Drummaul and united to the congregation of Ahoghill. The commissioners representing the disaffected members of Drummaul were Jon Nisbet and Wm Wining and, usefully, the names of those signing the petition were listed in the minutes of Synod (vol. 2, p. 240). This list distinguished between heads of families and young people, as follows:

Heads of families		Young people
Jas Walker	Saml Agnue	Adam Glass
Jas Ker	Jno Hillis	Jno Ker
Jas Bankhead	Jno Forbes	Jno Nisbet
Thos Doel	Jas Winning	Samuel Stuart
Jon Wallace	Stephen Harper	Jno Stuart
Mort Gallaway	Alexr Muron	Saml Wilson
Hugh Reny	Jno Marshall	Jno Wilson
Wm Gallaway	Jno Thomson	Jas Lemon
Christy Nelson	Wm Carson	Wm Craig
Saml Thomson	Jas Craig	Wm Anderwood
Robt Adair	Jas Gillespie	Alex Dumbar
Jos Thomson	Andr Clerk	Wm Graham
Robt Lyamon	Jas Montgomery	
Jas Henderson	Jas Willson	

There was a regional Sub-Synod of Derry and its minutes for 1706–36 and 1744 onwards, are available in the Presbyterian Historical Society. PRONI holds a copy of the minutes for 1706–36 (CR3/46/3/1).

Publications

There is no shortage of published works on Irish Presbyterianism. Two early histories of Presbyterianism in Ireland, written in the second half of the 1600s, were by Rev. Patrick Adair ('True narrative of the rise and progress of the Presbyterian Government in the north of Ireland') and Rev. Andrew Stewart ('Short account of the Church of Christ …'). Along with introductory essays and copious footnotes, these have been published as *Presbyterian History in Ireland: Two Seventeenth-Century Narratives*, edited by Robert Armstrong, Andrew Holmes, Scott Spurlock and Patrick Walsh (Ulster Historical Foundation, 2016).

In the nineteenth century several men, usually ministers, began to write detailed histories of Irish Presbyterianism. Foremost among them was James Seaton Reid who wrote the magisterial *History of the Presbyterian Church in Ireland*, edited by W. D. Killen (3 vols, 2nd edition, 1867). Others works include Thomas Witherow, *Historical and Literary Memorials of Presbyterianism in Ireland* (2 vols, 1879–80) and W. D. Killen, *History of the Congregations of the Presbyterian Church in Ireland* (1886). Some of these volumes can now be read on Google Books or Archive.org.

A very helpful book for understanding the relationship between Presbyterians and the state is J. C. Beckett, *Protestant Dissent in Ireland, 1687–1780* (1948). More recently, Finlay Holmes produced two excellent overviews of Presbyterianism: *Our Irish Presbyterian Heritage* (1985) and *The Presbyterian Church in Ireland: A Popular History* (2000). A handsomely-produced volume that provides a good overview of Irish Presbyterianism, along with a paragraph on each congregation and a photograph of each meeting house, is *Presbyterians in Ireland: An Illustrated History* by Laurence Kirkpatrick (2006).

Studies of the early history of Presbyterianism in Ireland include Richard L. Greaves, *God's Other Children: Nonconformists and the Emergence of Denominational Churches in Ireland, 1660–1700* (1997); and Phil Kilroy, *Protestant Dissent and Controversy in Ireland, 1660–1714* (1994). The most detailed study of the adherents of Presbyterianism in the north of Ireland in the late seventeenth and early eighteenth centuries is Robert Whan, *The Presbyterians of Ulster, 1680–1730* (2013). *The Shaping of Ulster Presbyterian Belief and Practice, 1770–1840* by Andrew Holmes (2006) is an excellent study of what Presbyterians believed and how they behaved, while Ian McBride, *Scripture Politics: Ulster Presbyterians and Irish Radicalism in the Late Eighteenth Century* (1998) provides an analysis of the role of Presbyterians in the period leading up to the 1798 Rebellion. It should be noted that these books take a broad approach to Presbyterianism and include information on the different denominations in existence in this period.

In his abovementioned book, Andrew Holmes has observed that there is a 'seemingly unique obsession of Ulster Presbyterians with writing and reading congregational histories'. To a large extent this is a reflection of the importance of the congregation within the Presbyterian system, and the way in which its identity is intertwined with its locality and the families who, often for generations, have been associated with it. A published history exists for many congregations and the best collection of these books is in the library of the Presbyterian Historical Society. Like other local publications, congregational histories can frequently include information that is not readily available elsewhere. For example, J. E. Mullin's *New Row: The History of New Row Presbyterian Church, Coleraine, 1727–1977* (1976) includes the names attached to a call to Rev. John Glasgow in 1795. A list of subscriptions to Millisle meeting house from 1773 is included in Thomas Kilpatrick's *Millisle and Ballycopeland Presbyterian Church. A Short History* (1934).

2.2.2 The Secession Presbyterian Church

Following a dispute in the Church of Scotland over the issue of patronage, a number of ministers seceded (hence their appellation Seceders) in 1733 and formed the Associate Presbytery. The conservative evangelicalism of the Seceders appealed to many Presbyterians in Ulster and from the 1740s onwards Seceder congregations were established here. As a general rule, it would appear that it was in those areas most strongly affected by the influx of families from Scotland in the years either side of 1700 that the Seceders made the greatest impact. The first Seceder congregation in Ireland was at Lylehill, County Antrim. In 1741, Presbyterians in this district appealed to the Associate Presbytery in Scotland to send them preachers. Occasional preaching supplies were provided for several years before Isaac Patton, a native of Myroe, near Limavady, was ordained their minister in 1746.

The Seceders in Scotland divided over the issue of the Burgess Oath, giving rise to the Burghers and Antiburghers. Though this division had little relevance to Ireland, nonetheless, the Seceders here separated into the two camps. The Irish Burghers established a Synod at a meeting in Monaghan in 1779 and the Antiburghers did so in Belfast in 1788. The two synods united in 1818. In 1840, the great majority of Secession congregations joined with the Synod of Ulster in forming the General Assembly of the Presbyterian Church. Some Secession congregations remained outside of this body, but in time most were received into the General Assembly, though a few joined the Reformed Presbyterian Church. Essential reading for an understanding of the Secession Church is David Stewart's *The Seceders in Ireland: With Annals of Their Congregations* (1950).

Surviving congregational records are listed in Appendix 1. Brief biographical details of Secession clergy appear in *Fasti of Seceder Ministers Ordained or Installed in Ireland 1746–1948*, arranged and edited by W. D. Bailie and L. S. Kirkpatrick, published by the Presbyterian Historical Society in 2005. Synod and presbytery records relating to the Secession Church in PRONI include the following:

> Typed copy of the minutes of the Associate (Antiburgher) presbytery
>   of Moira and Lisburn, 1774–86 – D1759/1D/22 (MIC637/6)
> Typed copy of minute book of Associate Synod, 1788–1818 –
>   D1759/1F/1 (MIC637/6)
> Typed copy of extracts from the minute book of the Scottish Secession
>   Synod including information relating to Ireland, 1736–82 –
>   D1759/1F/3 (MIC637/7)
> Extracts from Monaghan presbytery records, 1777–1820 –
>   D1759/2A/12 (MIC637/8)

The Presbyterian Historical Society holds the following Secession presbytery records:

> Down (Burgher) presbytery minutes, 1785–1842
> Moira and Lisburn (Antiburgher) presbytery minutes, 1774–86
> Monaghan Secession (Burgher) presbytery, 1773–1800 – PBY 33/2A/1–3

Union Theological College has acts and minutes of the Burgher Associate Synod of Ireland, 1779–1818, and acts and proceedings of the Antiburgher Associate Synod of Ireland, 1788–1818. Also worth reading are the copies of the affidavits against the Seceders in County Donegal held in PRONI (T808/14996); one for 1753 provides a long explanation of their doctrine and gives a good contemporary description and comment on them.

2.2.3 The Non-Subscribing Presbyterian Church

The origins of the Non-Subscribing Presbyterian Church can be traced to a dispute within the Presbyterian Church over the issue of subscription to the Westminster Confession of Faith, the statement of doctrine of the Presbyterian Church. Led by Rev. John Abernethy of Antrim, those who denied the necessity of subscribing to this work were known as 'New Light' Presbyterians or 'non-subscribers'. Failing to reach a consensus on the issue, in 1725 the Synod of Ulster placed the non-subscribing ministers in the Presbytery of Antrim (this did not mean that all of them were in County Antrim). In the following year the Synod decided that it could no longer 'maintain ministerial communion' with the Presbytery of Antrim. However, there continued to be a rather nebulous relationship between the Synod of Ulster and the Presbytery of Antrim.

The subscription controversy created rancour and division in some congregations. In Belfast the ministers of both the First and Second congregations were non-subscribers, which led to the formation of the Third Congregation in the early 1720s. Following the formation of the Presbytery of Antrim, a number of congregations divided. Abernethy's own congregation in Antrim split, leading to the creation of a separate congregation within the Synod of Ulster. Some congregations that had been placed in the Presbytery of Antrim reverted to the Synod of Ulster. For instance, the minister of Ahoghill was a non-subscriber and was, therefore, in the Presbytery of Antrim. However, following his death in 1731, his congregation rejoined the Synod of Ulster.

A century after the formation of the Presbytery of Antrim the issue of subscription again arose within the Synod of Ulster. Eventually this led to the withdrawal from the Synod of 17 ministers and the creation of the Remonstrant Synod of Ulster in 1830. As was the case a hundred years earlier, the disagreements led to splits in a number of congregations. For example, in 1835 the minister of Killinchy joined the Remonstrant Synod. Not all of the members agreed with him, however, which in the end resulted in the creation of two separate congregations. In 1910, the General Synod of the Non-Subscribing Presbyterian Church was formed by the Presbytery of Antrim and Remonstrant Synod. For a brief background to this denomination, see John Campbell, *A Short History of the Non-Subscribing Presbyterian Church of Ireland* (1914).

The complex origins of the Non-Subscribing Presbyterian Church need to be borne in mind when approaching its records. In particular it must be realised that nearly all of the congregations that are now part of the Non-Subscribing Presbyterian Church originated in the Synod of Ulster. In other words, those searching for ancestors in the seventeenth and eighteenth centuries should not discount examining the records of what are now Non-Subscribing congregations. Pre-1800 congregational records are listed in Appendix 1. Copies of the minutes of the Presbytery of Antrim, beginning in 1783, are available in PRONI (T1053).

2.2.4 The Reformed Presbyterian (Covenanter) Church

The Covenanter or Reformed Presbyterian Church was composed of those who adhered to the Covenants of 1638 and 1643 and who rejected the Revolution Settlement of 1691 in Scotland. The National Covenant of 1638 was a response to the attempts by Charles I to bring the Scottish Church into closer conformity with the episcopal Church of England and to introduce greater ritual and a prescribed liturgy to services. It established firmly the Presbyterian form of church government in Scotland, and bound the people to uphold the principles of the Reformation. The Solemn League and Covenant of 1643 was framed along similar lines and concerned England and Ireland as well as Scotland.

During the reigns of Charles II (1660–85) and James II (1685–8) there was considerable persecution of Covenanters, and many were executed or banished. Of critical importance for Reformed Presbyterians was the belief in the descending obligation of the Covenants from one generation to the next. Thus while the Revolution Settlement of 1689–90 established the Church of Scotland along Presbyterian lines, its failure to recognise the continuing validity of the Covenants resulted in a small minority rejecting the political and religious establishments. In 1743, these Covenanters were constituted as the Reformed Presbytery of Scotland, later the Reformed Presbyterian Church of Scotland.

In Ireland too, especially in the province of Ulster, there were groups of Covenanters, the product of successive waves of migration in the course of the seventeenth century and the accompanying spread of religious ideas. The Solemn League and Covenant was brought to Ireland in 1644 and subscribed to by many thousands in areas where Scottish settlement was most pronounced. In the 1670s and 1680s, during a period of intense persecution in Scotland, many individuals and families found refuge in the north of Ireland, strengthening numerically the position of the Covenanters on the island.

Of the early history of the Covenanters in Ireland very little is known, save that the denomination was small and scattered. Prior to the formation of regular congregations, Covenanters living in a particular district met in a group known as a 'society'. It was not until 1757 that the first Reformed Presbyterian minister, Rev. William Martin, was ordained in Ireland. A Reformed Presbytery was established in Ireland in 1763; due to a depleted ministry this was dissolved in 1779 though it was revived in 1792. By 1800 there were more than 20 congregations, mainly to be found in an arc stretching across the northern parts of Ulster from north Down to north Donegal. In 1811, a synod of the Reformed Presbyterian Church of Ireland met for the first time.

Very few Reformed Presbyterian records survive from the eighteenth century. This can be partly explained by the low number of congregations and the paucity of ministers in Ireland at this time. Many baptisms and marriages were performed by visiting ministers from Scotland, while in other instances Covenanters in Ireland crossed the North Channel to get married or to have their children baptised. A source worth checking is *Register of the Rev. John*

MacMillan: being a record of marriages and baptisms solemnised by him among the Cameronian Societies, edited by Henry Paton (1908), which covers the first half of the eighteenth century. A most interesting survival is the call that was issued in 1772 to Rev. William Stavely by the 'Covenanted electors between the Bridge of Dromore and Donaghadee in the County of Down', which was signed by over 90 individuals. A copy of the call is held in the Historical Library at the Reformed Theological College, Knockbracken, County Down.

A minute book of meetings of the session of Antrim (the congregations of Kellswater and Cullybackey) for the period *c.* 1789–1802 is available in PRONI and is revealing of the principles of the church at this time (CR5/9A/1). For example, because the Covenanters refused to accept the political status quo, they did not participate in elections. In 1792, the Antrim session was forced to deal with Robert Nickol. It was alleged that Nickol had accepted a bribe to leave the town of Antrim during an election, presumably to avoid voting. Shortly afterwards Nickol was summoned to appear before a court in Dublin to give evidence in a trial arising from this allegation. There he had sworn in an 'idolatrous way'. Afterwards he had returned to Antrim and taken an active part in the election there. He was publicly rebuked by session for his actions.

Another early minute book is that for Bready Reformed Presbyterian Church, which survives from the last decade of the eighteenth century (CR5/36/2/1/1). At this time the bounds of the congregation encompassed the Foyle Valley, taking in adjoining portions of counties Donegal, Londonderry and Tyrone. See William J. Roulston, *Foyle Valley Covenanters: A History of Bready Reformed Presbyterian Church, 1765–2015* (2015), which includes a list of the names appearing in the session book.

For background information on this denomination see *The Covenanters in Ireland: A History of the Reformed Presbyterian Church of Ireland* by Adam Loughridge (1984). Information on ministers in the Reformed Presbyterian Church can be found in *Fasti of the Reformed Presbyterian Church of Ireland*, compiled and edited by Adam Loughridge (1970). This *Fasti* has been incorporated into *The Covenanters in Ireland: A History of the Congregations* (2010). Rev. Samuel Ferguson's *Brief Biographical Sketches of Some Covenanting Ministers Who Laboured During the Latter Half of the Eighteenth Century* (1898) contains a great deal of useful information about the origins of the denomination. See also 'The origins of the Reformed Presbyterian Church of Ireland with some comments on its records' by William Roulston, published in *Familia* (2008), pp 86–110.

2.3 The Methodist Church

In 1747, John Wesley, the founder, along with his brother Charles, of the religious movement that acquired the name Methodism, made the first of many visits to Ireland. He travelled to Ireland a further 20 times and is believed to have preached in 30 of the 32 counties. His first visit to Ulster took place in

1756 when he preached in Newry, Lisburn, Belfast and elsewhere. Wesley's journals, published in various editions over the years, provide a vivid picture of eighteenth-century Ireland. For instance, in April 1762 he recorded the following entry in his journal about a visit to Lurgan, County Armagh:

> Mon. 26, in the evening I preached to a large congregation in the market-house at Lurgan. I now embraced the opportunity, which I had long desired, of talking with Mr Miller, the contriver of that statue, which was in Lurgan when I was there before. It was the figure of an old man, standing in a case, with a curtain drawn before him, over against a clock which stood on the other side of the room. Every time the clock struck, he opened the door with one hand, drew back the curtain with the other, turned his head, as if looking round on the company, and then said with a clear, loud, articulate voice, "Past one, two, three," and so on. But so many came to see this (the like of which all allowed was not to be seen in Europe) that Mr Miller was in danger of being ruined, not having time to attend his own business. So, as none offered to purchase it, or to reward him for his pains, he took the whole machine in pieces: nor has he any thought of ever making any thing of the kind again.

By the time of Wesley's final visit to Ireland in 1789 it was reckoned that over 14,000 people were associated with Methodist societies on the island. By the end of the century Methodist meeting houses, or chapels, had been established at a number of locations across Ulster, including Ballycastle and Lisburn, County Antrim; Downpatrick, Newry, Portaferry and Warrenpoint, County Down; and Togherdoo and Lisleen, County Tyrone. A copy of the lease for the Methodist chapel premises in the city of Armagh survives from 1796, which includes a number of names of preachers and followers of Methodism (T579/3).

It is important to realise, however, that even though many people attended separate meetings to hear Methodist preachers, they remained members of their own local congregations. Furthermore, it would appear that a majority of the followers of Methodism were members of the Established Church (Church of Ireland). In practice this meant that they continued to go to the parish church for baptisms, marriages and burials. It was not until the early nineteenth century that the adherents of a branch of Methodism in Ireland began to administer these rites and keep records of them. Therefore, for those who think their eighteenth-century ancestors may have sympathised with Methodism, the best place to begin looking for them is the local Church of Ireland register before moving on to the records of other denominations.

Original records relating to Irish Methodism can be found in the Public Record Office of Northern Ireland under reference CR6. These include:

Printed minutes of the Methodist Conference in Ireland, 1752–1819 – CR6/3/A/4/1

Journal of Conference, 1792–1812 – CR6/3/A/3/1

Private minutes of Conference, 1792–1846 – CR6/3/A/5/1
Registers of title to the property of the Methodist Church, 1743–1967 –
CR6/3/E (see also also MIC429/2)

See also *Minutes of the Methodist Conferences in Ireland, vol. 1, 1744–1819* (1864).

Historical accounts of Irish Methodism include Charles H. Crookshank, *History of Methodism in Ireland* (3 vols, 1885–8). This work includes much valuable information on early developments within Irish Methodism. The following extract appears under the year 1786:

> On the Charlemont circuit the blessed work continued to prosper greatly. The faithful itinerants stationed on this round preached in their turn at Portadown every second Sunday on their way from Kilmoriarty to Lurgan; and after some time were invited to the house of James Lemon, a chandler, where in spring a small class was formed, consisting of persons in very humble circumstances … The first leader was John Hamilton, who came from Newmills, near Gilford. About this time Messrs J. Noble and J. Heather began to visit Portadown, and preached in the house of Mr Richard Atkinson, a baker, who was friendly to Methodism, although not a member of the Society (vol. 1, p. 415).

A more recent work is Dudley Levingstone Cooney, *The Methodists in Ireland: A Short History* (2001). A booklet specifically aimed at those researching Methodist ancestors is Steven C. Ffeary-Smyrl, *Irish Methodists – Where do I start?* (No. 1 in the Exploring Irish Genealogy series published by the Council of Irish Genealogical Organisations). The Methodist Historical Society of Ireland maintains a library and archive at Edgehill College, 9 Lennoxvale, Belfast, BT9 5BY, which is open to the public at certain times during the week. The Society publishes a *Bulletin* and has a well established web presence (http://methodisthistoryireland.org).

2.4 The Moravian Church

The Moravian Church is a Protestant denomination that originated in what is now the Czech Republic and was introduced to Ireland in the middle of the eighteenth century. It is formally known as the Unitas Fratrum or Unity of the Brethren and occasionally Moravians are referred to as the United Brethren (not to be confused with the Plymouth Brethren). Principally through the missionary work of John Cennick, congregations were established at a number of places in Ulster, including Gracehill and Ballinderry in County Antrim, Gracefield in County Londonderry, Cootehill in County Cavan, and Kilwarlin in County Down.

The most successful Moravian community was that at Gracehill, where a planned village was laid out with the church building as its focus. To the rear of the church is one of the most unusual graveyards in Ulster – a long, rectangular plot of ground with a central path, with men buried on one side and women on the other. The memorials are small squarish stones laid flat on the ground (or raised at a slight angle to allow water to drain off them).

Moravians are very good record-keepers, and the information kept by them extends to a wide range of activities. For the Moravian church at Gracehill, in addition to baptisms, marriages and burials, there are elders' conference minutes beginning in 1755, congregational committee minutes beginning in 1788, and a register of members, 1755–91, with an index (MIC1F/3). The membership register for Ballinderry, County Antrim, also begins in 1755 (MIC1F/1), while for the congregation at Gracefield, near Magherafelt, County Londonderry, there are registers of members from 1759 onwards (MIC1F/31).

The records for Cootehill Moravian Church in County Cavan include a leather-bound volume with the title, 'Church Book of the Moravian Brethern Congregational at Cootehill' (MIC1F/5). This includes a record of members, giving such details as year of birth, date of admission to the Cootehill congregation and date of death or removal from the congregation. For example, on 6 July 1765 two men named John Wethered – distinguished as senior and junior and presumably father and son – were admitted to membership in Cootehill. The older man had been born in Ballinderry, County Antrim, in 1703; he had previously been a member of the Established Church; on 9 January 1772 he 'went happily to our Saviour' and was interred in the local Moravian burial ground. The younger man was born in 1739, also in Ballinderry. In November 1789 he and his family moved to Gracefield.

2.5 The Religious Society of Friends

The Religious Society of Friends, whose adherents were known as 'Friends' or, more popularly, 'Quakers', was founded in England in the mid-seventeenth century. The man who introduced the movement to Ireland was William Edmundson, who was originally from Westmoreland in the north of England. In 1652, he and his wife moved to Ireland and travelled north to Antrim where his brother, a soldier, was stationed and there Edmundson established a store-keeping business. Returning to England to acquire further goods for his shop in 1653, he came into contact with some leading Quakers and accepted the principles that they taught. In the following year he and his family moved to Lurgan, County Armagh, and it was there that they and some others established the first Quaker meeting in Ireland. The Quakers were particularly strong in the Lagan Valley and north Armagh – areas associated with significant English settlement – with further 'meetings' established at Ballyhagen, Cootehill, Hillsborough, Lisburn and elsewhere.

Quaker records

Almost from their first appearance in Ireland, Quakers were among the best record-keepers of any denomination on this island. These records include registers of births (Quakers do not practise baptism), marriages and deaths, minutes of a range of different meetings, accounts of sufferings and charity papers. Because their marriages were not recognised as legally valid by the state, Quakers went to great lengths to keep an accurate record of them. Those intending to marry would have to submit to enquiries to ensure that there was no impediment to them marrying, e.g. questions on whether a previous spouse was definitely dead. The record of the marriage was a lengthy document giving the names of addresses of the bride and groom, the date and venue of the marriage, and the signatures of those present (which could run to quite a few names). Those who did not live up to the high standards set by Quakers could find themselves disowned for a range of offences.

An excellent introduction to the records of the Society of Friends is *Guide to Irish Quaker Records, 1654–1860* by Olive C. Goodbody with a contribution on Northern Ireland records by B. G. Hutton (Irish Manuscripts Commission, 1967). This volume includes a section listing surnames extracted from Quaker registers (pp 193–207). The Friends Historical Library is located at Stocking Lane, Rathfarnham, Dublin (https://quakers-in-ireland.ie/historical-library). Many records relating to the Quakers in Ulster in the Friends Library in Lisburn were copied by PRONI and were originally given the reference T1062. These copied records can now be consulted on microfilm (MIC16). Records relating to particular Quaker meetings are listed in Appendix 1. Records relating to the Ulster province/quarterly meetings are set out below:

> Minutes of province/quarterly meetings, 1674–1823 – MIC16/1A–B
> Women's minutes of province/quarterly meetings, 1792–1801 –
>   MIC16/4
> Ministers' and elders' minutes of province/quarterly meetings, 1758–64 –
>   MIC16/4
> Marriage certificates, 1731–86 – MIC16/6
> Book of sufferings, 1748–1809 – MIC16/6
> Register of tithe sufferings, 1706–11 – MIC16/7

Other Quaker records include notes and accounts of losses from the time of the Williamite War, 1689–91, including goods seized by both the Jacobite and Williamite armies (D2224/1–6). For the Quaker meeting at Ballyhagen there are wills and inventories, 1685–1740, which have been analysed by J. R. H. Greeves, 'The will book of Ballyhagan meeting of the Society of Friends', *The Irish Genealogist*, 2 (1950), pp 228–39; and A. Gailey, 'The Ballyhagan inventories, 1716–1740', *Folk Life*, 15 (1977), pp 36–64. From an early stage, Quakers maintained their own separate burial grounds, though they eschewed erecting markers over their graves from the early eighteenth century through to the mid nineteenth century. The publication, *Lynastown Burial Ground, 1658–1993* (1993), includes a list of 200 interments in this burial ground between Lurgan and Portadown (over half of these are from the pre-1700 period).

Quaker sufferings

Because of their stance on many issues, Quakers frequently found themselves at odds with the civil and religious authorities. Among other things, they would not take up arms; they refused to swear oaths; and they would not pay tithes to the Established Church. As a result they faced persecution and records of their 'sufferings' were kept by Quakers. In addition to those that can be found in local records, several volumes of sufferings were published. The earliest of these was the book by Thomas Holmes and Abraham Fuller entitled, *A Brief Revelation of Some Part of the Sufferings of the True Christians, the People of God (in scorn called Quakers) in Ireland for these last eleven years, viz. from 1660 until 1671* (1673). This is organised by category, province, county and year. For example, the following entry appears under the heading of those who were persecuted for assembling together and concerns County Cavan in 1660:

> William Parker, Richard Faile, Miles Gray, Robert Wardell, Thomas Lunn and Thomas Moore with several other Friends, being met together, for the End aforesaid, in Belturbet, were ha[u]led out and committed to Prison four Days without Examination, by Order of Richard West, Provost; and because they could not pay Fees, having not broken any Law, some of them were stripped of their Cloaths, and then turned out.

Other printed books of sufferings include those by William Stockdale, covering the period 1671–83, and Joseph Besse, 1650–89 (this book concerns the British Empire and not just Ireland).

Publications

The story of the Quakers in Ireland has been chronicled in many books over the years. An early study is *A History of the Rise and Progress of the People called Quakers in Ireland* (1751), which was compiled initially by Thomas Wight and continued by John Rutty; this includes information on some of the earliest adherents of Quakerism in Ireland. Other studies include Isabel Grubb, *Quakers in Ireland, 1654–1900* (1927), Richard T. Vann, David Eversley, *Friends in Life and Death: British and Irish Quakers in the Demographic Transition* (2002), and Maurice J. Wigham, *The Irish Quakers: A Short History of the Religious Society of Friends in Ireland* (2nd ed., 2003). Richard S. Harrison is the author of *A Biographical Dictionary of Irish Quakers* (2nd ed., 2008), which includes details on some 300 Friends over a period of 350 years. A very useful book is David M. Butler, *The Quaker Meeting Houses of Ireland* (2004), which provides details on some 150 meeting house and 100 burial grounds across the island.

Steven W. Morrison has produced a number of important studies of Friends in Ulster. These include 'A Census of Early Ulster Quakers', *Familia* (2011), which includes an appendix listing over 200 names of late seventeenth-century Quakers extracted from 'suffering books'. He has also published 'The forgotten Ulster-English, using early Quaker records to fill the gaps', *DIFHR*, 35 (2012), which includes an appendix listing 180 Quakers. Quakers were among the earliest inhabitants of Ulster to seek a new life across the Atlantic and a useful book about Quaker emigration is A. C. Myers's *Immigration of the Irish Quakers into Pennsylvania, 1682–1750* (privately published, 1902).

2.6 The Roman Catholic Church

The Reformation in Ireland resulted in the conversion to Protestantism of no more than a fraction of the native population: nearly all continued to look to Rome for supreme authority in matters ecclesiastical. At an institutional level, however, the Roman Catholic Church suffered considerably as a result of the disruption caused by the plantations and wars of the late sixteenth and seventeenth centuries. Legislation in the form of the Penal Laws from the late seventeenth century onwards also had a significant impact, though in spite of these laws the Catholic Church was able to operate in most areas, even if clandestinely at different times. In the course of the eighteenth and nineteenth centuries the Catholic Church was able to establish new parochial structures. Since they were often based in the main on local demographics rather than on traditional boundaries, Catholic parishes do not necessarily follow the same pattern as civil and Church of Ireland parishes, and it is important for researchers to take this into consideration.

For the historical reasons briefly outlined above, very few Roman Catholic registers pre-date 1800. Among the earliest are those for Clonleigh and Camus, straddling the border between counties Donegal and Tyrone, and Castlerahan and Munterconnaught, Castletara, Killinkere, Lurgan and Mullagh, all in County Cavan, all of which have registers starting before 1780 (but no earlier than 1750). Unlike the records of other denominations, Catholic registers will often be in Latin, though this will generally only apply to forenames and a number of standard phrases. Baptismal registers record the names of the sponsors of the child who might be siblings of the parents or other close relatives. Marriage registers may include the names of witnesses who, again, might be related to either bride or groom.

PRONI and the National Library of Ireland hold microfilm copies of Catholic registers down to *c.* 1880. These have now been superseded by the online availability of these registers via the NLI website (http://registers.nli.ie). Most pre-1900 Catholic registers for Ulster are available on the Roots Ireland website (www.rootsireland.ie) as well as through other online providers.

Information on clergy
At present, biographical dictionaries of Catholic clergy in the northern dioceses are few in number. Those that do exist as published books include: *A Digest of the Historical Account of the Diocese of Down and Connor* (1945); and Edward Daly and Kieran Devlin (eds), *The Clergy of the Diocese of Derry: An Index* (2nd

ed., 2009). Details on clergy in the diocese of Clogher have been published in a series of articles (so far incomplete) in the *Clogher Record* entitled, 'Clogherici. A dictionary of the Catholic clergy of the diocese of Clogher (1535–1835)'.

Passed in the Irish Parliament in 1704, the 'Act for registering the popish clergy' obligated priests to register with civil magistrates. Fewer than 200 priests registered in Ulster (over 1,000 registered in all). Among other things, priests were required to provide their name, age, parish, place of residence and date of ordination. Usefully, in terms of the additional information listed, two named individuals were to stand surety for each priest. Looking at these names, it is clear that many of those who acted as sureties were Protestants. Some details for Derry diocese are reproduced below.

> Edmond MacCloskey, priest of Bovevy (Bovevagh) and Glendermott, sureties: John Conningham of Londonderry, merchant, and Neil McIlhinny of Glendermott
> John O'Cahan, priest of Cumber, sureties: Thomas Bawne (Bond) of Cumber and Charles Sterling of Bovevy (Bovevagh)
> Francis Brillaghan, priest of Maghera and Killilagh, sureties: William Jackson of Tobermore and James Lecky of Balteagh

The information gathered under this legislation was published in 1705 in *A list of the names of the Popish parish priests throughout the several counties in the kingdom of Ireland*. The names were reprinted in *The Complete Catholic Directory* of 1838 and have appeared in some publications since then, including some of the diocesan histories noticed below.

Diocesan records

Archives relating to the administration of Catholic dioceses are very limited in terms of the material available for the pre-1800 period. PRONI holds a small number of records for the diocese of Clogher from around 1800 (DIORC/1/8). These concern a number of different matters. For example, from 1800 is a bond of Michael Maginn of Avalreagh, Laurence McArdle of Corrakeen, Peter Flanagan of Drumquill, Charles Brennan of Muldrumman (all in the parish of Clontibret) for £200 borrowed from James Gallanders of Ballynagall, County Monaghan.

The Cardinal Tomás Ó Fiaich Memorial Library & Archive in Armagh has some pre-1800 material relating to the Catholic archdiocese of Armagh. Some fascinating material on Oliver Plunkett's period as archbishop of Armagh (1669–81) is found in John Hanly (ed.), *The Letters of Saint Oliver Plunkett, 1625–81* (1979). With regard to Raphoe, some material in Rome has been brought together in the publication *The Diocese of Raphoe (1773–1805): Documents illustrating the History of the Diocese from the Congressi volumes in the Archives of the Congregation de Propaganda Fide, Rome*, edited by Cathaldus Giblin (1980).

Publications
Background reading on Catholics and Catholicism in Ulster includes Oliver P. Rafferty, *Catholicism in Ulster, 1603–1983: An Interpretative History* (1994) and Marianne Elliott, *The Catholics of Ulster* (2000). An important study of the Church in early seventeenth-century Ulster is Brian Mac Cuarta, *Catholic Revival in the North of Ireland, 1603–41* (2007). Much useful information drawn from contemporary sources is presented in W. P. Burke, *Irish Priests in Penal Times (1660–1760)* (1914). For example, in 1744 the following was recorded about the clergy in the parish of Magheross, County Monaghan: 'Patrick Ginor resides with one Richard Hand of Carrickmacross and has a curate called Patrick Boyland who resides with one Bryan Byrn of Lurgann' (p. 295).

A number of diocesan histories are available. The most comprehensive of these is James O'Laverty's *Historical Account of the Diocese of Down and Connor*, published in five volumes between 1878 and 1895. Others include Edward Maguire, *A History of the Diocese of Raphoe* (2 vols, 1920); James E. McKenna, *Diocese of Clogher: Parochial Records* (2 vols, 1920), Phillip O'Connell, *The Diocese of Kilmore: Its History and Antiquities* (1937); Liam Kelly, *The Diocese of Kilmore, c.1100–1800* (2017); Henry A. Jefferies and Ciaran Devlin (eds), *History of the Diocese of Derry from Earliest Times* (2000); and Henry A. Jefferies (ed.), *History of the Diocese of Clogher* (2005).

2.7 Huguenots
The Huguenots were the French Protestant refugees who left France mostly after the revocation of the Edict of Nantes in 1685. Numbers of Huguenots came to Ireland, with the most important colony in Ulster at Lisburn, County Antrim. The names of many of the early Huguenot settlers in Lisburn appear in the Church of Ireland registers for Blaris parish and several of them have surviving memorials in the adjoining churchyard. Around 1700 a 'French church' catering for the spiritual needs of the Huguenot colony was built in Lisburn. It was demolished *c.* 1830 and, unfortunately, its registers have been lost. E. Joyce Best, *The Huguenots of Lisburn* (1997), includes biographical sketches of Huguenot families who settled in the area. See also Grace Lawless Lee, *The Huguenot Settlements in Ireland* (1936), and *The Huguenots & Ulster 1685–1985: Historical Introduction & Exhibition Catalogue* (1985).

3. Graveyards and gravestone inscriptions

Graveyards and gravestones have long held a fascination for those with an interest in the past. The Belfast merchant John Black wrote to his brother about how, in 1758, he had walked 'among our ancestor's tombs and inscriptions' in the former churchyard in High Street in the town. When Daniel Beaufort passed through the village of Ardstraw, County Tyrone, in 1787 'some neat tombs and a vault' in the old churchyard caught his eye. John Gamble, author of *A View of Society and Manners in the North of Ireland* (1812), wrote that he preferred to 'haunt church-yards' than spend time in the 'abodes of men', and that 'a church-yard is the best temple and a tomb-stone the best sermon'. Today, few visitors to Ireland in search of their roots are satisfied until they have identified the last resting place of their ancestors. Even if no headstone has survived, there is still something poignant about visiting the ancestral burial ground.

3.1 Graveyards

The number of graveyards in Ulster in use during the seventeenth and eighteenth centuries runs into the hundreds. Most of these burial grounds trace their origins to the medieval period and so pre-date the sixteenth-century Reformation. In graveyards of this antiquity it is usual to find burials of persons from across the religious divide, even if local demographics mean that Catholic interments considerably outnumber those of Protestants and vice-versa. There may be other reasons why a burial ground originating in the medieval period was used by people from only one religious denomination. For example, in the early seventeenth century the pre-Reformation graveyard in the parish of Faughanvale, County Londonderry, was not used by the Protestant settlers in the area because it had been used for the burial of unbaptised infants and persons who had committed suicide.

Following the Reformation, most parish churches were appropriated by the Protestant Church of Ireland. However, even though the church may have been used exclusively as a place of worship of the Church of Ireland, generally speaking, the graveyard attached to it continued to be used by the local Catholic population as well as the new Protestant community. In fact, many Church of

Ireland churches still stand on pre-Reformation sites. On the other hand, some pre-Reformation churches were abandoned altogether, but though they may no longer have been venues for public worship their grounds remained places of burial for the local population. Burials also took place in the curtilage of former monasteries. In 1698, the Irish Parliament passed a law that forbade burial in the vicinity of a disused monastery. This law was ignored by both Protestants and Catholics and many monastic sites continued to be used as places of interment.

Other burial grounds were created in the course of the seventeenth and eighteenth centuries. For the most part, these adjoined newly-constructed Church of Ireland places of worship. The graveyards adjoining these churches tended to be used either exclusively or at least mainly by Protestants. In the seventeenth and early eighteenth centuries the only religious denomination with its own distinct places of burial was the Religious Society of Friends (Quakers). Several Quaker graveyards can be identified from the late seventeenth century, though the practice of erecting headstones did not commence until the mid-nineteenth century. It was generally not until the late eighteenth century that Presbyterians began to lay out their own graveyards in the vicinity of their meeting houses. However, relatively few Presbyterian graveyards pre-date 1800. The same is true of graveyards adjoining Catholic churches. The earliest Moravian burial ground in Ulster is at Gracehill, near Ballymena, County Antrim, which was opened in the late 1750s; it is unusual in that men and women were buried separately on either side of a central path.

Clifton Street cemetery in Belfast was opened in the late 1790s by the Belfast Charitable Society, making it the oldest burial ground in Ulster not connected with a religious denomination. This graveyard superseded the burial ground adjoining the 'Corporation Church' in Belfast's High Street, which was closed by act of parliament in 1800; subsequently the churchyard was levelled and cleared, resulting in the loss of all but a handful of tombstones.

3.2 The place of burial

Usually the deceased was buried in a graveyard in the parish in which he or she lived. However, this was not always the case. In the 1750s Rev. George Bracegirdle, rector of Donagheady in County Tyrone, complained that the inhabitants of the neighbouring parish of Cumber were using a graveyard in his parish because the burial fees were lower. On many occasions the departed were taken back to the parish of their birth for interment in a family burial plot even if they were living somewhere else at the time that death occurred.

Wills frequently include instructions from the testator regarding his preferred place of burial. While these requests were not always followed, a will (assuming a copy or abstract survives: see Chapter 8 for more information on wills) can assist with identifying the burial place of an ancestor. Most of the time testators were very clear as to where they wished to be buried. For example, in 1716 Bartholemew Clark of Grange near Randalstown, County Antrim, requested 'my body to be buried in the burying place of the people called Quakers in the Grange with whom I live and die in fellowship' (T681/1, p. 315). In 1756, Arthur Magennis wrote in his will, 'as to my Body I order it to be Interred in the Burying place of my Ancestors either near my brother Constantine Magennis's grave at Donoghmore or near My Uncle Phelemy Magennis's Grave at Machera in case I dye in the County of Downe' (D2580/1).

Others were less specific. In his will of 1754 Rev. Edward Mathews requested burial in the churchyard of the parish in which he would die. However, he was clear that if his death occurred in Lisburn, 'my corps to be laid as near as may be to the grave of my dear deceased niece Alice Smyth (T681/1, p. 105). As Mathews's will indicates, even within the churchyard there were preferred places of burial. John Sterling of Killikean in County Cavan left instructions in his will of 1744 that he was to be buried in the churchyard attached to Kilmore cathedral close to the walk which enclosed the tomb of Bishop Bedell (T282/1, p. 5). In his will of 1777, Dr Theophilus McCartan, Catholic bishop of Down and Connor, included the following request: 'my body be buried with my parents in the churchyard of Clonalan (if I do not bring the tombstone to Loughanisland before that period)'. The bishop did indeed succeed in bringing the family tombstone to Loughinisland where it may still be seen.

While the majority of people were buried in a graveyard, those of status were often buried within the walls of a Church of Ireland church. In 1683, William Montgomery of Rosemount noted with regard to the church in Newtownards: 'None but persons of the best sort being buried in the said new-built church'. Those making a will would often stipulate where in the church they were to be buried. For example, Hugh Shaw of Killbright stipulated in his will of 1668 that he was to be 'buried in the parish church of Donaghadee under my nephew's seat of Belliganavie, and that to be our constant burial place'. In a number of instances a member of the landed gentry came to an agreement with the vestry over the location of his family burial place within the parish church. For instance, in 1700 John Hamilton of Caledon was granted the south aisle of Aghaloo parish church, County Tyrone, as a burial place for his family, he being responsible for its repair (D2602/1).

In the early eighteenth century there are indications that parishes were taking greater steps to control intramural burials. In 1710, the vestry of Donagheady instructed Alexander Mitchell to cover the unpaved part of the church with earth, clay or loam to quell the offensive smell and dangerous fumes that were rising from the graves inside the church (MIC1/35). The vestry also agreed that henceforth no-one would be allowed to bury within the church without the consent of the rector. Likewise in 1759 the vestry of Artrea issued the following ruling:

whereas it has been found by experience, that the custom of burying in the church has proved both unhealthful [sic] and inconvenient, the one arising from the dangerous smell of corpses to the living, the other from the destroying of the seats to the great prejudice and expense to the parishioners, it is unanimously agreed that the persons concerned hereafter in burying the dead shall pay to the minister for each corpse the sum of five pounds sterling for the repairs we also impower the sexton not to give the key to any without payment of the above sum.

In some new churches intramural burials were banned altogether. Moira parish vestry agreed to this on 3 May 1732 on the same day that the new church was consecrated (MIC1/79/1). Burial within churches was generally eschewed by Presbyterians in Ireland and rarely if ever took place within their meeting houses. However, an intriguing inscription from Islandmagee churchyard commemorates Henry Dunbar, son of Rev. James Dunbar, who died in June 1783 aged 21. Referring to Dunbar senior the inscription states, 'who was interd. in the body of the adjoining [Anglican] church, formerly Presbyterian clergyman of Island Magee'. It is known that Dunbar, a Scotsman, died on 26 April 1766, having been minister of First Islandmagee since 1758.

3.3 Gravestones
The value of gravestone inscriptions for ancestral research has long been recognised. The discovery of a single gravestone might provide more information on the history of a family than can be gleaned from a host of documentary sources. Prior to 1864, when official registration of deaths began in Ireland, and in the absence of burial registers, a gravestone inscription may be the only source for an individual's date of death. In the days when each tombstone was individually crafted by a mason, there was considerable variation in the form of memorials to the dead. In the seventeenth century gravestones tended to be ledgers laid flat on the ground. This format continued throughout the eighteenth century and into the nineteenth century. However, from the late seventeenth century, vertical headstones began to appear.

While there was a direct correlation between the wealth of the deceased's family and the elaboration of the memorial, it must not be thought that gravestones were entirely the preserve of the elite. From the late seventeenth century onwards an increasing number of headstones were erected by people from the middling strata of society. In counties Fermanagh and Monaghan there are hundreds of headstones from this era. Most of them bear Gaelic Irish names and are presumably to Catholics. These people could have been no more than tenant farmers. Interestingly, almost without exception the inscriptions are in English.

Inscriptions

The inscriptions on memorials from the seventeenth and eighteenth centuries frequently communicate more information about the departed than more recent headstones. Information about the deceased's life, occupation and place of residence will often be recorded. More unusual statements include the instructions inscribed on a Hamilton memorial in Bangor Abbey churchyard which, following the details of the deaths of several generations of the family between 1670 and 1785, concludes: 'posterity are desired not to burie any more under this stone'.

Some inscriptions incorporate a mini-biography of the deceased. Verse was also used to highlight the qualities of the deceased. The following inscription appears on a headstone in Greyabbey graveyard.

> HERE LYES JEAN HAY
> WHO NIGHT AND DAY
> WAS HONEST GOOD AND
> JUST HER HOP AND
> LOVE WAS FROM ABOVE
> IN WHICH PLACE WAS
> HER TRUST HER SPIRIT
> LEFT HER TERRANE
> PART WITH JOY TO
> GOD WHERE WAS HER
> HART ON THAT 4 DAY
>   OF JANY 170$^6/_7$

The format of the year of death on this stone is interesting. Possibly it represents an attempt to reconcile the difference in the date of the new year in Ireland and Scotland. Until 1752 the new year in England and Ireland began officially on 25 March, whereas in Scotland the new year began on 1 January. It may have been the case that Jean Hay died on 4 January 1706 under the English/Irish system, but 4 January 1707 under the Scottish.

Verse could also be used as a means of warning readers of their own mortality. The gravestone to Mathew Lyndsay (d. 1680) in Taughboyne churchyard, County Donegal includes the following lines:

> REMEMBER MAN AS
> THOW GOEST BY, AS
> THOW ARE NOW SO
> ONST WAS I, AS I AM
> NOW SO SHALT T
> HOW BE, REMEMBE
> R MAN THAT THO
> W MWST DYE

It will be noted that the letter 'w' was used for a 'u' as in thow/thou and mwst/must. Similar verses can be found in other graveyards across the English-speaking world.

On occasion the deceased lay in an unmarked grave for years before a memorial was erected. A particularly poignant example of this can be found in the burial ground adjoining Duneane Church of Ireland church, County Antrim. Here a sandstone headstone bears the following inscription:

> To the memory of John Bones, who died on the 1st of February 1799, aged 66 years, as a tribute of filial gratitude to one of the best of parents, this stone is erected by an affectionate son, who after a long absence from his native country visits the grave of his father with feelings of undiminished regret 1st September 1822.

John Bones was a Presbyterian tenant farmer with several sons. Which of them erected this headstone is not known for sure, but it may have been James who had been involved in United Irishmen and had taken part in an attack on Ballymena during the 1798 Rebellion. In 1810, James and his family emigrated to America and settled in Winnsboro, South Carolina. One can imagine him on a return visit to the land of his birth standing at the site of his father's burial place, reflecting on events over 20 years before, and feeling a sense of shame that no memorial had ever been erected. Spurred into action, he commissioned a mason to create the headstone and incise on it words that reflected his thoughts and feelings.

Circumstances of death

Occasionally the circumstances of death will be recorded on a gravestone. One of the few inscriptions referring to the 1641 rising can be read in Drumbeg Church of Ireland churchyard: 'Capt William Stewart, son of Lord Garlies, was killed at Kilcullin Bridge, he & his escort cut into pieces by a party of Roman Catholicks in 1641'. In 1772, the minister of Tullylish Presbyterian Church, Rev. Samuel Morrell, was, according to his inscription, killed when 'defending the house of Sir Richard Johnston of Gilford, Baronet, against the Insurgents called Hearts of Oak & Hearts of Steel.' John Barry of Ringneal (d. 1786) was, according to his inscription in Tullynakill graveyard, killed when the millstone of Ardmillan mill broke.

A number of memorials concern those who were caught up in the events of the turbulent 1790s. In the burial ground adjoining St Columb's Cathedral in Derry there is a tombstone that commemorates the life of Rev. William Hamilton, a minister of the Church of Ireland and a noted naturalist. The inscription records, 'He was assassinated at the house of Dr Waller, at Sharon, on the 2nd day of August 1793 [*recte* 1797], where he fell a victim to the brutal fury of an armed banditti in the fortieth year of his age.' Hamilton had been targeted due to his role as a magistrate in suppressing the United Irishmen. Several memorials commemorate those who were killed in the 1798 Rebellion. In Whitechurch graveyard near Ballywalter a stone was erected in memory of Hugh and David Maxwell of Ballywalter 'whose bodies are here interred. They fell in an attack made on the town of Newtownards the 10th of June 1798.' Other headstones allude to the rebellion without making explicit reference to it. Despite protesting his innocence, Archibald Wilson of Conlig was hanged for his suspected role in the rebellion and was buried in Bangor Abbey churchyard. The inscription on his headstone states that he was 'mart[y]red' and that on Judgement Day those who made false allegations against him would themselves be judged for what they had done.

In coastal areas graveyards abound in memorials to mariners and occasionally an eighteenth-century gravestone will refer to individuals lost at sea. In Saul Church of Ireland churchyard, County Down, a headstone featuring a carving of a woman mourning over a tomb commemorates Ambrose Lennon, who 'foundered in a hurricane in the West Indies on board his Majesty's ship Barbadoes with all the crew in the year 1780'. The memorial was erected by his son, Captain John Lennon.

British origins
A few memorials include the place of origin of those of British background. For example, the following inscription appears on a gravestone in Derg Church of Ireland churchyard in Castlederg, County Tyrone:

HERE LIETH INTERRED THE
BODY OF CORNET ARCHB
ALD JOHNSTON DECEND
ED OF THE ANCIENT F
AMILY OF LODERHAY IN
ANANDEAL IN THE KIN
GDOM OF SCOTLAND W
HO DECEASED THE [-] OF
MAR 167[-] AND ALSO MA
RGRET HIS WIFE DECEN
DED OF THE ANCIENT
FAMILY OF GRAHAMS
OF MUL WHO DECEASED THE
(inscription ends abruptly here)

The following inscription was recorded on a gravestone in the churchyard of St Salvator's in Glaslough, County Monaghan: 'Here lieth the body of Mungo Johnston Gent, of The Ancient House of Lockerby in Scotland who died the 2d of October, anno 1704'. The same desire to emphasise lineage can be found on the memorial to Oliver Anketill (d. 1666) in Monaghan Town which states that he was 'descended of the antient family of Shawstone in Dorcet Shire in England'. At times, however, some caution needs to be exercised in taking such claims at face value. For example, a memorial in Layd graveyard, near Cushendall, County Antrim, begins: 'In the Scotch army of Charles I in Ulster was Major Alex^r Macaulay from Ardincaple in Dumbarton Shire'. Despite these claims, this family was Irish and the Scottish origin may have been invented to distinguish this landowning branch of the family, which became Protestant, from relatives who remained Catholic and lived in more humble circumstances. (See Brian Turner's article in *DIFHR*, 38 (2015), p. 18.)

3.4 Gravestone decoration

Many memorials of this era display a range of decorative symbols from which we can learn much about our ancestors and their worldview. Gravestones to the elite very often include the family's coat of arms, reinforcing their status through the use of heraldry. However, in the eighteenth century many families of more modest means also added coats of arms to their headstones. A remarkable number of headstones featuring heraldic devices survive in graveyards in County Antrim, particularly in burial grounds along or near to the coast. While the accuracy and appropriateness of much of the heraldry on display in these graveyards can be called into question, there is no doubting its popularity. Rubbings of many of these headstones (including the inscriptions) were published in the *Ulster Journal of Archaeology* in the early 1900s. (See F. J. Bigger and H. Hughes, 'Armorial sculptured stones of the County Antrim', *UJA*, 2nd series, 6 (1900), pp 39–53, 90–104, 162–72, 231–44; 7 (1901), pp 58–61, 142–57; 8 (1902), pp 90–93; 9 (1903), pp 93–6, 131–7.)

Another form of decoration frequently found on gravestones of this period falls into the category of mortality symbolism. These symbols include a combination of a skull, crossed bones, hourglass, coffin, bell, Bible and sexton's tools, representing visually what the phrase *memento mori* – 'remember you must die' – communicated in words. Although mortality symbols are found on the memorials of individuals from all backgrounds, in the seventeenth century they are most frequently identified on the gravestones to Scottish settlers. One of the earliest is the gravestone to Thomas Goodlate (d. 1624) in Killyman Church of Ireland graveyard, County Tyrone, which depicts a skull clenching a longbone in its teeth. The use of mortality symbols continued into the eighteenth century, but by the close of the 1700s had more or less ceased as funerary symbolism began to reflect hope and the resurrection, rather than death.

Masonic symbols also appear on memorials, such as the late eighteenth-century Hannan gravestone in Cranfield graveyard, County Antrim, which depicts an arch and a representation of Pythagoras' theorem. Symbols associated with the trade of the deceased were also carved on memorials, though this occurred far less frequently in Ulster than it did in Scotland where it was quite widespread. The stone to William Stennors (d. 1626) inside Bangor Abbey, County Down, has representations of the symbols associated with the deceased's occupation of mason carved on it. In the churchyard adjoining Bangor Abbey is a headstone to James Armure which features a carving of a tanner's knife, one of the tools associated with the trade of the deceased. The inscription, with remarkable precision, records that Armure died on Thursday, 20 June 1672, at 12 o'clock. The gravestone in Friar's Bush graveyard in Belfast to John Gibson (d. 1717) features shears, suggesting that the deceased may have been involved in the cloth trade. Memorials to members of the Anglican and Catholic clergy sometimes include a representation of a chalice.

In Inver churchyard, Larne, the headstone to John Thom (d. 1767) features a carving of a man holding open a book and standing at a high desk, which has books resting on it. It seems likely that he was a schoolmaster. Symbols associated with a seafarer, including cannons, sextant and anchor, appear on the gravestone to Captain George Colvill in Bangor Abbey churchyard. Colvill was the commander of the private ship of war *Amazon* which was wrecked near Bangor on 25 February 1780. Another interesting memorial is the headstone to Alexander McCormick (d. 1781) in Ballyhalbert graveyard, County Down, which features a well-carved figure of a Volunteer at the top, on one side of which is a flag with a harp on it, and on the other side a small cannon and a drum. The inscription records that McCormick was an 'Echlinvale Volunteer' and that 'His Hon. Captain & Companie did him honour at his death & he was buried with ye honours of war' when he died aged just 15.

3.5 Locating inscriptions

The gravestone inscriptions from a large number of graveyards in Ulster have been transcribed and published. In the 1830s the compilers of the Ordnance Survey Memoirs occasionally noted down early and interesting inscriptions when drafting their parish studies. For example, the memoir for the parish of Ballinderry, County Antrim, includes the following inscription from the old graveyard beside Portmore Lough:

DSBR 1732
A husband kind,
A father dear;
A faithful friend,
Lieth here;
My days is spent,
My glass is run;
Children dear,
Prepare to come.
Cormick O'Dowd, aged 82 years.

The Memoirs were published in 40 volumes by the Institute of Irish Studies at Queen's University Belfast in the 1990s. Many Ulster inscriptions appeared in the *Journal of the Association for the Preservation of the Memorials of the Dead in Ireland*, published between 1888 and 1934. These recordings are particularly useful if the gravestone can no longer be found. A guide to the graveyards in Northern Ireland featured in this series is Ian Forsythe, 'An index to the *Memorials of the Dead*', *DIFHR*, 15 (1992).

In addition, the inscriptions from a large number of other graveyards in Ulster have been published in the journals of local historical societies such as *Clogher Record*, *Donegal Annual* and *Breifne*. Other volumes of inscriptions have been produced by some of the branches of the North of Ireland Family History Society. A local government initiative to publish inscriptions gave rise to the *Ballymena Borough Gravestone Series*. A number of parish and congregational histories will include a listing of gravestone inscriptions as an appendix. Many booklets of inscriptions from graveyards in counties Cavan, Donegal, Fermanagh, Monaghan and Tyrone have been produced by the Kabristan Archives. Some of these publications will simply list the inscriptions, though others will provide supplementary information on the families drawn from a range of other sources.

Increasingly, gravestone inscriptions are being made available online through various providers. The inscriptions recorded by some of the genealogy centres affiliated to the Irish Family History Foundation are available through RootsIreland (www.rootsireland.ie). The county source lists in John Grenham's *Tracing Your Irish Ancestors* (4th edition, 2012) include details of the availability of many collections of gravestone inscriptions, especially those published in local journals and inscription series as well as online. Collections of inscriptions made by genealogists and antiquarians can also be found in archives and libraries in Ireland. For example, PRONI holds the extensive McClay collection of inscriptions from many graveyards in counties Antrim and Londonderry (D3672).

Since 1966 the Ulster Historical Foundation has published 21 volumes of graveyard inscriptions for County Down, four for Belfast and four for County Antrim. A number of these volumes include source guides for the respective locality. The Foundation also holds recordings of gravestone inscriptions for many other graveyards in Ulster, which can be accessed via its website (free for members and pay-per-view for non-members). The Foundation's History from Headstones website (www.historyfromheadstones.com) includes maps identifying graveyards in the six counties of Northern Ireland. For each graveyard the Ordnance Survey grid reference is given, which can be used to pinpoint the burial ground's precise location.

In venturing out into the field, researchers should be aware that while many old graveyards in Ulster are well maintained by those charged with their care, a number are not. In a neglected graveyard it may be impossible to identify a particular gravestone in the undergrowth. Even if the graveyard is properly looked after, the family burial plot may be within railings that are impossible to climb over or squeeze between. An added problem is that many of the older memorials are largely if not completely illegible. Generally the inscription on a slate gravestone will have a much better survival rate than one on a sandstone memorial. Inscriptions carved in false relief will often survive better than incised inscriptions. At the same time, though a great deal of perseverance may be required, there are few things more satisfying for the family historian than locating the burial place of one's ancestors.

4. Seventeeth-century records

4.1 Pre-Plantation records

4.1.1 Fiants of the Tudor sovereigns

Fiants – from the Latin term, *Fiant litterae patentes* ('Let letters patent be made') – were warrants drawn up prior to the issue of letters patent. They concerned a broad range of matters, including pardons, grants of land, and political and religious appointments. The original fiants were lost in the destruction of the old Public Record Office of Ireland in 1922. However, soon after it was established in the late 1860s, the archivists in the Public Record Office began to prepare calendars of the fiants, 1521–1603, and these were published as appendices to the *Reports of the Deputy Keeper of the Public Records of Ireland* (1875–90). In 1994, the Dublin antiquarian bookseller, Eamonn de Burca, reproduced the fiants in three volumes with a fourth volume containing a comprehensive index under the title *The Irish Fiants of the Tudor Sovereigns during the Reigns of Henry VIII, Edward VI, Philip & Mary, and Elizabeth I*. This includes a helpful introduction by the historian Kenneth Nicholls.

Among the most valuable aspects of the fiants is the level of detail that they contain, with far fuller information recorded than in the actual letters patent issued in London. Some 120,000 individuals are named in the fiants, representing a high proportion of the total population of Ireland in this era. The pardons issued in the closing stages of the Nine Years' War are particularly helpful when researching families in Ulster at that time for they can include large numbers of names. For example, the pardon issued to Rory O'Donnell, lord of Tyrconnell (Donegal), and his followers in February 1603 (no. 6761) includes the names of *c.* 550 individuals, including some women, with almost 150 distinct surnames (by contrast, the published patent roll deriving from this fiant lists only ten individuals). Another pardon, that to Tirlagh McHenry O'Neale, 'chief of the Fues [Fews]', County Armagh, and his followers in June 1602 (no. 6662), contains *c.* 270 names, including the status or occupation for many of them, such as yeoman, husbandman and horseman.

4.2 Records relating to the Plantation period, 1610–40

4.2.1 Books on the Ulster Plantation

A historical background to the Ulster Plantation is given in the introductory essay of this book. In summary, it is important to note that the official scheme for the Ulster Plantation affected six of Ulster's nine counties – Armagh, Cavan, Donegal, Fermangh, Londonderry and Tyrone – while the remaining three counties – Antrim, Down and Monaghan – experienced British settlement to varying degrees. For those who wish to delve more deeply into this period, the following books will be helpful:

> Jonathan Bardon, *The Plantation of Ulster* (2011)
> Nicholas Canny, *Making Ireland British, 1580–1650* (2001)
> Raymond Gillespie, *Colonial Ulster: The Settlement of East Ulster, 1600–1641* (1985)
> George Hill, *An Historical Account of the Plantation in Ulster at the Commencement of the Seventeenth Century* (1877)
> Michael Perceval-Maxwell, *The Scottish Migration to Ulster in the Reign of James I* (1973)
> Philip Robinson, *The Plantation of Ulster* (1984)

A very helpful guide to early seventeenth-century records is R. J. Hunter (ed.), *Plantations in Ulster, 1600–41: A Collection of Documents*. First produced in 1975, a revised and expanded edition was prepared by Ian Montgomery and William Roulston and published in 2018 by the Public Record Office of Northern Ireland and the Ulster Historical Foundation. This volume includes reproductions of a series of documents along with transcriptions of them and additional commentary.

4.2.2 Plantation surveys

Between 1611 and 1622 the government commissioned four surveys to investigate the progress of the 'official' Plantation. These surveys and where they may be found are as follows:

1611: A survey carried out by Sir George Carew. Printed in *Calendar of the Carew Manuscripts, 1603–24*, pp 68–9, 75–9, 220–51. (Carew's account of Antrim, Down and Monaghan has been printed in *UJA*, 3rd series, 28 (1975), pp 81–2.)

1613: A survey carried out by Sir Josias Bodley. Printed in Historical Manuscripts Commission, *Hastings Manuscripts*, 4 (1947), pp 159–92.

1618–9: A survey carried out by Captain Nicholas Pynnar. Printed in George Hill, *An Historical Account of the Plantation of Ulster at the Commencement of the Seventeenth Century* (1877).

1622: A survey carried out by commissioners appointed by the government. The 1622 commission was the most detailed of all the investigations into the progress of the Plantation. In addition to the published reports there is a significant amount of original documentation relating to the 1622 survey in the National Library of Ireland (MSS 8013–8014), and to a lesser extent in the Huntingdon and Peterborough Record Office (Kimbolton Manuscripts, DD/M). This material includes many of the original certificates presented by the British landowners or their agents in counties Armagh and Tyrone. Names of tenants, often distinguishing between freeholders and leaseholders, are provided as well as information on the buildings on the estate and who had built them. The material arising from this commission has been collated in Victor Treadwell (ed.), *The Irish Commission of 1622* (2006), published by the Irish Manuscripts Commission.

4.2.3 R. J. Hunter Papers

R. J. (Bob) Hunter was one of the foremost historians of the Ulster Plantation. Following his death in 2007, his extensive collection of working papers was deposited in the Public Record Office of Northern Ireland (D4446). Microfilms acquired by him from the British Library and The National Archives (London) have been catalogued by PRONI under MIC721. Hunter's ambition, sadly unrealised, was to produce a major study of the English involvement in the Ulster Plantation and many of his papers relate to his research, much of it carried out in archives in England, into this subject. He was also interested in intellectual history, the book trade, and the built heritage of the Plantation.

With support from the R. J. Hunter Committee, in 2012–13 the Ulster Historical Foundation produced in book form Hunter's hitherto unpublished transcripts of the Ulster port books of 1612–15 and the muster roll of *c.* 1630 (see below). In addition, several other works by Hunter were issued: a new edition of *Strabane Barony during the Ulster Plantation, 1607–41*; his previously unpublished thesis, *The Ulster Plantation in the Counties of Armagh and Cavan 1608–41*; and a collection of his essays, *Ulster Transformed: Essays on Plantation and Print Culture c. 1590–1641.*

4.2.4 Ulster port books

The Ulster port books cover the years 1612–15 and include details of goods imported and exported through the ports of Londonderry, Coleraine and Carrickfergus as well as the ports in the barony of Lecale, County Down. They are an invaluable source of information on the nature of the economy in early seventeenth-century Ulster. The goods exported tended to be agricultural produce, such as salmon, beef and grain, while the imported commodities ranged from exotic foodstuffs to standard household items. The names recorded in the port books include masters of ships and merchants.

The port books were transcribed and published in R. J. Hunter (ed.), *The Ulster Port Books 1612–15*, prepared for publication by Brendan Scott (2012). This volume includes maps showing the various ports in the rest of Ireland, Britain and Continental Europe with which the Ulster ports traded. The original port books are in the Temple Newsam Manuscripts in the West Yorkshire Archive Service. Photocopies of these are available in the R. J. Hunter Papers in PRONI: D4446/B/6/1 (Carrickfergus); D4446/B/6/2 (Coleraine); D4446/B/6/3 (Lecale); and D4446/B/6/4–5 (Londonderry). R. J. Hunter's transcripts of these manuscripts can be found in D4446/A/6/20–21 (Londonderry); D4446/A/6/22 (Carrickfergus); D4446/A/6/28 (Coleraine); and D4446/A/6/29 (Lecale).

4.2.5 Ulster roll of gaol delivery

Rare survivals of the judicial system in early seventeenth-century Ulster are the extracts from what has been termed the 'Ulster roll of gaol delivery'. Some of the entries for the years 1613–18 were transcribed from the records of the Court of Exchequer in Dublin by James F. Ferguson and published in *UJA*, 1st series, 1 (1853), pp 260–70; 2 (1854), pp 25–9. Others appear in R. M. Young (ed.), *Historical Notices of Old Belfast* (1896), pp 30–39, and Thomas Gogarty, 'Ulster roll of gaol delivery', *Archivium Hibernicum*, 6 (1917), pp 83–93. See also Brian Gilmore, 'Assizes and inquisitions for counties Armagh, Tyrone, Monaghan, Cavan and Fermanagh in 1614–1615', *Duiche Neill*, 24 (2017), pp 38–57.

The extracts include the names of jurors, those charged with criminal behaviour and their alleged victims, and provide brief details of each case and the outcome. For example, a jury assembled in Downpatrick in 1613 dealt with the following case:

> … Murtagh Moder Magrane, late of Dromncknogher, county Down, yeoman, on the 20th of August, 1613, at Ballemullnany, stole a chestnut-coloured mare worth 40s. the property of John Prestly, of which he is found guilty; and the judgment of the Court is that he be brought back to the gaol by the gaoler and be disengaged from his chains, and that he be led from the gaol thro' the midst of the town of Down as far as the gallows, and there hung by the neck until he be dead, and the Sheriff of Down is commanded to carry this into execution.

4.2.6 Irish statute staple records

The Irish staple was created in the 1200s to regulate trade and by the early 1600s had become very important in the regulation of debt. Historians have used these records to analyse levels of indebtedness and the economic consequences of this. Surviving registers of the Dublin staple, 1596–1637 and

1664–78, are held in the Dublin City Archives. Related Chancery records are in the British Library. For more on these records see J. Ohlmeyer and É. Ó Ciardha (eds), *The Irish Statute Staple Books, 1596–1687* (1998). This book includes alphabetical listings of creditors and debtors (from across Ireland), including residence, status/occupation, date and monetary amount. The Staple Database was published as a CD-ROM accompanying the book.

4.2.7 Calendars of patent rolls

The original Irish patent rolls of the reigns of James I and Charles I, recording, among other things, grants of land or pardons issued, were destroyed in the Public Record Office of Ireland in 1922. Fortunately, some of the material had already been published in calendar form. Printed calendars of patent rolls exist for the reign of James I and the early part of the reign of Charles I. The *Calendar of the Patent Rolls of the Reign of James I* (1603–25) was prepared under the direction of the Irish Record Commission prior to 1830 and was printed before the Commission closed. The Irish Manuscripts Commission published a facsimile of the printed calendar in 1966. Among the most useful of items that it contains are the names of individuals who received grants of denization (see below). The calendar relating to the opening years of the reign of Charles I was published as *Calendar of the Patent and Close Rolls of Chancery in Ireland, of the Reign of Charles the First: First to Eighth Year, Inclusive*, edited by James Morrin (1863).

4.2.8 Denization and naturalisation records

Scottish settlers in early seventeenth-century Ulster did not automatically enjoy the same legal rights as the English. Naturalisation placed a Scot on the same footing as an English subject and was granted by the king or by an act of parliament. Many of the new Scottish landowners in Ulster were granted naturalisation by King James. In 1614, the Irish Parliament passed an act that allowed aliens of any nationality to acquire a grant of denization and in the following year the king wrote to his lord deputy in Ireland to implement this since 'many of the inhabitants of Scotland daily repair to Ireland'. By acquiring a grant of denization, the individual concerned was usually indicating a desire to stay in Ireland and protect his possessions using the existing legal safeguards.

The original grants of denization and naturalisation have not survived, but the abovementioned *Calendar of the Patent Rolls of the Reign of James I* includes lists of names of Scots in Ulster who received them, usually with the place of residence in Ulster of the individual concerned and occasionally the occupation. The lists may include the statement, 'all being of the Scotch nation or descent, to be free from the yoke of Scottish or Irish servitude, and to enjoy all the rights and privileges of English subjects'. Looking through the names of denizens, it is clear that they covered a broad spectrum of society and not simply the elite.

Rev. David Stewart, a Presbyterian minister and a very active local historian, extracted the names of several hundred Scots who were recorded as having been granted denization and naturalisation from the printed calendars, and published his findings in pamphlet form as *The Scots in Ulster: Their Denization and Naturalisation* (1954). In this work Stewart provided a historical background to the processes of denization and naturalisation. Much additional information from other seventeenth-century sources was also provided. Stewart's pamphlet was reprinted as an article in *Familia: Ulster Genealogical Review* in 1995 and in booklet form by the Presbyterian Historical Society of Ireland in 2015. See also William A. Shaw (ed.), *Letters of Denization and Acts of Naturalisation for Aliens in England and Ireland, 1603–1700*, Publications of the Huguenot Society of London, 18 (1911), which includes lists of Irish denizens from 1605 onwards.

4.2.9 Calendars of state papers

State papers concerning Ireland are preserved in The National Archives (formerly the Public Record Office) in London under SP 63. Calendars of the papers covering the period 1509–1670 were published in 24 volumes by the Public Record Office between 1860 and 1911 under the title *Calendar of the State Papers relating to Ireland*. An initiative to produce fuller versions of the sixteenth-century Irish state papers has so far resulted in the publication of several new volumes for the years 1547–53, 1566–7, 1568–71 and 1571–5. Each volume has a comprehensive index. Microfilm copies of the original State Papers, covering the period 1509–1782, can be found in PRONI (MIC223). The records can also be accessed via the internet at some libraries and archives through *State Papers Online*.

The State Papers concern the administration of Ireland during a period of enormous change. There is much information of interest about the Ulster Plantation and the issues arising from its implementation as well as the disruption caused by the wars of the 1640s. The documents cover a broad range of subjects. The following document in the State Papers dates from 15 September 1660 and provides an example of the type of information that can be found in these records:

> Copy of Record of a Coroner's Inquest held at Duncanalley [Dunkineely?] the 15th of September, 1660, be [by] Edmund [?] Collo McSweine, one of His Majesty's Coroners for the Co. Donegal, to inquire how Alexander and John Murray came to their deaths.
>
> The Jury are:—
> Wm Hamilton, foreman
> Alexr Montgomerie, gentleman
> Edward Creichtoune of Duncanalle
> Thomas Clerke of Drumrenny

Thomas Irving of Auchend
Thomas Cawnes of Burnecronen
John Paterson of Burnecronen
Francis Herries of Enver
James Scot of Courne
John Turbet of Calebegs [Killybegs]
John Warnenocke of Machrebollie
David Montgomerie of Killochtie
John Mulligan of Bellilocheny
Wm Watson of Auchend

They find the two dead men were murdered be [by] George Cunningham, Wm Cunningham, Andrew Cunningham, Alexr Cunningham, Charles Murray, James Lindsay, John Walker, Owen Roe McDonochy and John Craige, and that George Conningham and James Lindsay did fly for it (*CSPI, 1660–1662*, p. 37).

While the records generally concern matters of state and the civil administration, there are records that can be considered private papers. Of particular interest are the many documents relating to the management of the Conway (later Hertford) estate in south County Antrim in the 1650s and 1660s, mostly written by Sir George Rawdon, the agent to Lord Conway. For example, dated 8 July 1653 is a memorandum of a lease issued by Rawdon on behalf of Lord Conway and his son, which names the tenants to whom part of the townland of Ballinderry was leased: Samuel Dason, Andrew Bell, Arthur Smith, John Sizens, Patrick Magee, John Madder, Thomas Goffe and John Madders (*CSPI, 1647–1660*, p. 394).

After 1670 Irish material may be found in the *Calendar of the State Papers, Domestic Series*, also published by the Public Record Office; this series continues until the end of the reign of Queen Anne in 1714. Typescript copies of original state papers in London after 1714 and up to 1780 that relate to Ireland are available in PRONI. Also worth consulting for early material on the administration of Ireland is the *Calendar of the Carew Manuscripts: Preserved in the Archiepiscopal Library at Lambeth*, edited by J. S. Brewer and William Bullen (6 vols, 1867–73), covering the period 1515–1624.

4.2.10 Ulster inquisitions
In order to establish certain facts about a particular property in the seventeenth century, a jury was assembled which was composed of local men who investigated such matters as ownership, inheritance and leasing policy. The findings of these juries were printed in summary form in the *Inquisitionum in officio rotulorum cancellariae Hiberniae asservatarum repertorium*, published in two volumes in the 1820s with volume two covering Ulster. Many of the summaries are given in an abbreviated form of Latin, though it is usually

possible to get the gist of what is recorded. A significant number of the inquisitions name the tenants on individual estates. The following example is from the estate of Sir William Hamilton of Manor Elieston in County Tyrone, and dates from 4 May 1631:

> Bryen Roe McConmoy houldeth the balliboe of land called Tireamaddan for the term of two years from Andrew Hayes who houldeth the same from said Sir William. Morrise O'Ternan houldeth the balliboe of Litterbrett and Dorgragh from the said Sir William 'till the feast of all saints next, and dooth, plough, pasture and grass upon the same. Shane Roe O'Devin houldeth the ½ balliboe of Nonihicannon … from James Hamilton who houldeth the same from the said Sir William, and doe plough, pasture and grass the same 'till hallowtide next. Bryen McCrener and Rory O'Quyn hould the balliboe of Aghnacree from the said James Hamilton in manner aforesaid. Patrick Groome O'Devin hould the balliboe of Leath … from Thomas Petticreive whoe houldeth the same from the said Sir William, and doe plough, pasture and grass the same. The said Patrick houldeth ½ the balliboe of Loughes, in manner as aforesaid. Owen Modder McConmoy houldeth the ballebo of Gorten from the said Sir William, and also the balliboe of Leanamoor, in manner as aforesaid.

The names of the tenants of Scottish landlords recorded in the Ulster inquisitions were extracted by Rev. David Stewart and published by him in *The Scots in Ulster* (see above section 'Denization and naturalisation records' for more details on this publication).

4.2.11 Summonister rolls

Summonister rolls record, among other things, the names of people fined for non-attendance at the quarter sessions. Other offences are also recorded. For example, Henry O'Finnoghan in County Londonderry was fined for ploughing his land in the traditional Irish manner with the plough attached to the horse's tail (T808/15130). The papers of the genealogist Tenison Groves include transcripts of the names in these rolls for several counties. Most date from the early seventeenth century. These provide the names and residences of hundreds of individuals. In date order they are as follows:

Counties Cavan, Londonderry and Tyrone, 1610–24 – T808/15131
County Londonderry, 1611–69 – T808/15130
County Tyrone, 1615–38 – T808/15090
County Tyrone, *c.* 1615–21 – T808/15126
County Tyrone, *c.* 1618–38 – T808/15120
Counties Londonderry and Tyrone, *c.* 1637–40 – T808/15132
Counties Londonderry and Tyrone, *c.* 1640–70 – T808/15133
Counties Londonderry and Tyrone, 1656–62 – T808/15134

Counties Londonderry and Tyrone, 1623–38 – T808/15135
Counties not specified, *c.* 1620–84 – T808/15139

Further extracts from summonister rolls in PRONI can be found under reference T1365.

4.2.12 Muster rolls

A muster roll was a list of able-bodied men who were capable of military service. Several muster rolls survive for Ulster counties from the early seventeenth century. For example, a muster roll of Coleraine and Londonderry from 1622 was printed in *Londonderry and the London Companies*, edited by D. A. Chart (1928). The most important of the muster rolls of this period was that compiled between the spring of 1629 and the spring of 1633 by Lieut. William Graham, the muster-master of Ulster. Transcripts of this muster roll are available in PRONI (see D1759/3C/1–3 (MIC637/10–11) and T934/1) and some listings for individual counties have also been published (e.g. County Donegal in *Donegal Annual*, 10 (1972)). These have now been superseded by *Men and Arms: The Ulster Settlers, c. 1630*, edited by R. J. Hunter and prepared for publication by John Johnston (2012).

John Johnston provides the following information on this muster roll in his preface to this book:

> This muster roll is contained in a large, leather-bound volume in the British Library. The volume consists of 283 folio sheets on which are recorded the names of 13,147 men from the nine counties of Ulster. Each county forms a separate section of the volume and the men who mustered are listed under the names of their landlords; beside each man's name is a description of the weapons he was carrying or a note that he was unarmed. … Most of the men who mustered were English and Scottish settlers and, in the absence of comprehensive parish and estate records, the muster rolls is the nearest one has to a census of the British population of early seventeenth-century Ulster.

Hunter and Johnston's edition includes much supplementary information on the settlers, drawn from numerous contemporary sources, such as the Ulster inquisitions, state papers and the 1641 depositions. The weapons range from firearms (calivers, muskets and snaphances) to swords, pikes and halberds. Many men possessed more than one weapon, while a high proportion were unarmed, an indication of the degree of security that the settler community felt at this time. A handful of men were drummers and colour bearers. Unfortunately, a return does not survive for every estate. For instance, there are no names for the extensive Chichester and Conway estates in south County Antrim. Nonetheless, the muster roll can be used as a guide to the distribution of the settler population in Ulster *c.* 1630.

4.2.13 The Great Parchment Book

Compiled in 1639, the Great Parchment Book is a survey of the lands in County Londonderry that had been granted to the London livery companies and the Irish Society (a kind of umbrella organisation for these companies, but also a landowner in its own right) as part of the scheme for the Ulster Plantation. It was produced following the forfeiture of these lands to the Crown due to allegations that the Londoners had not fulfilled their obligations in Ulster. In March 1639 a commission was appointed to oversee the collection of all monies due to the King from the estates of the London companies and Irish Society and to agree new terms with the sitting tenants. Two of the members of the commission travelled to County Londonderry in the following month and completed their work in early October. The contracts they entered into were recorded in the Great Parchment Book.

For example, on 23 September 1639 the commissioners agreed terms with George Elliott, James Patterson, William Witty, and John Kennaday of Desert Lynn, all husbandmen, for the townland of Ballicromlargie, formerly part of the estate of the Salters' Company. This townland contained an estimated 112 Irish acres and for this Elliott and the others were to pay an annual rent of £14 stg. Among other obligations, they were required to build on the premises 'one sufficient and substantiall house of timber, stone or bricke after the manner of an Englishe house two stories high and conteining fower roomes att the least'.

The Great Parchment Book was damaged in a fire in 1786, but, following a major programme of conservation, it is now available to researchers. The original is held in the London Metropolitan Archives under reference CLA/049/EM/02/018. A full transcription of the volume, along with digital images of its pages, can be accessed online (www.greatparchmentbook.org).

4.3 Records relating to the 1641 rising and its aftermath

4.3.1 The 1641 depositions

The 1641 depositions are arguably the most controversial records in Irish history. They provide accounts of the events of the 1641 rising and its aftermath. The insurrection began in Ulster in October 1641 and soon spread to other parts of Ireland. The controversy associated with the depositions concerns the nature of the information that they contain for not only do they record the loss of personal possessions and the destruction of homes, they also contain accounts of atrocities, mainly perpetrated by the native Irish on the settler population. Contemporary propagandists seized on these reports and exploited them for their own ends, with wildly exaggerated accounts of the numbers killed appearing in books and news-sheets. This, together with the ways in which they have been used by others since then, has resulted in the depositions being either dismissed, ignored or challenged by many writers. Others, however, have recognised that the depositions are a rich source of information on economic, social and religious conditions in Ireland on the eve of the 1641 rising and provide an invaluable record of the people of Ireland caught up in the events of the insurrection.

Collecting the depositions

Essentially the depositions were collected in two distinct periods. In December 1641 a 'Commission for the Despoiled Subject' was established in Dublin to take witness statements from refugees. The eight members of the commission were all Anglican clergymen and they were led by Henry Jones, dean of Kilmore. Initially requested to record the losses suffered by those who had been robbed of their possessions, the commission's remit was extended soon afterwards to include instances of murder and apostacy. This commission concluded its work in September 1647, though most of the depositions collected by it were made in 1642 and 1643.

In 1652, under the Cromwellian regime, commissioners were appointed to gather information on those accused of murders and massacres. More than 70 commissioners across the island worked on this for around two years and the evidence they collected was used by the High Court of Justice to prosecute individuals charged with committing particular atrocities. See the article by Michael McCartan, 'The Cromwellian High Courts of Justice in Ulster, 1653', *Seanchas Ardmhacha*, 23:1 (2010), pp 91–161, which explores in some detail the cases of 30 individuals tried by these courts and subsequently executed.

The depositions

In all, there are around 8,000 depositions and associated documents, running to over 19,000 pages in 31 volumes. Since 1741 the originals have been held in what is now the Manuscripts & Archives Research Library of Trinity College Dublin (MSS 809–841). For the most part the depositions have been arranged by county, though some depositions have been wrongly assigned to a particular county. Furthermore, the county in which the events described by the deponent took place need not necessarily have been the county of residence at the time the testimony was given.

The depositions have been digitised and transcribed in full and can now be accessed on the 1641 Depositions website (1641.tcd.ie). The Irish Manuscripts Commission has begun publishing full transcriptions of the depositions in a series of 12 volumes. Each of these contains an essay explaining the background to the depositions as well as an introduction providing specific information on the counties included in that volume. The depositions for Ulster counties are found in the following volumes:

> Volume I: Armagh and Monaghan (also includes Louth)
> Volume II: Cavan and Fermanagh
> Volume III: Antrim, Down, Donegal, Londonderry and Tyrone

As will be clear from the above arrangement[, the number of depositions varies quite considerably from county to county. For instance, there are many more depositions for Cavan and Fermanagh than for Donegal and Londonderry. In part this reflected the fact that settlers in the former counties were more likely to seek refuge in Dublin than those in the latter, where Scotland provided a safe haven for people fleeing the disturbances. There are also clear regional variations between the numbers of depositions collected in the early 1640s compared with the early 1650s. The Antrim and Down depositions, for example, date overwhelmingly from 1653.

The information given
The depositions help us to understand the factors that led to the rising, such as the underlying tensions between planter and Gael that surfaced once the insurrection began. We also learn something of the course of events that followed the outbreak of the rising and the settler response to this, including the mobilisation of forces to defend the British population. What emerges from the depositions is that no general massacre of the settler population took place, though atrocities certainly occurred. While most of those who gave depositions were Protestants from the settler community, some Gaelic Irish Catholics also provided accounts of their experiences. The deponents came from diverse social backgrounds, with many farmers and tradesmen giving evidence as well as members of the Protestant clergy. With regard to the deponents themselves, the information recorded can include their place of residence, occupation or status, religion and age. Family members killed as a result of the rising might be recorded.

The material possessions of the settlers are revealed as they documented their losses. These ranged from livestock and farm buildings to clothing and books. Roger Markham, who was at Sir Thomas Staples' ironworks at Lissan on the Londonderry-Tyrone border when news of the rising came through, gave this statement on 15 February 1642 as to his personal losses:

> I have lost what I haue laboured for euer sence I was 17 or 18 yeares of age I have lost all my labours and study which I valued worth much when another would think them worth little[.] I have lost all my written hand Books both of Arithmaticke and Geometrie. I have Lost my Instruments both Arithmaticall and Geometricall. I lost all my Cloaths but what I had one my back (TCD, MS 839, fols 17r–23v).

In general, the depositions collected in the early 1640s are more interesting for their social and economic content than those of a decade later. However, all of the depositions are useful from a genealogical perspective. As with all records, a degree of caution must be exercised in using and applying them for research purposes. While much testimony was based on what the deponents had witnessed for themselves, there is also a considerable amount of hearsay.

The depositions are a very important source of information on the Gaelic Irish population in early seventeenth-century Ulster and in part make up for the fact that the Irish are often not to be found in other sources of this era. In his deposition of 14 April 1642 John Cairns of Parsonstown, County Tyrone, who stated that he was a 45-year-old Scotsman and Protestant, named the following individuals as persons he knew to be involved in robbing him and others in the barony of Clogher (original spelling and punctuation retained):

> Torlogh grome mccawell of altnerne gen & his sonnes donnell mccawell
> & Bryen mccawell
> Donnogh bane mcquire neer to blessingbane esqr
> Bryen oNeell gent [and] Henry o Neell gent both of Slate
> Shane mccawell of fenaghdrome gent
> Bryen mcsyane oge o Neell of the barrony of Clogher gent
> Bryen mcArte mcRory o Neell of the brady gent
> Doniell o daly of fernaghdrum yeoman
> James buy o donnelly of keadagh gent
> Patrik o hoane Late of Aughalen gent
> Shane o Neell Late of brade gen
> Patrik mcquire Late with the said donnoghy bane mcquire gentleman
> Richard mcgill Late of Aughor generall of the County of Tyron
> (TCD, MS 839, fols 33r–34v)

Whether those alleged to be the perpetrators of these crimes really were guilty is another matter entirely, but there is tremendous genealogical value in this list of names.

Further reading

There is no shortage of publications on the 1641 rising. Some recent volumes that researchers may find helpful include:

> Michael Perceval-Maxwell, *Outbreak of the Irish Rebellion of 1641* (1994)
> Brian Mac Cuarta (ed.), *Ulster 1641: Aspects of the Rising* (1997)
> Elaine Murphy, *Ireland and the War at Sea, 1641–1653* (2012)
> Eamon Darcy, Annaleigh Margey and Elaine Murphy (eds), *The 1641 Depositions and the Irish Rebellion* (2012)
> Eamon Darcy, *The Irish Rebellion of 1641 and the Wars of the Three Kingdoms* (2013)
> Micheál Ó Siochrú and Jane Ohlmeyer (eds), *Ireland: 1641. Contexts and Reactions* (2013)

4.3.2 Muster rolls

The 1640s was a period of warfare and devastation in Ireland. Several fighting forces were raised from among the settler population to defend their farms and families. For example, the Laggan army was raised among the settler population in the north-west and is the subject of Kevin McKenny's book, *The Laggan Army in Ireland 1640–1685: The Landed Interests, Political Ideologies and Military Campaigns of the North-west Ulster Settlers* (2005). In addition to locally raised forces, an army from Scotland was sent to Ulster in 1642 to assist the settlers. For information on the Scottish forces in Ireland in the 1640s, see Edward M. Furgol, *A Regimental History of the Covenanting Armies, 1639–1651* (1990).

A collection of muster rolls for the period 1642–5 is available in the papers of the genealogist Tenison Groves in PRONI (T808/15166–15177). The following is a selection from this collection.

> Muster roll of Sir Robert Stewart's regiment at Raphoe, County Donegal, 1642 – T808/15166 (transcribed by Len Swindley and published in *DIFHR*, 37 (2014), pp 13–19)
> Muster roll of foot companies of Chichester, Clanaboy, Clotworthy and Montgomery, and of the horse company of Col. Arthur Hill, 1642, *c.* 4,000 names – T808/15172
> Muster roll held at the city of Derry, 1642–3 – T808/15176
> Muster roll of Col. Audley Mervyn's company, 1643 – T808/15175, 15177

Other muster rolls from this period include:

> County Antrim muster roll, 1642 – T3726/2
> County Down muster roll, 1642–3 – T563/1
> Donaghadee muster roll, 1642 – T3726/1

See also Brian Mitchell, *Defenders of the Plantation of Ulster, 1641–1691* (2010), which includes a 'Muster Roll of Garrison in the City of Londonderry, 1642–1643'; this identifies 905 men in nine foot companies.

4.4 Records relating to the Cromwellian and Restoration land settlements

When order was restored in Ireland in the early 1650s following the turbulence of the previous decade, the Cromwellians began a programme of land confiscation which continued during the reign of Charles II. Records relating to this period are discussed below.

4.4.1 The proposed transplantation of Scots from Ulster
One of the issues faced by the Cromwellians was what to do with Ulster's disaffected Scottish Presbyterians. Commissioners appointed 'for settling and securing the province of Ulster' in April 1653 concluded that 'there is no visible expedient to preserve these parts in safety, but by transplanting all popular Scots into some other part of Ireland'. Lists of those to be transplanted to the counties

of Kilkenny, Tipperary and Waterford were drawn up, but in the end the proposal was not put into effect. The names of some 250 individuals in counties Antrim and Down, including a few men of English and Irish background, who were identified for transplantation were printed in *Historical Notices of Old Belfast and its Vicinity*, edited by R. M. Young (1896), pp 80–83. For the most part, these names are listed by 'quarter', i.e. 'Six Mile Water Quarters' and only rarely is a more precise address given for any of them.

4.4.2 The Civil Survey

The Civil Survey was carried out under the Cromwellian administration in Ireland between 1654 and 1656. An edition of the Civil Survey for counties Donegal, Londonderry and Tyrone – the only Ulster counties for which the survey survives in full – was published by the Irish Manuscripts Commission in 1937 under the editorship of R. C. Simington. The Civil Survey includes a good deal of topographical material through the detailed descriptions of the boundaries of many of the baronies and parishes and sometimes even individual properties. Lands that had been forfeited by the native Irish are listed separately, as are lands owned by the Church (i.e. the Church of Ireland). For each of the baronies in the three counties there is a personal name index, with an index to lands at the end of the volume.

The information contained in the Civil Survey for each parish is tabulated and includes for each denomination of land the name of the proprietor, the extent of profitable and unprofitable acres and the value of the lands in 1640. The proprietor was not always the outright owner of the land, since some freeholders and leaseholders were also included under this column. The ethnic background and religion of the individual is usually given and occasionally additional information about him. For example, Will More, a freeholder in the parish of Clogher, was a 'horseman at the Seidge of Derry'. This was a siege that took place in 1649 when an army of Presbyterians, angry at the execution of Charles I, briefly encamped around Derry before dispersing.

Supplementary information may be provided, such as details of tenure and rents paid by individuals leasing the lands from the proprietors. In County Donegal several leases were issued by the bishop of Raphoe in 1636 which included the proviso that the tenant was to pay a specified sum of money – in one case £250 – towards the cost of building the bishop's palace. The parish of Raphoe is especially well documented. Those who held property in the town of Raphoe typically possessed a house and garden along with a few acres and grazing rights.

With regard to the listings of forfeited lands, these are helpful in identifying native proprietors before the 1641 rising. The Civil Survey for the barony of Dungannon reveals that most of the Irish landowners were generally in possession of no more than one or two townlands. In addition, the Civil Survey reveals something of the transfer of lands from native Irish to settler that had occurred prior to the rising. For example, it was noted that Henry Thomson had been gifted Gortegerties in Faughanvale parish by his uncle Hugh Thomson, an alderman in Londonderry who died in 1630, who in turn had purchased these lands from Bryan O'Cahan.

4.4.3 Books of survey and distribution

The books of survey and distribution were compiled in the course of the Restoration land settlement of the 1660s and 1670s. They record the transfer of land ownership from forfeiting Irish landowners to new patentees who had been granted the confiscated lands by the Crown. The information in the books is given in tabular form by county. The name of the landowner in 1641 is stated, together with a list of the lands in his possession, as well as their value and extent. The name of the new owner is also given. A set of the books of survey and distribution can be found in the Annesley collection in PRONI under D1854/1 and MIC532.

4.4.4 Land grants

Printed abstracts of the land grants made at this time may be found in the *Reports of the Commissioners Appointed ... Respecting the Public Records of Ireland*, 11th–15th Annual Reports (1825). Also included in this volume is an index to the certificates of the Court of Claims (see below), indexes to Adventurers' and soldiers' certificates and an index to adjudications in favour of the 1649 officers. The Adventurers were individuals who, in the 1640s, subscribed money towards the war effort in Ireland, in return for which they were promised grants of land. The 1649 officers (or '49 Officers) were settlers who had supported the royalist cause in Ireland, mainly between 1648 and 1650, and who, to compensate them for their sufferings, were to receive grants of land. The abstracts of the land grants in the aforementioned *Reports* were based on the Lodge Manuscripts in the National Archives of Ireland (available in PRONI under MIC600). Guides to the manuscript material relating to the land settlements of this period may be found in the 55th and 56th *Reports of the Deputy Keeper of the Public Records in Ireland*.

4.4.5 Court of Claims

The Court of Claims was established to hear and deliberate on claims presented by Catholics attempting to prove their innocence of any wrongdoing in the previous 20 years and seeking to have their lands restored to them. The original records are in Armagh Robinson Library (formerly Armagh Public Library) and were brought together by Geraldine Tallon as *Court of Claims, Submissions and Evidence, 1663*, with an introduction by J. G. Simms (2006), published by the Irish Manuscripts Commission. In all, there are nearly 900 claims of innocence, which were heard between 28 January and 20 August 1663, though judgements were given in only *c*. 100 instances. The claims include details of property held and the history of its ownership, which can often provide vital family information. For example, the following claim concerns an Audley family in County Down.

> James Audley in his claim sets forth that James Audley, the claimant's grandfather, being seized in fee of and in the castle and townland of Audleystowne alias the Castletowne, and of the townland of Ballinerre, situate in the parish of Ballicultor, barony Lecale, county Downe, did by his deed dated 6 January 1633 [1634] convey the same to Nicholas Fitzsymons and others therein named … (pp 170–71).

The claim also notes that the claimant was the son of Robert Audley; an additional note records that Robert Audley of Audleystowne had been outlawed twice.

4.5 Name lists from *c.* 1660 to *c.* 1690

4.5.1 '1659 Census'
The so-called '1659 Census' is available for every county in Ulster with the exception of Cavan and Tyrone. However, it is not a census in the true sense of the word and in fact it has been suggested that it is is really an abstract of the poll tax returns of 1660–61. It contains only the names of individuals termed 'tituladoes' (mainly those with title to land) and the total number of English/Scots and Irish resident in each townland. It is organised primarily by barony and then by parish. At the end of each barony section there is a list of the principal Irish names in that barony along with numerical totals for each name.

An edition of the 'census' by Seamus Pender, entitled, *A Census of Ireland circa 1659, with Supplementary Material from the Poll Money Ordinances*, was published by the Irish Manuscripts Commission in 1939. It was reprinted in 2002 with a new introduction by William J. Smyth, which provided a detailed analysis of the 'census' and challenged many of the earlier notions about it. The published edition includes a breakdown of the figures for each county and an index of both personal names and place-names. It also includes the names of those appointed to collect the poll tax in each county in 1660 and 1661.

4.5.2 Poll books
Only a few parishes in Ulster have surviving poll books, listing those liable for the poll tax, from the the beginning of the 1660s, all of them in County Tyrone. The names are arranged by townland with the occupation of the taxpayer – usually farmer, servant or yeoman – noted and the amount payable. The poll tax was paid as follows: a gentleman 4 shillings, a yeoman or farmer 2 shillings, a servant or labourer 1 shilling, with the sum doubled if the individual was

married. Some caution should be exercised, however, regarding these designations. Crossle, who transcribed the poll tax roll for Aghaloo parish, commented: 'Although parties are entered as labourers, this is not a true description of their social standing – it was done principally to evade the tax'.

Comparisons with subsidy rolls (see below) reveal that many people classed as labourers or yeoman in the poll books paid a higher subsidy tax on their goods than some who were styled 'gentleman' or 'esquire'. It also seems to have been the case that some of the grown-up children of yeomen and gentry were classified as servants to avoid paying the higher tax. For example, in Ardugboy (present-day Mountcastle) townland in the parish of Donagheady, Archibald Galbraith and wife were classified as gentry, while a Christian Galbraith was listed as a servant. In all likelihood, however, Archibald was Christian's father.

Parish	Source
Aghaloo	T458/8
Donagheady	T1365/1; John Rutherford, *Donagheady Presbyterian Churches and Parish* (1953), pp 106–09
Termonmaguirk	Earl of Belmore, *A History of Two Ulster Manors* (1903), pp 305–09
Urney	T1365/1; T808/15089

4.5.3 Hearth money rolls

In 1662, as a means of raising revenue for the government, the Hearth Tax Act was passed. Under the terms of this legislation, an annual tax of two shillings was levied on 'every fire-hearth and other place used for firing, and stoves within every such house and edifice.' Those who lived on alms and 'not able to get his or her living by his or her work and labour' were exempted. Houses certified by two justices of the peace as being below the annual value of eight shillings were also exempted, though under a 1665 act only widows were able to avail of this. The hearth money rolls, arranged by parish and usually with townland locations, listed the names of householders paying this tax.

The original hearth money rolls were destroyed in Dublin in 1922, but copies, in many cases typescript versions, had been made of many of them prior to this. They survive for nearly half of the counties in Ireland, with coverage most complete in Ulster (all counties except Down). Most counties have more than one hearth money roll, but in some cases the hearth money roll is incomplete, with only a few parishes covered. Appendix 1 should be consulted to find out whether or not a particular parish has a surviving hearth money roll. Even for those parishes for which there is a hearth money roll, it cannot be taken as a complete record of every household liable for the tax for there seems to have been a degree of evasion. Transcripts of the hearth money rolls in PRONI, along with printed editions of these, are set out below.

County	Year	Source
Antrim	1666	T3022/4/1; S. T. Carleton (ed.), *Heads and Hearths* (1991)
Antrim	1669	T307/A; Carleton, *Heads and Hearths*
Armagh	1664	T604; *Seanchas Ardmhacha*, 3:1 (1958), pp 96–142
Armagh	1665	(incomplete) T808/14950; *Seanchas Ardmhacha*, 3:1 (1958), pp 96–142
Cavan	1664	(incomplete) T808/15142, 15143 (Urney, Cavan borough, Annagelliff, Templeport, Killeshandra, Annagh, Kildallan); *Breifne*, 1:3 (1960), pp 247–62 (Killeshandra, Kildallan, Templeport, Tomregan, Killinagh); *Breifne*, 7:25 (1987), pp 489–97 (Lurgan, Crosserlough, Castlerahan and Munterconnaught, Killinkere)
Donegal	1663	(incomplete) T808/15003
Donegal	1665	T283D; T307D; some parish returns published in *Donegal Annual,* various issues
Fermanagh	1665, 1666	(incomplete) T808/15042; *Clogher Record*, 2 (1957), pp 207–14
Londonderry	1663	T307A
Monaghan	1663, 1665	T808/15156; D. C. Rushe, *History of Monaghan* (1921), pp 291–338 (the 1996 reprint of this book lists the names alphabetically)
Tyrone	1664	(incomplete) T458/8, T1365/3
Tyrone	1666	T307A; T716/16

Heads and Hearths, edited by S. T. Carleton and published by the Public Record Office of Northern Ireland in 1991, provides a detailed analysis of the 1669 hearth money roll of County Antrim. The editor matched the townlands recorded in 1669 with those of the present day and identified where two or more parishes have been listed under the same heading. The book also lists names from the 1666 hearth money roll of County Antrim not found in the 1669 roll. The volume is particularly useful when dealing with the barony of Toome, where parishes are not named. Unfortunately, the book was published without an index. There is, however, an index to the hearth money rolls of Antrim, Londonderry and Tyrone under T307A. Many hearth money rolls can now be accessed online on a variety of different websites.

4.5.4 Subsidy rolls

Subsidy rolls from the 1660s list those of means in the community who were subject to the payment of subsidies, sanctioned by the Irish Parliament, which provided much needed revenue for the Crown. Transcripts of the subsidy rolls survive for most counties in Ulster and record the name of the person paying the subsidy, his or her address, and the amount paid. Because they include only the wealthier members of society, they are less useful than hearth money rolls. However, the County Down list is all the more valuable because of the absence of a hearth money roll for that county. Copies of subsidy rolls in PRONI include:

County	Year	Source
Antrim	1666	T808/14889
Cavan	1662	T808/15142
Donegal	1662	T808/14998
Donegal	1669	T808/15003
Down	1663	T307A
Fermanagh	1662	T808/15068 (Enniskillen town only)
Londonderry	1662	D4164/A/14; T716/4, 15; T1592/19
Tyrone	1664	T283/D/1; T808/15092
Tyrone	1668	T808/15097

4.5.5 Excommunications in Derry diocese

In 1667, a significant number of people in 14 parishes in Derry diocese were excommunicated by the Established Church, mostly for nonconformity. According to the order for their expulsion, nonconformity was defined as 'not only absence from church, but baptising by unlicensed ministers'. A number of individuals were excommunicated for refusing to contribute to the repair of the Church of Ireland place of worship in their parish. Another excommunicant, John Boyd of Ardstraw, was further charged with ploughing on Christmas Day and condemning the ecclesiastical government. The parishes in question were: Ardstraw, Balteagh, Bodoney, Cappagh, Clondermot, Clonleigh, Cumber, Donagheady, Donaghmore, Drumachose, Dungiven, Faughanvale, Tamlaght Finlagan and Termoneeny. The names of those excommunicated were transcribed by Canon J. B. Leslie and can be found in PRONI under T552.

4.5.6 Franciscan petition lists

Copies of these lists are in the Franciscan Library, Dún Mhuire, Killiney, County Dublin. The background to their creation is provided by P. J. Campbell in his article, 'The Franciscan petition lists: diocese of Armagh, 1670–71', published in *Seanchas Ardmhacha*, 15:1 (1992), pp 186–216. In summary, they relate to a dispute between the Franciscans and Dominicans going back to the 1640s over the rights to such things as the collection of alms and donations. Most of the clergy and laity in Ulster sided with the Franciscans. Campbell's article includes a transcription of the lists for the diocese of Armagh. The parishes from which petitions emanated are as follows.

County Armagh: Armagh, Creggan, Derrynoose, Drumbruchuis
    (thought to have been part of Keady), Kilclooney, Killevy, Kilmore,
    Loughgall, Loughgilly, Mullaghbrack, Tanathly (Ballymore), Tynan
County Tyrone: Aghaloo, Errigal Keerogue, Termonmaguirk

The Clogher diocese lists have been published in Cathaldus Giblin,
'The Franciscan ministry in the diocese of Clogher', *Clogher Record*, 7:2 (1970),
pp 193–203. These include a petition of 1665 signed by *c.* 500 inhabitants of
Fermanagh opposing the introduction of a new religious order into the county
as the people were already finding it difficult to support the diocesan clergy
and the Franciscans. Another list of *c.* 130 names is either a petition of 1669
or a continuation of the 1665 petition. Another petition, in this case undated,
was signed by *c.* 400 people from County Monaghan. This seems to have been
organised by parish, the parishes in question being: Clontibret, Donaghmoyne,
Killeevan, Magheracloone and Magheross.

4.5.7 Laggan presbytery representatives

This category of record properly belongs under Presbyterian Church records,
but has been included here because it provides an extensive list of names across
north-west Ulster for the late seventeenth century. The names are those of elders
and commissioners who represented their respective congregations at the
meetings the Laggan presbytery. They were extracted from the presbytery
minutes covering the period 1672–1700 and were published as an appendix to
Rev. A. G. Lecky's book, *In the Days of the Laggan Presbytery* (1908). The
following congregations are covered:

County Donegal: Burt, Donegal and Ballyshannon, Donoughmore,
    Fannet, Killygarvan (Rathmullan), Inishowen (Donagh, Moville,
    Culdaff, Redcastle), Letterkenny, Lifford (Ballindrait), Ramelton,
    Raphoe (Convoy), Ray, Stranorlar, Taboyn (Monreagh)
County Londonderry: Londonderry (Derry), Glendermott
County Tyrone: Ardstraw, Donagheady, Omagh (Drumra, Termon
    M'Gurk, Longfield, Cappagh, Badoney), Strabane, Urney

In addition, there are also names for Enniskillen, County Fermanagh, and Sligo,
County Sligo. Copies of the Laggan presbytery minutes are available in PRONI
(MIC637/6) and the Library of the Presbyterian Historical Society of Ireland.

4.5.8 Collectors' accounts

Several collectors' accounts may be found among the papers of the genealogist
Tenison Groves in PRONI. These date from 1683 to 1692 and are mainly
concerned with the collection of excise duties.

List of ale and wine licences, naming licensees, for Belfast, Malone,
    Whitehouse, Stranmillis, Carrickfergus, Ballynure, Islandmagee,

Larne, Curran, Glenarm, Dunmurry, Carnmoney, etc, 1683–4 –
T808/14891

Collectors [?] accounts for Coleraine, naming individuals and amounts
paid, 1689–91 – T456/1

Collectors' accounts naming person who owed arrears in Lisburn,
Glenavy, Hillsborough, Antrim and Ballymena Walks, 1690: over
500 names arranged by location – T808/14903

Collectors' accounts naming persons owing arrears for Lisburn Walk,
1691: over 400 names arranged by location – T808/14904
(T808/14902 is an alphabetical list of the names in this source)

Collectors' accounts, County Londonderry, 1692 – T808/15137

4.6 Records from the period of the Williamite War

Following a period of relative stability and recovery from the effects of the
troubles of the 1640s, Ireland again experienced the outbreak of open warfare
in the late 1680s, which was to have consequences at many different levels. A
very good introduction to the period and its artefacts is the Ulster Museum
publication, W. A. Maguire (ed.), *Kings in Conflict; The Revolutionary War in
Ireland and its aftermath* (1990). Other books on the subject include Richard
Doherty, *The Williamite War in Ireland, 1688–1691* (1998) and John Childs,
The Williamite Wars in Ireland (2007).

4.6.1 Jacobite corporations

In 1687 and 1688 the corporations that provided local government in over 100
towns and cities in Ireland were reorganised through the issuing of new charters
and the appointment of new burgesses. The intention was to bring these ruling
bodies more closely under Jacobite control and so ensure that they would return
MPs to the Irish House of Commons who were sympathetic to the policies of
James II. The result of these actions was the large-scale removal of Protestant
burgesses and their replacement with Catholic members. Unsurprisingly, this
provoked considerable alarm within the Protestant community. The names of
members of these corporations were published as an appendix in *The History
of the Life and Reign of William-Henry* (1749) under the heading, 'List of the
Constituent Members of the several new Corporations established by King
James II upon ruins of the old ones'. Looking at the names of those appointed
to the new corporations in Ulster, it is clear that men of Gaelic Irish background
predominated. However, individuals from the settler community can also be
found. By way of example, the names of the new members of the corporation
of Cavan are listed below.

Luke Reyly Esq., Sovereign   Richard Brady Esq.
Robert Fenly and Alexander   Miles Reyly Gent.
    Mac-Leland (Portreeves)   Robert Fenly merchant
Edmund Reyly Esq.   Charles Reyly Gent.

Philip Reyly Junior Esq.
Thomas Fleming Esq.
Philip Reyly Senior Esq.
Miles Reyly Esq.
John Reyly Esq.
Francis Bourke Esq.
Hugh Reyly Gent.

Alexander Mac Leland merchant
John Sheridan Gent.
John Price In[n]keeper
Edmund Lynch Gent.
Daniel Donelly Gent.,
    Recorder and Town Clerk Esq.

4.6.2 Names of those attainted by James II

In 1689, an 'Act for the Attainder of Divers Rebels, and for Preserving the Interest of Loyal Subjects' was passed in the Jacobite-controlled Irish Parliament. It listed the names of Irish Protestants considered to be disloyal to James II. Most of those listed were members of the landed gentry or substantial tenants. The names of those attainted (i.e. found guilty of treason) were published in *The State of the Protestants of Ireland under the late King James's Government* by William King (1713). A list of those attainted in County Monaghan appears in D. C. Rushe, *History of Monaghan for Two Hundred Years, 1660–1860* (1921), while the names of those attainted in County Armagh can be found in PRONI under T808/14985.

4.6.3 Protestant refugees from Ireland

Many Protestants fled Ireland as a result of the conflict, withdrawing to England or Scotland. Lists of names of some of these refugees survive in the Manuscripts & Archives Research Library at Trinity College Dublin and include:

> 'An alphabetical list of such protestants of Ireland as fled out of Ireland for safety of their lives under the Government of K. James 2d, their condition, families, estates'; gives names and numbers of children, etc – MS 847/1
> 'The briefe for the protest[ants] of Irel[and] at Chester 1689': alphabetical list names with position or profession and number of children and allowances paid to them; opposite some of the names are the names of other places, besides Chester, including Holyhead, Ruthen, Wigan and Manchester (the total number of names is *c.* 1,200) – MS 847/2

See also TCD, MS 1449 and Genealogical Office, MS 447. Names for counties Antrim and Down were published in George Benn, *A History of the Town of Belfast* (1877), pp 737–8. A copy of the list of Protestant refugees from County Armagh in England can be found in the Groves Collection in PRONI (T808/14988).

4.6.4 Participants in the war

For information on those who were involved in the siege of Derry in 1689 and events during the Williamite War in general, the best single source is W. R. Young, *Fighters of Derry, Their Deeds and Descendents, Being a Chronicle of Events in Ireland during the Revolutionary Period, 1688–91* (1932; reprinted 2016). This lists the names of some 1,660 individuals who defended Derry or were associated with William of Orange; for many of them brief biographical sketches are provided. This book provides a real insight into settler society, particularly in north-west Ulster, in the late seventeenth century. Young also compiled a list of 352 Jacobites, again with biographical sketches for many of them. See also Brian Mitchell, *Defenders of the Plantation of Ulster, 1641–1691* (2010).

An interesting document related to the siege is an indenture of 1691 empowering certain individuals to seek compensation for debts and expenses sustained during the siege (T1847/12). A copy of an 'account of particulars belonging to James Lenox which were made use of by the garrison of Derry in the time of the siege, and money expended by said James Lenox for the public use' is available (T3161/1/1).

Biographical information on the main protagonists on the Jacobite side can also be found in John D'Alton, *Illustrations, Historical and Genealogical: Of King James's Irish Army List (1689)* (1855). A small, but valuable collection in PRONI relating to this period can be found in the McCance Papers (D272). This comprises various items, including lists of soldiers buried at Carrickfergus (1691) and Lisburn (1689–91), and lists of debts due by soldiers and officers with names of creditors.

The Museum of Orange Heritage in Belfast has in its custody the 'Paymasters General's Book of Accounts', a volume kept by Thomas Coningsby and Charles Fox, who held jointly the position of Receiver and Paymaster-General of King William's army in Ireland. The book covers the period from June 1690 to March 1691 and includes records of a broad range of payments. Ordinary foot soldiers do not appear in the book, though several hundred officers are recorded as being the recipients of sums of money. A copy of the book is held by PRONI (T689/1). A collection of records from the late seventeenth and early eighteenth centuries relating to Thomas Coningsby can be found in PRONI (D638; use MIC413).

4.6.5 Williamite land settlement

Following the end of the Williamite War in 1691, there was a major redistribution of land in Ireland. Lands that had been confiscated from Jacobites were vested with the Trustees for the Sale of the Forfeited Estates. Sir Francis Annesley was one of the Trustees and played a major role in the deliberations over the sales. A large collection of depositions, minute books, accounts, etc relating to the work of the Trustees has survived among the Annesley Papers in PRONI (D1854; use MIC532). The information in this collection is less extensive for Ulster than for other provinces in Ireland. This was due to the fact that in Ulster most of the land had already passed to British landlords by the 1680s as a result of the Plantation scheme of the early seventeenth century and the Cromwellian and Restoration land settlements of the 1650s–70s.

Of particular interest is a volume entitled, *Printed rentals and particulars of sale of forfeited lands exposed for sale in Dublin with manuscript additions detailing the sales by cant giving purchasers names, addresses, date of sale, purchase price, method of sale etc.* (D1854/2/29a). Most of the sales took place in 1703 and we can assume that the rentals must have been drawn up shortly before this. The volume includes a rental of the manor of Strabane owned by the earl of Abercorn (the Catholic fourth earl had been a prominent supporter of James II). Names of tenants from a number of smaller estates owned by Jacobites are also given. The following extracts provide examples of the type of information recorded.

Loghtee barony, County Cavan

Denomination	Late proprietor	Tenant	Description
One tenement in the east side of Cavan	Bryan McCabe	Rob Johnson	This house stands in the market-place in the Town of Cavan, built of timber, and in good repair, the back part being newly built, containing 30 foot in front, backward 420 foot, and 60 foot broad in the garden.

Kinelarty barony, County Down

Denomination	Late proprietor	Tenant	Description
Ballymaglane Itragh with a tuckmill	John O'Hara	William Scott	In the parish of Magredrill [Magheradrool], distant from the parish church one mile, Downe and Hillsborough each 8 miles, Belfast 15. On it 5 farm-houses, with barns, stable and a small orchard; the land is arable, meadow and course shrubby pasture.

There are numerous handwritten annotations providing the name of the purchaser of the property and the amount of money paid for it. The parishes in the province of Ulster affected are as follows:

> County Antrim: Ballintoy, Ballymoney, Ballyrashane, Derrykeighan,
>   Drummaul, Killead, Layd, Loughguile, Racavan
> County Armagh: Creggan, Killevy, Loughgilly, Tynan
> County Cavan: Enniskeen, Urney
> County Donegal: All Saints (Taughboyne)

County Down: Ardglass, Ballyphilip, Bright, Magheradrool, Newry
County Londonderry: Ballinderry
County Monaghan: Muckno
County Tyrone: Ardstraw, Camus-juxta-Mourne, Urney

It should be acknowledged that, with a few exceptions, the number of townlands in each parish affected was fairly small, while the number of names of tenants will vary.

Another volume of interest is *A list of the claims as they are entered with the Trustees: at Chichester House on College Green, Dublin, on or before the tenth of August, 1700* (1701). The *List of the claims* runs to 355 pages and provides details on the names of the claimants, what they were claiming for, its value and where it was located, as well as the name of the forfeiting proprietor. The book was apparently never made available to the public because of the alarm expressed by the claimants over its contents. The government was forced to destroy the entire impression with the exception of copies already given to the Trustees. Therefore, only a few copies survive; they can be found in such places as the library of Queen's University Belfast, the National Library of Ireland and the National Archives of Ireland. See also a detailed list of lands forfeited by supporters of James II in County Antrim, 1690s (D207/15/30). Abstracts of the land grants made in this period may be found in the *Reports of the commissioners appointed ... respecting the public records of Ireland*, 11th–15th Annual Reports (1825).

5. Eighteeth-century records

5.1 'Census substitutes'

The following categories of record have been grouped together under the loose heading of 'census substitutes' and cover the full span of the eighteenth century. In a number of cases they are transcripts of records that were destroyed in Dublin in 1922.

5.1.1 'A view of the archbishopric of Armagh', 1703

Although this source properly belongs with the Armagh Church of Ireland diocesan archive, the original is closed on grounds of preservation, and instead a photostat version is available for consultation in PRONI (T848). The 'View' is a neatly written survey of the extensive property owned by the archbishop of Armagh which was prepared by Thomas Ashe at the beginning of the eighteenth century. These lands were mainly to be found in counties Armagh, Londonderry, Louth and Tyrone, with smaller portions in Antrim, Down and Meath. The information provided is of an incredibly detailed nature. The name of the tenant of each of the townlands is given, together with the names of the undertenants. In addition, the extent of the townland, the type of structures standing on it (such as dwellings, farm out-buildings, bridges, churches, taverns and mills), the degree of agricultural improvement and antiquities are noted.

For instance, the townland of Killin was the location of Clonoe Church of Ireland parish church; one of the undertenants was a Mr Elliott, the clerk of the parish, who kept an ale-house. In the townland of Kildress, also the location of a parish church, John McWhaw had a small tenement and a tuck mill. A resident of Outlackan was Thady Gallogly, a parish priest, who lived in a stone house. Daniel Christie was the tenant of an inn in Cookstown which bore the sign of the 'Blew Garter'. In Drumsallansoughtra John Bond had built at his own expense a very good farm house, stable, barn and cow house.

5.1.2 Lists of the nobility and gentry in each county, *c.* 1730

Lists of those 'generally esteemed' to be worth more than £100 per annum were compiled for each county *c.* 1730 (T3446/1). (Another list of *c.* 1720 can be found under reference T3374/1/1.) These lists show that the denominational bias was overwhelmingly in favour of the Church of Ireland, followed some distance behind by Presbyterians, with Catholics coming in third. Over 500 individuals are named in the lists for counties in Ulster, usually without indicating where they lived. The breakdown by county is as follows:

County	Church of Ireland	Presbyterian	Roman Catholic
Antrim	36	8	1
Armagh	54	3	0
Cavan	63	2	4
Donegal	64	1	1
Down	79	10	1
Fermanagh	44	3	1
Londonderry	34	1	0
Monaghan	67	4	0
Tyrone	49	9	0
Total	490	41	8

5.1.3 Religious census for Cary barony, County Antrim, 1734

For the barony of Cary in north County Antrim there is a religious census from 1734, which lists nearly 1,500 householders, giving townland and religious affiliation. The parishes included Armoy, Ballintoy, Billy (that part in Cary barony), Culfeightrin, Derrykeighan (part) and Ramoan. William Reeves prepared a list of the names from the original in Glenarm Castle which is in the Manuscripts & Archives Research Library of Trinity College Dublin (MS 1059). A copy of this is in the Séamus Ó Casaide manuscripts in the National Library of Ireland (MS 5456). The names from a number of parishes were transcribed by Harry Doyle and published in *The Glynns*:

> Culfeightrin – vol. 21 (1993), pp 65–76
> Armoy – vol. 22 (1994), pp 53–8
> Ramoan – vol. 23 (1995), pp 55–62
> Ballintoy – vol. 25 (1997), pp 30–37

Names for Ballycastle were published in *The Glynns* in 1980 (vol. 8, p. 17). The Groves Papers in PRONI include a list of householders from 'Part of the parish of Derrykeighan called Drumtullogh' in 1734 (T808/14905).

5.1.4 'Census of Protestant householders', 1740

The so-called 'census of Protestant householders' was compiled in 1740, apparently at the behest of the Irish Parliament. It runs to nearly 16,000 names and is particularly good for County Londonderry (nearly all parishes) and much of north and mid County Antrim. The original records of this survey were destroyed in Dublin in 1922, but transcripts made by the genealogist Tenison Groves are available in PRONI (T808/15258), and extracts also exist in other archives (e.g. the National Library of Ireland, MS 4173).

It would seem that the lists of names were based on returns made by the collectors of the hearth money. The collectors were given responsibility for a particular geographical area known as a 'walk' and some of the 1740 returns make reference to a 'walk' (e.g. the Loughbrickland walk). In his analysis of the returns, Bill Macafee has concluded that those responsible for the Toome walk, which included the barony of Loughinsholin in County Londonderry, were not as accurate in distinguishing between Protestants and Catholics and that many of the latter were listed. In fact, some 22% of names in Loughinsholin are Gaelic Irish, while the percentage for the other baronies is no more than 4%.

For the most part, the 'census' is a listing of names by parish. However, for the baronies of Inishowen in County Donegal and Keenaght and Tirkeeran in County Londonderry the names are listed by townland and parish. Bill Macafee believes that where personal names are not arranged by townland they are listed in geographical order – arising from the route taken by the hearth money collector on his 'walk' – and that sometimes it is possibly to work out the route taken by the collector.

The Name Search database on the PRONI website includes names from the following parishes:

> County Antrim – Ahoghill, Armoy, Ballintoy, Ballymena [Kirkinriola], Ballymoney, Ballyrashane, Ballywillin, Billy, Clough [Dunaghy], Culfeightrin, Derrykeighan, Drummaul, Duneane, Dunluce, Finvoy, Kilraghts, Loughguile, Manybrooks [Grange of Ballyscullion], Ramoan, Rasharkin and Rathlin
>
> County Armagh – Derrynoose, Mullaghbrack, Shankill and Tynan
>
> County Donegal – Clonca, Clonmany, Culdaff, Desertegny, Donagh, Fahan, Moville and Templemore
>
> County Down – Kilbroney and Seapatrick (Loughbrickland Walk)
>
> County Londonderry – all parishes except Agivey (possibly included with Aghadowey) and Arboe
>
> County Tyrone – Derryloran and Kildress

Further information – such as whether or not the townland is given – can be found under the heading *Census substitutes* within the relevant parish source guide in Appendix 1.

5.1.5 The religious census of 1766

In the spring of 1766 the Irish House of Lords issued instructions to Church of Ireland clergy to prepare returns of all householders in their respective parishes, indicating the religion of each householder, and giving an account of any Roman Catholic clergy active in their area. Most of the parish returns consist simply of numerical totals of the householders. However, some of the more diligent clergy submitted lists of names of householders, occasionally alongside the townland. With regard to the religious affiliation of the householder, the term Protestant was sometimes used in the general sense, though on other occasions it was applied exclusively to members of the Church of Ireland with the term Dissenters used for Presbyterians. Catholics were referred to as 'Papists' in the returns. All of the original returns were destroyed in the Public Record Office of Ireland in 1922, but transcripts are available in PRONI, notably in the Tenison Groves Collection (T808/15264, 15266 and 15267), and in other repositories, such as the National Archives of Ireland (M 207/8; M 2476) and the National Library of Ireland (MS 4173).

The following parish returns are included in the Name Search database on the PRONI website:

> County Antrim – Ahoghill, Ballintoy, Ballymoney and Ballynure
> County Armagh – Creggan
> County Cavan – Kinawley (partly in Fermanagh), Lavey, Lurgan and
>   Munterconnaught
> County Down – Inch, Kilbroney and Seapatrick
> County Donegal – Donaghmore, Inch, Leck and Raphoe
> County Fermanagh – Derryvullan, Devenish, Kinawley (partly in
>   Cavan), Rossorry
> County Londonderry – Artrea, Ballynascreen, Banagher, Bovevagh,
>   Cumber, Desertlyn, Desertmartin, Drumachose, Dungiven and
>   Magherafelt
> County Tyrone – Aghaloo, Artrea, Carnteel, Clonfeacle, Derryloran,
>   Donaghenry, Drumglass (also Dungannon Town and Corporation),
>   Errigal Keerogue, Kildress and Tullyniskan

Further information – such as whether or not the return includes all householders or those of only one religious affiliation – can be found under the heading *Census substitutes* within the relevant parish source guide in Appendix 1.

James O'Laverty, in his *An Historical Account of the Diocese of Down and Connor, Ancient and Modern* (5 vols, 1878–95), listed names, mainly of Catholics, from the 1766 religious census for a number of parishes in the diocese of Connor (mainly County Antrim and a small part of County Londonderry). In general, these parishes had low Catholic populations and so the number of names is fairly small. The parishes in question are:

> Heads of Catholic families in Ballynure (vol. 3, p. 294)
> Surnames of Protestant and Catholic families on Rathlin Island
>   (vol. 4, p. 388)
> Catholic heads of household in Milton [Ballywillin] and Singinton
>   [Ballyrashane] (vol. 4, p. xxix)
> Catholic heads of household in Coleraine, distinguishing between town,
>   suburbs and parish (vol. 4, pp xxix–xxx)

Catholic heads of household in Connor (including Kells) (vol. 4,
  p. xxviii)
Catholic heads of household in Glenwherry (vol. 4, p. xxviii)

5.1.6 Hearts of Steel memorials, 1771–2

The Hearts of Steel was a Protestant movement of agrarian protest that
originated on the Donegall estate in County Antrim over the general reletting
of farms in 1770. The movement spread to other parts of Ulster over the
following two years, with the protests concentrating on rent levels, evictions
and local taxation. Frequently these protests were violent and included the
burning of houses and the maiming of cattle. In response to the outrages, the
inhabitants of a large number of towns and parishes as well as a few townlands
drew up memorials declaring their abhorrence of the activities of the Hearts of
Steel. Many of these memorials, sometimes accompanied by a list of names,
were published in the *Belfast Newsletter*. The following is an extract from the
memorial drawn up by the inhabitants of Magherafelt, County Londonderry:

> We, the inhabitants of the town of Magherafelt, sensible of the danger of
> that spirit of riot and outrage which has so amazingly spread itself in this
> neighbourhood, and desiring to contribute all that in us lies to the
> preservation of order and the authority of the laws, do agree to each other
> not only to shun all such combinations and lawless practices ourselves, but
> also to take care that all under our influence shall also abstain from them.

The names from some 20 memorials were published in the *Belfast Newsletter*
in 1771 and 1772. Many more memorials were submitted to the editor of this
newspaper, but unfortunately these were printed without the list of names. The
areas for which the names of signatories are available, together with the issue
of the *Belfast Newsletter*, are as follows:

County Antrim
Ahoghill – 14 April 1772
Ballyeaston [Ballycor parish] – 11 October 1771
Ballymoney – 7 April 1772
Ballynure – 25 October 1771
Dunaghy – 17 March 1772
Island Magee Presbyterian congregation [Island Magee parish] –
  21 April 1772
Lisburn [Blaris parish] – 24 March 1772
Killead – 10 April 1772
Larne [probably including Inver], Kilwaughter and Raloo – 7 April
  1772
Magheragall (the tenants of James Watson of Brookhill) – 22 May 1772
Templepatrick – 6 September 1771

County Armagh
Lurgan [Shankill parish] – 11 December 1772

County Down
Ballyhalbert – 10 April 1770
Ballykeel in Dromore parish – 27 March 1772
Ballynahinch [Magheradrool parish] – 31 March 1772
Cluntagh in Annahilt parish – 3 April 1772
Drumlough in Dromore parish – 31 March 1772
Killinchy – 31 July 1772
Moneyrea Presbyterian congregation [Comber parish] – 3 April 1772
Saintfield – 25 August 1772

County Londonderry
Magherafelt – 17 March 1772
Tamlaght O'Crilly – 14 April 1772

A background to this period is found in F. J. Bigger, *The Ulster Land War of 1770* (1910), which incorporates a large amount of contemporary information drawn from newspapers and other sources, including summaries of selected trials from 1772 to 1777.

5.1.7 The flaxseed premiums of 1796

In 1796, as part of a government initiative to encourage the linen industry in Ireland, free spinning wheels or looms were granted to farmers who planted a certain acreage of their holdings with flax. The names of over 56,000 recipients of these awards have survived in printed form, arranged by county and parish (unfortunately, not by townland). Two copies of this book are known to exist, one in the Linen Hall Library in Belfast and the other in the Irish Linen Centre and Lisburn Museum in Lisburn, County Antrim. The Ulster Historical Foundation has indexed this source and it is available as a free searchable database on the UHF website (www.ancestryireland.com/scotsinulster). Nearly two-thirds of the names relate to Ulster and the following table breaks the totals down by county:

County	Names
Antrim	1,185
Armagh	3,161
Cavan	2,467
Donegal	7,455
Down	3,028
Fermanagh	2,345
Londonderry	5,144
Monaghan	4,555
Tyrone	7,049
Total	**36,389**

It is clear that there was considerable variation between counties as to the number of premiums claimed, reflecting in part the quantity of flax grown in each. The major flax-producing counties of Donegal and Tyrone head the list with over 7,000 claimants each.

5.2 Records arising from the Penal Laws

Legislation known as the Penal Laws was passed in the Irish Parliament between 1695 and 1728 to preserve the privileged position of the Anglican elite. The Penal Laws targeted Catholics in particular, though they also impacted upon nonconformist Protestants. This subject area is looked at in more detail in the historical essay at the start of this book.

5.2.1 Convert Rolls

The Convert Rolls list those converting from Roman Catholicism to the Established Church (i.e. the Church of Ireland). Following the *Act to prevent the further growth of popery* of 1703, a Catholic converting to the Church of Ireland had to provide proof of conformity. By conforming to the Established Church a Catholic was freed from the legal disabilities affecting property rights and membership of certain professions, etc, in force under the Penal Laws. To begin with, it was necessary for a convert to obtain a certificate of conformity from the Anglican bishop of the diocese in which he or she lived. A new law passed in 1782 made it possible for a member of the Church of Ireland clergy to issue a certificate. By 1800 over 5,000 enrolments had taken place, most of them in the period 1760–89. It is believed, however, that many Catholics who conformed to the Church of Ireland never enrolled certificates. The number of enrolments dropped significantly in the late eighteenth century as new legislation improved the position of Catholics in Ireland. It should be noted that a substantial minority of converts were women, very often because until they conformed their Protestant husbands were disbarred from voting.

The original Convert Rolls were lost in the destruction of the old Public Record Office in Dublin in 1922. Fortunately, a calendar of the rolls had been prepared. In addition, some other sources relating to converts have survived, including a list prepared by John Lodge, a former Deputy Keeper of the Rolls, prior to his death in 1774. The available information was brought together in a volume edited by Eileen O'Byrne and published by the Irish Manuscripts Commission in 1981 entitled, *The Convert Rolls*, the introduction to which provides a detailed background to the subject; a revised edition with additional information edited by Anne Chamney was published in 2005. The details available for each convert include typically the place of residence (though generally no more specific than the county or parish) and the dates of conformity and enrolment; the status or occupation of the individual is occasionally given. The website of the National Archives of Ireland includes a searchable database of the names in the Convert Rolls. A few certificates have survived in various collections. For example, there are more than a dozen certificates of conformity for the parish and town of Antrim from 1776 in the Foster/Massereene Papers in PRONI (D207/26).

5.2.2 Catholic Qualification Rolls

The gradual relaxation of the Penal Laws was enshrined in law through the passing of a series of acts of parliament. In 1773–4, *An Act to enable his Majesty's subjects of whatever persuasion to testify their allegiance to him* was passed in the Irish Parliament. Under the terms of this act, a Catholic was able to go before a judge of the King's Bench, a justice of the peace, or the magistrate of a corporate town and swear an oath of allegiance to the Crown.

There was little initial enthusiasm for taking the oath, not to mention considerable clerical opposition to the very idea of it. A transcript of the 'Test Book' for 1775–6, now in NAI, but copied from the original in the Public Record Office of Ireland prior to its destruction in 1922, includes just over 1,500 names, of which only a handful relate to counties in Ulster – 12 for Londonderry and one for Fermanagh. For more information on this volume, see the article in the *59th Report of the Deputy Keeper of the Public Records* (1962), pp 50–84. Subsequent legislation, however, made taking the oath much more advantageous and so the numbers doing so increased substantially.

The original Catholic Qualification Rolls were lost in 1922, but indexes to the rolls for 1778–90 and 1793–6 are available in the National Archives of Ireland and can now be searched via the institution's website. Generally speaking, they provide the name, residence and occupation of the individual concerned, as well as when and where the qualification oath was taken. Some names from a few counties have been published, including Seán Ó Domhnaill, 'County Donegal in the Catholic Qualification Rolls, 1778–1790', *Journal of the County Donegal Historical Society*, 1:3 (1949), pp 204–05; and P. Ó Gallachair, 'Catholic qualification rolls index. Fermanagh and Monaghan', *Clogher Record*, 2:3 (1959), pp 544–51. See also Patrick Fagan, *Divided Loyalties: The Question of an Oath for Irish Catholics in the Eighteenth-Century* (1997).

5.2.3 Petitions of Protestant Dissenters, 1775

In 1774, an act was passed in the Irish Parliament which restricted the voting rights of nonconformists at vestry meetings. This provoked a huge outcry from Ulster's Presbyterians and nearly 40 petitions protesting against this legislation were submitted to the government in October and November 1775. Most of these petitions emanated from Presbyterian congregations, though some members of the Established Church also voiced their opposition. In 1776, the act was repealed through a bill introduced by Thomas Conolly, whose own tenants in County Londonderry had been particularly vociferous in their opposition to the original act.

The original petitions were destroyed, but transcripts made by Tenison Groves are available in PRONI (T808/15307). Only the names of the petitioners are given, not where they lived. The names in these transcripts can now be searched via the PRONI Name Search database. The congregations and parishes for which there are petitions with names are set out below.

> County Antrim – Antrim Borough; Old Antrim [possibly the non-subscribing congregation]; Ballyclare town and neighbourhood; Ballymena town and neighbourhood; Belfast parish and town; Carnmoney parish; Carrickfergus town and county; Donagore, Kilbride and Nilteen; Dunmurry congregation in Drumbeg parish; Larne, Raloo, Carncastle, Kilwaughter, Glenarm & Ballyeaston; Lisburn town and neighbourhood
>
> County Armagh – Armagh parish; Clare congregation in Ballymore parish
>
> County Down – Ballee congregation; Comber parish; Dundonald parish; Dromore parish; Drumara parish; Drumballyroney and Drumgoolan parishes; Drumgooland; Killileagh parish
>
> County Londonderry – Coleraine and Killowen parishes; Londonderry City
>
> County Tyrone – Benburb town and neighbourhood; Coagh; Cookstown congregation; Dungannon barony; Dungannon town and neighbourhood; Strabane town and neighbourhood

5.3 Records relating to the United Irishmen and 1798 Rebellion

The historical essay at the beginning of this book outlined the developments in the tumultuous 1790s and their consequences for Ulster, from the formation of the Society of United Irishmen in 1791 to the 1798 Rebellion and its aftermath. A significant quantity of documentation relating to this period was created in final decade of the eighteenth century which provides a vast and, from a genealogical point of view, generally overlooked body of material that can be utilised for research purposes.

5.3.1 Records in the National Archives of Ireland

The records relating to this period in the National Archives of Ireland derive principally from the former State Paper Office in Dublin Castle. These were never in the old Public Record Office of Ireland and so escaped destruction in 1922. It should be noted that the categories of record discussed below may be of broader interest than simply the United Irishmen and 1798 Rebellion and many documents in these collections concern wider issues of law and order. Nonetheless, for the sake of convenience they have been grouped together in this section. (See Chapter 9 for more information on records relating to law and order.)

The Rebellion Papers

The most important source of information on the United Irishmen and the 1798 Rebellion – and more broadly the 1790s and opening years of the 1800s – is the collection of documents known as the 'Rebellion Papers'. While the records predominantly relate to the period 1796–1805, there are some from either side of those years. In 1853, these records were in the State Paper Office in Dublin Castle and were stored in two huge chests, which bore the words, 'secret and confidential not to be opened'. They were sorted subsequently into a series of cartons and today these are held by the National Archives of Ireland under reference 620. Researchers wishing to view these records now do so using microfilm.

An introduction to the Rebellion Papers by Deirdre Lindsay was published in *Ulster Local Studies*, 18:2 (Spring, 1997), pp 28–42. This includes a summary listing of the documentation available. An online version of this can be read on the website of the National Archives. See also L. M. Cullen, 'Politics and Rebellion: Wicklow in the 1790s' in K. Hannigan and W. Nolan (eds), *Wicklow: History and Society* (1994), which includes a helpful background to the records.

The Rebellion Papers are calendared in five volumes which are available on the open shelves of the Reading Room in the National Archives. The first two of these volumes cover subjects such as courts martial, 'State Prisoners' (i.e. those incarcerated because of their revolutionary activities, alleged or otherwise), and lists of prisoners in gaols or on ships. The remaining three volumes are primarily concerned with correspondence with the authorities in Dublin. This is particularly voluminous – for the years 1796–8 alone there are some 4,000 letters – and the correspondents range from army officers, clergymen and magistrates to government informers and local gossips. The correspondence, covering the period 1796–1804, is listed chronologically; the calendar entry typically provides the name and occasionally the address of the correspondent, together with the date and a short synopsis of the letter. Other search aids in the Reading Room of the National Archives include an index to the Rebellion Papers in seven volumes and a card index to the first two volumes of the calendar of this archive. There is as yet, however, no overall index to every personal name that appears in these records.

The material in the Rebellion Papers can include useful lists of names, occupations and addresses. For example, among the prisoners held in Belfast in September 1798 were the following individuals (RP 620/4/29/36):

> John Coulter of Collin, County Antrim, linen draper
> Robert Hunter of Belfast, ship broker
> Rev. William Steele Dickson of Portaferry, County Down, Presbyterian
>   minister
> Luke Teeling of Lisburn, County Antrim, linen draper

William Phillips of Bangor, County Down, apothecary
Alexander Clark of Belfast, watchmaker
John Dickey of Crumlin, County Antrim, shopkeeper
Francis Fallon of Donaghadee, County Down, innkeeper

With regard to records of trials, we may note that the witnesses called to give evidence at the trial of Richard Caldwell of Harmony Hill, near Ballymoney, held on 13–14 July 1798 (RP 620/2/8/8), were as follows:

James Clark, Ballamena, Revenue Officer
James Crosbie, Stranocum, servant to Lt Rd Hutchinson of the Dunluce
    Cavalry
Thomas McNeil, Ballymoney parish, linen weaver
Benjamin Cooper, Ballymoney, grocer
James Parks, Bushbank, attorney
Neil McLaughlin, Ballymoney, tobacco spinner
Robert Kelso, Ballymena, parish of Aghohill, linen draper
Lieut. Brady of the Dunluce Infantry
William Dickson, Ballamena, brewer

Caldwell was found guilty. Eventually, he was allowed to transport himself to America (along with the rest of his family) where he died on active service during the War of 1812. (See below for the Caldwell Papers in the Public Record Office of Northern Ireland.)

Among the letters in the Rebellion Papers is a particularly poignant one from Susan Wilson on behalf of her husband Dr Thomas Wilson (RP 620/48/9). Wilson, a doctor in Newtownards, County Down, was active in public life in the area. He was involved in the rebellion for which he was banished to America, sailing in May 1799, though without his family accompanying him. In October 1799 his wife Susan, whom he had married in February 1797, wrote to the authorities on his behalf, pointing out that before the rebellion Wilson had been of good character, but he had been led astray by 'artful and desperate men'. During his imprisonment his behaviour had been exemplary. His departure from America had left her and Wilson's three young children from his first marriage in a difficult situation for they did not have the means to join him. Mrs Wilson requested that her husband be allowed to return home and she assured the authorities that he would provide security for his continued good behaviour. Some time after this Dr Wilson returned to Ulster.

State of the Country Papers

The State of the Country Papers (SOC) concern matters relating to law and order across Ireland, especially subversive activities. They really belong with the Rebellion Papers, but were listed separately during the organisation of the records of the State Paper Office in the nineteenth and early twentieth centuries. The State of the Country Papers include intelligence reports and correspondence from various individuals, such as army officers, magistrates, clergymen and informers.

For example, from March 1796 we have a copy (SOC 1015/9A) of an examination of John McAllister of Garvagh, County Londonderry, who swore that on 19 February 1796 William McKeever alias Campbell of 'upper land' (Upperlands), near Maghera, had instructed him to come to the house of Manus O'Kane, an innkeeper in Garvagh. McAllister did so and after drinking beer with McKeever, the latter asked him to accompany him upstairs. There McKeever attempted to force McAllister to swear a seditious oath. McAllister further learned that Walter Graham of Crew, near Maghera, was one of the first United Irishmen in the county.

The State of the Country Papers are organised in two series: Series 1, covering the years 1796–1831 (arranged by year and county), and Series 2, covering 1790–1831 (arranged by year). This division seems to have been made for storage purposes only, rather than because of any difference in the nature of the material in each series. Finding aids in the National Archives of Ireland include a calendar for Series 1 and a card index for Series 2 for the years 1790–1808. There are ring-bound catalogues of entries for Ulster counties (except Donegal) in the Search Room in PRONI.

Official Papers

The collection known as the Official Papers (OP) contains correspondence relating to the Chief Secretary's Office. Series 1 covers material from 1790 to 1831 and is organised by year and subject. The items include memorials and petitions seeking redress for wrongs or compensation for losses incurred by victims of criminal activity. For example, in 1800 Christopher Palles, a Cavan magistrate, sought compensation for the destruction of his house at the hands of the United Irishmen in 1797; because the incident took place before the rebellion his request was turned down (OP 80/1). Of particular interest within the Official Papers are the 1803 agricultural census returns for County Antrim (see below).

Another series within the Official Papers is the class of records which has been termed Official Papers Miscellaneous and Assorted (OPMA). This varied collection of material begins around 1750. For example, from *c.* 1798 there is a list of names and addresses of persons living in the Fews barony, County Armagh, whose claims for damages were upheld at the quarter sessions held before James Dawson (OPMA 41). The names of the claimants were:

> James Toner senior, Hugh Bigham, Fergy McCartan, John Feghan,
> Teague Toner, Bryan Callaghan, Widow Gribben, John Connery,
> James Sherry, James Donelly, James Sherry junior, Owen Sherry,

Michael Connery, Hugh Feghan, Patrick Hagan, George McKeowen, Felix McKenna, Neale Molloy, Gordon O'Neile, Widow O'Neile, Nicholas Little, Owen Hagan, Owen Keenan, Terence Callaghan, John Kidd.

Prisoners' Petitions and Cases

These cover the period 1787–1836 and concern petitions sent to the authorities by, or on behalf of, prisoners seeking commutation or remission of sentences. The search aid is a card index in the Reading Room. These records have been included in the Transportation Database which is available through the website of the National Archives of Ireland. The information can include the crime, place of trial and sentence handed down to the prisoner, as well as his place of origin and something of his family circumstances. For example, in 1799 William Diffen submitted a petition. He had stood trial in Armagh and was found guilty of burglary for which he was sentenced to death. Diffen stated that his family had always lived under Lord Gosford in Markethill, County Armagh, and that he was a yeoman by trade (PPC 130).

Not all petitions sought clemency for the prisoner. From 1791 we have the case of Robert Flanagan who was prosecuted for robbing Thomas Harkness near Jonesborough in south County Armagh. (The *Belfast Newsletter* of 29 April–3 May 1791 reported that Flanagan had been found guilty of highway robbery at the Armagh assizes.) A letter was sent to Isaac Corry, a local magistrate, pointing out the seriousness of the crimes and insisting that Flanagan should not be pardoned, but should be transported to Australia; Corry was urged to use his influence to ensure that this happened (PPC 3880).

State Prisoners' Petitions

The State Prisoners' Petitions (SPP) relate to those who were incarcerated for their involvement, whether suspected or actual, in seditious activities. These cover the period 1796–9 and the index is found in a calendar in the Reading Room. The petitioners ranged from the prisoners themselves to those writing on their behalf. In a letter of 5 April 1797, Arthur Cole Hamilton of Gortin, a landowner and magistrate, wrote that Daniel McCullagh, then a prisoner in Omagh gaol, was 'an able resolute wicked fellow', who 'was in the artillery, but turned out a leader of the Defenders'; he was now prepared to enter into military or naval service (SPP 29).

Petitions seeking clemency for John Moore of Limavady were sent by 'an old resident of Newtown Limavady' to Lord Castlereagh on 24 July 1798 and to Lady Louisa Conolly by his parents, Thomas and Mary, both of whom were over 60 years old (SPP 225). Moore had been sentenced to transportation to Australia for alleged involvement in the United Irishmen. In the first petition the author wrote, 'America, My Lord, we request for his destination', and raised the issue of the expense of sending him to Botany Bay. The fact that two other men tried at the same time, James Long and John Cust, had had their sentence of transportation commuted to banishment to America was highlighted as a reason for extending the same to Moore. It is not clear if mercy was shown to him.

5.3.2 Records in the Public Record Office of Northern Ireland

The Public Record Office of Northern Ireland has a very large collection of records concerning this period. In the 1970s PRONI produced separate education facsimiles relating to the United Irishmen and the 1798 Rebellion. In 1998, it produced a source list of documents relevant to this period. Summarised below are some of the more valuable collections of records, followed by a selection of other items of interest.

Caldwell Papers
The Caldwell Papers include letters and various other documents concerning the involvement in the rebellion of members of the Caldwell family of Harmony Hill, near Ballymoney, County Antrim, and their subsequent emigration to America (T3541). A fascinating item in this collection is the reminiscences of John Caldwell junior entitled, 'Particulars of history of a North County Irish Family', which is available in typescript (T3541/5/3). In some detail, Caldwell recounted his family background, upbringing, education, business affairs, and his involvement in politics and the United Irishmen. Of particular interest is his description of his voyage across the Atlantic in 1799 on the *Peggy*, a ship that Caldwell had chartered to carry him and over 100 fellow United Irishmen to America. A study of this document is David A. Wilson, 'John Caldwell's memoir: a case study in Ulster-American radicalism' in David A. Wilson and Mark G. Spencer (eds), *Ulster Presbyterians in the Atlantic World: Religion, Politics and Identity* (2006), pp 104–28. PRONI also has copies of documents relating to the trial of Richard Caldwell (T3058/1). Other records relating to the Caldwell family can be found under reference D1518.

Cleland Papers
Letters and papers relating to the efforts at suppressing the United Irishmen by Rev. John Cleland, a County Down-based Anglican clergyman who served as Lord Londonderry's land agent, have been archived under reference D714 (some of the material has been microfilmed under reference MIC507). These include a series of espionage reports, made by Nicholas Magin, the 'Saintfield informer', which give details of meetings of the Provincial Committee of the Society of United Irishman, 1797–8, and a series of depositions made before Cleland. For example, on 22 July 1798 the following deposition was sworn before Cleland:

> Jas Petty of Carnilea, labourer ... made oath that Jas Gray of Bangor, muslin weaver, administered the Oath of United Irish Men to him at

Bangor about 2 years ago … and Witness says that on … 10th of June last, he saw Jas Simpson of Bangor, riding, who ordered him to get an instrument or pike … Witness … went into Bangor … was march'd to Conlig, Jas Francis of Bangor appeared to have the Command (D714/3/19).

Dobbs Papers

The Dobbs Papers (D162; MIC533) include a number of miscellaneous items relating to the period of the rebellion. These include a list of officers serving in the rebel army (D162/98); prisoners in the Donegall Arms in Belfast (D162/102); and various depositions concerning the rebellion, e.g. depositions taken at Newtownards and Saintfield against various persons alleged to be United Irishmen and to have been at the battles of Antrim and Ballynahinch (D162/100B).

Downshire Papers

Some of the landed estate collections in PRONI include correspondence relating to the United Irishmen and rebellion. For example, the Downshire estate collection (D607) includes numerous letters relating to the events leading up to and including the rebellion and its aftermath. For instance, a letter in the collection, written by H. Galbraith in Belfast to Edward Hull in Stranraer and dated 13 June 1798, includes details of those who had perished at Newtownards in the rebellion:

> The men killed on Sunday at Newtownards are James Kain of Ballyferis, John Morison, sailor, Ballywalter, two sons of David Maxwell of Ballywalter, one son of Stewart, a blacksmith of Ballywalter, and another wounded, Andrew Adams of Ballywalter killed, one sergeant and one man of the Yorks killed (D607/F/235).

The following letter, written by George Stephenson in Hillsborough to Lord Downshire on 17 June 1798, provides details from the aftermath of the rebellion:

> Yesterday I saw the rebel general, Munro, hanged at Lisburn, and his head is now fixed on the market house there. Birch of Saintfield is to be tried this day, and it is thought he will be hanged. Cowan of Carnew, James Wallace of Banbridge, Crawford near that place, two Harrisons of Dromore and Jeremiah Norwood of Ballylintagh and a Thomas Jameson of Larchfield, are all taken up by parties of our troop, and by them conveyed to Belfast, as also Roger Magenis of Baleely. Information is coming in very fast from all quarters. Arms are delivering up in thousands, of all kinds, particularly pikes. Hanna of Moira, who was a recruiting sergeant for the rebels, with young Carleton, the Quaker, that went to America, is taken up, and Priest Mooney of Moira is also lodged safe (D607/F/251).

Lowry, Cleland, Steele and Nicholson Papers
This set of papers (D1494; MIC506) comprises a range of different items relating to the 1798 period. These include a statement issued in the autumn of 1796 by the inhabitants of the town and parish of Newtownards 'assembled for the purpose of expressing our sentiments of attachment to the principles of the constitution at this alarming period, when a foreign enemy threatens our shores and suspicion and distrust distract the minds of people of every description' (D1494/2/24). Other documents include minutes of meetings of United Irishmen and various depositions relating to the activities of this organisation.

McCance Papers
The McCance Papers (D272; MIC575) comprise various documents, including lists from 1798–9 of persons confined by order of the government in Belfast, Carrickfergus and on the prison ship, *Postlethwaite*. There are also affidavits and depositions relating to United Irishmen. For example, on 8 August 1798 Widow Jane McAllen of Gloverstown, in the parish of Duneane, County Antrim, accused William Cook, a retailer of spirits in Gloverstown, of leading a party of insurgents through the village, giving them whiskey and that they drank his health (D272/5). Several of the depositions – by Patrick McHenty of Cregan, farmer; Mary Donaldson of Carnala, spinster; and Andrew Stewart of Drimnacole, yeoman – relate to the attempts by Rev. Robert Acheson, Presbyterian minister of Glenarm, to persuade people to give up their arms in the wake of the rebellion (D272/22).

The most interesting item in this collection is the 'Black Book of the Rebellion of the North of Ireland' (D272/1), which contains the names of some 200 individuals who were members or suspected to be members of the United Irishmen and some details of their appearance and activities. For example, James Maxwell of Monaghan was described as 'about 40 years of age, brown hair, but not very short & was once a prisoner in the Artillery Barracks'. Another very valuable source is a list of 82 tenants on the estate of the Right Hon. Charles Fitzgerald at Ardglass, County Down, who had offered their assistance to His Majesty's Service with cars and horses for transporting troops, baggage, etc (D272/18).

Other items
Further materials of interest held by PRONI include copies of 156 letters (with an index of persons, places and regiments) received by Generals Lake and Hewitt and others during the period December 1796–December 1798 (MIC67/1). These are in the form of detailed reports from local army commanders in various parts of Ireland and concern measures to deal with the United Irishmen and with the 1798 Rebellion. Some other items are listed below.

An account of the burning of Ballymoney, 1798 – D1518/1/12

Typed copy of a letter '... from an Irish Emigrant to his friend in the United States giving an account of the Commotions in Ireland ...' which was printed in Philadephia in 1799; the author was Rev. Thomas Ledlie Birch, formerly minister of Saintfield Presbyterian Church, County Down – D1759/3B/8; T2685/1

Notebook containing details on the rebellion, especially as it concerned Presbyterians and the Presbyterian clergy – D3300/5/1

Letter informing on persons in the Millisle and Carrowdore area of County Down involved in the rebellion and giving the names of loyal persons who, if threatened with loss of property, would give information about the rebels, 1798 – D3579/1

Typescript extracts from the Rebellion Papers in NAI, 1792–1806 – T759/1

Copies of R. R. Madden's transcripts of letters to and from Henry Joy McCracken, many written by his sister Mary Ann, which include names of prisoners and informers, 1797–8 – T1210

Printed notice issued by Sir George Nugent, Major-General commanding Northern District and containing a list of names of rebels – T2162/2/2

Copies of documents from the Rebellion Papers in NAI relating to County Armagh – T3194/2

5.3.3 Records in the National Library of Ireland

Bound into a single volume in the National Library of Ireland are returns from a number of Irish counties, including Antrim and Down, of those who suffered losses in the rising and who had 'given in their claims on or before the 6th of April, 1799, to the Commissioners for enquiring into the losses sustained by such of his Majesty's loyal subjects, as have suffered in their property by the rebellion' (reference JLB.94107 – available via the Manuscripts Department). These returns provide the name of each claimant along with his or her address, occupation, nature of loss and amount claimed. For County Antrim there are *c.* 140 claimants, while for County Down the figure is *c.* 180. The claims range from £2,915 sought by James Armstrong for losses concerning his grocery business in Ballynahinch, to £1 8s. 8d. claimed by Mary Millon of Ballygrooby, near Randalstown, for 'Cloaths'. The names for Antrim and Down were published in *DIFHR*, 40 (2017), pp 8–13.

NLI also holds a copy of the following printed source: *List of the Subscribers to the Fund for the Relief of Widows and Orphans of Yeomen, Soldiers, &c. who fell in suppressing the late rebellion. Together with the proceedings of the Committee entrusted with the distribution of the Fund, the several persons to whom relief was granted, and the hands through which the same passed* (1800). The recipients included widows of men in various military units including the Antrim Militia, Antrim Yeomanry, Armagh Militia and Ballymena Yeomanry. Those who received support through their connection to the Donegal Militia included:

Sarah Dougherty (widow of Bryan)
Grace Gallagher (widow of Bryan)
Hannah McCartney (widow of Daniel)
Bell McManamon (widow of Daniel)
Margaret Murphy (widow of Michael)
Hannah O'Donnell (widow of Hugh)

5.3.4 Catholics departing from Ulster in 1795–6

Due to considerable sectarian unrest in Ulster, and in particular in north
County Armagh, in the mid 1790s many Catholic families were forced to leave
Ulster. While some sailed to Scotland or across the Atlantic, the majority
travelled westwards to the province of Connacht, especially to County Mayo.
Information on the arrival in Mayo of families from Ulster, including lists of
names, was provided to the authorities in Dublin from various individuals.
Records relating to this episode are mainly to be found in the Rebellion Papers
in the National Archives of Ireland. They are discussed here because they
comprise an important set of documentation on a particular episode from this
decade.

Among those who supplied information to Dublin were Lord Altamont and
his brother Denis Browne who submitted several reports on the impact of this
influx. In July 1796 Altamont wrote, 'The emigration from the Northern
counties to these parts still continues and I consider it the more alarming
because the extent of it does not seem to be understood'. In November 1796
Denis Browne wrote, 'The emigration from the North continues; every day
families arrive here with the wreck of their properties.' In the following month
Captain James Cuffe of Deel Castle, Crossmolina, noted that the new arrivals
were 'all of the Roman Catholic religion and almost all of them are from County
Armagh and are weavers.'

Estimates of the numbers leaving Ulster vary, but it would appear that the
figure was perhaps upwards of 5,000. Some 1,350 names were supplied to the
Dublin administration in a series of lists, which have been reproduced in a
number of publications. See in particular the articles by Patrick Tohall, 'The
Diamond fight of 1795 and the resultant expulsions', Seanchas Ardmhacha, 3:1
(1958), pp 17–50; Patrick Hogan, 'The migration of Ulster Catholics to
Connaught, 1795–96', Seanchas Ardmhacha, 9:2 (1979), pp 286–301; and, by
the same author, 'The migration of Ulster Catholics to Connaught, 1795–96:
an addendum', Seanchas Ardmhacha, 12:1 (1986), pp 252–3. Not only do we
have personal names, but in many instances the parish, and even the townland,
from which they originated is recorded. While names from County Armagh
predominated, other refugees were drawn from counties Antrim, Down,
Londonderry, Monaghan and Tyrone.

Among other items is a petition, emanating from the Westport area of
County Mayo, bearing 101 signatures, which was sent to the lord lieutenant,

Lord Camden, stating that the subscribers, and several hundred others they were writing on behalf of, were

> … emigrants from the North of Ireland [who] have been forced to fly from their respective holdings and habitations in the Counties of Armagh, Tyrone and Londonderry, in consequence of a persecution carried against them on account of their religion, being of the Roman Catholic persuasion.

The petitioners had erected temporary huts for themselves, but looked 'forward to the approach of winter with great uneasiness and anxiety, having no fixed residence nor houses to protect themselves and families from the inclemency of the weather', and so sought relief from the lord lieutenant. See 'Petition of Armagh migrants into the Westport area', *Cathair na Mart*, 2:1 (1982), pp 47–8. Other studies of this episode include Desmond O'Neill, 'Ulster Migration to Mayo, 1795–1796' in Bernard O'Hara (ed.), *Mayo: Aspects of its Heritage* (1982), pp 84–7; and Tomas O Fiaich, 'Migration from Ulster to County Mayo in 1795–'96', *Ulster Local Studies*, 12:2 (Winter 1990), pp 7–19 (reprinted from the *North Mayo Historical Journal*, 2:3 (1990/91)). Liam Kelly, *A Flame Now Quenched: Rebels and Frenchmen in Leitrim, 1793–1798* (1998), pp 47–53, deals with the arrival of northern refugees in County Leitrim.

5.3.5 Published studies of the United Irishmen and 1798 Rebellion

Numerous books and articles have been written about the 1798 Rebellion. A superb account of the Ulster story is A. T. Q. Stewart, *The Summer Soldiers: The 1798 Rebellion in Antrim and Down* (1995). Other valuable works include: David Dickson, Daire Keogh and Kevin Whelan (eds), *The United Irishmen: Republicanism, Radicalism and Rebellion* (1993); Nancy Curtin, *The United Irishmen: Popular Politics in Ulster and Dublin, 1791–1798* (1994); Cathal Póirtéir (ed.), *The Great Irish Rebellion of 1798* (1998); and Thomas Bartlett, David Dickson, Daire Keogh and Kevin Whelan (eds), *1798: A Bicentenary Perspective* (2003). The bibliographies of these books should be consulted for additional published and unpublished material.

An excellent county study is Myrtle Hill, Brian Turner and Kenneth Dawson (eds), *The 1798 Rebellion in County Down* (1998). This includes an essay by Thomas Bartlett on 'Repressing the rebellion in County Down' (pp 187–210) which includes a 'Finding list of prisoners tried by courts martial for offences committed in county Down, 1798' as well as 'Miscellaneous reports of courts martial for which I have found no formal transcript'. These are based on the Rebellion Papers and include over 100 names, many with a place of residence and occupation. On this subject see also Patrick C. Power, *The Courts Martial of 1798–99* (1997). Another very detailed county study is Brendan McEvoy, *The United Irishmen in Tyrone* (1998), which was originally published in

Seanchas Ardmhacha. See also the *History and Society* series of county volumes by Geography Publications for further essays on this period, notably those by Réamonn Ó Muirí (Armagh), Liam Kelly (Cavan), Nancy Curtin (Down), and Brian McDonald (Monaghan).

Other local studies of the conflict include Kenneth Robinson, *North Down and Ards in 1798* (1998), Harry Allen, *Men of the Ards* (2004), and Séamas Mac Annaidh (ed.), *Fermanagh and 1798* (2000). A number of local societies devoted the 1998 edition of their journal to the rebellion. For example, *Dúiche Néill*, 12 (1998) featured much local information on the United Irishmen and rebellion, including a lengthy article by Brendan McAnallen on 'The Brantry Boys of '98'. Biographies of particular individuals include Kenneth L. Dawson, *The Belfast Jacobin: Samuel Neilson and the United Irishmen* (2017). A recently published volume that looks at the story of those who left for America around the time of the rebellion is Peter Gilmore, Trevor Parkhill and William Roulston, *Exiles of '98: Ulster Presbyterians and the United States* (2018).

While much of the focus of the 1790s is on the United Irishmen, there was another underground movement active at this time known as the Defenders. This was overwhelmingly Catholic as far as its membership was concerned. For information on this organisation, see Marianne Elliott, 'The Defenders of Ulster' in David Dickson, Daire Keogh and Kevin Whelan (eds), *The United Irishmen: Republicanism, Radicalism and Rebellion* (1993), pp 222–33. A detailed local study is Brendan McEvoy, 'The Peep of Day Boys and Defenders in the County Armagh', *Seanchas Ardmhacha*, 12:1 (1986), pp 122–63; 12:2 (1987), pp 60–127.

5.4 Post Rebellion records

5.4.1 Petitions relating to the Act of Union, 1799–1800

The Act of Union was passed in 1800 and came into force on 1 January 1801. The Irish Parliament was abolished and henceforth Irish MPs represented their constituents at Westminster. During the debates surrounding this legislation, petitions both for and against the Act of Union were drawn up across Ireland. Some of these petitions were county-based, while others were from parishes or manors and a number of them were published in the *Belfast Newsletter*:

County Antrim – 27 December 1799
County Armagh – 14 January 1800
County Donegal – 27, 31 December 1799 and 3, 7, 17 January 1800
County Londonderry – 27 September 1799
County Tyrone – 3, 6, 13 December 1799
City of Londonderry – 24 September 1799
Borough of Antrim – 11 October 1799
Manors of Richhill and Mullalelish, County Armagh – 20 December 1799

Roman Catholic inhabitants of Lower Creggan, County Armagh –
17 January 1800
Parish of St Andrews (Ballyhalbert), County Down – 31 January 1800
Parish of Bangor, County Down – 28, 31 January 1800
Landholders and inhabitants in and about Tandragee, County Armagh –
11 February 1800

Other petitions include:

Page of signatures from a petition against the Act of Union, *c.* 1799 –
T533/6
Printed Anti-Union petition from freeholders of County Armagh to
Parliament, 1799 – D207/10/4
Copy of the *Dublin Evening Post* of 1–4 February 1800, giving
a list of *c.* 2,000 signatures of Armagh anti-unionists – T2344/2
List of over 300 signatures, many with the townland of residence,
apparently relating to the anti-unionist address from County Down,
1800 – D607/H/5
Newspaper cutting containing a unionist address from the Provost and
Grand Jury of the town and corporation of Monaghan at their annual
court leet (with one dissentient) to Lord Cornwallis, and Cornwallis's
reply, 1799 – T3465/112

5.4.2 Emmet's Rebellion of 1803

In 1803, there was a further rebellion led by Robert Emmet, which was swiftly
suppressed. Thomas Russell, who had been the librarian of what is now the
Linen Hall Library in Belfast, attempted to enlist support from United Irish
sympathisers in Ulster, but with limited success. Both men were hanged for
their part in the rising, Russell at Downpatrick. For more information on this
episode, see Ruan O'Donnell, *Robert Emmet and the Rising of 1803* (2003).
Records relating to this insurrection can be found in the Rebellion Papers in
NAI. Some items relating to it are in PRONI, such as a bundle of 19 documents
concerning various individuals imprisoned in the gaol in Downpatrick for their
part in the rebellion (D2930/3/10). The records include: indictments for
treason against Michael Maguire, Thomas Russell, Fergus McCartan and James
Drake; examinations of Edward Smyth, Abraham Everal and James Carey;
statements by informers Hugh Maginnis, Patrick Murray, Henry Roland,
Henry Smith, and Robert Nelson; and a deposition of John Tate.

Among other valuable sources is a document in the Minto Papers in the
National Library of Scotland which has been transcribed and published: James
Kelly, 'Official list of radical activists and suspected activists involved in Emmet's
rebellion, 1803', *Analecta Hibernica*, 43 (2012), pp 129–200. This includes
descriptive information on individuals. For example, James Hope, who had
earlier been a leading figure in the 1798 Rebellion, was described as: 'About 5

feet 7 in[ches] high; black hair & eyes; long faced; ill looking; has a stoop in his shoulders. Speaks with the northern accent and is about 40 years old. Comes from the co[unty] Antrim somewhere near Belfast.' Additional information on particular individuals is provided in the footnotes. For instance 'Gen[era]l [John] O'Neil who is an old man' was John O'Neill (1737–1811), a native of Derrynoose, County Armagh; he fought in the Seven Years' War (1756–63) and in the West Indies during the American War of Independence and retired on a pension in 1799.

5.4.3 The agricultural census of 1803

The threat of an invasion of Great Britain and Ireland by France recurred periodically during the late 1790s and the early years of the nineteenth century. The government in London made plans in 1797 and 1798 to abandon coastal areas and introduced new legislation for defending the kingdom. This legislation required the lord lieutenant in each county to compile returns, especially from maritime parishes, enumerating livestock and the wagons and horses available for transport, and giving the quantity of 'dead stock' (crops stored). During a scare in 1803 about an invasion of Ireland, resulting from the planned but abortive insurrection of that year (see above), similar returns were made under the same legislation, which now, following the Act of Union, applied to Ireland. The surviving returns relate to many parishes in County Down and the northern parishes of County Antrim.

The surviving returns for County Antrim are in the National Archives of Ireland (Official Papers, 153/103/1–16) and a microfilm copy is available in PRONI (MIC678/1). The returns for County Down were made to the first marquess of Londonderry, the governor of the county, and are in the Londonderry Papers in PRONI (D654/A2). A detailed analysis of the returns for County Down is provided by Duncan Scarlett in *Researching Down Ancestors*, published by the Ulster Historical Foundation in 2004. This is essential reading for it notes gaps in the coverage and also highlights instances where the returns for some townlands have been placed incorrectly with those of another parish. In all, there are around 11,300 names for County Down. Additional information in some returns includes numbers of 'cars and carts', of people 'able to drive cattle and load carts' and of those 'willing to serve the Government gratuitously or for hire'. Details of the parishes covered by the 1803 agricultural census can be found in Appendix 1 of this book.

6. Landed estate records

U ntil the beginning of the twentieth century the most important unit of land organisation in Ireland was the estate. Very few farmers owned their farms outright, but rather leased them from a landlord. The early seventeenth-century Plantation of Ulster, followed by the Cromwellian, Restoration and Williamite land settlements of the 1650s through to the beginning of the eighteenth century all contributed to the evolution of the landed estate system. It was not until the passing of a series of acts of parliament in the late nineteenth and early twentieth centuries that these estates were broken up and an owner-occupier class of farmers was created.

6.1 Landed estates in Ulster
Landed estates in Ulster ranged in size from over 100,000 acres to under 1,000. There were thus considerable variations in the wealth and lifestyles of landowners, and to regard them as forming a single homogeneous group would be wrong. The owners of the largest estates were usually titled aristocrats and often owned properties in several parts of Ireland and in Britain. Their homes were generally built on a grand scale and were set within extensive demesnes. They exerted considerable control over representative politics in their respective counties. The smaller landowners, on the other hand, lived more modestly and in many cases were on the same level as many of the more substantial tenant farmers. One thing that most landowners shared was membership of the Church of Ireland. Only a small number of landed proprietors were Presbyterians, and even fewer were Roman Catholics.

Those in outright ownership of a landed estate could either manage it directly, with the assistance of agents, or they could lease the estate in its entirety to an intermediary known as a middleman. In these circumstances the tenant farmers held their farms from the middleman rather than from the outright owner of the estate. The use of middlemen was notable in County Londonderry where the estates of the London livery companies tended to be in the possession of middlemen. There was a sizeable estate attached to each Anglican bishopric and the normal practice was for these lands to be leased to middlemen. The fact that so much land was in the possession of such individuals was regarded as one of the major problems with landholding in Ireland. In 1782, one observer wrote 'there is no difficulty in believing that there are numbers of proprietors of estates who are ignorant of the severities practised on their tenants by that swarm of locusts, those middlemen or land-jobbers, as they are called, whose depredations are more destructive than all the plagues of Egypt' (T3649/2).

The number of published studies on Irish estates has increased considerably in recent times. Terence Dooley's volumes, *Sources for the History of Landed Estates in Ireland* (2000) and *The Big Houses and Landed Estates of Ireland: A Research Guide* (2007), provide an introduction to the value of estate collections and other records for studying landed estates. Case studies of individual estates and their owners include the following volumes on the Abercorn estate in counties Donegal and Tyrone: W. H. Crawford, *The Management of a Major Ulster Estate in the Late Eighteenth Century: The Eighth Earl of Abercorn and his Irish Agents* (2001) and William J. Roulston, *Abercorn: The Hamiltons of Barons Court* (2014). Local historical publications often include useful information relating to landed estates. For example, *Clogher Record*, the journal of the Clogher Historical Society, is a veritable treasure trove of information on landed estates in, for the most part, counties Fermanagh and Monaghan.

6.2 Locating estate papers

The documents generated by the management of landed estates are among the most valuable records for the local and family historian. Appendix 2 of this book provides details on some 350 collections of estate papers for the nine counties of Ulster. There are two main repositories for documentation relating to estates in Ulster: the Public Record Office of Northern Ireland and the National Library of Ireland.

Public Record Office of Northern Ireland

PRONI's extensive collections of estate papers relate not only to the six counties of Northern Ireland, but to other parts of Ireland as well, notably counties Donegal and Monaghan. What makes the estate records in PRONI stand out is the fact that most of them have been expertly catalogued making it relatively easy to discover what is available for a particular property. Detailed introductions have been prepared for many of the larger collections and these can now be read on the PRONI website. Most of these introductions were written by Dr A. P. W. Malcomson, a former Director of the institution and the leading authority on landed society in the eighteenth century, and they describe the history of the landowning family, the scope of the collection, and the way in which the records have been organised.

National Library of Ireland

The principal repository in the Republic of Ireland for landed estate records is the National Library in Dublin. Its holdings include many documents relating to estates in Ulster. Notable collections relating to Ulster include the records of the Farnham estate in County Cavan and those for the Leslie estate, which relate mainly to County Monaghan. In recent times considerable resources have been applied to cataloguing some of the more significant collections. These catalogues can be downloaded as PDFs from the website of the National Library.

Other repositories
A few items relating to Ulster estates can be found in the National Archives of Ireland. The Manuscripts & Archives Research Library of Trinity College Dublin holds extensive records relating to the property owned by the College in counties Armagh, Donegal and Fermanagh, as well as some records relating to other Ulster estates. County archives and libraries in the Republic of Ireland also hold collections of estate papers. The Registry of Deeds, which will be looked at in more detail in Chapter 7, is another important repository for information on the occupation of land. In addition to repositories on the island of Ireland, some archives in Britain and North America hold records relating to the management of landed estates in Ulster.

6.3 Identifying the relevant estate
Before delving into estate papers, it is first of all necessary to identify the collection of records relating to where your ancestor lived. There are various ways of doing this. First of all, if estate records are available for a particular parish this is indicated in Appendix 1 of this book. So, for example, for the parish of Ballynure in County Antrim the available collections include those for the following estates: the Adair estate; the Brice estate; the Dobbs estate; and the Donegall estate. Researchers should refer to the relevant entry in Appendix 2 for more information on each of these estate collections. This approach is helpful for those searching for records by parish. However, if looking for the landlord of an individual townland a different method will usually be required.

One way to identify the owner of a particular townland is to examine Griffith's Valuation of *c.* 1860 (available online at www.askaboutireland.ie/griffith-valuation) and note the name in the column headed 'Immediate Lessor' for the townland in question. While this may not always be the name of the owner of a landed estate, in many instances it will. For the researcher concentrating on the eighteenth century, however, there are clearly limitations with this approach. Although the family in possession of an estate in 1860 was often the same in 1760, and occasionally in 1660, in many cases it will not be. Sometimes this will not be a problem, as the records of successive owners will be found together in the same estate collection.

Searching the online catalogues of the different archives holding estate collections is another way to try to identify if records exist for a particular townland. This approach is particularly worthwhile when looking for documentation in PRONI using the eCatalogue since many of PRONI's collections have been catalogued down to townland level. The Freeholders' Records database on the PRONI website is also worth checking since many of the registers will give the name of the freeholder's landlord (see Chapter 10 for more on freeholders).

Even after trying these and other approaches, it may not be possible to identify a relevant estate collection. For one thing, it must be acknowledged that the records of many estates have not survived. Some were destroyed in the disturbances of the early 1920s; others were lost in the more recent 'Troubles'. Still others were burnt by their owners, who felt that they had no more use for them or wanted to clear space. Generally speaking, the larger the estate, the more likely it is that records have survived, usually because facilities were created to store securely the papers relating to the management of the property. Conversely, the records of smaller estates, those in the 1,000–3,000-acre range, have a much poorer survival rate. Finally, some collections remain in private custody, perhaps still awaiting 'rediscovery'.

6.4 The range of records
Some categories of estate papers are more useful to family historians than others. Title deeds are concerned with the legal ownership of an estate, and are generally of limited value to genealogists. The same can be said of mortgages. Wills and marriage settlements usually refer only to the members of the landowner's family. However, rentals, leases, lease books, maps, correspondence and manor court records can all be extremely helpful for those searching for their ancestors.

6.4.1 Leases
Typically the item most commonly found within a landed estate collection will be a lease. For some estate collections the number of surviving leases can run into the thousands. Most of these will be for farms, though a proportion will be for tenements in a town, and others for mills and fisheries, etc. The information contained in a lease can be considered under the following headings.

The names of lessor and lessee
A lease will name the parties to it. On the one hand, there will be the lessor (or grantor), i.e. the landowner, and on the other, the lessee (or grantee), i.e. the tenant. A lease granted by a landlord to a tenant gave him the right to take possession of the holding (the term for the area of land held by a lease). Two copies of the lease were usually prepared, with one copy retained by the landlord and the other by the tenant. Sometimes there may be more than one lessor, perhaps if the estate happened to be in the possession of trustees while the owner was a minor. There may also have been more than one

lessee for on many occasions several tenants – perhaps related to each other – joined together to take a lease.

The location of the farm

A lease will indicate the location of the farm. Sometimes this will be no more specific than the name of the townland or subdivision of the townland. Frequently, however, the lease will provide a written description of the position of the holding within the townland. For example, a lease of 1796 from Susanna Barton to John Johnston of Shanroe in Forkill parish, County Armagh, recorded that the holding was 'meared and bounded on the East by Mafoner River, on the West by the Road leading to Mafoner Bridge, on the South by Owen McNamee's Holding and on the North by Jas Bennitt's Holding' (D294/105A). Some leases include a small map showing the location of the farm.

The rent to be paid

The lease specified the rent that was due to the landlord by the tenant. The rent was usually paid twice a year on what were known as gale days, often 1 May and 1 November. The landlord's agent may have collected the rent in person or the tenant may have been required to appear at the estate office. The rent was usually a cash sum, often with additional 'in-kind' payments. The currency was frequently specified for there were separate English and Irish currencies in operation in Ireland. The rent need not have stayed the same throughout the duration of the lease for some leases included a clause that increased the rent after a specified period of time. In addition to the rent, other payments were demanded from the tenant, such as receiver's fees and duties. Occasionally the landlord might waive the rent for a tenant in straitened circumstances or who had carried out some particular service for him. There are also examples of a small nominal rent, known as a peppercorn rent, being charged.

The in-kind payments that formed part of the rent could include livestock, crops and so many days of service to the landlord. For instance, when Edward Edwards leased Maghernageeragh and Thainboy, County Tyrone, to William Caldwell in 1678 the rent comprised £5 10s. with 1½ barrels of good oats and one fat unshorn mutton and three days' work of 'man and horse' (D2281/1). An early seventeenth-century lease which is interesting because of its in-kind payments is that issued to Hugh Hamilton by the earl of Abercorn in 1615. In return for a lease of Lisdivin, County Tyrone, Hamilton was to pay either £6 or 'one hogshead of Gascoign wine, one pound of good pepper, four pounds of loaf sugar and a box of marmalade containing at least two pounds of the preserve' (D623/B/13/2A).

The practice of including in-kind payments in leases continued in the eighteenth century. A 1707 lease relating to Lord Massereene's estate in County Antrim stipulated that in addition to £9 the tenant should provide 'the work of two men for one day, in harvest or otherwise, and also two good fat Capons at Christmas, two good fat ducks at Lamas and two good fatt hens at Shrovetide yearly' or six pence in lieu of each (D2171/13). A 1731 lease for Edenagarry in the parish of Drumballyroney, County Down, required the tenant to provide one fat hog weighing one hundred pounds when killed and dressed or 12 shillings in lieu (D2653/1/3A). Under the terms of a lease of 1788, the rent for a farm in Goland, County Donegal, included the yearly delivery of 1,600 Lough Swilly oysters (Coventry History Centre, PA 1484/51/3). A 1770 lease for the same estate required the tenant of the mills in Drumboe and Callanoe to pay an additional one shilling per annum to promote a horse race in Ballybofey (PA 1484/54/1).

The conditions to be fulfilled by the lessee
Leases included a broad range of clauses requiring the tenant to carry out, or to desist from, various activities. It was usual for the landlord to stipulate the mill to which the tenant was to take his corn (oats). In other words, the tenant could not take his corn to the mill where he would receive the best price, but rather the mill his landlord directed him to use. Frequently this mill was referred to as the 'manor mill' and often it was leased directly to a miller by the landlord himself. Tenants were also required to do 'suit and service' to the manor court, which provided a forum for the administration of justice on the estate (see below for manor court records).

The conditions to be fulfilled by the lessee could include the construction of a house on his property, often with clear instructions as to its dimensions, wall thickness, roof covering, etc. For example, under the terms of a lease issued by the earl of Antrim in 1736 the tenant, James Calderwood, was required to build within three years a new house of brick or stone with a roof of oak or fir timber on his tenement in Ballymoney. Furthermore, the house was to be 27 feet in front (in other words, the full width of the tenement) and 17 feet high in the side wall (D2977/3A/3/2/10/69). Other leases, especially those for towns, specified that the chimney should be of stone or brick to limit the threat of fire. A lease for a tenement in Lisnaskea, County Fermanagh, included instructions that the house to be built on the property should have 'large sash windows on the streete side' (D1939/17/10/9).

The creation of gardens and orchards could also be promoted through the clauses contained in leases. When Sir John Magill leased a farm in Greenoge, County Down, to John Gibson in 1696 he required him to plant an orchard of 100 fruit trees (D2487/2). Other leases specified the type of fruit trees that were to be planted, apple and pear being the most common. Additionally, a tenant could be required to mark off the boundaries – the mears or mearings – of his farm in a certain way and to divide his farm up into fields and plant hedges to distinguish between those fields. A lease for lands in County Fermanagh from 1718 included the clause that the tenant should delineate 'the meares and ditches enclosing the premises and plant on such mears and ditches, trees of oak, ash, elm, birch or alder at 20 feet distance' (D1096/76/1).

Tenants often sub-let the property, or part of it, to a third party; this was known as a sub-lease. The third party became an undertenant, paying rent to the tenant, who continued to pay rent to the landlord. A lease generally included a clause concerning the subletting of the holding. Sometimes this was strictly forbidden, though on other occasions it was allowed on the payment of an additional sum of money to the landlord. (See more below on undertenants.) Some leases included a condition that the tenant should not set aside any part of his farm as a site for a Presbyterian or Catholic place of worship. Alternatively, a tenant could be allowed to do this, but only on the payment of an additional rent. For example, a lease issued in 1769 by James Hamilton Moore for a farm in Keenaghan in Killyman parish, County Tyrone, stipulated that an extra £30 per annum would be levied if the tenant allowed a 'Mass House' or 'Meeting House' to be built on his farm (D235/29).

Tenants who did not fulfil the conditions imposed on them – which were often time-limited – were liable to a penalty of one form or another. For example, in the above lease to James Calderwood there was a fine of £1 per annum in the event of him not building a house on his tenement in Ballymoney. Some leases included clauses that can be regarded as inducements to act or behave in a certain way. For instance, in a lease of 1700 granted by Viscount Charlemont the tenant was to have a reduction in the duty payments if he and his family and sub-tenants attended the Established Church on Sundays and other days appointed by the government (D859/6).

The tenure of the lease

The tenure – that is, the period for which the lease was valid – was also specified in a lease. Again, this could vary depending on the landlord's preferences and the circumstances of the time. A fee farm grant was effectively a lease in perpetuity. In the early 1600s, as part of the scheme for the Plantation of Ulster, landowers were obliged, under the terms of their patents, to lease a proportion of their lands in fee farm, the thinking being that those who received such grants would become the backbone of the tenantry, individuals who were secure in their title and ready to invest in their lands. Fee farm grants continued to be issued from time to time by many landlords. Generally speaking, later fee farm grants were issued in return for an up-front payment, which could be quite substantial, and were often created in response to financial difficulties for the landowner or to stimulate urban development. When John Cole of Florence Court, County Fermanagh, issued a fee farm grant to Alexander Nixon in 1758 the advance payment was £705 (D580/111).

Much more common than a fee farm grant was a lease for a determinate number of years. Such a lease would not expire until a specified period of time had elapsed. The number of years varied considerably, from fewer than five to upwards of 1,000. Leases for 21, 31 or 41 years were particularly common. It should be noted that for much of the eighteenth century the maximum duration of a lease issued to a Catholic was 31 years.

In the second half of the seventeenth century leases for lives became increasingly popular. A lease for lives would not expire until certain individuals, identified by name in the lease, had died. Usually a lease for lives also included a term of years. So one will find, for example, a lease for three lives or 21 years; the lease will last for whichever was the longer. The number of 'lives' inserted in a lease varied from one to four or even five, with three the most common. The choice of the lives seems mainly to have been the privilege of the tenant. Leases for lives are very useful for genealogists because a tenant often named members of his family as the lives. The ages of the persons named as lives were frequently stated, especially if they were children; this information is especially useful in the absence of church registers. On very rare occasions the date of birth of one of the lives may appear in a lease. For instance, a note appended to a 1751 lease for a farm in Lisnasure, County Down, recorded, 'Robert Beatty son of David Beatty one of the within named lives was born 29th of October 1746' (D778/94).

Young relatives were often named as lives in the hope that at least one of them would survive for many years and the lease could last potentially for upwards of half a century. Sometimes, it is possible to identify several generations of one family through the named lives. For example, the lives in a lease of 1800 from Lord Dungannon to William Moore senior of Toreagh, County Antrim, were Thomas, Ann and Patrick Moore, identified respectively as the son, neice and grandson of the lessee (D300/2/1/130/1). It must be acknowledged, however, that in quite a few instances the lives named in a lease were not family members, but rather members of the Royal Family, presumably on the basis that these individuals, with a better diet and health care, were more likely to reach old age.

Depending on the terms of the lease, a lease for lives could be updated on the fall of each life by inserting a new name on the payment of a renewal fine. The renewals might have been limited to a certain number of lives, though often they were renewable forever. Such a lease was in effect a grant in perpetuity so long as the tenant wished to renew it. When a new life was added to the lease details of the person's age and relationship to the lessee might be included.

For the tenant a lease for lives was a prized possession for it gave him and his family a greater degree of security. So long as his farm was above a certain value, a man in possession of a lease for lives was also entitled to vote (see Chapter 10). From the landlord's perspective, the issuing of leases for lives not only created a solid and generally contented tenantry, it also allowed him to flex his muscles in parliamentary elections. In other words, he could direct his tenants to vote for his preferred candidate (there was no secret ballot at this time). Problems could arise for the landlord in keeping track of the lives in a lease, especially if one or more of them emigrated. For a case study of the ramifications of this, see 'The lives lease system and emigration from Ulster: an example from Montgomery County, Pennsylvania' by Peter Roebuck, published in *DIFHR*, 18 (1995), pp 75–7.

Example of a lease
By way of example, the following extracts are taken from a 1783 lease for three lives for a farm in County Tyrone (D476/21).

> This indenture made the twenty-first day of November in the year of Our Lord, one thousand seven hundred and eighty three between the Right Honourable Thomas, Lord Baron Welles of Dungannon, in the County of Tyrone, of the one part, and Joseph Dickson of Mullaghbawn in the Parish of Donaghmore in the County of Tyrone aforesaid of the other part.
>
> Witnesseth that the said Thomas, Lord Baron Welles, for and in consideration of the yearly rents and covenants hereinafter reserved and expressed, hath demised, granted, set and to farm let unto the said Joseph Dickson all that part and parcel of land in the townland of Dristernan formerly in the possession of James McGinnis and partners and now in the actual possession of the said Joseph Dickson containing by Henry Long's survey thirty-six acres English Statute measure appertaining, situate, lying and being in the townland of Dristernan, parish of Donaghmore, barony of Dungannon, and county aforesaid.
>
> To have and to hold all and singular the said demised premises with the rights, members and appurtenances unto the said Joseph Dickson his heirs, executors, administrators and assigns, for and during the natural life and lives of the three following persons, and the survivors and survivor of them and each of them, to wit, the life of the said Joseph Dickson, part to these presents, Samuel Dickson, now aged about six years, and Mathew Dickson, now aged about two years, both sons of the said Joseph Dickson, commencing from the first day of November, one thousand seven hundred and eighty three from thenceforth fully should be complete and ended.
>
> Rent of 13 shillings per acre every year. Additional covenants concerning payment of duties, non-payment of rent, covenant by tenant to build a house, tenant to make enclosures, tenant bound to grind at the landlord's mill, tenant to plant an orchard, landlord's promise to tenant of quiet enjoyment of the premises.

6.4.2 Lease books

Lease books can be among the most useful of estate papers as far as genealogy is concerned. They record in summary form the information contained in the original leases, such as the name of the lessee, the date the lease commenced, the location and extent of the holding, and the rent payable on it. More detailed lease books can include the names of the lives in the leases and the status of those lives (i.e. whether alive or dead and, if alive, where resident). Often covering an entire estate, they can be a much quicker way of finding information on a tenant farmer than searching for the lease itself.

A good example of an eighteenth-century lease book is the volume that survives for the Caledon estate in County Tyrone (D2433/A/5/3). This includes a precis of the contents of each lease, giving the name of the tenant, the date the lease began, the conditions to be fulfilled by the lessee, and the names of the 'lives'. There are also annotations indicating the status of the lives. Several of these make reference to individuals who had emigrated – not always voluntarily – to America. Examples include:

> Tenement in Caledon: 'John Browne was transported as a Felon to
>   America in 1772'
> Tenement in Caledon: '1774 Sepr 24th rec'd an Acct that Robt Swan
>   dyed in America – he died at Caledon in October 1797'
> Mullaghmore: 'Wm Browne, son of ... Elizth is in America & supposed
>   dead'
> Crievelaght: 'Adam Kennedy went to America in Spring 1772'

6.4.3 Rentals

Rentals, rent rolls or rent books record the rent payments made by the tenants to their landlord. They are generally arranged by year (rents were usually paid half-yearly) or with several years covered by the same document. In their simplest form they may only include the total value of the rents collected in each townland, but more detailed rentals can include a broad range of information, such as the name of the tenant, the extent and location of the holding, and the date and tenure of the lease. It should be noted that a rental may not record the names of all the tenants of a particular holding. Often the name of a tenant in a rental will be followed by the term 'and partners' or something similar. It may be the case that a later rental will name all of the partners, but it must be accepted that these 'silent' partners often remain anonymous.

Occasionally rentals are annotated and may contain additional details such as a change in occupancy and the reason for this, or whether or not the tenants had fulfilled or failed to fulfil the covenants in their leases. For instance, a rent roll of the Balfour estate in County Fermanagh of 1770 (D1939/17/10/50) included a note that as part of his rent Thomas Armstrong was to pay five bottles of good wine and provide ten days' service of man and horse as well as build a good inn and keep it in repair; there was an additional comment that no inn had been built and neither the wine nor the days of work had been supplied. Some rentals include remarks about the conduct of a tenant. For example, in a rental and account book of the Montgomery estate at Fivemiletown, County Tyrone, covering the period 1789 to 1807, the following annotation appears: 'William Birney, son to Thos Birney, has been guilty of stealing a number of trees in this estate & is a very dishonest man & should not be looked upon as a proper tennant' (D627/48).

Others rentals may provide a broader perspective on the social and economic conditions then prevailing. For example, a rent roll of 1718 (D2094/21) of the Vintners' Company estate in County Londonderry, at that time leased in its entirety by William Conolly, the Speaker of the Irish House of Commons, includes various comments by its compiler, Amos Strettle, about conditions in the area at that time. For instance, Strettle noted that 'a great many of the inhabitants and tenants of that part of the country are going off to America and leaving their habitations and lands'. This exodus was having an impact on the rental value of the land.

A 1774 rental for the Langford estate in County Antrim gives the date each lease was granted and the terms of the lease (D2624/4A). Many of these leases were issued in 1726 and usefully the rental includes the names of the lives in these leases which were still in being in October 1775, with a few later annotations. For example, it was recorded Mary Kelso, a life in a lease for a farm in Craigarogan, died in March 1776, while there was a note that Hugh Brown, a life in a lease for a farm in Ballymather, had written a letter home from Philadelphia on 20 September 1775 – clearly the family had produced this letter as evidence that Hugh was still alive (and, therefore, the lease was still valid).

6.4.4 Maps

Maps form an important element in most estate collections. Early estate maps were often pictorial and included representations of houses, mills and other landscape features. Many can be considered important works of art in their own right as the cartographer showed off his skills. Archaeological sites might also be shown, such as megalithic tombs and ringforts, some of which may since have been destroyed through agricultural improvement schemes. From a genealogical perspective, maps that name tenants and identify the location of their farms are the most useful. The value of such maps lies in the fact that they can help a researcher to pinpoint the location of the farm in which an ancestor lived. Occasionally, estate maps have an accompanying 'terrier' that includes detailed information about each farm.

The earliest surviving detailed estates maps for Ulster are those prepared by Thomas Raven of the lands of the London companies in County Londonderry in 1622. These provide the names of the householders in the settlements founded by the companies. These maps and the names of householders were published in *Londonderry and the London Companies*, edited by D. A. Chart and published by the Public Record Office of Northern Ireland in 1928. Coloured replica drawings of the originals are in PRONI (T510), while the Ulster-Scots Agency has reproduced the maps on CD-ROM along with a commentary by Prof. Raymond Gillespie. In 1625, Raven prepared detailed maps of Sir James Hamilton's estate in north-east County Down, which name many of the tenants. The original set of maps is in North Down Museum, but a copy is available in PRONI (T870).

6.4.5 Surveys and valuations

A landlord keen to improve his estate in order to maximise his income from it might carry out a survey or valuation of it. Often these surveys contain little of genealogical interest, as they concentrate on land quality and use. For example, William Starrat of Strabane worked extensively as a surveyor in west Ulster in the first half of the eighteenth century, but there is little information on the tenant farmers in his surveys. Nonetheless, while not containing the sort of detail that will allow a family tree to be extended, such surveys can provide a glimpse into the world of our forebears and should still be consulted.

Other surveys and valuations do contain much of interest to the genealogist. A good example of a very detailed survey is that for the Murray of Broughton estate in west County Donegal, which was compiled *c.* 1730 (D2860/25/10). This includes detailed information on the tenants and their tenancies as the following extract demonstrates:

> Daniel Keeve holds from year to year one cabin and garden and one park which formerly was held by Brian O'Cain at 23s per annum and Keeve paid in the year ending at May 1728, 30s per annum and in the year 1729 he paid but 24s per annum as per the rentroll. This house and garden lies backward between Patrick Scott's and John Warren's and the park is near the head of the Lough joining to Fergal McAward's park.

Sometimes it might be possible to learn something of the challenges faced by a tenant. The following extract is from a valuation of the Ironmongers' estate in County Londonderry by John Hood in 1765, and relates to the townland of Ballinuntagh:

> James Collins an aged and infirm man whose ancestors has [*sic*] held a considerable deal of land in the proportion since the first settlement of Protestants in Ireland implores the compassion of the Governor and Company as he is unable to pay more rent than he at present pays (MIC145/8).

6.4.6 Correspondence

The correspondence between a landlord and his agent can be of immense genealogical value. Not only can it include details of the day-to-day running of the estate, and the issues facing the tenants, but mention is often made of those who worked on the estate. The best collection of eighteenth-century estate correspondence relates to the Abercorn estate in west Tyrone and east Donegal (D623/A). Most of the letters were written by the eighth earl of Abercorn and his estate agents, John McClintock, Nathaniel Nisbett, John Colhoun, John Sinclair, John Hamilton and James Hamilton. The eighth earl was an absentee landlord who lived most of his life in London and only rarely visited his Irish estate. However, few absentee landlords can have known more about their estate than the earl knew about his. The letters cover a broad range of subjects and relate to all aspects of the estate's management. The correspondence was transcribed primarily by Dr Brian Trainor, a former Director of PRONI, as part of his recuperation from an accident and the letters can now be read on the PRONI eCatalogue.

The following excerpt from a letter of November 1767 from John Hamilton to the eighth earl demonstrates how the lives of the tenants could be recorded in the minutest detail:

> Patrick Biglay, late of Brownhill [Leckpatrick parish], had three sons, Patrick, Thomas and George. Patrick, who was the eldest, got the half of his father's land several years ago. Thomas was taught the weaver trade and maintained in his father's house, notwithstanding would not leave his father or give up his claim to the land till George, who laboured the land and supported his aged father, was obliged to pay him five guineas upon which his father gave an article of the land to George, reserving some little part to himself. Patrick the father was a papist and his wife being a Protestant, all the sons went to church with the mother. Thomas never satisfied that George should get the land. To ingratiate himself into his father's favour returned to Mass, and the father upon that takes him again into his house and dispossess [sic] George. The father on his death bed made a will and left it to be divided equally between them. Now as Thomas has a trade and in good circumstances and George quite destitute, who made a fair bargain with the father, I think … that George has the best right (D623/A/37/105).

Difficulties between a landlord and his agent and the tenants on an estate are reflected in the following letter of 1779 from John Slade to Lord Hillsborough:

> The tenants require strict severity to make them pay their rents. Last week the sheriff gave me possession of Crawford's holding at Carrickfergus, but they were obliged to carry George McKinney's wife out by force. I have set the 20 acres that he was in possession of for the remaining part of this year for 24 guineas to a responsible tenant … I purpose to punish that old villain George McKinney somehow or other (D607/B/80).

The following letters relate to the Erne estate in County Fermanagh, and highlight why it may be necessary to read two or more letters in order to grasp the full story of a particular incident. On 19 May 1770, William Veaitch wrote to Lord Erne:

I am apprehensive that the lives of Kinoghtra lease are now extinct by the death of James Morton of Belturbett. John, James and George Lawrence, and George's son called George are all dead (D1939/11/7/4).

On 30 May 1770, Hume Jones wrote to Lord Erne:

I had a letter from Mr Veaitch by which he gives me to understand that your Lordship is informed my lease of Kenotrah is expired and that your Lordship is kind enough to give me liberty of treating with you for a renewall for which I am extreamly obliged to you, but I do assure your Lordship on my word and honour I never untill I gott Mr Veaitches note heard of George Lawrence's death nor do I yet believe he is dead as I think it nearly impossible he shoud be dead withoute my hearing of it as he is a relation of mine and lives in Dublin; he is the only life I now have of it, if he is dead my lease is certainly expired. If your Lordship would give yourselfe the trouble of ordering one of your servants to call at the lying in Hospitall his mother is a housekeeper there and he can readily find out whether he is living or not (D1939/11/7/5).

A sub-category within estate correspondence is tenants' petitions. These take the form of letters to the landlord, asking or even imploring him to consider a particular request, such as a rent abatement. Some petitions were presented by an individual tenant, while others were from a group of tenants, perhaps seeking redress for a grievance. There is a good run of petitions from tenants on the Savile estate in County Tyrone. For example, in 1776 William Robertson of Glenhoys petitioned his landlord seeking help in his present circumstances (Nottinghamshire Archives, DD/FJ/11/1/7/311). Robertson explained that he had been:

a tenant in Manor Cecil near fifty years and is now reduced low and helpless by the death of an industrious and active wife, the death of four cows and three horses, having no cow left now ... the giving away of his land to two of his eldest sons except about seven acres, together with three small children that the eldest can scare put on its cloths ... infirmities of age have rendered your poor petitioner unable to pay his rent as it become due till the arrears have amounted to[o] heavy for him.

6.4.7 Accounts

Frequently found in estate collections are sets of accounts. Often these are of limited genealogical value and relate primarily to expenditure by members of the landowning family. Occasionally, however, an item of real interest will turn up. Among the Perceval Maxwell of Finnebrogue Papers are accounts from the 1770s recording workmen's wages. One from 1774 lists the names and wages of workmen employed in weeding oak in 'Portilogh'. The names of the 31 workmen employed were:

Wm Pake	Nickles Richey	Nickles Flanigan
Wm Gibpson	John Whisker	James Cochren
James Law	James McCation	John Dornan
John Law	Daniel Casmey	Hugh Cochren
James McMullen	George Nelson	Patrick Fichpatrick
John McMullen	Fellmey McCrisshan	Brine Dorragan
James McComb	Henry McGraw	James Meglanen
James Calwal	Henry McLay	Archey Boyd
Edward Monen	John McLay	Daniel Blaney
John Melvin	Hugh Meglainen	
Wm Richey	Hugh Meglanen jun.	

Although no residences are given for these men, it may be assumed that they lived in the Finnebrogue area of County Down. Building accounts can also be found in some estate collections and these might name the masons and craftsmen who were employed to carry out some structural works on behalf of a landlord.

6.4.8 Manor court records

Many of the newly created estates in the seventeenth century were given the status of manors by royal patent. Under the provisions of such a patent, the landlord was empowered to hold manor courts to regulate the affairs of his estate. Tenants were obliged, under the terms of their leases, to attend the manor courts as directed. Surviving manor court records for Ulster are listed under the respective estate to which they belong in Appendix 2. Disappointingly, only a relatively small number of manor court records exist. The best collection is found in the records relating to the earl of Antrim's estate (D2977). A good introduction to these records and to the subject in general is Ian Montgomery's article, 'The manorial courts of the earls of Antrim', *Familia*, 16 (2000), pp 1–23, which discusses the range of manor court records and the functions of these courts.

The court leet, also known as a 'view of frank-pledge', was originally a meeting of the freeholders of the manor called to exercise criminal jurisdiction. With the development of the criminal justice system and the rise of the magistracy, the importance of the court leet declined so that it became an administrative body. The court baron dealt with a range of civil actions, ranging from the recovery of small debts to trespasses and claims for damages. Usually a limit of 40 shillings was placed on the claims that the court could deal with. However, if a landlord wished to extend the power of his court he could have it made a 'court of record', which could deal with larger claims. The courts were under the control of an official called a seneschal who was appointed by the landlord. The courts may have been held in a purpose-built structure or other public building, but often they were held in private homes or in the open air.

The manor courts held on the earl of Antrim's estate were Ballycastle, Dunluce, Glenarm and Oldstone (based, respectively, on the baronies of Cary, Dunluce, Glenarm and Kilconway). The important thing to note is that even after large swathes of the Antrim estate were conveyed to new landowners the jurisdiction of these courts continued to extend to the area comprising the original manor. Unfortunately, there are no surviving records relating to the manor of Ballycastle. For the other three manors there are at least some eighteenth-century documents relating to the manor courts – both courts of record and courts leet. The names recorded in the manor court books of the Antrim estate include those who were called to sit as a jury. It would appear that the jurors on the courts of record tended to be local farmers and merchants, rather than members of the gentry. In addition, the books kept of the meetings of the courts of record include the names of defendants and plaintiffs, as well as witnesses in the various cases that were heard.

By the middle of the eighteenth century the courts leet had assumed a role at local level akin to that of the county grand jury (see Chapter 9), leading to some local tensions and confusion over their respective areas of responsibility. The court leet for the manor of Oldstone (or Kilconway) for 1773–1819 (D2977/23/4/1) exercised the following functions: appointing petty constables and apploters; raising money for repairs to the court house in Clough; appointing inspectors of weights and measures; and paying the wages of the manor bailiff and the keeper of the manor goal. The equivalent book for Glenarm reveals the ways in which the court took responsibility for keeping the streets in the town of Larne free from rubbish (D2977/23/2/1). Non-attendance at the court when required to do so resulted in punishment as the following entry from the court leet book for the manor of Oldstone from 1775 demonstrates:

> We present the sum of five shilling sterl[ing] to be leivied of the goods of each of the undernamed persons for theire haveing contemptuously refused to attend at this court last after being duly summoned and the sarvice proved –
>> Stephen Holland of Carraragh
>> Allexr Ramage of Mullans
>> Petter Dunlop of Knockans
>> John Dunlop of same
>> Saml Arthurs of same

6.5 Undertenants and cottiers

Depending on the size of his holding, the tenant farmer might have been in a position to sub-let part of it to a sub-tenant or undertenant. A landlord might have attempted to regulate this through adding a clause to the lease which forbade subletting without permission and including a financial penalty for every undertenant on the property. The rent that the undertenant provided to the farmer was usually in the form of cash and/or labour. The term 'cottier' has been applied to those who worked for a farmer and in return were provided with accommodation and a plot of ground for cultivation and possibly some grazing rights (known as a 'cottake'). The labour provided to the farmer may have involved working outdoors in the fields or indoors at a loom. The economic position of undertenants and cottiers was often fragile and few enjoyed any form of secure tenure.

Given their status, records relating to undertenants and cottiers are usually hard to come by, but a few do exist in estate collections. For example, within the Downshire estate collection there is a 1758 list of the undertenants on farms possessed by tenants named Trimble and Maxwell, with details of the rents they paid (D607/A/181). Occasionally, they will turn up in estate correspondence. In January 1767 James Hamilton, the agent on the Abercorn estate, wrote to his employer, 'Hugh Rankin one of the undertenants of Tonagh with some of his neighbours came to me this day to inform me that they had been all this day served with ejectments' (D623/A/37/55). The names of undertenants may also be found in a lease for a property. For instance, a lease issued in 1740 by Dr James Dobbin to John Wilson, a carpenter, for property in Carrickfergus named the undertenants as William Johnston and William Low (D639/2).

6.6 Other sources of information on landed estates
A number of sources exist which can supplement existing estate papers or act as an alternative in the absence of records relating to a particular property. The Registry of Deeds is a major resource and is the subject of Chapter 7. It should also be noted that while this book concentrates on estate papers generated prior to the nineteenth century, post-1800 estate records often include retrospective information on tenants and tenancies.

Newspapers
The importance of newspapers when looking for information on the occupiers of land is highlighted in Chapter 12. To give one example here, on 1 May 1770 an advertisement appeared in the *Belfast Newsletter* announcing that Lord Dungannon's estate in the parish of Island Magee in County Antrim was 'out of lease, and to be let for terms of years'. The advertisement included the names of the sitting tenants by townland along with the size of their farms. This advertisement is the only known eighteenth-century document relating to Island Magee that lists farmers by townland.

Encumbered Estates Court
The Great Famine had a massive impact on the management and economic viability of landed estates. By an act of parliament of 1849 the Encumbered Estates Court was established with authority to sell estates on the application

of the owner or encumbrancer (one who had a claim on the estate). After the sale the court distributed the money among the creditors and granted clear title to the new owners. The functions of the court were assumed by the Landed Estates Court in 1858. In advance of the sale of an estate a printed rental was prepared. These rentals contain very detailed information, including on many occasions details of leases issued prior to 1800 giving the names of the lessees and, if relevant, the 'lives'. There are several sets of Encumbered Estates Court rentals which can be accessed at the National Library and National Archives, Dublin, and in PRONI (D1201), as well as on the Findmypast website.

Land Registry
The Land Registry archive at PRONI is a vast collection of documentation that was generated as the result of a series of acts of parliament passed in the late nineteenth and early twentieth centuries, which facilitated the transfer of land from landlord to tenant. Records created prior to 1922 was transferred from Dublin to Northern Ireland and subsequently deposited in PRONI along with material generated post-partition. The Land Registry archive in PRONI has been catalogued under LR1 and is organised by estate with the documentation broken down into administrative records, title deeds and testamentary papers (catalogued A, B and C, respectively). The Land Registry is not an easy archive to use and requires much patience and perseverance.

Land Purchase Commission
The Land Purchase Commission was established by the Northern Ireland Land Act of 1925 to complete the process of transferring land from landlord to tenant that had begun under earlier legislation. The Land Purchase Commission archive in the Public Record Office of Northern Ireland includes a collection of documents, ranging from testamentary papers to leases and deeds, which were used as evidence of title to property. There are some 400 items in this collection that date from the seventeenth and eighteenth centuries. The PRONI eCatalogue lists these documents under reference LPC.

7. The Registry of Deeds

7.1 The creation of the Registry of Deeds

The Registry of Deeds was established by an act passed in the Irish Parliament in 1707. The aim of the act was to provide one central office in Dublin 'for the public registering of all deeds, conveyances and wills that shall be made of any honours, manors, lands, tenements or hereditaments'. Furthermore, its purpose was 'for securing, purchasers, preventing forgeries and fraudulent gifts and conveyances of lands, tenements and hereditaments, which have been frequently practised in this kingdom, especially by Papists, to the great prejudice of the Protestant interest thereof.' By this it can be seen that the legislation that created the Registry of Deeds was part of the Penal Laws that were designed to preserve the privileged position of the Anglican elite by restricting the rights of Catholics.

The Registry of Deeds opened in 1708 and the first deed was registered on 29 March at 5 o'clock in the afternoon. Just over a week later the second deed to be registered was the first to concern property in Ulster, specifically lands in County Monaghan owned by the Cairnes family. Whatever may have been intended by the framers of the original legislation, in practice registration was not compulsory and it must be realised that the registered deeds represent only a proportion of all land transactions executed in the 1700s. Even so, the sheer number of deeds registered in the eighteenth century is incredible. By the early 1750s more than 100,000 deeds had been registered and by the end of the century this figure had increased to nearly 350,000. Furthermore, as an archive the Registry of Deeds survives intact. It is little wonder that one experienced researcher described the Registry of Deeds as the 'most important single source of genealogical information for the eighteenth century'.

The sections that follow provide an overview of the registration process, the indexes to the deeds, the range of material and the usefulness of the Registry of Deeds in researching Ulster ancestors. Other helpful studies of the Registry of Deeds include: P. B. Phair, 'Guide to the Registry of Deeds', *Analecta Hibernica*, 23 (1966), pp 257–76; Jean Agnew, 'How to use the Registry of Deeds', *Familia*, 6 (1990), pp 78–84; John Grenham, *Tracing Your Irish Ancestors* (4th edition, 2012), chapter 9; and Brian Nugent, *A Guide to the 18th Century Land Records in the Irish Registry of Deeds* (2013).

7.2 The registration process

The registration process can be summarised as follows: a deed was drawn up between two or more parties; one of those parties felt that it would be advantageous to register the deed in the Registry of Deeds in Dublin; a copy of the original deed was made, and this copy, known as a 'memorial', was verified by a justice of the peace; the memorial was then taken to the Registry of Deeds; here the memorial was given a unique reference number and was copied into a transcript volume by a clerk. The memorials were retained and these are stored in the vaults at the Registry of Deeds. Researchers should be aware that if a copy of a deed is ordered the item provided will be of the memorial not of the entry in the transcription book (unless the memorial is missing).

The transcript volumes – large and cumbersome books that have been called 'tombstones' – are available for public inspection. Several transcript volumes may have been in use simultaneously meaning that the deeds registered in one particular year may be found in several different volumes. It may be observed that the handwriting in the transcript volumes of the early eighteenth century tends to be more legible than that found in the books of the late 1700s. While registration generally took place fairly soon after the date of the transaction, it is not unusual to find deeds registered many years later, perhaps because of concerns about an impending legal dispute over title to the property in question. Unfortunately, very few of the registered deeds are of transactions completed any earlier than 1708.

7.3 The indexes

Two indexes to the transcripts of the memorials are available: an index of grantors and a lands index.

Index of grantors

Until 1833 the index of grantors provided no more than the surname and the forename of the grantor, followed by the surname only of the grantee, and then the volume, page number and memorial number. It is important to emphasise that the names listed alphabetically in this index are those of the person transferring the land rather than the individual to whom the property was transferred. Unfortunately, there is no index to grantees. Aristocrats tend to be listed under their title rather than their surname. Some of the volumes will include 'Names that admit of different spellings', listing alternative renderings of particular surnames. Until 1785, generally speaking, each index volume is specific to an initial letter, and covers a certain period of years: 1708–29, 1730–45 and so on. Deeds registered between 1786 and 1793 are in three volumes (A–E, F–L, M–Z), as are those for 1794 to 1799 (A–D, E–J, K–Z). Ten volumes cover the period from 1800 to 1809.

Lands index
The lands index is organised by county, with one or more counties per individual index volume. The entries are arranged alphabetically, but only with regard to initial letter. Each entry gives the surnames of the parties, the name of the denomination of land, and the volume, page number and memorial number. There is a column for the name of the barony and parish, though this is not always filled in; occasionally the name of the manor in which the property is located is given here. Chronologically, the lands index covering the eighteenth century is arranged in two periods: 1708–38 and 1739–1810. Deeds relating to corporate towns (see Chapter 9) are indexed separately from the rest of the deeds for a particular county. (However, for reasons that are not altogether clear, the corporate town of Killyleagh was not indexed separately from the rest of County Down.) Frequently the index will provide a more precise location for a property in a corporate town than for a rural landholding, including for example the name of the street, or the names of the occupiers of neighbouring tenements.

7.4 The range of documents registered

The legislation that created the Registry of Deeds was framed in such a way that it allowed for a range of different documents to be registered so long as they were concerned with the transfer of 'lands, tenements and hereditaments [i.e. property that can be inherited]' from one party to another. The legal jargon used means that it can be difficult to understand the exact purpose of the deed. A deed introduced as a 'lease and release' could have been a mortgage, while a deed described as a 'bargain and sale' may have been a lease. Furthermore, some deeds have many different parties and understanding how each of them relates to the transaction can be challenging. However, after reading through the contents of a memorial it is usually possible to work out what it entails or at least get the gist of what the framers of the deed intended. In any case, the genealogical information contained in the deed is often more important than the nature of the transaction itself.

Sales, assignments and leases
Outright sales of property were rare: a landowner usually wished to retain some interest, however minimal, in the land that was being transferred to the grantee. An assignment was the transfer of the interest in a property to another party. For example, in 1722 William Austin of Lurgan, County Armagh, and his wife Mary (née Nugent) assigned property in their possession in Lurgan to Ann Gilbert (40.7.23814). In this case, the memorial helpfully includes the details of the original transaction, reciting that the property in question had been, in 1721, leased by Hugh Matthews of Lurgan to Mary Nugent for three lives renewable forever (the original lives being his brothers, Alexander, John and William Mathews).

Much more common than transactions relating to the sale or assignment of property are deeds concerning the leasing of land. Often these were between persons of relatively similar social standing, rather than the landlord-tenant relationship. In fact, registered leases from landlord to tenant for the eighteenth century are not as common as might be hoped (see Chapter 6 for more on estate leases). For one thing, the legislation of 1707 specifically stated that it did not extend to leases 'for years not exceeding twenty-one years, where the actual possession goeth along with the said lease'. Since many leases did not fall into this category they were excluded from registration. (In practice, however, many shorter leases were registered.) For many landed estates, therefore, there are either no registered leases at all or else very few.

For some estates, however, there are useful runs of leases in the Registry of Deeds. For example, for the manor Ardstraw in County Tyrone, held by the McCausland family from the bishop of Derry in the early eighteenth century, there are over a dozen registered leases from the 1720s containing the names of around 100 tenant farmers (these were published in *DIFHR*, 24 (2001), p. 84). Information on the occupiers of churchlands in the eighteenth century is usually very hard to come by, making this collection all the more valuable. The fact that the McCauslands were perpetually in financial difficulties and uncertain about their future may account for the registration of so many of these leases.

Marriage settlements

A marriage settlement was the agreement made between the families of the prospective bride and groom prior to their wedding. The main aim was to provide financial security to the bride should she outlive her husband. The information in this type of deed varies, but can include the names and addresses of a large number of people from the two families involved. The first two parties to the deed will typically be the groom and the father of the bride. If the latter was dead, then the bride's guardian will be named.

A good example is the deed that was drawn up prior to the nuptials between Con O'Neill of Casshell, County Antrim, and Margaret Hamilton of Middletown, County Armagh (87.496.62791). This deed is interesting on many different levels. First of all it was made in 1723, but not registered until 1737 (or 1738 according to the current calendar). The marriage itself was between two people of very different background – a groom from a Gaelic Irish family and a bride of Scottish descent. The marriage settlement also provides information on additional members of the O'Neill and Hamilton families. The deed names the groom's father, Collo, and his brothers, Arthur, Charles and John. It also records that the landlord of the family's property was John O'Neill of Edenduffcarrick (Shane's Castle). With regard to the bride's family, the deed records that her father was named William and that she had a brother called John.

The marriage portion or dowry included in a marriage settlement provides an idea of the wealth of the bride's family. The marriage portion could be paid in one lump sum or in stages. Registered in February 1745 was the marriage settlement of John Walker of Terconnelly, Donagheady parish, County Tyrone, a Presbyterian tenant farmer, and Mary Gillaspy of Minlougher, County Donegal (117.232.80596). Under the terms of the settlement the bride's parents, Thomas and Elizabeth Gillaspy, agreed to pay an initial marriage portion of £50 with an additional £25 to be paid on each of their deaths.

Occasionally, a marriage settlement can contain unexpected information of immense value. For example, the marriage settlement of 1734 involving Lord Mountjoy included a list of tenants on his Newtownstewart estate in County Tyrone, details that are not available from any other source (these names were published in *DIFHR*, 24 (2001), p. 84).

Mortgages and rent charges
In the era before the creation of a reliable banking system, mortgages were commonly used as a ready means of raising capital, particularly by merchants and those seeking to acquire additional land. Mortgages can be usually be recognised by the inclusion of the rate of interest and a clause of redemption, though these may not always appear in the memorial. Rent charges were annual payments issuing from specified lands and were used to pay off debts or to provide for family members without an adequate income.

Wills
The parliamentary act that established the Registry of Deeds provided for the registering of wills of testators who died after 25 March 1708. A will can be easily identified in the index to grantors by the phrase 'His Will' or 'Her Will' appearing where the surname of the grantee would otherwise have been written. A will may have been registered if there were concerns that it was going to be contested. Some of the wills were transcribed in full, while others were recorded in a more abbreviated format. The Irish Manuscripts Commission published three volumes of abstracts of over 2,000 wills registered between 1708 and 1832 (P. Beryl Eustace and Eilish Ellis (eds), *Registry of Deeds, Dublin: Abstracts of wills*, 1954–88). These abstracts provide the names, addresses and occupations of the various individuals named (e.g. beneficiaries and witnesses) and the testator's property that was mentioned in the will.

By way of example, the will of Rev. Alexander Hutcheson of Drumalig in the parish of 'Tonaghneeve' (Saintfield), dated 25 September 1711, was registered on 26 January 1725 [1726] (47.311.30761). This names his only son John and grandsons Francis (later to become Professor of Moral Philosophy at Glasgow University) and Robert Hutcheson; his daughter Beatrix Wallace and her son William; and his daughter Mary Young and her son John. The witnesses are also named and interestingly one of them, Hugh Fisher, was of Edenderry, County Armagh, when the will was made and of South Carolina at the time the will was registered.

Bills of discovery

Bills of discovery were issued against Catholics holding lands on terms forbidden under the Penal Laws. The Protestant filing the bill was able to claim the lands affected. In many cases the bill was filed by a Protestant friend of the Catholic in order to pre-empt a less sympathetic discovery. The following deed makes reference to a bill of discovery relating to lands in County Fermanagh (107.297.73998).

> A memorial of an assignment bearing date the 27th day of April 1742 between Rowland Kane of Desertmartin, in the County of Londonderry, gent., and Hugh Montgomery of Derrygonnelly, in the County of Fermanagh, Esq.; reciting that the said Rowland Kane hath exhibited his bill in his Ma[jes]ties Couty of Exchequer in Ireland on or about the 16th day of February last past against Hugh O'Donnell of Mullaghbane in the County of Fermanagh aforesaid, Esq., and John Cole of Florence Court within said County, Esq., as a Protestant Discoverer to be decreed to the benefit of a lease or term of years of the town and lands commonly called & known by the names of Aghagilgulman [there follows a long list of place-names] situated in the barony of Glenawley & County of Fermanagh aforesaid made by the said John Cole to the said Hugh O'Donnell who is disabled to take such lease term or int. by the laws and statutes inforce in this kingdom. [Kane then assigned the lands in question to Montgomery for the sum of 5 shillings.]

7.5 The value of research in the Registry of Deeds

A popular misconception of the Registry of Deeds is that it is of little value for those researching families below the level of the elite. In actual fact, a significant number of deeds, even in the first half of the eighteenth century, concern directly or make reference to tenant farmers, merchants and tradesmen. At the same time, it must be acknowledged that large swathes of Irish society, both for economic and social reasons, will generally not be found in the Registry of Deeds.

In terms of their genealogical value, the registered deeds provide the researcher with the names, addresses and occupations of the parties involved. Sometimes several generations of one family can be found in a single deed. A conveyance of July 1763 concerning a property in Strabane, County Tyrone, serves as a good example of the depth of information that can be found in a deed (225.575.147907). The parties to this transaction were as follows:

> Elizabeth Hunter, formerly Tredennick, of Omagh, widow, eldest daughter of George Tredennick, late of Strabane
> Robert Baird and George Baird of Strabane, husband and son to Jane Tredennick, second daughter of the aforementioned George Tredennick
> John Orr of Strabane, merchant, and Martha, his wife, third daughter of the aforementioned George Tredennick

Samuel Gormaly, then in America, and Margaret, his wife, of Strabane,
    fourth daughter of the aforementioned George Tredennick
John Vance of Strabane, merchant

The property in question was a tenement in the town of Strabane which,
according to the deed, had been granted to Edward Tredennick, father of
George Tredennick, by the sixth earl of Abercorn in 1704. George had
presumably inherited the tenement from his father Edward and he in turn must
have bequeathed it jointly to his daughters. It therefore required the consent of
all his daughters and their husbands before the property could be conveyed to
John Vance. As this example also shows, deeds referring to emigrants can be
found occasionally. Generally, these relate to property in which the migrant
had a residual interest. Much rarer are deeds that concern the disposal of
property by someone intending to emigrate.

Deeds will also include the names, addresses and occupations of those who
acted as witnesses and these may provide other avenues of research. Two sets of
witnesses will appear: one set witnessed the original transaction, while the other
witnessed the memorial. At least one of the witnesses to the memorial had
witnessed the original deed. For example, the witnesses to an assignment of 1722
(40.7.23814) concerning property in Lurgan, County Armagh, were as follows:

Jonathan Gilbert of Lurgan, shopkeeper
Henry Dobson of Lurgan, shoemaker
John Ditchers of Lurgan, brazier
Joseph Willson of Lurgan, pewterer
Stephen Gilbert of Lurgan, shopkeeper (who also witnessed the memorial)
John Keney of Tynan, County Armagh, butcher

Neither is it true that Catholic tenant farmers are excluded altogether from the
Registry of Deeds. The following slightly abridged deed relates to County
Armagh (36.4.20880).

A memorial of an indenture dated 24 December 1719 between Roger
o fferan of Tonnywalton, County Armagh, yeoman, of the one part, and
Bryan o ffearan of the said town and county of the other part.

    Whereby the said Roger fferan to farm let to the said Bryan Fearan
that parcel of the townland of Tonnywalton containing 34 acres as also
another parcel part Pagan's farm containing 20 acres, 22 roods and
3 perches, likewise another parcel of land part of Barkley's farm containing
10 acres, 3 roods, all situate in the Manor of Clare, County Ardmagh, to
hold to the said Bryan o ffearan from November 1 last past for the term
of 31 years at the yearly rent of £11 5s. 4d. above all taxes.

    Said lease witnessed by Cornelius Calter of Cornescribe, County
Ardmagh, Arthur Devlin, John McGrune and John FitzPatrick, all

of Tavanawalton, County Ardmagh. This memorial witnessed by Cornelius Calter aforesaid and by Bryan Rogers of Portadown, County Ardmagh.

Cornelius Calter swears as to the witnessing on 26 May 1722 at Richhill, County Ardmagh, before Andrew Charleton in the presence of J. Richardson and Andrew Charleton, JPs.

7.6 Access to the Registry of Deeds

Initially, the Registry of Deeds was located in a private house in Dublin, before new premises were acquired in Lower Castle Yard. In 1805, the registry was transferred to Inns Quay, which was convenient to the Four Courts. Since the early 1830s the Registry of Deeds has been located in a large Georgian building in Henrietta Street (the main entrance faces on to Constitution Hill). The Registry of Deeds is open to the public free of charge each week from Monday to Friday, 10.00am to 4.30pm. Researchers sign in at the reception desk and then make their way to the top floor of the building where the indexes and transcript volumes are available for inspection. Information can be noted down from these volumes, but photography is strictly forbidden; copying facilities are available.

Microfilm copies of the indexes and memorial volumes are available through various institutions, such as the National Library of Ireland and the Public Record Office of Northern Ireland. A major development has been the release online of digitised versions of these microfilms by FamilySearch.org. A Registry of Deeds Index Project has been running for a number of years and many thousands of index entries have been created (http://irishdeedsindex.net).

Although the layout of the building can be confusing, the arrangement of the records somewhat haphazard, the transcript volumes undoubtedly heavy and cumbersome, the handwriting often testing, and the legalese frequently bewildering, the Registry of Deeds is unlike any other archive in Ireland. While access to its resources is possible through other means – and increasingly so via the Internet – it is still well worth a visit during a research trip to Dublin, if only for the experience of using it.

8. Wills and testamentary records

Wills are among the most valuable sources of information for the family historian. A single will can provide the names of the testator's spouse, children, grandchildren, siblings, cousins, friends, servants and neighbours. Details on the testator's possessions, both personal belongings and land, can be recorded. Family members living elsewhere in Ireland or abroad might be mentioned, which can be helpful in trying to identify persons who emigrated. Prior to 1858 the Church of Ireland was responsible for testamentary matters. It must not be thought, however, that just because the Church of Ireland was responsible for administering wills, only persons who belonged to that particular denomination left wills. Nonconformist Protestants and Roman Catholics also left wills; if they did not it was principally for economic rather than religious reasons. The nature of the property laws in operation during this period meant that most testators were men. Women making wills tended to be widows or spinsters. Unfortunately, virtually all original wills probated before 1858 were lost in the destruction of the old Public Record Office of Ireland in 1922. However, as will be discussed in more detail below, this loss is partly compensated by the survival in one form or another of many testamentary papers.

8.1 The administration of testamentary matters

Until 1858 a Consistorial Court in each diocese was responsible for granting probate and conferring on executors the authority to administer a testator's estate. The authority of the Consistorial Court was generally limited to persons who were resident in the diocese in which the court was held and who had no personal estate in another diocese. These courts also dealt with wills drawn up by individuals who died outside of Ireland, but whose personal estate related to only one diocese. An exception to this established practice concerned what was known as the Exempt Jurisdiction of Newry and Mourne where authority over ecclesiastical and testamentary matters lay not with a bishop, but with a secular lord. The background to this complex story is discussed by Fred Rankin in *Familia*, 14 (1998), pp 68–86. The parishes in question were Kilcoo, Kilkeel and Kilmegan in County Down and Newry, which straddled the boundary between counties Armagh and Down.

If a testator's estate included effects worth more than £5 in another diocese the will was dealt with at the Prerogative Court. This operated under the authority of the Anglican archbishop of Armagh. While the testamentary affairs dealt with by this court tended to concern the wealthier members of society, it must not be thought that the Prerogative Court was solely the preserve of the landed gentry and aristocracy. The wills of many merchants, tradesmen, medical practitioners and farmers, among others, were dealt with at this court. For example, testators from Lurgan, County Armagh, included men who followed these professions: linen draper, innholder, distiller, apothecary and shopkeeper.

In the absence of a will, the Consistorial Courts and the Prerogative Court had the power to appoint individuals to administer an estate. Those to whom this authority was given were usually close family members of the deceased or those to whom he owed money. In return they lodged bonds (essentially guarantees that they would discharge their duties responsibly) with the respective court. The original administration bonds were also destroyed in Dublin in 1922.

8.2 Indexes to testamentary records

Following the opening of the Public Record Office in Dublin in the late 1860s, original wills were transferred here from each of the courts noted above. It must be acknowledged, however, that some testamentary papers had been lost before this time. Those that had made the transfer were then transcribed into will books. Manuscript indexes to the wills probated in each court were also prepared and these survived the destruction of 1922, though some were damaged. These are now in the National Archives of Ireland with copies of some of them in PRONI.

The information in each of these diocesan will indexes varies. Typically they include the name of the testator, his or her address, and the year of probate (or sometimes the year in which the will was made). The year can be a guide to when the testator died, though it should be borne in mind that occasionally a will was not probated until many years after the death of the testator. The address given is usually the townland in which the testator resided, though it might be simply the parish. Occasionally the testator's occupation is given.

Some of these will indexes have been published. For example, a published index to the prerogative wills of Ireland, edited by Sir Arthur Vicars, covers the period 1536–1810. A number of diocesan indexes were published by Phillimore in the early part of the twentieth century. These include Dromore and the Exempt Jurisdiction of Newry and Mourne (vol. 4, 1918), and Derry and Raphoe (vol. 5, 1920). An index to Kilmore wills was edited and published by Patrick Smythe-Wood in 1975.

There are also surviving indexes to administration bonds in PRONI and NAI. These include similar information to the will indexes (i.e. name of deceased, address, year and sometimes occupation), though they are arranged chronologically under each initial letter.

Surviving will and administration bond indexes

Diocese	Counties in Ulster (all or part of)	Wills from	Administration bonds from
Armagh	Armagh, Londonderry, Tyrone	1666	
Clogher	Donegal, Fermanagh, Monaghan, Tyrone	1661	1660
Connor	Antrim, Down, Londonderry	1636	1636
Derry	Donegal, Londonderry, Tyrone	1612	1698
Down	Antrim, Down	1646	1635
Dromore	Antrim, Armagh, Down	1678	1742
Kilmore	Cavan, Fermanagh	1682	1728
Newry and Mourne	Armagh, Down	1727	post-1800
Raphoe	Donegal	1684	1684

The National Archives of Ireland website includes an index to the diocesan will indexes. The online PRONI Name Search database includes the unpublished indexes to pre-1858 wills and administration bonds for dioceses covering Northern Ireland. The index to prerogative administrations is available in PRONI under T490.

8.3 The availability of testamentary records

As noted above, original wills in the old Public Record Office were almost totally destroyed in 1922. With a couple of exceptions, both from the nineteenth century, this was also the case with the diocesan will books. Some will books of the Prerogative Court survived destruction and are available for inspection in the National Archives of Ireland. For the pre-1800 period these cover the following years: 1664–84, 1706–08 (A–W), 1726–8 (A–W), 1728–9 (A–W) and 1777 (A–L). Furthermore, the Armagh diocesan collection, now on deposit in PRONI, includes a series of volumes containing extracts from wills with charitable bequests which were proved at the Prerogative Court (DIO/4/9/14/1–7); these cover the years 1771–83 (handwritten) and 1801–04 (printed). Copies of wills can also be found in the Registry of Deeds in Dublin (see Chapter 7).

In addition, thousands of abstracts and even full copies of original wills survive in many archives and also in private possession. Abstracts or copies of administration bonds can also be found. Many of these abstracts were made by genealogists working in the old Public Record Office of Ireland prior to 1922, which are now available in various collections. Copies of original wills, often used as evidence of title to property, can be found in landed estate collections and solicitors' papers, among other places. Transcripts of wills, or extracts from them, have been published in many local and family histories. For example, Amy Young, *300 Years in Innishowen* (1929) contains over 40 will abstracts for County Donegal.

The principal repositories in Ireland all have substantial collections of wills and will abstracts. An index of over 13,000 pre-1858 surviving wills and will abstracts is available in PRONI and can be searched via the Name Search database. It must be acknowledged, however, that this does not include every abstract or copy of a will in PRONI. An 'Index of will abstracts in the Genealogical Office, Dublin' was published in *Guide to the Genealogical Office, Dublin* (Irish Manuscripts Commission, 1998; reprinted from *Analecta Hibernica*, 17 (1949)), though this is not complete; it does not include, for example, the Betham sketch pedigrees discussed below. The collections of abstracts and copies of wills in the National Archives of Ireland can be searched via various card indexes. These NAI indexes were digitised by Eneclann and published as a CD-ROM: *Index of Irish Wills, 1484–1858* (now available through Findmypast.ie). A helpful guide to the survival of Irish wills can be found in John Grenham's *Tracing Your Irish Ancestors* (4th edition, 2012).

Betham's Manuscripts
Sir William Betham's manuscripts are an invaluable source of genealogical information. Arriving in Ireland in the early 1800s, Betham went on to become Ulster King of Arms, holding this position until his death in 1853. He undertook the herculean task of organising the records of the Ulster Office and in the process created a vast quantity of documentation arising from his explorations of these materials. Over many years he worked his way through the wills of the Prerogative Court up to 1800. The National Archives of Ireland has Betham's notebooks in which he recorded information extracted from these wills. Based on his notes he sketched out thousands of pedigrees which are to be found in more than 30 volumes in the Genealogical Office in Dublin. While based principally on data extracted from the Prerogative Court wills, these include additional information derived from other sources. The level of detail in each pedigree depends mainly on the amount of information recorded in the original will. Occasionally there is an attempt to link several generations of one family together through information extracted from two or more wills. The Genealogical Office also has Betham's correspondence on genealogical matters as well as further extracts from testamentary records made by him. For more on Betham and his papers, see P. B. Phair, 'Sir William Betham's Manuscripts', *Analecta Hibernica*, 27 (1972), pp 1–99.

Burke's Pedigrees
PRONI holds records that have been termed 'Burke's Pedigrees' – so-called because they were compiled by or for Sir Bernard Burke, Betham's successor as Ulster King of Arms (T559). Running to 42 volumes, these are based on information extracted from the Prerogative Court wills. Essentially these are the same as Betham's sketch pedigrees, noted above, though more neatly presented. However, they lack the supplementary information found in the sketch pedigrees.

Testamentary papers in England and Scotland
Researchers should consider the possibility that if someone had property on the other side of the Irish Sea there may be a copy of a will in a repository in England or Scotland. The Prerogative Court of Canterbury was particularly important in this regard. The wills that it dealt with are in The National Archives, Kew, and transcripts of these have been digitised and can be accessed via the institution's website. Testamentary papers for Scotland are held by the National Records of Scotland and can be accessed via the ScotlandsPeople website.

8.4 The information in a will

There were essentially two types of will. One was a will that was written down either by the testator himself or by someone else on his behalf, such as a clerk or attorney, which he then signed. The other type of will was much rarer. This was a nuncupative or verbal will. In other words, before a number of witnesses the testator declared audibly his intentions. A record of these may have been made subsequently. For example, PRONI has a memorandum of the nuncupative will of John Lowry of Aghenis, County Tyrone, made during the siege of Derry of 1689, from shortly before his death (D3007/A/4/2). The executors appointed to carry out the instructions in a will were often close family members. The names of witnesses should also be noted, for even if there is no apparent relationship, this may be revealed with further searching.

Wills generally followed a fairly standard format. The testator often began by committing his soul to God. These expressions were often formulaic, but occasionally it is possible to discern a genuine religious devotion on the part of the testator as he or she prepared for death. The preferred place of burial was often stated (see Chapter 3 for more on this). This could be more specific than the name of the church or churchyard. For example, in 1717 Walter Dawson left instructions in his will that he was to be buried in the cathedral of Armagh 'in the south aisle in the grave where my d[ea]r daughter Ann Dawson lies, it joining my dear father and son Walter Dawson' (D3053/1/2/3).

Some form of provision was usually made for the testator's wife. This might be an annual sum of money to be paid to her by the principal beneficiary of the will. On other occasions it was something of practical use. For instance, in his will of 1775 James Hogg, a Lisburn merchant, left his wife 'the use of my cloth press in new lapping room with all the utensils' (D847/1/9). The family home or part of it might be left to the wife and any unmarried daughters in the family. If the testator was on good terms with his children, all of them could expect to receive a bequest from him, unless they had already been provided for. Unmarried daughters might be left a sum of money which could be used as a dowry. Some wills include instructions that the sons and daughters of the testator should only marry with the consent of their mother or the executors.

If the testator was a farmer he would usually leave the farm to his eldest son. Even if he did not own the land outright he could still leave the 'interest' in the farm to his son. Unless the testator was in possession of several landholdings, the other children usually received bequests of money, though it may be noted that in 1710 William Knox of Ashmoyne, County Donegal, left a two-year-old colt to each of his three sons, and to each of his unmarried daughters a cow in calf (D3045/4/1/25). The testator's personal possessions, such as clothing, riding equipment, books or watch, may also have been divided out among family members.

Relatives living overseas may be mentioned in wills. For example, in 1783 John Dunlap of Strabane, a saddler, left instructions that his 'wife may continue to live in the back house in which we lived for some time as long as it may be pleasing to my son John now in America' (T1336/1/17); the son was the famous John Dunlap, printer of the American Declaration of Independence. The inevitability that at some of his family would emigrate is captured in the 1778 will of John Boreland of Kilraughts parish, who wrote, 'if any of my Sons choose to go abroad … my Exec[uto]rs shall prepare them for their voyage'. At the same time, Boreland was anxious that those of his family who remained at home would 'all live together in the same amicable and Christian manner they now live under me Industriously and sociably working together' (T2880/1).

Other beneficiaries of a will could include the testator's servants – a will may be the only mention anywhere of their existence. In 1634, Sir Marmaduke Whitchurch of Loughbrickland left his servant Pdk Madden McRathy 'two cows & a garron [horse] & an old doublet & hose of mine' (D765/1). The will of George Macghee of Strabane, dated 25 October 1741, includes bequests to the following poor people: Widow O'Quin, Widow Mackroddian, Mary Robison alias Widow Monroe, Meve the lame woman, 'Bigg Margret' and Jos Dowler (LPC/1325).

Charitable bequests also feature in many wills, especially those of the upper classes and merchant community, though some farmers also left money to help those in need. Sums of money could be left to the poor of the parish in which the testator resided, or perhaps another parish with which he or she had some connection. In 1691, the wealthy merchant George McCartney bequeathed £40 'for ye use of ye poor old decayed inhabitants of ye towne of Belfast' (D1184/1A). Some testators could be very specific about those who would benefit from their generosity. In 1788, Nathaniel Willson, a cotton manufacturer in Belfast, left £600 to the Belfast Charitable Society to allow it to admit six poor cotton weavers into the Poor House so long as they had been 'sober honest industrious tradesmen, and that they never sold or embezzled any yarn cotton or other material of manufacture' (D1824/C/1/1/1/15). Some charitable bodies were founded on the basis of bequests in wills (see Chapter 14).

The will of Charles McKenna of Tandergee, County Tyrone, provides a particularly detailed insight into the circumstances of one farming family in rural Ulster at the end of the eighteenth century, and is quoted here in full. This will is found in the Lowry of Pomeroy estate collection in PRONI (D1132/1/81).

In the Name of God, Amen, I, Charles McKenna, of Tandergee, parish of Pomeroy and County of Tyrone, being frail in body and calling to mind my state of mortality do make and publish this my last will and testament in maner following: first I leave and bequeath my soul to God who gave it and my body to be buried in a Christian maner in the church yard of Donaghmore; secondly I leave and bequeath to my grandson, Charles McKenna, second son of Patrick McKenna of said Tandergee now deceased the full half of the farm in said Tandergee which half I now possess, my daughter-in-law, Sarah McKenna, possessing the other half as her husband, my son, and I was [sic] joyned in lease equally for said farm; also to Charles my grandson my old dwelling house which is now made a barn of with my pot, crock, & tongs; also I will to my daughter Alis McKenna, otherwise Donaghy, one shilling sterling. Lastly I nominate and apoint Thomas Kinaghan of said Tandergee executor of this my will in trust to see it executed according to the true intent and meaning of it, making void all other wills made or done by me.

In witness whereof I have put my hand and seal this twenty second day of Aught in the year of our Lord eighteen hundred 1800.

Signed sealed & delivered in presence of being first duly read, Henry Long, Kennedy Long, John Hughes.

[Charles McKenna made his mark.]

9. Records relating to government and the legal system

The question of authority and who exercised it was one of the key issues confronting society in early modern Ulster. Authority was represented and experienced in different ways by the various sections of the population. Most by reason of birth and social status were excluded altogether from the machinery of government in its various forms, whether central, local or parochial, while others were able to participate, but only in a limited way. This chapter looks at records generated by official bodies that relate to governance and justice.

9.1 Records of the Irish Parliament

Until the Act of Union of 1800 abolished the Irish Parliament, each county in Ireland, along with a large number of boroughs, returned two MPs to the House of Commons in Dublin. In addition to the Commons, there was also the House of Lords which was composed of those who held Irish peerages. The definitive study of the Irish Parliament in the eighteenth century is the six-volume *History of the Irish Parliament, 1692–1800*, edited by E. M. Johnston-Liik (Ulster Historical Foundation, 2002). In addition to providing a political survey and a summary listing of all statutes passed, the work also includes studies of every constituency and biographies, many quite detailed, of some 2,300 individuals who were returned to the Irish House of Commons in this period. Studies of earlier MPs include two unpublished theses by Bríd McGrath: 'The Membership of the Irish House of Commons, 1613–1615' (MLitt, TCD, 1985); 'The Membership of the Irish House of Commons, 1640–1' (University of Dublin, PhD thesis, 1997).

The *Journals of the House of Commons of the Kingdom of Ireland* for the period 1613–1800 were published in a series of editions. A wide variety of information is included in these volumes, ranging from petitions from individuals or bodies to information on law and order, road-building projects and industrial ventures. The appendices to volume 7 (first edition) include the names of individuals transported from Ireland between 1735 and 1743 for various crimes ranging from being a felon or vagabond to forgery and sheep-stealing. This information, including names from every county in Ulster, was published in Frances

McDonnell, *Emigrants from Ireland to America, 1735–43. A Transcription of the Report of the Irish House of Commons into Enforced Emigration to America* (1992). The appendices to volume 17 (fourth edition) of the House of Commons journal, published in 1798, include schedules of prisoners brought to trial in each of the Ulster counties in 1797–8, as well as lists of prisoners still in gaol. This is followed by a list of JPs appointed since 1 June 1789 and a list of JPs superseded (i.e. dismissed or retired) in the same period. Unfortunately, the indexes to these volumes are not sufficiently comprehensive to allow a search for a specific name.

The laws passed by the Irish Parliament are contained in *The Statutes at Large, Passed in the Parliaments Held in Ireland.* Occasionally these can include useful lists of names. For example, *An Act for the Relief of Insolvent Debtors,* 1777–8, lists names of those imprisoned across Ireland on account of debt (*The Statutes at Large*, vol. 11 (1782), pp 131–49). Those in Down County Gaol in Downpatrick were named as Arthur Hughs, James Emerson, Samuel McMullan, Rev. Robert Smyth, Thomas Chambers, Robert Gaff, Arthur Waterson and Thomas Parkinson; Robert Smyth was possibly the Presbyterian minister of Ardglass.

For those interested in the Lords, see Francis G. James, *Lords of the Ascendancy: The Irish House of Lords and its Members, 1600–1800* (1995). The *Journals of the House of Lords, 1634–1800* were published in eight volumes between 1779 and 1800. Also of value is the three-volume set of *Proceedings of the Irish House of Lords, 1771–1800*, edited by James Kelly (Irish Manuscripts Commission, 2008). See also Dermot Englefield, *The Printed Records of the Parliament of Ireland, 1613–1800* (1978) and also Coleman A. Dennehy, 'Some manuscript alternatives to the printed Irish parliamentary journals', *Parliaments, Estates and Representation*, 30 (2010), pp 129–43.

9.2 Grand jury records

Until the reorganisation of local government in Ireland at the end of the nineteenth century the most important administrative body in each county was the grand jury. Various laws passed in the course of the eighteenth century helped to clarify the powers of the grand jury and to remove areas of confusion in terms of its responsibilities. The grand jury was selected by the high sheriff and was, by accepted convention, composed of at least 12 and not more than 23 men. An act of 1708 excluded Catholics from serving on the grand jury unless there were insufficient numbers of suitably qualified Protestants (a few Catholics in Ulster are known to have served as grand jurors); these restrictions were removed in 1793. Presbyterians were not expressly forbidden from serving on grand juries.

There was no specific property qualification for sitting on the grand jury and landlord's agents, tenant farmers and merchants served as grand jurors. However, in the course of the eighteenth century the membership of the grand jury came to be dominated increasingly by the county's landed elite (though those holding peerages were excluded). The grand jury met twice a year at the same time as the assizes. Service on the grand jury was voluntary, though there were two full-time salaried officials to assist in the performance of the required duties – a treasurer and a clerk of the Crown. Useful background reading on the role and remit of the grand jury can be found in Neal Garnham, 'Local élite creation in early Hanoverian Ireland: the case of the county grand jury', *Historical Journal*, 42 (1999), pp 623–42.

Presentment books

The grand jury had the authority to raise money through the levying of a tax known as the county cess. The money raised could be applied to a variety of initiatives, such as the construction and maintenance of roads and bridges, as well as courthouses, hospitals and other public buildings. Prior to the assizes, preliminary investigations were carried out to identify the works that were required and the costs of these. Proposals, known as presentments, were then submitted to the grand jury, which had the power to accept, reject or modify them. The presentments that were accepted were then passed for approval to the justice of the assize.

The grand jury presentment books provide a record of the presentments that had been approved at each assize along with a brief statement of the works to be undertaken, the names of those entrusted to oversee the completion of the task in question, and the money that had been apportioned to cover the cost of this. There might also be a note to indicate whether the works had been completed and perhaps even the signature of the overseer to confirm that the payment had been made. In addition to major public works, the grand jury could raise money for a range of other activities, including the apprehension of criminals and the killing of vermin.

To illustrate something of the information recorded, several entries from a County Antrim grand jury presentment book (ANT/4/2/1/1) concerning the repair of roads in the upper half barony of Belfast are given below:

> 28 March 1776 – £39 1s. 2d. paid to John Alexander of Cogry and John Alexander of Doagh to cover the cost of repairing 124 perches of the Antrim-Larne road from the junction with the Belfast-Ballymena road and Robert Mitchell's land.
>
> 16 August 1776 – £21 paid to William Swan and William Houston to repair 80 perches of the Antrim-Carrickfergus road from George Young's farm to John Minise's march ditch.
>
> 16 August 1776 – £11 3s. 2d. paid to James McCluney and Andrew Moore to cover the cost of repairing 25 perches of the road from Ballymena to Dunsilly between Arthur McAnerry's house and Andrew Moore's march ditch.

From a genealogical point of view, the value of this information derives not only from the identification of the individuals responsible for overseeing the work, but also from the fact that the names of householders and farmers were used as a guide to the stretch of road due for repair.

Occasionally it is possible to weave together something of a story from various entries in a grand jury presentment book, as the following extracts from the presentment book for County Antrim, 1711–21, relating to Eneas or Neice O'Haghion, reveal.

> 21 July 1721 – £15 to Daniel Phillips of Ballymacscanlan and £5 to Mr John Hawkins 'for apprehending and bringing to justice Neice O'Haghion, a proclaimed Tory robber and rapparee'.
>
> 7 April 1722 – £1 6s. 1d. paid to John McQuown for, *inter alia*, repairing 'some breaches made in the gaol by Eneas O'Haghian'.
>
> 7 April 1722 – £1 paid to Francis Clements, high sheriff of County Antrim, for transferring 'Neeice O'Haghian' from Belfast to Carrickfergus.
>
> 17 July 1722 – £5 2s. 6d. paid to Francis Clements 'to reimburse him the like sume expended in procureing him a strong guard of sixty men when Eneas O'Haghion and six other men were executed and for fixing the said Haghion's head on the gaole'.

As the above entries make clear, the grand jury could authorise expenditure relating to the enforcement of the law. In addition, the grand jury might approve compensation for those who had lost possessions as a result of criminal activity. In 1797, the County Down grand jury ordered that £100 should be raised off the parish of Tullylish and paid to John Doake, Thomas Anderson, William Cherry, John Montgomery and John Fowler 'to reimburse them for damages sustained by the burning of the meeting house of Newmills'. Other items of expenditure that turn up in presentment books include the payments made to the families of men serving in the Downshire Militia recorded in the County Down presentment books for the 1790s (DOW/4/4/1).

Registers of trees planted

Concerns about deforestation in Ireland and the consequent shortage of timber led to a series of acts being passed from 1698 onwards to encourage tree-planting. One of these, *An Act for Encouraging the Planting of Timber Trees* of 1765, allowed a tenant to retain the trees he had planted on his farm on the expiration of his lease or claim the value of them. In order to avail of these provisions, the tenant was required to lodge a certificate listing the location, number and type of trees with the clerk of the peace of the county within six months of the planting. The legislation required the clerk to keep these certificates and record their details in a separate book. A few of these registers of trees have survived from the eighteenth century for counties in Ulster. The register for County Londonderry has been published by PRONI as *A Register of Trees for Co. Londonderry, 1768–1911*, edited by Eileen M. McCracken and Donal P. McCracken (1984), which contains much useful background material on the subject.

Indictment books
Grand juries had an important role in the administration of justice during the assizes. The grand jury examined bills of indictment and the evidence presented in support of them relating to criminal charges and deliberated on whether a particular bill should be rejected or considered a 'true bill', in which case the case would proceed to a full trial. The County Armagh indictment books, covering the period 1735–97, extend to more than 1,000 pages and provide the names of the grand jurors, prosecutors and defendants, the nature of the crimes (though with few details of specific incidents), and the findings of the grand jury. In the ten years between 1751 and 1761 the County Tyrone grand jury dealt with bills against more than 1,200 individuals.

Surviving grand jury records

County Antrim
Presentment books, 1711–21 (available in typescript in PRONI on request and in Ballymena Central Library), 1727–67, 1775–84, 1796–1804 – ANT/4/1/1–7
Grand warrant books: baronies of Upper and Lower Antrim, 1776–93, 1794–1804 – ANT/4/2/1/1–2
Grand warrant books: baronies of Upper and Lower Dunluce, 1776–92, 1792–1804 – ANT/4/2/2/1–2
Grand warrant books: baronies of Kilconway and Cary, 1776–92, 1793–1804 – ANT/4/2/3/1–2
Grand warrant books: baronies of Upper and Lower Massereene, 1776–92, 1792–1804 – ANT/4/2/4/1–2
Grand warrant books: baronies of Upper and Lower Belfast, 1775–92, 1792–1804 – ANT/4/2/5/1–2
Grand warrant books: baronies of Upper and Lower Glenarm, 1776–94, 1794–1816 – ANT/4/2/6/1–2
Grand warrant book: baronies of Upper and Lower Toome, 1791–1804 – ANT/4/2/7/1
Grand warrant book: Carrickfergus, 1766–1817 – ANT/4/2/8/1
Printed presentment book, 1778–1800 – ANT/4/4/1
Grand Jury resolution book with account, 1780–1824 – ANT/4/7/1
Cash account book and ledger, 1739–52 – ANT/7/8/1
Grand Jury lists, 1613–1803 – T1110/1

County Armagh

Assize indictment books, 1735–75, 1776–97 – MIC650/1 (originals in Armagh Robinson Library)

Extracts from Grand Jury records, 1735–75, providing names of prosecutors, persons indicted and reason; lists of jurors, 1735–98 – T636/1, pp 85–100

Grand Jury lists, 1735–97 – T647

Treasurers receipt and payment book, c. 1750–1796 (assizes), c. 1760– (presentments) – D2523/2/1

Presentment books, beginning in 1758 – ARM/4/1

Presentment book, 1790 – D288/1

Assize indictment book, 1797–1822 – ARM/1/2/A/1

Grand Jury presentments, 1800–10 – T636/46

County Cavan

Ledger containing accounts kept by the county treasurer, c. 1794–1817 – Cavan Archives Service, GJ/1

Registers of trees planted, 1779–1911 – NAI

County Donegal

Grand Jury presentments, 1753–69, 1768–83, 1769–78, 1793–8 – Donegal County Archives Service

Grand Jury presentments, baronies of Boylagh and Banagh, 1772, 1784–98 – NLI, MS 12,910 (MIC352/1)

Grand Jury queries, 1772–83, presentments, 1784–98 – NLI, n.5374, p.5505

Grand Jury book, Kilmacrenan barony, 1772–98 – D2428/1 (MIC73/1; also NAI, MFA 1/1)

Grand Jury books for the General Assizes, baronies of Raphoe and Inishowen, 1769–83 – T2352/1/1, /2

Grand Jury books: queries, 1768–98, 1766–98 – T2352/1/3, /4

See also Raymond Blair, 'An analysis of the Donegal grand jury presentment book for the years 1753 to 1762', *Donegal Annual*, 36 (1984), pp 61–74

County Down

Presentment books, beginning in 1778 – DOW/4/2

Grand Jury record books, beginning in 1780 – DOW/4/4

Register of trees planted, 1769–99 – DOW/7/3/2/1

Presentments at assizes, 1714–96 – T808/15015

Treasurer's presentment book recording paid and unpaid presentments, 1781–1810 – DOW/4/5

Bound volume containing, *inter alia*, notes on Grand Jury presentments, 1778–1822 – D3030/R/1

Extracts from Grand Jury presentments listing sums of money to be 'raised off the parish of Tullylish', to reimburse various individuals for damages by fire, robbery, etc, 1796–9 – T426/1, p. 44

See also F. J. Bigger, 'Old county of Down presentments', *UJA*, 2nd series, 13:3 (August 1907), pp 109–16

County Fermanagh
Presentment book for the county at large, 1792–1819 – FER/4/3/1
Grand Jury bill book containing a register of bills of indictment brought before the Grand Jury at the assize courts, 1792–1861 – FER/4/8/1

County Londonderry
Copy of presentment made at the assizes held at Londonderry, 1759 – T420/1, pp 111–14
Presentment books, beginning in 1788 – LOND/4/1
Register of trees planted, 1773–1894 – LOND/7/7/1
Printed presentments for the City and County of Londonderry, 1785–92 – D644/1–11
Grand jury lists for County Londonderry, 1614–1819, and a printed copy of the grand jury valuation of the county, 1697 –T1113/1–2

County Monaghan
Highway presentments at Clones, 1697 – MIC170/1
Highway presentment at Monaghan quarter sessions, 1709 – MIC170/5
Printed copy of Grand Jury presentments, Monaghan assizes, 1784 – D1150/4/6
Grand Jury bill book, 1784–1820 – MIC309/1

County Tyrone
Presentment books, beginning in 1799 – TYR/4/1
Grand Jury indictment book, 1745–1809; also notes and resolutions of the Grand Jury, presentments made at spring assizes 1745 and occasionally thereafter – TYR/4/2/1 (badly damaged)

9.3 Corporation records

Prior to 1841, local government in over 20 towns and cities in Ulster was controlled by a corporation. The corporations of Carrickfergus and Downpatrick had been established initially in the medieval period, but the rest were were seventeenth-century creations, mostly of the years 1610–13. The issuing of charters marked the beginning of formal municipal government in these towns. Furthermore, corporate towns were empowered to return two MPs to the Irish House of Commons in Dublin. For information on the development of towns in the early seventeenth century, see R. J. Hunter, *Ulster Transformed: Essays on Plantation and Print Culture, c. 1590–1641* (2012).

Records relating to some 18 corporations have survived and include minute books, lists of freemen, and information on the possessions of the corporation. Many entries in corporation minute books are fairly uninformative, at times being little more than a record that a meeting did take place and listing only the names of those present. On other occasions, however, there will be information of real value. For example, on 5 October 1745 the corporation of Hillsborough decided to appoint a town watch and issued it with the following instructions: 'That once in each hour one half of the said Guard shall patrole from the house of Patrick Jackson to the house of Moses Green in Hillsborough'. The watch was to last from 10pm to 6am, and anyone found out after 11pm was to be arrested. For the corporation of Bangor there is a register of elections of provosts, burgesses and freemen, 1716–68 (LA/20/1/CA/1A–B). As an example of its contents, on 30 May 1728 William Pickerin and John Reed, carpenters, John Stewart and Alexander Gibbson, shoemakers, John Kennedy, innkeeper, and Joseph Brown, weaver, were admitted as freemen of the corporation.

The following extract is from the Limavady corporation book for 2 July 1716 and highlights the fact that information in corporation records is not necessarily restricted to those living in the town itself:

> Edward Dymock of Faughanvale bought from Teague O'Harken of Dunmore, two Black cows at £2 7s. 8d., and vouched the same to be lawfully come. Robert Martin of Crindle, voucher. Shane O'Garakell of Arnogunog, in the Parish of Clondermott, and County of Londonderry, hath sold this day to William Ransdly of Magilligan, twenty sheep at 2s. 6d. per sheep; and David McFall of Clady, in the Parish of Cumber, and Owen O'Galaher of Glendermott, vouch that they are honestly come.

The minutes of the Londonderry corporation begin in 1673 and these have been digitised and made available as downloadable PDFs on the PRONI website. Also available electronically are the registers of the city's freemen. The minutes cover a broad range of subjects, such as the regulation of markets and customs duties, the appointment of corporation officials, the admission of freemen, and the provision of assistance for the poor. The minutes of 1696 include a resolution condemning a plot to assassinate William III, which has the names of 226 subscribers. Among the items of interest in the Coleraine corporation minutes is the entry of the meeting of 2 October 1797, at which the Coleraine Yeomanry were made freemen of the town. This order is followed by a list of the officers and men of the Yeomanry.

The following table lists the corporate towns in Ulster with surviving records for the seventeenth and eighteenth centuries. Information on what is available is listed under the heading *Corporation records* under the relevant parish in Appendix 1. It should be noted that some corporation records have been published, and others remain in local custody.

Corporation	Parish	County
Armagh	Armagh	Armagh
Bangor	Bangor	Down
Belfast	Shankill	Antrim
Belturbet	Annagh	Cavan
Carrickfergus	Carrickfergus	Antrim
Cavan	Urney	Cavan
Clogher	Clogher	Tyrone
Coleraine	Coleraine	Londonderry
Dungannon	Drumglass	Tyrone
Enniskillen	Enniskillen	Fermanagh
Hillsborough	Hillsborough	Down
Killyleagh	Killyleagh	Down
Lifford	Clonleigh	Donegal
Limavady	Drumachose	Londonderry
Londonderry	Templemore	Londonderry
Monaghan	Monaghan	Monaghan
Newtownards	Newtownards	Down
Strabane	Camus-juxta-Mourne	Tyrone

Researchers should also be aware of the parliamentary investigations into Irish corporations from the 1830s. The *First report of the commissioners appointed to inquire into the municipal corporations in Ireland* of 1835 includes sections on the existing state of municipal corporations, defects in their constitutions, the privileges of freemen and other members, their jurisdiction and powers in the administration of justice, and the nature of their tolls and customs. The massive appendix to the report (published in 1835–6) provides details on such things as the charters of each town, the fairs and markets held there, and the property owned by the corporation. Information can be found that relates to the seventeenth and eighteenth centuries. For instance, the section dealing with Enniskillen includes some material about the letting of corporation lands in the 1700s as well as accounts for 1749–50, which include payments to persons who carried out various tasks on behalf of the corporation (e.g. Edward Kernan for work at the market-house) and those in need who received financial support from the body. See also *Reports from Commissioners, Municipal Corporations Boundaries (Ireland)* of 1837, which includes maps showing corporation boundaries.

9.4 Records relating to the legal system

There were a number of tiers to the Irish legal system. In Dublin there were four superior courts – Chancery, Common Pleas, Exchequer and King's Bench. The assize courts were the most important criminal courts in provincial Ireland. They were presided over by two judges and were held biannually, at lent and summer. The assize courts were organised by circuit: the Northeast Ulster assize circuit comprised counties Antrim, Armagh, Down and Monaghan; the remaining Ulster counties (along with counties Longford and Westmeath) were within the Northwest Ulster circuit. Quarter sessions were convened four times a year and were presided over by one or more justices of the peace. Their jurisdiction extended to the county in which they were held. It was not until the 1820s that a formal network of petty sessions courts began to be established across Ireland. Manor courts were held under the authority of the landlord and dealt with various matters concerning his estate; the records generated by these courts are covered in Chapter 6.

The best guide to the Irish legal system in the seventeenth and eighteenth centuries is Neal Garnham, *The Courts, Crime and the Criminal Law in Ireland, 1692–1760* (1996). See also his essay 'Crime, policing, and the law, 1600–1900' in *Ulster Since 1600: Politics, Economy, and Society*, edited by Liam Kennedy and Philip Ollerenshaw (2013). Though, as the title indicates, Brian Griffin's book, *Sources for the Study of Crime in Ireland, 1801–1921* (2005), is concerned primarily with the nineteenth century, it does include useful information on some sources that originated in the late eighteenth century.

Records at the National Archives of Ireland
A range of different records relating to law and order can be accessed in the National Archives of Ireland in Dublin. To a large extent, these originated in the State Paper Office and especially from the class of records that derived from the Chief Secretary's Office. The State Paper Office was established in 1702 as the repository for documentation relating to the Lord Lieutenant and Chief Secretary for Ireland and was based in Dublin Castle. Records created before *c.* 1790 were moved to the old Public Record Office of Ireland and so were lost in 1922. The surviving records from *c.* 1790 onwards are now available in NAI. Several categories of these records, such as the Rebellion Papers and State of the Country Papers, are discussed in Chapter 5 in the section looking at the period of the United Irishmen and 1798 Rebellion.

Mention may be made here of the Privy Council Office Proclamations in NAI. These are listed in a calendar arranged chronologically beginning in 1652 with an alphabetical index by surname and place-name. By way of example, no. 65, dated 24 December 1717, concerns 'Tories, Robbers and Rapparees' in County Antrim who are named as Paul McSevenagh, Glenbush; Bryan Agnew, near Stony-foord; Evear Magee, Braid; Duncams O'Kelly, Glenarm Glen; Daniel Magee, Braid; Allester Buoy McKey, Glenclewe; and Gilbert Agnew, Stony-foord. Another, no. 101, from 9 June 1735, concerns Roger O'Cahan and William Boyd of Kilrea, yeomen; Andrew Gray of Agivey, yeoman; Bryan Oge O'Dempsey of Drumcal; Donaghy O'Cahan of Moneysaney, all of County Londonderry. See also *The Proclamations of Ireland, 1660–1820*, edited by James Kelly with Mary Ann Lyons (5 vols, Irish Manuscripts Commission, 2014).

Court records
Most of the early records relating to the courts seem to have been lost in 1922 with the destruction of the old Public Record Office. However, a few records,

or at least copies of them, survive. For example, pages from a 'Crown Book' concerning the County Antrim summer assizes of 1766, held at Carrickfergus, list more than 100 indictments for a range of offences, including murder, assault and theft (D207/19/109). The names recorded include those of the individuals charged with the crimes, their victims and persons providing bail. Addresses and occupations are often provided. For example, the following individuals were charged with destroying chairs, mugs, bowls, etc belonging to John Dillon at Ballyclare on 30 November 1765: John Allen, John Kindlorn(?), Nathaniel McAlester, Hugh Kirkwood, James Robinson and Margaret McAlester. Similar records for Antrim from lent 1769 and Londonderry from summer 1773 include, respectively, 76 and 40 indictments. A few gaol calendars are also available, which provide the names of prisoners and their crimes, and when these offences were committed.

Extracts from court records made prior to 1922 exist in various collections as well as records deriving from other sources, such as solicitors' archives. For example, the genealogist Tenison Groves made great use of court records in carrying out research in the old Public Record Office and his transcripts are available in PRONI (T808). For instance, his notes on the Baird family include extracts from an Exchequer bill of 5 February 1731 [1732] which involved, on the one hand, George McGee of Strabane and on the other, several parties including Rebecca Baird, daughter and only child of James Knox and widow of John Baird (T808/884). The latter was stated to have been formerly of Strabane and then of Christian (Christiana) Hundred, New Castle County, in what is now the state of Delaware. According to this bill, Hugh Edwards of Castlederg leased Creeduff in perpetuity to James Knox in 1685; Knox in turn bequeathed this property to his daughter Rebecca. Around seven years earlier (i.e. c. 1725) Rebecca and her husband John Baird had emigrated to America and settled at Christian Hundred. In 1728, Rebecca and her son Robert returned to Strabane to sell Creeduff and some other properties. In July of that year Creeduff was sold to George McGee for £200, after which Rebecca and Robert returned to America. However, difficulties arose resulting in the legal proceedings.

Newspapers routinely carried reports of the assizes and quarter sessions (see Chapter 12). The more sensational trials generated much public interest and accounts of the proceedings made it into print. Among the more notorious court cases of the early 1700s were the 'Islandmagee Witch Trials'. An account of the trials was published as *The Islandmagee witches: A narrative of the sufferings of a young girl called Mary Dunbar, who was strangely molested by spirits and witches, at Mr. James Hattridge's house, Islandmagee, near Carrickfergus, in the county of Antrim and province of Ulster in Ireland, and in some other places to which she was removed during the time of her disorder, as also of the aforesaid Mr. Hattridge's house being haunted with spirits in the latter end of 1710 and the begining of 1711*, edited by Samuel McSkimmin (1822). The depositions made by those giving evidence were printed in R. M. Young (ed.), *Historical Notices of Old Belfast* (1896), pp 161–4. A recent study of this episode is Andrew Sneddon's book, *Possessed by the Devil: The Real History of the Islandmagee Witches & Ireland's Only Mass Witchcraft Trial* (2013). The trial records include a wealth of local information for east County Antrim. Usefully, Sneddon provides brief biographical sketches of the main characters involved in this case.

Local history publications can also include details of court cases and some of these draw on records that were lost in 1922. For instance, D. C. Rushe, *Monaghan in the Eighteenth Century* (1916) includes many extracts from records relating to law and order, a number of which are no longer extant. For example, at the summer assizes of 1711 the high sheriff of County Monaghan, Alexander Montgomery, issued the following proclamation:

> We present Patrick Glass O'Connolly, late of Cornaglare, Parish of Kilmore, James O'Connolly, late of Cornaglare aforesaid, formerly in Sligo Gaol, married to Reggie O'Connolly, daughter of Patrick Glass O'Connolly's sister, Peter O'Connolly, son of James O'Connolly's brother married to Paralone O'Connolly's daughter, and Peter and Jas O'Connolly, reputed sons of John O'Connolly, formerly in the Gaol of this County, to be dangerous Robbers, Tories and Rapparees out upon their keeping, in arms and not amenable to the laws, but robbing and plundering His Majesty's good subjects.

King's Inns, Dublin

Originating in the reign of Henry VIII, King's Inns is the oldest legal institution in Ireland. In 1629, membership of King's Inns was made compulsory for counsellors (barristers) and attorneys in Dublin and in 1635 this rule was extended to all counsellors in Ireland. King's Inns has been located in Henrietta Street, Dublin, since the beginning of the nineteenth century. Open carts were used to transport the records to Henrietta Street around 1804 with the unfortunate result that many papers were lost. The admission papers include such details as the name, residence and occupation of the father of the applicant, as well as the name (usually including the maiden name) of his mother. The names of those who entered this institution were published by the Irish Manuscripts Commission in *King's Inns Admission Papers, 1607–1867*, edited by Edward Keane, P. Beryl Phair and Thomas U. Sadleir (1982). See also Colum Kenny, *King's Inns and the Kingdom of Ireland: The Irish 'Inn of Court', 1541–1800* (1992).

Surviving records relating to law and order

Surviving records relating to the administration of justice include the following items in PRONI.

County Antrim

Fines in the Court of Wards, Lower Antrim, 1637: *c.* 30 names –
T808/14884

Extracts from assize and quarter session records, 1721–40 –
T808/14895

Summaries of cases at assizes, 1717–30 – T808/14896

Examinations and reports of cases of 18th-century County Antrim
assizes relating largely to Tories and Hearts of Steel outrages –
T808/14910

'Crown Book' comprising several unbound sheets being the pleas of
the Crown at Carrickfergus assizes, with details of charges of murder,
assault, and stealing of linen, etc, summer 1766 – D207/19/109
(use MIC511)

'A calendar of prisoners remaining in the gaol of the said County
[Antrim] since last Assizes, and since committed, to said gaol, with
their names, crimes, by whom, and when, committed, discharged, by
whom, and when, this 21st day of August 1766', summer 1766 –
D207/19/110 (use MIC511)

Notes of evidence given before the County Antrim assizes, with a special
reference to the theft of rum from the cellars of Campbell &
Donaldson's in Belfast – D207/19/111 (use MIC511)

Pleas of the Crown at County Antrim assizes held at Carrickfergus,
spring 1769 – D207/19/125 (use MIC511)

County Armagh

Depositions concerning a riot in 'Scotch Armagh', 17 March 1717,
naming rioters, victims and witnesses – T552, p. 140; T808/14937

Depositions relating to the burning of Freeduff Presbyterian meeting
house, 1743 – T1392/1, T808/14925

List of indictments at lent assizes, 1771 – T808/14951

County Down

Copy of case for the Crown relating to certain indictments at
Downpatrick assizes, April 1772, which concerned the murder of Rev.
Samuel Morrell (Presbyterian minister of Tullylish), the destruction of
Richard Johnston's house at Gilford, and the tendering of 'oaths and
solemn engagements and other felonys against the late Acts', 1773 –
D207/1/12 (use MIC511)

Bound volume containing, *inter alia*, notes on various cases of petty
crime, made by Rev. John Cleland in his capacity as a magistrate,
1778–1822 – D3030/R/1

County Londonderry

Miscellaneous Londonderry court records beginning in 1763, including
the names of justices to attend the quarter sessions at Londonderry
and Magherafelt, 1798 – D1509

Crown Pleas at the city and county of Londonderry assizes, summer
  1773 – D207/19/139 (use MIC511)
Gaol calendar for the city and county of Londonderry assizes, 13
  September 1773 – D207/19/140 (use MIC511)
Copy deed of delivery of gaol prisoners from one set of high sheriffs
  to another, 1786 – D1453/14
Sixteen bonds, recognisances and sworn examinations in cases of theft
  and assault relating to Alexander Orr JP [of Landmore, Aghadowey],
  1800–10 – D664/O/5

County Tyrone
Extracts from early 17th-century Chancery and Exchequer inquisitions,
  etc relating to County Tyrone sessions and assizes – T1365/1
Warrant issued to constables of Dungannon concerning persons in
  Arboe parish, 1660 – D1618/15/2/21
'A calendar of the Crown Prisoners in the gaol of Omagh'; this relates
  to the County Tyrone summer assizes, 1774 – D207/19/144 (use
  MIC511)

High sheriffs and justices of the peace

The high sheriff of the county was originally a lifetime appointee chosen by
the King. By the seventeenth century he was appointed annually. A justice of
the peace (JP) played an important role in the administration of local justice.
Some records relating to these offices are set out below.

Lists of high sheriffs for every county in Ireland (with the exception of
  Londonderry), 14th–19th centuries – D302/1
Lists of sheriffs for counties Antrim, Armagh, Carlow, Cavan, Donegal
  and Down, 1343–1864 – T3374/2

County Antrim high sheriffs, 1663–1790 – T1306/2
County Antrim JPs in the 17th century – T808/14893–4
County Antrim magistrates, 1773 (53 names) – D4164/A/3
County Armagh high sheriffs, 1593–1969 – T2704/1
County Armagh JPs, 1655 – T808/1495
County Donegal high sheriffs, 1607–1814 – T808/14995
County Down high sheriffs, 1400–1874 – Alexander Knox,
  A History of Down (1875), pp 91–8
County Down high sheriffs, 1663–1790 – T1306/2
County Fermanagh JPs, 1663–1844 – T517/1
County and city of Londonderry sheriffs from early 1600s onwards –
  D2807/1, D3703/A/1/1, T3324/1, T3402/18
County Monaghan JPs in 1758 – D3053/8/4/1
County Tyrone high sheriffs, 1606–1895 – T808/15116

10. Parliamentary election records

10.1 The electorate

Prior to the abolition of the Irish Parliament under the terms of the Act of Union of 1800, each county constituency and each borough in Ireland could return two MPs to the Irish House of Commons in Dublin. (See Chapter 9 for more on the Irish Parliament.) Before 1768 there was no law limiting the duration of Irish parliaments and nothing to compel the government to hold a general election except the death of the reigning monarch. The *Act for limiting the duration of parliaments* of 1768 (popularly known as the Octennial Act) stipulated that a general election should be held at least every eight years. However, many constituency elections were uncontested and parliamentary representation remained firmly in the hands of a small number of powerful landed families in each county.

Throughout the seventeenth and eighteenth centuries the right to vote in parliamentary elections for county constituencies was closely linked to land tenure. The franchise was restricted to adult males in possession of freehold land, that is, land owned in fee simple or leased for a term of life. The freehold itself had to be worth at least 40 shillings a year once the rent and other duties had been paid. The majority of Ulster's tenant farmers who were qualified to vote fell under the heading of '40-shilling freeholders'. Under the terms of the *Act for the further regulating the election of members of Parliament*, passed in 1728, a freeholder had to register his freehold at least six months before an election in which he intended to vote. In 1795, freeholders were required to re-register every eight years (unless their freehold was worth £50 or more a year). It is worth emphasising the point that the possession of a lease for years, no matter how many years, did not entitle one to vote.

The numbers of freeholders in existence at any one time depended on a number of factors. To begin with, under the provisions of the abovementioned act of 1728 Catholics were expressly forbidden to vote and it was not until 1793 that the franchise was restored to them. On the other hand, Presbyterians and other nonconformist Protestants were never specifically denied the right to vote in parliamentary elections. The leasing policy of an individual landowner also had an impact on the numbers of voters. Some landlords, for economic reasons and/or political apathy, rarely issued leases for lives and so the numbers of freeholders among their tenantry were small or non-existent.

However, politically ambitious landlords used their power to create freeholds to increase their electoral clout. There was no secret ballot in this era and the way an individual cast his vote was public knowledge. A landlord could direct his tenants to vote for a particular candidate with ramifications for them if they disobeyed him. Inevitably, therefore, much of the impetus for the registration of freeholders came from landlords who were anxious to use the votes of their tenants to influence the outcome of elections. It is also worth noting that the bishops of the Church of Ireland, despite being in possession of some of the largest estates in Ulster, were not allowed to issue leases for lives to their tenants.

10.2 Election records

Election records come in two main forms: poll books and freeholders' registers. Introduced in 1696 in an effort to curb disputes over election results, poll books record the names of voters and the candidates for whom they voted. Freeholders' registers were designed to provide evidence of the authenticity of a particular individual's claim to have the right to vote. In most of these records the information provided about the voter or prospective voter is fairly basic – his name and the location of his freehold. The latter need not necessarily have been the same as his place of residence and so some lists will also give the freeholder's abode. The name of the freeholder's landlord is sometimes recorded and this can be helpful in trying to identify relevant estate papers (see Chapter 6).

Occasionally, some additional information of interest is provided. In a list of Armagh freeholders of *c.* 1710–37 the names of the lives in the lease are often recorded (D1928/F/1A). For example, the entry for William Lyndsay reveals that he held his freehold of Cargans from Oliver St John by virtue of a lease of 10 June 1726 for the lives of himself and his sons John and Thomas. Many of the annotations to election records are in the form of challenges to the right of a particular individual to vote or to be registered to vote. In the Armagh poll book of 1753 Robert Jones was objected to 'for being seen at Mass and giving offerings to the priest', while Silas Hamilton was objected to on the grounds that he was a 'rioter'.

The 'Deputy Court Cheque Book' for County Antrim of 1776 contains many annotations relating to whether or not an individual was suitably qualified to vote (D1364/L/1). For example, Robert Peerece of Aughnahough was 'Objected to for want of freehold – the last surviving life in the lease being a soldier & went to Africa about four years ago, since which there was no account from him, altho' he regularly wrote to his mother before that time & soe is dead so long – rejected.' Other annotations provide useful family history information. For instance, it was noted that William Tate of Morusk 'comes to vote under his father John Tate's registry & that the lease was made to his father about 30 years ago & that he is dead from 6 to 10 years & that he had no brothers or sisters living'. A selection of other extracts from this source is given below.

John Stevenson, Ballynamaddy, 'wou'd not swear – a Covenanter'

John Cooper, Artresna, 'objected to as a Papist'

William Gleghorn, Sixteen Towns, 'not duly registered, being reg'd in his father-in-law James Fleming's name'

Robert Lusk, Larne, 'holds by an assignment from his grandfather executed about 8 years ago'

James Maginn, Targreacy, 'his name not Maginn, but Magill'

John Forbes, Aghaleck, 'married to a Papist – rejected'

William Crawford, Ballygilbert, 'reg'd by his father Thomas Crawford 22 years ago – father dead 5 years'

10.3 Surviving election records

The survival of election records for Ulster varies considerably from county to county, with coverage best for counties Armagh and Down. A list of the records is set out below.

County Antrim

Belfast voters, 1744 – printed in R. M. Young (ed.), *The Town Book of the Corporation of Belfast* (1892), pp 215–17

Some County Antrim freeholders, 1768 – T808/14900

Deputy Court Cheque Book, 1776 – D1364/L/1 (an index was printed in *DIFHR*, 22 (1999), pp 72–80)

Voters, 1790 (3,538 names) – printed in *A collection of all the authenticated public addresses, resolutions, and advertisements, relative to the late election of Knights of the Shire for the County of Antrim: Together with a correct list of the poll, alphabetically arranged, shewing at one view how and when each elector voted*, by 'a member of the Independent Committee' (Belfast, 1790); copy in PRONI, D3300/133/1

County Armagh

Freeholders list, *c*. 1710–37 – D1928/F/1A (also T2731/1)

Freeholders list, 1738 – NLI, p.206

Freeholders register, 1753 – D1928/F/1B

Armagh poll book, 1753 – T808/14936; MIC353/1

Objections to voters in poll book of 1753 – T808/14949

List of freeholders from the Portadown district, 1747–1802 – D2394/3/5; T281/5

Memorial from freeholders and merchants of Oneilland West barony, 1763 – *Belfast Newsletter*, 2 Aug. 1763

Draft address of the high sheriff, grand jury, gentlemen, clergy, and freeholders of the County Armagh to the Lord Lieutenant, [1772?] – NLI, MS 38,725

Registered freeholders in the Portadown district, 1792–1802 – T281/6

County Cavan
Poll book, 1761 – T1522 (an index was printed in *DIFHR*, 23 (2000), pp 93–101)

County Donegal
Poll book, 1761–75 – T808/14999; MIC353/1 (an index was printed in *DIFHR*, 20 (1997), pp 70–76)
Freeholders, 1775–81, 1789–90 – T808/15006
Copy of a series of 11 freeholders' affidavits taken at the quarter sessions at Lifford, 1786 – T2430/2

County Down
Election 'cheque book' for freeholders with surnames A–G arranged alphabetically, 1746–89 – D654/A3/1/1A
List of 40-shilling freeholders and £10 leaseholders on the Sharman estate, Banbridge, 1765 – D856/B/6/1
List of over 400 signatures of tenants on the Needham estate, Newry, election of 1768 – NLI, MS 8163
Registers of freeholders, 1777, 1780–85 – DOW/5/3/1
Registers of freeholders, 1790–95 – DOW/5/3/2
Index book of electors for the borough of Downpatrick, *c*. 1783 – D2223/21/1
'Deputy Court cheque book', 1789 – D654/A3/1/1B
Freeholders, Lecale barony, *c*. 1790 – T393/1
Freeholders, Lecale barony, 1795–9 – T808/15012
Freeholders, Lecale barony, 1795–1800 – T808/15018
Lists of freeholders, Upper and Lower Iveagh baronies, 1796–1811 – D654/A3/1C–X
Draft list of freeholders who support and oppose union, 1799 – D3030/960

County Fermanagh
Poll book, 1747–68 – T808/15063 (an index was printed in *DIFHR*, 21 (1998), pp 58–69)
Register of freeholders arranged alphabetically, *c*. 1788 – D1939/3/1
Poll book, 1788 – T543/1; T808/15075; MIC353/1
Freeholders register, 1796–1802 – D1096/92
Lists of freeholders, no dates given [18th century] – John Rylands Library, Manchester, B 3/26/1–145

County Londonderry
Names of those who voted at the County Londonderry by-election of 1697 – T3161/1/4
Freeholders in Cumber parish, 1761–81, 1791, 1796 – printed in John Rutherford, *Cumber Presbyterian Church and Parish* (1939), pp 117–25
Freeholders in Tamlaght Finlagan parish, 1774 (136 names and addresses) – D2094/46

County Monaghan
Extracts from County Court of Monaghan giving lists of freeholders,
    1692: *c.* 70 names – MIC170/5

County Tyrone
Freeholders, Dungannon barony, 1763 – *Belfast Newsletter*, 30 Aug. 1763
Freeholders, Cookstown area, 1768–95 – T808/15127
Freeholders, Dungannon barony, 1795–8 – TYR/5/3/1
Freeholders in the manor of Blessingburn, *c.* 1790 – D627/56

The majority of eighteenth-century election records have been indexed by
PRONI and are available as a searchable database on its website
(www.nidirect.gov.uk/proni).

11. Military records

For a general background to the armed forces and military service, see Thomas Bartlett and Keith Jeffery (eds), *A Military History of Ireland* (1997). Researchers should also be aware of the Military History Society of Ireland, which was founded in 1949. The society's journal, *The Irish Sword*, includes numerous articles of interest for those researching ancestors in Ulster who served in the military. Articles of interest are listed in the relevant sections below. See also D. C. Linehan, 'Index to the manuscripts of military interest in the National Library of Ireland', *Irish Sword*, 2 (1954), pp 33–9; and K. P. Ferguson, 'Military manuscripts in the Public Record Office of Ireland', *Irish Sword*, 15 (1982), pp 112–15, which refers to material in what is now the National Archives of Ireland.

11.1 The regular army

Most of the information that has survived about those who served in the regular army will be found in the War Office (WO) papers in The National Archives (TNA), Kew (formerly the Public Record Office). These records comprise commissions, muster rolls, pensions, discharges, regimental papers, etc. The TNA website (www.nationalarchives.gov.uk) has detailed guides on what is available and how it can be accessed. A helpful published guide is Simon Fowler, *Tracing Your Army Ancestors: A Guide for Family Historians* (3rd edition, 2017). Increasingly, records of those in the armed forces are being digitised and made available through a variety of providers.

There was a separate military establishment in Ireland, which comprised British regiments stationed on the island, and which was paid for out of the Irish Revenue. A proclamation of 1701 prohibited Catholics from serving and, while inevitably many slipped through, it was not until the 1770s that cautious approval for Catholic recruitment was given. Likewise, except during critical manpower crises, Irish Protestants were supposed to be excluded from the ranks (though not the officer class). From the 1740s onwards, however, it would seem that the presence of members of the Church of Ireland in the ranks was accepted, though it was not until 1780 that Presbyterians and other Protestant nonconformists were allowed officially to enlist.

Of some interest for those researching soldiers in regiments on the Irish establishment are the registers of in- and out-pensioners of the Royal Hospital Kilmainham, beginning in 1704 (WO 118), as well as certificates of service of pensioners, 1757–1849 (WO 119). The details recorded can include the age and place of birth of the pensioner, as well as a brief description of the individual himself, his service record and why he was discharged from the army. Microfilm copies of the Kilmainham records are available in the National Archives of Ireland. Many men from Ulster also served in regiments on the English establishment and so may appear in the records of the Royal Hospital Chelsea (including WO 23, WO 97, WO 116, WO 120 and WO 121).

The online Discovery catalogue of The National Archives, Kew, includes summary details of soldiers extracted from some of the Chelsea and Kilmainham records. Typically these will record the soldier's place of birth, the regiment in which he served, and the year in which he was discharged as well as his age at that time. Some examples are set out below:

> Edward Evans, born Belturbet, County Cavan, 76th Foot Regiment, discharged aged 41, 1760 (WO 97/873/49)
> James McQuillan, born Portadown, County Armagh, 5th Dragoons, discharged aged 47, 1777 (WO 119/5/232)
> Thomas Walker, born Raphoe, County Donegal, 16th Foot Regiment, discharged aged 40 after 4 years of service, 1787 (WO 121/2/148)
> Edward Blair, born Letterkenny, County Donegal, 4th Dragoon Guards, discharged aged 41, 1792 (WO 97/20/2)
> Francis Money, born Clones, County Fermanagh, Royal Irish Invalids, discharged aged 34, 1794 (WO 97/1201/258)
> David Wright, born Hillsborough, County Down, 10th Foot Regiment, discharged aged 31 after 18 years of service, 1798 (WO 121/32/271)

The originals of some of the Kilmainham and Chelsea records have been digitised and made available through a partner organisation (the TNA website will provide the relevant link).

Few records relating to the personnel of the regular army in the eighteenth century are to be found in the Public Record Office of Northern Ireland. The Groves Collection includes some extracts from the regular army muster rolls, 1741–80 (T808/15196). A somewhat unusual item is a copy of a list of signatures of captured 'Convention Troops' (British soldiers taken prisoner at Saratoga, New York, after the surrender of General Burgoyne to the Patriots in October 1777) giving Ireland as their place of origin (T3699/1). The names include:

> William Jordan, Dromore, County Down
> John Reily, Inniskilling, County Fermanagh
> John Foster, Billy, County Antrim
> William Blead, Munamore [Moneymore], County Londonderry

11.2 The militia

The tradition of raising local defence forces in response to particular threats, both from within and without, can be traced back to the period of the Ulster Plantation. From the early 1690s there were attempts to reform and regulate the militia system on a more formal basis and eventually, in 1716, an act of parliament was passed which established the force on a legal footing. This legislation was designed to 'make the militia of this kingdom more useful'. All Protestant men aged between 16 and 60 were liable for service and they were required to take part in exercises four times a year. Nonconformist Protestants could serve in the militia, but it was not until 1756 that they were allowed to hold commissions. In 1776, the authority for raising a militia lapsed and although new legislation concerning the militia was passed in 1778 it was not implemented. Unfortunately, very few records of the pre-1793 militia survive. There is a list of militia officers for all counties in Ireland in 1761 (T808/15235). Other records potentially of assistance to researchers are listed below.

The *Act for amending and reducing into one act of parliament the laws relating to the militia in Ireland* of 1793 was a radical overhaul of the militia system. Lists of eligible men aged 18 to 45 were drawn up in each county and then a ballot was held until the requisite number was reached. Those selected were enrolled in the militia for four years. Anyone who did not wish to serve was allowed to put forward a substitute. The militia was also open to volunteers. Those exempted from the militia included those already serving in the armed forces, clergymen, seamen and fathers of three living children. Subsequent legislation further regulated the organisation and financing of this force as well as providing financial support for the families of militiamen. Unlike the previous militia, the rank and file of the post-1793 militia was mainly Catholic, though the officers were nearly all Protestants. At times the militia was prone to poor discipline when sent to disturbed areas. For example, on 12 July 1797 the Kerry Militia was involved in fight with Orangemen in Stewartstown, County Tyrone, with the result that several of the militiamen were killed. Furthermore, the authorities were concerned that the force was being infiltrated by the Defenders and United Irishmen. However, the militia played an effective role in suppressing the rebellion in 1798.

Late eighteenth-century militia muster rolls and pay lists are in the War Office records at The National Archives, Kew (WO 13). These list alphabetically the names of officers and men by company. The places of residence of the men are not given, but the name of the commanding officer can act as a guide to the district from which the soldiers in a particular company were drawn. There are occasional comments, such as 'sick', 'absent', 'deserted' or 'dead'. The lists for certain years have been copied by PRONI for counties Antrim, Armagh, Donegal, Down and Fermanagh. The major work on the militia in Ireland is Neal Garnham, *The Militia in Eighteenth-Century Ireland:*

In Defence of the Protestant Interest (2012), which focuses mainly on the pre-1793 force. See also Sir Henry McAnally, *The Irish Militia, 1793–1816* (1949) and Ivan Nelson, *The Irish Militia, 1793–1802: Ireland's Forgotten Army* (2007).

11.3 The Volunteers

One of the most celebrated military organisations in Irish history is the Volunteers. This part-time defence force was raised in the late 1770s at a time when the regular army in Ireland had been reduced in size due to the transfer of troops to America to take part in the Revolutionary War. From the spring of 1778 Volunteer companies were raised locally to maintain law and order and to guard against invasion. The membership of the Volunteers was dominated by middle class Protestants, with Presbyterians playing influential roles. Volunteering developed into a powerful movement, advocating reforms of the political system including the legislative independence of the Irish Parliament (which was conceded by London in 1782). The movement's role at a national level declined in 1784. There was a revival in Volunteering in the early 1790s, but legislation passed in 1793, banning the import of arms and the calling of an assembly demanding changes in the law, effectively ended the movement.

Surviving records relating to the Volunteers include some membership rolls and minute books. Taking the minute book of the Rathfriland Volunteers as an example, we may note that it includes the names of some 70 subscribers to the set of rules drawn up by the company on 12 September 1779. Of these, only nine made their mark rather than sign in their own hand. One of the subscribers, Andrew Hart, died just over a month later, while another, John Martin, was in the navy. The original captain of the company was Rev. Samuel Barber, the Presbyterian minister in Rathfriland. Subsequent minutes record details of new members of the company, as well as those expelled for various offences, such as insolence and refusing to attend exercises. An entry of 29 January 1781 recorded that it had been unanimously agreed that William Hood should be discharged from the company with the added note 'and that three chears was given on the ocation'. Those signing to indicate receipt of arms are recorded on several occasions and in March 1781 there is a list of names of those who were proposing to purchase their own weapons.

The historian T. G. F. Paterson published numerous articles on the Volunteers, listing the different companies and their commanding officers, etc. His work on the Armagh Volunteers was particularly extensive. In addition, he published a series of articles in *The Irish Sword* entitled, 'The Volunteer Companies of Ulster, 1778-93', which dealt with the remaining Ulster counties. Details of his publications on the Volunteers are set out below. Pádraig Ó Snodaigh (Oliver Snoddy) has also carried out considerable research into the eighteenth-century Volunteers; see his *The Irish Volunteers, 1715-1793: A List of the Units* (1995). See also Peter Smyth, 'The Volunteers and Parliament' in Thomas Bartlett and D. W. Hayton (eds), *Penal Era and Golden Age: Essays in*

Irish History, 1690–1800 (1979), pp 113–36. It is also worth mentioning that the correspondence of James Caulfeild, first earl of Charlemont, on deposit in the Royal Irish Academy in Dublin includes much about the Volunteers.

11.4 The Yeomanry

The Yeomanry was formed in September 1796 at a time of intense political excitement in Ireland, with the twin threat of domestic rebellion and invasion from France. The Yeomanry was a part-time defence force composed of local volunteers. It was led by the gentry and its membership was predominantly Protestant. For the most part the Yeomanry was financed by a parliamentary grant, which covered the cost of uniforms, equipment and weapons, as well as pay. The force played an important role in suppressing the 1798 Rebellion. In the aftermath of the rebellion Lord Cornwallis wrote, 'The Yeomanry are in the style of the loyalists of America, only much more numerous and powerful, and a thousand times more ferocious'.

The Yeomanry Office records were lost in the destruction of the old Public Record Office in Dublin in 1922. Some early records have survived from a variety of other sources and these are listed below. For a detailed account of the yeomanry, see Allan Blackstock, *Ascendancy Army: The Irish Yeomanry, 1796–1834* (1998). Dr Blackstock is also the author of *Double Traitors: The Belfast Volunteers and Yeomen, 1778–1828* (2000).

11.5 Surviving records of the militia, Volunteers and Yeomanry, 1691–1800

The following records have been arranged chronologically by county. For muster rolls from the first half of the seventeenth century, see Chapter 4. Records relating to combatants in the Williamite War in Ireland, 1689–91, are also covered in Chapter 4.

County Antrim

READ
T. G. F. Paterson, 'The Volunteer Companies of Ulster, 1778–93'
    [Antrim] – *Irish Sword*, 7:27 (Winter 1965), pp 90–116

MILITIA
Militia officers, 1691 – T808/15185
Notes on the County Antrim militia, 1760, Volunteers, 1780–84, and
    militia and yeomanry, 1793–1810 – T3374/1/4
Militia pay lists and muster rolls, 1793–1800 – TNA, WO 13/2574,
    /2575, /2576 (PRONI has copies for 1799–1800: T1115/1A–B
    and MIC15A/95)

VOLUNTEERS
Roll of the Belfast First Volunteer Company, 1778–81 – printed in
    George Benn, *A History of the Town of Belfast* (1877), pp 754–5

Protest by individuals who had determined to secede from the Lisburn
Volunteers, 1780 – *Belfast Newsletter*, 1–5 Sept. 1780

YEOMANRY

Lisburn Yeomanry, 1798 – names printed in *These Hallowed Grounds*,
vol. 2 (2005), p. 281

Declaration of allegiance by officers of Carrickfergus Yeomanry Infantry,
n.d. [*c*. 1803] – D162/103 (MIC533/3)

Roll of the Cary Yeomanry, 1797 – printed in S. Leighton, *History of
Freemasonry in the Province of Antrim* (1938), p. 75

County Armagh

READ

T. G. F. Paterson, 'The County Armagh Volunteers of 1778–93', *UJA*,
3rd series, 4 (1941), pp 101–27; 5 (1942), pp 31–61; 6 (1943),
pp 69–105; 7 (1944), pp 76–95

MILITIA

Militia lists by parish in the barony of Oneilland West, 1793–5 –
D1928/Y/1

Muster rolls, Armagh Militia, 1793–7 – D183/1

Militia pay lists and muster rolls, 1793–1800 – TNA, WO 13/2603,
/2604, /2605, /2606 (PRONI has copies for 1798–1800:
T1115/2A–C and MIC15A/95)

VOLUNTEERS

Miscellaneous notes on County Armagh Volunteers – D3696/A

Roll of First Company of Armagh Volunteers, n.d. – T636/1, p. 339

Documents relating to the Volunteers in County Armagh, especially
the Armagh First Company – Armagh Robinson Library (see
Paterson, 'County Armagh Volunteers', *UJA*, 3rd series, 7 (1944),
for more)

YEOMANRY

Ardress Yeomany Book, *c*. 1796 – D296

Churchill Yeomanry Book, *c*. 1796 – D321/1

Roll of the Armagh corps of Supplementary Yeomanry, 1798–1803 –
T808/15248

County Cavan

READ

T. G. F. Paterson, 'The Volunteer Companies of Ulster, 1778–93'
[Cavan, Donegal] – *Irish Sword*, 7:29 (Winter 1966), pp 308–12

Pádraig Ó Snodaigh, 'Notes on the Volunteers, militia, yeomanry and
Orangemen of County Cavan', *Breifne*, 3:11 (1968), pp 320–39

MILITIA

Militia pay lists and muster rolls, 1794–1800 – TNA, WO 13/2647, /2648, /2649

County Donegal

READ

T. G. F. Paterson, 'The Volunteer Companies of Ulster, 1778–93' [Cavan, Donegal] – *Irish Sword*, 7:29 (Winter 1966), pp 308–12

Pádraig Ó Snodaigh, 'Notes on Volunteers, Militia, Yeomen and Orangemen of Co. Donegal', *Donegal Annual*, 8 (1969), pp 49–73

MILITIA

Papers relating to the Donegal Militia, 1794 onwards – NLI, MS 36,054–36,059

Militia pay lists and muster rolls, 1793–1800 – TNA, WO 13/2751, /2752, /2753 (PRONI has copies for 1799: T1115/3 and MIC15A/96)

YEOMANRY

Return of Yeomanry corps, naming captains, 1803 – D623/A/161/12

County Down

READ

T. G. F. Paterson, 'The Volunteer Companies of Ulster, 1778–93' [Down] – *Irish Sword*, 7:28 (Summer 1966), pp 204–30

MILITIA

Receipts for guns and bayonets to be used in Robert Maxwell's troop of militia, Inch parish, 1746 – D1556/16/15/1–14

Men in the parish of Inch who have subscribed towards finding substitutes for the Militia, 1793: *c.* 150 names – T1023/139

Royal Downshire Militia correspondence and order book, 1799–1804 – D374/1

Royal Downshire Militia courts martial book (recording 228 disciplinary cases), 1793–6 – D374/4

Militia pay lists and muster rolls, 1793–1800 – TNA, WO 13/2776, /2777, /2778, /2779, /2797 (PRONI has copies for 1799–1800: T1115/4A–C and MIC15A/95, /96)

VOLUNTEERS

Minute book for the men of Mourne Volunteer Corps, 1778–92 – T1317

Minute book of the 1st and 2nd Volunteer companies of Newtownards, 1787 – D3030/R/1

Minute books of Newry 1st Volunteer company, 1778–93 – T3202/1A

Minute books of Newry [2nd] Volunteer company, 1778–87 – T3202/2A

Minute book of the Rathfriland Volunteers, 1779 – Ulster Museum,
603–1914 (see Andrew Morrow, 'The Rev. Samuel Barber, A.M., and
the Rathfriland Volunteers', *UJA*, 2nd series, 14 (1908), pp 104–19,
which includes extracts from this minute book, including the names
of *c*. 70 original members of the corps as well as those who joined
subsequently), 15 (1909), pp 29–35, 125–33, 149–57

Names of members of 'Captain Hamilton's company' (presumably the
First Killinchy Volunteers), 1780–81 – MIC583/10

Roll of the Rathfriland Volunteers, 1781, in Rev. Samuel Barber's
common-place book – PHSI

Copy of Volunteer order, County Down, with extract of Volunteer
muster roll, 1782 – T441/1

Miscellaneous notes on County Down Volunteers – D3696/A

YEOMANRY

Signatures of those in Inch parish prepared to form the Inch Infantry,
'having taken the Oath prescribed in the Yeomanry Act', *c*. 1796 –
T1379/1

Signatures in relation to the formation of a Yeomanry corps in Inch
parish, 1797: around 200 names – T1023/144–5

Address by First Company of Lower Iveagh Yeomen, 1798: over 70
names – D607/F/22

Oath and list of names of Ballyculter Supplementary Corps, 1798 –
T1023/153

Killyleagh Yeomanry list, 1798 – D303/3

Names of those proposing to form a cavalry unit to act with the Inch
infantry and to be known as Inch Legion, *c*. 1798: 18 names –
T1023/163

Records relating to the Yeomanry of Dromore – Bodleian Library,
Oxford, MS Percy.c.6, ff 70–75

County Fermanagh

READ

T. G. F. Paterson, 'The Volunteer Companies of Ulster, 1778–93'
[Fermanagh, Monaghan] – *Irish Sword*, 8:31 (Winter 1967), pp 92–7

MILITIA

Various militia lists, 1689–1756 – printed in W. C. Trimble, *The History
of Enniskillen* (3 vols, 1919–21), vol. 3, pp 684–99

Papers about Enniskillen Light Horse commanded by Sir James
Caldwell, 1759–65 – John Rylands Library, Manchester, B 3/23/1–31

Militia pay lists and muster rolls, 1793–1800 – TNA, WO 13/2861,
/2862, /2863 (PRONI has copies for 1793–9: T1115/5A–C and
MIC15A/96)

Officers in the Fermanagh Militia, 1799, printed, with additional notes, in
Séamas Mac Annaidh (ed.), *Fermanagh and 1798* (2000), pp 118–20

YEOMANRY
Yeomanry muster rolls, 1797–1804 – T808/15244
County Fermanagh military, yeomanry and volunteer infantry, 1797–
1834 – T808/15244

County Londonderry

READ
T. G. F. Paterson, 'The Volunteer Companies of Ulster, 1778-93'
[Londonderry] – *Irish Sword*, 8:30 (Summer 1967), pp 23–32

MILITIA
Order from the Commissioners of the Army and Militia for the County
of Londonderry to the constables of the parishes of Magilligan and
Aghanloo that certain named individuals (*c.* 70) appear 'with their
best arms' at Limavady, 1666 – T640/103
Names of men enlisted in the barony of Loughinsholin militia, 1745 –
D1449/11/1
Miscellaneous 18th-century papers about counties Londonderry and
Tyrone militias, including lists of officers – D1449/9
Militia pay lists and muster rolls, 1793–1800 – TNA, WO 13/3039,
/3040, /3041

VOLUNTEERS
Coleraine Volunteers (1st Company), 1776–82 – D4164/A/23,
pp 5597–8

YEOMANRY
Coleraine Yeomanry, 1796 (116 names) – D4164/A/12
Coleraine Yeomanry, 1797 – LA/25/2AA/2
Yeomanry muster rolls, 1797–1804 – T1021/3
Muster roll of Louisa and Muff Cavalry, 1800 – printed in B. Mitchell,
Historic Eglinton (1994), p. 83

County Monaghan

READ
T. G. F. Paterson, 'The Volunteer Companies of Ulster, 1778–93'
[Fermanagh, Monaghan] – *Irish Sword*, 8:31 (Winter 1967), pp 92–7
Pádraig Ó Snodaigh, 'Notes on the Volunteers, militia, yeomanry,
and Orangemen of County Monaghan', *Clogher Record*, 9:2 (1977),
pp 142–66

MILITIA
Militia pay lists and muster rolls, 1793–1800 – TNA, WO 13/3160,
/3161, /3162

County Tyrone

READ

T. G. F. Paterson, 'The Volunteer Companies of Ulster, 1778–93'
[Tyrone] – *Irish Sword*, 8:32 (Summer 1968), pp 210–17

MILITIA

Miscellaneous 18th-century papers about counties Londonderry and
Tyrone militias, including lists of officers – D1449/9
Militia pay lists and muster rolls, 1793–1800 – TNA, WO 13/3264,
/3265, /3266

VOLUNTEERS

Notes on the Gortin Volunteers, 1782 – T808/15114, /15121

YEOMANRY

Muster roll of Cookstown Cavalry and Loughrey Infantry, 1797 –
T808/15242

11.6 Continental armies

Many Irishmen served in the armies of the Continental powers in the
seventeenth and eighteenth centuries. Eoghan Ó hAnnracháin has carried out
extensive research on Irish soldiers who were admitted to the Hôtel Royal des
Invalides in Paris and has published a number of articles providing the names
and brief biographical details of Ulstermen. These include 'Irish veterans at the
Hôtel Royal des Invalides (1692–1769)', *Irish Sword*, 21 (1998–9) and 'Some
early Wild Geese at the Invalides', *Irish Sword*, 22 (2001), as well as a series of
county studies:

Antrim – *Seanchas Ard Mhacha*, 23:2 (2011)
Armagh – *Seanchas Ard Mhacha*, 19:2 (2003)
Cavan – *Breifne*, 10:38 (2002)
Donegal – *Donegal Annual*, 54 (2002)
Down – *Seanchas Ard Mhacha*, 22:2 (2009)
Fermanagh and Monaghan – *Clogher Record*, 19:3 (2005)
Londonderry – *Seanchas Ard Mhacha*, 21:1 (2006)
Tyrone – *Seanchas Ard Mhacha*, 20:1 (2004)

Virtually all of those admitted to the Hôtel Royal des Invalides were Catholics
of Gaelic background. There were, however, some Protestants, such as William
Swan from 'Slivstenn', County Tyrone, admitted in 1786 at the age of 38;
a soldier in Viscount Galmoy's company, he had been injured in Tobago.

12. Newspapers and books

12.1 Eighteenth-century Ulster newspapers

It has long been recognised that newspapers have the potential to be excellent sources of information on family history. The time-consuming nature of using them for research purposes has been a major drawback to exploiting their riches. In recent years, however, digitisation is providing ever greater access to old newspapers, dramatically improving the ease with which they can be used. Two major online providers are the British Newspaper Archive (www.britishnewspaperarchive.co.uk) and the Irish Newspaper Archives (www.irishnewsarchive.com).

A comprehensive record of the availability of Irish newspapers in archives and libraries in the British Isles is contained in the NEWSPLAN database. The repositories include the Public Record Office of Northern Ireland, National Library of Ireland, British Library, universities and public libraries. The information in NEWSPLAN can be accessed via the website of the National Library of Ireland (www.nli.ie/en/catalogues-and-databases-printed-newspapers.aspx) and researchers should refer to this for fuller details of what survives and where it can be accessed. The focus of what follows is primarily the availability of pre-1800 newspapers in the Public Record Office of Northern Ireland and the Linen Hall Library in Belfast. Around a dozen newspapers are known to have been published in Ulster in the eighteenth century, though most of these were fairly short-lived. Two, however, survive to the present day.

Belfast Newsletter, 1737–present
By far the most important newspaper printed in Ulster in the eighteenth century was the publication that first appeared in September 1737 as the *Belfast News-Letter and General Advertiser*. It is still being published today as the *News Letter*, making it the longest continuously published newspaper in Ireland and one of the oldest in the British Isles. Originally a single sheet, the newspaper was increased to four pages in February 1739 and so continued for the rest of the eighteenth century. The original publisher and editor of the *Belfast Newsletter* (as it will be referred to in this book) was Francis Joy, who was of French Huguenot ancestry. Its readership extended far beyond Belfast to include much of Ulster. A volume listing over 2,000 subscribers, 1795–7, is available in PRONI (T2771/4).

The most complete set of eighteenth-century editions of the *Belfast Newsletter* is available in the Linen Hall Library, having been presented to it in 1838 by a member of the Joy family. For the period prior to 1756 the following periods are covered: 1738 (3, 6 October, 12, 22 December) 1739 (January-August); 1740 (February-March); 1746 (June-November, imperfect); 1747 (5 May, 30 October); 1750; 1752 (June-December, imperfect), 1753 (January-September); 1754; and 1755 (January-May, October-December). From 1756 onwards the run is reasonably complete. Both the Linen Hall Library and PRONI have microfilm copies of the surviving editions, though PRONI's set, available under MIC19, is missing the years 1759, 1764 and 1787.

A comprehensive index to the surviving issues of the *Belfast Newsletter* from 1738 to 1800 is available on the web (www.ucs.louisiana.edu/bnl). This index, running to nearly 300,000 entries, includes every significant word and date in the 20,000 surviving pages. In addition there is an index to the pre-1800 birth, marriage and death notices in the Linen Hall Library and at PRONI (T1584).

Belfast Courant, 1745–6
This newspaper was published for a short period in the mid 1740s. No known copies of it survive, though the Ulster Museum's History Department photographic collection has a lantern slide photograph of a page from the edition of 22 April 1746 (Y14137).

Belfast Mercury or Freeman's Chronicle, 1783–7
This newspaper began in August 1783 and ran through to June 1786 when it changed ownership and was renamed the *Belfast Evening Post*, which continued until the autumn of 1787. It can be consulted at PRONI (MIC401).

Northern Star, 1792–7
Appearing in January 1792, the *Northern Star* was published by Belfast's radicals. It continued until soldiers from the Monaghan Militia attacked the print-works in Wilson's Court in May 1797. The *Northern Star* minute book, 1791–3, is in the Rebellion Papers in the National Archives of Ireland (620/15/8/1). See John Gray, 'A tale of two newspapers: the contest between the *Belfast News Letter* and the *Northern Star* in the 1790s' in John Gray and Wesley McCann (eds), *An Uncommon Bookman: Essays in Memory of J .R .R. Adams* (1996). Copies of the *Northern Star* are available in the Linen Hall Library and in PRONI (MIC403). See also *Index to County Down and Lisburn items in the Northern Star, 1792–7*, prepared by J. McCoy and published by the South Eastern Education and Library Board (1992).

Londonderry Journal, 1772–present
Only one other Ulster newspaper founded in the eighteenth century survives to this day. Now called the *Derry Journal*, it was published originally as the

Londonderry Journal, the first issue appearing in 1772. It can be consulted in PRONI (MIC60), though the reel covering June 1773–June 1776 is missing; furthermore, there are no issues for 1797. See also *Irish Genealogical Abstracts from the Londonderry Journal, 1772–84*, edited by Donald Schlegel (1990).

Newry Journal, c. 1761–c. 1776
There were several newspapers named the *Newry Journal* in the 1760s and 1770s: *Carpenter's*, founded *c.* 1761, *Jones's, c.* 1770, and *Stevenson's, c.* 1774. The Linen Hall Library has a copy of the issue of 28 November 1776.

Gordon's Newry Chronicle, 1777–c. 1797
This was the most successful of Newry's newspapers in the late eighteenth century. Microfilm copies of the issues from May 1792 to April 1793 are available in PRONI (MIC56/1). PRONI also holds extracts of births, marriages and deaths taken from *Gordon's Newry Chronicle*, 1778–9 (T699/6) and holds a few issues of the newspaper, including 31 December 1796–4 January 1797, 25–29 March 1797, and 17–20 January 1782 (D3165/1).

Strabane Journal or the General Advertiser, 1771–c. 1801
Strabane was an important centre of printing in the late eighteenth century and the *Strabane Journal* was one of two newspapers known to have been published in the town in that period. Issues from May 1785 to April 1787 are in the Linen Hall Library. A list of notices extracted from the *Strabane Journal*, 1785–7, was published in *DIFHR*, 15 (1992), p. 65. The other eighteenth-century newspaper printed in Strabane was the *Strabane Newsletter*, which ran from *c.* 1788 to *c.* 1810, but no surviving copies of it are believed to exist.

12.2 The range of material in newspapers
Material of genealogical value in newspapers comes in a number of forms. Some of the more helpful of these are summarised below.

Family matters
First of all, there are birth, marriage and death notices. In the eighteenth century few births were announced in newspapers, and those that did appear were generally for families from the upper reaches of society. In any case, these notices tend to be rather uninformative, with the child's name and also that of the mother often omitted. Though they also relate primarily to the upper classes, marriage notices usually provide more information, such as the place of residence of each party and the name of the father of the bride, though the bride herself will often be identified simply as 'Miss ...'. Death notices occasionally provide a brief sketch of the life of the deceased. For example, the following notice appeared in the *Londonderry Journal* on 1 January 1773.

A few days since died in the parish of Ardstraw and County of Tyrone, Robert McCreary aged 106. He came over as a soldier with King William; he had three wives [and] a number of children and grandchildren; he was married to his third wife nine years ago by whom he has left three children, the youngest of which is but two years old. He was very healthy and retained his senses to the last.

Occasionally disgruntled spouses placed notices in newspapers warning readers to exercise caution in dealing with their marriage partner. The following examples are taken from the *Belfast Newsletter* of 23 and 27 March 1750. (Note that the old calendar, where the New Year did not begin until 25 March, was still in operation at this time.)

Whereas Mary Watson, the wife of John Watson of Drumanamo, in the parish of Shankill and county of Armagh, doth refuse to live peaceably with me, and watches all opportunities to waste and embezzle my substance, and will carry on a separate trade against my will and consent. I therefore give this notice that no person from henceforward give her any credit on my account, for I will not pay for any thing she contracts. Given under my hand, this 10th day of March, 1749–50. John Watson.

Whereas I Mary Watson, wife to John Watson of Dromonomoe, near Lurgan, do think it proper in my own vindication, to certify that my said husband has at sundry times abused and turned me out of his house, having four fatherless children, and will not allow me nor them maintenance, so that I am obliged to follow trade on my own credit for their support: and further, that I never have, nor will make use of his credit, neither have I embezzl'd any of his goods; but that he, on the contrary, has drawn part of my substance out of my hands, and has ruined my trade; and very lately forcibly pick'd my pocket of a considerable sum of money. This therefore to give notice to all persons, that I will pay my own debts punctually for all goods I have bought, or will hereafter buy. Given under my hand this 25th day of March, 1750. Mary Watson.

Business
A high proportion of each edition of a newspaper comprised advertisements. These can be of assistance to researchers, particularly if they provide details of local businesses. Often a new business owner would advertise his existence through the press. On the other hand, the bankruptcy of a businessman could also be reported. Lists of names of those involved in the linen industry appear on a regular basis. For example, the *Belfast Newsletter* of 7 July 1758 included a list of registered linen lappers that had been issued by the Linen Board. This comprised 117 names from County Antrim; 129 names from County Armagh; 31 names from County Cavan; 6 names from County Donegal; 106 names

from County Down; 4 names from County Dublin; 1 name from County Fermanagh; 28 names from County Londonderry; 4 names from County Louth; 28 names from County Monaghan; and 30 names from County Tyrone.

Estate management
Advertisements relating to the sale or letting of land can also be of great help to those researching eighteenth-century ancestors. Often such notices included a list of the sitting tenants, perhaps also indicating the size of each farm and the rent that was to be paid. Such news items are particularly helpful if the papers relating to a particular estate are few or perhaps even non-existent. For instance, the pre-1800 records for the O'Neill of Shanes Castle estate in County Antrim were almost entirely destroyed in the early 1800s. However, in the mid eighteenth century the O'Neills made great use of the *Belfast Newsletter* in advertising lands for letting and these advertisements generally listed the sitting tenants. A selection of newspaper items, mainly from the *Belfast Newsletter*, giving details of tenants are listed under the relevant estate in Appendix 2 of this book.

Law and order
Reports of criminal activities, such as murder, theft, arson, etc, featured regularly in newspapers, while accounts of trials can include the names of perpetrators, victims and witnesses, as well as details of convictions. Such news items make up in part the loss of actual court records (see Chapter 11). Lists of those who had subscribed to a reward for information on a crime also make regular appearances in newspapers. Many of these have been listed under the respective parish in Appendix 1. Reports of army deserters were also published in the press and these can include a surprising amount of detail on the men who had absconded. For example, in the *Belfast Newsletter* of 29 June–3 July 1781 the following deserters from Lieut. Bristow's recruiting party of the 46th Regiment of Foot were listed:

> Bernard McKernan, labourer, born in Finvoy parish, County Antrim, aged 19
> John Robson, weaver, born in Ahoghill parish, County Antrim, aged 21
> John Johnson, ferrier, born in Dromara parish, County Down, aged 15
> John Moore, weaver, born in Derryloran parish, County Tyrone, aged 18
> Robert Skillen, labourer, born in Killinchy parish, County Down, aged 18
> Nicholas Maxwell, tinker, born in 'Balyleg' [Ballyclug?] parish, County Antrim, aged 19
> John McIlravey, weaver, born in Clough [Dunaghy] parish, County Antrim, aged 25
> Daniel Morgan, flax-dresser, born in Tamlaght parish, County Londonderry, aged 24

Details of the height, complexion, and colour of eyes and hair were also given for each individual, as well as the place of desertion.

Petitions and declarations

Lengthy petitions and declarations relating to contemporary events often appear in eighteenth-century newspapers. The *Belfast Newsletter* of 16 April 1756 carried a statement from the inhabitants of a district in the Ards peninsula in which they declared:

> We the inhabitants of the parishes of Ballywalter, Ballyhalbert, and St Andrews, and county of Down, whose named are underneath subscribed, roused by a just sense of our apparent danger from our most treacherous enemies the French, have unanimously agreed that we will to the utmost of our power now and ever, support our most gracious King and happy constitution.

This was produced at a time of rising tensions between Britain and France, which would very soon lead to the Seven Years' War. Nearly 80 names were appended to the above declaration. Petitions relating to agrarian unrest in 1763 and again in the early 1770s were published in the *Belfast Newsletter* (see Hearts of Steel memorials in Chapter 5). Declarations of loyalty also appeared in the press in the 1790s when political tensions were particularly high. The *Londonderry Journal* of 9 October, 1792 carried the following announcement:

> Mr Printer we have not without surprise seen certain late publications in your Journal positively asserting that the Roman Catholics of this part have either refused or altogether neglected to subscribe the Declaration of the Catholics of Ireland. Now Mr Printer we are members of that communion; we are inhabitants of this city and its suburbs; we subscribed the Declaration some months ago and have been happy to embrace so public an opportunity of disclaiming and disavowing the odious tenets and principles disclaimed and disavowed in the Declaration – tenets and principles which we never learned in our catechisms, imbibed from our parents nor have they been conveyed to us by public or private instructions. ...
> [Signed by] Law. McShane Jun., Edward Sweeny, And. McShane, Neal Boyle, Jeffry Finlay, John Gillespie, Philip Smith, Pat. Holladay, Pat. Adair, Dan Holladay.

In 1799–1800 many petitions concerning the Act of Union were published in newspapers (see Chapter 5). The published declarations of passengers on transatlantic vessels satisfied with the conduct of the ship's captain may also be mentioned here (see Chapter 13).

12.3 Other newspapers in Ireland and Britain

News about events and happenings in Ulster were reported in newspapers published elsewhere in Ireland and indeed across the Irish Sea in Britain. In addition to online access to these newspapers through the providers noted above, helpful indexes in traditional format include Henry Farrar, *Irish marriages: being an index to the marriages in Walker's Hibernian Magazine, 1771 to 1812* (2 vols, 1897; new edition 1972), and the index to marriages and deaths in *Pue's Occurrences* and the *Dublin Gazette*, 1730–40, in the National Library of Ireland (MS 3197).

Two official publications that researchers should be aware of are the *London Gazette* and the abovementioned *Dublin Gazette*. In November 1665, when the Royal Court was in Oxford, having fled London because of the plague, the first edition of an official government publication was issued. Known initially as the *Oxford Gazette*, it was renamed the *London Gazette* on the return of the Royal Court to the capital. The publication's website (www.thegazette.co.uk) provides access to past issues back to 1665. Occasionally, the *London Gazette* included items relating to Ulster as the following example from the edition of 24 April 1679 demonstrates:

> Dublin, April 9. This morning the Lord Lieutenant signed a Warrant for the Pardon of Lawry, a Scotch man, Minister in the County of Fermanagh and his five Servants, for killing five notorious Tories in that Countrey, wounding two others to death, as is believed, and taking the eighth. The Parson killed three of them with his own hand; and while another of the Tories was going to-draw the Trigger of his Gun to shoot him, his Hand was cut off by one of the Parsons Servants.

In 1705, the *Dublin Gazette* was established and it continued to be published until 1922. It included a broad range of items, including both official announcements and what can be considered more general news. While it may be thought that there will be little for the genealogist in a publication of this nature, occasionally material of real interest will be found. A notice carried in the *Dublin Gazette* of 9 January 1738/9 begins:

> We the under-named William Docherty, David Lindsay, Neal McKay, John McDougale, James Douthitt, John Gardner, and John Morrison, creditors of John Mullin of Coleraine in the County of Londonderry, mason, now a prisoner in the Marshalsea of Coleraine ...

The National Library of Ireland holds the most complete set of issues of the *Dublin Gazette*, while online access is available for certain periods through a number of providers, including the website of the Oireachtas Library & Research Service (www.oireachtas.ie/parliament/about/libraryresearchservice).

12.4 Publications of the seventeenth and eighteenth centuries

Printing in Ulster can be dated to the mid 1690s when two Scots, Patrick Neil and James Blow, settled in Belfast and established a print-works. By 1800 over 160 books had been printed in Ulster, most of them on religious subjects, though some volumes of poetry and history had also appeared. Ulster writers also authored or made contributions to works that were published elsewhere in Ireland and in Britain. Though publications of this era may not be the most obvious place to look for an ancestor, their increasing availability through, among others, Google Books, HathiTrust and Archive.org, means that many volumes published in the seventeenth and eighteenth centuries can now be searched and read online.

Many books published in the eighteenth century included lengthy lists of subscribers. While only representing a fraction of the total population, these subscription lists can be useful in identifying individuals and where they lived. To some extent at least the names of subscribers reflected the personal contacts of the author as well as the publisher's hinterland. For example, a significant proportion of the subscribers to the Newry-published volume, *Odes and elegies, descriptive and sentimental, with The Patriot, a poem*, by John Corry, were from Newry and its vicinity.

A volume of tremendous genealogical value is *The sure way to heaven, being a new volume, such never before published in English on the truths of salvation*, by Rev. James Mathew MacCary, Catholic rector of Carrickfergus and Larne, which was published in 1797. The list of subscribers runs to over 450 names. From the addresses given, it is clear that many were from his own congregation, while others were from his home area in North Antrim. Others were from further afield. Several priests were resident in Lisbon in Portugal and one or more of them may have been colleagues from MacCary's own time there. Over 90 of the subscribers were named MacCary suggesting the author had made full use of his family networks in securing support for his volume. A number of these MacCarys were resident overseas, in Glasgow, Whitehaven and Philadelphia. It is also clear that some of the subscribers to this book were Protestants.

Books to aid travellers through Ireland appeared in increasing numbers from the late eighteenth century onwards. The well known volume *Taylor and Skinner's Maps of the Roads of Ireland, surveyed 1777* (1778) not only shows the major routes through the island, but also names the major houses and their owners. A potentially very helpful book for those researching ancestors in the parish of Ballyculter, County Down, is *An account of the trial of Edward Smyth, late curate of Ballyculter, in the Diocese of Down*, which was published in Dublin in 1777. Smyth had been accused of holding unorthodox religious views and in particular of sympathising with Methodism. The book includes a great deal of information on the inhabitants of Ballyculter, including the names of tenants of Lord Bangor.

Occasionally information of the most unexpected nature can be uncovered. The following paragraphs, which refer to some of the present writer's own ancestors, are taken from *Philosophical Transactions, Giving Some Accompt of the Present Undertakings, Studies, and Labours of the Ingenious in Many Considerable Parts of the World, Volume 48, Part I. For the Year 1753* (London, 1754), pp 1–2.

> Given under my hand this 21 day of October, 1752
> William Henry, D. D.
> Rector of the Parish of Urney.

'An Account of an extraordinary Stream of Wind, which shot thro' Part of the Parishes of Termonomungan and Urney, in the County of Tyrone, on Wednesday October 11, 1752'.

The air for the whole day was serene and calm; sometimes a gentle breeze from the south-east. About four of the clock in the afternoon, the sky seemed to open; and there was a flash of lightning from the south-east. In the space of half an hour after, there was heard thunder, as at a great distance, from the same point. About five the sky was a little overcast with clouds; but the air continued in a dead calm. On a sudden there was heard a violent rustling noise; the sky seemed to open, and emitted a flash of lightning, but no noise of thunder; and a stream of wind instantly ensued, the violence of which nothing could resist.

This stream of wind, so far as can be traced by the effects, arose from a glin called Allgolan, and continued its course for three miles from south-east to north-west. The violent current of it seemed to be confined to a space about 16 feet in breadth, and the whole body of the air in motion did not exceed sixty feet, as may be computed from some of the following particulars, which happened in the little village of Lisnacloon in the parish of Termonomungan, and the edge of the parish of Urney.

At the distance of a mile to the south-east of this village, it cut a line thro' several clamps of turf, which were standing in a bog, and tumbled down all the clamps in this line. Thence it cross'd the river Derge, in the same line, and dash'd up the water with great noise and violence, as was observed by **John Kyle**, who has mills on the river, and several others. Thence, in the same line, and at the space of half a mile, it took the village of Lisnacloon, where there are 13 dwelling-houses, beside officehouses, belonging to farmers and cottagers, scattered irregularly.

1st, It dashed down an hay-stack belonging to **Wm. Montieth**, which was the first object in its way; and stripped intirely twelve feet off the roof of his dwelling-house.

2dly, It knocked down **Henry Carolan's** turf-stack, and carried some of the turf above 300 yards over the cabbins into the fields.

3dly, At the distance of 69 paces, it took **Henry Crawford's** house. Full in the broadside of which, it stripped 59 feet, leaving each of the ends, above and below the stream of air, quite unmoved. This particular points out its utmost breadth. At the back of this house it overset an hay-rick, which stood in its line; but did not ruffle any of the corn-stacks, which stood within a few yards to the north fide.

4. It knocked off eight feet of the roof of **Solomon Folliot's** kiln, which stood in its line.

5. It levelled 55 feet of **David Montieth's** garden-ditch.

6. It levelled, in the same direct line, **Wm Folliot** the younger's hay-stack, which stood south-east from his house.

7. It burst with incredible violence thro' his cowhouse, and cut a passage of 16 feet quite thro' it, and carried some of the ribs of the house before it 400 yards into the field: The rest of the house was a little ruffled. His wife, who was gone into the cowhouse a minute before, was knocked down by one of the ribs falling. She declared, that it was a dead calm the minute before; when, on a sudden, she saw a flash of lightning, and heard and felt the violent storm; but heard no thunder.

Old **William Folliot**, aged 93, who was walking in the field, at the back of the house, was blown down, and grievously bruised. He saw the lightning, but heard no thunder.

Solomon Folliot, being in the same field (but out of the line, in which the stream of wind passed) felt no wind, but heard a mighty rushing noise, and saw the timber, thatch, turf, and dust of the houses, fly by him, at the distance of forty yards. He saw a flight of rooks dashed down in the same field.

In this village are several other inhabited houses, both on the north and south sides of the course of this stream, none of which were in the least ruffled. The air continued still, among these houses; and the inhabitants stood astonished, on seeing the sudden devastation so near them.

After passing this village, the stream was continued in the same line, but with less violence, to a large hill in the parish of Urney, which is called Muckle; and, on the north side of the hill, at the distance of a mile from Lisnacloon, burst open the door of **John Ranking**, a weaver, and broke down a web in his loom. As at this last place it entered a large bog which is extended for three miles, it could be traced no farther.

The time, in which this stream passed thro' the village of Lisnacloon, was about five minutes. It was succeeded immediately by a torrent of rain.

Having been informed of this extraordinary phænomenon, that I might have the more perfect knowledge of all particulars, I took with me two gentlemen, **Dr. Michael Law**, a physician of note, and the reverend **Charles Rhea**, on the 20th instant, from Strabane, and view'd and measur'd on the spot the course of this violent stream, as it appeared by the marks; and at the same time examined minutely the several inhabitants of the village of Lisnacloon, who were eye-witnesses of this fact; and from their united testimonies, and my own ocular observations, collected the above account.

13. Records relating to emigration from Ulster

It is a sad truth that for the great majority of the tens of thousands of people who left Ulster in the seventeenth and eighteenth centuries no documentation survives concerning their departure from these shores. Official records of people leaving Ireland do not exist for this period – and in fact do not begin until 1890. For a number of years in the 1770s there are weekly returns of emigration from ports in England, which give the names and other details of emigrants; some of those departing were originally from Ireland, but unfortunately no specific location is provided for the Irish emigrants (PRONI, MIC462/1, /2). However, information pertaining to emigration from Ulster can be found in a range of sources. It is the purpose of this chapter to highlight some of the collections in archives in Ireland where this information *might* be found. Consideration should also be given to the possibility that there could be relevant records in the country of arrival relating to the immigration of families from Ulster.

To begin with, researchers should be familiar with the Irish Emigration Database (IED) created and maintained by the Mellon Centre for Migration Studies (MCMS) at the Ulster American Folk Park, Omagh, County Tyrone. The IED is a computerised collection of over 30,000 records drawn from a variety of mainly eighteenth- and nineteenth-century sources, including emigrant letters, newspaper articles and shipping advertisements. It can be accessed for free via the DIPPAM website (www.dippam.ac.uk). Some of the records discussed below, especially items from newspapers and correspondence, have been included in this database.

13.1 Background reading

Numerous publications consider emigration from Ulster in the late seventeenth and eighteenth centuries and what follows can only be regarded as a selection of these. R. J. Dickson was the author of what has come to be regarded as the classic study of the movement of people from the north of Ireland to the New World in the eighteenth century; *Ulster Emigration to Colonial America, 1718–1775* (1966) was the first book to be published by the Ulster Historical Foundation and has been reprinted on a regular basis ever since. The most recent reprinting, for the fiftieth anniversary in 2016, includes a new introduction by Paddy Fitzgerald, which evaluates Dickson's work in the light of more recent scholarship.

For the earlier migration story, see Graeme Kirkham, 'Ulster emigration to North America, 1680–1720', published in H. T. Blethen and C. W. Wood (eds), *Ulster and North America: Transatlantic Perspectives on the Scotch-Irish* (1997). Emigration after 1775 is considered in Maldwyn A. Jones, 'Ulster emigration, 1783–1815' in E. R. R. Green (ed.), *Essays in Scotch-Irish History* (1969), pp 46–68; and Trevor Parkhill, 'Between revolution and famine: patterns of emigration from Ulster 1776–1845' in John Gray and Wesley McCann (eds), *An Uncommon Bookman: Essays in Memory of J. R. R. Adams* (1996), pp 59–73.

For an overview of Ireland's migration story, with much of interest for those seeking Ulster ancestors, see Patrick Fitzgerald and Brian Lambkin, *Migration in Irish History, 1607–2007* (2008) and Kerby A. Miller, *Emigrants and Exiles: Ireland and the Irish Exodus to North America* (1985). Also strongly recommended is Patrick Griffin, *The People with No Name: Ireland's Ulster Scots, America's Scots Irish, and the creation of a British Atlantic World, 1689–1764* (2001), which presents a large amount of evidence drawn from sources in Ulster; the American story is focused mainly on Pennsylvania. An analysis of the numbers of immigrants can be found in Marianne S. Wokeck, *Trade in Strangers: The Beginnings of Mass Migration to North America* (1999); see also her article 'Irish immigration to the Delaware Valley before the American Revolution', *PRIA*, 96C (1996), pp 103–35.

Much of the focus of Rankin Sherling's book, *The Invisible Irish: Finding Protestants in the Nineteenth-Century Migrations to America* (2016), is on the migration of Presbyterian ministers from Ulster to America from the late 1600s onwards and a consideration of what that can tell us about the broader story of the transatlantic movement of Presbyterians. Narrower in focus is *Ulster Presbyterians and the Scots Irish Diaspora, 1750–1764* by Benjamin Bankhurst (2013). *Ulster to America: The Scots-Irish Migration Experience 1680–1830*, edited by Warren R. Hofstra (2012), is a fine collection of essays that focuses primarily on the American aspects of the story. A detailed study of one group of mainly Reformed Presbyterian migrants from Ulster is Jean Stephenson, *Scotch-Irish Migration to South Carolina, 1772 (Rev. William Martin and His Five Shiploads of Settlers)* (1971). See also Trevor Parkhill, 'With a little help from their friends: assisted emigration schemes, 1700–1845' in Patrick Duffy and Gerard Moran (eds), *To and From Ireland: Planned Migration Schemes c. 1600–2000* (2004), pp 57–78.

In the early twentieth century several major works on the movement of families and individuals from Ulster to America were published. These included Charles A. Hanna, *The Scotch-Irish, or the Scot in North Britain, North Ireland and North America* (2 vols, 1902); Charles K. Bolton, *Scotch-Irish Pioneers in Ulster and America* (1910); and Henry Jones Ford, *The Scotch-Irish in America*

(1915). It is easy to be critical of earlier works on this subject and to dismiss them at least in part on account of their filio-pietistic tone and lack of objectivity. Nonetheless, much material of interest was gathered which is still of value to researchers today. In America, the most influential mid twentieth-century work on Ulster and America was James G. Leyburn's *The Scotch-Irish: A Social History* (1962).

The above works are concerned overwhelmingly with what became the United States of America. There are comparatively few studies that consider the movement of families from Ulster to Canada prior to 1800. Helpful will be Cecil J. Houston, William J. Smyth, *Irish Emigration and Canadian Settlement: Patterns, Links, and Letters* (1990); Richard K. MacMaster, 'Emigration from Ulster to Prince Edward Island, 1770–1790', *Familia*, 12 (1996), pp 14–32; Donald Harman Akenson, *The Irish in Ontario: A Study in Rural History* (1999); Brendan O'Grady, *Exiles and Islanders: The Irish Settlers of Prince Edward Island* (2004); and Lucille H. Campey, *Atlantic Canada's Irish Immigrants: A Fish and Timber Story* (2016). It should be borne in mind that many people with Ulster roots moved into Canada from America, some through settlement schemes and others as 'United Empire Loyalists' during or after the War of Independence.

Most studies of the Irish in Britain are concerned with the Victorian period and twentieth century. Relatively few look at the period prior to 1800. Those that do include Donald MacRaild, *Irish Immigrants in Modern Britain, 1750–1922* (1999) and Craig Bailey, *Irish London: Middle-class Migration in the Global Eighteenth Century* (2013). With regard to the experiences of the Irish on the European Continent, see Hector McDonnell, *The Wild Geese of the Antrim MacDonnells* (1996); Thomas O'Connor (ed.), *The Irish in Europe, 1580–1815* (2001); Thomas O'Connor, Mary Ann Lyons (eds), *Irish Migrants in Europe after Kinsale, 1602–1820* (2003); Thomas O'Connor, Mary Ann Lyons (eds), *Irish Communities in Early Modern Europe* (2006); and Mary Ann Lyons, Thomas O'Connor (eds), *Strangers to Citizens: The Irish in Europe, 1600–1800* (2008).

13.2 Newspapers and emigration

Occasionally, newspapers can include information on emigrants from Ulster (see Chapter 12). These can take the form of declarations of thanks from passengers for the conduct of the captain of the ship on which they had crossed the Atlantic. Published in the *Belfast Newsletter* on 26 November 1771 is a letter from the passengers of the *Philadelphia* thanking their captain, James Malcom, for his good conduct towards them on their voyage from Belfast to Philadelphia. In particular he 'distributed a greater variety of provisions than was promised; which, with his humane usage, helped much to the rendering the voyage unhurtful and agreeable'. The signatories to the letter, which was penned at Delaware Bay on 4 July 1771, were as follows:

John McCollough	John McClughan	Hugh Ramsey
Thos Alexander	Samuel Irwin	Samuel Colvin
James McHenry	John Storry	Robert Bell
Michael Rankin	Richard McQuon	Wm Meek
Francis Lee	James Campbell	David Fairservise
James Boyd	John Hill	Wm Patterson
Adam Johnston	Thos Hill	David Parkinson
Wm Thompson	Samuel Long	Hans Woods
Daniel Young	James Duncan	John Cairns
John Gallaway	Samuel Duff	John Cooper
James Laird	David Leathin	John Clark
Wm Watson	Wm Hallyday	James Laird
Matthew McCauley	Robert Corry	Samuel Allan
Hugh O'Quin	Alex Boyse	George Willson
Joseph Wilson	Henry Hannah	
Hamilton Potts	Wm Stirling	

Similar announcements were found in the following issues, among others, of the *Belfast Newsletter*:

Buchannan, Newry to New York – 22 Oct. 1765
Britannia, Newry to New York – 21 Nov. 1766
Britannia, Belfast to Savannah – 13 March 1772
Britannia, to Charleston – 1 Sept. 1772
Agnes, Belfast to New Castle, Delaware, 7–10 Sept. 1773
Waddell – 14–17 June 1774

Occasionally, these announcements concerned the passage of ships from America to Ireland. For instance, the *Belfast Newsletter* of 24–27 April 1792 included a notice of thanks to Captain Hugh Makee of the ship *Canton*, which had sailed from Philadelphia. Helpfully, this provides an Ulster address (usually the county) for each of the passengers, all of whom, according to the notice, intended to return to America. Newspapers in America can also include information of this nature. For a good illustration of what may be found, see Gary T. Hawbaker, 'Passenger lists and other references to Irish immigrants from early Wilmington, New Castle County, Delaware newspapers', *Familia*, 23 (2007), pp 65–83.

13.3 Estate papers and emigration

Estate papers (see Chapter 6) can be a very helpful source of information on the departure of people for America. Annotations in rentals, endorsements on the back of leases and updates in lease books can all include references to persons who had emigrated. These may have been the tenants themselves or they could have been persons named as lives in leases. For instance, a lease book for the Caledon estate in County Tyrone contains several references to emigration, including, with regard to the townland of Crievelaght, 'Adam Kennedy went to America in Spring 1772' (D2433/A/5/3). A most unusual inclusion in a lease can be found in that issued to Patrick McGawgey of Fernaghandrum, County Tyrone, in 1769 which included the proviso that the lease was to be surrendered to the lessee's brother, Phelemy McGawgey, if he returned from America (T3381/4/5).

The correspondence between a landlord and his agent can include references to the impact of emigration on an estate. Few documents are as valuable as the one that William Conolly received from his agent, Robert McCausland, in August 1718 which listed the names of tenants in the manor of Limavady and in the Grocers' Company estate (which Conolly leased) who were 'Gon and Going to New England', as well as the new occupiers of their farms. All of these names were published in Richard MacMaster, 'Emigrants to New England from the Conolly estates, 1718', *Journal of Scotch-Irish Studies*, 1 (Spring 2000), pp 8–23.

The correspondence relating to the Abercorn estate in counties Donegal and Tyrone includes numerous letters that make reference to emigration. A few extracts are provided below:

> James Hamilton to earl of Abercorn, 1 March 1771 (D623/A/39/107)
> Adam Murray of Tillywhisker who pays £3 12s. 6d. rent intends goeing
>   to America, and has agreed to sell his holding to Jeremiagh Alcorn his
>   neighbour at £50 who desired I should let him know, if your
>   Lordship consents to it.

> James Hamilton to earl of Abercorn, 5 May 1772 (D623/A/40/32)
> Daniel McMorriss of Gortmellan and William Sproul of Mt Castle,
>   came to me some considderable time ago; Sproul told me he had
>   letters from relations in America, encourageing him to bring over
>   his family with him there, and that he agreed to sell his lease to
>   McMorriss, who resolved fixing his son in it.

> Earl of Abercorn to James Hamilton, 17 Dec. 1783 (D623/A/25/130)
> If Arthur McGonagle is serious, in wishing to go to America, and has a
>   prospect of subsisting there, pay his passage, and give him something
>   in his pocket.

Petitions to landlords can also include details concerning the migration stories of individual tenants. For example, in 1775 William Little of Askermore in the Savile estate, County Tyrone, wrote to his landlord to explain that he had been one of his tenants, but had gone to America to improve his situation in life. Having made his fortune, he decided to return to Ireland, but was shipwrecked in Wales. As a result he had had to borrow money at interest in order to resume farming, but this debt now had to be repaid and Little hoped that Savile would look kindly on him in his predicament (Nottinghamshire Archives, DD/FJ/11/1/7/299).

Some landowners, because of their rank and influence, received letters from those planning to emigrate who were not necessarily of their own tenantry. For example, from December 1790 there is a letter from Robert Hewitt, who was in charge of the Post Office in Ballymena, County Antrim, to Lord Hillsborough, in which he complained that he was unable to support his family on his income from the Post Office (D607/B/286). Hewitt asked for a better position or for assistance to emigrate to Nova Scotia; his brother lived near St John, New Brunswick.

13.4 Church records and emigration

Records kept by religious denominations, especially the Presbyterian churches and Quakers, can include information on emigrants (see Chapter 2 for more on church records). While registers of baptisms, marriages and burials will only very occasionally make reference to persons living overseas – for example, the baptism of a child whose father was abroad – administrative records of the Presbyterian churches can include information on those who had emigrated or were about to do so. For instance, those planning to emigrate often sought a testimonial setting out their credentials as good Presbyterians. This would enable them to join a Presbyterian congregation in America without having to undergo a rigorous examination of their character and religious beliefs. While a request for a testimonial may have been dealt with at congregational level, it could also have been brought to the attention of the local presbytery. A copy of the testimonial – often referred to as a certificate of disjunction – carried by the Ralston family of Ballymoney, County Antrim, to Pennsylvania in 1736 is available in PRONI (T1177/1). This noted that James and Mary Ralston had 'lived within the bounds of this Cong'on from their infancies and behaved themselves christianly, honestly, soberly, inoffensively and free of Scandal known to us'.

Disappointingly few requests for testimonials are recorded in the surviving eighteenth-century minutes of congregations and presbyteries in Ireland. As an example, of what may be found, in December 1718 John Alison came before the presbytery of Strabane desiring a testimonial as he was preparing to emigrate (CR3/26/2/1). Presbytery decided not to issue him with one until just before he was ready to leave, and then only on condition of his continued good behaviour. The records of American churches are worth checking to see if they include references to individuals being received into membership on the basis of testimonials issued in Ireland. For instance, the records of the First Church of Wells, Maine, include an entry from 10 April 1720 that Andrew Symington was received on the recommendation of the presbytery of Strabane, the testimonial having been signed by Nehemiah Donaldson, minister at Derg (Castlederg), County Tyrone.

Material relating to emigration can be found in the records of the Religious Society of Friends (Quakers). Friends intending to emigrate would seek a 'certificate of removal', which, like Presbyterian testimonials noted above, would confirm the good standing of the person in possession of it. For example, in 1729 Olivia McCool was given a certificate of removal by the Men's Meeting at 'Belnacree' (Ballynacree), near Ballymoney, County Antrim. This was addressed to 'Friends in America or Elsewhere' and declared that Mrs McCool was the widow of John McCool and that she intended to 'Transpoarte herself, In Ordr to Settle in America'. The certificate noted that she had 'Beheaved her Self Orderly, liveing In Good Unity & Fellowship with us, and doth Leave this In the Same, being also free from Debt'. For more on the transatlantic movement of Friends, see A. C. Myers, *Immigration of the Irish Quakers into Pennsylvania, 1682–1750* (1902).

13.5 Emigrant's letters/journals

The letters sent back and forth between emigrants and individuals back home form an invaluable resource for those researching Ulster ancestors. The Public Record Office of Northern Ireland has an outstanding collection of letters written by or to Ulster emigrants, which was built up over many decades. Researchers should consult PRONI's eCatalogue to identify material of potential relevance. The Irish Emigration Database (see above) is also worth checking for it includes transcriptions of many of the emigrants' letters in PRONI. Other archives have collections of such letters, while further correspondence remains in private possession.

A remarkable volume is Kerby A. Miller, Arnold Schrier, Bruce D. Boling, David N. Doyle, *Irish Immigrants in the Land of Canaan: Letters and Memoirs from Colonial and Revolutionary America, 1675–1815* (2003). Running to more than 800 pages, it includes a large number of letters and other documents written by Irish immigrants in America, many of whom originated in Ulster. Other studies include E. R. R. Green, 'Ulster emigrants' Letters' in *Essays in Scotch-Irish History* (1969), pp 87–103; and Trevor Parkhill, 'Philadelphia here I come: a study of the letters of Ulster immigrants in Pennsylvania, 1750–1875' in Blethen and Wood's aforementioned volume, *Ulster and North America*, pp 118–33.

Letters sent back from America included information about how families were settling into their new surroundings as well as new developments, such as the appearance of a new generation. On 21 January 1799 Hester Habersham of Savannah, Georgia, wrote to her sister, Helen Lawrence of Coleraine, County Londonderry, with news of her family, (D955/15; MIC516):

> My two daughters are happily married to gentlemen of good fortune. Each of them have two daughters. My eldest daughter Polly Maxwell has had

three sons but has lost them. My daughter Hetty who married a Mr Elliott three years ago has had only these two girls who are still living. My eldest son James is Deputy Collector of this part under his uncle Major John Habersham. Aleck is going to finish his studies, and John my third son now seventeen is at school in Philadelphia.

Letters from home kept emigrants informed of local happenings and family news back in Ulster. The following letter was written by Andrew Gibson of Lisnagirr, Cappagh parish, County Tyrone, to Robert Love, near Gastonia, North Carolina, on 2 June 1788 (T3610/1):

> ... My daughter Martha is married about a year ago and has got a young daughter. Her husband is John Irwin's youngest son (Robert). My son John is just about to take shipping for Philadelphia. He expects to see you perhaps in another season but not having a proper opportunity of a vessel for Carolina, and being afraid of the unknown shores, he thought proper to try first the more northerly part of America. Your brother Hugh and family, sister Eleanor and her family are all well and nothing remarkable among them. ... Among the rest my brothers Andrew and William Gibson with their families intend this year taking shipping at Belfast for Charlestown [South Carolina]. If they come across you your advice to them would surely be necessary.

Occasionally, journals kept by emigrants have survived. For example, PRONI holds a journal kept by John Moore of Carrickfergus, chronicling his journey to and life in America during the 1760s (D3165/2/1). A few extracts are given below:

> On the 15 May [1760] my sister and I proceed from Carrickfergus (our native place) to Larne in order to embark from thence to New York in N. America. Here we remain till Saturday the 24th then in the afternoon went on board the Snow *Cape Breton*, Robert Wilson captain, and sailed with a fair wind and I hope under the guidance and protection of Heaven. 35 passengers on board besides my sister and me. ... We entered New York harbour ... [24 July 1760]. We got along side the wharf. Thanks and praise be unto God who had thus brought us all in safety and health to our intended port after a voyage of 9 weeks, having met with no storms nor difficulties, but as agreeable as it was reasonable to expect. My sister and me received very kindly by my Uncle Robert and his wife. My uncle having some sugar to dispose of, which he brought lately from Jamaica, purposes to go to Albany to sell it, accompanying me so far on my journey to my Uncle James now at Crown Point sutling for the army [25 July 1760]. ... I had the pleasure of seeing Mr Alexander Cobham, a cousin of mine and born and bred in Carrickfergus. He is now purser of a 50 gun ship called the *Norwich* [26 July 1760].

13.6 Other sources of information on emigration

There are many other contemporary sources that can include information on Ulster emigrants, some of which are highlighted elsewhere in this book, e.g. gravestone inscriptions (see Chapter 3), testamentary papers (see Chapter 8), and Freemasons' minute books (see Chapter 16). A somewhat unusual item is a list of Irish people who departed from Bordeaux, France, in the eighteenth century (T3421/1).

A remarkable document relating to emigration from Ulster is the petition bearing the date 26 March 1718, which was addressed to Samuel Shute, the Governor of Massachusetts and New Hampshire. This was signed by over 300 'Inhabitants of the North of Ireland' who expressed 'our sincere and hearty inclination to transport ourselves to that very excellent and renowned plantation' on being given 'suitable encouragement'. The petition, which is now in the custody of the New Hampshire Historial Society, was carried to Boston by Rev. William Boyd of Macosquin. How many of the signatories actually emigrated is not clear – of the nine Presbyterian ministers to sign it, not one left Ireland. The names of the signatories have been printed in Bolton's abovementioned book, *Scotch-Irish Pioneers* (pp 324–30).

Business records also contain information relating to individuals and families of Ulster origin overseas. The commercial aspects of the relationship between Ulster and America are dealt with in great detail by Richard MacMaster in his book, *Scotch-Irish Merchants in Colonial America* (2009); see also his essay, 'James Fulton: a Philadelphia merchant and his customers', *Familia*, 17 (2001), pp 23–34. Another valuable study is T. M. Truxes (ed.), *Letterbook of Greg & Cunningham, 1756–1757: Merchants of New York and Belfast* (2001), which, in addition to the contents of the letters, includes much additional biographical material of interest. The correspondence relating to the linen business of the Greer family of east County Tyrone includes letters from merchants in America, occasionally giving items of news about individuals who had crossed the Atlantic. For example, we find the following news item in a letter of 1769 from the Morton brothers in Philadelphia to Thomas Greer in Dungannon: 'Brother Samuel who was in Charlestown, S. Carolina, tells me that William Johnson who kept a school there, and was from your "parts" has died' (D1044/176).

Passports of this period are exceptionally hard to come by and if they do survive are likely to be in private possession. A rare example is the passport that was issued by a County Antrim justice of the peace to the Stewart family in 1762 (T2439/2). This records that

> William Stewart, Linen Weaver and Ann Stewart, (otherwise Park), his wife, have lived several years in this Town of Clough and said County, with very fair characters and good reputation. Having behaved themselves very honestly and inoffensively, and as they have got encouragement to remove with their family to Pennsylvania, in America, Permit them therefore, the

said William Stewart, and Ann Sewart with their family of children to Pass and Repass from hence to New Castle or any part of His Majesty's British Dominions in America or Europe without let hindrance or molestation, they behaving themselves as becometh good subjects. Given under my Hand and Seal at Clough and said County this, 7th day of July 1762. Geo. Rogers.

See also the article by Mary Jane Kuffner Hirt, 'James Leech's 1763 passport unlocks family migration story: Ulster to Colonial America', *Familia*, 33 (2017), pp 58–102.

13.7 Transportation

The transportation of convicted felons from Ireland to the New World can be traced to the 1650s, though it would appear to have been carried out on an intermittent basis until the eighteenth century. In 1703, the Irish Parliament passed a law that formalised the removal of certain classes of criminals; subsequent legislation over the next decades further regularised the process. The designated ports in Ulster for the transportation of criminals were Belfast and Londonderry. The outbreak of the War of Independence in 1775 interrupted, but did not bring an end to the shipping of convicts to North America, which continued into the 1780s. In all, it is believed that perhaps as many as 11,000 criminals were transported from Ireland between the years 1703 and 1789.

Most official records relating to the transportation of convicts to North America have not survived. However, details concerning over 1,900 convicts ordered to the transported between 1736 and 1743 were published in the *Journals of the House of Commons of the Kingdom of Ireland* (1st edition, vol. 7, pp 562–614). Of these, 334 were from Ulster. This information, including names from every county in Ulster, was published in Frances McDonnell, *Emigrants from Ireland to America, 1735–43. A Transcription of the Report of the Irish House of Commons into Enforced Emigration to America* (1992).

In 1791, the first convicts were transported from Ireland to Australia. The first ship, the *Queen*, set sail in April of that year with 133 male and 22 female convicts on board, including individuals from several Ulster counties who had been found guilty of various crimes. Transportation registers survive from 1836 onwards. Information on those sentenced to transportation prior to that year can be found in the petitions they submitted to the authorities. These petitions can be found in the National Archives of Ireland under Prisoners' Petitions and Cases, and State Prisoners' Petitions (see Chapter 5).

For example, the State Prisoners' Petitions include one from 7 January 1799 concerning the following individuals held prisoner in Enniskillen: John McCann, Michael Reilly, John Tute, Patrick McEnroe, Patrick Grawny and Nicholas Grawny, all of whom were natives of the parish of Munterconnaught, County Cavan. They had been found guilty of having pike heads in order to join the rebellion and they had been sentenced to transportation (SPP/362). See Rena Lohan, 'Sources in the National Archives for research into the transportation of Irish convicts to Australia (1791–1853)', *Irish Archives: Journal of the Irish Society for Archives* (Spring 1996). The surviving records have been digitised as the Ireland-Australia Transportation Database, which can be searched on the website of the National Archives of Ireland (www.nationalarchives.ie).

Newspapers can include reports of individuals sentenced to transportation. For example, the *Belfast Newsletter* of 13 April 1739 carried the following news item:

> At the Assizes at Monaghan ... one Henry Crone of Scarnageragh in said County of Monaghan, who is thought to be worth 700*l.* was tried for several Felonies, and found guilty of one to the Value of 4*s.* 6*d.* upon which the Court order'd him to be forthwith transported to his Majesty's Plantations in America.

For more on the subject of transportation, see Patrick Fitzgerald, 'A sentence to sail: the transportation of Irish convicts and vagrants to Colonial America in the eighteenth century' in Patrick Fitzgerald and Steve Ickringill (eds), *Atlantic Crossroads: Historical Connections between Scotland, Ulster and North America*, (2001), pp 114–29; James Kelly, 'Transportation from Ireland to North America, 1703–1789' in David Dickson and Cormac Ó Gráda (eds), *Refiguring Ireland: Essays in Honour of L. M. Cullen* (2003), pp 112–35; and Bob Reece, *The Origins of Irish Convict Transportation to New South Wales* (2001). For Australia, see also Anne-Maree Whitaker, *Unfinished Revolution: United Irishmen in New South Wales, 1800–1810* (1994) and Liam Kelly, 'Convicts from Leitrim & Cavan transported to Botany Bay in the 1790s', *Breifne*, 9:37 (2001), pp 375–401.

14. Education, charity and hospital records

14.1 Education records

The provision of education in the seventeenth and eighteenth centuries took many forms. The Church of Ireland in each parish was obliged to maintain a school, but this requirement was not always put into practice. Vestry minutes can provide the name of the schoolmaster, but little else is known about the way these schools were conducted. There were many instances of a Presbyterian minister conducting a school in his own home, often with a view to preparing his pupils for a university education. Again, information on these schools is limited. In addition, hundreds of informal 'hedge schools' were conducted across the countryside. Though particularly associated with the Catholic population, 'hedge schools' also provided an education for Protestants. The term derived from the original setting in which many such schools were held, i.e. under the shelter of a hedge, especially during those periods when the prohibition of teaching by anyone not of the Established Church was more strictly enforced.

Royal schools
'Royal' schools were established in a number of Ulster counties in the early 1600s. Dr Michael Quane researched these and other schools in some detail and his papers are on deposit at the National Library of Ireland (see the NLI Sources Catalogue for more details). For example, for Raphoe Royal School, County Donegal, the records include documents relating to the school's estate at Townavilly, near Donegal Town; included is a survey and valuation from 1798 (NLI, MS 17,960). See also Dr Quane's articles, 'Raphoe Royal School', *Donegal Annual*, 7:2 (1967), pp 148–211, and 'Portora Royal School, Enniskillen', *Clogher Record*, 6:3 (1968), pp 500–54.

With regard to pupils educated at the Royal schools, names are listed in the following sources:

Armagh Royal School, County Armagh
Register of the Royal School, Armagh, compiled by Major M. L. Ferrar (1933)

Dungannon Royal School, County Tyrone
Alphabetical list of boys with notes on their careers, names of fathers, etc,
   c. 1648–1920 – MIC29/1

Enniskillen (Portora) Royal School, County Fermanagh
Names of pupils who matriculated at Trinity College Dublin – printed
   in W. C. Trimble, *The History of Enniskillen* (3 vols, 1919–21), vol. 3,
   pp 828–31

Charter schools

In 1734, the Incorporated Society for Promoting English Protestant Working
Schools in Ireland received its charter. The purpose of this society was to provide
the children of the poor with educational opportunities within the context of
the Church of Ireland. By 1750 charter schools had been established at the
following places in Ulster: Ballynahinch, Castlecaulfield, Creggan, Ballycastle,
Killough, Newtowncorry, Ray (Raymoghy) and Strangford. Records relating
to the Incorporated Society are on deposit in the Manuscripts & Archives
Research Library of Trinity College Dublin. Essential reading on these schools
is Kenneth Milne, *The Irish Charter Schools, 1730–1830* (1997).

Belfast Academy

Belfast Academy (now Belfast Royal Academy) was founded by Rev. Dr James
Crombie, minister of First Presbyterian Church, and opened in 1786. The
academy was established along the lines of a Scottish collegiate institution and
drew pupils from far beyond Belfast. The early history of the school is very well
dealt with in A. T. Q. Stewart, *Belfast Royal Academy: The First Century, 1785–
1885* (1985), which includes the names of the original patrons/subscribers in
1785 (pp 102–03). A copy of the first minute book of the academy, covering
the years 1786–1834, is in PRONI (T3101/1). The most notorious incident
in the early history of the school was the 'barring-out' of April 1792. This was
in response to the abolition of the Easter holidays and the curtailing of others.
Seven boarders (C. Auchinleck, I. Stouppe, F. McMinn, C. and P. Rially, A.
Atkinson, J. Verner, J. Arbuckle) and two day pupils (J. Crombie and W.
Cunningham) barricaded themselves into the school with food and firearms.
A number of shots were discharged, but eventually the boys surrendered.

The names of pupils receiving awards for good examination results
occasionally appeared in the *Belfast Newsletter*. For example, the results of the
Christmas examinations of 1796 were published in the *Newsletter* of 19–23
December. Those receiving premiums and certificates included the following:

Writing Greek Prose and Latin Verse – Certificate, W. Curry (Aughnacloy)
Writing Greek Prose – W. Phillips
Logic – Premium, W. Curry (Aughnacloy); certificate for good Answering,
   A. Barklimore (Ballyclare)

Greek – A. Kennedy and G. Tomb

Latin – J. Apsley, G. Tomb, James Stewart (Gracehill), T. J. Smyth (Lisburn), R. Orr (High Street), R. Holmes, J. L. Drummond, Richard Hill (Bellaghy) and G. Law (Dublin)

Coleraine Free School

Records relating to Coleraine Free School include the names of boys 'on the foundation' and 'not on the foundation' in 1731, giving names, ages and when admitted; two of the boys have the comment 'left the school' beside their names; a further bundle of documents survives for the years 1791–6 (D668/N/1). Material relating to the school can also be found in the records of the Irish Society of London (the landlord of Coleraine), which are available on microfilm in PRONI (MIC9A). In his book *Coleraine in Georgian Times* (1977), T. H. Mullin printed a letter of 1728 from the Irish Society concerning the list of pupils provided to it by the master:

> ... Jno. Campbell, menconed in sd list, left the achool above two years ago, that Wm Carlisle, therin also menconed, was a boy imployed by you to look after your cattle, and no scholar, that James O'Boylan therein menconed, is brother to your said late Usher ... and went away about March last, that neither Jno. Wanlock, Gorges Kinkead nor Sam Kinkead was ever schollars there, that James Dunlap left school at Whitsun last and Robert Hendrickson in May last, that Thos Squire hath not been at school since ye 24 June last, so that of all ye persons menconed in your said list or certificate you had no more schollars in July last, no have since, than Alexr McCreely, Jos. Wilson, Robt Church, Wm Church, whom you teach in a back house belonging to yourself ... (p. 42)

Lurgan Free School

Of the few school records surviving from the eighteenth century, the most interesting relate to Lurgan Free School, established by the town's landlords, the Brownlows, to provide an education for the children of the poor in Shankill parish, County Armagh. Among the surviving records of this school is a book giving the names of the pupils who attended as well as the names of their parents, their religious denomination and age. Also provided are comments, such as when the pupil left the school and their educational attainments at the time of doing so. The book covers the period 1786–95 and can be found among the Brownlow Papers in PRONI (D1928/S/1/1). A transcription of the names in this register by Florence Gracey was printed in *DIFHR*, 33 (2010), pp 4–12.

Vaughan Charity School

The Vaughan Charity School was established under the terms of the will of George Vaughan and was located at Tubrid, near Kesh in County Fermanagh. The school opened in 1787 with 30 boys and from that date onwards there is a register of pupils (D433/5). This records the name of the pupil, his age, religion, parish, county, date of certificate, by whom recommended, and a column titled 'Observations'. The last of these contains some interesting information about the fate of the boys. For example, John Finlay, who started the school in 1787, was apprenticed to Felix Magee, a shoemaker in Ardess, Magheraculmoney parish. Neal McCourt, who began his education there in 1788, was 'taken away by his mother rather than let him be ap[prentice]d to a Protestant master'. Other pupils at the school simply ran away. A list of the original pupils at the school and their addresses was published in *Clogher Record*, 12 (1986), p. 178. There is also a minute book of the governors of the school, 1776–1884 (D433/1).

Weymouth School, Carrickmacross
Some papers about Lord Weymouth's school at Carrickmacross, County Monaghan, founded in 1711, are on deposit in PRONI (DIO/4/8/11/1–4). There are no details on eighteenth-century pupils, but the names of teachers and the occupiers of the properties used to endow the school are recorded. See also Michael Quane, 'Viscount Weymouth grammar school, Carrickmacross', *JRSAI*, 86 (1956), pp 27–51.

Other schools
Occasionally, information about a school will turn up in estate correspondence. For instance, in 1797 a school teacher named James Moorhead wrote from Edenderry to Lord Downshire explaining why he was unable to pay his rent and giving his plans for clearing the debt. The letter was signed by several of the parents of his pupils: H. Lambart, Thomas Jackson, Thomas Grattan MD, Robert Jackson, William Baines, and John White (D607/A/544B). As the example of Belfast Academy demonstrated, records relating to schools will also appear in the press. For example, the *Belfast Newsletter* of 19–23 December 1796 includes the results of an examination held in Mr Mawhinny's English School in Belfast. This particular school educated both boys and girls.

University education
Opportunities for higher education were limited. Generally, only the sons of the landed classes, clergy, wealthy merchants and better-off tenant farmers received a university education. Nearly all Ulster Presbyterians who availed of a third level education did so in Scotland, mainly at the University of Glasgow. Records of students at this institution can be found in the following publications:

> *Munimenta Alme Universitatis Glasguensis: Records of the University of Glasgow from Its Foundation Till 1727*, edited by Joseph Robertson and Cosmo Innes (4 vols, 1854)
> *The Matriculation Albums of the University of Glasgow from 1728 to 1858*, transcribed and annotated by W. Innes Addison (1913)

For students at the University of Edinburgh, see *A Catalogue of the Graduates in the Faculties of Arts, Divinity, and Law, of the University of Edinburgh, Since its Foundation* (1858). Those studying medicine tended to do so in Edinburgh; for information on those doing so, see *List of the Graduates in Medicine in the University of Edinburgh from MDCCV to MDCCCLXVI* (1867).

Anglican families in Ulster tended to send their sons to Trinity College Dublin. Lists of students are found in *Alumni Dublinenses: A Register of the Students, Graduates, Professors and Provosts of Trinity College, in the University of Dublin*, edited by George Dames Burtchaell and Thomas Ulick Sadleir (1924). A new edition with a supplement was published in 1935. In addition to the name of the student, the name and occupation of the father and the name of the schoolmaster under whom the youth previously studied are routinely given.

14.2 Charity records

Information on charitable giving can be found in surviving wills and will abstracts. Vestry minutes can also include details of the distribution of charitable donations. For example, the vestry book for Killaghtee parish, County Donegal, gives the names of poor parishioners receiving alms through the provisions of a bequest. A number of charitable bodies were established in the seventeenth and eighteenth centuries in response to particular needs. The records of several of these bodies survive and are discussed below.

Belfast Charitable Society
The Belfast Charitable Society was founded in 1752 to provide assistance to Belfast's poor. Many of Belfast's leading residents were involved in the society. In 1768, a site at the north end of Donegall Street was acquired from the earl of Donegall for 'a Poor House, Infirmary, Hospital, Workhouse or other buildings for charitable purposes'. The foundation stone was laid in 1771 and the Poor House (now Clifton House) opened in 1774. In the 1790s the Belfast Charitable Society opened a burial ground to the rear of the Poor House, which was known as the New Burying Ground and is now generally referred to as Clifton Street Cemetery (or Graveyard). Essential reading is R. W. M. Strain, *Belfast and its Charitable Society: A Story of Urban Social Development* (1961).

The records of the Belfast Charitable Society are held in Clifton House and can be examined with the permission of the Archivist. A summary listing of the society's records can be found in *DIFHR*, 36 (2016), pp 26–8. Early records include:

Minute books beginning in 1752 (gap 1794–1800)
Cash book, 1795–1811
Orderly book, 1775–8
Register of plots sold by Belfast Charitable Society, 1798–1859
Register of plots in the Poor House Burial Ground, 1798–1860

The records of the society are also available on microfilm at the Public Record Office of Northern Ireland (MIC61).

Gill's Charity, Carrickfergus, County Antrim

This charity was established through the will of Henry Gill, an alderman of Carrickfergus, who died in 1761. Its purpose was to provide 'for the annual support and maintenance for ever of fourteen aged men, decayed in their circumstances ... that have been either living or inhabitants of the Town of Carrickfergus'. PRONI holds the minute book (a large leather-bound volume) of the charity (D4064/1; use MIC602). This volume includes records of payments to individuals on the charitable list from 1768 onwards, occasionally with additional information of interest, such as date of death, occupation and residence. When vacancies arose on the charitable list others were elected to fill them. The volume also includes a rent roll of the late Mr Gill's real estate and accounts detailing rent payments from 1761 onwards.

Grove charitable gift, Letterkenny, County Donegal

A manuscript volume among the records of Church of Ireland parish of Conwal details payments to the local poor from a fund established by Thomas Grove of Castle Shannahan in 1677. Grove dedicated 40 shillings a year out of certain lands belonging to him towards the 'relief of the poor inhabitants of Letterkenny ... English inhabitants of ye town to be preferred ... next widows and those undertaking ye charge of orphans'. The money was to be entrusted to the churchwardens of Conwal parish and the names of those benefitting from the fund were to be 'entered in a parchment book'. The surviving volume details payments to individuals from 1678 to 1748 (with gaps). By 'English inhabitants' Grove may have meant members of the Anglican Church (Church of Ireland). Certainly those of Irish background were beneficiaries of the fund, though they may have been converts to the Church of Ireland. A microfilm copy of the volume is in the National Library of Ireland (n.4704, p.4692). The names have been transcribed and published: J. C. T. McDonagh, 'A seventeenth century Letterkenny manuscript, containing A true copy of the Deed of Gift to the poor of the parish of Conwall, by Thomas Grove, dated May, 1695', *Donegal Annual*, 3:2 (1956), pp 139–42.

Hutchinson charitable fund

'The First Report of Francis Dobbs ... of the Names and Degrees of Kindred of such Claimants as have established their right before him, to a share of said Fund' is in many ways an astonishing document for its level of detail (MIC123/1). It concerns a charitable fund established under the will of Archibald Hutchinson. Hutchinson, who was from Stranocum in Ballymoney parish, County Antrim, died in London in 1740 and left a substantial sum of money to invest in land for the support of members of his wider family. For various reasons there was a lengthy delay in implementing the full provisions of his will. When eventually, in 1790, the trustees advertised for claimants over 18,000 people responded. This led to the passing of *An Act to Enable Certain Trustees to Execute the Charitable Intentions Expressed: In the Will of Archibald Hutchinson, of the Middle Temple, London, Esquire, Deceased* in the Irish Parliament, which limited the degree of kinship of claimants and stipulated that they should receive a lump sum rather than an annuity.

Francis Dobbs, the barrister appointed to investigate the claims, prepared a lengthy report running to over 100 pages, which seems to have been issued by February 1797. Included in this report are details of the testator's relatives, on both the paternal and maternal sides, to the sixth degree of kindred. Names and relationships are given, though not dates and only occasionally places of residence. Dobbs also included brief family histories of both the paternal and maternal lines as well as a section on rejected claims. Anyone researching a family in north County Antrim should consider this source, though it is of wider relevance as well. A copy of Hutchinson's will is in PRONI (T1531/4). J. A. I. McCurdy, *The Hutchinson Bequest* (2001) includes a transcription of the report by Dobbs and an index of surnames.

Southwell Charity, Downpatrick, County Down
This charity was founded by Edward Southwell, the landlord of Downpatrick, in 1733. It was originally designed to provide support for six old men and six old women and instruction for 12 poor girls and 12 poor boys. In addition, eight orphan boys and eight orphan girls were to be provided with accommodation and an education. The records include a book giving names, etc of men and women taken into almshouses and boys and girls admitted to schools and to trade on leaving, 1780–1844, though this includes only a few names of individuals received prior to 1800, all female (D2961/2/2/1).

Jackson Trust, Forkhill, County Armagh
The Jackson Trust was established through the will of Richard Jackson (1722–87), the conscientious owner of the Forkill estate in south County Armagh. His will proved complex and required an act of parliament and the appointment of a board of trustees to fulfil its instructions. The records relating to the Trust include:

Bound volume entitled 'First Minutes of Proceedings of the Trustees of Charitable Donations of Richard Jackson of Forkhill, Esq.', 1789–1830 – D4338/1/1/1

Bound volume of accounts relating to the Education Fund, 1791–1822 – D4338/3/2/1

Bound volume of accounts relating to the Old Farmers Fund, 1791–1822 – D4338/3/3/1

The minutes include the names of 'old men … selected for the objects of the charity' in particular years and the names of boys to be apprenticed to suitable masters. The Education Fund accounts record, *inter alia*, payments to schoolmasters and to masons and other tradesmen for work on school-houses.

14.3 Hospital records

For a general look at medical provision in Ireland in this period, see James Kelly, Fiona Clark (eds), *Ireland and Medicine in the Seventeenth and Eighteenth Centuries* (2013). Prior to the second half of the eighteenth century medical provision in Ulster was extremely limited. A major step forward occurred in 1766 when the Irish Parliament passed *An Act for Erecting and Establishing Publick Infirmaries or Hospitals in this Kingdom*. As a result of this legislation a number of hospitals were established in Ireland, including several in Ulster. The available records are listed below.

> *County Antrim Infirmary*
> Resolutions and minutes of the Governors, 1767–1854 – HOS/7/3/1/A/1
> Extracts from the minute books of the Standing Committee of the Board of Governors, 1767–1805 – HOS/7/3/1/B/1
>
> *County Armagh Infirmary*
> Minutes of the Governors beginning in 1767 – Armagh County Museum
> See D. R. M. Weatherup, 'The foundation of the Armagh County Infirmary' in A. J. Hughes and W. Nolan (eds), *Armagh: History and Society* (2001), pp 713–43
>
> *County Down Infirmary*
> Printed list of subscribers to the County Down Infirmary, 1770 – D1556/16/11
> Minutes of meetings of the Governors, 1767–1848 – HOS/14/2/1/A/1
> See *The Bi-Centenary of the Down County Infirmary (now Downe Hospital), 1767–1967* (1967)

In addition to the Governors, those named in the minutes tend to be members of staff and suppliers of goods and services. On 6 November 1769, the Governors of the Antrim Infirmary agreed that Catherine Cunningham, a maidservant, should be paid half a guinea 'as a reward for her extraordinary care & trouble after the death of the late housekeeper'. The minutes of the Down Infirmary of 4 June 1792 include the following statement:

> Resolved that thanks of this Board be given to Mrs Johnston for her very great attention, care and attendance during the course of twenty-four years to the patients in this House and faithfull discharge of her trust, and that the governors lament very much of so good a Housekeeper, and as a token

of their approbation of her conduct they request her to receive and accept with her next payment a present of Twenty Guineas.

Only rarely are patients mentioned. For example, in the minutes of the Antrim Infirmary of 3 November 1767 it was agreed that Dorothy Johnson, 'late a patient in the Infirmary', should be employed as a servant in the institution. Rules and regulations are also noted in the minutes. In 1768, the rules of the Down Infirmary included: 'No patient shall smoke tobacco in the Infirmary unless the Physician shall judge it proper or necessary for his or her health, and even in that case, they should do it in the kitchen only.'

Medical practitioners
Biographical information on doctors and surgeons can be found in R. S. J. Clarke, *A Directory of Ulster Doctors (who qualified before 1901)* (2 vols, 2013). An example of the type of information provided in this source is given below.

> HAMILTON, WILLIAM (fl c 1765–90), Naval Medical Service, Strabane, county Tyrone, and Londonderry; son of Thomas Hamilton of Gortavea, county Tyrone; joined the Naval Medical Service, serving in the West Indies but resigned c 1769 because of ill health; surgeon in Gortavea, Strabane, 'earning a precarious living by inoculating children against smallpox'; applied for the post of surgeon in Lifford Hospital in 1774 and 1779 but was unsuccessful; apothecary in Londonderry c 1782 and wrote to the Earl of Abercorn in November 1783 expressing a desire to 'settle with his brother in Gortavea to keep some medicines and practise as surgeon'; did not move and was still living and working there in March 1786.

Records kept by individual medical practitioners in this period are few in number. A rare example is the medical case book of 1763 of Dr Marcus Boyd relating to the Limavady area of County Londonderry, which gives the names and ages of patients, details of their symptoms and treatment, and progress of their illnesses (T3657/1).

Information on apothecaries in the late eighteenth century can be found in a series of returns made to the British Parliament in 1829. These returns are:

> *A return of the names of each person in each year since the 24th of June 1791, who has been examined by the governor and directors of the Apothecaries' Hall in Dublin and who has received a certificate of his proper qualification to become an apprentice to learn the business of an apothecary.*

> *A return of the name of each person in each year since the 24th June 1791, who has been examined by the governor and directors of the Apothecaries' Hall in Dublin, and who has received a certificate of his proper qualification to become an assistant or journeyman to the business of an apothecary.*

A return of the name of each person in each year since the 24th June 1791, who has been examined by, and received a certificate from the governor and director of the Apothecaries' Hall in Dublin, of his qualification to open a shop and practise as an apothecary in Ireland.

A return of the number of prosecutions, the name of the person prosecuted, the date of each prosecution, together with the offence committed against the Act 31 Geo. III from the 24th June 1791, until the 25 March 1829; also the number of penalties, with the name of the person from whom recovered, and the date of recovery of said penalty.

15. Business and occupation records

15.1 The range of business records

Business records from this period are comparatively few in number and vary considerably in their usefulness for genealogical research. Some will contain detailed listings of customers and clients, while others may be a series of unintelligible digits. Very helpfully, some of the volumes kept by merchants include an index of customers' names. Many of the surviving records relate to the linen industry and researchers should refer to the writings of W. H. Crawford in particular for background information on it. See especially his volumes *The Handloom Weavers and the Ulster Linen Industry* (1994), and *The Impact of the Domestic Linen Industry in Ulster* (2005), the latter being a collection of his most important essays on the subject.

While many business records are very local in focus, others relate to trade conducted beyond Ulster, not only with the rest of Ireland and Britain, but also with Continental Europe and North America including the Caribbean. On the trading links between Ulster and North America, see Thomas M. Truxes, *Irish-American Trade, 1660–1783* (2004) and Richard MacMaster, *Scotch-Irish Merchants in Colonial America* (2009).

Early business records include the letter-books of a number of Belfast merchants in the second half of the seventeenth century, among them George McCartney and David Butle. For more on these individuals, see Jean Agnew, *Belfast Merchant Families in the Seventeenth Century* (1996). From the eighteenth century there are extensive records relating to the business of Daniel Mussenden and his son William. These include indentures of apprenticeship, promissory notes, drafts, receipts, and correspondence, reflecting the Mussendens' extensive trading links, with Britain, Europe and North America. A couple of individual records of particular interest are: a bond of obligation of John Fowler, master of the Bruerton of Liverpool, to Daniel Mussenden of Belfast, to deliver servants to Philadelphia, giving the names of 32 servants, 1729 (D354/477); and a deposition made in 1738 by Malcolm McNeal of Rathlin Island, master of the brig *Antrim*, on behalf of James McDonnell, Ballypatrick, owner of the *Antrim* (D354/1011). The latter takes the form of a protest against Robert Miller, Coleraine, Robert Byrtt, sovereign of Belfast, William Chorley, waterbailiff of Belfast, and Richard Finley, a town sergeant of Belfast, relating to the arrest of the *Antrim* on its entry into Belfast Lough.

While the records listed below are nearly all of private businesses, documentation relating to a number of other bodies, such as the Belfast Chamber of Commerce and the Lagan Navigation, has also been included here. A few farm account books survive and these have also been incorporated into this summary listing. Records relating to trade guilds in Ulster are virtually non-existent. However, from the late eighteenth century there is the minute book of the Belfast Journeymen Cabinet Makers, which is said to be 'the oldest surviving building trade union document in the British Isles' (see J. W. Boyle, *The Irish Labor Movement in the Nineteenth Century* (1988), p. 11). The union was founded in 1788 and had 20 members originally. The minute book names the officers and members of the committee and gives the names of those admitted to the union (D1050/15/1).

15.2 Business records relating to Ulster, 1600–1800

Adams, Chequer Hall, Ballyweaney, County Antrim
Bundle of linen and household accounts of John Adams, *c.* 1780–*c.* 1810 – D1518/2/2
Cash book of John Adams, Chequer Hall, Ballyweaney, linen merchant (bought yarn to give out to weavers in their cottages), 1782–6 – D1518/2/3
Cash account book, John Adams, Ballyweaney, 1789–1803 – D1518/2/4

Alexander, Limavady, County Londonderry
Bonds of John and Lesley Alexander, 1757–64 and 1801; accounts re linen trade, bills of exchange and wines and spirits, 1764–7 – D1491/1

Andrews, Comber, County Down
Records of the Andrews family, linen merchants, bleachers and millers, Comber, including:
Letter books, 1771–6, 1776–83, 1797–1802 – T3124/A/1–3
Day books, 1756–62, 1770–74, 1772–5, 1785–7 – T3124/B/1–4
Account book, 1763–5 – T3124/C/1
Invoice books, 1771–4, 1780–85 – T3124/C/2, /4
Ledger books, 1776–8, 1786–91 – T3124/C/3, /5
For more on this family and business, see Sydney Andrews, *Nine Generations: A History of the Andrews Family, Millers of Comber*, edited by J. Burls (1958)

Anon., Drumlee, County Down
Rent account book for Drumlee, County Down, 1766–74 – T1550/1

Atkinson, Belfast and Moy, County Tyrone
Account book: part I (pp 1–147A) is a day book of a Belfast wine and spirit merchant [T. and M. Atkinson?], 1792–3 (these pages were originally sewn together); part II (pp 1–157) is a ledger of Robert Atkinson, linen merchant, Green Hall, Moy, 1798–1806 (this section starts about the centre of the book) – D1721/1

Ballycastle merchant (anon.), County Antrim
Account book of a Ballycastle merchant, 1751–4 – T1044

Bartley, Ballybay, County Monaghan
Volume containing, *inter alia*, some rough and sparse accounts of a linen draper, 1790–95, probably kept by George Bartley of Ballybay; also some scattered domestic accounts of the Bartley family, 1770–79 – D178/1

Belfast Journeymen Cabinet Makers
Minute Book of the Belfast Journeymen Cabinet Makers, 1788–1832: names officers and committee, names of those admitted and those to whom tickets were issued – D1050/15/1

Belfast Chamber of Commerce
The Belfast Chamber of Commerce was founded in 1783 and the first minute book of General and Council meetings is available for 1783–94, though the opening pages are missing (D1857/1/AB/1). George Chambers' book, *Faces of Change: The Belfast and Northern Ireland Chambers of Commerce and Industry, 1783–1983* (1983), includes a great deal of biographical information on the 'founding fathers' of the Chamber of Commerce.

Belfast Harbour
Nineteenth-century copy of customs register of ships entering the port of Belfast: includes the names of ships, their ports of departure, date of arrival in Belfast, masters' names, details of cargoes, etc, 1682–7 – HAR/1/G/1/13/1 (entry from 11 May 1685 concerning Jean Grey, Jennett Stephenson, Margarett Miller, servants from Scotland, who had been issued with a pass)

Blair, Newry, County Down
Letters from Mrs Blair, Newry, to her son James Blair, St Eustatius, West Indies, describing local affairs in Newry, difficulties with tenants on her lands at Baven and issues relating to her business as a shopkeeper in Newry; also accounts, bills of exchange, letters, etc concerning the activities of James Blair as a general merchant in the West Indies (1780–1795), 1773–96 – D717

Black, Belfast and Bordeaux
Extensive collections of letters from the 1670s onwards relating to the business of the Black family of Belfast and Bordeaux – D719, D1950, D4457

Bradshaw, Dublin and Milecross, County Down
Volume containing the out-correspondence, accounts and memoranda of Robert Bradshaw of Dublin and Milecross near Newtownards; the early years provide details of Bradshaw's interest in the flaxseed trade but eventually the entries become concerned exclusively with Quaker trust affairs, 1784–92 – MIC99/1

Brady, Omagh, County Tyrone
Farm and household account book of John Brady, Omagh area, 1757–66 – T2748/1

Brakinridge, Ballykeel, County Down
Rent and farm account book of the Brakinridge family, Ballykeel [Dromore parish?], *c.* 1779 – T1344/2

Brice, Belfast
Account book of Edward Brice, merchant and shipowner, *c.* 1686–1696 – D1556/16/7

Butle, Belfast
Out-letter book of David Butle, merchant and shipowner, 1696–1703 – D1449/13/1

Canavan, Dunsilly, County Antrim
Cash account book of the Canavan family, Dunsilly, Antrim, 1765–1832 – T2188/1

Casement, Sheepland Beg, County Down
Farm account book/diary recording the management of a farm owned by Robert and William Casement in the townland of Sheepland Beg, Dunsfort parish, 1799–1833: it is mainly concerned with recording the names, wages and terms of employment of a series of labourers, both regular and occasional – D3034/1

Castlewellan merchant (anon), County Down
Day book of a merchant in Castlewellan, dealing mainly in tobacco, but also in wines, spirits and linen; also includes details of household expenses, the purchase of materials for a bleach green, etc, 1791–5 – D1202/1

Clark, Upperlands, County Londonderry
Records relating to William Clark & Sons Ltd, Upperlands, including miscellaneous 18th-century documents – MIC638/1
For more on this family and business, see Wallace Clark, *Linen on the Green: An Irish Mill Village, 1730–2008* (1982, 3rd ed. 2008)

Courtenay, Benburb, County Tyrone
Domestic, farm and rent account book of the Courtenay family, Benburb area, 1776–1806 – D1179/1

Cowan, Londonderry
Trading accounts and receipts belonging to Robert Cowan, including some household accounts, and a list of goods shipped back to Mrs Mary Cowan, Londonderry (1727), 1705–29 – D654/B/1/5M

Erskine, Dunaverney, County Antrim
Account book of William Askin (Erskine) Dunaverney, Ballymoney: includes genealogical notes on the Erskine family as well as accounts of the selling and purchase of yarn, livestock, potatoes and payments to hired servants, etc, *c.* 1800 – T2082/1

Faulkner, Gortalowry and Wellbrook, County Tyrone
Around 100 letters mainly from Hugh Faulkner, Gortalowry, Wellbrook and Savile
Park, to Samuel Faulkner, Dublin, about various matters, including the building
of a bleach green and mill; linen industry; estate business, leases, rents, etc;
finances; also includes family news and local events concerning the Cookstown
and Dungannon areas; also household accounts, 1764–90 – MIC21/1
Cloth account of Hugh Faulkner, Gortalowry, recording transactions with various
people and with firms in London, 1762–3 – MIC21/2
Typescript history of the Faulkner family, entitled 'The Praying Angel, by Amy
Monahan, written *c*. 1960 – MIC21/2
For more on this family and business, see Amy Monahan, 'An eighteenth century
family linen business: the Faulkners of Wellbrook, Cookstown, Co. Tyrone',
Ulster Folklife, 9 (1963).

Ferguson, Belfast
Account book of James Ferguson, Belfast, linen merchant, 1771–83 – D468/1

Ferguson, Londonderry
Outward letter books of Andrew Ferguson, Londonderry, general merchant, 1775–
80, 1783–7 – D1130/1–2 (MIC460/1)

Greer, Rhone Hill and Tullylagan, County Tyrone
Over 800 18th-century letters relating to the Greer family, many of them
concerning the linen industry – D1044
Thomas Greer's market book covering the purchase of cloth in the markets of
Dungannon, Stewartstown, Caledon, Moneymore, Monaghan and Cootehill,
1758–9; contains over 700 names of sellers – T1127/4. For a discussion of this
document, see W. H. Crawford, 'The market book of Thomas Greer, a
Dungannon linendraper 1758–9', *Ulster Folklife*, 13 (1967), pp 54–60.
Thomas Greer's account book giving miscellaneous customers accounts, 1785–
1840 – D1044/872B

Greg & Cunningham, Belfast
T. M. Truxes (ed.), *Letterbook of Greg & Cunningham, 1756–1757: Merchants of
New York and Belfast* (2001): in addition to the contents of the letters, this volume
includes much additional biographical material

Holmes, Benburb, County Tyrone
Farm account and stock book, possibly kept by a Holmes family: includes details
of wages paid and money lent to various people etc, Benburb area, *c*. 1780–*c*. 1821
– D1782/3

Lagan Navigation
In 1753, *An Act for making the River Lagan navigable and opening a Passage by Water
between Lough Neagh and the Town of Belfast* was passed in the Irish Parliament. By
the mid 1760s the River Lagan had been made navigable to a point beyond

Lisburn. In 1779, the 'Company of Undertakers of the Lagan Navigation' was established and in late 1793 Lough Neagh was reached. The Lagan Navigation records are a rich source of information for those associated with this waterway. The minute book includes such entries as: 'Willm Stewart & Jas Agnew recommend Matw Burke as Lock Keeper for No. 7 and will be security for his good behaviour' (11 Nov. 1793).

Map of the Lagan Navigation, naming proprietors of mills along the River Lagan, 1768 – T1129/248; T2125/20/44

Ledger of the Lagan Navigation, 1792–1810: mainly financial in detail – COM/1/3/1/1

Lagan Navigation minute book, 1793–1811, containing minutes, copies of letters, and an account of spirits distilled and of ale and beer brewed in the Lagan district, 1789–95, etc – COM/1/1/1

Letter-book of the secretary to the Lagan Navigation and Ulster Canal Companies, 1809–26, with nine folios of shipping invoices recording the names of merchants and masters of vessels for 1799–1801 at the back of the volume – COM/1/2/1

Debentures of Lagan Navigation stock and documents of transfer, 1777–1825 – COM/1/5/6

Debentures of Lagan Navigation stock, 1777–1938 – COM/1/5/9

Lurgan weaver, County Armagh
Weaver's cash book, possibly Lurgan, County Armagh, *c.* 1795 – D1673/1/1

Martin, Ballooly, County Down
James Martin's farm workers' wages book, Ballooly, 1779–1817 – D2722/1

McCartney, Belfast
Letter-books of 'Black' George McCartney, merchant and shipowner, 1661–8, 1679–81 – MIC19/1–2 (originals in the Linen Hall Library)

Letter-book of Isaac McCartney (son of above), merchant and shipowner, 1704–06 – D501/1 (MIC459/1)

McCance, Ballyclare, County Antrim
Account book of William McCance, linen merchant, Ballyclare, 1796–1805 – D823/1–2

McClenaghan, Newry, County Down
Volume recording transactions with merchants to whom goods were shipped and from whom materials were imported, and also with local businessmen who purchased the goods on arrival in Newry, 1797–1824 – D3025/A/7/1 (see also MIC492)

McCrea, Foyle Valley
Cash book of William McCrea, salaried linen buyer, operating in the markets of Strabane, Newtownstewart, Omagh and Londonderry, 1765–80 – D664/O/1 (see also **Orr, Aghadowey** below)

McGildowney, Ballycastle, County Antrim
Letters and accounts relating to the Ballycastle colliery, 1778–82 – D1375/3/29
Letters and accounts between Edmund and John McGildowney, some relating to the colliery and others to additional commercial activities, including two sloops which seem to have been fishing ships, 1783–97 – D1375/3/31

McHendry, Sixtowns, County Londonderry
Account book of the McHendry family, particularly Thomas, relating to their tanyard business in Sixtowns, Draperstown, 1797–1883 – T3232/1

McNeill
Account book of a shoe-maker [William Mc Neill], 1776–84 – D1518/4/1

Mitchell, Ballymena, County Antrim
Cash book of Alexander Mitchell, hardware merchant, Ballymena: accounts with various people mainly in the Ballymena area, but also some in Belfast, Dublin and other parts of Ireland, 1776–1817: index of customers – D1364/G/1
Day book of Alexander Mitchell, 1783–7 (with some entries up to 1797) – D1364/G/3
For a discussion of these sources, see W. H. Crawford, 'A Ballymena business in the late eighteenth century' in J. Gray and W. McCann (eds), *An Uncommon Bookman: Essays in Memory of J. R. R. Adams* (1996), pp 23–33.

Montgomery, Inniskeel, County Donegal
Account book compiled at Inniskeel [Inishkeel] by a Donegal merchant/agent, possibly named Montgomery, [1770]–1800; mainly relating to Donegal, but some references to Swanlinbar and Cavan Town, County Cavan; includes an alphabetical index of clients and customers – TCD, MS 10,713

Mussenden, Belfast
Extensive 18th-century records relating to the business of Daniel Mussenden and his son William, including indentures of apprenticeship, promissory notes, drafts, receipts, etc – D354
Two pages from an account book of 'Mussenden, Bateson & Co.' Belfast, wine and spirit merchants, 1726–7 – T2687/1

Orr, Aghadowey, County Londonderry
Ledger kept by Alexander Orr, Landmore, Aghadowey, linen merchant, 1784–*c.* 1807 – D2356/1
Copy letter book kept by Alexander Orr, Landmore, concerning his business as a linen buyer and bleacher with occasional mentions of personal matters, 1797–9 – D664/O/2A
Notebook containing details of money lent (with payment of interest and sometimes repayment of the loan) begun by one of the Orr family of Gorton in 1782 and carried on by Alexander Orr until 1828 – D664/O/16
Cash book containing the accounts of William McCrea, a salaried linen buyer operating in the markets of the North-West, 1765–80 (see **McCrea, Foyle Valley**

above); also includes accounts of bleaching expenses in Gortan and Mullahinch greens, Aghadowey parish, 1788–1792, and some copy letters relating to the Orr family – D664/O/1

Orr, Glasdrumman, County Down
Farm and household account book of the Orr family, Glasdrumman, Annalong: includes details of the hire of domestic and farm labour and household accounts, 1731–1861 – T3301/1

Rea, Lifford, County Donegal
Copy out-letter book of John Rea of Lifford, relating to his business interests in Jamaica and also to the wine trade, 1778–80 and 1787 – D642/A/2

Reynolds, Ballymoney, County Antrim
Flyleaf pages from a farm account book of the Reynolds family of Drumafevy [Drumnafivey?], Ballymoney, *c.* 1800 – D1013/2/1

Richardson, Lisburn, County Antrim
Cash account book, recording, *inter alia*, wages paid, of the linen firm of the Richardsons of Lisburn, 1784–9 – MIC120/1

Ross, Ballymoney, County Antrim
Ledger of John Ross, Ballymoney, merchant, early 18th century – Ballymoney Museum

Smyly, Strabane, County Tyrone
Cash book relating to Robert Smyly, Camus, Strabane, 1762–74 – D1075/1

Thom(p)son, Belfast
Copy out-letter book of a discount company in Belfast; letters are signed initially by Peter Golan and Robert Thompson, and then by B. Maziere and Robert Thomson, 1772–85 – D3439/2
Copy out-letter book of a discount company in Belfast; letters are signed initially by Robert Thomson & Co., then by Gilbert or McIlveen & Co., and later by John Turnley, 1798–1814 – D3439/3

Watt, Ramelton, County Donegal
Correspondence relating to the Watt family of Ramelton, including material concerning their trade with the West Indies, 1790–1850 – MIC135/1

15.3 Trade tokens

Trade tokens were used by merchants and were especially popular for a period in the second half of the seventeenth century. The number of trade tokens surviving for a town has been used an indicator of the relative size of that settlement's merchant community. In Ulster the largest number of surviving tokens for the period 1653–79 is for Belfast with 26 issuers, followed by Derry with 18. There are 11–14 tokens for Antrim, Coleraine and Lisburn. Between four and seven tokens survive for Armagh, Ballymoney, Ballymena, Carrickfergus,

Downpatrick, Dromore, Enniskillen, Killyleagh, Newry and Strabane. Typically, the tokens include the name of the merchant and the town in which he was based. Many of them also include the year they were issued and sometimes the family arms will appear. While many of them list the occupation of the issuer simply as merchant, other tokens are more specific. For example, Matthew Bethell of Antrim was 'POSTMSTR' (Postmaster), while Robart Young of the same place was a dyer. Listings of trade tokens relating to Ulster can be found in the following works:

G. Benn, 'Notices of local tokens issued in Ulster', *UJA*, 1st series, 2 (1854), pp 29–31, 230–32; 3 (1855), pp 172–5; 4 (1856), pp 239–41

G. C. Williamson, *Trade Tokens issued in the Seventeenth Century* (3 vols, 1889–91; reprinted 1967)

R. A. S. Macalister, 'A catalogue of the Irish traders' tokens in the collection of the Royal Irish Academy', *PRIA*, 40C (1931), pp 19–185

Peter Seaby, *Coins and Tokens of Ireland* (1970)

Brian de Breffny, 'Businessmen who issued tokens in Ireland, 1653–79', *Irish Ancestor*, 10:1 (1978), pp 51–60

15.4 Occupations

Information on occupations can be found in many different places and what follows is only a sample of these. The importance of newspapers is again emphasised. Of particular help are the fascicles prepared for a number of Ulster towns in the *Irish Historic Towns Atlas* series. These include:

Armagh (Catherine McCullough, W. H. Crawford, 2005)

Belfast, part I, to 1840 (Raymond Gillespie, Stephen Royle, 2003)

Carrickfergus (Philip Robinson, 1986)

Derry-Londonderry (Avril Thomas, 2005)

Downpatrick (R. H. Buchanan, 1997)

Each fascicle includes topographical information derived from a variety of sources and covering such subject areas as manufacturing, trades and services, and education. Within these subject areas the names of the owners of mills, tradesmen and teachers, to name a few, can be found. For example, we learn from the *Irish Historic Towns Atlas* for Derry-Londonderry that William Patterson had a brewery in the city in 1776, that Alexander Cummin was a cabinet maker there in 1772, and that Mrs Macklin and Mrs Boggs each ran a school in 1777–8.

Architects

Architects, as we understand the term today, were something of a rarity in Ireland in the seventeenth and eighteenth centuries. See Rolf Loeber, *Biographical Dictionary of Architects in Ireland, 1600–1720* (1981) and also the online Dictionary of Irish Architects database (www.dia.ie).

Clergymen
Sources for studying the lives of the clergy of the various religious denominations are discussed in Chapter 2.

Doctors, surgeons and apothecaries
Sources for studying medical practitioners are highlighted in Chapter 14.

Engineers
For engineers, see Rolf Loeber, 'Biographical dictionary of engineers in Ireland, 1600–1730', *Irish Sword*, 13 (1977–9), pp 30–44, 106–22, 230–55, 283–314.

Lawyers and attornies
Information on those who worked in the legal profession is discussed in Chapter 9.

Millers
Information on millers can be found in estate collections (see Chapter 6).

Paper-makers
See Alison Muir, 'The eighteenth-century paper-makers of the north of Ireland', *Familia: Ulster Genealogical Review*, 20 (2005), pp 37–73.

Printers and booksellers
A number of publications deal with those involved in printing in eighteenth-century Ulster. In the early 1900s, Ernest Reginald McClintock Dix researched and wrote widely on the subject in a series of articles, many of them appearing in *The Irish Book Lover*. Dix was also a contributor to *A Dictionary of the Printers and Booksellers who were at work in England, Scotland and Ireland from 1726 to 1775* (1930). Other studies include A. A. Campbell, *Literary History of Strabane* (1902) and more recently J. R. R. Adams, *The Printed Word and the Common Man: Popular Culture in Ulster 1700–1900* (1987). See also Chapter 12.

Soldiers
Records relating to the armed forces are discussed in Chapter 11.

Surveyors and cartographers
Surveyors and cartographers were employed by landowners to survey or map out their estates (see Chapter 6). They may also have been employed by grand juries (see Chapter 9). Biographical information can be found in Peter Eden (ed.), *Dictionary of Land Surveyors and Local Cartographers of Great Britain and Ireland, 1550–1850* (1975), and Sarah Bendall (ed.), *Dictionary of Land Surveyors and Local Map-makers of Great Britain and Ireland 1530–1850* (2 vols, 1997).

Teachers
Sources of information on teachers are discussed in Chapter 14.

16. Records of organisations, clubs and societies

The eighteenth century witnessed the creation of a number of organisations, clubs and societies, each with its own aims and objectives, and each generating various types of records. For more information on this subject area in general, see James Kelly and M. J. Powell (eds), *Clubs and Societies in Eighteenth-Century Ireland* (2010), especially the chapters by Eoin Magennis ('Clubs and societies in eighteenth-century Belfast') and Allan Blackstock ('Loyal clubs and societies in Ulster, 1770–1800'). Two major fraternal organisations that were formed in the eighteenth century, the Freemasons and the Orange Order, are considered in more detail below.

16.1 The Freemasons

Freemasonry in Ireland can be traced to the seventeenth century and by 1725 the Grand Lodge of Freemasons had been founded. From the early 1730s the Grand Lodge began to issue warrants to named individuals allowing them, in an official sense, to hold a lodge. The first warrant granted for a location in Ulster was that issued to Enniskillen in 1733. Other early Ulster warrants included Cootehill (1734), Newry (1737), Cavan (1738), Armagh (1739) and Lisburn (1739). It should be noted that these were the years in which warrants were granted; there may have been lodges operating at these places prior to these years. By the end of the 1750s there was at least one lodge with a Grand Lodge warrant in each county in Ulster and over 40 in all in the province. As an example, the warrant granted to lodge no. 138 in Coleraine records that it was issued to Henry Brumhall, John McAllester and Alexander Sinclare on 9 September 1743 (D668/O/1)

Freemasons' Hall in Dublin maintains an archive of Masonic records. Minutes of Grand Lodge survive from 1780 and those of the Committee of Charity from 1795. A membership register, organised in several series, commences in 1760. The first series, running from 1760 to 1800, is available in three large volumes (a fourth has been lost). This lists by lodge the names of members returned to Grand Lodge along with the date of the return. Save for some entries from the early years, the register does not record occupations and neither does it provide places of residence. Nearly 14,000 Ulster Masons are recorded in the first series of the register (1760–1800). Of these, over 1,100 belonged to Belfast lodges, while Antrim and Tyrone had the highest county totals, with some 2,360 registered Masons for each. Research has shown, however, that there was a significant discrepancy between the numbers of Masons registered with Grand Lodge and the actual number of lodge members; it has been estimated that there were at least 20,000 Masons in Ulster in 1800. It must also be realised that at this time many Catholics were Masons.

The records kept by local lodges include minute books, which record various details, including the admission of new members (which occasionally included a member's occupation). Minute books also record the raising of members through the different degrees of Freemasonry – apprentice, fellow craft and master mason (after which an individual qualified as a full member of a lodge), as well as various higher degrees. In addition, support for widows and orphans, charitable activities, and assistance extended to those in need of help, not necessarily fellow Masons, might be recorded. For example, a lodge in Downpatrick offered support to William Moor of 'Balygigin' in the late 1780s following the burning of his house and shop. Preparations for social occasions, such as dinners and parades, were also noted. In addition, disciplinary matters were recorded. Members who stepped out of line could be suspended for minor offences or expelled for more serious transgressions; expulsions of significance were sometimes reported in the press.

Lodge minutes can also include information on members planning to emigrate. Those intending to do so could request a certificate testifying to their membership of a particular lodge. Others might be raised to a higher degree within their lodge prior to departure so that they would leave as full members. The minute book of the lodge in Raphoe includes such an entry from May 1784 when 'Mr John McCausland, entered apprentice, being destined for America and having made the same known to this lodge and the ship being in waiting for the first fair wind' was raised to the second and third degrees of Freemasonry. Some of these early certificates survive. For example, the following certificate was issued by a Coleraine lodge on 13 March 1783 (D668/O/1):

> We the Master Wardens & Brethren of Lodge No. 235 of Free and Excepted Masons of the Town of Coleraine in the County of Londonderry and Kingdom of Ireland do Certify that our Trusty & well beloved Brother Felix O'Neale was by us regularly made A Registerd Master Mason and continued in our Body as Sitting Member for the Space of 7 months and by the Confidence and Trust reposed in Him we do Recommend him to all Honest Brethren round the Globe whom this may reach.
> [signed by Cornelius Moore, John Bradley and James Criswell]

Accounts are also available for some lodges. These may be found within the minute books or in separate volumes. Generally these will record the payment of membership fees and expenses associated with lodge activities, but occasionally these can include information on a range of other matters. For example, accounts for a Masonic lodge in Coleraine include the following entry: 'Paid B[rothe]r Holmes for a Great Coat given to James Patterson in New York' (D668/O/1).

Essential reading on this subject, and the source of much of the above text, is Petri Mirala, *Freemasonry in Ulster, 1733–1813: A Social and Political History of the Masonic Brotherhood in the North of Ireland* (2007). This volume provides a detailed analysis of Freemasonry, covering such topics as its organisation and structures, social composition, and the contribution of Masons to political developments in the late eighteenth century. See also C. G. Horton, 'The records of the Freemasons of Ireland', *Familia*, 2 (1986), pp 65–9, which helpfully includes a map showing the location of Masonic lodges in Ireland in 1770.

Other works that provide invaluable information include John Heron Lepper and Philip Crossle, *History of the Grand Lodge of Free and Accepted Masons of Ireland*, vol. 1 (1925), and Philip Crossle, *Irish Masonic Records* (1973). The 'Lodge of Research' has been active in researching Masonic history and its published transactions include much of interest. See, for example, Thomas W. R. Milner, 'Donegal Masonry as practised at Raphoe during the late eighteenth and early nineteenth centuries, 1762–1823', *The Lodge of Research No. CC. Transactions, for the Years 1934–38* (1947), pp 189–208. See also the volume in PRONI containing manuscript notes on the history of Freemasonry compiled by Colonel Wallace, *c.* 1900–14 (D1889/7/2).

Records relating to individual lodges that are currently held in Freemasons' Hall in Dublin are listed under the parish in which the lodge met in Appendix 1. (However, bear in mind that the members of a lodge could have been drawn from a much wider area than the immediate environs of the meeting place.) In addition, Mirala, in his abovementioned book *Freemasonry in Ulster*, made use of records in local custody. These included:

> Downpatrick Masonic Hall – records of Lodge 367, 1765–
> Provincial Grand Lodge of Armagh – records of Lodge 409 (Armagh),
> 1791– ; records of Lodge 623 (Armagh), 1791– ; transcripts of
> records of Lodge 459 (Clare), 1797–
> Provincial Grand Lodge of Antrim – records of Lodge 418 (Drumbridge),
> 1784– ; records of Lodge 432 (Ballycastle), 1778– ; Lodge 465 (Crew,
> County Tyrone), 1790– ; Lodge 529 (Antrim), 1775–

In 2017, the records of the Provincial Grand Lodge of Antrim were transferred to the Public Record Office of Northern Ireland.

16.2 The Orange Order

The Orange Order was founded in north Armagh in September 1795 during a period of economic and social unrest and political excitement. The movement spread rapidly and in 1798 the Grand Orange Lodge of Ireland was established.

A number of studies have looked at the origins and early history of the Orange Order. A volume which contains much valuable source material is *The Formation of the Orange Order, 1795–1798: The Edited Papers of Colonel William Blacker and Colonel Robert H. Wallace* edited by Cecil Kilpatrick (1994). See also David W. Miller, 'The origins of the Orange Order in County Armagh' in A. J. Hughes and William Nolan (eds), *Armagh: History and Society* (2001), pp 583–615.

Unfortunately, it is generally difficult to trace ancestors who were members of the Orange Order unless the name of the lodge to which they belonged is known and even then it depends on the survival of the records. Many records remain in local custody and very few survive from as far back as the closing years of the eighteenth century. An archive is maintained at the Museum of Orange Heritage in Belfast (www.orangeheritage.co.uk/archives), which includes a range of material, though primarily the records date from the 1830s onwards. The original Grand Lodge minute book covers the period 1798–1818. The matters dealt with ranged from the issuing of warrants to queries concerning masters of local lodges. The minute book also includes lists of warrants issued by Grand Lodge. The details given are the warrant number, geographical district in which the lodge was located, county, and the person to whom the warrant was issued. With regard to the records of individual lodges, the earliest known minutes date from 1796 and concern Ballyleaney Purple Star, Richhill, County Armagh. Other very early records include the minute/roll book of the 'Fort Edward Body of Orangemen', Killymaddy, County Tyrone. This volume, covering the period 1798–9, includes a list of the names and addresses of the members and some details on those who were subsequently admitted or who were expelled for such offences as non-attendance and misconduct.

Some early Orange Order records are available in PRONI. These include a notebook of the Coleraine District Lodge of the Orange Order naming members of lodges in and near Coleraine in 1799 (D668/O/1). This includes the names of the officers within each lodge, the parish of residence of the members, the date of admittance, and the religion of each member (recorded as Protestant or 'Desenter', i.e. Presbyterian). PRONI holds the papers of Aiken McClelland, the former librarian at the Ulster Folk and Transport Museum, who was an active researcher of the history of the Order and had identified much material of interest (D3815). Extracts from lodge records can be found in local histories. For example, J. J. Marshall's *Annals of Aughnacloy* (1925 and 2009 editions) includes extracts from the minute book of Aughnacloy Orange Lodge (no. 156) beginning in 1797.

An interesting item found in the Home Office records (see Chapter 1) in The National Archives, Kew, is a printed booklet containing the rules and regulations of the 'Boyne Society, commonly called Orange Men, of the County of Antrim' which had been issued to Member No. 121, Thomas Briggs of Broomhedge (HO 42/41/71, fos 218–224). The booklet included the resolutions of the quarterly meeting of the Masters of the Orange Societies in

the County Antrim District, held in Mr Henry Moore's, Belfast, on 15
September 1797. The resolutions included the appointment of Dr William
Atkinson of Belfast as Grand Master and Treasurer for the District and the
following Masters as a General Committee: William Hart of Lisburn, Stephen
Daniel of Belfast, Michael Boomer of Derriaghy, James Law of Belfast, James
Innes of Lisburn, David McCall of Lambeg, William McDowell of Lisburn,
Isaac McNiece of Glenevy [Glenavy], William Johnson of Ballinderry, William
Tinsley of Broomhedge, and William Murphy of Maghragell [Magheragall].

16.3 Other organisations
Surviving records relating to other organisations in existence in the eighteenth
century are listed below.

Ballymena Hunt
Records relating to the Ballymena Hunt, including minutes (1799–
1803) and accounts (1799–1804) – D2109/2/2B (see also T1252/3)

Belfast Reading Society
The minutes of the Belfast Reading Society, founded in 1788, are in
the Linen Hall Library. Extracts from the minutes can be found in John
Anderson, *History of the Belfast Library and Society for Promoting
Knowledge, commonly known as the Linen Hall Library, chiefly taken from
the minutes of the Society, and published in connection with the centenary
celebration in 1888* (1888), which also includes the names of the
founding and earliest members of the Reading Society.

Down Royal Corporation of Horse-Breeders
Minute book, 1740–1801 – D3276/A/1
Treasurer's account book, 1740–1892, including a list of subscribers
　　from 1723 – D3276/B/1
Copy of the resolution and subscription list concerning the Maze which
　　acknowledges that the course is Lord Downshire's private property,
　　1798 – D607/F/144
Subscription list for the Maze Races, 1798 – D1556/18/7/17
Printed volumes: 'Annals of The Downe Hunt' – D2229/9, /10A

Newry Snug Club
Minutes of the Newry Snug Club, 1778–99 (including an index of
names) – T3202A

Northern Whig Club
Founded in 1790, a list of original members of this club can be found
in Henry Joy, *Historical Collections Relative to the Town of Belfast* (1817),
pp 341–2.

17. Diaries, journals, memoirs and correspondence

A number of pre-1800 diaries, journals, memoirs and collections of correspondence survive and are either available in published form or are on deposit in various repositories. Listed below is a selection of this material. The correspondence highlighted here is primarily of a personal nature, rather than letters of a more formal nature relating to business, government or estate management. Diaries and correspondence concerning the clergy are discussed in Chapter 2, while the value of emigrant's letters is highlighted in Chapter 13.

Anon., County Down
Small bound diary entitled 'Memorabilia 1779' by an author whose identity cannot be determined, but who was probably from County Down, 1779–1811 – D3873/1

Anon., Belfast to Liverpool
Diary of a linen merchant travelling between Belfast and Liverpool, 1779 – T1763/3

Ash, Ashbrook, Londonderry
Thomas Ash, *A Circumstantial Account of the Siege of Londonderry* (1792); reprinted in *Two Diaries of Derry in 1689*, edited by Thomas Witherow (1888)
Thomas Ash, *The Ash MSS, written in the year 1735*, edited by Edward T. Martin (1890)

Black, Belfast and Bordeaux
Extensive collections of letters from the 1670s onwards concerning the Black family of Belfast and Bordeaux – D719, D1950, D4457

Bruce, Holywood, County Down
Correspondence involving the Bruce and Traill families of Holywood and Killyleagh, County Down, including Rev. William Bruce's journal of a tour in the north in 1783 – T3041

Caldwell, Harmony Hill, Ballymoney, County Antrim
Bundle of documents including typescript copies of letters, 1798–9, from John
    Parks, Dublin and Harmony Hill, near Ballymoney, County Antrim, to his
    father-in-law, John Caldwell senior, linen merchant, in New York State, USA,
    and his brother-in-law, John Caldwell junior – T3541
Typescript copy of the reminiscences of John Caldwell junior entitled 'Particulars
    of history of a North County Irish Family', which describes in some detail
    the author's life in Ireland, involvement with the United Irishmen and exile
    in America, 1850 – T3541/5/3 (for a discussion of this work, see David A.
    Wilson, 'John Caldwell's memoir: a case study in Ulster-American radicalism'
    in David A. Wilson and Mark G. Spencer (eds), *Ulster Presbyterians in the
    Atlantic World: Religion, Politics and Identity* (2006), pp 104–27).

Chesney, Ballymena, County Antrim; South Carolina; Annalong, County Down
Diary of Alexander Chesney – D2260/1 (T1095/3/1–79 is copy of this
document)
    Chesney was born in Dunclug, near Ballymena, County Antrim, in 1755.
He emigrated with his family to South Carolina in 1772, took part in the War
of Independence, and returned to Ireland in 1782, spending most of the rest
of his life near Annalong, County Down. The opening of his diary provides a
great deal of information about his family background of which the following
is an extract:

> My father, Robert Chesney or McChesney was only son to Alexander
> Chesney of Dunclug, aforesaid, and of Jane Fulton his wife, his sisters
> were Ann married to William Purdy of Glenravil who was brother of
> my mother, as she was a sister to my Father; they are now with their
> Family settled in South Carolina. Second Martha Chesney married to
> Matthew Gillespy who went also to Carolina and died there shortly
> after their arrival, about the year 1768; her husband is married again
> and lives near Enoree-River, South Carolina. Third Sarah Chesney who
> married James Archbold a pensioner and lives in County Antrim. My
> grandfather Chesney had several brothers, I recollect to have seen some
> of their sons who came from County Tyrone, and near the Bann River.

The diary was published as E. Alfred Jones (ed.), *The Journal of Alexander
Chesney, a South Carolina Loyalist in the Revolution and After* (1921) and Bobby
Gilmer Moss (ed.), *Journal of Capt. Alexander Chesney: Adjutant to Major Patrick
Ferguson* (2002).

Cunningham, Belfast to Boston
Journal of a voyage on the board the *America* from Belfast to Boston by
John Cunningham, 1795 – D394/2 (extracts published in D. H. Akenson and

W. H. Crawford (eds), *Local Poets and Social History: James Orr, Bard of Ballycarry* (1977), pp 105–09)

Delaney, County Down
Angelique Day (ed.), *Letters from Georgian Ireland: The Correspondence of Mary Delaney, 1731–68* (1991); Mrs Delaney was the wife of Patrick Delaney, Anglican dean of Down (1744–68).

Drennan-McTier, Belfast, etc
The Drennan-McTier Letters, edited by Jean Agnew (1998–9), published by the Irish Manuscripts Commission in three volumes (1776–1793, 1794–1801, 1802–19). Between 1776 and 1819 William Drennan and his sister Martha McTier exchanged over 1,400 letters covering a broad range of different subjects. They were the children of Rev. Thomas Drennan, a Presbyterian minister in Belfast, and William Drennan, a medical doctor, was one of the founders of the United Irishmen in 1791. This edition includes copious footnotes.

Ferguson, Londonderry
Letters to Dr John Ferguson from his son Andrew and also the bishop of Derry and Lady Sarah Napier, 1781–95 – T1638/5

Galt, Coleraine, County Londonderry
Diaries of John Galt, Coleraine, County Londonderry, general merchant, 1796–1837 (gap 1803–17) – D561

Greer, Rhone Hill and Tullylagan, County Tyrone
Numerous 18th-century letters relating to the Greer family, many of them business-related, but others concerning family matters – D1044

Hamilton, County Down
Towards the end of the seventeenth century a member of the Hamilton family prepared an account of the history of his family line beginning with Rev. Hans Hamilton, the vicar of Dunlop in Ayrshire, whose descendants, notably his son Sir James Hamilton (1st Viscount Claneboye), were to play important roles in Ulster in the seventeenth century. An addition of these papers was edited by T. K. Lowry and published as *The Hamilton Manuscripts* (1867). Lowry added numerous footnotes, providing additional information, including transcripts of contemporary letters and a detailed rental of the Hamilton estate in 1681.

Hamilton, Newtownhamilton, County Armagh
Leather-bound diary of Alexander Hamilton, QC, LLD, of Newtownhamilton, County Armagh, and Dublin, 1793–1807 – NLI, MS 49,371

Harris, Moymucklemurray, County Londonderry
Letters received by John Harris, surgeon, Botany Bay and Paramatta, New South Wales, Australia, from his parents in Moymucklemurray, Desertlyn parish, County Londonderry, 1793–4 – T3752

Heyland, Coleraine, County Londonderry
Letters by Elizabeth Heyland of Castleroe and Coleraine, County Londonderry, 1784–7: some written from Clonfeacle, County Tyrone, the home of her relative, Rev. William Richardson – D4058/D/1

Jellet, Moira, County Down
Typescript copy of 'The Anecdotical Recollections of Morgan Jellet', *c.* 1830 – T2777/1A–1B
    Jellet was born in Moira, County Down, in 1769, the son of Morgan Jellet, Steward to Lord Moira and his second wife, Brilliana Mason. During the 1798 Rebellion he served in the Belfast Yeoman Cavalry and then, in the spring of 1799, emigrated to America and soon afterwards brought out his wife. They lived near Baltimore for six years and then returned to Ireland where he became a gentleman farmer.

Kennedy, Cultra, County Down
Recollections of Elizabeth Kennedy (née Cole) containing the most important features of her life and including dates of birth and death and some notes of the activities of many members of the Kennedy family, 1766–1823 – D686/2

Leathes, Belfast
Extracts from a journal kept by Robert Leathes, merchant, late 1600s/early 1700s – Linen Hall Library, Joy MS 7

Lenox, Londonderry
Letter-book of the Len(n)ox family, concerning various family and other matters, 1738–45 – D1449/12/51 (contents summarised in PRONI catalogue)

Macky, River Bann
Diary of John Macky, water bailiff on the River Bann, 1791–1809 – T925/1
    This diary has been published as *The Diary of an Irish Water Bailiff*, edited by E. J. Malone (2008). Macky was the Inspector of Waterkeepers for the Bann fisheries and his diary provides a fascinating insight into the nature of his responsibilities and the keepers over whom he had charge. His diary also reveals the impact of contemporary political events on his activites, especially in the period 1796–8.

McClintock, Londonderry
Letters to Mrs Catherine McClintock, Ferry Quay Street, Londonderry, from various members of her family, 1740–98 – T1638/3

McKee, Rathfriland, County Down
Diary of William McKee, Rathfriland, County Down, including rent memoranda relating to an unidentified estate in County Monaghan, 1758–85 – T1322/1

McNaught, Burt, County Donegal
A series of letters, beginning in 1796, written to William McNaught who emigrated from Grange in the parish of Burt, County Donegal, in the summer of 1791, has been published by Gary T. Hawbaker as *Dear William: Letters From Home, 1796–1826* (2008). Most of the letters were written by John Patton, a farmer and brewer in Ramelton and William McNaught's brother-in-law. Others were written by McNaught's siblings still living on the home farm.

Montgomery, County Down
Towards the end of his life William Montgomery (1633–1707) of Rosemount, Greyabbey, County Down, began to prepare memoirs of the various branches of the Montgomery family, looking at, among other things, their contribution to seventeenth-century Ulster. The surviving manuscripts were brought together by George Hill and published as *The Montgomery Manuscripts* (1869). Hill's edition includes copious footnotes containing a huge amount of additional information of value on families that settled in Ulster, especially County Down, in the 1600s. His notes to Montgomery's detailed description of the funeral of his grandfather, Sir Hugh Montgomery (1st Viscount Ards), in 1636 are a good example of the thoroughness of his own approach. Additional writings by William Montgomery can be found in the Savage-Nugent Papers in PRONI (D552).

Moore, Carrickfergus, County Antrim
Journal kept by John Moore of Carrickfergus chronicling his journey to and life in America, 1760–70 – D3165/2/1 (see also MIC481)

Morrison, Crookedstone, County Antrim
Diary of William Morrison, Crookedstone, Killead parish, County Antrim, farmer, recording day to day events – D3300/109

Nevin, Ballywarren, County Down
Extracts from the diary of James Nevin, Ballywarren, Down parish, County Down, 1767–97 – *Lecale Review*, 14 (2016), pp 24–7 (reproduced from *Down Recorder*, 3 April 1920)

Pilson, Downpatrick, County Down
Memoranda from the diaries of Aynsworth Pilson, 1775–1862 – D365/1
Abstract of diary of Aynsworth Pilson, 1799–1849 – D365/3
See also Aynsworth Pilson, *Memoirs of Notable Inhabitants of Downpatrick*,
   edited by Reginald W. H. Blackwood, Colm Rooney and W. Gordon
   Wheeler (2016).

Rainey, Belfast
Extracts from the diary of William Rainey, merchant, early 1700s – Linen Hall
Library, Joy MS 10

Reford, Antrim, County Antrim
Copies of letters from Lewis Reford, Antrim, to Frances Walker, 1725–8 –
D3300/96/1

Tennent, Roseyards, County Antrim; Coleraine, County Londonderry; Belfast
Extensive material relating to the Tennent family is available in PRONI under
reference D1748. Rev. John Tennent, a native of Scotland, was the minister of
the Secession congregation of Roseyards in north County Antrim from 1751
to his death in 1808. His sons William, Robert and John became prominent
figures in business and politics in Belfast. The material can be summarised as
follows:

> Correspondence and papers of Rev. John Tennent, 1764–1806 –
>   D1748/A
> Correspondence and papers of William Tennent, 1783–1832 –
>   D1748/B
> Correspondence and papers of Robert Tennent, *c.* 1784–1837 –
>   D1748/C
> Correspondence and papers of John Tennent, 1790–97 – D1748/D

Within these categories the documentation ranges far and wide to include
letters, diaries, account books, receipts and leases, etc. The records relating to
John Tennent include, for instance, a large journal titled, 'Journal during his
apprenticeship to Samuel Givin in Coleraine, July 1786 to July 1790'
(D1748/D/2/2). A few extracts from 1789 illustrate the range of material
contained in this journal.

> 15 February 1789: Samuel Givin, on N[ancy] Kelly leaving him, hired a
>   woman of the name of Sarah McLaughlin (an old woman) and so was
>   Nancy Kelly for he never hires any but old women.
> 5 April 1789: Francis Neilson of this town, Hatter, died.
> 11 May 1789: James Simpson (son of the Revd John Simpson's) closed his
>   shop on Saturday night never more to open it, and went off on Sunday

evening to go to America. He was about two years in business but he did not pay proper attention to his business, but followed after whoring and drinking, till he brought himself to ruin.

16 May 1789: John Begly, tobacconist of this town, departed this life after a very tedious illness. He was a Roman Catholic.

11 December 1789: A paragraph appeared in this evening's Belfast paper which shows how cautious people ought to be in crediting newspaper reports: viz, "Died at Coleraine after an illness of a few days, Mr John Searson, Superintendent of the free school of that place." Now the man is living and well.

There is also a small notebook, containing, among other things, accounts from the period of John Tennent's apprenticeship in Coleraine (D1748/D/2/3).

Thomson, Carngranny, County Antrim
Known as the 'Bard of Carngranny', Thomson was a schoolmaster and poet based between Mallusk and Templepatrick in County Antrim. See Jennifer Orr (ed.), *The Correspondence of Samuel Thomson (1766–1816): Fostering an Irish Writers' Circle* (2012), which is based primarily on Thomson's correspondence in Trinity College Dublin (MS 7257).

Traill, Killyleagh, County Down
Extracts from the diary of James Traill of Killyleagh, County Down, *c.* 1690–1742 – D1460/1
See also **Bruce**

Weir, Stewartstown, County Tyrone
Letters from America to members of Weir family of Stewartstown, County Tyrone, 1771 onwards – D1140 (MIC561)

APPENDIX 1

Records relating to parishes in Ulster

This appendix provides a summary listing of genealogical sources for every civil parish in the nine counties of Ulster for the period 1600–1800. Of all the administrative divisions in use in this era the civil parish provides the most convenient way of organising the available records. The parish was an important unit in civil administration and many sources, such as the 'census substitutes' noted below and elsewhere in this book, were organised by parish.

At the same time, researchers should be aware of a number of issues that arise from this approach. The most important of these concerns the listing of church records by parish. While the network of civil parishes was aligned closely with the network of Church of Ireland parishes, the arrangement of Catholic parishes differed somewhat (though for the period under discussion the precise nature of these differences is not an easy one to establish). Furthermore, Presbyterians were organised by congregation and the bounds of an individual congregation could cross more than one parish boundary. The best approach for researchers is to examine sources for both the parish of primary interest and its nearest neighbours.

Each parish entry includes a range of information and the level of detail presented depends on the volume of surviving material. To begin with, some geographical information on each parish is provided. After this the main records are categorised under the following headings: *Church records, Estate papers, Census substitutes, Business records, Corporation records, Freemasonry records, Other records* and *Publications*. Not every parish has entries for all of these categories and, unfortunately, some parishes have very few pre-1800 records of genealogical interest.

Geographical information
The geographical details listed for each parish include the county (found in the parish heading), barony and diocese within which the parish falls, as well as the main places in the parish and the graveyards. A number of parishes crossed county boundaries and on the southern fringes of Ulster a few parishes extended beyond the province of Ulster into the province of Leinster. In these instances, the records concentrate on resources specific to the portion of the parish within Ulster.

The civil parish network in Ulster has been subject to change over the last four centuries. If a parish came into existence during the period 1600–1800 the year in which this occurred, if known, is stated, along with the name of the parish or parishes from which the new entity was formed. For example, the parish of Keady in County Armagh was created out of Derrynoose parish in 1773. Researchers interested in Keady should also refer to the entry for Derrynoose for additional source material. A number of new parishes were formed in the first half of the nineteenth century. For example, the County Antrim parishes of Craigs and Portglenone were created out of Ahoghill. Post 1800 parishes are listed below with the names of the original parishes from which they were created.

The name of the barony (or baronies, for many parishes were divided between two or more baronies) will be helpful when using grand jury records (see Chapter 9) and the Registry of Deeds (see Chapter 7). A parish will always be found entirely within one diocese. Knowing the name of the pre-1800 diocese will be useful in identifying, among other things, the correct diocesan will index (see Chapter 8). The places listed range from major towns to hamlets, as well as some districts.

With regard to the listing of graveyards, it has not been possible to identify with certainty every burial ground in existence today that was in use in the period 1600–1800. The focus is primarily on graveyards that originated in the pre-Reformation period, which were used by all sections of society, as well as others that had been opened by the latter part of the eighteenth century. Researchers should be aware that a graveyard might be known by more than one name and the name used here may not be the only one in use. The term 'Old' usually applies to a burial ground that dates from the medieval period and which is often now in the care of a local authority. Many other graveyards are in the custody of a religious denomination – the abbreviations used are the same as those listed below under *Church records* – though it is important to bear in mind that the graveyard was not necessarily used exclusively by the members of that denomination. See Chapter 3 for a fuller discussion of graveyards in Ulster.

Church records

Available church records for the period 1600–1800 are listed under this heading. Most church records for Ulster are available in the Public Record Office of Northern Ireland, though others can be found in the Presbyterian Historical Society of Ireland and the Representative Church Body Library. A few records remain in the custody of the church in question. The references given for Catholic records are those of the microfilms in PRONI, though it should be noted that digitised scans of these are now available on the website of the National Library of Ireland (www.nli.ie). The abbreviations for the different religious denominations under the heading of *Church records* are as follows:

CI – Church of Ireland
MOR – Moravian
NSP – Non-Subscribing Presbyterian
P – Presbyterian
RC – Roman Catholic
RP – Reformed Presbyterian
RSF – Religious Society of Friends

Estate papers

If estate records are available for a particular parish, this is indicated by providing the name of the estate owner. For fuller information on the scope of each estate collection, the reader should refer to Appendix 2, where surviving records are set out in some detail. It must be understood that there is no guarantee that pre-1800 records survive for all of the townlands owned by an individual landowner.

Census substitutes

For convenience, several categories of sources from the seventeenth and eighteenth centuries have been grouped together as 'census substitutes'. Each of these sources is discussed in more detail in Chapters 4 and 5. The abbreviations used for these 'census substitutes' are as follows:

AC – Agricultural census of 1803
CPH – 'Census of Protestant Householders', 1740
DE – Derry diocese excommunicants, 1667
DP – Dissenters' petition, 1775
FL – Flaxgrowers' list (flaxseed premiums), 1796
FP – Franciscan petition lists, 1665–71
HMR – Hearth money rolls, 1660s
HSM – Hearts of Steel memorials, 1771–2
LP – Laggan presbytery representatives, 1672–1700
PB – Poll book, c. 1662
RCC – Religious census for Cary barony, 1734
RelC – Religious census of 1766
VAA – 'View of the archbishopric of Armagh', 1703

Business records
Surviving records relating to businesses in Ulster are listed in Chapter 15. Here the name of the business (usually a family name) is given as well as the place from which the business operated. It is important to remember that while the business may have been based in a specific town or parish, its customer base may have extended much further.

Corporation records
Surviving administrative records for corporate towns are listed under this heading. For more on corporation records, see Chapter 9.

Freemasonry records
Listed here are records held in the archive at Freemasons' Hall in Dublin as well as records available in other archives. For records held elsewhere as well as a discussion of Masonic records, see Chapter 16.

Other records
Miscellaneous sources for a parish are listed individually under this heading. These materials may include items that do not fit conveniently under other headings, such as a collection of document relating to particular location or family. Other records included here derive from lists of names found in newspapers, such as subscription lists.

Publications
Published materials of potential interest are listed under this heading, focusing in particular on books, though occasionally referencing relevant articles from journals. This listing is not exhaustive and researchers should consult library catalogues for further information. Particularly helpful in this regard are the catalogues of the National Library of Ireland, Libraries Ireland, Libraries NI, and the Linen Hall Library.

AGHABOG PARISH, COUNTY MONAGHAN

Aghabog was created out of **Galloon** parish in 1767.

Barony: Dartree
Diocese: Clogher

Estate papers
Barton estate; Dawson estate; Forster estate; Ker estate; Rossmore estate

Census substitutes
HMR, FL

Publications
Seamus McPhillips, *Aghabog Parish. An Outline History* (n.d.)
David Nesbitt, *The Drumkeen Story: A Story of Aghabog Presbyterians, 1803–2003*
    (2003)
*From Carn to Clonfad, Killeevan Heritage Group takes a Journey through some Pages out
    of the History of Currin, Killeevan and Aghabog* (2 vols)

AGHADERG PARISH, COUNTY DOWN

Barony: Iveagh Upper (Upper Half)
Diocese: Dromore
Places: Glascar, Loughbrickland, Scarva
Graveyard: Aghaderg CI

Church registers
CI Aghaderg
Vestry minutes, 1747–   Local custody

P Glascar (originally Secession)
Baptisms, 1780– ; marriages, 1781–98   MIC1P/63

Session minutes, 1760–1818   PHSI

Estate papers
Downshire estate; Hall estate, Strangford and Lower Iveagh; Innis estate; Johnston
estate; Meade estate; Sharman estate; Whyte estate

Census substitutes
FL

Publications
G. N. Little, *Historical Highlights, Parish of Aghaderg* (1989): includes inscriptions
    from Aghaderg Church of Ireland graveyard and a list of churchwardens from 1746
J. J. Sands, 'Pre-Famine poverty in the parish of Aghaderg', *'Before I Forget ... ':
    Journal of the Poyntzpass and District Local History Society*, 3 (1989), pp 49–55

AGHADOWEY PARISH, COUNTY LONDONDERRY

Barony: Coleraine
Diocese: Derry
Places: Aghadowey, Ringsend
Graveyard: Aghadowey CI

Church records
CI Aghadowey
Vestry minutes, 1774–   Local custody

P Aghadowey
Session minutes, 1702–61   PHSI

Estate papers
Beresford estate; Derry bishopric estate; Du Pré estate; Heyland estate; Ironmongers'
Company estate; Jackson estate; Mercers' Company estate; Merchant Taylors'
Company estate; Richardson estate; Rowley estate

Census substitutes
HMR, CPH, FL

Business records
Orr, Aghadowey

Other records
Notebook containing notification of registering arms, including residents of
    Aghadowey, 1796 – D668/N/1
Subscribers to a reward fund relating to a libel against the Bovagh Cavalry, 1798 –
    Londonderry Journal, 9 Jan. 1798

Publications
T. H. Mullin, *Aghadowey: A Parish and its Linen Industry* (1972): includes names
from Pyke's survey of 1725 and Alsop's survey of 1765, both of the Ironmongers'
Company estate

AGHAGALLON PARISH, COUNTY ANTRIM

Barony: Massereene Upper
Diocese: Connor
Place: Aghagallon
Graveyards: Aghagallon Old, Magheranagaw

Estate papers
Conway estate

Census substitutes
HMR

Other records
Subscribers to a reward fund 'Given under our Hands at Aghagallon' (over 220 names)
– *Belfast Newsletter*, 2–6 March 1781 (see also the issue of 27–30 March 1781)

AGHALEE PARISH, COUNTY ANTRIM

Barony: Massereene Upper
Diocese: Dromore
Places: Aghalee, Soldierstown
Graveyards: Aghalee CI, Aghalee Old

Estate papers
Conway estate

Census substitutes
HMR

Other records
Subscribers to a reward fund following a robbery in Aghalee parish, 1786 – *Belfast
Newsletter*, 5–9 May 1786

Publications
S. J. Brennan, *Aghalee Parish Tercentenary, 1677–1977* (1977)

AGHALOO PARISH, COUNTY TYRONE
The boundaries of the parishes of Aghaloo, Carnteel and Killeeshil were reorganised
in 1680.

Barony: Dungannon Lower
Diocese: Armagh
Places: Brantry, Caledon, Dyan, Minterburn
Graveyard: Aghaloo CI

Church records
CI Aghaloo or Caledon

Baptisms, 1791–5; marriages, 1792–5, 1800– ;	T679/286, 290
burials, 1792–5, 1800– ; vestry minutes, 1691–	(MIC583/25);
	MIC1/326A/1; D2602/1

The vestry minutes have been published as *The Vestry Records of the Church of St John
Parish of Aghalow, Caledon, Co. Tyrone, 1691–1807*, edited by J. J. Marshall (1935);
the footnotes in this volume contain much valuable information; records of
applotments for repairing roads in the 1780s contain upwards of 20 names.

Estate papers
Armagh archbishopric estate; Caledon estate

Census substitutes
PB, HMR, FP, VAA, RelC (Protestants and Catholics), FL

Other records
Petition from the parishioners of Aghaloo and Carnteel for the removal of
Archdeacon Michael Hewetson, 1700 – DIO/4/32/A/2/4/1–3

Publications
J. J. Marshall, *History of the Territory of Minterburn and Town of Caledon (formerly
    Munter Birn, and Kenard, Co. Tyrone)* (1923)
R. Buick Knox, *The Presbyterian Church in Ireland: Minterburn Congregation, 1657–
    1957* (1957)
The Book of Eglish: Where the Oona Flows (2011): at over 500 pages this book contains
    a wealth of information about the area

AGHALURCHER PARISH, COUNTIES FERMANAGH AND TYRONE

Baronies: Magherastephana (Fermanagh portion), Clogher (Tyrone portion)
Diocese: Clogher
Places: Cooneen, Lisnaskea, Maguiresbridge
Graveyards: Aghalurcher Old, Lisnaskea CI, Tullynageeran

Church records
CI Aghalurcher
Baptisms, 1788–   T679/25 (MIC583/3)

Vestry minutes, 1747–   Local custody

Estate papers
Brooke estate; Clogher bishopric estate; Erne estate; Montgomery estate

Census substitutes
HMR (incomplete), FL

Publications
Vicky Herbert, *The Lisnaskea Story: People and Places* (2001)
Patrick McKay, *Place-names of Northern Ireland. Vol. 8, County Fermanagh 1:
    Lisnaskea and District: The Parish of Aghalurcher* (2004)

AGHANLOO PARISH, COUNTY LONDONDERRY

Barony: Keenaght
Diocese: Derry
Place: Artikelly
Graveyard: Aghanloo Old

Estate papers
Beresford estate; Derry bishopric estate; Haberdashers' Company estate;
McClelland/Maxwell estate

Census substitutes
HMR, CPH (includes townlands), FL

Other records
Names of men from Aghanloo parish ordered to appear 'with their best arms' at
Limavady, 1666 – T640/103

AGHANUNSHIN PARISH, COUNTY DONEGAL

Barony: Kilmacrenan
Diocese: Raphoe
Graveyard: Aghanunshin Old

Church records
CI Aghanunshin
Vestry minutes, 1788–   MIC1/214

Estate papers
Raphoe bishopric estate; Wray estate

Census substitutes
HMR, FL

Publications
L. R. Lawrenson, *The Parish of Conwall, Aughanunshin and Leck* (1943)

AGHAVEA PARISH, COUNTY FERMANAGH

Barony: Magherastephana
Diocese: Clogher
Place: Brookeborough
Graveyard: Aghavea CI

Church records
CI Aghavea
Vestry minutes, 1762– , including poor list, 1774   MIC1/229D/1–2
(name and address of poor person plus name of
person making recommendation), names of persons
appointed to sit on a committee to decide on the
poor, 1774

Estate papers
Brooke estate; Clogher bishopric estate; Erne estate

Census substitutes
FL

Publications
Jack Johnston (ed.), *The Brookeborough Story: Aghalun in Aghavea* (2004)

AGHNAMULLEN PARISH, COUNTY MONAGHAN

Barony: Cremorne
Diocese: Clogher
Graveyards: Aughnamullen CI, Killahear, Templemoyle

Church records
CI Aughnamullen
Descriptive notes and extracts from the parish   D3531/A/4
registers, 1775–1801 [in catalogue, but not located]

Estate papers
Barton estate; Clogher bishopric estate; Crofton estate; Dawson estate; Leslie of
Ballybay estate; Massereene estate

Census substitutes
HMR, FL

Publications
Seámus O Draoda, *History of Latton O'Rahilly's Club and Parish* (1986)

AGIVEY PARISH, COUNTY LONDONDERRY
In the medieval period, Agivey was a grange of **Aghadowey** parish. Subsequently, it
was recognised as a civil parish.

Barony: Coleraine
Diocese: Derry
Graveyard: Agivey

Estate papers
Derry bishopric estate; Du Pré estate; Ironmongers' Company estate

Census substitutes
HMR (under Aghadowey), FL

Other records
Commonplace book, late 17th/early 18th centuries: belonged in 1696 to Samuel
   Hyndman of Milltown, Agivey; appears to have been in the possession of others
   subsequently, possibly including Rev. James McGregor – PHSI
Notebook containing notification of registering arms, including residents of Agivey,
   1796 – D668/N/1

AHOGHILL PARISH, COUNTY ANTRIM

In former times this parish was also known as Magherahoghill (spelled variously). In the early nineteenth century the parishes of Craigs and Portglenone were created out of Ahoghill.

Baronies: Antrim Lower, Toome Lower, Toome Upper
Diocese: Connor
Places: Ahoghill, Cullybackey, Galgorm, Gracehill, Portglenone
Graveyards: Ahoghill Old; Aughnahoy Old; Gracehill Moravian, Portglenone CI

Church records
MOR Gracehill

Diaries that record baptisms, marriages and deaths   MIC1F/3
as well as the movement of members, 1750– ;
baptisms, 1749– ; marriages, 1758– ; burials, 1766– ;
elders' conference minutes, 1755– ; congregational
committee minutes, 1788– ; congregational council
minutes, 1790–95; lot conference minutes, 1755–91;
register of members with an index, 1755–91

P Cullybackey

Baptisms, 1726– ; marriages, 1727–92   PHSI

Names of members of Cullybackey Presbyterian
Church who subscribed to a reward fund, 1773 –
Belfast Newsletter, 8 Jan. 1773

RP Cullybackey

Session minutes of the Antrim Meeting   CR5/9
(Kellswater and Cullybackey), *c.* 1789–

Estate papers
Adair estate; Davy estate; Hunter estate; Hutchinson estate, Portglenone; Moore estate, Ballynacree; Mount Cashell estate; Mount Stafford estate; O'Neill estate

Census substitutes
HMR, CPH, HSM, FL

Other records
Typescript history of the Presbyterian congregation and ministers at Ahoghill and a
    notebook containing anecdotes relating to the history, folklife and superstitions
    of the Ahoghill area – MIC43/B
Papers relating to the Raphael family of Galgorm, beginning in 1724 – D3751
Personal account book kept by a member of the O'Hara or Hamilton family,
    Portglenone, possibly Charles Hamilton, a grandson of Bishop Hutchinson,
    1763-7 – DIO/1/22/4A

Indictments at spring assizes in 1772 of a large number of people from the
  Cullybackey area – printed in F. J. Bigger, *The Ulster Land War of 1770* (1910),
  pp 147–8

Publications
A History of Gracehill [1977]: includes extracts from 18th-century Moravian records
The 1798 Rebellion as Recorded in the Diaries of Gracehill Moravian Church (1998)
W. H. A. Lee, *The Parish Church of St Colmanell* (n.d.)
Adam Loughridge, *The Covenanters of Cullybackey 1789–1989* (1989)
Jane Megaw, *The Sun-Dialled Meeting Houses, Cullybackey: A Short History of the
  Cuningham Memorial Presbyterian Church and its Predecessor* (2004)
William Shaw, *A Short History of the Reformed Presbyterian Congregation, Cullybackey*
  (1912)
William Shaw, *Cullybackey: The Story of an Ulster Village* (1913)
Joseph Thompson, *The Meeting House on the Shining Bann: The Story of First
  Presbyterian Church Portglenone* (1972)
Joseph Thompson, *First Ahoghill Congregation from 1654* (2008)

ALL SAINTS PARISH, COUNTY DONEGAL
This parish was formed out of Taughboyne at some point in the eighteenth century.

Barony: Raphoe North
Diocese: Raphoe
Place: Newtowncunningham
Graveyard: All Saints CI

Church records
CI All Saints
Vestry minutes, 1773–   Local custody

P Crossroads (originally Secession)
Church history, *c.* 1780–1885   MIC1P/259

Estate papers
Forward estate; Hamilton estate, Castle Cunningham; Stewart estate, Ballylawn

Census substitutes
HMR (under Taughboyne); FL

Other records
A map of 'Rochan' glebe, 1769, attached to a printed lease of the glebe, 1771 – RCB,
MS K 27

Publications
Guide to the Districts of St Johnston, Carrigans and Newtowncunningham (1979)
S. M. Campbell, *The Laggan and its People* (n.d.)
D. W. T. Crooks, *In the Footsteps of St Baithin. A History of Taughboyne Group* (1992)

ANNACLONE PARISH, COUNTY DOWN
Alternative spellings include Anaghclone and Annacloan(e).

Barony: Iveagh Upper (Upper Half)
Diocese: Dromore
Place: Annaclone
Graveyard: Ardbrin Old

Estate papers
Downshire estate; Meade estate; Waring estate, Ballynafern; Sharman estate

Census substitutes
FL

Publications
Annaclone & Drumballyroney Local History (2010)

ANNAGELLIFF PARISH, COUNTY CAVAN

Barony: Loughtee Upper
Diocese: Kilmore
Graveyard: Annagelliff Old

Church records
For CI records see **Urney**

Estate papers
Annesley estate; Farnham estate; Lanesborough estate; Saunderson estate

Census substitutes
HMR, FL

ANNAGH PARISH, COUNTY CAVAN

Baronies: Loughtee Lower, Tullygarvey
Diocese: Kilmore
Places: Belturbet, Cloverhill, Redhills
Graveyards: Annagh CI, Annagh Old, Killoughter Old

Estate papers
Annesley estate; Lanesborough estate; Saunderson estate

Census substitutes
HMR, FL

Corporation records: Belturbet
The following records were formerly in NAI (and are still available there on microfilm), but are now held by the Cavan County Archives Service:

Corporation minute book or entry book, 1657–*c.* 1730s – BC/1

Fragment of corporation minute book, 1660–64 – BC/2

Volume containing records of the corporation, including accounts relating to charitable bequests and donations to the poor of Belturbet, 1737–1834 – BC/3

Court book of the corporation, 1740–1888 – BC/4

Volume which mainly contains records of elections held to select provosts and burgesses, 1778–1840 – BC/5

Surveys of property belonging to the corporation (includes a map of lands belonging to Rev. Samuel Madden listing names of occupiers), 1723, 1735, 1773 – NLI, MS 8105

See also *The Town Book of the Borough of Belturbet 1657–1840*, compiled and transcribed by Shane McGovern (2007).

Freemasonry records
Minute book of Masonic lodge no. 560 (Belturbet), 1787–98 – GLI

Other records
Papers concerning property in Belturbet, *c.* 1750 – NLI, MSS 28,823/2, 28,827/3

Publications
Belturbet: A Chequered History, compiled by George Morrissey and edited by Therese Conway (2006)

Jonathan Cherry, *Cloverhill: A Church of Ireland Parish in County Cavan, c. 1720–2010* (2010)

William Gamble, *History of Killoughter Parish, Co. Cavan* (1914)

ANNAHILT PARISH, COUNTY DOWN

Baronies: Iveagh Lower (Lower Half), Kinelarty
Diocese: Dromore
Place: Annahilt
Graveyard: Annahilt CI

Church records
CI Annahilt

Baptisms, 1784–91; marriages, 1777; burials, 1784; vestry minutes, 1777– , including the names of overseers appointed for each townland (1–2 names per townland), 1789, 1793	MIC1/101/1

P Annahilt see under **Hillsborough**

Estate papers
Annesley estate; Downshire estate

Census substitutes
HSM, FL

Publications
Ivan McAuley, *Loughaghery Presbyterian Church: A Chronological List of Events and Developments in the Life of the Congregation during its First 250 Years* (2000)

ANTRIM PARISH, COUNTY ANTRIM

Baronies: Antrim Upper, Toome Upper
Diocese: Connor
Places: Antrim, Milltown
Graveyards: Antrim CI, Moylinny (Muckamore) Quaker

Church records
CI Antrim

Baptisms, 1700–55, 1785– ; marriages, 1700–56, 1788– ; burials, 1700–54; 1786–	T679/133, 134 (MIC583/11, 12); MIC1/328A/1–2

P 1st Antrim (Millrow)

Baptisms, 1677–1733 (including index), 1753–85, 1791–2; marriages, 1675–1736 (including index); family records for the late 18th and 19th centuries	MIC1P/3; CR3/2A/1

See also W. S. Smith, 'Early register of the old Presbyterian congregation of Antrim', *UJA*, 2nd series, 5 (Sept. 1899), pp 180–90; 6 (Jan. 1900), p. 60

RSF Antrim see under **Grange of Ballyscullion**

Estate papers
Donegall estate; Massereene estate, Reford estate

Census substitutes
HMR, DP (Antrim Borough and Old Antrim)

Business records
Canavan, Dunsilly

Other records
Documents relating to the Quaker burial ground at Moylinny – T3029
Offer of a reward in relation to the burning of a house on the lands of Connor, County Antrim: 42 names of the principal inhabitants of Antrim, 1756 – *Belfast Newsletter*, 16 Jan. 1756
List of subscribers from Antrim town offering a reward: over 150 names, 1761 – *Belfast Newsletter*, 27 Jan. 1761
Certificates of conformity, Antrim parish and town, 1776 – D207/26
Memorial of the inhabitants of the borough of Antrim, 1778 – *Belfast Newsletter*, 21–25 Aug. 1778

Borough of Antrim petition in relation to Act of Union, 1799 – *Belfast Newletter*,
    11 Oct. 1799

Publications
Thomas West, *A Historical Sketch of First Antrim Presbyterian Church* (1902)
M. Majury, *First Antrim Presbyterian Church: Gleanings from over 300 years of
    Presbyterianism in Antrim* (1934)
Alastair Smyth, *The Story of Antrim* (1984)
George Hughes, *Hewn from the Rock: The Story of First Antrim Presbyterian Church*
    (1996)

ARBOE PARISH, COUNTIES LONDONDERRY AND TYRONE
This parish name is also spelled Ardboe.

Baronies: Loughinsholin (Londonderry portion), Dungannon Upper (Tyrone
    portion)
Diocese: Armagh
Places: Arboe, Moortown
Graveyards: Arboe CI, Arboe Old

Church records
CI Arboe
Baptisms, 1775– (including index); marriages,   T679/111
1773– (including index); burials,   (MIC583/10); D1278
1776– ; vestry minutes, 1773–

The earliest records are in a single volume, which also includes a census by townland
of the Protestant inhabitants of Arboe in 1775; includes comments such as 'removed
out of the parish'. Other lists of names include children receiving prayer books, 1773;
lists of the poor, 1789, 1794; and a list of those appointed to collect
the parish cess (over 40 names), 1803.

Estate papers
Armagh archbishopric estate; Castle Stewart estate; Drapers' Company estate;
Stewart estate, Killymoon

Census substitutes
HMR, VAA, FL

Other records
Warrant issued to Constables of Dungannon concerning persons in Arboe parish,
    1660 – D1618/15/2/21
Survey listing tenants in townlands in Arboe parish, n.d. [early 18th century?];
    rental of same, n.d. [late 18th century?] – D668/A/16

Publications
J. Baxter, *St Colman's Parish Church, Ardboe* (1989)

W. J. Crossley Mercer, *Ballygoney Presbyterian Church, 1762–1962* (1962)
William J. Roulston, 'An agreement to build a new church in Arboe parish in 1710',
    UJA, 3rd series, 61 (2002), pp 148–51

ARDCLINIS PARISH, COUNTY ANTRIM

Barony: Glenarm Lower
Diocese: Connor
Place: Carnlough
Graveyards: Ardclinis Old; Killycrappin (Nappan)

Estate papers
Antrim estate

Census substitutes
HMR

Publications
Felix McKillop, *Glencloy: A Local History (including Carnlough)* (1996)

ARDGLASS PARISH, COUNTY DOWN

Barony: Lecale Lower
Diocese: Down
Place: Ardglass
Graveyard: Ardglass CI

Estate papers
Kildare estate; Leslie estate; Ward estate

Census substitutes
FL, AC

Publications
James McCabe Napier, *The Story of Ardglass* (1966)
Duane Fitzsimons, *Under the Shade of Our Lady's Sweet Image: The Story of a Unique
    Coastal Parish in the Diocese of Down and Connor* (2016)
A Harvest of History from Dunsford and Ardglass (2014–)

ARDKEEN PARISH, COUNTY DOWN

Barony: Ards Upper
Diocese: Down
Place: Kirkistown
Graveyard: Ardkeen Old

Church records
CI Ardkeen

Baptisms, 1745– ; marriages, 1748– ; burials,	T679/121
1746– (all with gaps); confirmations, 1745–	(MIC583/10); T1065/28/1

Estate papers
Magill estate, Ards; Montgomery estate, Rosemount; Savage estate, Ardkeen

Census substitutes
FL, AC

Other records
Two lists of inhabitants of the manor of Ardkeen, 1779 and 1783, in a small volume
– D2223/15/10

ARDQUIN PARISH, COUNTY DOWN

Barony: Ards Upper
Diocese: Down
Graveyard: Ardquin CI

Church records
For CI records see **Ballyphilip**

Estate papers
Mount Ross estate; Savage-Nugent estate

Census substitutes
FL

ARDSTRAW PARISH, COUNTY TYRONE

Baronies: Omagh West, Strabane Lower
Diocese: Derry
Places: Ardstraw, Baronscourt, Douglas Bridge, Garvetagh, Newtownstewart
Graveyards: Ardstraw CI (Newtownstewart), Ardstraw Old, Pubble, Scarvagherin

Estate papers
Abercorn estate; Castle Stewart estate; Derry bishopric estate; Huntingdon estate;
McCausland estate; Mountjoy estate

Census substitutes
HMR, DE, LP (Ardstraw), FL

Freemasonry records
History of Masonic lodge no. 547, Newtownstewart, including a photograph of the
original warrant issued to the lodge in 1777 – T3453/1

Publications
William John Bradley, *Gallon: The History of Three Townlands in County Tyrone* (2000)
John H. Gebbie, *Ardstraw (Newtownstewart): Historical Survey of a Parish, 1600–1900* (1968)
T. P. Donnelly, *A History of the Parish of Ardstraw West and Castlederg* (n.d.)
The Parish of Ardstraw East: 1785–1985 (1985)
Wesley and Anna Millar, *On the Banks of the Douglas Burn* (2010)

ARMAGH PARISH, COUNTY ARMAGH

Barony: Armagh
Diocese: Armagh
Place: Armagh
Graveyards: Armagh CI Cathedral, Armagh P (formerly 2nd), Kildarton Old

Church records
CI Armagh

Baptisms, 1750–58, 1775– ; marriages, 1750–58, 1776– ; burials, 1750–58, 1770–75	T679/140 (MIC583/12)
Vestry minutes, 1791–	Local custody

P 1st Armagh

Baptisms, 1707–28, 1796– (including index); marriages, 1707–28, 1796– (including index); copies of session accounts, 1707–32, with a list of session members, 1707	MIC1P/4, D1759/1B/1 (MIC637/1); T636/1, pp 277–337
Session minutes, 1707–29; session accounts, 1707–32	PHSI
Typescript copy of registers of baptisms and marriages of the First Presbyterian Congregation of Armagh, with indexes, 1707–29, 1796–1809	NLI, MS 1395

'A list of Presbyterian marriages copied from The Session-Book of the Congregation of Armagh, 1707–28', *JRSAI*, 5th series, 8 (1898), pp 345–51

Extracts from session minutes and accounts in T. G. F. Paterson, 'Presbyterianism in Armagh' *Seanchas Ardmhacha*, 19:2 (2003), pp 140–63

RC Armagh

Baptisms, 1796–	MIC1D/41

Estate papers
Armagh archbishopric estate; Burges estate; Dawson estate; Lenox-Conyngham estate; Whaley estate

Census substitutes
HMR, FP, DP, FL

Corporation records: Armagh
Corporation records, 1731–1840, including borough books, 1731–76, 1738–1818, 1776–1816; corporation book, 1792; pipe water book, 1796–1833 – Armagh Robinson Library
Miscellaneous papers about Armagh corporation, 1686–92, 1747–1824 – DIO/4/40/1/1/1–21
Lists of burgesses of Armagh, 1747–96 – DIO/4/40/1/1/11–13
Extracts from Armagh corporation minute books, 1731–1818 – T808/14932, /14983, /15318
Lists of Armagh city grand jurors, 1731–1833 – T808/15319
Notes from Armagh city pipe water book giving personal names, 1796 – T808/14983
Names of jurors extracted from corporation records, 1731–75, 1776–1815 – T636/1, pp 103–12, 114–21

Other records
Depositions concerning a riot in 'Scotch Armagh', 17 March 1717, naming rioters, victims and witnesses – T552, p. 140; T808/14937
Householders in Armagh, 1770 – T389, T1228/1, T808/14977
Lease of Methodist chapel premises in Armagh, 1796: includes many names – T579/3

Publications
L. A. Clarkson and E. M. Crawford, *Ways to Wealth: The Cust Family of Eighteenth-Century Armagh* (1985)
G. Temple Lundie, *First Armagh Presbyterian Church, 1673–1973* (1973)
Catherine McCullough and W. H. Crawford, *Irish Historic Towns Atlas: Armagh* (2007)
James Stuart, *Historical Memoirs of the City of Armagh* (1819)

ARMOY PARISH, COUNTY ANTRIM

Baronies: Cary, Dunluce Upper
Diocese: Connor
Place: Armoy
Graveyard: Armoy CI

Church records
CI Armoy
Vestry minutes, 1758–   MIC1/334D/1

The vestry minutes include a list of parishioners providing security (for road repairs?), *c.* 1760.

Estate papers
Antrim estate; Macartney estate

Census substitutes
HMR, RCC, CPH, FL, AC

Publications
Dorothy Arthur, *St Patrick's Church Graveyard, Armoy* (2017)

ARTREA PARISH, COUNTIES LONDONDERRY AND TYRONE
The name of this parish is also spelled Ardtrea.

Baronies: Loughinsholin (Londonderry portion), Dungannon Upper (Tyrone portion)
Diocese: Armagh
Places: Ballyronan, Gracefield, (The) Loup, Moneymore
Graveyards: Artrea CI, Ballyeglish Old, Gracefield Moravian (former), Woods
    Chapel CI

Church records
CI Artrea
Vestry minutes, 1724–   MIC1/319D/1

The vestry minutes include a list of schoolmasters in the parish on the arrival of
the new rector, Rev. John Shadwell, in 1724 with list of names (cess-payers?) by
townland; a list of the poor 'with ye Protestant Dissenting Congregation of [–?]',
c. 1728; a list of the poor of the parish allowed to receive badges, 1729.

CI Woods Chapel
(also known as Lisnamorrow Chapel)
Vestry minutes, 1792–   MIC1/97

MOR Gracefield
Diaries, 1759– (with gaps); baptisms,   MIC1F/3
1750– ; burials, 1765– ; register of members
with an index, 1759– (with gaps)

Estate papers
Armagh archbishopric estate; Dawson estate; Drapers' Company estate; Graves
estate; Lenox-Conyngham estate; Lindesay estate; Salters' Company estate; Stewart
estate, Killymoon

Census substitutes
HMR, CPH, RelC (Anglicans, Presbyterians and Catholics; includes townlands), FL

Other records
Notes from various 17th- and 18th-century sources for Artrea parish – T716
Rental of Ballymilligan [Ballymulligan], 1752 – D3300/5/1

Publications
R. J. N. Porteus, *A Brief History of Ardtrea Parish Church* (1979)

AUGHNISH PARISH, COUNTY DONEGAL

Barony: Kilmacrenan
Diocese: Raphoe
Place: Ramelton
Graveyards: Killydonnell Friary; Tullyaughnish Old (Ramelton)

Church records
CI Aughnish or Tullyaughnish, including Tullyfern
Baptisms, 1798– ; marriages, 1788– ; burials, 1798–   MIC1/167A/1

P 1st Ramelton
Leather-bound sermon notebook   MIC1P/455/1
of Rev. Seth Drummond, 1705–07

Estate papers
Raphoe bishopric estate; Stewart estate, Fortstewart

Census substitutes
HMR, LP (Ramelton)

Business records
Watt, Ramelton

Other records
Bundle of badly damaged letters and receipts to Cairnes Edwards of 'Rathmelton',
     1741–7 – D1618/15/5/1

Publications
Brian Smeaton, *The Parish of Tullyaughnish, Ramelton* (1997)
Mary Haggan, *Ramelton: An Illustrated Guide to the Town* (2nd edition, 2004)
Áine Ní Dhuibhne (ed.), *Rathmullan, Ramelton & Raphoe Diocese: At the Time of the
     Flight of the Earls* (2007)

BADONEY see BODONEY

BAILIEBOROUGH PARISH, COUNTY CAVAN
The circumstances in which this parish was created are not entirely clear. According to
one account, this parish was formed in 1778 by detaching 29 townlands from the parish
of Killan (now **Shercock**), including the town of Bailieborough, and uniting them to
the old parish of **Moybologue**, which extended into County Meath in the province of
Leinster. It is said that the practice grew up of calling the Ulster section Bailieborough
and the Leinster section Moybologue with the result that the two sections were
eventually made into separate parishes. A small portion of Moybologue remains in
Cavan, however.

Baronies: Castlerahan, Clankee
Diocese: Kilmore
Place: Bailieborough
Graveyards: Bailieborough Old, Killan

Estate papers
Armagh archbishopric estate; Kilmore bishopric estate; Stewart Corry estate

Census substitutes
FL

Other sources
Typescript copy of a history of Bailieborough parish by W. G. Coleman – RCB,
    MS K 39
Inhabitants of the town of Bailieborough, 1805 – listed in the Appendix to Thomas
    Hall, 'The history of Presbyterianism in East Cavan and a small portion of Meath
    and Monaghan' (1912): a copy of this unpublished study is in Johnston Central
    Library in Cavan Town and on the library's website

Publications
J. A. Coleman, *Bailieborough: Historic Sketch* (1914)
Leslie McKeague, *Bailieborough: A Pictorial Past* (2010)
Leslie McKeague, *Trinity Presbyterian Church Bailieborough: The First 125 Years
    1887–2012 (Incorporates the Churches of 2nd Bailieborough and Seafin)* (2013) –
    the origins of 2nd Bailieborough (also known as Urcher) can be traced to the
    latter part of the 1700s
Leslie McKeague, *First Bailieborough Presbyterian Church (Corglass): 300 Years of
    Worship (1714–2014)* (2014)
Warren Porter, *'In Old Corglass': An Outline of 250 years in First Bailieboro'
    Presbyterian Church* (1964)

BALLEE PARISH, COUNTY DOWN

Barony: Lecale Lower
Diocese: Down
Graveyard: Ballee CI

Church records
CI Ballee
Baptisms, 1792–   T679/157
                                                        (MIC583/14)

Estate papers
Dickson estate; Fitzgerald estate; Leslie estate; Southwell estate; Ward estate

Census substitutes
DP (Ballee NSP), FL, AC

Publications
View book of the great tithes of the deanery of Down, 1732 – D1145/D/1

BALLINDERRY PARISH, COUNTY ANTRIM

Barony: Massereene Upper
Diocese: Connor
Places: Lower Ballinderry, Upper Ballinderry
Graveyards: Ballinderry Middle, Portmore, Templecormac

Church records
CI Ballinderry   T679/167
Vestry minutes, 1790–   (MIC583/14)

MOR Ballinderry
Baptisms, 1754– ; marriages, 1784– ; register   MIC1F/1
of members, 1755– ; ministers' diary, 1768

Estate papers
Conway estate

Census substitutes
HMR

Publications
Violet Best, *A History of Ballinderry Moravian Church* (2000)

BALLINDERRY PARISH, COUNTIES LONDONDERRY AND TYRONE

Baronies: Loughinsholin (Londonderry portion), Dungannon Upper (Tyrone
     portion)
Diocese: Armagh
Graveyards: Ballinderry Old, Eglish

Church records
CI Ballinderry
Vestry minutes, 1773–   Local custody

Estate papers
Armagh archbishopric estate; Drapers' Company estate

Census substitutes
HMR, CPH, FL

Publications
J. Baxter, *Ballinderry Parish Church: A Miscellany* (1984)
Kevin Johnston, *O'Neill's Own Country: A History of the Ballinderry Valley* (2009)

BALLINTEMPLE PARISH, COUNTY CAVAN

Barony: Clanmahon
Diocese: Kilmore
Graveyard: Ballintemple Old

Estate papers:
Coyne estate; Farnham estate; Pole estate; Saunderson estate

Census substitutes
FL

Publications
Tom Sullivan (ed.), *Drumkilly: From Ardkill Mountain to Kilderry Hill* (2001)

BALLINTOY PARISH, COUNTY ANTRIM
Ballintoy was created out of **Billy** parish in 1670.

Barony: Cary
Diocese: Connor
Places: Ballintoy, Portbraddan
Graveyards: Ballintoy CI, Templastragh

Church records
CI Ballintoy
Vestry minutes, 1712–   T679/68, 69
                                                        (MIC583/6, 7);
                                                        MIC1/111

The vestry minutes include the seating arrangement in the church (some names, but mainly organised by townland); names and addresses of the poor, 1790 (with later annotations); a census, 1803 (including the maiden name of wives).

Estate papers
Antrim estate; Fullerton estate; Stewart estate, Ballintoy; Stewart/Trail estate

Census substitutes
HMR (included under Billy parish), RCC, CPH, RelC (Protestants and Catholics; includes townlands), FL, AC

Other records
Letters of Rev. James Smyth, Beardiville and Ballintoy, 1713–24 – NLI, MS 41,582/2–4

Publications
George Hill, *The Stewarts of Ballintoy: With Notices of Other Families of the District in the Seventeenth Century* (1865, reprinted 1976)

BALLYAGHRAN PARISH, COUNTY LONDONDERRY

This parish is also known as Agherton.

Barony: North-East Liberties of Coleraine
Diocese: Connor
Place: Portstewart
Graveyard: Agherton Old

Estate papers
Antrim estate; Bacon estate

Census substitutes
HMR, CPH, FL

Other records
Leases for land in North Bellemont, 1763, 1792, 1803 – T3482/2
Notebook containing notification of registering arms, including residents of
    Ballyaghran, 1796 – D668/N/1
Notebook naming members of various Orange lodges in and near Coleraine
    including 'Ballyagherton', 1799 – D668/O/1

BALLYBAY PARISH, COUNTY MONAGHAN

Ballybay parish was formed in 1798 out of the parishes of **Aghnamullen** and
Tullycorbet.

Baronies: Cremorne, Monaghan
Diocese: Clogher
Place: Ballybay

Church records
P 1st Ballybay
Baptisms, 1799–   PHSI

Estate papers
Barton estate; Leslie estate, Ballybay; Massereene estate; Templetown estate

Business records
Bartley, Ballybay

Publications
David Nesbitt, *Full Circle: A Story of Ballybay Presbyterians* (1999)
James and Peadar Murnane, *At the Ford of the Birches: The History of Ballybay,*
    Its People and Vicinity (1999)

BALLYCLOG PARISH, COUNTY TYRONE

Barony: Dungannon Upper
Diocese: Armagh
Graveyard: Ballyclog Old

Estate papers
Armagh archbishopric estate; Castle Stewart estate; Charlemont estate; Drelincourt Charity estate; Maxwell estate

Census substitutes
HMR, FL

Other records
Applotment of Ballyclog parish, 'of sixty pounds towards the reparation of the parish church', n.d. (late 1600s) – D1618/15/2/55

Publications
R. S. Fisher, *The Brigh: Worship and Service over 375 Years* (1990)

BALLYCLUG PARISH, COUNTY ANTRIM

Barony: Antrim Lower
Diocese: Connor
Place: Moorfields
Graveyard: Ballyclug Old

Estate papers
O'Hara estate

Census substitutes
HMR

Publications
F. J. Mitchell, *A Short History of the Parish of Ballyclug* (1944)

BALLYCOR PARISH, COUNTY ANTRIM

Barony: Antrim Upper
Diocese: Connor
Place: Ballyeaston
Graveyards: Ballycor Old, Ballyeaston Old

Estate papers
Donegall estate; Forsythe estate

Census substitutes
HMR (included under Rashee parish), HSM, DP (Larne, Raloo, Carncastle, Kilwaughter, Glenarm and Ballyeaston)

Publications
Wilbert Garvin, *A History of Second Ballyeaston Presbyterian Church: Celebrating 250 Years, 1763–2013* (2013)

Jim Wilson, *His House of the Hill: A History of First Ballyeaston Presbyterian Church 1676–2004* (2005)

BALLYCULTER PARISH, COUNTY DOWN

Barony: Lecale Lower
Diocese: Down
Places: Raholp, Strangford
Graveyards: Ballyculter CI, Oldcourt CI

Church records
CI Ballyculter
Baptisms, 1777–   T679/176 (MIC583/15)

Estate papers
Hall estate, Strangford and Lower Iveagh; Kildare estate; Southwell estate; Ward estate

Census substitutes
FL, AC

Other records
View book of the great tithes of the deanery of Down, 1732 – D1145/D/1
Oaths of the Ballyculter Supplementary Corps, *c.* 1798: 63 names – T1023/153

Publications
Brian S. Turner, *Aspects of Audleystown: A Townland in Lecale* (2014)
W. E. Kennedy, *The Bangors and Ballyculter: An Historical Sketch of the Parish of Ballyculter (Strangford)* (1980)
An Account of the Trial of Edward Smyth, Late Curate of Ballyculter, in the Diocese of Down (1777): includes considerable detail on the parishioners, including the names of tenants of Lord Bangor

BALLYHALBERT PARISH, COUNTY DOWN
This parish is also known as St Andrew's.

Barony: Ards Upper
Diocese: Down
Places: Ballyhalbert, Glastry, Portavogie
Graveyards: Ballyhalbert Old

Church records
For CI records see **Inishargy**

P Glastry
Baptisms, 1728– ; marriages, 1750–   MIC1P/111

Estate papers
Allen estate; Bailie estate; Blackwood estate; Hamilton (Claneboye and Clanbrassil) estate; Echlin estate; Holmes estate; Ross estate, Portavo

Census substitutes
HSM, FL (listed as 'St Andrew')

Other records
Petition from inhabitants of Ballywalter and Ballyhalbert in response to the threat of danger from 'our most treacherous enemies the French', 1756: 78 names – *Belfast Newsletter*, 16 April 1756
Parish of St Andrews (Ballyhalbert) petition in relation to Act of Union, 1800 – *Belfast Newsletter*, 31 Jan. 1800

Publications
W. D. Bailie, *The Story of Glastry Congregation (formerly Ballyhalbert), 1721–1977* (1977)

BALLYKINLER PARISH, COUNTY DOWN

Barony: Lecale Upper
Diocese: Down
Place: Ballykinler

Estate papers
Downshire estate; Gibbons estate

BALLYLINNY PARISH, COUNTY ANTRIM

Barony: Belfast Lower
Diocese: Connor
Graveyard: Ballylinny Old

Estate papers
Donegall estate; Ellis estate

Census substitutes
HMR (included under Ballynure parish)

Other records
Subscribers to a reward fund, 1771 – *Belfast Newsletter*, 20 Sept. 1771

BALLYMACHUGH PARISH, COUNTY CAVAN

Barony: Clanmahon
Diocese: Ardagh
Place: Ballyheelan
Graveyard: Ballymachugh CI

Estate papers
Farnham estate; Pole estate

Census substitutes
FL

Publications
Bríd Donohoe, Nicholas Baxter (eds), *Ballymachugh and Drumloman South: Our Home Place by Sheelin's Side* (2008)

BALLYMARTIN PARISH, COUNTY ANTRIM

Baronies: Belfast Lower, Belfast Upper
Diocese: Connor

Estate papers
Upton estate

Other records
Names of tenants in Ballypallady townland, 1784 – *Belfast Newsletter*, 3–6 Feb. 1784

BALLYMONEY PARISH, COUNTIES ANTRIM AND LONDONDERRY

Baronies: Dunluce Upper, Kilconway (Antrim portion), North-East Liberties of Coleraine (Londonderry portion)
Diocese: Down
Places: Ballymoney, Balnamore, Bendooragh, Garryduff, Stranocum
Graveyards: Ballymoney Old, Roseyards P

Church records
P 1st Ballymoney
Baptisms, 1751–71 (with gaps); session   MIC1P/373; CR3/1
minutes, *c.* 1733–4; poor accounts, 1751–9

Session minutes, 1800–23   UTC

See also the call to Rev. Benjamin Mitchell, 1800, available as an online database at www.ballymoneyancestry.com

P Roseyards (originally Secession)
Volume entitled 'An Universal Book for ye use   D1748/A/2/3/1
of ye Session & Cong'n of Roseyards', including
collectors' accounts, 1777–81, marriages, 1780–91,
1798, seatholders, 1783, young communicants,
1781–1805

Covenant signed by members of the Roseyards   D1748/A/2/2
congregation, 1764, with a renewal, 1780

Various loose papers, including marriage certificates,   D1748/A/2/3
testimonials, etc, mainly late 1700s

Rev. John Tennent's account book, 1751–1807   D1748/A/2/1/3

Estate papers
Antrim estate; Caldwell estate; Dunlop estate; Legge estate; Hutchinson estate,
Stranocum; Leslie estate; McAulay estate; Magenis estate; O'Hara estate, O'Hara
Brook; Rowan estate, Ballymoney

Census substitutes
HMR, CPH, RelC (Anglicans, Presbyterians and Catholics), HSM, FL, AC

Freemasonry records
Extracts from the records of Ballymoney Masonic lodge no. 240, 1761–1849, which
include lists of members of the lodge and names of members expelled for their
involvement in the 1798 Rebellion – T1177/19/3–8

Business records
Erskine, Dunaverney; Reynolds, Ballymoney

Other records
Map of the town of Ballymoney, naming householders, 1734 – T935/1
Tithe-payers, 1780–95, giving names and townlands – T1177/19/16–20 (duplicate
    at T1177/17/32–5, but dates given as 1780–85)
Subscribers to a reward fund, Ballymoney, 1792 – *Northern Star*, 11–14 April 1792
Ballymoney applotment, 1795 – T1177/19/35–8
Notebook containing notification of registering arms, including residents of
    Ballymoney, 1796 – D668/N/1
Resolution of the inhabitants of Ballymoney, 1798 – *Belfast Newsletter*, 27 April 1798
Various manuscripts: account of the burning of Ballymoney, 1798; and notes on
    Hamilton's army in Ballymoney, 1798; the Coleraine attack; notes on Ballymoney
    history and the history of the linen market there – D1518/1/12

Publications
Dorothy Arthur, *Ballymoney Old Church Graveyard* (2008)
A. H. Dill, J. B. Armour, D. D. Doyle and J. Ramsay, *A Short History of the
    Presbyterian Churches of Ballymoney* (1898)
S. Alexander Blair, *The Meetinghouse Near the Cross: A History of Drumreagh
    Presbyterian Church* (1988)
S. Alexander Blair, *The Big Meetinghouse: A History of First Presbyterian Church,
    Ballymoney* (1996)

BALLYMORE PARISH, COUNTY ARMAGH

Barony: Orior Lower
Diocese: Armagh
Places: Acton, Clare, Poyntzpass, Tandragee, Tyrone's Ditches
Graveyards: Acton Old, Ballynaback, Ballymore CI, Terryhoogan (Relicarn)

Church records
CI Acton

Vestry minutes, 1793–	Local custody

CI Ballymore

Baptisms, 1783– ; marriages, 1783– ; burials, 1783– ; vestry minutes, 1771–	T679/52, 271 (MIC583/5, 24); MIC1/324A/1
Extracts from vestry minutes, 1771–1810	T2706/6, pp 125–42

The vestry minutes regularly include the names of the directors and overseers of road repairs from the early 1770s onwards.

P Tyrone's Ditches (originally Secession)

Baptisms, 1793– ; marriages, 1794– ; deaths, 1800– ; stipend collected, 1790– (the foregoing are all loose-leaf bundles of pages)	MIC1P/457

Estate papers
Armagh archbishopric estate; De Salis estate; Hamilton estate; Manchester estate; St John estate; Sandwich estate; Stewart estate

Census substitutes
HMR, FP, DP (Clare congregation), FL

Freemasonry records
Accounts for Masonic lodge no. 315, Tandragee, 1778–1827 – GLI

Other records
Map of Tandragee naming tenants in town, 1750 – T1224/1
Subscribers to a reward fund, 1777 – *Belfast Newsletter*, 16–20 May 1777
Landholders and inhabitants in and about Tandragee, County Armagh, petition about Act of Union – *Belfast Newsletter*, 11 Feb. 1800

Publications
C. F. McGleenon, 'Patterns of settlement in the Catholic parishes of Ballymore and Mullaghbrack in the 17th and 18th centuries', *Seanchas Ardmhacha*, 15:2 (1993), pp 51–83

Michael Anderson, *St Joseph's Church, Poyntzpass: Its Parish Priests and Curates 1788–1996: Parish of Ballymore and Mullabrack* (1996): includes a copy of the 1792 lease for the site of the Catholic church and a discussion of the 24 parishioners who were party to this deed

BALLYMYRE PARISH, COUNTY ARMAGH

This parish, also called Ballymoyer, was detached from **Armagh** *c.* 1770.

Barony: Fews Upper
Diocese: Armagh
Place: Whitecross
Graveyard: Ballymoyer Old

Estate papers
Armagh archbishopric estate

BALLYNASCREEN PARISH, COUNTY LONDONDERRY

The name of this parish is more generally spelled Ballinascreen.

Barony: Loughinsholin
Diocese: Derry
Places: Draperstown, Moneyneany, Sixtowns, Straw
Graveyard: Ballynascreen CI, Ballinascreen Old

Estate papers
Derry bishopric estate; Drapers' Company estate; Rowley estate; Skinners' Company estate

Census substitutes
HMR, CPH, RelC (Protestants), FL

Business records
McHendry, Sixtowns

Publications
J. A. Coulter, *Ballinascreen* (1953)
John McHugh, *Far from Ballinascreen: The Story of 18th and 19th Century Emigration from South Derry to Loretto (Cambria County) and the Development of it, and Other New Settlements in Western Pennsylvania*, edited by Joe Bradley and Graham Mawhinney (2012)
Townlands of the Parish of Ballinascreen: An Introductory Study (2015)

BALLYNURE PARISH, COUNTY ANTRIM

Barony: Belfast Lower
Diocese: Connor
Places: Ballynure, Straid
Graveyard: Ballynure Old

Estate papers
Adair estate, Loughanore; Brice estate; Dobbs estate; Donegall estate

Census substitutes
HMR, RelC (Catholics), HSM, DP (plus an Established Church petition)

Publications
Old Families of Carrickfergus & Ballynure from Gravestone Inscriptions, Wills and
    Biographical Notes, compiled by George Rutherford and edited by R. S. J. Clarke
    (1995)
Ernest McAlister Scott, *Ballynure: A Look at the History and Happenings in the Village*
    and Parish Over the Last 400 Years (2004)
Ernest McAlister Scott, *Neither Lost Nor Stolen But Straid (Ballyclare)* (2007)

BALLYPHILIP PARISH, COUNTY DOWN

Barony: Ards Upper
Diocese: Down
Place: Portaferry
Graveyard: Templecraney

Church records
CI Ballyphilip
Baptisms, 1745– ; marriages, 1746– ; burials, 1745–   T679/218, 219
                                                              (MIC583/17, 18)

Vestry minutes, 1751–   Local custody

P Portaferry
Baptisms, 1699–1786; marriages, 1750–84   MIC1P/137/1

Marriages, 1785–1822; committee minutes, 1739–98   PHSI

Estate papers
Brice estate; Mount Ross estate; Savage-Nugent estate

Census substitutes
FL

Other records
Deposition by Catherine McTimpany naming persons attending Mass [in Portaferry?],
    c. 1671 – D552/B/4/2/1
Charles Savage, Portaferry, wine cellar account, 1777 – D733/1
Subscription list of merchants of Portaferry concerning theft from shipwrecks, 1780
    – *Belfast Newsletter*, 18–22 Feb. 1780
Subscribers to a reward fund, Portaferry, 1784 – *Belfast Newsletter*, 10–13 Feb. 1784

Subscribers to a reward fund, Portaferry, 1786 – *Belfast Newsletter*, 24–28 March 1786
Notebook containing rent receipts paid to the Savage family by Abraham Matthews
    and Widow Matthews for property in New Row, Portaferry, 1771–1802 – T3043

Publications
'Court-martial held two centuries ago, at Portaferry, County Down', *UJA*, 1st series,
    8 (1860), pp 62–9
W. D. Bailie, *Portaferry Presbyterian Church, 1642–1992* (1992)
*Souvenir of the Bi-Centenary of St Patrick's Church Ballyphilip Portaferry: Sunday, 21st
    October, 1962* (1962)
The *Journal of the Upper Ards Historical Society* contains much of interest.

BALLYRASHANE PARISH, COUNTIES ANTRIM AND LONDONDERRY
This parish has also been known as St John's Town or Singinton.

Baronies: Dunluce Lower (Antrim portion), North-East Liberties of Coleraine
    (Londonderry portion)
Diocese: Connor
Graveyard: Ballyrashane CI

Church records
P Ballyrashane
Petty cash book of Rev. Samuel Boyce   MIC139/1
(minister of Ballyrashane, 1746–60), 1731–60

Estate papers
Antrim estate; Legge estate; McNaghten estate

Census substitutes
HMR, CPH, RelC (Catholics), FL, AC

Other records
Notebook containing notification of registering arms, including residents of
Ballyrashane, 1796 – D668/N/1

Publications
T. H. Mullin and J. E. Mullin, *The Kirk and Parish of Ballyrashane since the Scottish
    Settlement* (1957): includes the Antrim rent roll, 1641 (pp 176–8); freeholders,
    1790 (pp 179–80); names of persons born before 1800 on tombstones in the old
    graveyard (pp 186–8); tenants from the Beardiville estate map, 1713 (p. 63)
T. H. Mullin, *Families of Ballyrashane* (1969): a very detailed study of the families

BALLYSCULLION PARISH, COUNTY LONDONDERRY
One townland (Ballyscullion East) in this parish is in County Antrim.

Barony: Loughinsholin
Diocese: Derry

Place: Bellaghy
Graveyards: Ballyscullion CI, Church Island

Estate papers
Conolly estate; Dawson estate; Derry bishopric estate; Graves estate; Salters'
Company estate; Strafford estate; Vintners' Company estate

Census substitutes
HMR, CPH, FL

Other records
Petition of the parishioners of Ballyscullion concerning the ruinous state of their
    church, 1664 – D683/160 (printed in Moody and Simms, *Bishopric of Derry and
    the Irish Society of London*, vol. 1, p. 376)
Notices concerning the linen market at Bellaghy, naming, *inter alia*, drapers and
    manufacturers, 1763–4 – *Belfast Newsletter*, 6 May 1763, 25 May 1764

BALLYTRUSTAN PARISH, COUNTY DOWN

Barony: Ards Upper
Diocese: Down
Graveyard: Ballytrustan

Church records:
For CI records see **Ballyphilip**

Estate papers
Mount Ross estate; Savage-Nugent estate

BALLYWALTER PARISH, COUNTY DOWN

Barony: Ards Upper
Diocese: Down
Place: Ballywalter
Graveyard: Whitechurch

Church records
For CI records see **Inishargy**

Estate papers
Allen estate; Bailie estate; Blackwood estate; Hamilton (Claneboye and Clanbrassil)
estate; Ross estate, Portavo

Other records
Petition from inhabitants of Ballywalter and Ballyhalbert in response to the threat
of danger from 'our most treacherous enemies the French', 1756: 78 names – *Belfast
Newsletter*, 16 April 1756

Publications
Derek A. Patton, *Settlers by the Sea, 1626–1989: Ballywalter and its Presbyterians* (1989)
David Stewart, *An Historical Account of Ballywalter 1626–1926* (1928)

BALLYWILLIN PARISH, COUNTIES ANTRIM AND LONDONDERRY
This parish has also been known as Milton or Milltown.

Baronies: Dunluce Lower (Antrim portion); North-East Liberties of Coleraine (Londonderry portion)
Diocese: Connor
Place: Portrush
Graveyard: Ballywillin Old

Church records
CI Ballywillin
Vestry minutes, 1710–55   MIC1/287D/1
                                                      (RCB, MS E. 15)

The vestry minutes include lists of the poor, 1729, 1750s; and names of cess payers, *c.* 1734, 1735, 1736.

Estate papers
Antrim estate; Bacon estate; McNaghten estate

Census substitutes
HMR, CPH, RelC (Catholics), FL, AC

Other records
Book of vicarial tithes for the parish of 'Ballywoolen' (Ballywillin), listing tithe-payers by townland, 1783 – D668/B
Notebook containing notification of registering arms, including residents of Ballywillin, 1796 – D668/N/1

Publications
T. W. R. Milner, *A History of the Church of Ireland in the Parish of Ballywillan (Portrush)* (1972)
Julia E. Mullin, *The Kirk of Ballywillan since the Scottish Reformation* (1961)
H. G. McGrattan, *To Lovingly Make Known: Ballywillan Presbyterian Church from 1661* (2013)

BALTEAGH PARISH, COUNTY LONDONDERRY

Barony: Keenaght
Diocese: Derry

Place: Drumsurn
Graveyard: Balteagh Old

Estate papers
Beresford estate; Derry bishopric estate

Census substitutes
HMR, DE, CPH (includes townlands), FL

Other records
Exchequer bill naming 12 tenants in the townland of Cloghan, 1727 – T808/11353

Publications
J. S. P. Black, *Speaking Yet: Limavady Presbyterians and Balteagh* (1986)

BANAGHER PARISH, COUNTY LONDONDERRY

Baronies: Keenaght, Tirkeeran
Diocese: Derry
Place: Feeny
Graveyards: Banagher Old, Straid

Estate papers
Derry bishopric estate; Fishmongers Company estate; Skinners' Company estate

Census substitutes
HMR, CPH (includes townlands), RelC (Protestants), FL

Publications
Philip Donnelly, *The Parish of Banagher* (1996)

BANGOR PARISH AND TOWN, COUNTY DOWN

Baronies: Ards Lower, Castlereagh Lower
Diocese: Down
Places: Ballyholme, Bangor, Conlig, Crawfordsburn, Groomsport
Graveyard: Bangor Abbey

Church records
CI Bangor
Vestry minutes, 1788–   CR1/87/D/1

List of churchwardens of Bangor parish, 1720–82, printed in *UJA*, 2nd series,
7 (July 1901), pp 126–7

P 1st Bangor
Minutes, 1792, 1797–1801   PHSI

Estate papers
Allen estate; Blackwood estate; Brice estate; Hamilton (Claneboye and Clanbrassil) estate; Moor estate; Perceval-Maxwell estate; Ross estate, Portavo

Census substitutes
FL

Corporation records: Bangor
Register of elections of provosts, burgesses and freemen, 1716–68 – LA/20/1/CA/1A–B

Other records
Memorial from inhabitants, 1771 – *Belfast Newsletter*, 25 Jan. 1771
Subscribers to a reward fund, 1778 – *Belfast Newsletter*, 29 May–2 June 1778
Rev. James Hull's rent roll for Rathgill (Rathgael), 1780 – MIC506/1
Parish of Bangor petition in relation to Act of Union – *Belfast Newsletter*, 31 Jan. 1800 (printed in *DIFHR*, 29 (2006), p. 89)

Publications
David Irwin, *Tides and Times in the 'port: A Narrative History of the Co. Down Village of Groomsport with Particular Reference to the 150 Years of Groomsport Presbyterian Church* (1993)
William Wilson, *1623–1973: 350th Anniversary of First Bangor Presbyterian Church* (1973)

BARR OF INCH OR MINTIAGHS see MINTIAGHS OR BARR OF INCH

BELLEEK PARISH, COUNTY FERMANAGH
This parish was formed out of **Templecarn** in 1791.

Barony: Lurg
Diocese: Clogher
Places: Belleek, Castle Caldwell
Graveyards: Castle Caldwell (Rosbeg), Keenaghan

Estate papers
Caldwell estate

Census substitutes
FL

Publications
J. B. Cunningham, *A History of Castle Caldwell and its Families* (1980)
J. B. Cunningham, 'The landlord, the minister, the tenant and the tithe in Belleek in 1758', *Clogher Record*, 13 (1989), pp 84–90

BILLY PARISH, COUNTY ANTRIM

The parish of **Ballintoy** was created from Billy in 1670.

Baronies: Cary, Dunluce Lower
Diocese: Connor
Places: Bushmills, Dunseverick, Liscolman
Graveyard: Billy CI

Estate papers
Antrim estate; Dunlop estate; Macartney estate; Stewart/Trail estate; Wray estate

Church records
CI Billy
Vestry minutes, 1787–   CR1/29/A/1

The vestry minutes include lists of the poor, with townlands, 1793 (*c.* 30 names), 1795 (over 50 names); 40 names appended to the minutes of 1796.

Census substitutes
HMR, RCC, CPH, FL, AC

Publications
Adam A. Johns, *Short History of the Parish of Billy* (1982)
H. Barkley Wallace, *Bushmills Presbyterian Church, 1646–1996* (1996)

BLARIS PARISH, COUNTIES ANTRIM AND DOWN

Baronies: Massereene Upper (Antrim portion), Castlereagh Upper, Iveagh Lower
    (Upper Half) (Down portion)
Diocese: Connor
Places: Culcavey, Lisburn, Ravernet
Graveyards: Blaris Old, Christ Church Cathedral, Kilrush, Lisburn Friends

Church records
CI Lisburn (Christ Church Cathedral)
Baptisms, 1637, 1639–41, 1643–6, 1655– ;   T679/112
baptisms of Huguenot children, 1707–36;   (MIC583/10);
marriages, 1639–41, 1643–6, 1664– ; burials,   MIC1/3–5; CR1/35
1639–41, 1661– ; burials in Lisburn Cathedral
churchyard, 1670– ; vestry minutes, 1675– ;
confirmations, 1667, 1675, 1678; notebook
of Rev. Thomas Haslam, *c.* 1675–95

The earliest registers have been published as *Register of the Church of St Thomas, Lisnagarvey, Co. Antrim, 1637–1646* (1996).

The vestry records include churchwardens' accounts for 1668–9 and a number of subsequent years; there are also lists of the poor, 167[4], 1727.

P 1st Lisburn

Baptisms, 1692–1732, 1736–64, 1779– ; marriages,   MIC1P/159; CR3/11
1688–96, 1711–19, 1782– ; session minutes,
1688–1709, 1711–63; subscription list for the
new meeting house, 1764–5; seat lists and pew
rents, 1764– ; accounts, 1775–

'Session books of first Lisburn Presbyterian congregation', *UJA*, 2nd series, 6 (1900), p. 183

'The M'Cracken Correspondence', *JRSAI*, 5th series, 16 (1906), pp 51–8: transcripts of letters, 1707–13, by Rev. Alexander McCracken, minister of 1st Lisburn (not concerning members of his congregation)

Call to Rev. Andrew Craig, 1782 – printed in *These Hallowed Grounds*, vol. 2, p. 281

RSF Lisburn

Men's monthly meeting minutes, 1675– ;   MIC16/7–23
women's monthly meeting minutes, 1793–1800;
ministers' and elders' minutes, 1791– ; births,
1781– ; marriages, 1731–86 ; removal certificates,
1766– ; register of members, 1794– ; disownment
records, 1703– ; account book, 1789– ; register of
tithe sufferings, 1706–11

Estate papers
Downshire estate; Conway estate; Wallace estate

Census substitutes
HMR, HSM, DP, FL (one name: Robert Fowler)

Business records
Richardson, Lisburn

Freemasonry records
Minute book of Masonic lodge no. 683 (Ballykeel Edenagonnell), 1793–1813 – GLI

Other records
List of tenants of Lisnegarvey (Lisburn), 1630 – T808/14909
Map of Lisnegarvey (Lisburn) with details of tenements, 1632 – T343
Collectors' accounts for Lisburn Walk, 1691: over 400 names arranged by place –
    T808/14904 (T808/14902 is an alphabetical list of these names)
Rent roll of those receiving piped water in the town of Lisburn, 1768 – D195/1

Subscribers to a reward fund, 1771 – *Belfast Newsletter*, 23 Aug. 1771
Subscribers to a reward fund, 1777 – *Belfast Newsletter*, 1–5 Aug. 1777
Protest by individuals who had determined to secede from the Lisburn Volunteers, 1780 – *Belfast Newsletter*, 1–5 Sept. 1780

Publications
H. Bayley, *A Topographical and Historical Account of Lisburn* (1834)
'An autobiographical sketch of Andrew Craig, 1754–1833. Presbyterian minister of Lisburn', *UJA*, 2nd series, 14 (May-Aug. 1908), pp 10–15, 51–5
W. P. Carmody, *Lisburn Cathedral and its Past Rectors* (1926)
T. G. F. Paterson, 'Lisburn and neighbourhood in 1798', *UJA*, 3rd series, 1 (1938), pp 193–8
W. I. Craig, *Presbyterianism in Lisburn from the Seventeenth Century: First Lisburn Presbyterian Church* (1960)
William Richer, *Despair to Resurrection: First Lisburn Presbyterian Church 1688–1988* (1988)
Raymond Gillespie, 'George Rawdon's Lisburn', *Lisburn Historical Society Journal*, 8 (1991), pp 32–6
These Hallowed Grounds: Lisburn gravestone inscriptions and additional genealogical materials, vol. 1 (2001), vol. 2 (2005)
Arthur G. Chapman, *Quakers in Lisburn – Four centuries of Work and Witness* (2009)
The *Lisburn Historical Society Journal* contains much material of interest.

BODONEY PARISH, COUNTY TYRONE
This parish, also spelled Badoney, was divided into Upper and Lower sections in 1774.

Barony: Strabane Upper
Diocese: Derry
Places: Cranagh, Glenelly, Glenhull, Gortin, Greencastle, Plumbridge, Rousky
Graveyards: Bodoney Lower CI, Bodoney Upper CI, Corrick

Estate papers
Belmore estate; Derry bishopric estate; Hamilton estate, Dunnamanagh; Hamilton estate, Manor Elieston

Census substitutes
HMR, DE, FL

Other records
Names of masters of families, 1699 – T542
Miscellaneous 18th-century extracts from the Registry of Deeds – T808/15112
Deeds relating to various townlands, 18th century – D3733

Publications
Meetings and Memories in Lower Badoney, vol. 1 (1995), vol. 2 (2000)
Sean Clarke, *Broughderg: A Place and its Peoples* (n.d.)

BOHO PARISH, COUNTY FERMANAGH

Baronies: Clanawley, Magheraboy
Diocese: Clogher
Place: Boho
Graveyard: Boho RC

Estate papers
Clogher bishopric estate; Cooper estate; Erne estate

Other records
An account of the tithes in the parishes of Devenish and Boho, 1695: long list of names – printed in W. B. Steele, *The Parish of Devenish, County Fermanagh: Materials for its History* (1937), pp 78–80

Publications
E. G. Elliott, *The Parish of Devenish and Boho* (1990)
Edel Bannon, Louise McLaughlin and Cecilia Flanagan (eds), *Boho Heritage: A Treasure Trove of History and Lore* (2009)

BOVEVAGH PARISH, COUNTY LONDONDERRY

Barony: Keenaght
Diocese: Derry
Places: Burnfoot, Gortnahey
Graveyard: Bovevagh Old

Church records
CI Bovevagh
Vestry minutes, 1777–   Local custody

P Bovevagh
Transcripts of marriages, 1761–7 (12 entries)   PHSI

Estate papers
Beresford estate; Derry bishopric estate

Census substitutes
HMR, CPH (includes townlands), RelC (Anglicans, Presbyterians and Catholics; includes townlands), FL

Other records
Various documents concerning the MacClurg (McClorg) family, Templemoyle, from various locations in USA, 1767–1847 – T1227, T1229

Publications
Philip Donnelly, 'The Catholic parish of Bovevagh', *Seanchas Ardmhacha*, 19:1 (2002), pp 138-67

BRIGHT PARISH, COUNTY DOWN

Barony: Lecale Upper
Diocese: Down
Graveyard: Bright CI

Church records
CI Bright
Vestry minutes, 1770–   MIC1/115/1

The vestry minutes record the names of those to whom seats were distributed, 1792.

Estate papers
Gibbons estate; Kildare estate; Lascelles estate; Southwell estate; Ward estate

Census substitutes
FL, AC

Other records
View book of the great tithes of the deanery of Down, 1732 – D1145/D/1

BURT PARISH, COUNTY DONEGAL
This parish was created in 1809 out of **Templemore**.

Barony: Inishowen West
Diocese: Derry
Places: Burnfoot, Burt
Graveyard: Burt Old (Castlecooly), Drumhaggart, Grange

Church records
P Burt
Session minutes, 1676–1719 [currently missing]   UTC

Transcripts from session minutes of baptisms,   PHSI
1677–83; marriages, 1678–80, 1690–1716;
elders, 1691–8 (plus index)

Estate papers
Donegall estate; Forward estate

Census substitutes
LP (Burt)

Publications
D. W. T. Crooks, *In the Footsteps of St Baithin. A History of Taughboyne Group* (1992)
Seoirse Ó Dochartaigh, *Inis Eoghain: The Island of Eoghan: The Place-Names of
    Inishowen* (2011)
Seoirse Ó Dochartaigh, *The Great Name Book of Inishowen* (2016)

CAMLIN PARISH, COUNTY ANTRIM

Barony: Massereene Upper
Diocese: Connor
Place: Crumlin
Graveyards: Camlin Old, Crumlin NSP

Church records
For CI records see **Glenavy**

Estate papers
Conway estate; Langford estate

Census substitutes
HMR (included under Glenavy parish)

Publications
Charles Watson, *The Story of the United Parishes of Glenavy, Camlin and Tullyrusk* (1892)

CAMUS-JUXTA-MOURNE PARISH, COUNTY TYRONE

Barony: Strabane Lower
Diocese: Derry
Place: Strabane
Graveyards: Patrick Street (Strabane), Camus Old

Church records
P Strabane
'Diary of Rev. William Homes of Chilmark, Martha's Vineyard, 1689–1746',
New England Historical and Genealogical Register, 48 (1894), pp 446–53; 49 (1895), pp 413–16; 50 (1896), pp 155–66: Homes (or Holmes) was minister of Strabane from 1692 to 1714; the information recorded during his time in Strabane mainly concerned his wider family

For RC records see **Clonleigh**

Estate papers
Abercorn estate; Derry bishopric estate; Erne (Lady) estate; Hamill estate

Census substitutes
HMR, LP (Strabane), DP (Strabane), FL

Corporation records: Strabane
Corporation council minutes, 1755–1812; corporation minutes, accounts and borough court proceedings, 1769–1850; jury book, 1773–1810: the records include

a list of over 100 individuals upon whom quarterage was levied, 1773, and a list of 66 townspeople fined 6½d. each for various misdemeanours, 1787 – MIC159/1

Business records
Smyly, Strabane

Other records
Names of inhabitants of the town of Strabane from the Registry of Deeds, 1708–38, published in *DIFHR*, 24 (2001), pp 83–4
Names of *c.* 40 inhabitants of Strabane in a letter by the eighth earl of Abercorn, 1745 – D623/A/12/5
Petition from inhabitants of Strabane to the eighth earl of Abercorn, 1768: *c.* 85 names – D623/A/38/28
Memorial from the inhabitants of Strabane to the first marquess of Abercorn, 1790: *c.* 50 names – D623/A/151/47

Publications
Jim Bradley et al., *The Fair River Valley: Strabane through the ages*, edited by John Dooher and Michael Kennedy (2000)
Michael Cox, *Overlooking the River Mourne: Four Centuries of Family Farms in Edymore and Cavanalee in County Tyrone* (2006)
David Killen, *Through All the Days: A Presbyterian Heritage, Strabane, 1659–1994* (1994)
E. E. K. McClelland, *Friendly Strabane: A Glimpse at the History of the Town and of the Presbyterian Church* (1959)
William J. Roulston, *Restoration Strabane: Economy and Society in Provincial Ireland, 1660–1714* (2007)

CAPPAGH PARISH, COUNTY TYRONE

Barony: Strabane Upper
Diocese: Derry
Places: Campsie, Erganagh, Mountfield, Mountjoy, Omagh
Graveyards: Dunmullan (Cappagh Old)

Church records
CI Cappagh
Baptisms, 1753– ; marriages, 1752– ;   T679/4, 303, 328
burials, 1758– ; vestry minutes, *c.* 1758–   (MIC583/1, 27, 30)

Estate papers
Derry bishopric estate; Huntingdon estate; McCausland estate, Omagh; Mervyn estate; Mountjoy estate

Census substitutes
HMR, DE, FL

Other sources
Names of masters of families, 1699 – T542

Publications
Reflections on Cappagh: 'Within the Sound of the Bell' (2013)

CARNCASTLE PARISH, COUNTY ANTRIM
The name of this parish is also spelled Cairncastle.

Barony: Glenarm Upper
Diocese: Connor
Places: Ballygally, Carncastle
Graveyard: Carncastle CI

Estate papers
Agnew estate; Antrim estate; Moore and Stewart Moore estate; Richardson estate

Census substitutes
HMR, DP (Larne, Raloo, Carncastle, Kilwaughter, Glenarm and Ballyeaston)

Publications
Harold R. Allen, *A History of Cairncastle Presbyterian Church 1832–1990* (1990)

CARNMONEY PARISH, COUNTY ANTRIM

Barony: Belfast Lower
Diocese: Connor
Places: Carnmoney, Glengormley, Whiteabbey, Whitehouse
Graveyard: Carnmoney CI

Church records
CI Carnmoney

Baptisms, 1788– ; marriages, 1791–	T679/332
	(MIC583/29)

P Carnmoney

Baptisms, 1708– ; marriages, 1708– ;	MIC1P/37/4–9;
session minutes, 1686–1748, 1767– ;	T1013/1
poor lists, 1716–84; names of those who	
transferred from other congregations, 1708–25	

Notebook giving marriages, births and deaths	T1013/2A–B
of various families with an index, 1708–1917	

See also Bonar, *Nigh on Three and a Half Centuries*, including a call to Rev. John
Thomson sen., 1730 (pp 328–9) and a call to Rev. John Thomson jun. (pp 330-31);

and William Fee McKinney, 'Old session books of Carnmoney, County Antrim, 1686–1821', *UJA*, 2nd series, 6 (Jan. 1900), pp 6–11

Estate papers
Donegall estate; Mussenden estate

Census substitutes
HMR, DP (plus Established Church petition)

Other records
Tithe book, Carnmoney parish, listing tithe-payers by townland, 1789 – D852/1

Publications
Robert Armstrong, *Through the Ages to Newtownabbey* (revised edition, 1994)
Robert H. Bonar, *Nigh on Three and a Half Centuries. A History of Carnmoney Presbyterian Church* (2004)
E. V. Scott, *The Carnmoney Connection: A History of Carnmoney Parish from 1796– 1985* (1985)

CARNTEEL PARISH, COUNTY TYRONE
The boundaries of the parishes of Aghaloo, Carnteel and Killeeshil were reorganised in 1680.

Barony: Dungannon Lower
Diocese: Armagh
Places: Aughnacloy, Ballyreagh, Carnteel
Graveyards: Aghaloo Old, Carnteel CI, Carnteel Old

Church records
CI Carnteel
Vestry minutes, 1712–   T679/355 (MIC583/31)

P Aughnacloy
Finance committee book, 1743–82   PHSI

Estate papers
Armagh archbishopric estate; Stewart estate, Killymoon; Verner estate

Census substitutes
HMR, RelC (Protestants and Catholics)

Other records
Petition from the parishioners of Aghaloo and Carnteel for the removal of Archdeacon Michael Hewetson, 1700 – DIO/4/32/A/2/4/1–3
Printed resolution of the members of the Orange lodges in the neighbourhood of Clogher, Augher, Ballygawley and Aughnacloy, with names appended, 1798 – D2085/6

Publications
J. J. Marshall, *Annals of Aughnacloy and of the Parish of Carnteel, County Tyrone*
    (1920; 2nd edition 1925; 3rd edition 2009): includes extracts from the minute
    book of Aughnacloy Orange Lodge (no. 156) beginning in 1797
Ministries in Miniature: Aughnacloy Presbyterian Church, 1697–1990 (1938), revised
    and updated by Cecil Givan (1993)
The Book of Eglish: Where the Oona Flows (2011): at over 500 pages this book is a
    wealth of information about the area

CARRICK PARISH, COUNTY LONDONDERRY
This parish was created as a perpetual curacy in 1846 out of portions of the parishes
of **Balteagh**, **Bovevagh** and **Tamlaght Finlagan**.

CARRICKFERGUS PARISH, COUNTY ANTRIM

Barony: Belfast Lower
Diocese: Connor
Places: Boneybefore, Carrickfergus, Eden, Greenisland, Woodburn
Graveyard: Carrickfergus CI (St Nicholas)

Church records
CI Carrickfergus

Baptisms, 1740–99; marriages, 1740– ; burials, 1740–1800	T679/323 (MIC583/28)
Accounts relating to the construction of the church spire, 1778–9	CR1/25/5/1

Estate papers
Brice estate; Brytt estate; Dalway estate; Donegall estate; Kirk estate; Macartney
estate; Saunders estate; Vesey estate

Census substitutes
HMR, DP

Corporation records: Carrickfergus
Volume of *c.* 90 pages containing information about Carrickfergus corporation,
    c. 1568–*c.* 1689 – D162/1. It shows that in 1683 there were 105 freemen and 41
    burgesses, of whom 17 were aldermen. Also included is a rental of Carrickfergus
    for the half year ending May 1674.
Memoranda on elections of burgesses, 1672–1702 – D162/5
List of burgesses and freemen of the corporation, n.d. (pre-1706): over 250 names,
    with occupations – D162/18
Records of Carrickfergus as copied from the old books of records by Richard Dobbs,
    1569–1801 – T707/1

Miscellaneous collection relating to the borough of Carrickfergus, 1609–1874 – D3860/F

Other records
Leases, etc for Carrickfergus, starting in 1596 – T686
Premiums awarded to pupils at Carrickfergus School, master Mr McCloskey, 1800 – *Belfast Newsletter*, 18 April 1800

Publications
James Mathew MacCary [Catholic rector of Carrickfergus and Larne], *The Sure Way to Heaven, being a new volume, such never before published in English on the truths of salvation* (1797): the list of subscribers runs to over 450 names and from the addresses given, it is clear that many were from the author's own congregation (names printed in *DIFHR*, 35 (2012), pp 3–6)
Old Families of Carrickfergus & Ballynure from Gravestone Inscriptions, Wills and Biographical Notes, compiled by George Rutherford and edited by R. S. J. Clarke (1995)
D. J. McCartney, *Nor Principalities Nor Powers: Or Three Hundred and Seventy Years of Presbyterianism: A History of First Presbyterian Church, Carrickfergus* (1991)
Samuel McSkimin, *The History and Antiquities of the County of the Town of Carrickfergus* (1811; new edition 1909 with notes and appendix by E. J. McCrum): provides a huge amount of detail on Carrickfergus and its families; includes names of corporation tenants in 1674 and 1731, and a rent roll for Carrickfergus, 1709
Philip Robinson, *Irish Historic Towns Atlas: Carrickfergus* (1986)
See also the *Carrickfergus & District Historical Journal*

CASTLEBOY PARISH, COUNTY DOWN
This parish is also known as St Johnstown.

Barony: Ards Upper
Diocese: Down
Place: Cloghy

Church records
For CI records see **Ballyphilip**

Estate papers
Echlin estate; Savage-Nugent estate

Census substitutes
AC

Other records
Recovery of lands of Castleboy, 1708 – D466/1

CASTLEKEERAN see **LOUGHAN OR CASTLEKEERAN**

CASTLERAHAN PARISH, COUNTY CAVAN

Barony: Castlerahan
Diocese: Kilmore
Place: Ballyjamesduff
Graveyard: Castlerahan Old

Church records
RC Castlerahan and Munterconnaught
Baptisms, 1752–71, 1773–6; marriages, 1751–71,   MIC1D/81
1773–5; deaths, 1751–8, 1761–9, 1773–5

Estate papers
Coyne estate; Farnham estate; Massereene estate; Nugent estate

Census substitutes
FL

Publications
Sara Cullen, *Castlerahan* (1981)
Ballyjamesduff: Past and Present (n.d.)

CASTLETERRA PARISH, COUNTY CAVAN
The name of this parish is also spelled Castletarra and Castletara.

Barony: Loughtee Upper
Diocese: Kilmore
Places: Ballyhaise, Butlers Bridge
Graveyard: Castleterra Old

Church records
RC Castletara
Baptisms, 1763– ; marriages, 1763–93   MIC1D/83–4

Estate papers
Annesley estate; Lanesborough estate; Richardson estate

Census substitutes
FL

Publications
Ballyhaise and Castletara: Past and Present (1983)
*Ballyhaise Agricultural College 1906–2006 including a History of Ballyhaise House and
    Estate from 1610* (2006)
P. J. Dunne, *Butlersbridge: A History* (2012)

CLEENISH PARISH, COUNTY FERMANAGH

Baronies: Clanawley, Magheraboy, Magherastephana, Tirkennedy
Diocese: Clogher
Places: Arney, Belcoo, Bellanaleck, Holywell, Letterbreen, Lisbellaw
Graveyards: Cleenish CI (Bellanaleck), Cleenish Old, Holywell (Templerushin),
    Lisbellaw CI, Templenaffrin

Estate papers
Clogher bishopric estate; Enniskillen estate; Erne estate; Hassard estate;
Huntingdon estate

Census substitutes
FL

Publications
Joe Crawford, *Lisbellaw: "The Hard Rocks"* (1992)
If Only: Historical Sketches of the Belcoo Area (1996)

CLOGHER PARISH, COUNTY TYRONE

Barony: Clogher
Diocese: Clogher
Places: Augher, Clogher, Eskra, Fivemiletown
Graveyards: Clogher CI Cathedral, Fivemiletown CI

Church records
CI Clogher

Baptisms, 1763– ; marriages, 1777–8, 1796– ; burials, 1783, 1798– ; list of churchwardens, 1713– ; vestry minutes, 1713–95 (with gaps)	MIC1/22, 23

The vestry minutes reveal that there were over 30 signatories to the meeting of
30 Dec. 1766.

List of churchwardens of Clogher parish, 1713–1900	T2655/4/1

Extracts from the baptism register, 1763–1812	T2655/4/2

'Some christenings, marriages and burials in the parish church of Clogher, Co.
Tyrone in 1666 with some notes' by Jack Johnston, *Clogher Record*, 14 (1992),
    pp 63–5

'Clogher parish – some early sidesmen 1662–1734' by Jack Johnston, *Clogher Record*,
(1991), pp 89–91

P Clogher (Carntall)
Call to Rev. Andrew Millar from the session and   T2655/4/3
congregation of Carntall, 1773: 76 signatories

Estate papers
Cairns estate; Clogher bishopric estate; Forbes estate; Gorges estate; Leslie estate,
Glaslough; Mervyn estate; Montgomery estate; Mountjoy estate; Moutray estate;
Speer estate; Story estate

Census substitutes
HMR, FL

Corporation records: Clogher
The corporation book is kept in the Diocesan Archive Room in Clogher Cathedral.
Extracts from the corporation book, 1783–98 – T1566

Other records
Printed resolution of the members of the Orange lodges in the neighbourhood of
Clogher, Augher, Ballygawley and Aughnacloy, with names appended, 1798 –
D2085/6

Publications
J. I. D. [Jack] Johnston, *Clogher Cathedral Graveyard* (1972): includes a wealth of
    information about the families buried there
Jack Johnston, *Glenhoy: The First 200 Years* (1979): includes a chapter providing brief
    biographical notes on the families associated with Glenhoy Presbyterian Church
    and appendices including a rental of the Savile (Foljambe) estate from 1738 and
    leaseholders in the manor of Cecil in 1769
Jack Johnston, *From Annahoe to Fivemiletown: Orangeism in the Clogher Valley, 1795–
    1995* (1995)
Jack Johnston, *The Clogher Story* (2015): includes a map of the demesne belonging to
    the see of Clogher, 1745, naming tenants in tenements in the town of Clogher
J. J. Marshall, *Clochar na Righ (Clogher of the Kings): being a history of the town of and
    district of Clogher, in the county of Tyrone. Also some account of the parish of Errigal
    Keeroge, in the county of Tyrone, and the parish of Errigal Truagh, in the county of
    Monaghan* (1930)
H. B. Murphy, *Three Hundred Years of Presbyterianism in Clogher* (1958)

CLOGHERNY PARISH, COUNTY TYRONE
This parish, also spelled Clogherney, was created in 1732 out of **Termonmaguirk**.

Barony: Omagh East
Diocese: Armagh
Places: Beragh, Gortaclare, Seskinore
Graveyards: Clogherny CI, Donaghanie

Estate papers
Armagh archbishopric estate; Belmore estate; Gorges estate; Perry estate

Census substitutes
HMR, FL

Publications
J. W. Lockington, *A History of Clogherney Presbyterian Church* (2010)
P. J. McCusker, 'Ballentaken: Beragh in the 17th century', *Seanchas Ardmhacha*, 10:2
    (1982), pp 455–501

CLONALLAN PARISH, COUNTY DOWN
The name of this parish is also spelled Clonallon; around 1840 the parish of
Warrenpoint was detached from Clonallan.

Barony: Iveagh Upper (Upper Half)
Diocese: Dromore
Places: Burren, Mayobridge, Narrow Water, Warrenpoint
Graveyard: Clonallan CI

Estate papers
Downshire estate; Dungannon estate; Hall estate, Narrow Water; Meade estate

Census substitutes
FL

Publications
Padraic Keenan, *Clonallon Parish: Its Annals and Antiquities* (1942)

CLONCA PARISH, COUNTY DONEGAL
See also **Culdaff** parish.

Barony: Inishowen East
Diocese: Derry
Places: Ballygorman, Malin
Graveyards: Clonca Old, Lag(g)

Church records
CI Cloncha
Vestry minutes, 1693–1707   D803/1

These vestry minutes are found in a volume that is mainly concerned with **Culdaff**
parish.

Estate papers
Derry bishopric estate; Donegall estate; Hart estate

Census substitutes
HMR, CPH (includes townlands), FL

Publications
Brian Bonner, *Our Inis Eoghain Heritage: The Parishes of Culdaff and Cloncha* (1984)
Seoirse Ó Dochartaigh, *Inis Eoghain: The Island of Eoghan: The Place-Names of Inishowen* (2011)
Seoirse Ó Dochartaigh, *The Great Name Book of Inishowen* (2016)

CLONDAHORKY PARISH, COUNTY DONEGAL

Barony: Kilmacrenan
Diocese: Raphoe
Places: Creeslough, Doe Castle, Dunfanaghy, Faugher, Portnablagh
Graveyards: Doe Castle, Clondahorky Old, Cloon

Estate papers
Hart estate; Raphoe bishopric estate; Stewart estate, Ards; Vaughan estate

Census substitutes
HMR

Publications
C. W. P. MacArthur, *Dunfanaghy Presbyterian Congregation and its Times* (1978)
Brian Moriarty, *Built Upon a Hill. The Story of St John's Church, Ballymore, 1732–2002* (2004)

CLONDAVADDOG PARISH, COUNTY DONEGAL
The name of this parish has been spelled in a number of different ways, including Clondevaddock.

Barony: Kilmacrenan
Diocese: Raphoe
Places: Portsalon, Rosnakill
Graveyard: Clondevaddock CI

Church records
CI Clondevaddock
Baptisms, 1794– ; marriages, 1794– ;   MIC1/164A/1
burials, 1794– ; census, 1796

The census of 1796 is arranged by townland and names the head of each household, indicating the relationship of others in the household to him/her (e.g. spouse, children, servants); the census concerns the Anglican population in the parish, but indicates if a member of a household was affiliated to another denomination.

Estate papers
Clements estate; Raphoe bishopric estate; Stewart estate, Fortstewart

Census substitutes
HMR, FL

Publications
Hugh Doherty, *Oughterlin to Lough Swilly: A Local History* (2015)
John Fitzgerald and John McCreadie, *Glenvar and Oughterlin* (1986)

CLONDERMOT PARISH, COUNTY LONDONDERRY
This parish is also known as Glendermott.

Barony: Tirkeeran
Diocese: Derry
Places: Ardmore, Derry-Londonderry (The Waterside), New Buildings
Graveyards: Enagh, Glendermott Old

Estate papers
Conolly estate; Derry bishopric estate; Goldsmiths' Company estate; Grocers'
Company estate; Ponsonby estate

Census substitutes
HMR, DE, LP (Glendermott), CPH (Glendermot, includes townlands), FL

Other records
Names of those from the manor of Goldsmiths summoned to appear at a court leet,
1716: over 200 names – MIC9B/12A

Publications
Glendermott Presbyterian Church, 1654–1954 (1954)
In the Shadow of the Tail of the Fox: A History of New Buildings & District (2002),
    includes extensive information on townlands, including details taken from
    18th-century sources
Samuel Ferguson, *Some Items of Historic Interest about the Waterside* (1902)
Trevor Magee, *Planted by a River: Two Hundred Years of Covenanter Witness at
    Faughan Bridge 1790–1990* (1990)

CLONDUFF PARISH, COUNTY DOWN

Barony: Iveagh Upper (Upper Half)
Diocese: Dromore
Place: Hilltown
Graveyards: Clonduff CI, Clonduff Old

Church records
CI Clonduff
Baptisms, 1782– ; marriages, 1786– ; burials, 1787–   T679/17 (MIC583/2)

Estate papers
Annesley estate; Close estate; Downshire estate; Meade estate

Census substitutes
FL, AC

Publications
Padraic Keenan, *Brief Historical Sketch of the Parish of Clonduff* (1941)

CLONES PARISH, COUNTIES FERMANAGH AND MONAGHAN

Baronies: Clankelly (Fermanagh portion), Dartree, Monaghan (Monaghan portion)
Diocese: Clogher
Places: Aghadrumsee, Clones, Magheraveely, Rosslea, Smithborough
Graveyards: Clones Abbey, Clones CI, Clones Round Tower, Magheraveely, Uttony

Church records
CI Clogh
Marriages, 1792–   MIC1/288

CI Clones
Baptisms, marriages and burials, 1667–70   Printed in Shirley,
    Monaghan, pp 591–5
    (reprinted in *DIFHR*,
    36 (2013), pp 3–10)

Baptisms, 1682– ; marriages, 1682–1788,   MIC1/147; CR1/58/1, 2
1792– ; burials, 1682–1704, 1709, 1722–5,
1733–4; vestry minutes, 1688–

The vestry minutes include: names of subscribers to church repairs, 1692; allocation of ground within the church for seats for particular families, 1694; around 140 signatures appended to a meeting in 1715 to discuss where a chapel of ease should be built; lists of seatholders, 1735; over 40 names of the poor to whom badges could be issued, along with the person vouching for each one, 1741 (with updates); 'A regulation of seats made at a vestry in Clones … [in 1735] and newly transcribed now out of that former registry … [in 1783]', includes information on the reallocation of seats between 1735 and 1783.

Estate papers
Barrett Lennard estate; Clogher bishopric estate; Dawson estate; Erne estate; McClintock estate; Madden estate; Massereene estate

Census substitutes
HMR (listed under 'Ballytraboy or Rosslea' as well as Clones), FL

Freemasonry records
Minutes of Masonic lodge no. 881, Clones, 1800–26 – GLI

Other records
Map of the lands of Streneniogh, parish of Clones, 1733: townlands included are
    Corflough, County Fermanagh, Coolnamarrow, County Fermanagh and Scrabby,
    County Cavan – NAI, M/319
Map of Clones town with a list of tenants, 1768 – MIC170/4
Resolution of principal inhabitants of Clones concerning danger of invasion and
    affirming their loyalty, 1796: *c.* 170 names of those present at the meeting –
    MIC170/5

Publications
A Clones Miscellany (2004)
Clogher Record includes numerous articles about Clones

CLONFEACLE PARISH, COUNTIES ARMAGH AND TYRONE

Baronies: Armagh, Oneilland West (Armagh portion), Dungannon Middle (Tyrone
    portion)
Diocese: Armagh
Places: Benburb, Blackwatertown, Eglish, Moy, Moygashel
Graveyards: Clonfeacle CI, Clonfeacle Old, Eglish RC, Gorestown, Grange Friends,
    Moy CI

Church records
CI Clonfeacle
Typed extracts from vestry minutes, 1763–   T679/43 (MIC583/4)

P Benburb
Diary of Rev. John Kennedy, 1714–37,   PHSI
and other notebooks kept by him

RSF Grange
Men's monthly meeting minutes, 1726–70,   MIC16/34–8
1776–9, 1787–95; record book of testimonies
against Quakers, 1686–1784; family record
books, 1653–1814, 1725–1805; testimonies
of disownment, 1755–84; accounts, 1733–40

Estate papers
Armagh archbishopric estate; Caledon estate; Charlemont estate; Dawson estate;
Ker estate; Knox estate; MacGeough-Bond estate; Powerscourt estate; Stewart estate,
Killymoon; Verner estate

Census substitutes
HMR, DP (Benburb), FL

Freemasonry records
Minutes of Masonic lodge no. 557, Benburb, 1778–1837 – GLI

Business records
Atkinson, Moy; Courtenay, Benburb; Holmes, Benburb

Other records
Map of Moy, 1771, naming tenants – D291/3

Publications
W. D. Bailie, *Benburb Presbyterian Church 1670–1970* (1970)
George R. Chapman, *An Historical Sketch of Grange Meeting: Issued in the Tercentenary Year 1960* (1960)
J. J. Marshall, *Benburb: Its Battlefields and History; With an Account of Blackwater-Foot and Coney Island* (1924)
The Book of Eglish: Where the Oona Flows (2011): at over 500 pages this book is a wealth of information about the area
Duiche Neill, the journal of the O'Neill Country Historical Society, contains numerous articles of interest.

CLONLEIGH PARISH, COUNTY DONEGAL

Barony: Raphoe North
Diocese: Derry
Places: Ballindrait, Lifford
Graveyards: Ballybogan, Clonleigh CI, Clonleigh Old, Kilmonaster (Churchminster)

Church records
CI Clonleigh
Vestry minutes, 1788–   MIC1/179

The vestry minutes include cess applotments for most years of the 1790s.

P Ballindrait (Lifford)
Address by the Presbyterians of Newcastle,   T3762/1
Pennsylvania, 1706; 'the greatest number of us
born and educated in Irland under the ministry
of one William Traill a presbiterian minister
formerly of Liford'

RC Clonleigh and Camus
Baptisms, 1773–95; marriages, 1778–81   MIC1D/61

Estate papers
Derry bishopric estate; Erne estate

Census substitutes
HMR, DE, LP (Lifford/Ballindrait), FL (listed under Lifford)

Corporation records: Lifford
Extract from the charter of Lifford, 1611 – D1939/18/15/1
Petition of corporation to bishop of Derry, 1682 – printed in Moody and Simms,
   Bishopric of Derry and the Irish Society of London, vol. 2, p. 51
Court and borough book, 1716–83 – D1939/18/6/9 (see also the article by Brian
   Hutton in *Donegal Annual*, 5:1 (1961), pp 67–9)
Extract from the 'Book containing the records of the Corporation of Lifford' giving
   details of tenures and rents, 172[?] – D1939/18/14/5
Letter of 14 June 1748 giving the names of the warden and 12 burgesses of Lifford
   in 1727 – D1939/18/15/9

Freemasonry records
Minute book of Masonic lodge no. 569, Lifford, 1782–97 – GLI (see Walter J.
Hobbs, 'An Irish lodge minute book, 1782–1797', *Quatuor Coronati Lodge*, 34
(1921), pp 74–124)

Business records
Rea, Lifford

Other records
Petition of parishioners of Lifford to the bishop of Derry about the parish
schoolmaster, 1664: 80 signatories – D683/163 (printed in Moody and Simms,
Bishopric of Derry and the Irish Society of London, vol. 1, pp 380–81)

Publications
Margaret Giblin, *Lifford Legends & Condensed History* (2007)
G. A. Heatley, *Clonleigh Parish Church, Lifford (St Lugadius)* (1947)
Belinda Mahaffy, *A History of Ballindrait* [Presbyterian] *Church and its People* (2008)
Billy Patton, *Lifford, Seat of Power* (2008)

CLONMANY PARISH, COUNTY DONEGAL

Barony: Inishowen East
Diocese: Derry
Places: Ballyliffin, Clonmany
Graveyard: Straid (formerly Clonmany CI)

Estate papers
Derry bishopric estate; Donegall estate

Census substitutes
HMR, CPH (includes townlands), FL

Publications
Seoirse Ó Dochartaigh, *Inis Eoghain: The Island of Eoghan: The Place-Names of Inishowen* (2011)
Seoirse Ó Dochartaigh, *The Great Name Book of Inishowen* (2016)

CLONOE PARISH, COUNTY TYRONE

Barony: Dungannon Middle
Diocese: Armagh
Places: Clonoe, Coalisland, Killen, Mountjoy, Washing Bay
Graveyard: Clonoe CI

Church records
CI Clonoe
Vestry minutes, 1783–   MIC1/11

Estate papers
Annesley estate; Armagh archbishopric estate; Drelincourt Charity estate

Census substitutes
HMR, FL

Publications
Wilfred Dilworth, *The History of St Michael's Church, Clonoe, and Notes on the Parish* (2012)
Austin Stewart, *Coalisland, County Tyrone, in the Industrial Revolution, 1800–1901* (2002)
James Walshe and Wilfred Dilworth, *The Faire Field* (2012)

CLONTIBRET PARISH, COUNTY MONAGHAN

Barony: Cremorne
Diocese: Clogher
Place: Clontibret
Graveyard: Clontibret CI/Old

Church records
CI Clontibret
Vestry minutes, 1711, 1749–   MIC1/149; D2365/1

The vestry minutes include a poor list, 1752 (loose sheet); and the names of those repairing roads in the parish, 1761–4.

Estate papers
Barton estate; Blayney estate; Clogher bishopric estate; Templetown estate

Census substitutes
HMR, FP, FL

Publications
Gary Carville, *Parish of Clontibret* (1984)
Brendan Ó Dufaigh, *The Book of Clontibret* (1997)

COLERAINE PARISH, COUNTY LONDONDERRY

Barony: North-East Liberties of Coleraine
Diocese: Connor
Place: Coleraine
Graveyard: Coleraine CI

Church records
CI Coleraine

Baptisms, 1769– ; marriages, 1769– ; burials, 1769– ; vestry minutes, 1769–	MIC1/7A
Extracts from vestry minutes, 1769–1816	D4164/A/28

The vestry minutes include a list of 31 persons to be issued with badges, 1774.

P 1st Coleraine

Call to minister from congregation of Coleraine, 1673	T525/1
Accounts, 1719–28	PHSI
Stipend book, 1768–92 with an index of names at start [previously listed for Lylehill]	PHSI

P 2nd Coleraine (New Row)

Extracts from treasurers' book, 1774–1834	T1069/9–11
Call to Rev. John Glasgow, 1795 – names printed in Mullin, *New Row*, p. 51	

Estate papers
Bacon estate; Curtis estate; Heyland estate; Irish Society estate

Census substitutes
HMR, RelC (Catholics); DP, FL

Corporation records: Coleraine
Acts of the Corporation of Coleraine, 1623–1669, edited by Bríd McGrath (2017)
Minute books of the court of common council of the corporation of Coleraine,
    1672–1707, 1707–10, 1792–1840 (originals and copies) – LA/25/2AA/1A–2
Freemen of the corporation, 1715–1830 – *Return of persons admitted or elected in*
    corporation of Coleraine (1832)
Box of miscellaneous 18th-century papers relating to the corporation, including a
    list of members of the corporation in 1783 – D668/N/1

Other records
A large collection of notes of historical and genealogical interest relating to the
    Coleraine area may be found among the papers of Max Given – D4164/A; for
    more on this collection, see Robert Forrest's article in *The Bann Disc*, 9 (2003),
    pp 8–23.
Collectors' [?] accounts for Coleraine, naming individuals and amounts paid,
    1689–91 – T456/1
Tithes for Coleraine parish, 1690–91 – D2096/1/13
Some Coleraine residents, 1729, 1783, 1791 – D4164/A/26
Map of the town lots of Coleraine, 1758, naming tenants – T837/1
Resolution of inhabitants of Coleraine and Killowen, 1787 – *Belfast Newsletter*,
    2–6 Feb. 1787
Tithe book, Coleraine parish, including arrears, 1789–93 – D668/B
Returns of pupils at the Free School in Coleraine, 1790/91–6 – D668/N/1
Church cess list, the country part of Coleraine parish, listing names and acreages
    held, 1792 – D668/A/16
Diaries of John Galt, Coleraine, County Londonderry, general merchant, 1796–
    1837 (gap 1803–17) – D561
Valuation of houses and lands in the suburbs of Coleraine, 1797 (plus details from
    1777 and 1794) – D668/N/1
Coleraine Yeomanry, 1796: 116 names – D4164/A/12
'Notification of Registering Arms taken by Mr Lyle & the Mayor [of Coleraine]',
    1796: over 250 names for residents of Coleraine and surrounding parishes –
    D668/N/1
List of members of an Orange Lodge in Coleraine (no. 316), 1797–9 – D668/O/1
Notebook of the Coleraine District Lodge of the Orange Order naming members of
    lodges in and near Coleraine, 1799 (nos 316, 487, 735, 769, 917 and 930) –
    D668/O/1

Freemasonry records
Account book of Masonic lodge no. 138, Coleraine, 1756–73 – D668/O/1
Minutes of Masonic lodge no. 754, Coleraine, 1794–1812 – GLI

Publications
David Clarke, *Others Have Laboured: Terrace Row Presbyterian Church, 1796–1996*
    (1996)

Andrew Kane, *The Town Book of Coleraine* (2016): includes supplementary
information from 18th-century leases; Acre tenants, 1738; Town tenants, 1738–58;
and a rent roll, 1777 (with additional information from a 1794 rent roll)
J. E. Mullin, *New Row. The History of New Row Presbyterian Church, Coleraine,
1727–1977* (1976)
T. H. Mullin, *Coleraine in By-gone Centuries* (1976): includes a chapter on 17th-
century Coleraine families
T. H. Mullin, *Coleraine in Georgian Times* (1977): has appendices providing brief
biographical sketches of Coleraine families

COMBER PARISH, COUNTY DOWN

Baronies: Castlereagh Lower, Castlereagh Upper
Diocese: Down
Places: Ballygowan, Comber, Moneyrea(gh)
Graveyards: Comber CI, Moneyrea NSP

Church records
CI Comber
Baptisms, 1683– ; marriages, 1683– ;   T679/411–13, 415B
burials, 1683– ; vestry minutes, 1700–   (MIC583/36, 37)

The vestry minutes include the names of those who contributed to the fund in aid of
the Vaudois (Waldensians), 1699 (over 300 names); collectors, etc for road repairs
regularly listed from 1778 onwards; collectors, etc of parish cess, 1799.

Extracts from registers, 1712–   T921/1

P Moneyreagh
The congregation is now in the Non-Subscribing Presbyterian Church.

Trust deed, 1719, giving a few names   T1627/1

Estate papers
Blackwood estate; Hamilton (Claneboye and Clanbrassil) estate; Downshire estate;
Dungannon estate; Londonderry estate; Montgomery estate, Donaghadee

Census substitutes
HSM, DP, FL, AC

Business records
Andrews, Comber

Other records
Account book of expenses compiled on a return journey from Comber to Glasgow,
1792–3 – D1889/9/1

Publications
Len Ball and Desmond Rainey, *A Taste of Old Comber: The Town and its History*
  (2002)
Gilbert A. Cromie, *A History of Granshaw Presbyterian Church 1801–2001* (2004)
William McMillan, *A History of the Moneyreagh Congregation, 1719–1969* (1969)
W. G. Simpson, *Masonry of the Olden Time in the Comber District, County Down*
  (1926)

CONNOR PARISH, COUNTY ANTRIM

Barony: Antrim Lower
Diocese: Connor
Places: Connor, Kells, Kellswater
Graveyards: Connor CI, Kells Abbey (Templemoyle)

Church records
P Connor
Session minutes, 1693, 1699–1735; accounts, 1787–91   PHSI

RP Kellswater
Session minutes of the Antrim Meeting   CR5/9
(Kellswater and Cullybackey), *c.* 1789–

Estate papers
Massereene estate; Mount Cashell estate; O'Hara estate

Census substitutes
HMR, RelC (Catholics)

Other records
Subscribers to a reward fund, 1756: 74 names of inhabitants of Kells and Connor –
Belfast Newsletter, 16 Jan. 1756

Publications
Robert Buchanan, *Kellswater Reformed Presbyterian Church, Co. Antrim: A Short
History*, edited by Eull Dunlop (1989)

CONVOY PARISH, COUNTY DONEGAL
Convoy parish was created out of **Raphoe** in 1773.

Barony: Raphoe South
Diocese: Raphoe
Place: Convoy

Publications
T. H. Mullin, *The Kirk and Lands of Convoy since the Scottish Settlement* (1960):
  includes names of elders, early vestry appointments (from the Raphoe vestry

book), diocesan wills, prerogative wills, 'citizenship' (denization) grants, muster roll of 1631, hearth money roll of 1665 and freeholders in 1768

Aodh Gallagher and Marie Slevin, *Convoy Village: Its People and Townlands* (1996)

CONWAL PARISH, COUNTY DONEGAL

Baronies: Kilmacrenan, Raphoe South
Diocese: Raphoe
Place: Letterkenny
Graveyards: Conwal CI, Conwal Old, Templedouglas

Estate papers
Chambers estate; Gore estate; Hart estate; Raphoe bishopric estate

Census substitutes
HMR, LP (Letterkenny), FL

Other records
Notebook relating to the charity established by Thomas Grove in 1677 for the poor of the parish of Conwal, with names of beneficiaries, 1678–1748 – NLI, n.4704, p.4692 (see Chapter 14 for more on this charity and also J. C. T. McDonagh, 'A seventeenth century Letterkenny manuscript …', *Donegal Annual*, 3:2 (1956), pp 139–42, for the names of those who received assistance)

Publications
L. R. Lawrenson, *The Parish of Conwall, Aughanunshin and Leck* (1943)
Edward Maguire, *Letterkenny Past and Present* (192[-])
S. Fleming, *Letterkenny Past and Present* (n.d.)
Joan Slater, *Conwal Parish Letterkenny Church 1636–1986* (1986)
A. J. Weir, *Letterkenny Congregations, Ministers, & People: 1615–1960* (1960)

CRANFIELD PARISH, COUNTY ANTRIM
This parish is now composed of the solitary townland of Cranfield. See also **Drummaul** and **Duneane** parishes.

Barony: Toome Upper
Diocese: Connor
Graveyard: Cranfield

Census substitutes
HMR

CREGGAN PARISH, COUNTIES ARMAGH AND LOUTH

Barony: Fews Upper (Armagh portion)
Diocese: Armagh

Places: Ballsmill, Creggan, Crossmaglen, Cullaville, Cullyhanna, Silverbridge
Graveyards: Creggan CI, Creggan (Freeduff) P

Church records
P Creggan (or Freeduff)
List of the original seatholders, 1765; list of   MIC1P/444/1
subscribers, 1795; notes on the early history of the
congregation from 1734, including 'A Concise
Historical Retrospect of the Parish of Creggan'

Depositions relating to the burning of   T1392/1; T808/14925
Freeduff Presbyterian meeting house, 1743

RC Upper Creggan (Crossmaglen)
Baptisms and marriages, 1796–   MIC1D/43

Estate papers
Armagh archbishopric estate; Ball estate; Hall estate, Fews; MacGeough-Bond estate

Census substitutes
HMR, FP, RelC (Protestants and Catholics; includes townlands), FL

Other records
Petition about Act of Union from Roman Catholic inhabitants of Lower Creggan,
    1800 – *Belfast Newsletter*, 17 Jan. 1800
Manuscript history of Creggan parish, 1611–1840, by Rev. Simon Nelson – T541
Gravestone inscriptions from Creggan (Freeduff) Presbyterian churchyard –
    T808/14922

Publications
John Donaldson, *A Historical and Statistical Account of the Barony of the Upper Fews
    in the County of Armagh, 1838* (1923)
L. P. Murray, Isaac Dobson, W. Frankland and J. Southey, 'The history of the parish
    of Creggan in the 17th and 18th centuries', *Journal of the County Louth
    Archaeological Society*, 8:2 (1934), pp 117–63
Kevin McMahon, *Guide to Creggan Church & Graveyard* (1988)
Tomás Ó Fiaich, *The O'Neills of the Fews* (2003)
Sean Farrell, 'The burning of Freeduff Presbyterian Church, 1743', *New Hibernia
    Review/Iris Éireannach Nua*, 9:3 (Autumn, 2005), pp 72–85

CROSSERLOUGH PARISH, COUNTY CAVAN

Baronies: Castlerahan, Clanmahon, Loughtee Upper
Diocese: Kilmore
Place: Kilnaleck
Graveyards: Crosserlough Old, Kill

Estate papers
Farnham estate

Census substitutes
FL

Publications
Tom Sullivan (ed.), *Drumkilly: From Ardkill Mountain to Kilderry Hill* (2001)
Crosserlough: Through the Ages (2013)

CULDAFF PARISH, COUNTY DONEGAL

Barony: Inishowen East
Diocese: Derry
Places: Culdaff, Gleneely
Graveyards: Ardmore, Culdaff CI

Church records
CI Culdaff
Baptisms, 1668–*c.* 1790 (with gaps);   D803/1
marriages, 1713–21, 1770–82; burials,
1714–18; vestry minutes, 1693–1803

The above records are bound into a single volume, the pages much conserved, along
with an accompanying folder of loose sheets. The pre-1700 baptisms are concerned
with the Young family. The early vestry minutes also concern the parish of Clonca.
The documentation includes a number of cess applotments and lists of parishioners
dating from 1697 and various years in the late eighteenth century and the start of the
nineteenth century (see also below under *Other records*).

Estate papers
Derry bishopric estate; Donegall estate

Census substitutes
HMR, CPH (includes townlands), FL

Other records
Cess applotments, 1778, 1782 (published in Young, *Three Hundred Years in
    Innishowen*, pp 159–60), *c.* 1792, 1800, 1802 – D3045/7/1/3 (MIC586/14)
Names of parishioners, arranged by families with ages of children given, *c.* 1802 –
    D3045/7/1/3 (MIC586/14)

Publications
Brian Bonner, *Our Inis Eoghain Heritage: The Parishes of Culdaff and Cloncha* (1984)
Amy Young, *Three Hundred Years in Innishowen* (1929)
Seoirse Ó Dochartaigh, *Inis Eoghain: The Island of Eoghan: The Place-Names of
    Inishowen* (2011)
Seoirse Ó Dochartaigh, *The Great Name Book of Inishowen* (2016)

CULFEIGHTRIN PARISH, COUNTY ANTRIM
See also **Ramoan** parish.

Barony: Cary
Diocese: Connor
Places: Ballyvoy, Cushendun
Graveyards: Bonamargy, Culfeightrin CI

Estate papers
Antrim estate; Boyd estate; Caledon estate; McCollum estate; McGildowney estate

Census substitutes
HMR, CPH, FL, AC

Publications
H. A. Boyd, *Parish of Culfeightrin, Diocese of Connor: The Story of a Little Country Parish Church* (1958)

CUMBER PARISH, COUNTY LONDONDERRY
This parish was divided into Upper Cumber and Lower Cumber in 1789.

Barony: Tirkeeran
Diocese: Derry
Places: Claudy, Killaloo, Park, Tullintrain
Graveyard: Cumber Old

Estate papers
Conolly estate; Derry bishopric estate; Fishmongers' Company estate; Goldsmiths' Company estate; Grocers' Company estate; Skinners' Company estate

Census substitutes
HMR, DE, FL

Other records
Depositions, 1693–4, concerning incidents in Cumber parish in 1693 (*c.* 30 names) – D683/234, 237 (printed in Moody and Simms, *Bishopric of Derry and the Irish Society of London*, vol. 2, pp 145–9, 152–3)
Various documents concerning Lettermuck, including maps of 1734, 1771, 1773 and 1791 – D2298/102/2

Publications
John Rutherford, *Cumber Presbyterian Church and Parish* (1939): marriages and baptisms for Cumber parish extracted from the 17th-century registers of St Columb's cathedral in Derry; subsidy roll, 1662; hearth money roll, 1663; Protestant householders, 1740; freeholders' registers, 1761–81, 1791, 1796; flax seed premiums awarded in 1781; Cumber Yeomanry Cavalry, 1797; Cumber wills, 1720–1857; students from Cumber educated at Trinity College Dublin and elsewhere

CURRIN PARISH, COUNTIES FERMANAGH AND MONAGHAN
This parish was created out of **Galloon** in 1795.

Baronies: Clankelly (Fermanagh portion), Dartree (Monaghan portion)
Diocese: Clogher
Places: Drum, Scotshouse

Estate papers
Dawson estate; Madden estate

Census substitutes
HMR, FL

Publications
P. O Mordha, 'Some transactions in Currin parish in the first quarter of the
  eighteenth century', *Clogher Record*, 16 (1997), pp 162–5
*From Carn to Clonfad, Killeevan Heritage Group takes a Journey through some pages
  out of the history of Currin, Killeevan and Aghabog* (2 vols)

DENN PARISH, COUNTY CAVAN

Baronies: Castlerahan, Clanmahon, Loughtee Upper
Diocese: Kilmore
Place: Carrickaboy
Graveyard: Denn Old (Carrickaboy)

Estate papers
Annesley estate; Farnham estate; Richardson estate; Saunderson estate

Census substitutes
FL

Publications
Tom Sullivan (ed.), *Drumkilly: From Ardkill Mountain to Kilderry Hill* (2001)

DERRYAGHY PARISH, COUNTY ANTRIM
The name of this parish is also spelled Derriaghy.

Baronies: Belfast Upper, Massereene Upper
Diocese: Connor
Places: Derriaghy, Stoneyford
Graveyard: Derriaghy CI

Church records
CI Derriaghy

Baptisms, 1696–1763, 1771– ; marriages,	CR1/1; MIC1/32, 33;
1696–1746, 1772; burials, 1696–1738, 1772–3;	T679/35 (MIC583/4)

vestry minutes, 1709–58, 1794– ; volume of
accounts and receipts, 1768–78

A typescript version of the vestry minutes for 1700–58 is available in the PRONI
calendar. The vestry minutes include a list of 'parishioners who have fined the
primat's [Primate's] lease' giving rent and fine, undated, but between minutes of
1736 and 1739 (over 200 names); the Primate refers to the Anglican archbishop of
Armagh, the owner of an estate in the parish. The minutes also include a list of
persons confirmed in Derriaghy and Lambeg, 1705; a list of cess-payers in 'Derriaghy
Constablewick', 1772 (found between minutes of meetings held in 1721).

Estate papers
Armagh archbishopric estate; Conway estate

Census substitutes
HMR

Publications
W. N. C. Barr, *Derriaghy: A Short History of the Parish* (1974)
John L. Spence, 'Life in early eighteenth century rural Ulster as reflected in a parish
    record book', *UJA*, 3rd series, 6 (1943), pp 35–8

DERRYBRUSK PARISH, COUNTY FERMANAGH
Prior to its reorganisation in 1856, this was a small and fragmented parish.
Researchers should also refer to sources available for neighbouring parishes.

Baronies: Magherastephana, Tirkennedy
Diocese: Clogher

Estate papers
Belmore estate; Clogher bishopric estate

Census substitutes
FL

Other records
'Cash rec'd by Mr Armar from ye parishioners', 1747–52: covers parishes of
    Derrybrusk and Enniskillen, gives names and in many cases residences – D627/14
    (volume broken into several sections, with an index of names for one section at
    the front)
Tithes received by Mr Armar out of Derrybrusk and Enniskillen parishes, *c.* 1750:
    over 140 names, but no residences – D627/15

DERRYKEIGHAN PARISH, COUNTY ANTRIM
See also **Grange of Drumtullagh**.

Barony: Dunluce Lower
Diocese: Connor

Places: Derrykeighan, Dervock
Graveyard: Derrykeighan Old

Estate papers
Antrim estate; Hutchinson estate; Legge estate; Macartney estate; Montgomery estate; Moore and Stewart Moore estate; Rowan estate, Ballymoney; Stewart/Trail estate

Census substitutes
HMR, RCC, CPH, FL, AC

Publications
Dorothy Arthur, *Derrykeighan Old Church Graveyard* (2012)
Thomas Camac, *History of the Parish of Derrykeighan for Three Centuries* (1908)
J. D. Trevor McCauley, *A Covenant Heritage: Historical Sketch of Dervock Reformed Presbyterian Church, 1783–1983* (1983)
Hugh McNeill, *The Annals of the Parish of Derrykeighan, from AD 453 to AD 1890* (1910; reprinted 1993)

DERRYLORAN PARISH, COUNTIES LONDONDERRY AND TYRONE

Baronies: Loughinsholin (Londonderry portion), Dungannon Upper (Tyrone portion)
Diocese: Armagh
Place: Cookstown
Graveyard: Derryloran Old

Church records
CI Derryloran
Baptisms, 1795– ; marriages, 1797– ; burials, 1797–   MIC1/15/1

Estate papers
Armagh archbishopric of estate; Castle Stewart estate; Drapers' Company estate; Lindesay estate; Staples estate; Stewart estate, Killymoon

Census substitutes
HMR, RelC (Protestants and Catholics; includes townlands), DP (Cookstown), FL

Freemasonry records
Minutes of Masonic lodge no. 668, Donarisk and Cookstown, 1787–1809 – GLI

Business records
Faulkner, Gortalowry

Other records
Miscellaneous extracts from the Registry of Deeds for the Cookstown area – T808/15103

Description by Theodore Martin, rector of Desertlyn, of an encounter with the 'Green Boys' at Cookstown in 1763 – T1442/6

Publications
Henry L. Glasgow, *History of Cookstown* (2008) [historical notes reprinted from the *Mid-Ulster Mail*, 1924–6]
W. J. H. McKee, *Aspects of Presbyterianism in Cookstown* (1995)

DERRYNOOSE PARISH, COUNTY ARMAGH
In 1773, a portion of this parish was detached to form the parish of **Keady**.

Baronies: Armagh, Tiranny
Diocese: Armagh
Places: Derrynoose, Madden
Graveyards: Derrynoose CI, Derrynoose Old, Maghery

Church records
CI Derrynoose

Baptisms, 1710–46 (with gaps);	MIC1/14; T679/10
marriages, 1712–43; vestry minutes, 1709–	(MIC583/2)

The attendance at some vestry meetings was in excess of 20 persons; torn list of the poor, 1715? (found in minute book between minutes of meetings held in 1730); list of nearly 50 names, numbered, possibly list of the poor/persons to be badged, *c.* 1750.

Estate papers
Armagh archbishopric estate; Irwin estate; Maxwell estate

Census substitutes
HMR, FP, VAA, CPH, FL

Other records
Subscribers to a reward fund, 1784 – *Belfast Newsletter*, 6–9 April 1784
Tithe account, 1785–7, naming tithe-payers by townland – T636/1, pp 235–40

DERRYVULLAN PARISH, COUNTY FERMANAGH
This parish is split into two separate portions, sometimes referred to as North and South.

Baronies: Lurg, Tirkennedy
Diocese: Clogher
Places: Irvinestown (Lowtherstown), Lisnarick, Tamlaght
Graveyards: Derryvullan Old, Irvinestown Old, Lisnarick

Estate papers
Archdale estate; Belmore estate; Clogher bishopric estate; Cooper estate; Enniskillen estate

Census substitutes
RelC (Protestants and Catholics; includes townlands), FL

Publications
Breege McCuster, *Irvinestown Through the Years* (1984)

DESERTCREAT PARISH, COUNTY TYRONE
The name of this parish is also spelled Desertcreight.

Barony: Dungannon Upper
Diocese: Armagh
Places: Rock, Sandholes, Tullyhogue
Graveyards: Desertcreat CI, Donarisk (Donaghrisk)

Church records
CI Desertcreat
Burial (1 entry), 1791; vestry minutes, 1740–   MIC1/9/1

The vestry minutes include a list of the poor (places of residence given for most of them), 1784.

Estate papers
Armagh archbishopric estate; Hamilton Moore estate; Hill estate; Lindesay estate; Lowry estate, Pomeroy; Richardson estate, Tullyreavy; Sanderson estate; Stewart estate, Killymoon

Census substitutes
HMR, FL

Freemasonry records
Minutes of Masonic lodge no. 668, Donarisk and Cookstown, 1787–1809 – GLI

Business records
Greer, Tullylagan

Publications
John Edwin Barr, *History of Sandholes Presbyterian Church, Including the Arrival of Presbyterianism in East Tyrone* (1994)

DESERTEGNY PARISH, COUNTY DONEGAL

Barony: Inishowen West
Diocese: Derry
Graveyards: Desertegny CI (Linsfort), Greenhill

Estate papers
Derry bishopric estate; Donegall estate

Census substitutes
HMR, CPH (includes townlands), FL

Publications
Seoirse Ó Dochartaigh, *Inis Eoghain: The Island of Eoghan: The Place-Names of Inishowen* (2011)
Seoirse Ó Dochartaigh, *The Great Name Book of Inishowen* (2016)

DESERTLYN PARISH, COUNTY LONDONDERRY
The name of this parish is also spelled Desertlynn.

Barony: Loughinsholin
Diocese: Armagh
Place: Moneymore
Graveyards: Desertlyn Old (Ballymully), Desertlyn Old (Moneymore)

Church records
CI Desertlynn
Baptisms, 1797– ; marriages, 1797– ; burials, 1798–   MIC1/10A

Estate papers
Armagh archbishopric estate; Drapers' Company estate; Salters' Company estate

Census substitutes
HMR, RelC (Protestants and Catholics), FL

Publications
James Stevens Curl, *Moneymore and Draperstown: The Architecture and Planning of the Estates of the Drapers' Company* (1979)

DESERTMARTIN PARISH, COUNTY LONDONDERRY

Barony: Loughinsholin
Diocese: Derry
Places: Cranny, Desertmartin
Graveyard: Desertmartin Old

Church records
CI Desertmartin
Baptisms, 1785– ; marriages, 1784– ;   MIC1/16; T679/6
burials, 1783, 1788; vestry minutes, 1751– ,   (MIC583/1)
with some baptisms for 1752

The vestry minutes include a list of the poor by townland who are entitled to exemption from the hearth tax, 1793 (*c.* 200 names); also a list of 'Persons married after publication of the banns in Desertmartin Church who had been clandestinely married before', 22 Oct. 1794 (18 couples).

List of tithes, 1794   Local custody

Estate papers
Conolly estate; Derry bishopric estate; Drapers' Company estate; Salters' Company
estate; Strafford estate; Vintners' Company estate

Census substitutes
HMR, CPH, FL

Other records
Map of Dromore and part of Killymuck, glebe-lands, 1802, with details of
tenements – D360/1

Publications
Norman McAuley, *To God be the Glory: The History of Lecumpher Presbyterian Church
1795–1995* (1995)

DESERTOGHILL PARISH, COUNTY LONDONDERRY
See also **Errigal** parish.

Barony: Coleraine
Diocese: Derry
Place: Moneydig
Graveyard: Desertoghill Old

CI Desertoghill
List of subscribers to Desertoghill Church of Ireland   D1514/1/1/52
church with account of church expenses, 1775–8

An account for £500 concerning Desertoghill   D1514/1/1/54
Church of Ireland church, 1776–7

Estate papers
Beresford estate; Derry bishopric estate; Du Pré estate; Ironmongers' Company
estate; Mercers' Company estate; Rowley estate

Census substitutes
HMR, CPH, FL

Other records
Notebook containing notification of registering arms, including residents of
Desertoghill, 1796 – D668/N/1

Publications
R. W. Patterson, *Garvagh: A Town and Two Parishes* (1999)

DEVENISH PARISH, COUNTY FERMANAGH

Barony: Magheraboy
Diocese: Clogher
Places: Garrison, Monea
Graveyards: Devenish CI (Monea), Devenish Island

Church records
CI Devenish
Baptisms, 1706, 1798, 1800– ;   MIC1/31; CR1/84/A/1
marriages, 1800– ; vestry minutes, 1739–

The vestry minutes include information on the allocation of space for seats within the parish church, 1744; and the seating arrangements in 1802.

Estate papers
Archdale estate; Clogher bishopric estate; Ely estate; Huntingdon estate; Montgomery estate; O'Brien estate

Census substitutes
HMR, RelC (Protestants and Catholics), FL

Other records
An account of the tithes in the parishes of Devenish and Boho, 1695 (long list of names) – printed in Steele, *The Parish of Devenish*, pp 78–80
Copy memorial of the 'Protestant Inhabitants of the Parishes of Kilbarren and Garrison, also (Innismac)saint who live nearer Belleek than any other church', *c.* 1788 – DIO/2/9/660A
Memorial from the '… Protestant Inhabitants of the Extreme end of the Parish of Devenish …', *c.* 1790 – DIO/2/9/449

Publications
W. B. Steele, *The Parish of Devenish, County Fermanagh: Materials for Its History* (1937)
E. G. Elliott, *The Parish of Devenish and Boho* (1990)
P. McGuinness, *Garrison: A Frontier for Two Thousand Years* (1998)

DONACAVEY PARISH, COUNTY TYRONE
This parish, also spelled Donaghcavey, is also known as Fintona.

Baronies: Clogher, Omagh
Diocese: Clogher
Place: Fintona
Graveyards: Donacavey Old, Fintona Old

Church records
CI Donacavey or Fintona
Baptisms, 1800– ; baptisms for the Eccles   MIC1/45/2; CR1/101
and Dickson families, 1777–91; marriages,
1800– ; burials, 1800– ; vestry minutes, 1779–

Notes from the vestry book, 1778–1802   D1048/4

The vestry minutes include lengthy lists of the poor (with addresses) from 1783
onwards.

Estate papers
Belmore estate; Clogher bishopric estate; Eccles estate; Mervyn estate

Census substitutes
HMR, FL

Publications
Samuel Burdy, *The Life of Philip Skelton*, edited by Norman Moore (1914): Skelton
    was Prebendary of Donacavey from 1766 to 1787
P. O Gallachair, *Old Fintona: A History of the Catholic Parish of Donaghcavey in
    County Tyrone* (1974)

DONAGH PARISH, COUNTY DONEGAL

Barony: Inishowen East
Diocese: Derry
Place: Carndonagh
Graveyard: Donagh CI

Church records
CI Donagh
Vestry minutes, 1782–   Local custody

Estate papers
Derry bishopric estate; Donegall estate; Ferguson estate

Census substitutes
CPH (includes townlands), FL

Publications
Seoirse Ó Dochartaigh, *Inis Eoghain: The Island of Eoghan: The Place-Names of
    Inishowen* (2011)
Seoirse Ó Dochartaigh, *The Great Name Book of Inishowen* (2016)

DONAGH PARISH, COUNTY MONAGHAN

Barony: Trough
Diocese: Clogher
Places: Emyvale, Glaslough
Graveyards: Donagh CI, Donagh Old

Church records
CI Donagh
Baptisms, 1736, 1796– ; marriages, 1736, 1797– ;   MIC1/127
burials, 1736, 1797– ; vestry minutes, 1731–

The vestry minutes include the names of the poor who received tickets (and in some
cases the names of those who recommended them), *c.* 1742; lists of the poor, 1773,
1774, 1775 and 1778.

Estate papers
Anketell estate; Clogher bishopric estate; Dawson estate; Leslie estate, Glaslough;
Rossmore estate; Singleton estate

Census substitutes
HMR, FL

Publications
J. B. D. Cotter, *A Short History of Donagh Parish* (n.d.)
Seymour Leslie, *Of Glaslough in the Kingdom of Oriel* (1913)

DONAGHADEE PARISH, COUNTY DOWN

Barony: Ards Lower
Diocese: Down
Places: Ballycopeland, Carrowdore, Donaghadee, Millisle
Graveyards: Copeland Island, Donaghadee CI, Templepatrick

Church records
CI Donaghadee
Baptisms, 1771– ; marriages, 1772– ;   CR1/54; MIC1/17;
burials, 1771– ; vestry minutes, 1779–   T679/44 (MIC583/5)

The vestry minutes include what seems to be a cess applotment, giving the name of
each householder, residence and occasionally occupation, 1797 (*c.* 600 names); the
minutes also include regular lists of overseers of road repairs.

P Ballycopeland (originally Secession)
Baptisms, 1773–6   PHSI

P 1st Donaghadee

Baptisms, 1793– ; session and   MIC1P/167
committee minutes, 1783–

P Millisle

Baptisms, 1777– ; list of elders and members, 1777   MIC1P/230/7;
                                                   MIC1P/382A/1

List of subscriptions to Millisle meeting house, 1773 (pp 2–7), a list of seats let to members, 1776 (pp 9–13), and names subscribed to a call to Rev. Andrew Greer, 1777 (pp 17–18) in Kilpatrick, *Millisle and Ballycopeland Presbyterian Church*

Estate papers
Brice estate; Montgomery estate, Donaghadee; Reid estate

Census substitutes
AC

Freemasonry records
Transcript of minutes of Masonic lodge 29/699, Donaghadee, beginning in 1786 – GLI

Other records
Plan of lands near Donaghadee, 1728 – T2845/11
Report from State Papers of the forcible taking of people from Skye to America on board the *William* of Donaghadee, 1739: the ship put in at Donaghadee and the report contains an account of this – T827/1
Subscribers to a reward fund, 1782 – *Belfast Newsletter*, 24–27 Dec. 1782
Letter informing on persons in the Millisle and Carrowdore area involved in the 1798 Rebellion and giving the names of loyal persons who, if threatened with loss of property, would give information about the rebels – D3579/1
Notes on occupants, Donaghadee area, *c.* 1800 – T2845/13

Publications
Harry Allen, *Donaghadee: An Illustrated History* (2006)
Peter Carr, *Portavo: An Irish Townland and its Peoples* (2 vols, 2003, 2005)
George M. Eagleson and Tom Johnston, *First Presbyterian Church, Donaghadee, 1642–1992: A Historical Review* (1992)
Thomas Kilpatrick, *Millisle and Ballycopeland Presbyterian Church. A Short History* (1934)

DONAGHCLONEY PARISH, COUNTY DOWN
The name of this parish is also spelled Donacloney.

Barony: Iveagh Lower (Upper Half)
Diocese: Dromore
Places: Blackskull, Donaghcloney, Waringstown
Graveyards: Donaghcloney CI, Donaghcloney Old

Church records
CI Donaghcloney
Baptisms, 1697– ; marriages, 1697– ;   CR1/103; MIC1/92, 93
burials, 1697– ; vestry minutes, 1772– ;
parish accounts, 1745–8; 'Scheme of
Provision for the Widows of Clergymen
in Diocese of Dromore', 1773–1825

The vestry minutes include the names and townlands of those 'thought worthy' to be
badged, 1801 (46 names). The parish accounts relate in part to building work at the
church and include the names of many of those employed on this.

P Donacloney
Baptisms, 1798– ; subscription list for the   MIC1P/342
new meeting house, 1795

Estate papers
Clanwilliam estate; Downshire estate; Fortescue estate; Waring estate

Census substitutes
DP (Seapatrick, Tullylish and Donochclony)

Other records
Subscribers to a reward fund from inhabitants of Waringstown and neighbourhood,
    1779: over 70 names – *Belfast Newsletter*, 12–15 Jan. 1779
Material relating to the history of Donaghcloney – D4161

Publications
E. D. Atkinson, *An Ulster Parish: Being a History of Donaghcloney (Waringstown)*
    (1898): includes a valuation of Waringstown, 1696
S. J. W. Cooper, *Something to Celebrate: Parish of Donaghcloney, 1681–1981* (1981)
J. Haddock, *A Parish Miscellany: A Review of Donaghcloney Parish from the Earliest
    Times to the Present Day* (1940)
Joseph Magill and William Harold McCafferty, *Donacloney Meeting: An Historical
    Survey* (1950): includes the names of subscribers to a meeting house fund, 1795

DONAGHEDY PARISH, COUNTY TYRONE
The name of this parish is usually spelled Donagheady.

Barony: Strabane Lower
Diocese: Derry
Places: Bready, Dunnalong, Dunnamanagh (Donemana)
Graveyards: Donagheady Old, Grange

Church records
CI Donagheady
Baptisms, 1697–1723, 1753–65; marriages,   MIC1/35–6

1697–1726, 1754–64; burials, 1698–1726, 1754–7;
vestry minutes, 1697–1723, 1754– ; confirmation list,
1701; poor lists, 1726–38

RP Bready
Session book, *c.* 1790–1800   CR5/36/2/1/1

Estate papers
Abercorn estate; Belmore estate; Derry bishopric estate; Hamilton estate,
Dunnamanagh; Hamilton estate, Manor Elieston

Census substitutes
PB, HMR, DE, LP (Donaghadie), FL

Other records
Account and vouchers for Donagheady rents: James Galbraith to the earl of Bristol,
1794 – D1514/1/1/98

Publications
E. T. Dundas, *The History of Donagheady Parish* (1979)
William J. Roulston, *The Parishes of Leckpatrick and Dunnalong: Their Place in
    History* (2000)
William J. Roulston, *Three Centuries of Life in a Tyrone Parish: A History of
    Donagheady from 1600 to 1900* (2010)
William J. Roulston, *Foyle Valley Covenanters: A History of Bready Reformed
    Presbyterian Church* (2015)
John Rutherford, *Donagheady Presbyterian Churches and Parish* (1953)

DONAGHENRY PARISH, COUNTY TYRONE

Barony: Dungannon Middle
Diocese: Armagh
Place: Stewartstown
Graveyards: Donaghenry CI, Donaghenry Old

Church records
CI Donaghenry or Donaghendry
Baptisms, 1733–4, 1754–68; marriages,   T679/331 (MIC583/29)
1733–5, 1754–68, 1763– ; burials, 1735,
1754–68; vestry minutes, 1738–

The vestry minutes include a list of names and addresses under the heading, 'A return
of the sess [sic] that ought to have been pay'd me', 1785.

Estate papers
Armagh archbishopric estate; Castle Stewart estate; Charlemont estate; Lindesay
estate; Stewart estate, Killymoon

Census substitutes
HMR, RelC (Anglicans, Presbyterians and Catholics), FL

Other records
Subscribers to a reward fund, Stewartstown, 1790 – *Belfast Newsletter*, 21–24 Dec.
1790 (also 21–25 Jan. 1791)

Publications
James Glendinning, *On the Meeting House Steps: Two Hundred Years of
   Presbyterianism in Stewartstown, 1788–1988* (1988)
See also *The Bell*, the journal of the Stewartsown Historical Society, including
   'The United Irishmen in East Tyrone', (vol. 7, pp 3–45), which includes detailed
   information on events and individuals in east Tyrone in the 1790s, and 'A View of
   Stewartstown, 1750–1800' (vol. 13, pp 23–7), which is a compilation of material
   from the *Belfast Newsletter*.

DONAGHMORE PARISH, COUNTY DONEGAL

Barony: Raphoe South
Diocese: Derry
Places: Castlefinn, Cross Roads, Killygordon
Graveyard: Donaghmore CI

Estate papers
Conolly estate; Derry bishopric estate; Gage estate; Hamilton estate, Castlefinn;
Hamilton estate, Cavan; Lifford estate; McCausland/Gage estate; Mansfield estate

Census substitutes
HMR, DE, LP (Donoughmore), RelC (Protestants, Seceders and Catholics), FL

Publications
S. P. Kerrigan, 'Castlefin – at the base of the Lagan', *Donegal Annual*, 10 (1956)

DONAGHMORE PARISH, COUNTY DOWN

Barony: Iveagh Upper (Upper Half)
Diocese: Dromore
Graveyard: Donaghmore CI

Church records
CI Donaghmore
Baptisms, 1783– (including index); marriages, 1795   MIC1/54/2
(including index); burials, 1784– (including index)

P Donaghmore
Subscribers to a reward fund from the 'Protestant
Dissenting Congregation' of Donaghmore –
Belfast Newsletter, 6–9 Feb. 1776

Estate papers
Armagh archbishopric estate; Innis estate; Meade estate; Vaughan estate

Census substitutes
FL, AC

Publications
J. Davison Cowan, *An Ancient Irish Parish Past and Present Being the Parish of Donaghmore, County Down* (1914)

DONAGHMORE PARISH, COUNTY TYRONE

Barony: Dungannon Middle
Diocese: Armagh
Places: Carland, Castlecaulfield, Donaghmore
Graveyards: Donaghmore CI, Donaghmore Old

Church records
CI Donaghmore

Baptisms, 1748– ; marriages, 1741– ; burials, 1741–; vestry minutes, 1781–2	T679/19 (MIC583/2); MIC1/106/1–2
Typescript copy of baptisms, 1748– ; marriages, 1741– ; burials, 1741– (with indexes); vestry minutes, 1778, 1781–2	MIC1/106/3
Vestry minutes, 1783–	Local custody

P Carland

Baptisms, 1759–99; marriages, 1770–1802	MIC1P/28
Session minutes, 1754–1801	PHSI

Estate papers
Armagh archbishopric estate; Burges estate; Charlemont estate; Knox estate; Lowry estate, Pomeroy; Verner estate

Census substitutes
HMR, VAA, FL

Other records
Notes consisting of pieces of transcription of 'The History of Carland Congregation from its first establishment 1648 to 1826', written by the Rev. William Kennedy McKay (minister of 1st Portglenone, 1826–59) – D2594/2A–F
Minute/roll book of the 'Fort Edward Body of Orangemen', Killymaddy, 1798–9 – Museum of Orange Heritage

Publications
Ynyr A. Burges, *History of St Michael's Church, Castle Caulfield* (1936, revised ed.
    1966)
R. J. McLean, *The Old Meeting House at Carland: Being a History of Carland
    Presbyterian Church, 1646–1996* (1996)
Eamon Ó Doibhlin, *Domnach Mor (Donaghmore). An Outline of Parish History* (1969)
Samuel Stewart, *Historical Outline of the Presbyterian Congregation of Carland* (copied
    by Stewart Carse, 1847)

DONAGHMOYNE PARISH, COUNTY MONAGHAN

Barony: Farney
Diocese: Clogher
Graveyard: Donaghmoyne CI

Estate papers
Bath estate; Clogher bishopric estate; Essex estate; Kane estate, Donaghmoyne;
Shirley estate

Census substitutes
HMR, FP, FL

Publications
Daig Quinn, *St Anne's Church Drumcatton & Blackstaff 1796 to 1996* (1996)

DONEGAL PARISH, COUNTY DONEGAL
This parish was created in 1722 out of **Drumhome**.

Barony: Tirhugh
Diocese: Raphoe
Place: Donegal
Graveyard: Donegal Friary

Estate papers
Trinity College Dublin estate

Census substitutes
LP (Donegal and Ballyshannon), FL

Other records
'Account of monies laid out at Donegal 1795': accounts relating to building works
at the harbour and in the town with some names of those involved – T3200/5/2

DONEGORE PARISH, COUNTY ANTRIM

Barony: Antrim Upper
Diocese: Connor

Place: Parkgate
Graveyard: Donegore CI

Church records
P 1st Donegore

Extracts from the minutes of the Antrim presbytery	D1759/1/A/3
relating to the congregation of Donegore, 1687–91	(MIC637/1)

Estate papers
Donegall estate

Census substitutes
HMR, DP (Donegore, Kilbride and Nilteen)

Publications
Donald Alexander, *The Parkgate Presbyterians: People and Kirk over Four Centuries: The First Donegore Story* (2012)
Margaret Bell, *A History of St John's Church, Donegore* (1988)
William A. Gawn, *A History of Second Donegore Presbyterian Church* (2008)

DOWN PARISH, COUNTY DOWN

Barony: Lecale Upper
Diocese: Down
Place: Downpatrick
Graveyards: Down Cathedral, Downpatrick CI, Downpatrick NSP

Church records
CI Down or Downpatrick

Baptisms, 1733–4, 1750– ; marriages, 1701– ;	MIC1/38, 39; CR1/33
burials, 1718–36, 1752– ; vestry minutes, 1704–	

The vestry minutes include a 'list of the poor widows & objects … in order to be exempted from hearth money', 1733 (over 150 names by townland); distribution of money to the poor, *c.* 1769; list of the poor to be badged, 1773; and a protest by the churchwardens and parishioners in relation to a cess, 1791 (*c.* 70 names).

Copy of baptisms, marriages and burials, 1752–	T684/1

Copy of baptisms, 1733– ,	D1759/1D/3
marriages, 1701– , and burials, 1719–	(MIC637/2)

Plan of Downpatrick Parish Church, made in 1734–5,	D1889/5/1
showing the distribution of the pews, with the names	
of the parishioners to whom they were allotted; printed	

booklet entitled *Memoirs of Downpatrick and its Parish Church* by Aynsworth Pilson, Jan. 1852. The booklet gives biographical sketches of the proprietors of the

several pews as displayed on the earlier plan and also lists
all the deans, archdeacons, curates and churchwardens
associated with the church throughout its history.

Rental relating to the houses of Clergymen's Widows, containing minutes, transcribed leases, copy letters, lists of subscribers and accounts, 1730–1827	MIC1/341/1

Rental relating to the houses of Clergymen' Widows, also including minutes, lists of subscribers and rent rolls, 1791–1890	MIC1/341/2

E. Parkinson, 'The vestry books of the parish of Down', *UJA*, 2nd series, 14 (1908), pp 145–155; 15 (1909), pp 20–28, 79–86

Memoirs of seatholders in 1735, printed in Parkinson, *The City of Downe*, pp 62–76

NSP Downpatrick
This congregation was placed in the non-subscribing Presbytery of Antrim in 1725.

Notebook containing stipend and other accounts, 1781–1811; seat account book, 1760–67; poor account book, 1795–1803; notebook recording families in Saul, Struell, Tobermoney, Ballymote, Clogher, Ballyrenan, etc, with dates of birth and burials, *c.* 1782–*c.* 1887; notebook recording families in Rathmullan, Inch, Tullyveery, Ballydonnell, Glovet, Ballyrenan, etc, with dates of birth and burials, *c.* 1796–*c.* 1889; notebook recording families in Downpatrick with dates of birth and burials, *c.* 1789–*c.* 1877	CR4/8; MIC1B/12

Memoranda and account books, *c.* 1740–	T1268/1/1–6

Estate papers
Ardglass estate; Forde estate; Gibbons estate; Leslie estate; Maxwell estate; Southwell estate; Ward estate

Census substitutes
FL

Freemasonry records
Transcript of minutes of Masonic lodge no. 367, Downpatrick, 1784–93, 1791–1800, 1794–1806 – GLI (Mirala, *Freemasonry in Ulster*, also lists records held locally for 1765–83, 1784–93, 1791–1800)

Other records

Obituaries, Downpatrick area, 1693–1853 – T684/3–8

Copy of a survey of the town carried out in 1708 – D1759/2A/8 (MIC637/8); this consists of a list of each of the named premises, naming principal tenant

Hardback volume of surveys, maps, etc, relating to Downpatrick town and demesne, including a later copy of the survey of the town of Downpatrick of 1708 – D1889/8/1

Marriages in the Downpatrick area, 1727–1853 – T684/2, 9

View book of the great tithes of the deanery of Down, 1732 – D1145/D/1

Extracts from the diary of James Nevin, Ballywarren, 1767–97 – *Lecale Review* 14 (2016), pp 24–7 (reproduced from *Down Recorder*, 3 April 1920)

Subscribers to a reward fund, 1782 – *Belfast Newsletter*, 6–10 Dec. 1782

Names of inhabitants and householders of Downpatrick in 1790, compiled by Aynsworth Pilson and published in the *Downpatrick Recorder*, 4 Feb. 1860 (reprinted in *DIFHR*, 32 (2009))

Papers of Aynsworth Pilson of Downpatrick, including memoranda from his diaries, his memoirs, abstract of his diary, 1775 onwards – D365/1–3

Minute book of the Committee of Subscribers for the Relief of the Poor in Downpatrick, 1801 – D1889/9/2; D2223/11/36

Publications

Old Families of Downpatrick & District from Gravestone Inscriptions, Wills and Biographical Notes, edited by R. S. J. Clarke (1993)

R. H. Buchanan, *Irish Historic Towns Atlas: Downpatrick* (1997)

E. Parkinson, *The City of Downe from Its Earliest Days*, edited by R. E. Parkinson (1928): contains a printed copy of the 1708 survey

Aynsworth Pilson, *Memoirs of Downpatrick and Its Parish Church* (1852)

Aynsworth Pilson, *Memoirs of Notable Inhabitants of Downpatrick*, edited by R. W. H. Blackwood, Gordon Wheeler and Colm Rooney (2016)

L. A. Pooler, *Down and Its Parish Church* (1907)

J. F. Rankin, *Down Cathedral* (1997)

Mary Stewart, *The History of the First Presbyterian (Non-Subscribing) Church, Downpatrick* (2011)

Anthony M. Wilson, *Saint Patrick's Town: A History of Downpatrick and the Barony of Lecale* (1995)

DROMARA PARISH, COUNTY DOWN

Baronies: Iveagh Lower (Lower Half), Iveagh Upper (Lower Half)
Diocese: Dromore
Places: Dromara, Finnis
Graveyards: Dromara CI, Dromara 1st P, Finnis RC

P 1st Dromara

Baptisms, 1762– ; marriages, 1799–1802; session minutes, 1763– ; accounts, 1762–99	MIC1P/89; T1447
History of the church, 1713–1913	D2453/85

Estate papers
Annesley estate; Downshire estate; Dungannon estate; Forde estate; Johnston estate; Magenis estate, Dromara; Mathews estate; Rawdon estate; Sharman estate

Census substitutes
DP, FL, AC

Publications
Aiken McClelland, *A Short History of First Dromara Presbyterian Church* (1963)
W. G. Glasgow, *The Story of the First Dromara Presbyterian Church, 1713–1913* (1913)
S. E. Long, *A Short History of the Parish of Dromara* (1979)

DROMORE PARISH, COUNTY DOWN

Barony: Iveagh Lower (Lower Half)
Diocese: Dromore
Places: Dromore, Kinallen
Graveyard: Dromore CI Cathedral

Church records
CI Dromore
Baptisms, 1784– ; marriages, 1784– ; burials, 1784–   T679/395 (MIC583/35)

Estate papers
Clanwilliam estate; Dromore bishopric estate; Hall estate, Strangford and Lower Iveagh; Lambert estate; Magenis estate, Dromara; Mathews estate

Census substitutes
HSM, DP, FL

Business records
Brakinridge, Ballykeel (Dromore parish?)

Other records
Map and survey of the town of Dromore, 1790, providing details of tenants – T2372/1A–C

Publications
Andrew Doloughan, *Our Great Inheritance* (2 vols, 1995): vol. 1 covers the Cathedral Church, Dromore, and vol. 2 deals with Dromore cathedral parish
W. D. Patton, *The Church on the Hill: A Short History of First Dromore Presbyterian Church 1660–1981* (1982)

DROMORE PARISH, COUNTY TYRONE

Barony: Omagh East
Diocese: Clogher

Place: Dromore
Graveyard: Dromore Old

Church records
CI Dromore
Vestry minutes, 1762–   Local custody

Estate papers
Belmore estate; Cooper estate; Huntingdon estate; Kane estate; Lowry estate,
Drumragh; Mervyn estate

Census substitutes
HMR, FL

Other records
Names of male Protestants aged 17 and over, 1785 – T808/15259

DRUMACHOSE PARISH, COUNTY LONDONDERRY

Barony: Keenaght
Diocese: Derry
Places: Bolea, Limavady (also once known as Newtownlimavady)
Graveyards: Drumachose CI, Drumachose Old

Church records
CI Drumachose
Baptisms, 1730–52; marriages, 1728–53;   T679/3, 394
burials, 1730–36; vestry minutes, *c.* 1728–1777,   (MIC583/1, 35)
1787, 1794–

The vestry minutes are incredibly detailed and include a wealth of information
about the parish. They include: list of the poor and their badge numbers, *c.* 1728;
collection and distribution of money to the poor, 1728; list of names (reason unclear),
1746; distribution of money to the poor, 1750 and subsequent years; subscribers to
the fund for rebuilding the church, 1753; list of names for Easter Day, 1754
(attendees at church?); list of the poor, *c.* 1787; applotment of the 'Six Towns of
Newtown', 1787. In 1766, the vestry met to discuss the raising of a cess for the poor;
the minutes of the meeting are followed by two lists: one listing those in favour of the
cess and the other, the longer, those against it (*c.* 80 names in total); the minutes
conclude with a lament about 'the cruel opposition against the cause of God's poor'.

Estate papers
Beresford estate; Conolly estate; Derry bishopric estate; Phillips estate

Census substitutes
HMR, DE, CPH (includes townlands), RelC (Anglicans, Presbyterians and
Catholics; includes townlands), FL

Corporation records: Limavady
Corporation minute books, 1659–1736, 1736–68, 1771–81, 1781–1808 –
  D663/2–5 (published as *Records of the Town of Limavady, 1609 to 1808*, edited
  by E. M. F.-G. Boyle (1912; reprinted 1989)
Miscellaneous corporation records, 17th and 18th centuries – D663 *passim*

Business records
Alexander, Limavady

Other records
18th-century deeds, etc relating to the Alexander family of Limavady – D1118/3
Petition of the inhabitants of Limavady, 1796 – *Londonderry Journal*, 18–25 Oct.
  1796

Publications
Douglas Bartlett, *An Illustrated History of Limavady and the Roe Valley: From
  Prehistoric to Modern Times* (2010)
T. H. Mullin, *Limavady and the Roe Valley* (1983): includes brief notes on some
  90 families

DRUMBALLYRONEY, COUNTY DOWN

Barony: Iveagh Upper (Lower Half)
Diocese: Dromore
Places: Ballyroney, Katesbridge
Graveyard: Drumballyroney CI

Estate papers
Annesley estate; Downshire estate; Close estate; Meade estate; Sharman estate

Census substitutes
DP (Drumballyroney and Drumgoolan), FL, AC

Publications
John Lockington, *Ballyroney: Its Church and People* (1977)
Annaclone & Drumballyroney Local History (2010)

DRUMBEG PARISH, COUNTIES ANTRIM AND DOWN

Barony: Belfast Upper (Antrim portion), Castlereagh Upper (Down portion)
Diocese: Down
Places: Drumbeg, Dunmurry, Finaghy, Hillhall
Graveyards: Drumbeg CI, Dunmurry NSP

Church records
NSP Dunmurry
Notes about the history of the church, *c.* 1686–1820   CR4/1/B/1

Burials in the churchyard, 1781–1954   T1602

Census substitutes
HMR (portion in County Antrim only, included under heading 'Dunmurry
Liberty'), DP (Dunmurry), AC

Publications
Robert Common, *Some Observations on Dunmurry's Past* (1999)
Matthew Neill, *Ecclesia de Drum: Recollections of the Parish of Drumbeg, Diocese of
Down* [c. 1995]

DRUMBO PARISH, COUNTY DOWN

Barony: Castlereagh Upper
Diocese: Down
Places: Baileysmills, Ballylesson, Carryduff, Drumbo, Edenderry
Graveyards: Drumbo, Knockbracken RP

Church records
CI Drumbo
Baptisms, 1791– ; marriages, 1791– ;   MIC1/41
burials, 1792– ; vestry minutes, 1788–

The vestry minutes include a number of lists of names of overseers of road repairs
and collectors of the parish cess in the 1790s.

P Drumbo
Baptisms, 1699–1723, 1764–73, 1781–92;   MIC1P/291;
marriages, 1706–21, 1772, 1782–83, 1786–91   D1759/1D/1
                                                        (MIC637/2)

Printed history of the congregation   CR3/54
from the early 17th century

Session minutes, 1701–34 [missing]

Estate papers
Downshire estate; Dungannon estate; McNeill estate

Census substitutes
AC

Publications
J. Fred Rankin, *The Heritage of Drumbo* (1981): includes names of subscribers to
    the new Church of Ireland church, 1789–91, and names of churchwardens and
    sidesmen from 1791 onwards

C. I. Reid, *The Past Revisited: A History of Drumbo Presbyterian Church* (1991): includes names of collectors and sub-collectors by aisle, plus names of seatholders in east aisle, 20 May 1706

George A. Bowsie and Graham Murphy, *Carryduff 2000* (2000)

J. B. Wallace, *A History of Drumbo Presbyterian Church 1655–1956* (1956)

DRUMCAW PARISH, COUNTY DOWN

This parish was united with Loughinisland in the early 1700s: see **Loughinisland** parish.

DRUMCREE PARISH, COUNTY ARMAGH

Barony: Oneilland West
Diocese: Armagh
Places: Portadown, Scotch Street
Graveyard: Drumcree CI

Church records
CI Drumcree
Baptisms, 1788– ; vestry minutes, 1767–   MIC1/21, /42, /43

The vestry records include lists of Protestants and Catholics in receipt of aid from the parish from 1765 onwards; there is also detailed information on road repairs and those responsible for them.

Estate papers
Armagh archbishopric estate; Brownlow estate; Burges estate; Jenny estate; Manchester estate; Obins estate; Obre estate; Workman estate

Census substitutes
HMR, FL

Other records
'An Inventory of the Goods and Chattels of the Rev. Mr Robert Letherbarrow, late Retcor [sic] of the Parish of Drumcree in the County of Armagh Decd., together with a Return of the debts due to him for rents and Tythes in said Parish, and also the small dues, due to him out of the Parish of Killdress and County of Tyrone ...', 1737 – D2395/9 (also T808/15298)

Notes on Drumcree parish, including: state of the parish in 1796, list of Protestant householders of the parish in 1740, list of freeholders of the parish in 1753 and subsidy roll of 1634 – CR1/116/10/1 [digital copy only available, original held by church]

Publications
Historical Sketch of Drumcree Parish, Diocese of Armagh: Compiled from Original Sources (1927)
Isobel Carrick, *Historical Sketch of Drumcree Parish: An Appendix* (1991)

DRUMCRIN PARISH, COUNTIES FERMANAGH AND MONAGHAN

This parish was created out of Drummully and Galloon in 1773. However, it ceased to exist in the early 1800s when it was divided between the parishes of **Currin** and **Drummully**.

DRUMGATH PARISH, COUNTY DOWN

Barony: Iveagh Upper (Upper Half)
Diocese: Dromore
Place: Rathfriland
Graveyards: Drumgath CI, Drumgath Old

Church records
P 1st Rathfriland

Marriages, 1782–	MIC1P/131; D1759/1D/14 (MIC637/4); T1037/1
Common-place book of Rev. Samuel Barber, 1781–1811, including names of the Rathfriland Company of Volunteers, 1781 (with comments) and marriages, 1782–1811	PHSI
Visiting book of Rev. Samuel Barber, listing families by townland, pre-1798	PHSI

Estate papers
Annesley estate; Close estate; Downshire estate; Meade estate

Census substitutes
DP (Rathfriland), FL, AC

Other records
Diary of William McKee, Rathfriland, including rent memoranda relating to an unidentified estate in County Monaghan, 1758–85 – T1322/1
Scheme for the improvement of the estate and town of Rathfriland by Henry Waring, 1764: does not name occupiers of property – T1181/1 (copy at T2125/11/3)
Minute book of the Rathfriland Volunteers, 1779 – Ulster Museum, 603–1914
Rent receipt book of Geo. Newell, Rathfryland, 1787–95, including miscellaneous notes on cash transactions, etc – D2071/6
Original cash account book with list of 'bad debts', Rathfriland, Newry area, 1796 – D1759/2/A/4 (MIC637/7)
John A. McCracken, 'Rathfriland in bygone days' (typescript possibly written in the 1960s) – NLI, 2B 236

Publications
David Magee, *A Story Worth Telling: Historical Sketch of Rathfriland Reformed Presbyterian Church, 1777–1977* (1977)
R. G. A. Morrison, 'A *Household of Faith': A Historical Survey of the First Rathfriland Presbyterian Congregation* (1962)
Andrew Morrow, 'The Rev. Samuel Barber, A.M., and the Rathfriland Volunteers', *UJA*, 2nd series, 14 (1908), pp 104–19 (which includes the names of *c.* 70 subscribers to the rules of the company in 1779 as well as those who joined subsequently); and 15 (1909), pp 29–35, 125–33, 149–57

DRUMGLASS PARISH, COUNTY TYRONE

Barony: Dungannon Middle
Diocese: Armagh
Place: Dungannon
Graveyard: Drumglass Old

Church records
CI Drumglass (Armagh)
Baptisms, 1665–1767, 1774–1802; marriages,   MIC1/18; MIC1/36
1677–1766, 1791–2, 1799–1804; burials,
1672–1767; vestry minutes, 1693–

The vestry minutes, the earliest of which are in very poor condition, also cover Tullyniskan parish, which did not have its own parish church for most of the 1700s. The minutes include a list of names and acres (in the Corporation lands?), *c.* 1780; the minutes of a meeting in 1795 concerning funds for erecting a spire on the new Church of Ireland church included over 50 signatories; plans of the new church showing the allocation of seats, undated [*c.* 1797].

P 1st Dungannon
Baptisms, 1790– ; marriages and notices of   MIC1P/3A
marriages with rebukes for irregular marriages, 1789–

Estate papers
Armagh archbishopric estate; Knox estate; Stewart estate, Killymoon

Census substitutes
HMR, RelC (Protestants and Catholics; townlands included), DP (Dungannon town and neighbourhood + Dungannon barony), FL

Corporation records: Dungannon
Corporation minute book, 1695–1840 – MIC547/1

Publications
W. R. Hutchison, *Tyrone Precinct: A History of the Plantation Settlement of Dungannon and Mountjoy to Modern Times* (1951)

E. W. Monteith, *A History of The Parish of Drumglass* (n.d.): includes extracts from early vestry minutes
Dungannon Presbyterian Church: A Short Memoir to Mark the 250th Year of the Congregation's History (1966)

DRUMGOOLAND PARISH, COUNTY DOWN

Barony: Iveagh Upper (Lower Half)
Diocese: Dromore
Places: Ballyward, Drumlee, Leitrim, Moneyslane
Graveyards: Deehommed, Drumadonnell

Church records
CI Drumgooland
Baptisms, 1779–92; marriages, 1779–91   MIC1/40A/1

Extracts from the Drumgooland vestry book, 1790–1828 in *Journal of the Royal Historical and Archaeological Association of Ireland*, 4th series, 9:81 (Oct. 1889–Jan. 1890), pp 318–24

Estate papers
Annesley estate; Dungannon estate; Meade estate

Census substitutes
DP (Drumgooland + Drumballyroney and Drumgoolan), FL, AC

Publications
C. R. J. Rudd, *A Short History of Drumgooland Parish* (n.d.)

DRUMGOON PARISH, COUNTY CAVAN

Baronies: Clankee, Tullygarvey
Diocese: Kilmore
Place: Cootehill
Graveyards: Church Street (Cootehill), Cootehill Moravian, Cootehill Quaker, Drumgoon Old

Church records
MOR Cootehill
Baptisms, 1765– ; marriages, 1769– ; reception   MIC1/F/5
register, 1765– , recording details of baptisms back
to 1700, former religious denomination of new
members, date of confirmation and communion,
marital status, date of death from 1767 onwards and
occurrences, for example, of emigration or movement
to other societies.

RSF Cootehill
Men's monthly meeting minutes, 1766–96   MIC16/45

Estate papers
Coote estate

Census substitutes
FL

Publications
Aogán Ó Fearghail (ed.), *An Maide Bán: Maudabawn* (1991)
Patrick Cassidy, 'Religious diversity in Cootehill in the eighteenth century', *Breifne*,
    36 (2000), pp 243–58
[Patrick Cassidy, 'Cootehill: an eighteenth century Ulster linen town', National
    University of Ireland Maynooth thesis (1998)]

DRUMHOME PARISH, COUNTY DONEGAL
The name of this parish is also spelled Drumholm.

Barony: Tirhugh
Diocese: Raphoe
Places: Ballintra, Laghy, Rossnowlagh
Graveyard: Drumhome Old

Church records
CI Drumhome
Baptisms, 1719–20, 1739–48, 1764, 1783– ;   MIC1/148
marriages, 1691–1718, 1764, 1783– ;
burials, 1696–1715, 1764, 1783–

Vestry minutes, 1783–   Local custody

Estate papers
Conolly estate; Hamilton estate, Brownhall; Raphoe bishopric estate

Census substitutes
HMR, FL

Publications
Keith Corcoran, *Drumhome Stepping Back in Time* (2016)
Bernard Egan, *Drumhome* (1986)
T. H. Trimble, *The Legacy that is Laghey Community and Church* (2000)

DRUMKEERAN PARISH, COUNTY FERMANAGH
This parish was created out of **Magheraculmoney** *c.* 1774.

Barony: Lurg
Diocese: Clogher
Graveyard: Drumkeeran CI

Church records
CI Drumkeeran
Vestry minutes, 1794–   Local custody

Estate papers
Archdale estate; Barton estate; Lenox estate; Vaughan estate

Census substitutes
FL

DRUMLANE PARISH, COUNTY CAVAN

Barony: Loughtee Lower
Diocese: Kilmore
Place: Milltown
Graveyard: Drumlane Abbey

Estate papers
Annesley estate; Farnham estate; Lanesborough estate; Pleydell estate

Census substitutes
FL

DRUMLUMMAN PARISH, COUNTY CAVAN
The name of this parish is also spelled Drumloman and Drumlummon.

Barony: Clanmahon
Diocese: Ardagh
Place: Kilcogy
Graveyard: Drumlummon CI (former)

Estate papers
Annesley estate; Coyne estate; Farnham estate

Census substitutes
FL

Publications
Bríd Donohoe, Nicholas Baxter (eds), *Ballymachugh and Drumloman South: Our Home Place by Sheelin's Side* (2008)
Edward J. Boylan, *The Parish of Mullahoran (Drumlumman North and Loughduff)* (1977)

DRUMMAUL PARISH, COUNTY ANTRIM

Barony: Toome Upper
Diocese: Connor
Places: Caddy, Groggan, Randalstown, Shane's Castle
Graveyards: Drummaul CI, Drummaul Old, Shane's Castle

Church records
P Drummaul (Randalstown)
Heads of families and names of young people   *RGSU*, vol. 2, p. 240
wishing to separate from the congregation, 1738   (see pp 58–9 of this book)

Estate papers
O'Neill estate

Census substitutes
HMR, CPH

Other records
Subscribers to a reward fund, 1772 – *Belfast Newsletter*, 7 April 1772

Publications
Randalstown Presbyterian Church (Old Congregation) Tercentenary, 1655–1955 (1955)
Robert Allen, *Three Centuries of Christian Witness, Being the History of First Randalstown Presbyterian Church* (1955)
H. A. Boyd, *Drummaul Parish Church: Historical Sketch* [*c.* 1943]
Patrick O'Kane, *Sweet Drummaul. The Catholic Parish of Drummaul, Randalstown* (1991): includes 18th-century names on headstones in Shanes Castle graveyard (p. 24)

DRUMMULLY PARISH, COUNTIES FERMANAGH AND MONAGHAN
See the note under **Galloon** parish for more information on the bounds of this parish.

Baronies: Dartree (Monghan portion), Coole (Fermanagh portion)
Diocese: Clogher
Place: Wattlebridge
Graveyard: Drummully Old

Church records
CI Drummully
Vestry minutes, 1779–   MIC1/51/1

These vestry minutes concern the parish of Drummully prior to the parochial reorganisation of the early 1800s and so relate to what became the parish of Galloon (see **Galloon** for more information).

Estate papers
Clogher bishopric estate; Dawson estate

Census substitutes
FL

DRUMRAGH PARISH, COUNTY TYRONE

Barony: Omagh East
Diocese: Derry
Places: Gillygooly, Omagh
Graveyard: Drumragh Old

Church records
CI Drumragh
Vestry minutes, 1792–   MIC1/40C/1

RC Drumragh
Printed history of the parish   CR2/9/1
from the 17th century to *c.* 1900

Estate papers
Derry bishopric estate; Huntingdon estate; Kane estate; Lowry estate, Drumragh; Mervyn estate; Stewart estate

Census substitutes
HMR, FL

Business records
Brady, Omagh

Other records
Masters of families, 1699 – T542
Publication of a loyal resolution by the Roman Catholics of Omagh and its vicinity, dated 14 June 1798, indicating their willingness to join the Volunteers or Supplementary Yeomanry, *c.* 60 names, printed in Brendan McEvoy, *The United Irishmen in County Tyrone* (1998), p. 90

Publications
Audrey Hodge, *"A Congregation in the Omey": The Story of First Omagh Presbyterian Church* (1997)
John McCandless and Claire McElhinney, *The People of Trinity Presbyterian Church, Omagh 1754–2004* (2004)

DRUMREILLY see TEMPLEPORT

DRUMSNAT PARISH, COUNTY MONAGHAN

Barony: Monaghan
Diocese: Clogher
Place: Threemilehouse
Graveyard: Drumsnat Old

Estate papers
Blayney estate; Clogher bishopric estate; Evatt estate

Census substitutes
HMR, FL

Publications
Eamonn Mulligan and Brian McCluskey, *'The Replay': A Parish History* (1984):
a history of the parishes of Kilmore and Drumsnat

DRUNG PARISH, COUNTY CAVAN

Barony: Tullygarvey
Diocese: Kilmore
Graveyards: Drung Old, Magherintemple

Church records
CI Drung (Kilmore diocese)
Baptisms, 1759– ; marriages, 1785– ; burials, 1774–   MIC1/300

Estate papers
Annesley estate

Census substitutes
FL

DUNAGHY PARISH, COUNTY ANTRIM

Barony: Kilconway
Diocese: Connor
Places: Cargan, Clough, Glenravel
Graveyard: Clough (Dunaghy) Old

Church records
CI Dunaghy
Notebook of Rev. Andrew Rowan, 1672–80   T796/1 (MIC691/1)

Analyses of this volume can be found in D. A. Chart, 'An account book of the Rev. Andrew Rowan, rector of Dunaghy, County Antrim, *c.* 1672–1680', *UJA*, 3rd series, 5 (1942), pp 67–76, and R. Gillespie, 'The world of Andrew Rowan: economy and society in Restoration Antrim' in B. Collins, P. Ollerenshaw and T. Parkhill (eds), *Industry, Trade and People in Ireland, 1650–1950. Essays in Honour of W. H. Crawford* (2005), pp 10–30.

Estate papers
Adams estate; Antrim estate; Mitchell estate; Moore and Stewart Moore estate; O'Hara estate; Rowan estate, Mullans

Census substitutes
HMR, CPH, HSM, FL

Other records
18th-century deeds for Ballybogy – D2223/15/56

Publications
Felix McKillop, *Along the Ravel and Clough Water* (2012)

DUNBOE PARISH, COUNTY LONDONDERRY

Barony: Coleraine
Diocese: Derry
Places: Articlave, Castlerock, Downhill
Graveyards: Dunboe CI, Dunboe Old

CI Dunboe
Vestry minutes, 1783–   MIC1/135D/1

The vestry minutes include some baptisms, 1790–91, 1795; lists of 'reduced housekeepers', 1783–5.

P 1st Dunboe
Memorandum book of Rev. William Knox,   T2646/3
Presbyterian minister of Dunboe (1765–1801),
including accounts and details of the births of
his children, 1746–*c.* 1769

Stipend list, 1801   Local custody

Estate papers
Clothworkers' Company estate; Derry bishopric estate; Hervey/Bruce estate; Jackson estate; McClelland/Maxwell estate; Merchant Taylors' Company estate; Richardson estate

Census substitutes
CPH, FL

Other records
Surveys of Articlave, n.d. [probably late 18th century] – D668/N/1
Memorandum book for Dunboe parish, 1769–70: detailed information on tenants and farms – D668/C/1
Notebook containing notification of registering arms, including residents of Dunboe, 1796 – D668/N/1

Publications
James Mark, *First Dunboe: An Historical Sketch* (1915)
A. P. Chamberlain, *History of Dunboe Parish* (n.d.)
Alison A. McCaughan, *Heath, Hearth and Heart: The Story of Dunboe and the Meeting House at Articlave* (1988)

DUNDONALD PARISH, COUNTY DOWN

Barony: Castlereagh Lower
Diocese: Down
Place: Dundonald
Graveyard: Dundonald CI

Church records
P Dundonald
Session book, 1678–1716, including baptisms,   PHSI
1678–98, and marriages, 1678–93

For extracts, see 'The old session book of the Presbyterian congregation at Dundonald', *UJA*, 2nd series, 3 (July 1893), pp 227–32; 4 (Oct. 1897), pp 33–66

Estate papers
Annesley estate; Armagh archbishopric estate; Hamilton (Claneboye and Clanbrassil) estate; Londonderry estate; Ross estate, Portavo

Census substitutes
DP, FL

Publications
Alexander Hanna, *These Three Hundred and Forty Years of Witness. An Historical Outline of Dundonald Presbyterian Congregation, 1645–1985* (1985)
Peter Carr, *'The Most Unpretending of Places': A History of Dundonald, County Down* (1988)

DUNEANE PARISH, COUNTY ANTRIM

Barony: Toome Upper
Diocese: Connor
Places: Moneyglass, Staffordstown, Toome (Toomebridge)
Graveyard: Duneane CI

Estate papers
O'Neill estate

Census substitutes
HMR, CPH

DUNGIVEN PARISH, COUNTY LONDONDERRY

Barony: Keenaght
Diocese: Derry
Places: Dungiven, Glenshane, Scriggan
Graveyards: Dungiven CI, Dungiven Priory

Church records
CI Dungiven

Baptisms, 1795– ; marriages, 1795– ; vestry minutes, 1778–	T679/70 (MIC583/7)

There were over 30 signatories to the vestry minutes of 1787.

Baptisms, 1778–94; marriages, 1778–94	Local custody

Estate papers
Beresford estate; Derry bishopric estate; Skinners' Company estate

Census substitutes
HMR, DE, CPH (includes townlands), RelC (Protestants), FL

Publications
The magazines *Benbradagh* and *The Winding Roe* contain much of historical interest.

DUNLUCE PARISH, COUNTY ANTRIM

Barony: Dunluce Lower
Diocese: Connor
Places: Ballybogy, Bushmills, Portballintrae
Graveyard: Dunluce Old

Church records
CI Dunluce

Vestry minutes, 1778–	MIC1/90/1

The vestry minutes include applotments for the upper and lower 'constablewicks' of the parish, 1779–81; subscribers to a petition discouraging drunkenness at funerals, 1801 (over 40 names).

P Dunluce
Call to Rev. John Cameron, 1755 – printed in Mullin, *Dunluce Presbyterian Church*, pp 83–4

Estate papers
Antrim estate; McNaghten estate; Montgomery estate

Census substitutes
HMR, CPH, FL, AC

Other records
Account of a disturbance at Dunluce fair on 2 Nov. 1663 – D2977/5/1/2/43

Publications
Julia E. Mullin, *A History of Dunluce Presbyterian Church* (1995)
Colin Breen, *Dunluce Castle: Archaeology and History* (2012)

DUNSFORT PARISH, COUNTY DOWN
The name of this parish is also spelled Dunsford.

Barony: Lecale Lower
Diocese: Down
Places: Ballyhornan, Chapeltown
Graveyards: Dunsfort CI, Dunsfort RC

Estate papers
Hall estate, Ballyhornan; Kildare estate; Ward estate

Census substitutes
FL, AC

Business records
Casement, Sheepland Beg

Publications
Duane Fitzsimons, *Under the Shade of Our Lady's Sweet Image: The Story of a Unique Coastal Parish in the Diocese of Down and Connor* (2016)
G. Rice, *St Mary's Roman Catholic Church, Dunsford, 1791–1991* (1991)
A Harvest of History from Dunsford and Ardglass (2014–)

EGLISH PARISH, COUNTY ARMAGH
This parish was created out of **Armagh parish** in 1720.

Baronies: Armagh, Tiranny
Diocese: Armagh
Places: Carrickaness, Navan
Graveyard: Eglish Old

Estate papers
Armagh archbishopric estate; Burges estate; Charlemont estate; Houston estate;
Johnston estate, Eglish; Ker estate; MacGeough-Bond estate; Whaley estate

Publications
J. M. Batchelor, 'List of burials in the Old Eglish churchyard, Co. Armagh', *Duiche Neill*, 5 (1990): information extracted from Armagh CI records, 1750–57 and 1770–75

EMATRIS PARISH, COUNTY MONAGHAN
This parish was created around 1730 out of the parish of **Galloon**.

Barony: Dartree
Diocese: Clogher
Place: Rockcorry
Graveyards: Edergole, Ematris CI

Church records
CI Ematris
Vestry minutes, 1767– , with baptisms,   MIC1/132
1753–91, and marriages, 1753–75

The vestry minutes include details about seating arrangements in the parish church, 1786; and the names of applotters for each townland, 1803 (over 60 names).

Estate papers
Clogher bishopric estate; Dawson estate; Moore estate

Census substitutes
HMR, FL

Publications
Peter McKenna, *A History of Rockcorry St Mary's in 'The Emetresse'* (1991)

ENNISKEEN, COUNTY CAVAN

Barony: Clankee
Diocese: Meath

Place: Kingscourt
Graveyard: Enniskeen Old

Estate papers
Pratt estate

Census substitutes
FL

Other records
List of Protestant inhabitants, 1802 – printed in *The Irish Ancestor*, 5 (1973)

Publications
John Gilmore, *Kingscourt: A History* (2012)

ENNISKILLEN PARISH, COUNTY FERMANAGH

Baronies: Magheraboy, Tirkennedy
Diocese: Clogher
Places: Clabby, Enniskillen, Garvary, Tempo
Graveyards: Enniskillen CI (St Macartin's Cathedral), Inishkeen Island, Pubble

Church records
CI Enniskillen (now St Macartin's Cathedral)

Vestry minutes, 1731–	MIC1/110/1; D2296/1
Extracts of baptisms, 1667–1789, marriages, 1668–1794, and burials, 1667–1781	CR1/21A/1
Extracts from baptism, marriage and burial registers, 1666–1826	T3548/1
Printed copy of *Old Enniskillen Vestry Book*, with extracts of births, marriages and deaths, 1666–*c*. 1797	D3007/T/578
Extracts from vestry minutes, 1666–1912, which include some baptisms, marriages and burials	D1588/6

'The Old Enniskillen vestry book (1666–1797). …', *UJA*, 2nd series, Special Volume (1903), pp 136–86

Estate papers
Belmore estate; Clogher bishopric estate; Cooper estate; Enniskillen estate; Erne estate; Lendrum estate; Montgomery estate; Maguire estate

Census substitutes
HMR, LP (Inniskillen), FL (also listed under 'Tempo')

Corporation records
Information about the corporation of Enniskillen and its members, 1718–79 –
D3007/T/582

Other sources
'Account of the losses of the inhabitants of Enniskillen delivered to me [Sir Michael
Cole] by the Provost, July 1705' – D1702/12/1 (printed in Trimble, *History of
Enniskillen*, vol. 3, pp 747–8); this comprises a long list of names and losses
following the devastating fire in Enniskillen in 1705
'Cash rec'd by Mr Armar from ye parishioners', 1747–52: covers parishes of
Derrybrusk and Enniskillen, gives names and in many cases residences – D627/14
(volume broken into several sections, with an index of names for one section at
the front)
Tithes received by Mr Armar out of Derrybrusk and Enniskillen parishes, *c.* 1750:
over 140 names, but no residences – D627/15
Map of Enniskillen, 1772: names tenements, not tenants – D53/1

Publications
W. H. Bradshaw, *Enniskillen Long Ago* (1878)
W. H. Dundas, *Enniskillen, Parish and Town* (1913)
Samuel B. Morrow, *The Church of Ireland Parishes of Clabby and Tempo* (2002),
includes churchwardens (from 1697 onwards, with gaps) and sidesmen (from
1681 onwards, with gaps) who served the country part of Enniskillen parish
(pp 26–7)
W. C. Trimble, *The History of Enniskillen* (3 vols, 1919–21)

ERRIGAL PARISH, COUNTY LONDONDERRY

Barony: Coleraine
Diocese: Derry
Places: Ballerin, Garvagh, Glenullin
Graveyards: Errigal CI, Errigal Old

Church records
P 1st Garvagh
Baptisms, 1795– ; marriages, 1795– ;   MIC1P/257
census of congregation, 1796

Estate papers
Beresford estate; Canning estate; Derry bishopric estate; Heyland estate;
Ironmongers' Company estate; Merchant Taylors' Company estate; Richardson
estate; Rowley estate

Census substitutes
HMR, CPH, FL

Other records
Petition of Protestant inhabitants of Errigal concerning their wish to build a church
    at Garvagh, *c.* 1665 – D683/121 (printed in Moody and Simms, *Bishopric of
    Derry and the Irish Society of London*, vol. 1, pp 185–6)
Notebook containing notification of registering arms, including residents of Errigal,
    1796 – D668/N/1
Rent account book recording rent payments by the Clinton family to the Canning
    family and others for lands at Garvagh, etc, 1742–1833 – D2171/31

Publications
Glimpses of the Past 1641–1991 [First Garvagh Presbyterian Church] (1991)
R. W. Patterson, *Garvagh: A Town and Two Parishes* (1999)

ERRIGAL KEEROGUE PARISH, COUNTY TYRONE

Barony: Clogher
Diocese: Armagh
Places: Ballygawley, Garvaghey
Graveyards: Errigal Keerogue CI, Errigal Old

Church records
CI Errigal Keerogue
Parish valuation, 1757 (only a few names)   MIC1/2/1

Estate papers
Armagh archbishopric estate; Foljambe estate; Leslie estate, Glaslough; Verner estate

Census substitutes
HMR, FP, RelC (Protestants and Catholics; includes townlands), FL

Other records
Printed resolution of the members of the Orange lodges in the neighbourhood of
Clogher, Augher, Ballygawley and Aughnacloy, with names appended, 1798 –
D2085/6

Publications
J. J. Marshall, *Clochar na Righ (Clogher of the Kings): being a history of the town of and
district of Clogher, in the county of Tyrone. Also some account of the parish of Errigal
Keeroge, in the county of Tyrone, and the parish of Errigal Truagh, in the county of
Monaghan* (1930)

ERRIGAL TROUGH PARISH, COUNTIES MONAGHAN AND TYRONE

Baronies: Trough (Monaghan portion), Clogher (Tyrone portion)
Diocese: Clogher
Graveyard: Errigal Old

Church records
CI Errigal Trough
Baptisms, marriages and burials, 1671–2;   MIC1/125A/1
1719–20, 1722–3, 1728–9

Estate papers
Anketell estate; Barton estate; Clogher bishopric estate; Crofton estate; Dawson estate; Kane estate; Leslie estate, Glaslough; Massereene estate; Mervyn estate; Moutray estate; Singleton estate; Verner estate

Census substitutes
HMR, FL

Other records
Names of male Protestants aged 17 and over, 1785 – T808/15259

Publications
J. J. Marshall, *Clochar na Righ (Clogher of the Kings): being a history of the town of and district of Clogher, in the county of Tyrone. Also some account of the parish of Errigal Keeroge, in the county of Tyrone, and the parish of Errigal Truagh, in the county of Monaghan* (1930)

FAHAN PARISH, COUNTY DONEGAL
This parish was divided into Upper Fahan and Lower Fahan in 1794.

Barony: Inishowen West
Diocese: Derry
Places: Buncrana, Fahan
Graveyard: Fahan Old

Church records
CI Fahan (later Fahan Upper)
Baptisms, 1762– ; vestry minutes, 1792–   MIC1/180D/1

The vestry minutes include poor lists from 1793 onwards, and an alphabetical list of the poor, 1802.

Estate papers
Derry bishopric estate; Hart estate

Census substitutes
HMR, CPH (includes townlands), FL

Other records
Declaration by the inhabitants of the 'Town of Buncranagh, quarterlands of Ardaravin, Tollydush, Ballymacarry, Ballymagan, Monyworry, and Tullyarvill',

expressing their abhorrence at cattle-maiming, 1773: 89 names – *Londonderry Journal*, 17 Aug. 1773

Publications
David Dickson, 'Buncrana and Derry in 1744', *Donegal Annual*, 9 (1970), pp 233–7
Seoirse Ó Dochartaigh, *Inis Eoghain: The Island of Eoghan: The Place-Names of Inishowen* (2011)
Seoirse Ó Dochartaigh, *The Great Name Book of Inishowen* (2016)
H. P. Swan, *Buncrana Presbyterian Church, 1861–1961* (1960)

FAUGHANVALE PARISH, COUNTY LONDONDERRY

Barony: Tirkeeran
Diocese: Derry
Places: Eglinton (formerly Muff), Greysteel
Graveyards: Eglinton Old (Faughanvale CI), Faughanvale Old

Church records
CI Faughanvale
Census, 1803   MIC1/7B

Estate papers
Conolly estate; Derry bishopric estate; Fishmongers' Company estate; Grocers' Company estate

Census substitutes
HMR, DE, CPH (includes townlands), FL

Other records
Depositions giving the names of the occupiers of certain lands in Faughanvale parish, 1665 – D683/169 (Moody and Simms, *Bishopric of Derry and the Irish Society of London*, vol. 1, pp 392–3)
Subscribers to a reward fund relating to a fire in 'Carnimuff', Faughanvale parish, 1798 – *Londonderry Journal*, 16 Jan. 1798

Publications
Brian Mitchell, *Historic Eglinton: A Thriving Ornament* (1994): includes a Yeomanry muster roll of the Louisa and Muff Cavalry, 1800 (p. 83)
J. R. White, *The Meeting House at Tullanee. A History of Faughanvale Presbyterian Church* (1994)

FINVOY PARISH, COUNTY ANTRIM

Barony: Kilconway
Diocese: Connor
Place: Dunloy
Graveyards: Caldanagh (Ballymacaldrack), Finvoy CI, Knockans, Vow

Church records
CI Finvoy
Vestry minutes, 1791–   Local custody

Estate papers
Bateson estate; Magenis estate, Dromara; Moore estate, Ballynacree; Rowan estate, Mullans; Stewart estate, Finvoy

Census substitutes
HMR, CPH, FL

Other records
Typescript notes relating to the history of Finvoy parish, compiled *c.* 1950 – T1397/1

Publications
Mary McLean, *Dunloy Past & Present* (1990)
Joseph Thompson, *The Story of Finvoy Presbyterian Church* (1990)

FORKILL PARISH, COUNTY ARMAGH
This parish, also spelled Forkhill, was created in 1771 out of **Loughgilly**, with an addition made to it in 1773 from **Killevy**.

Barony: Orior Lower
Diocese: Armagh
Places: Forkill, Mullaghbawn
Graveyards: Forkill CI, Mullaghbawn RC

Church records
CI Forkill
Vestry minutes, *c.* 1793   MIC1/112/1

Note: the vestry minutes are listed in the PRONI catalogue under Creggan parish.

Estate papers
Armagh archbishopric estate; Jackson estate

Publications
Kick Any Stone: Townlands, People and Stories of Forkhill Parish, compiled and edited
    by Úna Walsh and Kevin Murphy (2003)
Kyla Madden, *Forkhill Protestants and Forkhill Catholics, 1787–1858* (2006)

GALLOON PARISH, COUNTY FERMANAGH
The network of parishes in the area straddling the boundary between counties Fermanagh and Monaghan has a particularly complex history. The parish of Galloon in the early 1700s was almost entirely within County Monaghan. In the course of the eighteenth century the parishes of Aghabog, Currin, Ematris and Killeevan were

created out of it. The present parish of Galloon was created in the early nineteenth century. The area now covered by Galloon included a portion of the pre-1800 parish of Drummully, including the site of the parish church in Newtownbutler. See J. B. Leslie, *Clogher Clergy and Parishes* (1929), pp 273–8, for more information. It should be clear, therefore, that research in this area is not without its difficulties. The sources listed below concern primarily the parish of Galloon as constituted in the early 1800s. However, if looking for ancestors from Galloon, researchers should also consult records for the following parishes: **Aghabog, Currin, Drummully, Ematris** and **Killeevan**.

Baronies: Clankelly, Coole, Knockninny
Diocese: Clogher
Places: Donagh, Newtownbutler
Graveyards: Donagh, Galloon CI (Newtownbutler), Galloon Old

Church records
CI Galloon
Baptisms, 1798– ; marriages, 1798– ;   MIC1/51/1
burials, 1798– ; vestry minutes, 1779–

The vestry minutes (and presumably the earliest registers) concern what was in the late 1700s the parish of Drummully and the vestry meetings were held in the parish church located in Newtownbutler. They include a detailed list of seatholders in the parish church, 1787.

Estate papers
Clogher bishopric estate; Erne estate; Lanesborough estate; Madden estate

Publications
Barbara Chapman, *A History of Newtownbutler* (2005)
Dermot Maguire, *Drumlone at the Crossroads: A Country Area in Co. Fermanagh* (2005)
Dermot Maguire, *A Townland Miscellany: History-Memory-Story* (2014)

GARTAN PARISH, COUNTY DONEGAL

Barony: Kilmacrenan
Diocese: Raphoe
Places: Churchill, Glenveagh
Graveyard: Gartan Old

Estate papers
Gore estate; Keys estate; Raphoe bishopric estate

Census substitutes
HMR, FL

Publications
Frank McHugh, *Gleanings from Glendowan, Gartan, Glenveagh* (2017)

GARVAGHY PARISH, COUNTY DOWN

Baronies: Iveagh Upper (Lower Half), Iveagh Lower (Lower Half)
Diocese: Dromore
Places: Ballooly, Waringsford
Graveyard: Garvaghy CI

Estate papers
Waring estate, Garvaghy

Census substitutes
FL, AC

Business records
Martin, Ballooly

Publications
George Musgrave and Paul Thompson, *A Rough Field: The Story of Garvaghy Parish,*
    Co. Down [1999]
J. A. Todd, *Garvaghy Presbyterian Church, 1800–1954: An Historical Record* (1954)

GLENAVY PARISH, COUNTY ANTRIM

Barony: Massereene Upper
Diocese: Connor
Place: Glenavy
Graveyard: Glenavy CI

CI Glenavy

Baptisms, 1707– ; marriages, 1707– ;	T679/1 (MIC583/1);
burials, 1707– ; vestry minutes, 1707–	MIC1/43, 44

These records also cover the parishes of Camlin and Tullyrusk. The vestry minutes
include a list of 81 individuals from Glenavy, Camlin and Tullyrusk who were
confirmed in Ballinderry church, *c.* 1720; names of seatholders in the church, 1725;
subscriptions for the relief of the poor (organised by district), 1800.

Estate papers
Conway estate

Census substitutes
HMR

Publications
Patrick J. McKavanagh, *Glenavy: The Church of the Dwarf, 1868–1968* (1968)
Jean Totten, *Gleanings from Glenavy Parish* (1980)
Charles Watson, *The Story of the United Parishes of Glenavy, Camlin and Tullyrusk*
    (1892)

GLENCOLUMBKILLE PARISH, COUNTY DONEGAL

The name of this parish has been spelled in different ways, including Glencolumbcille.

Barony: Banagh
Diocese: Raphoe
Places: Carrick, Glencolumbkille, Teelin
Graveyard: Glencolumbkille CI

Estate papers
Murray of Broughton estate; Raphoe bishopric estate

Census substitutes
HMR

Publications
'The Glencolmcille Tradition of Prince Charles Edward', *Irish Sword*, 7:28 (Summer 1966), pp 196–203: reprinted from *Dublin University Magazine* of Sept. 1860 recounting supposed events of *c.* 1746; includes a number of local names
Conall Mac Cuinneagáin, *Glencolmcille: A Parish History* (2002)

GLENWHIRRY PARISH, COUNTY ANTRIM

Also spelled Glenwherry, the orgins of this parish are not entirely clear. It was described in Lewis's *Topographical Dictionary of Ireland* (1837) as 'an extra-parochial district'. In earlier times it seems to have been counted as part of **Racavan** parish.

Barony: Antrim Lower
Diocese: Connor

Estate papers
Mountcashell estate

Census substitutes
HMR (included under Racavan), RelC (Catholics)

GLYNN PARISH, COUNTY ANTRIM

Barony: Belfast Lower
Diocese: Connor
Places: Glynn, Magheramorne
Graveyard: Glynn Old

Church records
For CI records see **Inver**

Estate papers
Donegall estate

Census substitutes
HMR (included under heading 'Parish of Magheramorne')

GRANGE PARISH, COUNTY ARMAGH
This parish was created out of **Armagh** parish in 1776.

Barony: Armagh
Diocese: Armagh
Graveyard: Grange CI (Salters Grange)

Church records
CI Grange
Baptisms, 1780– ; marriages, 1780– ; burials, 1783–   MIC1/65/1

Estate papers
Armagh archbishopric estate; Charlemont estate; Houston estate; Ker estate;
MacGeough-Bond estate

Other sources
Subscribers to a reward fund concerning a robbery from a house at Cabragh near
Armagh, 1792 – *Northern Star*, 9–13 June 1792

GRANGE OF BALLYROBERT, COUNTY ANTRIM
See also **Templepatrick** parish.

Barony: Belfast Lower
Diocese: Connor
Places: Ballyrobert

Estate papers
Donegall estate

GRANGE OF BALLYSCULLION, COUNTY ANTRIM
This parish has also been called Manybrooks.

Barony: Toome Upper
Diocese: Connor
Places: Grange, Millquarter
Graveyards: Millquarter Quaker (The Green Garden), Templemoyle

Church records
**RSF Antrim or Grange (Grange, Ballynacree,
Toberhead, Coleraine and Antrim)**
Men's monthly meeting minutes, 1740– ; women's   MIC16/43
monthly meeting minutes, 1794–1800; volume
containing testimonies of disownment, etc, 1758–1800;
marriages, 1768–77; births, 1751–1800; deaths, 1741–97

Estate papers
Massereene estate

Census substitutes
HMR, CPH (under heading of 'Manybrooks')

GRANGE OF BALLYWALTER, COUNTY ANTRIM
See also **Ballylinny** parish.

Barony: Belfast Lower
Diocese: Connor

Estate papers
Donegall estate

GRANGE OF DOAGH, COUNTY ANTRIM

Barony: Antrim Upper
Diocese: Connor
Places: Ballyclare, Cogry, Doagh
Graveyard: Doagh

Estate papers
Agnew estate; Donegall estate; Wilson estate

Census substitutes
HMR (included under Rashee parish), DP (Ballyclare)

Business records
McCance, Ballyclare

Publications
R. R. Cox, *A History of the Parish of Kilbride* (1959)
[William Roulston], *'An Old World Place': An Introduction to the History of Doagh*
    [2013]

GRANGE OF DRUMTULLAGH, COUNTY ANTRIM
See also **Derrykeighan** parish.

Barony: Cary
Diocese: Connor
Places: Moss-side

Estate papers
Antrim estate; Dunlop estate

Census substitutes
HMR (included under Armoy parish), RCC

Other sources
List of householders from 'Part of the parish of Derrykeighan called Drumtullogh' indicating their religion, 1734 – T808/14905

Publications
J. D. C. Marshall, *Whar or ye frae? Family Names in the District of Mosside* (2007)
J. D. C. Marshall, *Discovering Mosside: The History of an Ulster Scots Village* (2008)
L. F. Quigg, *'The Wee Church on the Hill': A History of Drumtullagh Church, 1841– 1991* [1991]

GRANGE OF DUNDERMOT, COUNTY ANTRIM
See also **Dunaghy** parish.

Barony: Kilconway
Diocese: Connor

Estate papers
Antrim estate

Census substitutes
HMR (included under Dunaghy parish)

GRANGE OF INISPOLLAN, COUNTY ANTRIM
See also **Layd** parish.

Barony: Glenarm Lower
Diocese: Connor

Estate papers
Antrim estate

Census substitutes
HMR (included under Layd parish)

GRANGE OF KILLYGLEN, COUNTY ANTRIM
See also **Carncastle** parish.

Barony: Glenarm Upper
Diocese: Connor

Census substitutes
HMR (included under Carncastle)

GRANGE OF LAYD, COUNTY ANTRIM
See also **Layd** parish.

Barony: Glenarm Lower
Diocese: Connor

Estate papers
Antrim estate

Census substitutes
HMR (included under Layd parish)

GRANGE OF MALLUSK, COUNTY ANTRIM
See also **Templepatrick** parish.

Barony: Belfast Lower
Diocese: Connor
Place: Mallusk
Graveyard: Mallusk

Estate papers
Donegall estate; Langford estate

GRANGE OF MUCKAMORE, COUNTY ANTRIM

Barony: Massereene Lower
Diocese: Connor
Place: Muckamore
Graveyard: Muckamore Old

Estate papers
Massereene estate

Census substitutes
HMR

GRANGE OF NILTEEN, COUNTY ANTRIM

Barony: Antrim Upper
Diocese: Connor
Place: Dunadry

Estate papers
Donegall estate

Census substitutes
HMR (included under Donegore parish), DP (Donegore, Kilbride and Nilteen)

GRANGE OF SHILVODAN, COUNTY ANTRIM

Barony: Toome Upper
Diocese: Connor

Estate papers
O'Neill estate

Census substitutes
HMR

GREY ABBEY PARISH, COUNTY DOWN
The name of this parish is sometimes rendered Greyabbey.

Barony: Ards Lower
Diocese: Down
Places: Greyabbey, Mount Stewart
Graveyard: Greyabbey (within the abbey complex and to the east of the ruins)

Church records
CI Greyabbey
Vestry minutes, 1789–   MIC1/49/1

The vestry minutes include overseers of roads (names plus townlands), 1801.

Estate papers
Allen estate; Londonderry estate; Montgomery estate

Other records
Map of Greyabbey graveyard with key to burials, 1857 – T1619/1

Publications
S. M. Stephenson, *An Historical Essay on the Parish and Congregation of Grey-Abbey; Compiled in the Year 1827* (1828)

HILLSBOROUGH PARISH, COUNTY DOWN

Barony: Iveagh Lower (Upper Half)
Diocese: Down
Place: Hillsborough
Graveyards: Hillsborough, Hillsborough Friends (within the grounds of
    Hillsborough Castle)

Church records
CI Hillsborough
Baptisms, 1686–95, 1763–9, 1772– ;   MIC1/62A, B
marriages, 1688–95, 1772–4, 1782– ;
burials, 1688–1735, 1772–3, 1784;
vestry minutes, 1709– (gap *c.* 1711–*c.* 1730)

The vestry minutes include a list of names plus acreages by townland, *c.* 1764; a list of the poor of the parish, 1772 (*c.* 40 names); details of persons involved with road repairs in late 1700s.

Register of marriages by licence, 1796–   D1944/8/1

P Annahilt
Baptisms, 1780–   MIC1/360A/1

Estate papers
Downshire estate

Census substitutes
FL

Corporation records: Hillsborough
Corporation books, 1740–74 and 1773–1841 – D671/O/1

Freemasonry records
Minute book (photocopy) of Masonic lodge no. 683, Ballykeel Edenagonnell, 1792–1806 – GLI

Other records
Turnpike Trust Board minute book, for Hillsborough, with accounts, 1762–87 – D671/O/3/1
Subscribers to a reward fund, 1770 – *Belfast Newsletter*, 24 April 1770

Publications
J. Barry, *Hillsborough: A Parish in the Ulster Plantation* (1962)

HOLYWOOD PARISH, COUNTY DOWN

Barony: Castlereagh Lower
Diocese: Down
Places: Cultra, Holywood
Graveyard: Holywood Old

Estate papers
Hamilton (Claneboye and Clanbrassil) estate; Ker estate; Ross estate, Portavo; Ward estate

Census substitutes
FL

Other sources
A copy of the Solemn League and Covenant signed at Holywood in 1644 is in the collection of the Ulster Museum.

Publications
Thomas Bruce, *An Outline of the History of Presbyterianism in Holywood* (1909)
J. A. Lamont, *Presbyterianism in Holywood* (1965)
James Robinson (with Heather Walker and Janet Taylor), *Presbyterianism in Ulster
    1613–c. 1865: A Regional Study with Particular Reference to Holywood, Co. Down*
    (2015)

INCH PARISH, COUNTY DONEGAL
This island parish was created in 1809 out of **Templemore**.

Barony: Inishowen West
Diocese: Derry
Place: Inch Island
Graveyard: Strahack

Church records
For CI records see **Templemore**

Estate papers
Donegall estate

Publications
Seoirse Ó Dochartaigh, *Inis Eoghain: The Island of Eoghan: The Place-Names of
    Inishowen* (2011)
Seoirse Ó Dochartaigh, *The Great Name Book of Inishowen* (2016)

INCH PARISH, COUNTY DOWN

Barony: Lecale Lower
Diocese: Down
Place: Annacloy
Graveyard: Inch Old

Church records
CI Inch

Baptisms, 1767– ; marriages, 1764, 1791– ; burials, 1788– ; vestry minutes, 1757–	MIC1/49; MIC1/311/1, 7
Manuscript copy of baptisms, marriages and burials, 1796–1933	D1759/1D/4 (MIC637/3)

Estate papers
Ardglass estate; Perceval Maxwell estate; Southwell estate

Census substitutes
RelC (Protestants and Catholics; includes townlands), FL

Other records

Receipts for guns and bayonets to be used in Robert Maxwell's troop of militia, 1746 – D1556/16/15/1–14

Men in the parish of Inch who have subscribed towards finding substitutes for the militia, 1793: *c.* 150 names – T1023/139

Return of 23 inhabitants of the parish, 1793 – T1023/140

Signatures in relation to the formation of a Yeomanry corps in the parish, 1797: around 200 names – T1023/144–5

List of names by townland in Inch parish, *c.* 1798: over 190 names – T1023/162

Names of those proposing to form a cavalry unit to act with the Inch infantry and to be known as Inch Legion, *c.* 1798: 18 names – T1023/163

Names of men who have sworn that they are not United Irishmen, *c.* 1798 – D1556/18/8/17; T1023/164

Publications

M. Donnelly, *Inch Abbey and Parish* (1979)

INISHARGY PARISH, COUNTY DOWN

Barony: Ards Upper
Diocese: Down
Places: Glastry, Kircubbin
Graveyards: Inishargy CI, Inishargy Old

Church records

CI Inishargy

Baptisms, 1783– ; marriages, 1783; burials, 1783– ;	T679/278
vestry minutes, 1706–84, which include baptisms,	(MIC583/24);
1728–69, marriages, 1728–69 and burials, 1769–71;	MIC1/96/1
vestry minutes, 1783–	

The vestry minutes include regular poor lists from 1749 onwards (some from the 1770s are tabulated and include addresses); names of cess collectors, 1768, 1769; detailed information on road repairs, 1785, 1787; parish cess collection giving names of overseers 'in their own townland' with power to levy cess (usually two individuals per townland), 1786 (and subsequent years).

'Vestry book of the united parishes of Ballywalter, Ballyhalbert and Inishargie in the Ardes, County Down, 1706', *UJA*, 2nd series, 5 (1899), pp 95–9

P Glastry see under **Ballyhalbert**

P Kircubbin

Baptisms, 1778– ; marriages, 1781– ;	MIC1P/396;
collections and accounts, 1777–87	D1759/1D/12
	(MIC637/4)

Index to baptisms (1778–1921), marriages (1781–1920)   CR3/72/A/1

Estate papers
Allen estate; Hamilton (Claneboye and Clanbrassil) estate; Holmes estate; Ross estate, Portavo

Publications
J. C. Beckett et al., *St Andrew's, Inishargy, Balligan* (1966)

INISHKEEL PARISH, COUNTY DONEGAL
The name of this parish is also spelled Inniskeel.

Baronies: Banagh, Boylagh
Diocese: Raphoe
Places: Doochary, Fintown, Glenties, Narin, Portnoo
Graveyards: Glenties Old, Inishkeel Island, Kiltooris

Church records
CI Inishkeel
Baptisms, 1699–1700, marriages, 1699;   CR1/51/1–3
burials, 1699–1700; confirmations, 1715, 1723

Estate papers
Murray of Broughton estate; Raphoe bishopric estate

Census substitutes
HMR

Business records
Montgomery, Inniskeel

Publications
Liam Briody, *Glenties and Inniskeel* (1986)
P. J. McGill, *History of the Parish of Ardara* (1970)

INISHKEEN PARISH, COUNTIES LOUTH AND MONAGHAN
The name of this parish is also spelled Inniskeen.

Barony: Farney (Monaghan portion)
Diocese: Clogher
Place: Inniskeen
Graveyard: Inishkeen CI

Estate papers
Bath estate; Clogher bishopric estate

Census substitutes
HMR, FL

Publications
Matt Kearney, *Inniskeen Past and Present* (2014)

INISHMACSAINT PARISH, COUNTIES DONEGAL AND FERMANAGH

Baronies: Tirhugh (Donegal portion), Magheraboy (Fermanagh portion)
Diocese: Clogher
Places: Bundoran, Churchill, Derrygonnelly
Graveyards: Carrick, Derrgonnelly Old, Finner, Church Hill, Inishmacsaint Island, Slawin (Slavin Old)

Church records
CI Inishmacsaint
Vestry minutes, 1765–   MIC1/50/1

The vestry minutes include the names of seatholders in part of the church, 1772

Extracts from baptisms, 1660–72,   T808/15274–6
marriages, 1663–72, and burials, 1662–72

Extracts from baptisms, marriages and burials,   T3548/2
1660–1814

Extracts from baptisms, marriages and burials,   CR1/7
1660–1866

Estate papers
Archdale estate; Clogher bishopric estate; Conolly estate; Ely estate; Montgomery estate

Census substitutes
HMR (Donegal portion only), FL (Fermanagh portion listed under 'Churchill')

Other records
Copy memorial of the 'Protestant Inhabitants of the Parishes of Kilbarren and Garrison, also (Innismac)saint who live nearer Belleek than any other church', *c.* 1788 – DIO/2/9/660A

Publications
P. O Gallachair, *Where Erne and Drowes Meet the Sea: Fragments from a Patrician Parish* (1961): history of Bundoran and neighbourhood
W. K. Parke, *Glimpses of Old Derrygonnelly* (1978)
W. K. Parke, *The Parish of Inishmacsaint* (1982)

INVER PARISH, COUNTY ANTRIM

Barony: Belfast Lower
Diocese: Connor
Place: Larne
Graveyard: Inver CI

Church records
CI Inver (Connor)
Vestry minutes, 1763–   T679/59 (MIC583/6);
                                                       MIC1/49/1

The vestry also had responsibility for the parishes of Glynn and Raloo; the minutes include payments to persons for charitable purposes, 1768; cess payers in Raloo parish, 1769–70; list of the poor, 1800.

Estate papers
Donegall estate

Census substitutes
HMR (included under heading 'Parish of Magheramorne'), HSM

Publications
J. A. Fair, *To This You Belong* (n.d.): a history of Larne and Inver Church of Ireland, including extracts from vestry minutes, 1763–1904 (pp 46–53), a list of churchwardens, 1707–1978 (pp 117–21)
Old Families of Larne and District from Gravestone Inscriptions, Wills and Biographical Notes, compiled by George Rutherford and edited by R. S. J. Clarke (2004)

INVER PARISH, COUNTY DONEGAL

Barony: Banagh
Diocese: Raphoe
Places: Frosses, Inver, Mountcharles
Graveyard: Inver Old

Church records
CI Inver
Vestry minutes, 1782–   MIC1/159C/1

The vestry minutes include the names of cess collectors, 1793.

Estate papers
Murray of Broughton estate; Raphoe bishopric estate

Census substitutes
HMR, FL

Publications
Helen Meehan, *Inver Parish in History* (2005): a massive work containing a wealth of information

ISLAND MAGEE PARISH, COUNTY ANTRIM
The name of this parish is often spelled Islandmagee.

Barony: Belfast Lower
Diocese: Connor
Graveyards: Ballykeel, Ballypriormore, Island Magee CI

Estate papers
Donegall estate; Dungannon estate

Census substitutes
HMR, HSM

Other records
List of lands and tenants of Lord Dungannon on Island Magee, 1770 – *Belfast Newsletter*, 13 Feb. 1770

Publications
D. H. Akenson, *Between Two Revolutions: Islandmagee, County Antrim, 1798–1920* (1979)
Dixon Donaldson, *Historical, Traditional and Descriptive Account of Islandmagee* (1927)
Andrew Sneddon, *Possessed by the Devil: The Real History of the Islandmagee Witches and Ireland's Only Mass Witchcraft Trial* (2013)

JONESBOROUGH PARISH, COUNTY ARMAGH
This parish was created out of **Killevy** parish in 1760.

Barony: Orior Lower
Diocese: Armagh
Places: Flurrybridge, Jonesborough
Graveyard: Jonesborough CI (former)

Church records
CI Jonesborough
Vestry minutes, 1799–   Local custody

Other records
Petition and memorial of the Protestant parishioners of Jonesborough complaining that for several years the parish has been without any resident curate, [1785] – DIO/4/32/J/1/4

KEADY PARISH, COUNTY ARMAGH

This parish was created out of **Derrynoose** parish in 1773.

Barony: Armagh
Diocese: Armagh
Places: Darkley, Keady, Tassagh
Graveyards: Keady CI, Keady 1st P (The Temple), Tassagh Old

Church records
CI Keady
Baptisms, 1780– ; marriages, 1780–   T679/8A (MIC583/1);
                                                  MIC1/51/1

Estate papers
Armagh archbishopric estate; Charlemont estate; Irwin estate

Census substitutes
FL

Publications
Henry J. Dobbin, *Keady: One Hundred Years Ago. With Extracts From the Parish
    Records, 1780–1870* (1922)
Matthew Banks Hogg, *Short History of Keady Parish: Its Church & People* (1928)
F. X. McCorry, *Parish Registers: Historical Treasures in Manuscript* (2004): includes
    information from the Keady CI registers
William Monaghan (ed.), *The History of Darkley* (2014)
Florence Nicholson and Carole Trimble, *The Temple Meeting House: History of 1st
    Keady Presbyterian Church, 1702–2002* (2002)

KILBARRON PARISH, COUNTY DONEGAL

Barony: Tirhugh
Diocese: Raphoe
Place: Ballyshannon
Graveyards: Assaroe Abbey, Kilbarron CI, Te(e)tunny/Teightunny

CI Kilbarron
Baptisms, 1785–93; marriages, 1785– ; burials, 1785–   MIC1/156A/1

Vestry minutes, 1691–1781   Local custody

Estate papers
Conolly estate; Delap estate; Folliott estate; Raphoe bishopric estate; Trinity College
Dublin estate

Census substitutes
HMR, LP (Donegal and Ballyshannon), FL

Freemasonry records
Minute book of Masonic lodge no. 287, Ballyshannon, 1786–95 – GLI

Other records
'Copy memorial of the Protestant Inhabitants of the Parishes of Kilbarren and Garrison, also (Innismac)saint who live nearer Belleek than any other church', *c.* 1788 – DIO/2/9/660A

Publications
Hugh Allingham, *Ballyshannon: Its History and Antiquities* (1937)
Anthony Begley, *Ballyshannon and Surrounding Areas: History, Heritage and Folklore* (2009)
Geraldine Carville, *History of the Parish of Kilbarron, Ballyshannon: A Sense of Place – A Sense of Time* (2012)
Ivan and Mark Knox, *A Hundred Years of Rossnowlagh Presbyterian Church 1906– 2006 and a History of Ballyshannon Congregation since 1674* (2006)
Edward Maguire, *Ballyshannon, Past and Present* [*c.* 1930]

KILBRIDE PARISH, COUNTY ANTRIM

Barony: Antrim Upper
Diocese: Connor
Graveyard: Kilbride Old

Estate papers
Agnew estate; Donegall estate; Owens estate

Census substitutes
HMR (included under Donegore parish), DP (Donegore, Kilbride and Nilteen)

Publications
R. R. Cox, *A History of the Parish of Kilbride* (1959)

KILBRIDE PARISH, COUNTIES CAVAN AND MEATH
Most of this parish is in County Cavan.

Barony: Clanmahon (Cavan portion)
Diocese: Meath
Place: Mountnugent
Graveyard: Kilbride Old

Estate papers
Armagh archbishopric estate; Coyne estate; Farnham estate; Nugent estate

Census substitutes
FL

Publications
The Heritage and History of Kilbride and Killeagh (2006)
John Brady, *Mountnugent* (1944)
Philip O'Connell, 'The parish and district of Kilbride' (4 parts), *Riocht na Midhe*,
    2–3 (1962–5)

KILBRONEY PARISH, COUNTY DOWN

Barony: Iveagh Upper (Upper Half)
Diocese: Dromore
Places: Killowen, Rostrevor
Graveyards: The Crag (former Kilbroney CI), Kilbroney Old

Church records
CI Kilbroney
Vestry minutes, 1798–   MIC1/87/1

Extract from parish registers, 1784–1867 [missing]   DIO/1/14/1

Estate papers
Hall estate, Narrow Water; Needham estate; Ross estate, Rostrevor

Census substitutes
CPH, RelC (Protestants and Catholics), FL

Publications
W. H. Crowe, *Village in Seven Hills: The Story and Stories of Rostrevor, Co. Down*
(1972)

KILCAR PARISH, COUNTY DONEGAL

Barony: Banagh
Diocese: Raphoe
Place: Kilcar
Graveyard: Kilcar Old

Estate papers
Murray of Broughton estate; Raphoe bishopric estate

Census substitutes
HMR, FL

KILCLIEF PARISH, COUNTY DOWN

Barony: Lecale Lower
Diocese: Down
Graveyard: Kilclief CI

Estate papers
Hall estate, Strangford and Lower Iveagh; Kildare estate; Leslie estate; Ward estate

Census substitutes
FL, AC

KILCLOONEY PARISH, COUNTY ARMAGH
The name of this parish is also spelled Kilcluney.

Baronies: Fews Lower, Orior Lower
Diocese: Armagh
Place: Cladymore
Graveyard: Kilclooney Old

Church records
For CI records see **Mullaghbrack**

Estate papers
Armagh archbishopric estate; Charlemont parish; Gosford estate; MacGeough-Bond estate

Census substitutes
HMR, FP, VAA

Publications
Edward D. Smyth, *The House on the Hill: The Redrock Story 1799–1987* (1987)

KILCOO PARISH, COUNTY DOWN

Barony: Iveagh Upper (Lower Half)
Diocese: Down/Exempt Jurisdiction of Newry and Mourne
Places: Bryansford, Newcastle
Graveyard: Kilcoo Old

Church records
CI Kilcoo
Baptisms, 1786–   T679/57 (MIC583/5);
                                                     MIC1/55/1

Estate papers
Annesley estate; Downshire estate; Mathews estate

Census substitutes
FL, AC

Publications
Countess of Roden, *Kilcoo Parish Church, Bryansford* (1971)

KILCRONAGHAN PARISH, COUNTY LONDONDERRY

Barony: Loughinsholin
Diocese: Derry
Place: Tobermore
Graveyard: Kilcronaghan Old

Church records
CI Kilcronaghan
Baptisms, 1790– ; marriages, 1748–   MIC1/52/1

Vestry minutes, 1749–   Local custody

Estate papers
Derry bishopric estate; Drapers' Company estate; McCausland estate; Rowley estate;
Salters' Company estate; Vintners' Company estate

Census substitutes
HMR, CPH, FL

Other records
Names of some tenants in Kilcronaghan, 1680 – printed in Moody and Simms,
Bishopric of Derry and the Irish Society of London, vol. 2, p. 42

Publications
Hilary Richardson, *Kilcronaghan Parish Church* (2008)

KILDALLAN PARISH, COUNTY CAVAN
The name of this parish is also spelled Kildallon.

Barony: Tullyhunco
Diocese: Kilmore
Graveyard: Kildallon CI

Church records
P Killeshandra (also known as Cro(a)ghan)
Baptisms, 1743–81, 1799; marriages, 1741–76;   MIC1P/164/1–3
register of members, *c.* 1835, with dates of birth
of children in each family, the earliest being in 1790;
accounts, 1743–80

Estate papers
Annesley estate; Craige estate; Farnham estate; Stanford estate

Census substitutes
HMR, FL

Publications
Beneath Slieve Rushen's Slopes: Kildallan-Tomregan … (2000)

KILDARTON PARISH
This parish was formed in 1840 as a perpetual curacy out of **Armagh**, **Lisnadill**, **Loughgall** and **Mullaghbrack** parishes.

KILDOLLAGH PARISH, COUNTIES ANTRIM AND LONDONDERRY

Baronies: Dunluce Upper (Antrim portion), North-East Liberties of Coleraine
   (Londonderry portion)
Diocese: Connor
Graveyard: Loughan (Kildollagh Old)

Church records:
For CI records see **Coleraine**

Estate papers
Bacon estate

Census substitutes
HMR (listed with Ballyrashane)

KILDRESS PARISH, COUNTY TYRONE

Barony: Dungannon Upper
Diocese: Armagh
Places: Dunnamore, Orritor
Graveyard: Kildress Old

Church records
CI Kildress
Baptisms, 1794– ; marriages, 1794– ;   MIC1/107/1
vestry minutes, 1709–

Estate papers
Armagh archbishopric estate; Castle Stewart estate; Richardson estate; Stewart estate, Killymoon

Census substitutes
HMR, VAA, CPH, RelC (Protestants and Catholics; includes townlands), FL

Business records
Faulkner, Wellbrook

Other records
'An Inventory of the Goods and Chattels of the Rev. Mr Robert Letherbarrow, late Retcor [sic] of the Parish of Drumcree in the County of Armagh Decd., together with a Return of the debts due to him for rents and Tythes in said Parish, and also the small dues, due to him out of the Parish of Killdress and County of Tyrone ...', 1737 – D2395/9 (also T808/15298)

KILDRUMSHERDAN PARISH, COUNTY CAVAN
Other spellings of the name of this parish include Killersherdoney and Kilsherdany.

Barony: Tullygarvey
Diocese: Kilmore
Place: Kill
Graveyard: Kill Old

Church records
CI Killersherdoney
Baptisms, 1796– ; marriages, 1796– ; burials, 1797–   MIC1/281A/1

Estate papers
Clements estate; Coote estate

Census substitutes
FL

Publications
John Quinn (ed.), *Kilsherdany, its History and its People* (1977)

KILKEEL PARISH, COUNTY DOWN
This parish has also been known as Mourne.

Barony: Mourne
Diocese: Down/Exempt Jurisdiction of Newry and Mourne
Places: Annalong, Attical, Ballymartin, Greencastle, Kilkeel
Graveyards: Kilkeel Old, Tamlaght

Church records
MOR Kilkeel
Diary of the Moravian congregation, 1799–1853   D1052/1

Estate papers
Bagenal estate; Needham estate; Mathews estate

Census substitutes
FL, AC

Business records
Orr, Glassdrumman

Publications
H. S. Irvine, *The Big Meeting: The History of Mourne Presbyterian Church, 1696–1996* (1997)

KILLAGAN PARISH, COUNTY ANTRIM

Barony: Kilconway
Diocese: Connor
Place: Cloughmills

Estate papers
Antrim estate; Hamilton estate, Cloughmills; Moore estate, Ballynacree; Wray estate

Census substitutes
HMR (included under Dunaghy)

Publications
H. A. Boyd, *The Parishes of Craigs, Dunaghy and Killagan* (1991)

KILLAGHTEE PARISH, COUNTY DONEGAL

Barony: Banagh
Diocese: Raphoe
Places: Bruckless, Dunkineely
Graveyard: Killaghtee Old

Church records
CI Killaghtee
Vestry minutes, 1748–   DIO/3/40

The vestry minutes include the names of the poor receiving alms arising from a bequest, 1765, 1777; statistics of families, giving religion and literacy, though no names, 1779; and a list of householders by townland, 1794.

Estate papers
Murray of Broughton estate; Raphoe bishopric estate

Census substitutes
HMR, FL

Publications
Killaghtee (2001)
Brid Ward, *St John's Point County Donegal: In Former Days and Now* (2010)

KILLAN PARISH, COUNTY CAVAN
See also **Bailieborough** and **Shercock** parishes.

KILLANEY PARISH, COUNTY DOWN

Barony: Castlereagh Upper
Diocese: Down
Place: Boardmills
Graveyards: Boardmills 1st P, Killaney Old

Church records
For CI records see **Saintfield**

P 1st Boardmills

Baptisms, 1782– ; marriages, 1782– ; session minutes, 1784– ; private censures, 1784–	MIC1P/72
Copy of baptisms and marriages, 1724–54, 1782–	D1759/1D/1–2 (MIC637/2)

Estate papers
Downshire estate

Publications
First, Second Boardmills and Killaney Presbyterian Churches: 'The Church in the Rolling Hills', 250th Anniversary Celebration, 1748–1998 (1998)

KILLANNY PARISH, COUNTIES LOUTH AND MONAGHAN

Barony: Farney (Monaghan portion)
Diocese: Clogher
Graveyard: Killanny Old (in County Louth)

Estate papers
Bath estate; Clogher bishopric estate; Shirley estate

Census substitutes
HMR, FL

KILLEA PARISH, COUNTY DONEGAL

Barony: Raphoe North
Diocese: Raphoe
Place: Carrigans
Graveyard: Killea CI

Church records
CI Killea
Vestry minutes, 1788–   Local custody

Census substitutes
HMR (under Taughboyne), FL

Publications
Guide to the Districts of St Johnston, Carrigans and Newtowncunningham (1979)
S. M. Campbell, *The Laggan and its People* (n.d.)
D. W. T. Crooks, *In the Footsteps of St Baithin. A History of Taughboyne Group* (1992)

KILLEAD PARISH, COUNTY ANTRIM

Barony: Massereene Lower
Diocese: Connor
Places: Aldergrove, Loanends
Graveyards: Carmavy, Killead CI, Killead P

Estate papers
Allen estate; Henry estate; Langford estate; Massereene estate; Moore estate,
Cloverhill; Owens estate

Census substitutes
HMR, HSM

Other records
Diary of William Morrison, Crookedstone, County Antrim, farmer, recording day to
    day events – D3300/109/1 (/2 is a transcript)
Tithe roll for townlands of Ballyrobin, Ballysculty, Ballymather and Kilcross, 1776 –
    D2624/5
Subscribers to a reward fund, 1776 – *Belfast Newsletter*, 6–10 Dec. 1776

Publications
W. J. Baird, *Two Hundred and Seventy Years of Presbyterianism in Killead, 1625–1895*
    (1896)
W. D. Weir, and H. Campbell, *Presbyterianism in Killead, 1630–1980* (1980)

KILLEESHIL PARISH, COUNTY TYRONE

The boundaries of the parishes of Aghaloo, Carnteel and Killeeshil were reorganised in 1680.

Barony: Dungannon Lower
Diocese: Armagh
Place: Cabragh
Graveyard: Killeeshil CI

Estate papers
Armagh archbishopric estate; Stewart estate, Killymoon; Verner estate

Census substitutes
HMR (included under Aghaloo and Carnteel), VAA, FL

Publications
J. W. Fleck, *A History of the Clonaneese Presbyterian Churches, 1728–2010* (2010): includes a list of the 12 men who were trustees of the meeting house in 1754 (p. 38)

KILLEEVAN PARISH, COUNTY MONAGHAN

This parish was created in 1795 out of **Galloon**.

Barony: Dartree
Diocese: Clogher
Place: Newbliss
Graveyards: Drumswords, Killeevan Old

Estate papers
Barton estate; Blayney estate; Clogher bishopric estate; Forster estate; Ker estate; Leslie estate, Glaslough; Massereene estate; Rossmore estate

Census substitutes
HMR, FP, FL

Publications
From Carn to Clonfad, Killeevan Heritage Group takes a Journey through some pages out of the history of Currin, Killeevan and Aghabog (2 vols)

KILLELAGH PARISH, COUNTY LONDONDERRY

Barony: Loughinsholin
Diocese: Derry
Place: Swatragh
Graveyard: Killelagh Old

Estate papers
Conolly estate; Derry bishopric estate; Mercers' Company estate; Strafford estate; Vintners' Company estate

Census substitutes
HMR, CPH, FL

KILLESHANDRA PARISH, COUNTY CAVAN

Barony: Tullyhunco
Diocese: Kilmore
Places: Arvagh, Killashandra/Killeshandra
Graveyard: Killeshandra Old

Church records
CI Killeshandra
Baptisms, 1735; marriages, 1735– ; burials, 1735–   MIC1/220

Estate papers
Craige estate; Farnham estate; Gosford estate

Census substitutes
HMR, FL

Publications
Francis J. McCaughey, *Arva: Sources for Local History* (1998)
Maura Nallen, 'A Study of eight townlands in the parish of Killeshandra, 1608–1841', *Breifne*, 35 (1999), pp 5–84
Kevin O'Neill, *Family and Farm in Pre-Famine Ireland: The Parish of Killashandra* (1984)
Tomás Ó Raghallaigh, *Turbulence in Tullyhunco: Killeshandra, Kildallan, Arva, Gowna, Cornafean before, during and after the Ulster Plantation* (2010)

KILLESHER PARISH, COUNTY FERMANAGH

Barony: Clanawley
Diocese: Kilmore
Places: Florencecourt, Mackan
Graveyard: Killesher

Church records
CI Killesher
Baptisms, 1798– ; marriages, 1798–   T679/48 (MIC583/5);
                                          MIC1/56/1
Estate papers
Enniskillen estate; Erne estate

Census substitutes
FL

KILLEVY PARISH, COUNTY ARMAGH
This parish has also been known as Kilsleve.

Baronies: Orior Upper, Orior Lower
Diocese: Armagh
Places: Camlough, Bessbrook, Drumintee, Jerrettspass, Meigh, Mullaghglass
Graveyards: Drumbanagher CI, Killevy Old, Mullaghglass Old

Estate papers
Armagh archbishopric estate; Charlemont estate; Hall estate, Narrow Water;
Johnston estate, Drumbanagher; Stewart estate

Census substitutes
HMR, FP, VAA, FL

KILLINAGH PARISH, COUNTY CAVAN

Barony: Tullyhaw
Diocese: Kilmore
Places: Blacklion, Dowra
Graveyard: Killinagh Old

Estate papers
Pleydell estate

Census substitutes
HMR

Other sources
'The humble petition of the protestant tenants of Largey and parishioners of
Killynagh to Owen Wynne Esq.', *c.* 1739 – MIC666/2. This includes some two
dozen original signatures, complaining that there were '26 families and 122 souls',
all Protestants, in the parish and that the neglect of their clergyman was in danger
of causing defections to the Roman Catholic Church.

Publications
A. Leaden and Jim Nolan, *The History of Killinagh Parish, Blacklion* (1996)

KILLINCHY PARISH, COUNTY DOWN

Baronies: Castlereagh Lower, Castlereagh Upper, Dufferin
Diocese: Down
Places: Balloo, Killinchy
Graveyards: Kilcarn, Killinchy CI, Killinchy P

Church records
CI Killinchy

Vestry minutes, 1716–57, 1779, 1800–12;	CR1/16; T679/109, 109a
accounts, 1778–90; tithe survey, 1794	(MIC583/10)

The abovementioned accounts do not appear to necessarily relate to parish business; for 1780–81 there are over 60 names listed alongside the caption 'Captain Hamilton's company' (presumably the First Killinchy Volunteers).

P Killinchy
In 1835, this congregation divided over the Arian controversy and is now represented by Killinchy Presbyterian Church and Killinchy Non-Subscribing Presbyterian Church.

Pew rent book, *c.* 1785; accounts, 1781–	CR4/17; D1759/1D/9
	(MIC637/3)

Copy of manuscript history of	PHSI
congregation by James Gourley	

Estate papers
Blackwood estate; Hamilton (Claneboye and Clanbrassil) estate; Gordon estate; Londonderry estate; Macartney estate; Pollock estate

Census substitutes
HSM, FL, AC

Other records
Small early 18th-century notebook containing rent and other payments to Hewitt family of Killinchy – MIC721/1

Publications
David Stewart, *Killinchy Presbyterian Church, 1630–1930, With a History of the Parish* (1930)
C. W. McKinney, *Killinchy: A Brief History of Christianity in the District, with Special Reference to Presbyterianism* (n.d.)

KILLINKERE PARISH, COUNTY CAVAN

Baronies: Castlerahan, Loughtee Upper
Diocese: Kilmore
Graveyard: Gallon

Church records
RC Killinkere

Baptisms, 1766–90; marriages, 1766–89	MIC1D/82

Estate papers
Farnham estate; Saunderson estate

Census substitutes
HMR, FL

Publications
Killinkere: Its History and Heritage (1984)

KILLOWEN PARISH, COUNTY LONDONDERRY
See also **Coleraine** parish.

Barony: Coleraine
Diocese: Derry
Place: Coleraine (Waterside)
Graveyard: Killowen CI

Church records
CI Killowen
Vestry minutes, 1747–   Local custody

Extracts from vestry minutes, 1747–1872   D4164/A/23

Estate papers
Clothworkers' Company estate; Derry bishopric estate; Heyland estate; Jackson estate; McClelland/Maxwell estate; Rowley estate

Census substitutes
HMR, CPH, DP (Coleraine and Killowen), FL

Other sources
Valuation and plan of tenements in Killowen, 1781 – D668/N/1
Tithe book, Killowen parish, 1785 – D668/B
Resolution of inhabitants of Coleraine and Killowen, 1787 – *Belfast Newsletter*, 2–6 Feb. 1787
Rev. Robert Hezlet's tithe and rent book, Killowen parish, 1788 – D668/B
Notebook containing notification of registering arms, including residents of Killowen, 1796 – D668/N/1
Surveys of Parks of Killowen/Fields of the Waterside, n.d. [probably late 18th century] – D668/N/1

Publications
D. MacLaughlin, *Short Sketch of the History of the Parish Church of St John the Evangelist, Killowen, Coleraine* (1900)
Desmond Mullan and Philip Donnelly, *St John's Coleraine* (1992)

KILLYBEGS PARISH, COUNTY DONEGAL
For civil purposes this parish was divided into Upper and Lower sections.

Baronies: Banagh, Boylagh
Diocese: Raphoe
Places: Ardara, Killybegs
Graveyards: Killybegs Old (St Catherine's); Kilrean (Kilrain)

Church records
CI Killybegs

Baptisms, 1787–96	Local custody
Vestry minutes, 1788–	RCB

Estate papers
Conyngham estate; Murray of Broughton estate; Raphoe bishopric estate

Census substitutes
HMR, FL

Publications
Charles Conaghan, *History and Antiquities of Killybegs* (1974)
Pat Conaghan, *Bygones: New Horizons on the History of Killybegs* (1989)

KILLYGARVAN PARISH, COUNTY DONEGAL

Barony: Kilmacrenan
Diocese: Raphoe
Place: Rathmullan
Graveyards: Killygarvan Old; Rathmullan Priory

Church records
CI Killygarvan

Vestry minutes, 1706– (including some baptisms, 1706–8, 1725–7, 1737–8, 1785, 1788, 1790, 1792–3; marriages, 1706–8, 1725–6, 1737; burials, 1706–8, 1727–8, 1786–7, 1793, 1796, 1799); typescript list of 18th-century baptisms, marriages and burials extracted from vestry minutes	MIC1/166

The vestry minutes also include the names and addresses of persons exempted from the hearth tax, 1793 (50+ names).

Estate papers
Raphoe bishopric estate; Stewart estate, Fortstewart

Census substitutes
HMR, LP (Killygarvan/Rathmullan), FL

Publications
John Fitzgerald and John McCreadie, *Glenvar and Oughterlin* (1986)
Áine Ní Dhuibhne (ed.), *Rathmullan, Ramelton & Raphoe Diocese: At the Time of the Flight of the Earls* (2007)

KILLYLEAGH PARISH, COUNTY DOWN

Baronies: Castlereagh Upper, Dufferin
Diocese: Down
Places: Derryboy, Killyleagh, Shrigley
Graveyards: Killaresey, Killyleagh CI, Killyleagh Old, Killyleagh 1st P

Church records
CI Killyleagh
Vestry minutes, 1787–   MIC1/58B/1

The vestry minutes includes details of road repairs with the names of collectors and overseers.

P Killyleagh
Baptisms, 1693–1757; marriages, 1692–1757;   MIC1P/53;
minute books, 1725–32   D1759/1D/11
                                                         (MIC637/4)

Estate papers
Blackwood estate; Hamilton (Claneboye and Clanbrassil) estate; Clewlow estate; Forde estate; Maxwell estate; Southwell estate

Census substitutes
DP, FL, AC

Corporation records
Material regarding the Corporation and Commons of Killyleagh, and the property of James Moor, 1652–1707 – D1071/B/B/2
Extract from records of Killyleagh corporation making John Carr a free member of the Corporation, 1738 – D2930/8/2
Note: deeds for Killyleagh are not listed separately in the Registry of Deeds place-name index.

Other records
List of Killyleagh Yeomanry of Captain Gavin Hamilton, 1798 – D303/3
Bundle of rent receipts for Ringdufferin, Ballymacarron and Killyleagh, 1800–20 – T1868/1

Publications
Alexander McCreery, *The Presbyterian Ministers of Killyleagh: A Notice of Their Lives and Times* (1875)
400 Years of Christianity in Killyleagh (2000)

KILLYMAN PARISH, COUNTIES ARMAGH AND TYRONE

Baronies: Oneilland West (Armagh portion), Dungannon Middle (Tyrone portion)
Diocese: Armagh
Places: Killyman, Laghey
Graveyards: Church Hill, Killyman CI, Killyman RC

Church records
CI Killyman
Baptisms, 1745– ; marriages, 1741– ;   T679/383–5
burials, 1745– ; vestry minutes, 1756–   (MIC583/33, 34)

The vestry minutes include registries of seats in the Church of Ireland church, 1765 and 1786, and a registry of seats in the gallery of the church, 1795.

Estate papers
Armagh archbishopric estate; Hamilton Moore estate; Stewart estate, Omagh; Verner estate

Census substitutes
HMR, VAA, FL

Business records
Greer, Rhone Hill

Publications
W. A. Macafee, 'Pre-Famine population in Ulster: evidence from the parish register of Killyman' in P. O'Flanagan, P. Ferguson and K. Whelan (eds), *Rural Ireland: Modernisation and Change, 1600–1900* (1987), pp 142–61

KILLYMARD PARISH, COUNTY DONEGAL

Barony: Banagh
Diocese: Raphoe
Graveyard: Killymard Old

Estate papers
Murray of Broughton estate; Raphoe bishopric estate

Census substitutes
HMR, FL

Publications
H. Trimble, *Killymard: Ancient & Modern* (2001)

KILMACRENAN PARISH, COUNTY DONEGAL

Barony: Kilmacrenan
Diocese: Raphoe
Places: Cranford, Kilmacrenan, Termon
Graveyards: Kilmacrenan Old and Friary

Estate papers
Clements estate; Gore estate; Grove estate; Raphoe bishopric estate; Trinity College
Dublin estate; Wray estate

Census substitutes
HMR, FL

Publications
Brian Smeaton, *The Parish of Kilmacrennan Now and Then* ... [1996/7]

KILMEGAN PARISH, COUNTY DOWN

Baronies: Kinelarty, Lecale Upper
Diocese: Down/Exempt Jurisdiction of Newry and Mourne
Places: Annsborough, Castlewellan, Dundrum
Graveyard: Kilmegan CI

Estate papers
Annesley estate; Downshire estate; Forde estate; Mathews estate

Census substitutes
FL, AC

Business records
Castlewellan merchant (anon.)

Publications
Patsy Mullen, *The Ins, Outs and Whereabouts of Castlewellan* (1986)

KILMOOD PARISH, COUNTY DOWN
The name of this parish is also spelled Kilmud.

Barony: Castlereagh Lower
Diocese: Down
Graveyard: Kilmood CI

Church records
CI Kilmood
Burials, 1793–   MIC1/59A

Earlier in the 1700s the **Saintfield** vestry had responsibility for Kilmood.

Estate papers
Adair estate; Blackwood estate; Downshire estate; Gordon estate; Londonderry estate

Other records
Offer of reward from inhabitants of Ballymonistrogh and Tullynagee, Kilmood
parish, 1756: 29 names – *Belfast Newsletter*, 29 June 1756

KILMORE PARISH, COUNTY ARMAGH

Barony: Oneilland West
Diocese: Armagh
Places: Ahorey, Ballyhagen, Bottlehill, Kilmore, Richhill, Vinecash
Graveyards: Kilmore CI, Money (Monie) Quaker, Mullavilly CI

Church records
CI Kilmore
Baptisms, 1789–95, 1799– ; marriages,   MIC1/8/1
1799– ; vestry minutes, 1733–79

Extracts from vestry minutes, 1732–79   T476/1; T636/1,
                                                          pp 73–80

The vestry minutes include detailed information on those responsible for road repairs.

P Vinecash
History of the church, 1697–1923   MIC1P/348

RSF Ballyhagen (includes Richhill)
Family lists with details of births and burials,   MIC16/39
c. 1680–1814 (Ballyhagen and Richhill); marriage
certificates, 1692–1789 (Ballyhagen); testimonies of
disunity, 1708–1813 (Ballyhagen and Richhill);
wills and inventories, 1685–1740 (Ballyhagen);
account book of Ballyhagen monthly meetings,
1714–66; minutes of men's meetings, 1705–43

Extensive extracts from these records appear in Chapman, *History of Ballyhagan and
Richhill Meetings*, while the wills are discussed in J. R. H. Greeves, 'The will book of
Ballyhagan meeting of the Society of Friends', *The Irish Genealogist*, 2 (1950),

pp 228–39; and A. Gailey, 'The Ballyhagan inventories, 1716–1740', *Folk Life*, 15 (1977), pp 36–64.

RSF Richhill and Grange
Men's minutes, 1793–   MIC16/42

Estate papers
Armagh archbishopric estate; Cope estate; De Salis estate; Johnston estate, Gilford; Magenis estate, Dromara; Manchester estate; Richardson estate, Richhill; Sachervell estate; Verner estate

Census substitutes
HMR, FP, VAA, FL

Freemasonry records
Minutes of Masonic lodge no. 527, Ballintaggart, 1775–1808 – GLI

Other records
List of those willing to attend linen market at Richhill, 1762: 122 names – *Belfast Newsletter*, 28 May 1762
Resolution of inhabitants of Richhill, 1763 – *Belfast Newsletter*, 5 Aug. 1763
Manors of Richhill and Mullalelish petition in relation to Act of Union – *Belfast Newsletter*, 20 Dec. 1799

Publications
George Chapman, *The History of Ballyhagan and Richhill Meetings* (1979)
Benedict Fearon, *A History of the Parish of Kilmore* [*c.* 2003]

KILMORE PARISH, COUNTY CAVAN

Baronies: Clanmahon, Loughtee Upper
Diocese: Kilmore
Places: Ballinagh/Bellananagh, Kilmore
Graveyards: Kilmore Cathedral; Trinity Abbey (Trinity Island)

Church records
CI Kilmore (Kilmore diocese)
Baptisms, 1702– ; marriages,   MIC1/255A/1
1702– ; burials, 1702–

Estate papers
Annesley estate; Farnham estate; Nesbitt estate; Story estate

Census substitutes
FL

Publications
Wendy Swan, *'All Lovely Kilmore': Kilmore Parish, Co. Cavan: Its Churches, People and Heritage* (2002)

KILMORE PARISH, COUNTY DOWN

Baronies: Castlereagh Upper, Kinelarty
Diocese: Down
Places: Crossgar, Kilmore, Listooder
Graveyards: Killybawn, Kilmore Old, Rademon NSP

Estate papers
Forde estate; Maxwell estate; Montgomery estate, Donaghadee; Southwell estate

Census substitutes
FL

Other records
Subscribers to a reward fund, 1771 – *Belfast Newsletter*, 11 June 1771

Publications
J. W. S. Lowry, *Historical Account of the Lissara Presbyterian Church, Crossgar, containing a biographical sketch of each minister from its origin to the present* (1883)
David Stewart, *The Story of Kilmore Presbyterian Church Told as a Centenary Commemoration of its Founding August 6th, 1832 with a History of the Parish* (1932)

KILMORE PARISH, COUNTY MONAGHAN

Barony: Monaghan
Diocese: Clogher
Place: Threemilehouse
Graveyard: Kilmore CI

Estate papers
Barton estate; Blayney estate; Clogher bishopric estate; Dawson estate; Leslie estate, Glaslough; Rossmore estate

Census substitutes
HMR, FL

Publications
Eamonn Mulligan and Brian McCluskey, *'The Replay': A Parish History* (1984): a history of the parishes of Kilmore and Drumsnat

KILRAGHTS PARISH, COUNTY ANTRIM
The name of this parish is also spelled Kilraughts.

Barony: Dunluce Upper
Diocese: Connor
Graveyard: Kilraughts Old

Estate papers
Agnew estate; Antrim estate; Hutchinson estate; Magenis estate, Derrykeighan;
Montgomery estate

Census substitutes
HMR, CPH, FL, AC

Publications
Dorothy Arthur, *Kilraughts Old Church Graveyard* (2014)
S. Alexander Blair, *Kilraughts: A Kirk and Its People* (1973)
Adam Loughridge, *Two Hundred Years of Witness: The story of Kilraughts Covenanting
    Church* (1983)

KILREA PARISH, COUNTY LONDONDERRY

Baronies: Coleraine, Loughinsholin
Diocese: Derry
Places: Kilrea, Movanagher
Graveyard: Kilrea Old

Church records
CI Kilrea
Vestry minutes, 1733– ; notes on the   MIC1/55/1
history of the parish, 1607–1947

Included in the vestry minutes are the names of the inhabitants of Kilrea and
Tamlaght O'Crilly who subscribed to a loyal declaration, 1745–6: over 130 names

Estate papers
Derry bishopric estate; Mercers' Company estate

Census substitutes
HMR, CPH, FL

Other records
Notice from distillers in Coleraine district, Kilrea Survey, 1766: 25 names – *Belfast
Newsletter*, 9 Dec. 1766

Publications
Jane Clark, *The Story of the Presbyterian Church at Kilrea* (1897)
J. W. Kernohan, *Two Ulster Parishes: Kilrea and Tamlaght O'Crilly* (1912; reprinted

1993): includes loyal declaration by the inhabitants of Kilrea and Tamlaght O'Crilly, 1745–6

J. H. McIlfatrick, *The Scots Kirk, Kilrea* (1990)

KILROOT PARISH, COUNTY ANTRIM

Barony: Belfast Lower
Diocese: Connor
Graveyard: Kilroot

Estate papers
Brice estate

Census substitutes
HMR

Publications
Charles McConnell, *The History of the Parish of Kilroot: Including the St Colman's Church* (2003)
D. H. Rankin, *A Short History of the Parish of Kilroot* (1982)

KILSKEERY PARISH, COUNTY TYRONE

Barony: Omagh East
Diocese: Clogher
Places: Kilskeery, Trillick
Graveyard: Kilskeery Old

Church records
CI Kilskeery
Baptisms, 1767– ; marriages, 1778– ;   MIC1/6/1
burials, 1796–

Indexes to baptisms, 1767–1844, marriages, 1778–1841, and burials, 1796–1841 are in the PRONI Search Room.

Estate papers
Clogher bishopric estate; Cooper estate, Rossfad; Mervyn estate

Census substitutes
HMR (listed under Magheracross), FL

Publications
Michael McCaughey, *Around Trillick Way* (1990)
B. O'Daly, 'Material for a history of the parish of Kilskeery', *Clogher Record*, 1:1 (1953), 1:2 (1954), 1:3 (1955), 5:2 (1964)

KILTEEVOGE PARISH, COUNTY DONEGAL

This parish was created out of **Stranorlar** in 1773.

Barony: Raphoe South
Diocese: Raphoe
Place: Cloghan
Graveyard: Kilteevoge Old

Estate papers
Styles estate

Census substitutes
FL

KILWAUGHTER PARISH, COUNTY ANTRIM

Barony: Glenarm Upper
Diocese: Connor
Graveyard: Kilwaughter Old

Church records
For CI records see **Inver**
For NSP records see **Larne**

Estate papers
Agnew estate

Census substitutes
HSM, DP (Larne, Raloo, Carncastle, Kilwaughter, Glenarm and Ballyeaston)

Publications
James Kennedy, *Historical Sketch of the First Presbyterian Congregation of Larne,
    now known as the Old Presbyterian Congregation of Larne and Kilwaughter* (1889)
Classon Porter, *Congregational Memoirs of the Old Presbyterian Congregation of Larne
    and Kilwaughter*, edited and updated by R. H. McIlrath and J. W. Nelson (1975)
*Old Families of Larne and District from Gravestone Inscriptions, Wills and Biographical
    Notes*, compiled by George Rutherford and edited by R. S. J. Clarke (2004)

KINAWLEY PARISH, COUNTIES CAVAN AND FERMANAGH

Baronies: Tullyhaw (Cavan portion), Clanawley, Knockninny (Fermanagh portion)
Diocese: Kilmore
Places: Aghalane, Derrylin, Swanlinbar, Teemore
Graveyards: Callowhill, Killaghaduff, Kinawley Old

Church records
CI Kinawley
Baptisms, 1761–3, 1768–83, 1794– ; marriages,   MIC1/76; CR1/62A/1
1761–3, 1768– ; burials, 1768– ; vestry minutes
with accounts, 1775–

CI Swanlinbar
Baptisms, 1798– ; marriages, 1798– ; burials, 1799–   MIC1/212

Estate papers
Crofton estate; Enniskillen estate; Erne estate

Census substitutes
RelC (Protestants and Catholics), FL

Publications
Dan Gallogly, 'Swanlinbar and its ironworks from the Registry of Deeds', *Breifne*, 21
    (1982)
Joseph McKiernan, *By Claddagh's Banks: A History of Swanlinbar and District from
    Earliest Times* (2000)

KIRKINRIOLA PARISH, COUNTY ANTRIM
The name of this parish has also been spelled Kilconriola.

Barony: Toome Lower
Diocese: Connor
Place: Ballymena
Graveyards: Ballymena Old, Kirkinriola Old

Church records
CI Kirkinriola
Baptisms, 1789– ; burials, 1780, 1792;   T679/192 (MIC583/16);
vestry minutes, 1777–   MIC1/327A/1;
          CR1/78A/1

Estate papers
Adair estate; Mitchell estate; Mount Cashell estate

Census substitutes
HMR, CPH (listed as Ballymena), DP (Ballymena), FL (one name: Rev. Richard
Babington)

Business records
Mitchell, Ballymena

Other records
18th-century documents concerning property of the Campbell family of Ballygarvey
    (including Drumfane) – D2179/6

Memorial of inhabitants of the town and neighbourhood of Ballymena, 1773 –
  Belfast Newsletter, 20 April 1773
Subscribers to a reward fund, Ballymena, 1780 – *Belfast Newsletter*, 1–5 Sept. 1780
Records relating to the Ballymena Hunt, including minutes (1799–1803) and
  accounts (1799–1804) – D2109/2/2B (see also T1252/3)
William Reeves, 'Historical memoir of the parish of Kilconriola, Co. Antrim', 1845 –
  DIO/1/24/19/1

Publications
Nicola Pierce, *Ballymena: City of the Seven Towers* (2011)
Old Ballymena: A History of Ballymena during the 1798 Rebellion (reprinted 1998):
  includes a list of churchwardens, 1778–1855 (pp 81–4)
See also the various publications of the Mid-Antrim Historical Group.

KNOCKBREDA PARISH, COUNTY DOWN
Knockbreda is an amalgamation of the medieval parishes of Knockcolumcille and
Breda.

Barony: Castlereagh Lower, Castlereagh Upper
Diocese: Down
Places: Belfast, Castlereagh, Gilnahirk, Newtownbreda
Graveyards: Breda, Castlereagh P, Knock, Knockbreda CI

Church records
CI Knockbreda
Baptisms, 1785– ; marriages, 1784– ;   MIC1/57/1
burials, 1787– ; vestry minutes, 1791–

The vestry minutes include the names of overseers of road repairs, 1791–5, and a list
of the poor by townland, 1801.

P Gilnahirk (originally Secession)
Baptisms, 1797–   MIC1P/432

Copy of lease of Gilnahirk Presbyterian Church, 1759   D3300/164/1

Estate papers
Hamilton (Claneboye and Clanbrassil) estate; Downshire estate; Dungannon estate;
McNeill estate; Ross estate, Portavo

Census substitutes
FL (listed under 'Castlereagh'), AC

Other records
Papers concerning Knockbreda parish, *c.* 1733 – DIO/4/26/7/2/1, /2, /3
Resolution of inhabitants of Knockbreda, presented to Arthur Trevor, 1763 – *Belfast
  Newsletter*, 1 July 1763

Publications
W. P. Carmody, *History of the Parish of Knockbreda* (1929)
James Little, *Castlereagh Presbyterian Church, 1650–1950* [addendum by his son,
    D. J. Little] (1950)
H. C. Miller, *The Church on the Stye Brae: Gilnahirk Presbyterian Church 1787–1987*
    (1987)

KNOCKBRIDE PARISH, COUNTY CAVAN

Barony: Clankee
Diocese: Kilmore
Graveyard: Knockbride Old

Church records
P Coronary (originally Secession)
Baptisms, 1764– ; marriages, 1768–87; session   MIC1P/179
minutes, 1764–87; history of the congregation
and details of Sunday collections, 1769–89

Estate papers
Haig estate

Census substitutes
FL

Publications
Eugene P. Markey and John Clarke, *Knockbride: A History* (1995)

LAMBEG PARISH, COUNTIES ANTRIM AND DOWN

Baronies: Belfast Upper (Antrim portion), Castlereagh Upper (Down portion)
Diocese: Connor
Place: Lambeg
Graveyard: Lambeg CI

Estate papers
Conway estate

Census substitutes
HMR

Other records
Accounts concerning Lord Conway's expenses at Lambeg, 1740 – MIC257/1
Subscribers to a reward fund, 1779 – *Belfast Newsletter*, 16–20 July 1779

Publications
H. C. Marshall, *The Parish of Lambeg* (1933)

William Cassidy, *Lambeg Churchyard, Lisburn, Co. Antrim: Inscriptions on Old Tombstones (1626–1837) and on Those of Special Interest Up to the Present Day With Notes* (1937)

LARAH PARISH, COUNTY CAVAN

Baronies: Loughtee Upper, Tullygarvey
Diocese: Kilmore
Place: Stradone
Graveyard: Larah Old

Estate papers
Annesley estate; Saunderson estate

Census substitutes
FL

Publications
Terence P. Cunningham, *The Ecclesiastical History of Larah Parish* (1984)

LARNE PARISH, COUNTY ANTRIM

Barony: Glenarm Upper
Diocese: Connor
Place: Larne

Church records
For CI records see **Inver**

NSP Larne and Kilwaughter
Baptisms, 1720–69, 1796; marriages, 1721–69;   MIC1B/6
session minutes, 1720–48; discipline cases,
1721–49; poor accounts, 1720–57

Session minutes, 1699–1701 [current whereabouts uncertain]

Estate papers
Agnew estate; Antrim estate

Census substitutes
HMR, HSM, DP (Larne, Raloo, Carncastle, Kilwaughter, Glenarm and Ballyeaston)

Other sources
Map of the 'Old Town of Lairn als Gardenmore', 1735, listing nearly 80 tenants' names – D2977/36/2/1 (see also T982/1 for a list of names extracted from this map)
Text on 'The Oakboys, the Hearts of Steel, the Volunteers and the United Irishmen of Larne and neighbourhood' – D2095/18

Publications
First Larne Presbyterian Church: A People on the Move (2015): includes an appendix
    by Eric V. Stewart on the early history of the congregation
James Kennedy, *Historical Sketch of the First Presbyterian Congregation of Larne, now
    known as the Old Presbyterian Congregation of Larne and Kilwaughter* (1889)
Historical Sketch of the Gardenmore Presbyterian Church, Larne, 1769–1894 (1894)
Felix McKillop, *History of Larne and East Antrim* (2000)
D. J. McNeilly and William Burns, *Into a New Century: Gardenmore Presbyterian
    Church, Larne 1769–2003* (2003)
Classon Porter, *Congregational Memoirs of the Old Presbyterian Congregation of Larne
    and Kilwaughter*, edited and updated by R. H. McIlrath and J. W. Nelson (1975)
*Old Families of Larne and District from Gravestone Inscriptions, Wills and Biographical
    Notes*, compiled by George Rutherford and edited by R. S. J. Clarke (2004)

LAVEY PARISH, COUNTY CAVAN

Barony: Loughtee Upper
Diocese: Kilmore
Graveyard: Lavey Old

Estate papers
Annesley estate; Saunderson estate

Census substitutes
RelC (Protestants), FL

Piblications
Terence P. Cunningham, *The Ecclesiastical History of Lavey Parish* (1984)

LAYD PARISH, COUNTY ANTRIM
The name of this parish is also spelled Layde.

Barony: Glenarm Lower
Diocese: Connor
Places: Cushendall, Glenariff, Knocknacarry, Red Bay, Waterfoot
Graveyards: Kilmore, Layd Old

Estate papers
Antrim estate; Edwards estate; McCollum estate; Rowan estate, Mullans

Census substitutes
HMR, FL

Other records
Subscribers to a reward fund, 1772 – *Belfast Newsletter*, 14 April 1772

LEARMOUNT PARISH, COUNTY LONDONDERRY
This parish was created in 1831 out of **Banagher**, **Cumber** and **Donaghedy**.

LECK PARISH, COUNTY DONEGAL

Baronies: Raphoe North, Raphoe South
Diocese: Raphoe
Graveyard: Leck Old

Estate papers
Hayes estate; Raphoe bishopric estate

Census substitutes
HMR, RelC (Protestants), FL

Publications
L. R. Lawrenson, *The Parish of Conwall, Aughanunshin and Leck* (1943)

LECKPATRICK PARISH, COUNTY TYRONE

Barony: Strabane Lower
Diocese: Derry
Places: Artigarvan, Ballymagorry, Cloghcor, Glenmornan
Graveyard: Leckpatrick Old

Estate papers
Abercorn estate; Derry bishopric estate; Hall estate

Census substitutes
HMR, FL

Publications
William J. Roulston, *The Parishes of Leckpatrick and Dunnalong: Their Place in History* (2000)

LETTERMACAWARD PARISH, COUNTY DONEGAL

Barony: Boylagh
Diocese: Raphoe
Place: The Rosses
Graveyard: Lettermacaward CI

Estate papers
Conolly estate; Raphoe bishopric estate

Census substitutes
HMR

LISNADILL PARISH, COUNTY ARMAGH

This parish was created out of **Armagh** in 1772.

Baronies: Armagh, Fews Lower, Fews Upper
Diocese: Armagh
Places: Ballymacnab, Lisnadill, Milford
Graveyard: Lisnadill CI

Estate papers
Armagh archbishopric estate; Charlemont estate; Johnston estate, Eglish;
MacGeough-Bond estate; Whaley estate

LISSAN PARISH, COUNTIES LONDONDERRY AND TYRONE

Baronies: Loughinsholin (Londonderry portion), Dungannon Upper (Tyrone portion)
Diocese: Armagh
Places: Broughderg, Churchtown
Graveyard: Lissan CI

Church records
CI Lissan
Baptisms, 1753–95; marriages, 1744–94;   T679/9a (MIC583/1)
burials, 1753–95; vestry minutes, 1734–

Estate papers
Armagh archbishopric estate; Drapers' Company estate; Staples estate

Census substitutes
HMR, CPH, FL

Publications
The Townlands of Lissan, parts 1 and 2 (2002–)
Sean Clarke, *Broughderg: A Place and its Peoples* (n.d.)

LONGFIELD PARISH, COUNTY TYRONE

Also known as Langfield, this parish was divided into Upper and Lower (or East and
West) in 1795/6.

Baronies: Omagh East, Omagh West
Diocese: Derry
Place: Drumquin
Graveyard: Longfield Old (Lackagh)

Estate papers
Boyle estate; Castle Stewart estate; Derry bishopric estate; Huntingdon estate;
Mervyn estate

Census substitutes
HMR, FL

Other sources
Letter concerning seditious activities involving individuals from Longfield parish, 1763 – T3019/4670
Subscribers to a reward fund relating to Longfield, 1770 – *Belfast Newsletter*, 4 Dec. 1770

Publications
F. D. Creighton, *A Brief History of Langfield Parish* (1992)

LOUGHAN OR CASTLEKEERAN PARISH, COUNTIES CAVAN AND MEATH
Most of this parish is in County Meath.

Barony: Castlerahan
Diocese: Meath
Graveyard: Derver (Dervor)

Estate papers
Plunkett estate

LOUGHGALL PARISH, COUNTY ARMAGH

Barony: Oneilland West
Diocese: Armagh
Places: Annaghmore, Ardress, Charlemont, Loughgall
Graveyards: Legar Hill, Loughgall Old

Church records
CI Loughgall
Baptisms, 1706–29, 1779– ; marriages,   MIC1/59C; D54/1
1706–29, 1779– ; burials, 1706–29,
1779–94; vestry minutes, 1774–1809

The vestry minute book includes a list of the proprietors of seats, 1775; detailed lists of those charged with responsibility for repairing roads (that for 1777 has over 50 names); regular lists of persons placed on the parish list (i.e. the poor); names of persons appointed as trustees to lay out money, 1791 (over 30 names).

Extracts from the registers, 1709–1841   T636/1, p. 101

Estate papers
Armagh archbishopric estate; Charlemont estate; Cope estate; Molyneux estate; Verner estate

Census substitutes
HMR, FP, VAA, CPH, FL

Other records
Subscribers to a reward fund, 1778 – *Belfast Newsletter*, 1–4 Sept. 1778

Publications
Pat Reilly, *Loughgall: A Plantation Parish* (1995): includes a muster roll of the estate
  of Antony Cope, 1630 (pp 177–9), hearth money roll, 1664–5 (pp 180–85),
  churchwardens, 1773–1995 (pp 165–73), inhabitants of Loughgall to whom
  money was owed by Camboon's regiment in King William's Army, 1689–96
  (p. 186) and seatholders in the parish church, 1775 and 1803 (pp 189–90)
Joseph Thompson, *Three Hundred Years in God's Orchard: The Story of Loughgall
  Presbyterian Church* (2004)

LOUGHGILLY PARISH, COUNTY ARMAGH

Barony: Orior Lower
Diocese: Armagh
Places: Belleeks, Kingsmills, Loughgilly, Mountnorris, Mowhan, Tullyherron
Graveyard: Loughgilly CI

Church records
CI Loughgilly
Vestry minutes, 1797–   Local custody

P Tullyallen (originally Secession)
Baptisms, 1792–1834   Local custody

Estate papers
Armagh archbishopric estate; Charlemont estate; Magenis estate, Dromara; Stewart
estate

Census substitutes
HMR, FP, VAA, FL

Publications
Beatrice Elliott and Jennifer Lundy, *History of Kingsmills Presbyterian Church 1788–
1988* (1988)

LOUGHGUILE PARISH, COUNTY ANTRIM

Baronies: Dunluce Upper, Kilconway
Diocese: Connor
Places: Corkey, Lissanoure, Loughguile
Graveyard: Loughguile Old

Church records
CI Loughguile
Extracts from vestry minutes, *c.* 1701–*c.* 1730   DIO/1/24/3/1–13

Estate papers
Adams estate; Allen estate; Antrim estate; Boyd estate; Legge estate; Macartney estate

Census substitutes
HMR, CPH, FL, AC

Business records
Adams, Chequer Hall

Publications
Robert M'Cahan, *Loughguile Parish and the Macartney Family*, reprinted in
M'Cahan's Local Histories. A Series of Pamphlets on North Antrim and the Glens (1923)
(1988)

LOUGHINISLAND PARISH, COUNTY DOWN

Barony: Kinelarty
Diocese: Down
Places: Annadorn, Clough, Drumaroad, Seaforde
Graveyards: Clough P, Loughinisland CI (Seaforde), Loughinisland Old

Church records
CI Loughinisland
Baptisms, 1760– , with index; marriages,   D1407; T1
1760– , with index; burials, 1760–93,
with index; vestry minutes, 1773–

P Clough
Following a division *c.* 1830, this congregation is now represented by Clough
Presbyterian Church and Clough Non-Subscribing Presbyterian Church.

Baptisms, 1791/2– ; marriages, 1791–   T1701/1; MIC1P/308

Estate papers
Annesley estate; Bailie estate; Forde estate; Ker estate; Rawdon estate

Census substitutes
FL

Other sources
Historical account of Loughinisland parish mainly from the 17th century, written
by Rev. Hugh Smyth Cum(m)ing, *c.* 1844 – DIO/1/24/14; Linen Hall Library,
Blackwood Pedigrees, vol. 94 (also PRONI, MIC315/13)

Publications
R. W. H. Blackwood, 'Query concerning the vestry minutes of the parish of
   Loughinisland, County Down for the period 1772–1870', *UJA*, 2nd series, 15
   (Nov. 1909), p. 186
R. W. H. Blackwood, *Some Biographical Notices of the Rectors of Loughinisland: 1609–
   1911* (1911)
R. W. H. Blackwood, *Loughinisland: Its Legends and History* (1923)

LURGAN PARISH, COUNTY CAVAN

Barony: Castlerahan
Diocese: Kilmore
Place: Virginia
Graveyard: Lurgan Old

Church records
RC Lurgan (Virginia)
Baptisms, 1755–95 (with gaps, 1778–9 and   MIC1D/80–81
1785–6); marriages, 1755–70, 1773–80

Estate papers
Farnham estate; Headfort estate; Plunkett estate

Census substitutes
HMR, RelC (Protestants), FL

Other records
Chancery bills, answers, etc relating to Virginia, *c.* 1638–1670 – NLI, MS 8023

Publications
John O'Donohoe, *Virginia in the Bygone Days, 1607–2007* (2007)
Patrick Cassidy (ed.), *Virginia: A Portrait. Celebrating 400 Years 1612–2012* (2012)
Jim Gammons, *Virginia Then and Now: A Look at Virginia and Virginians* (2004)
Jim Gammons (ed.), *Virginia 400: A Ramble through History and Back to the Present*
   (2009)
Chris Kirk, *Virginia: One for the Road, Rediscovering the Past 400 Years* (2010)

MACOSQUIN PARISH, COUNTY LONDONDERRY
This parish is also known as Camus-juxta-Bann.

Barony: Coleraine
Diocese: Derry
Places: Macosquin, Somerset
Graveyards: Camus Old, Macosquin (Camus-juxta-Bann) CI

Estate papers
Clothworkers' Company estate; Derry bishopric estate; Du Pré estate; Heyland estate; Ironmongers' Company estate; Jackson estate; Merchant Taylors' Company estate; Richardson estate; Rowley estate

Census substitutes
HMR, CPH, FL

Other records
Names of some inhabitants of the parish, 1675 – printed in Moody and Simms, *Bishopric of Derry and the Irish Society of London*, vol. 2, pp 10–11
Notebook containing notification of registering arms, including residents of Macosquin, 1796 – D668/N/1

Publications
W. W. Reid, *Crossgar: The Meeting-house and its People* (1987)
Victor Whyte, *Macosquin Presbyterian Church* (1970)
David H. A. Wright, *Ballylaggan Reformed Presbyterian Church: Two Hundred and Fifty Years of Covenanter Witness in Bannside, 1763–2013* (2014)

MAGHERA PARISH, COUNTY DOWN

Barony: Iveagh Upper (Lower Half)
Diocese: Down
Place: Tollymore
Graveyard: Maghera CI

Estate papers
Mathews estate

Census substitutes
FL, AC

MAGHERA PARISH, COUNTY LONDONDERRY

Barony: Loughinsholin
Diocese: Derry
Places: Culnady, Curran, Fallagloon, Gulladuff, Maghera, Upperlands
Graveyard: Maghera Old

Church records
CI Maghera
Baptisms, 1785– ; marriages, 1798–   MIC1/20, 77

Estate papers
Conolly estate; Derry bishopric estate; Graves estate; Mercers' Company estate; Strafford estate; Vintners' Company estate

Census substitutes
HMR, CPH, FL

Business records
Clark, Upperlands

Other records
Three emigrant letters, two from Job Johnson and the third from William and Job Johnson in Pennsylvania, to their brothers in Slaghtybogy, 1766–84 – D4618/1/1; T3700

Publications
W. A. Macafee, 'The colonisation of the Maghera region of south Derry during the seventeenth and eighteenth Centuries', *Ulster Folklife*, 23 (1977), pp 70–91
Wallace Clark, *Linen on the Green: An Irish Mill Village* [Upperlands], *1730–2008* (1982, 3rd ed. 2008): includes information on early inhabitants of Upperlands
S. Sidlow McFarland, *Presbyterianism in Maghera: A Social and Congregational History* (1985)

MAGHERACLOONE PARISH, COUNTY MONAGHAN
The name of this parish has also been spelled Magheraclooney and Magherclune(y).

Barony: Farney
Diocese: Clogher
Graveyard: Magheracloone CI

Estate papers
Brownlow estate; Clogher bishopric estate; Shirley estate

Census substitutes
HMR, FP, FL

Other records
Names of male Protestants aged 17 and over, 1785 (Protestants [i.e. Anglicans] and Presbyterians listed separately) – T808/15259

MAGHERACROSS PARISH, COUNTIES FERMANAGH AND TYRONE

Baronies: Lurg, Tirkennedy (Fermanagh portion), Omagh (Tyrone portion)
Diocese: Clogher
Place: Ballinamallard
Graveyards: Magheracross CI, Magheracross Old

Church records
CI Magheracross
Baptisms, 1800– ; marriages, 1800– ; burials, 1800–   MIC1/78

Estate papers
Clogher bishopric estate; Conolly estate; Lendrum estate; Mervyn estate

Census substitutes
HMR, FL

Publications
Ballinamallard: A Place of Importance (2005)

MAGHERACULMONEY PARISH, COUNTY FERMANAGH
Around 1774 the parish of Drumkeeran was created out of **Magheraculmoney.**

Barony: Lurg
Diocese: Clogher
Places: Ederny, Kesh, Lack
Graveyards: Kiltierney, Magheraculmoney CI (Ardess)

Church records
CI Magheraculmoney

Baptisms, 1767– ; marriages, 1767– ; burials, 1767– ; vestry minutes, 1763–	MIC1/67–68

The vestry minutes include regular lists of the poor, distinguishing between Protestants and Catholics, from 1769 onwards.

Estate papers
Archdale estate; Clogher bishopric estate; Vaughan estate

Census substitutes
FL

Publications
F. A. Bailie, *A Short History of Magheraculmoney Parish* (1984)

MAGHERADROOL PARISH, COUNTY DOWN
The name of this parish is also spelled Magheradroll.

Barony: Kinelarty
Diocese: Dromore
Places: Ballynahinch, Drumaness, Spa
Graveyard: Magheradrool Old

Church records
P Ballynahinch

Baptisms, 1696–1735; marriages, 1696–1733; collections and disbursements, 1704–24; testimonials	CR3/69/A/1

and certificates, 1715–34; notes on the history
of Ballynahinch, Dromara, Kilmore and Drumcaw
Presbyterian congregations, compiled *c.* 1832

Estate papers
Annesley estate; Forde estate; Ker estate; Rawdon estate

Census substitutes
HSM, FL

Other records
Subscribers to a reward fund, 1775 – *Belfast Newsletter*, 8–12 Dec. 1775

Publications
W. D. Bailie, *Bi-centenary History of Edengrove Presbyterian Church, 1774–1974
(formerly Second and Third Ballynahinch)* (1974)

MAGHERAFELT PARISH, COUNTY LONDONDERRY

Barony: Loughinsholin
Diocese: Armagh
Places: Castledawson, Magherafelt
Graveyard: Magherafelt Old

Church records
CI Magherafelt
Baptisms, 1718–93, 1799– ; marriages,   MIC1/1A
1720– ; burials, 1716–71, 1799;
vestry minutes, 1718–95, 1798–

There were over 30 signatories of the minutes of a vestry meeting in 1763; other
meetings had 20+ signatories; list of over 20 individuals recommended for badges,
giving name, townland and name of person making the recommendation, *c.* 1790.

P Castledawson (Dawson's Bridge)
Baptisms, 1703–6   MIC1P/90

P 1st Magherafelt
Baptisms, 1771–80; marriages, 1769–82; session   MIC1P/450/1;
minutes, 1703–82; short history of the Presbyterian   CR3/13/C/5
congregation of Magherafelt intended to be used
as an introduction to a new session book, 1853

Estate papers
Armagh archbishopric estate; Dawson estate; Graves estate; Salters' Company estate;
Vintners' Company estate

Census substitutes
HMR, VAA, CPH, RelC (Anglicans, Presbyterians and Catholics), HSM, FL

Other records
Subscribers to a reward fund, Castledawson and district, 1769 – *Belfast Newsletter*,
28 April 1769

Publications
Some account of the town of Magherafelt and manor of Sal, in Ireland belonging …
    to the Worshipful Company of Salters (1842)
W. H. Maitland, *History of Magherafelt* (1916, reprinted Moyola Books, 1988 and
    1991)
Valerie Morgan, 'Mortality in Magherafelt, County Derry, in the early eighteenth
    century', *Irish Historical Studies*, 19:74 (Sept. 1974), pp 125–35
William Macafee, Valerie Morgan, 'Mortality in Magherafelt, County Derry, in
    the early eighteenth century reappraised', *Irish Historical Studies*, 23:89 (May
    1982), pp 50–60

MAGHERAGALL PARISH, COUNTY ANTRIM

Barony: Massereene Upper
Diocese: Connor
Graveyard: Magheragall CI

Church records
CI Magheragall
Baptisms, 1776– ; marriages, 1772– ;   MIC1/75/1
burials, 1772–81; vestry minutes, 1771–

The vestry minutes include detailed information on the repair of roads; a list of
subscribers for slating and repairing the roof of the parish church, 1780 (100+
names); and a declaration in response to the prevailing political situation, 1796
(*c.* 150 names).

Estate papers
Conway estate; Rawdon estate

Census substitutes
HMR, HSM

Other records
Correspondence and related material of Rev. W. H. Dundas, relating to family
    history and Magheragall churchyard – D260/B/1
File of typed extracts relating to the history of Magheragall parish compiled by
    Canon Dundas, *c.* 1930 – T1398/12

MAGHERAHAMLET PARISH, COUNTY DOWN
This parish was formed out of **Dromara** in the 1800s.

MAGHERALIN PARISH, COUNTIES ARMAGH AND DOWN
In 1722, the parish of **Moira** was created out of Magheralin.

Baronies: Oneilland East (Armagh portion), Iveagh Lower (Upper Half) (Down
portion)
Diocese: Dromore
Places: Dollingstown, Magheralin
Graveyard: Magheralin Old

Church records
CI Magheralin

Baptisms, 1692– ; marriages, 1692–1782, 1785– ; burials, 1692– ; vestry minutes, 1692– ; churchwardens' accounts, including details of money given to the poor, 1766–94	CR1/97; T679/365, 368, 376, 380 (MIC583/32, 33); MIC1/18/1
Annotated transcript of the vestry minute book, 1702–1855	CR1/97/D/1
Churchwardens' accounts, 1766–94	CR1/97/E/1
Extracts from parish registers, 1784–1853 [missing]	DIO/1/14/6

Estate papers
Brownlow estate; Clanwilliam estate; Downshire estate; Dungannon estate; Hall
estate, Strangford and Lower Iveagh; Patterson estate; Rawdon estate

Census substitutes
FL

Publications
Eileen Cousins, *Like an Evening Gone: The Church of the Holy and Undivided Trinity
Magheralin* (1991): includes extracts from the 18th-century CI registers and vestry
minutes
F. X. McCorry, *Parish Registers: Historical Treasures in Manuscript* (2004): includes
information from the Magheralin CI registers

MAGHERALLY PARISH, COUNTY DOWN

Barony: Iveagh Lower (Lower Half)
Diocese: Dromore
Graveyard: Magherally Old

Church records
CI Magherally
Extracts from parish registers, 1784–91 [missing]   DIO/1/14/7

P Magherally
Account books relating to stipends,   MIC1P/211D/1
collections and expenses, 1788–

Estate papers
Downshire estate; Fortescue estate

Census substitutes
FL

Publications
R. S. J. Clarke (ed.), *The Heart of Downe. Old Banbridge Families from Gravestone Inscriptions, Wills and Biographical Notes* (1989)
Mary Martin, *Magherally Presbyterian Church, 1656–1982* (1982)

MAGHERAMESK PARISH, COUNTY ANTRIM

Barony: Massereene Upper
Diocese: Connor
Place: Maghaberry
Graveyards: Maghaberry (Ballynalargy) Quaker, Trummery

Estate papers
Conway estate

Census substitutes
HMR

MAGHEROSS PARISH, COUNTY MONAGHAN

Barony: Farney
Diocese: Clogher
Place: Carrickmacross
Graveyard: Magheross Old

CI Magheross or Carrickmacross
Baptisms, marriages and burials, 1660–67   Printed in Shirley,
    Monaghan, pp 595–8

Baptisms, 1796– ; marriages, 1798– ;   MIC1/173A/1
burials, 1798–

Petition concerning the poor condition   D3531/A/4; *Clogher Record,*
of the church building, 1777   6 (1966), pp 119–25

Estate papers
Bath estate; Clogher bishopric estate; Essex estate; Shirley estate

Census substitutes
HMR, FP, FL

Other sources
Names of male Protestants aged 17 and over, 1785 – T808/15259

Publications
Pádraig Breathnach, *A Heritage Guide to Carrickmacross* (1996)

MAGILLIGAN PARISH, COUNTY LONDONDERRY
This parish is also known as Tamlaghtard.

Barony: Keenaght
Diocese: Derry
Places: Bellarena, Magilligan
Graveyard: Tamlaghtard Old

Church records
CI Tamlaghtard
Baptisms, 1747–68; marriages, 1747–53;   MIC1/86/1
burials, 1768–75; vestry minutes, 1747–

The vestry minutes include lists of the poor (one of the lists concerns those to be issued with badges), 1773; for subsequent years there are records of payments to the poor. From 1780 there is a record of a meeting that discussed raising money to build a new Church of Ireland church; two lists of names (over 30 in total) are appended to the minutes of this meeting (one for raising money for this purpose, and the other, the longer, against).

Estate papers
Bacon estate; Hervey/Bruce estate; Derry bishopric estate; Gage estate; McNeal estate

Census substitutes
HMR, CPH (includes townlands), FL

Other records
Names of men from Magilligan parish ordered to appear 'with their best arms' at Limavady, 1666 – T640/103

Publications
Bobby Forrest, *Historical Gleanings from the Parish of Magilligan, County Derry,*
    1600–1800 (2008): includes extracts from church registers, census substitutes and
    estate papers
Robert Innes, 'An Account of the Great Variety of Plants, Shell-stones and many
    other Curiosities in Parish of Magilligan in County of Londonderry …' [1725] in
    Miscellaneous Letters on Several Subjects (1732)

MEVAGH PARISH, COUNTY DONEGAL

Barony: Kilmacrenan
Diocese: Raphoe
Places: Carrigart, Downings, Glen
Graveyards: Mevagh CI; Mevagh Old

Estate papers
Clements estate; Raphoe bishopric estate

Census substitutes
HMR, FL

Publications
L. W. Lucas, *Mevagh Down the Years* (1972): includes extracts from estate papers

MINTIAGHS OR BARR OF INCH PARISH, COUNTY DONEGAL
See also **Clonmany.**

Barony: Inishowen West
Diocese: Derry

Estate papers
Donegall estate; Ferguson estate

Publications
Seoirse Ó Dochartaigh, *Inis Eoghain: The Island of Eoghan: The Place-Names of*
Inishowen (2011)
Seoirse Ó Dochartaigh, *The Great Name Book of Inishowen* (2016)

MOIRA PARISH, COUNTY DOWN
This parish was created in 1722 out of **Magheralin.**

Barony: Iveagh Lower (Upper Half)
Diocese: Dromore
Place: Moira
Graveyard: Moira CI

Church records
CI Moira

Baptisms, 1725–56; marriages, 1725–56;   MIC1/79, 80
burials, 1725–56; vestry minutes, 1725–55,
1758– ; accounts, 1745–8

The minutes of the early vestry meetings can have up to 30 signatures appended; from 1780–84 there are detailed lists of those appointed to act as directors, overseers, applotters and collectors with regard to repairing roads.

Extracts from parish registers, 1784–1860 [missing]   DIO/1/14/8

P Moira
Call to Rev. Andrew Craig from   PHSI
Moira congregation, 1778

Estate papers
Downshire estate; Rawdon estate

Other records
Subscribers to a reward fund, 1779 – *Belfast Newsletter*, 2–5 Nov. 1779

MONAGHAN PARISH, COUNTY MONAGHAN

Barony: Monaghan
Diocese: Clogher
Places: Castleshane, Monaghan
Graveyards: Monaghan CI, Rackwallace

Church records
CI Monaghan
Baptisms, marriages and burials,   Printed in Shirley,
1671–2 (includes Tehallen)   *Monaghan*, pp 590–91

Estate papers
Barton estate; Blayney estate; Clermont estate; Clogher bishopric estate; Dawson estate; Rossmore estate; Verner estate

Census substitutes
HMR, FL

Corporation records
Negative of map of the town and corporation of Monaghan, 1789, accompanied by a typescript list of corporation property leases (tenants' names, terms of leases, comments): lands of Aughanmy, Ballymickfarben, Drumgost, Killygoan,

Mullaghadun, Mullaghcroghery, Mullaghmatt, Mullaghmonaghan, Rooskey, Tully, Turkeenan – T3801/1

Other records
List of tenants in Monaghan Town, 1791 – MIC426/1

Publications
L. T. Brown, *Shepherding the Monaghan Flock: The Story of First Monaghan Presbyterian Church, 1697–1997* (1997)
Theo McMahon, *Old Monaghan, 1785–1995* (1995)
Sean Murphy, *Ardaghey Past & Present* [1991]

MONTIAGHS PARISH, COUNTY ARMAGH
The parish of Montiaghs was created from **Seagoe** in 1765.

Barony: Oneilland East
Diocese: Dromore
Places: Bannfoot, Charlestown, Derrytrasna
Graveyard: Montiaghs (Ardmore) CI

Church records
CI Montiaghs or Ardmore
Extracts from parish registers, 1789–1863 [missing]   DIO/1/14/9

Estate papers
Brownlow estate

Publications
Material of interest in *Review: Journal of Craigavon Historical Society.*

MOVILLE PARISH, COUNTY DONEGAL
This parish was divided into Upper and Lower sections in 1781.

Barony: Inishowen East
Diocese: Derry
Places: Greencastle, Moville
Graveyards: Cooley, Redcastle

Church records
CI Moville Lower
Vestry minutes, 1773–   MIC1/138; DIO/3/24

The vestry minutes include a cess list of 1774 containing a very lengthy list of names by townland.

Estate papers
Alexander estate; Derry bishopric estate; Donegall estate

Census substitutes
HMR, CPH (includes townlands), FL

Other records
An account of subscriptions to and expenses of Moville glebe house, 1775–8 –
D1514/1/1/53

Publications
Henry Montgomery, *A History of Moville and its Neighbourhood* (1991)
Seoirse Ó Dochartaigh, *Inis Eoghain: The Island of Eoghan: The Place-Names of Inishowen* (2011)
Seoirse Ó Dochartaigh, *The Great Name Book of Inishowen* (2016)

MOYBOLGUE PARISH, COUNTIES CAVAN AND MEATH
This parish, also known as Moybologue, originated in the medieval period. Parochial reorganisation in the late eighteenth century resulted in it becoming part of a new parish called Bailieborough (often referred to as Bailieborough alias Moybologue). It is not entirely clear why a small portion in County Cavan retained a separate identity as the parish of Moybolgue, at least in nineteenth-century valuations. See **Bailieborough** for further possible sources.

Barony: Clankee
Diocese: Kilmore
Graveyard: Moybologue Old

Estate papers
Kilmore bishopric estate

MUCKNO PARISH, COUNTY MONAGHAN

Barony: Cremorne
Diocese: Clogher
Places: Castleblayney, Oram
Graveyards: Muckno CI, Mullandoy

Estate papers
Blayney estate; Clogher bishopric estate; Templetown estate

Census substitutes
HMR, FL

Publications
Peadar Livingstone, 'The parish and townlands of Muckno', *Clogher Record*, 6:1 (1966), pp 137–90
Paula McGeough, *Beyond the Big Bridge: A History of Oram and Surrounding Townlands* (2000)

MUFF PARISH, COUNTY DONEGAL
This parish was created in 1809 out of **Templemore**.

Barony: Inishowen West
Diocese: Derry
Place: Muff
Graveyards: Eskaheen (Iskaheen); Muff CI

Church records
For CI records see **Templemore**

Estate papers
Donegall estate; Hart estate

Publications
Seoirse Ó Dochartaigh, *Inis Eoghain: The Island of Eoghan: The Place-Names of Inishowen* (2011)
Seoirse Ó Dochartaigh, *The Great Name Book of Inishowen* (2016)

MULLAGH PARISH, COUNTY CAVAN

Barony: Castlerahan
Diocese: Kilmore
Place: Mullagh
Graveyards: Raffony; Templekelly (Teampall Cheallaigh)

Church records
RC Mullagh
Baptisms, 1760– ; marriages, 1766–   MIC1D/82

Estate papers
Farnham estate; Plunkett estate

Census substitutes
HMR

Publications
Brendan Clarke, *The Townlands of the Parish of Mullagh* (2013)
Seámas P. O Mordha (ed.), *Portrait of a Parish: Mullagh* (1988)

MULLAGHBRACK PARISH, COUNTY ARMAGH
The name of this parish has also been spelled Mullabrack.

Barony: Oneilland West
Diocese: Armagh
Places: Hamiltonsbawn, Markethill
Graveyard: Mullabrack CI

Church records
CI Mullabrack

Baptisms, 1764–83, 1799– ; marriages,   MIC1/83/1
1767–83, 1798– ; vestry minutes, 1764–89

Typescript copy of marriages, 1767–83,   CR1/72B/1
1798–1811, plus 5 entries of death, 1732–1762,
and birth dates of the children of Squire Barker
and Sara Bury, 1730–50

P 1st Markethill
Resolution signed by nearly 200 members of Markethill Presbyterian Church, 1763
– *Belfast Newsletter*, 9 Aug. 1763

Estate papers
Armagh archbishopric estate; Charlemont estate; Gosford estate; Hamilton estate,
Hamiltonsbawn; Simpson estate; Whaley estate

Census substitutes
HMR, FP, VAA, CPH, FL

Freemasonry records
Transcripts of minutes of Masonic lodge no. 393, Hamiltonsbawn, 1786–1834 –
GLI

Other records
Commonplace book of Rev. Squire Barker, *c.* 1750–*c.* 1770: this contains much
    information about the inhabitants of the parish as well as marriage banns relating
    to Mullaghbrack – D943/1
Application by linen merchants for the establishment of a weekly linen market in
    Markethill, 1791 – D3857/1
Printed booklet about the parish of Mullabrack, 1953 – D3000/149/3

Publications
H. H. Moore, *Three Hundred Years of Congregational Life: The Story of the First
    Presbyterian Church, Markethill* (1909)
James M. Reaney, *The Kirk at Markethill: A Short History of First and Second
    Markethill Presbyterian Church* (1981)

MUNTERCONNAUGHT PARISH, COUNTY CAVAN

Barony: Castlerahan
Diocese: Kilmore
Graveyard: Munterconnaught Old

Church records
For RC records see **Castlerahan**

Estate papers
Plunkett estate

Census substitutes
HMR, RelC (Protestants), FL

Publications
Noel McEnroe (ed.), *Munterconnaught Uncovered: Heritage of a Rural Cavan Community* (2008)

NEWRY PARISH, COUNTIES ARMAGH AND DOWN
Note: there are some detached townlands belonging to this parish in counties Armagh and Down.

Baronies: Oneilland West, Orior Upper (Armagh portion), Lordship of Newry,
    Upper Iveagh (Lower Half) (Down portion)
Diocese: Dromore/Exempt Jurisdiction of Newry and Mourne
Place: Newry
Graveyards: Newry CI (St Patrick's), Newry RC (St Mary's)

Church records
CI Newry

Marriages, 1784– ; vestry minutes, 1775–	MIC1/47A/1; D2034/2/1–2, /4/1
Index to marriages, 1784	D2034/1/1

P Newry
In 1828, this congregation divided over the Arian controversy and is now represented by 1st Newry (Sandys Street) Presbyterian Church and 1st Newry (Non-Subscribing) Presbyterian Church.

Baptisms, 1779–97; marriages, 1781–95	T699/7

Estate papers
Bagenal estate; Downshire estate; Needham estate

Census substitutes
DP (plus Established Church petition), FL, AC

Business records
Blair, Newry; McClenaghan, Newry

Freemasonry records
Short historical account from *c.* 1890 of the history of St Patrick's Masonic Lodge, Newry, including a list of its membership from its foundation in 1737 – MIC249/2 (see also R. E. Parkinson, *Historical Sketch of St. Patrick's Masonic Lodge: No.77, Newry 1737–1937* (1936))

Other records

Extensive material of genealogical interest, much of it relating to Newry, was collected by Francis Crossle and his son Philip and can be found in PRONI (T618 and T699) and NLI (MSS 2202–34).

Map of Ballywholan [Ballyholland], 1776 plus a list of holdings in 1792 – T1101/10/1

Minutes of the Newry Snug Club, 1778–99: includes an index of names – T3202A

Publications

Tony Canavan, *Frontier Town: An Illustrated History of Newry* (1989)

R. S. J. Clarke (ed.), *Old Families of Newry & District from Gravestone Inscriptions, Wills and Biographical Notes* (1998)

M. Comer, *St Mary's and its People* (1990)

John Corry, *Odes and Elegies, Descriptive and Sentimental: With The Patriot, a Poem* (1797): published in Newry and with many local subscribers

F. C. Crossle, *Notes on the Literary History of Newry* (1897)

S. J. Heasley, *St Patrick's Parish Church, Newry, 1578–1978: A Short Historical Guide* (1978)

David S. McIlwrath, *Sandys Street, 1828–1978: A Hundred and Fifty Years of Congregational Life* (n.d.)

W. G. Strahan, *First Newry (Sandys Street) Presbyterian Congregation: Its History and Relationships* (1904)

NEWTOWNCROMMELIN PARISH, COUNTY ANTRIM

This parish was formed *c.* 1830 from **Dunaghy**.

NEWTOWNARDS PARISH, COUNTY DOWN

Baronies: Ards Lower, Castlereagh Lower
Diocese: Down
Places: Craigantlet, Newtownards, Scrabo
Graveyards: Killysuggan, Movilla, Newtownards Priory

Estate papers
Londonderry estate

Census substitutes
FL

Corporation records: Newtownards
Corporation minute book, 1741–75 – LA/60/2AB/1
Borough act book, 1742–75 – T433/1
Minute book of the grand jury of the corporation, 1756–1833 – LA/60/2AA/1 (see also T1874/1)

Business records
Bradshaw, Milecross

Other records
Map of the town of Newtownards, 1720, naming tenants, but very faded – D952/1
Subscribers to a reward fund, 1782 – *Belfast Newsletter*, 27–31 Dec. 1782
Statement issued by the inhabitants of the town and parish of Newtownards
    'assembled for the purpose of expressing our sentiments of attachment to the
    principles of the constitution', 1796 – D1494/2/24 (MIC506/1).

Publications
First Presbyterian Church, Newtownards: A History of the Congregation (1944)
John Brown, *Second Presbyterian Church Newtownards: A History of the Congregation
    1753–1953* (1953)
Trevor McCavery, *Newtown: A History of Newtownards* (1994, reprinted 2013)
Trevor McCavery, *A Covenant Community: A History of Newtownards Reformed
    Presbyterian Church* (1997)

NEWTOWNHAMILTON PARISH, COUNTY ARMAGH
This parish was created in 1773 out of **Creggan.**

Barony: Fews Upper
Diocese: Armagh
Place: Newtownhamilton
Graveyard: Tullyvallan Old

Estate papers
McCombe estate; Tipping estate

Census substitutes
FL

Other records
Leather-bound diary of Alexander Hamilton, QC, LLD, of Newtownhamilton and
Dublin, 1793–1807 – NLI, MS 49,371

Publications
J. B. A. Bell, *A History of Clarkesbridge and First Newtownhamilton Presbyterian
Churches* (1969)

POMEROY PARISH, COUNTY TYRONE
This parish was created in 1775 out of **Donaghmore.**

Barony: Dungannon Middle
Diocese: Armagh
Places: Altmore, Cappagh, Galbally, Pomeroy
Graveyard: Pomeroy CI

Estate papers
Forster estate; Lowry estate, Pomeroy; Stewart estate, Killymoon

Other sources
Names of the Pomeroy Corps of Infantry, 1798: *c.* 90 names – *Belfast Newsletter*, 16 March 1798

Publications
Feach: Essays on Local History in the Newsletter of Pomeroy Parish between 1987 and 1993 (1999)

PORTGLENONE PARISH, COUNTY ANTRIM
This parish was created in 1840 out of **Ahoghill**.

RACAVAN PARISH, COUNTY ANTRIM

Barony: Antrim Lower
Diocese: Connor
Places: Braid, Broughshane, Buckna, Slemish
Graveyards: Broughshane 1st P, Racavan

Estate papers
Mountcashell estate; O'Neill estate

Census substitutes
HMR, FL

Publications
Margaret E. Millar, *Presbyterianism in Buckna, 1756–1992: The History of a People in the Braid* (1992)
Felix McKillop, *The Valley of the Braid: A Local History* (2010)
First Broughshane Presbyterian Church 1655–1936 (1936)

RALOO PARISH, COUNTY ANTRIM

Barony: Belfast Lower
Diocese: Connor
Places: Glenoe, Mount Hill
Graveyard: Raloo Old

Church records:
For CI records see **Inver**

Estate papers
Dungannon estate; Neale estate

Census substitutes
HMR (included under heading 'Parish of Magheramorne'), HSM, DP (Larne, Raloo, Carncastle, Kilwaughter, Glenarm and Ballyeaston)

Other records
Raloo tithes, 1769–71 – printed in *DIFHR*, 29 (2006), p. 82
Map of Raloo parish, naming tenants, 1770 – D1954/6/1

RAMOAN PARISH, COUNTY ANTRIM

Barony: Cary
Diocese: Connor
Place: Ballycastle
Graveyard: Ramoan Old

Estate papers
Antrim estate; Boyd estate; McGildowney estate

Census substitutes
HMR, RCC, CPH, FL, AC

Freemasonry records
Much information on early Freemasonry in Ballycastle is given in Samuel Leighton, *History of Freemasonry in the Province of Antrim, Northern Ireland* (1938).

Business records
Ballycastle merchant (anon.); McGildowney, Ballycastle

Publications
Cahal Dallat, 'Ballycastle's 18th century industries', *The Glynns*, 3 (1978), pp 7–13
H. A. Boyd, *A History of the Church of Ireland in Ramoan Parish* (1930)
H. A. Boyd, 'An old Ballycastle account book', *The Glynns*, 8 (1980), pp 13–19: includes names of householders in Ballycastle in 1734 distinguishing between Church of Ireland, Presbyterian and Roman Catholic
A. W. G. Brown, *Ramoan Presbyterian Church: A Short History* (1997)

RAPHOE PARISH, COUNTY DONEGAL
In 1773, the parish of **Convoy** was created out of Raphoe.

Barony: Raphoe North
Diocese: Raphoe
Place: Raphoe
Graveyard: Raphoe CI Cathedral

Church records
CI Raphoe (St Eunan's Cathedral)
Baptisms, 1771–83; marriages, 1771– ;   MIC1/95/1
burials, 1771–83; vestry minutes, 1673–

The vestry minutes include the names of those in charge of planting trees, 1702/03; details of the disposal of seats in the cathedral, 1766.

Estate papers
Abercorn estate; Abraham estate; Gleadowes estate; Hamilton estate, Cavan; Hayes estate; McClintock estate; Raphoe bishopric estate

Census substitutes
HMR, LP (Raphoe/Convoy), RelC (Protestants), FL

Freemasonry records
Minutes of Masonic lodge no. 346, Raphoe, 1763–1826 – GLI

Other records
Map of part of the parish of Raphoe, naming tenants and showing type and acreage of land each holds, *c.* 1659 – T2444/2

Publications
About Raphoe (1998)

RASHARKIN PARISH, COUNTY ANTRIM

Barony: Kilconway
Diocese: Connor
Place: Rasharkin
Graveyard: Rasharkin Old

Estate papers
Antrim estate; Bateson estate; Leslie estate

Census substitutes
HMR, CPH, FL

Publications
Stephen Gaston, *Two Hundred Years of Presbyterianism in Killymurris* (1997)

RASHEE PARISH, COUNTY ANTRIM

Barony: Antrim Upper
Diocese: Connor
Graveyard: Rashee Old

Estate papers
Donegall estate

Census substitutes
HMR

RATHLIN PARISH, COUNTY ANTRIM

This island parish was created in 1722 by detaching it from **Ballintoy**.

Barony: Cary
Diocese: Connor
Graveyard: Rathlin CI

Church records
CI Rathlin
Vestry minutes, 1769–95   T861/1

These minutes are available in typescript; in general, those present at vestry meetings made their mark rather than signing their name.

Estate papers
Antrim estate; Gage estate

Census substitutes
HMR, CPH, RelC (surnames of Protestants and Catholics), AC

Other records
'Book of Rathlin' recording sales of household goods, meal and seed to the islanders, 1783–94 (index at front of volume to islanders: over 200 names) – D1375/11/1

Publications
Mrs Gage, *A History of the Island of Rathlin* (1851)
H. A. Boyd, *Rathlin Island* (1947)
Wallace Clark, *Rathlin: Its Island Story* (1971, reprinted 1988)
Wes Forsythe and Rosemary McConkey (eds), *Rathlin Island: An Archaeological Survey of a Maritime Landscape* (2012)

RATHMULLAN PARISH, COUNTY DOWN

Baronies: Lecale Lower, Lecale Upper
Diocese: Down
Places: Killough, Minerstown, Rossglass
Graveyards: Killough CI, Rathmullan CI

Estate papers
Banks estate; Gibbons estate; Leslie estate; Ward estate

Census substitutes
FL, AC

RAYMOGHY PARISH, COUNTY DONEGAL
This parish is also known as Ray and Raymochy.

Barony: Raphoe North
Diocese: Raphoe
Place: Manorcunningham
Graveyards: Balleeghan, Ray Old

Estate papers
Abercorn estate; Forward estate; Raphoe bishopric estate, Sanderson estate; Stewart estate, Ballylawn; Stewart estate, Mount Stewart

Census substitutes
HMR, LP (Ray), FL

Publications
Glimpses of Our Past: Raymochy Parishes Historical Society (2014 and subsequent years)
May McClintock, *The Heart of the Laggan* (1990)

RAYMUNTERDONEY PARISH, COUNTY DONEGAL

Barony: Kilmecrenan
Diocese: Raphoe
Place: Falcarragh
Graveyard: Ray Old

Estate papers
Clements estate; Hart estate; Raphoe bishopric estate; Stewart estate, Ards

Publications
Gerry McLaughlin, *Cloughaneely: Myth and Fact* (2002)

ROSSORRY PARISH, COUNTY FERMANAGH
The name of this parish is also spelled Rossory.

Baronies: Clanawley, Magheraboy
Diocese: Clogher
Place: Enniskillen
Graveyard: Rossorry Old

Church records
CI Rossory
Baptisms, 1796–7, 1799– ; marriages, 1799– ;   MIC1/22/1
burials, 1799– ; vestry minutes, 1763–

The vestry minutes include payments to the poor of the parish, 1764.

Estate papers
Clogher bishopric estate; Enniskillen estate; Huntingdon estate

Census substitutes
RelC (Protestants and Catholics), FL

Publications
M. Rogers, *A Short History of Rossory Parish* (n.d.)

SAINTFIELD PARISH, COUNTY DOWN
This parish was also known as Tonaghneeve (many variant spellings).

Barony: Castlereagh Upper
Diocese: Down
Place: Saintfield
Graveyards: Saintfield CI, Saintfield 1st P

Church records
CI Saintfield

Baptisms, 1724–57, 1793– ; marriages, 1724–57, 1798; vestry minutes, 1730–	MIC1/69/1

For at least part of the 1700s the vestry also represented the neighbouring parishes of Killaney and Kilmood. The vestry minutes include the names of collectors by townland (typically two collectors per townland), 1797; subscriptions for the relief of the poor (names of subscribers arranged by townland), 1801.

P 1st Saintfield
Call to Rev. Henry Simpson, 1799: over 100 names – printed in *Saintfield Heritage*, 4 (1994), pp 57–8

Estate papers
Hamilton (Claneboye and Clanbrassil) estate; Downshire estates; Hutcheson estate; Maxwell estate; Price estate; Wallace estate

Census substitutes
HSM, FL, AC

Other records
List of those from the Saintfield area who claimed for compensation after the 1798 Rebellion – D1759/3/B/8 (MIC637/10)
'Annals of Saintfield' in connection with William Spratt (1768–1846) – T1665/1

Publications
M. C. Perceval-Price, *Saintfield Parish under the Microscope* (n.d.)
David Stewart, *Historical Memoirs of First Saintfield Congregation (Tonaghneave), through three centuries, 1658–1958, with notices of the history of the parish, and development of the town of Saintfield* (1958)

SAUL PARISH, COUNTY DOWN

Barony: Lecale Lower
Diocese: Down
Graveyard: Saul CI

Church records
For early CI records see **Down**

Estate papers
Ardglass estate; Leslie estate; Southwell estate; Ward estate

Census substitutes
FL, AC

SCRABBY PARISH, COUNTY CAVAN
This parish has also been known as Ballimackelleny (spelled variously).

Barony: Tullyhunco
Diocese: Ardagh
Place: Loch (or Lough) Gowna (formerly Scrabby)
Graveyard: Loch Gowna CI

Estate papers
Borrowes estate; Gosford estate

Census substitutes
FL (it is possible that names from Scrabby have been listed under 'Columkil')

Other records
Map of the lands of Streneniogh, parish of Clones, 1733: townlands included are
Corflough, County Fermanagh, Coolnamarrow, County Fermanagh and Scrabby,
County Cavan – NAI, M/319

Publications
Edward J. Boylan, *The parish of Mullahoran (Drumlumman North and Loughduff)*
    (1977)
Edward J. Boylan, *Scrabby and Colmcille East (Lough Gowna and Mullinalaghta)*
    A History (1992)
Frank Columb, *The Lough Gowna Valley* (2002)
Niall J. Sloane *A History of Loch Gowna Parish Church* (2001)

SEAGOE PARISH, COUNTY ARMAGH
The parish of **Montiaghs** was detached from Seagoe in 1765.

Barony: Oneilland East
Diocese: Dromore

Places: Knocknamuckly, Portadown
Graveyards: Lynastown Quaker, Seagoe Old

CI Seagoe

Baptisms, 1672–1731, 1735– ; marriages,   MIC1/73, 74A, 75
1672–1731, 1735– ; burials, 1672–1731,
1735– ; vestry minutes, 1683–

The vestry minutes include over 130 names arranged by townland of those required
to plant trees, 1709; and a series of poor lists beginning in 1691 (some of which
distinguish between Protestant and Catholic poor).

Typescript indexes to baptisms, marriages and burials, 1672–1919, are available in
the Search Room in PRONI and in the UHF library

Analysis of registers of baptisms,   T2588
marriages and burials, 1672–1904

Estate papers
Brownlow estate; Burges estate; MacGeough-Bond estate; Magenis estate, Dromara;
Manchester estate; Richardson estate, Bocombra

Census substitutes
HMR, FL

Freemason's records
Lodge Roll of Tartaraghan, Portadown, and Eglish [Masonic?] lodges, 1793–1828 –
D871/7

Other records
List of those willing to attend linen market at Portadown, 1761: 37 names plus
residences – *Belfast Newsletter*, 4 Dec. 1761

Publications
Arthur G. Chapman, *100 Years and More – History of Friends in Portadown* (2005)
F. X. McCorry, *Seagoe: A Parish History* (1987)
F. X. McCorry, *Parish Registers: Historical Treasures in Manuscript* (2004): includes
    information from the Seagoe CI registers
Material of interest can be found in *Review: Journal of Craigavon Historical Society*

SEAPATRICK PARISH, COUNTY DOWN

Barony: Iveagh Upper (Upper Half)
Diocese: Dromore
Place: Banbridge
Graveyards: Banbridge 1st P (NSP), Seapatrick Old

Church records
P Banbridge
This congregation divided in the late 1820s over the Arian controversy and is now
represented by Banbridge Non-Subscribing Presbyterian Church and Scarva Street
Presbyterian Church.

Baptisms, 1754–94; marriages, 1756–94	CR4/6/B/1; T2995/1
Memorandum book, *c.* 1728–40, of Rev. Archibald Maclaine, minister of this congregation 1720–40: some personal family records, comment on contemporary events, including emigration, theological discussions, with additional entries by his son Archibald who emigrated to America in 1750	Wilson Library, University of North Carolina at Chapel Hill, MS 2313 (digitised copy on university's website)

Estate papers
Downshire estate; Dungannon estate; Fortescue estate; Whyte estate

Census substitutes
CPH, RelC (Protestants and Catholics), DP (Seapatrick, Tullylish and
Donochclony), FL

Freemasonry records
Papers of Masonic lodge no. 336, Banbridge, including an indexed account book
giving members' names and subscriptions, and other accounts, 1786–1828 – MIC249

Publications
R. Linn, *A History of Banbridge*, edited by W. S. Kerr (1935)
R. Stephens, *The Parish of Seapatrick* (n.d.)
R. S. J. Clarke (ed.), *The Heart of Downe. Old Banbridge Families from Gravestone
    Inscriptions, Wills and Biographical Notes* (1989)

SHANKILL PARISH, COUNTY ANTRIM

Baronies: Belfast Upper, Belfast Lower
Diocese: Connor
Places: Belfast, Ligoniel, Malone, Stranmillis
Graveyards: Friar's Bush, New Burying Ground (Clifton Street), Shankill

Church records
CI St Anne's, Shankill

Baptisms, 1745– ; marriages, 1745; burials, 1745–69, 1784– ; indexes to baptisms, marriages and burials, 1745–	T679/224, 225, 237, 238, 256 (MIC583/18, 22, 23); MIC178A/12–18
Typed copy of marriages, 1745–99	D1759/1C/2 (MIC637/2)
Typed transcript of burial registers, 1745–71	MIC583/19, 22

Register of the Parish of Shankill, Belfast,
1745–1761, edited by Raymond Gillespie
and Alison O'Keeffe (2006)

NSP First Congregation, Rosemary Street, Belfast
Baptisms, 1757– ; marriages, 1790– ; burials,   CR4/5/1/1–3
1712–36, with funeral accounts, lists of
members, 1760, 1775, 1781, 1783, 1790

See Gordon, *Historic Memorials of the First Presbyterian Church of Belfast* which
includes: baptisms, 1757–90 (pp 58–63), funeral register, 1712–36 (pp 64–94), lists
of members, 1760, 1775, 1790 (pp 97–8, 101), list of subscribers to the building
fund of the meeting house, 1781 (pp 99–100), list of 'The Ladys of Belfast' who
subscribed for the new pulpit, 1783 (p. 100)

Funeral Register of Rosemary Street Non-Subscribing Presbyterian Church (known as the
First Presbyterian Church of Belfast), 1712–36, edited by Jean Agnew (1995).

Subscribers to the meeting house building fund, 1781 – printed in Stewart, *Belfast*
Royal Academy, pp 104–05

NSP Second Congregation, Rosemary Street, Belfast (now All Souls)
Baptisms, 1782–92; marriages,   CR4/9/A/1
1771–87; poor accounts, 1792–

P Third Congregation, Rosemary Street, Belfast (now Rosemary)
Baptisms, *c.* 1723– (including index); marriages,   CR3/32/B/1/10;
c. 1741– (including index); pew rent books,   MIC1P/7/1–2; 1726–73,
1788–96; lists of communicants, 1728–42;   T654/1–3, 6–7
lists of catechisable persons, 1725–6;
committee minutes, 1774– ; accounts,
1721–70; stipend book, 1789–

Typed copy of marriages, 1741–61, with index   D1759/1C/1 (MIC637/2)

RC Belfast (originally St Mary's)
Baptisms, 1798– ; marriages, 1798– ;   MIC1D/66–67; CR2/20
printed history, 1784–1984

Estate papers
Banks estate; Donegall estate; Haliday estate; Legg estate; Saunders estate

Census substitutes
HMR, DP

Corporation records: Belfast
The corporation minutes of Belfast have been published as *The Town Book of the*
Corporation of Belfast, 1613–1816, edited by R. M. Young (1892), including the

roll of freemen, 1635–1796 (pp 246–300). See MIC131/1 for a microfilm of the original.

Manuscript assembly book, 1751–1824 – LA/7/2/AA/1 (extracts printed in Samuel Shannon Millin, *Sidelights on Belfast History* (1932), pp 1–12)

Minute Book of the Police Committee, 1800–04 – LA/7/2/BA/1/1

Business records
Atkinson, Belfast; Belfast Cabinet-Makers; Belfast Chamber of Commerce; Belfast Harbour; Black, Belfast and Bordeaux; Brice, Belfast; Butle, Belfast; Ferguson, Belfast; Greg & Cunningham, Belfast; McCartney, Belfast; Mussenden, Belfast; Thom(p)son, Belfast

Freemasonry records
Notes on the Orange [Masonic] Lodge of Belfast (no. 257), including names of members, 1782–3 in Millin, *Sidelights on Belfast History*, pp 167–72

Other sources
List of names of lessees on the Donegall estate in Belfast, 1750–1815: arranged by occupation with nearly 400 names in all – T1641

List of free and independent inhabitants of Belfast, 1754: *c.* 120 names – *Belfast Newsletter*, 26 Feb. 1754

Depositions relating to properties in the Mill Street and Millfield areas of Belfast, 1757 – NLI, MS 17,847

Names of merchants, traders and inhabitants of Belfast, 1774: *c.* 60 names – *Belfast Newsletter*, 26–29 July 1774

Report of a meeting of the Marine Society whose membership was drawn from those presently or lately masters of ships, 1782 – *Belfast Newsletter*, 22–26 Nov. 1782 (also 3–7 Jan. 1783)

List of Belfast inhabitants who subscribed to a request for information on missing artillery pieces, 1798: *c.* 151 names – *Belfast Newletter*, 5 June 1798

Publications
There are numerous books on the history of Belfast. The following is a select list

Jean Agnew, *Belfast Merchant Families in the Seventeenth Century* (1996)
George Benn, *The History of the Town of Belfast* (1823)
George Benn, *A History of the Town of Belfast*, 2 vols (1877–80)
Hugh T. Combe, *The Dowry of the Past: The Story of Berry Street Presbyterian Church, Belfast, c. 1770–1969* (1969)
Roger Courtney, *Second Congregation Belfast, 1708–2008* (2008)
Raymond Gillespie, *Early Belfast: The Origins and Growth of an Ulster Town to 1750* (2007)
Raymond Gillespie and Stephen Royle, *Irish Historic Towns Atlas: Belfast Part I, to 1840* (2003)

A. G. Gordon, *Historic Memorials of the First Presbyterian Church of Belfast* (1887)
J. W. Kernohan, *Rosemary Street Presbyterian Church: A Record of the Last 200 Years* (1923)
James McConnell, *Presbyterianism in Belfast* (1912)
Samuel Shannon Millin, *History of the Second Congregation of Protestant Dissenters in Belfast, 1708–1896* (1900)
Samuel Shannon Millin, *Sidelights on Belfast History* (1932), includes: facsimile of the petition of the 'Merchant Importers' of Belfast, 1777 (p. 52), facsimile of the petition of the 'Merchants, Linen Drapers & Linen Manufacturers' in and near Belfast, 1780 (p. 56), facsimile of the petition of the 'Merchants, Traders and Principal Inhabitants' of Belfast, 1785 (pp 58–9), facsimile of one page of signatures from the petition of the 'Merchants, Traders and Inhabitants' of Belfast, 1800 (p. 68)
Samuel Shannon Millin, *Additional Sidelights on Belfast History* (1938)
Tom Moore, *A History of The First Presbyterian Church Belfast, 1644–1983* (1983)
A. T. Q. Stewart, *Belfast Royal Academy: The First Century, 1785–1885* (1985)
R. W. Wilde, *Three Hundred Years of Worship, Work and Witness, 1644–1944* (1944)
Robert M. Young (ed.), *Historical Notices of Old Belfast and its Vicinity* (1896)

SHANKILL PARISH, COUNTIES ARMAGH AND DOWN

Baronies: Oneilland East (Armagh portion), Iveagh Lower (Upper Half) (Down portion)
Diocese: Dromore
Place: Lurgan
Graveyard: Shankill Old

Church records
CI Shankill
Baptisms, 1681– ; marriages, 1676– ;   MIC1/18, 24, 25
burials, 1675– ; vestry minutes, 1672–

The vestry minutes include: lists of the poor receiving alms on various dates; list of cess-payers for Lurgan, 1693; seatholders in the new parish church in 1725 with notes on the later disposal of seats; valuation of houses in Lurgan, 1782, 1795.

Churchwardens' accounts, 1790– ;   Local custody
list of churchwardens, 1760–

Seat-holders in parish church, 1725 – printed in *North Irish Roots*, 4:1 (1993), pp 4–6

P 1st Lurgan
Baptisms, 1746– (including index);   MIC1P/71
marriages, 1746, 1754, 1759

RSF Lurgan

Births, 1632– ; marriages, 1632– ; burials, 1632– ;   MIC16/24–33
minutes of men's meetings, 1675– ; minutes of
women's meetings, 1794– ; removal certificates,
1796– ; testimonies of disownment, 1688–96;
testimonies against Quakers, 1673–1700

Estate papers
Brownlow estate

Census substitutes
HMR, CPH, HSM

Freemasonry records
Transcripts of minutes, 1789–1804, and accounts, 1742–1843, of Masonic lodge
    no. 134, Lurgan – GLI
Minutes of Masonic lodge no. 394, Lurgan, 1763–1826 – GLI

Other records
List of tenants in the manor of Brownlow's-Derry, *c.* 1670–1799 (572 names plus
    occupations and residences) – compiled by W. H. Crawford and printed in
    Familia, 16 (2000), pp 51–60
Lurgan Free School records, 1786–95 – D1928/S (transcribed by Florence Gracey
    and printed in *DIFHR*, 33 (2010), pp 4–12)

Publications
Arthur G. Chapman, *History of the Religious Society of Friends in Lurgan* (1997)
F. X. McCorry, *Lurgan: An Irish Provincial Town, 1610–1970* (1993)
F. X. McCorry, *Parish Registers: Historical Treasures in Manuscript* (2004): includes
    information from the Shankill CI registers and Lurgan Quaker records
Material of interest can be found in *Review: Journal of Craigavon Historical Society*.

SHERCOCK, COUNTY CAVAN
This parish is also known as Killan(n). In the late eighteenth century a portion of it
was detached to form the parish of **Bailieborough**.

Barony: Clankee
Diocese: Kilmore
Places: Glasleck, Shercock

Estate papers
Fitzherbert estate; Kilmore bishopric estate

Census substitutes
FL (as Killan)

SKERRY PARISH, COUNTY ANTRIM

Barony: Antrim Lower
Diocese: Connor
Places: Aughafatten, Martinstown
Graveyard: Skerry Old

Estate papers
Mount Cashell estate; O'Neill estate

Census substitutes
HMR, FL

Publications
Felix McKillop, *The Valley of the Braid: A Local History* (2010)
Felix McKillop, *Along the Ravel and Clough Water* (2012)

SLANES, COUNTY DOWN

Barony: Ards Upper
Diocese: Down
Graveyard: Slanes

Church records
For CI records see **Ballyphilip**

STRANORLAR PARISH, COUNTY DONEGAL

Barony: Raphoe South
Diocese: Raphoe
Places: Ballybofey, Stranorlar
Graveyard: Stranorlar CI

Estate papers
Hayes estate; Lifford estate; McCausland estate; Raphoe bishopric estate

Census substitutes
HMR, FL

Other records
Petition from the poor of Ballybofey and Stranorlar, 1801', *Donegal Annual*, 6:1
(1964), p. 91: no names

Publications
Ivan and Mark Knox, *Centenary Celebrations: Stranorlar Presbyterian Church* (2006)

TAMLAGHT PARISH, COUNTIES LONDONDERRY AND TYRONE

Baronies: Loughinsholin (Londonderry portion), Dungannon Upper (Tyrone portion)
Diocese: Armagh
Place: Coagh
Graveyard: Tamlaght CI

Church records
P Coagh
Names of some members, 1709   *RGSU*, vol. 1, p. 176
(see p. 58 of this book)

Estate papers
Armagh archbishopric estate; Drapers' Company estate; Lenox-Conyngham estate

Census substitutes
HMR, CPH, DP (Coagh), FL

Publications
Ivor Smith, *Three Hundred Years and Still Praising: Coagh Presbyterian Church Tercentenary* (2008)

TAMLAGHT FINLAGAN PARISH, COUNTY LONDONDERRY

Barony: Keenaght
Diocese: Derry
Places: Ballykelly, Drumraighland, Glack, Myroe
Graveyards: Tamlaght Old, Walworth

Church records
CI Tamlaght Finlagan
Baptisms, 1796– ; marriages, 1796– ;   MIC1/38/1
burials, 1796 – ; vestry minutes, 1748–

Index to the registers, 1796–1861   CR1/8/1

The vestry minutes include the names of those who broke into the church in 1774 and added their own statement to the book; there were over 20 signatories to a meeting in 1801

P Ballykelly
Baptisms, 1699–1709 (including index);   MIC1P/208
marriages, 1699–1740 (including index)

Estate papers
Conolly estate; Derry bishopric estate; Fishmongers' Company estate; Grocers' Company estate; Phillips estate

Census substitutes
HMR, DE, CPH (includes townlands), FL

Other records
Freeholders from Tamlaght Finlagan parish, 1774: 136 names and addresses –
D2094/46

Publications
James Stevens Curl, *The History, Architecture and Planning of the Estates of the
    Fishmongers' Company in Ulster* (1981)
Harold Gough, *Tamlaghtfinlagan: 'An Historic Church'* (1995)
R. J. Hunter, 'The Fishmongers' Company of London and the Londonderry
    Plantation, 1609–41' in G. O'Brien (ed.), *Derry & Londonderry: History and
    Society* (1999) pp 205–58 (reprinted in R. J. Hunter, *Ulster Transformed: Essays
    on Plantation and Print Culture, c.1590–1641* (2012))

TAMLAGHT O'CRILLY PARISH, COUNTY LONDONDERRY
This parish was divided into Upper and Lower sections in 1775.

Baronies: Coleraine, Loughinsholin
Diocese: Derry
Places: Bovedy, Churchtown, Clady, Glenone, Inishrush
Graveyards: Tamlaght O'Crilly Lower CI, Tamlaght O'Crilly Upper CI

Estate papers
Beresford estate; Conolly estate; Derry bishopric estate; Mercers' Company estate;
Rowley estate; Strafford estate; Vintners' Company estate

Census substitutes
HMR, CPH, HSM, FL

Other records
Loyal declaration by the inhabitants of Kilrea and Tamlaght O'Crilly, 1745–6: over
130 names – MIC1/55

Publications
J. W. Kernohan, *Two Ulster Parishes: Kilrea and Tamlaght O'Crilly* (1912; reprinted
1993): includes loyal declaration by the inhabitants of Kilrea and Tamlaght O'Crilly,
1745–6

TARTARAGHAN PARISH, COUNTY ARMAGH

Barony: Oneilland West
Diocese: Armagh
Places: The Birches, Maghery, Tartaraghan
Graveyards: Maghery, Tartaraghan CI, Toby Hole

Estate papers
Armagh archbishopric estate; Atkinson and Hoop(e) estate; Brownlow estate; Charlemont estate; Nicholson estate; Obre estate; Roe estate; Verner estate

Census substitutes
HMR, VAA, FL

Freemasonry records
Lodge Roll of Tartaraghan, Portadown, and Eglish [?Masonic] lodges, 1793–1828 – D871/7

Other records
Petition of the inhabitants of Tartaraghan against the proposal of the archbishop of Armagh to annex them to the parish of Loughgall, 1700 – DIO/4/32/T/2/6

Publications
H. W. Coffey, *A History of Milltown Parish, The Birches, North-West Armagh* (1950)

TAUGHBOYNE PARISH, COUNTY DONEGAL

Barony: Raphoe North
Diocese: Raphoe
Place: St Johnston
Graveyards: St Johnston Old, Taughboyne CI

Church records
CI Taughboyne
Vestry minutes, 1796   MIC1/174D/1

Estate papers
Abercorn estate; Forward estate; Raphoe bishopric estate

Census substitutes
HMR, LP (Taboyn/Monreagh), FL

Publications
Guide to the Districts of St Johnston, Carrigans and Newtowncunningham (1979)
S. M. Campbell, *The Laggan and its People* (n.d.)
D. W. T. Crooks, *In the Footsteps of St Baithin. A History of Taughboyne Group* (1992)
Bertie Roulston, *A History of Monreagh Presbyterian Church, 1644–1994* (1994)

TEDAVNET PARISH, COUNTY MONAGHAN
The name of this parish is also spelled Tydavnet.

Barony: Monaghan
Diocese: Clogher
Places: Ballinode, Ballyalbany, Scotstown, Tydavnet
Graveyard: Tedavnet Old

Church records
P Ballyalbany (originally Secession)
List of over 160 names of individuals who subscribed to a call for a minister for Ballyalbany Presbyterian Church in 1751 and a list of seatholders in the church in 1804 – printed in Orr and Haslett, *Historical Sketch of Ballyalbany Presbyterian Church*, pp 10–12, 64–9

Estate papers
Blayney estate; Clogher bishopric estate; Crofton estate; Evatt estate; Rossmore estate

Census substitutes
HMR, FL

Publications
S. Lyle Orr and Alex Haslett, *Historical Sketch of Ballyalbany Presbyterian Church* (1940)

TEHALLAN PARISH, COUNTY MONAGHAN
The name of this parish is also spelled Tyholland.

Baronies: Cremorne, Monaghan
Diocese: Clogher
Graveyard: Tyholland CI

Church records
CI Tyholland
Baptisms, marriages and burial, 1671–2 (see under **Monaghan**)

Vestry minutes, 1712–   Local custody

Estate papers
Clogher bishopric estate; Leslie estate, Glaslough

Census substitutes
HMR, FL

TEMPLECARN PARISH, COUNTIES DONEGAL AND FERMANAGH

Barony: Tirhugh
Diocese: Clogher
Place: Pettigo
Graveyards: Caldragh, Carn

Church records
CI Templecarn
Vestry minutes, 1777–   Local custody

Estate papers
Caldwell estate; Clogher bishopric estate; Lenox estate; Leslie estate

Census substitutes
HMR, FL

Publications
P. O Gallachair, *The Parish of Carn* (n.d.)
M. L. Thompson, *'The Meeting-House Beside the Big Bush': A History of Pettigo Presbyterian Church* (2000)

TEMPLECORRAN PARISH, COUNTY ANTRIM

Barony: Belfast Lower
Diocese: Connor
Places: Ballycarry, Red Hall, Whitehead
Graveyard: Templecorran Old

Church records
P Ballycarry
In 1829, this congregation divided over the Arian controversy and is now represented by Ballycarry Presbyterian Church and the Old Presbyterian Church (Non-Subscribing), Ballycarry.

Session minutes, 1704–80   CR3/31/1–2; CR4/18/1

Estate papers
Edmonstone estate

Census substitutes
HMR (included under heading 'Brode Island Parish')

Publications
Avy Dowlin, *Ballycarry in Olden Days* (1963)
G. A. J. Farquhar, *Ballycarry Presbyterian Church 1613–2013: Memories Fresh and Old* (2013)
J. W. Nelson, *Ballycarry Old Presbyterian Church. A Brief History of the Present Church Building 1710–2010* (2010)

TEMPLECRONE PARISH, COUNTY DONEGAL

Barony: Boylagh
Diocese: Raphoe
Places: Annag(a)ry, Arranmore Island, Burtonport, Dungloe, Kincasslagh, Rannafast, The Rosses
Graveyard: Templecrone Old

Church records
CI Templecrone
Vestry minutes, 1776–   Local custody

Estate papers
Murray of Broughton estate; Raphoe bishopric estate

Census substitutes
HMR

Other records
Protestant householders, 1799, with churchwardens from 1775 onwards – printed in
The Irish Ancestor, 16 (1984), pp 78–9

Publications
Wes Forsythe, 'Improving landlords and planned settlements in eighteenth-century
    Ireland: William Burton Conyngham and the fishing station on Inis Mhic an
    Doirn, Co. Donegal', *PRIA*, 112C (2012), pp 301–32
Ben O'Donnell, *The Story of the Rosses* (1999)

TEMPLEMORE PARISH, COUNTIES DONEGAL AND LONDONDERRY

Until the nineteenth century Templemore also included what are now the parishes of
Burt, **Inch** and **Muff** in County Donegal.

Baronies: Inishowen West (Donegal portion), North-West Liberties of Londonderry
    (Londonderry portion)
Diocese: Derry
Places: Creggan, Culmore, Derry-Londonderry
Graveyards: Culmore CI, Killea, Long Tower RC, St Augustine's CI, St Columb's
    Cathedral

Church records
CI St Columb's Cathedral
Baptisms, 1642– ; marriages, 1649– ;   MIC1/18, 19, 20,
burials, 1642–1775; vestry minutes, 1741–93   26, 27, 28

The parish registers have been published as:
Registers of Derry Cathedral, 1642–1703 (1910)
Register of the Cathedral Church of St Columb, Derry, 1703–32 (1997)
Register of the Cathedral Church of St Columb, Derry, 1732–75 (1999)

The vestry minutes are very detailed with high attendances at vestry meetings (over
40 signatories was not unusual). There are extensive lists of cess payers for the parish
for many years from 1741 onwards (see below for transcripts). The records also
include information on the allocation of vacant seats in the cathedral, including a
plan of the cathedral showing the seating arrangements, 1746–7. Detailed

information is given on the allocation of church funds, e.g. a list of 34 orphans who were to be maintained, 1779.

Parish cess applotments and lists, 1742–53: includes the city and suburbs of Londonderry, Burt, Elough (Elagh), Muff and the Upper and Lower Liberties	T1020/1–2
Extracts from vestry book, 1772–84	T945/1; T946/1

P 1st Derry

Harvey Fund account book, 1790–1926	T2711/3B/1

Estate papers
Derry bishopric estate; Hart estate; Irish Society estate

Census substitutes
HMR, LP (Londonderry), CPH (includes townlands), DP (Londonderry plus Established Church petition), FL

Corporation records: Londonderry
Minute books of the corporation, 1673–1841 (with gaps) – LA/79/2AA/1–11B (available on the PRONI website); the minutes of 1696 include a resolution condemning a plot to assassinate William III, which has the names of 226 subscribers
Names of occupiers of corporation lands, 1694 – D683/238 (printed in Moody and Simms, *Bishopric of Derry and the Irish Society of London*, vol. 2, pp 155–8)

Business records
Ferguson, Londonderry; McCrea, Foyle Valley

Other records
'A particular of the howses and familyes in London Derry', 15 May 1628 – D683/42 (MIC517/1) (printed in printed in C. S. King (ed.), *A Particular of the Howses and Famylyes in London Derry, May 15 1628* (1936) and in Moody and Simms, *Bishopric of Derry and the Irish Society of London*, vol. 1, pp 154–60)
Indenture made between the 'Mayor, Comonaltie and Citizens' of Londonderry and Robert Rochfort, David Cairnes and John Mogridge; the latter were to act on behalf of the former in seeking compensation for their debts and disbursements sustained in the recent siege, 1691: over 200 names, both men and women – T1847/12
Newspaper cutting of *c.* 1920 which included the names of the members of Ferry-Quay Ward Yeomanry corps, 1798 – T1638/6/12
Inhabitants of the city of Londonderry who subscribed to a petition in relation to the proposed legislative union of Great Britain and Ireland, 1799 – printed in *DIFHR*, 24 (2001), pp 87–9

Second half of a list of names and addresses of people living in or near Londonderry, n.d. [late 18th century]: over 80 names – D2798/3/87

Publications
Brian Lacy, *Siege City: The Story of Derry and Londonderry* (1990)
Brian Mitchell, *Derry: A City Invincible* (2018)
Seoirse Ó Dochartaigh, *Inis Eoghain: The Island of Eoghan: The Place-Names of Inishowen* (2011)
Avril Thomas, *Irish Historic Towns Atlas: Derry-Londonderry* (2005)
J. D. Young, *First Derry Presbyterian Church. A History of the Church, 1642–1992* (1993)

TEMPLEPATRICK PARISH, COUNTY ANTRIM

Baronies: Belfast Upper, Belfast Lower
Diocese: Connor
Places: Lyle's Hill, Templepatrick
Graveyards: Templepatrick Old, Umgall

Church records
P Lylehill (originally Secession)
Pew rent book (?), 1798–1806   PHSI

[A stipend book, 1768–92, in PHSI previously listed for Lylehill is now thought to relate to 1st Coleraine.]

P Templepatrick
Around 1830 this congregation divided and is now represented by Templepatrick Presbyterian Chuch and Templepatrick Non-Subscribing Presbyterian Church.

Baptisms, 1796– ; marriages, 1797– ;   MIC1B/11/1;
accounts, 1799– ; session minutes, 1646–1743;   CR4/12B/1
farm accounts, 1799–1812

Baptisms (extracts only), 1758– ; marriages, 1797–   PHSI

Extensive extracts from the session records are included in 'The old session-book of Templepatrick Presbyterian Church', edited by W. T. Latimer, *JRSAI*, 5th series, 5 (1895), pp 130–34; 11 (1901), pp 162–75

Estate papers
Upton estate

Census substitutes
HMR, HSM

Other records
Names of tenant farmers, 1768–9 – *Belfast Newsletter*, 26 July 1768, 15 Nov. 1768, 28 March 1769

Publications
A. McN. R. McBride, *Lylehill Presbyterian Church 1741–1941* (1940)
S. M. Stephenson, *A Historical Essay on the Parish and Congregation of Templepatrick* (1825)
S. E. Adair, *Templepatrick 1619–1969: The Story of the Congregation* (1969)

TEMPLEPORT PARISH, COUNTY CAVAN

Barony: Tullyhaw
Diocese: Kilmore
Places: Ballymagauran, Bawnboy
Graveyard: St Mogue's Island

Estate papers
Annesley estate; Armagh archbishopric estate; Farnham estate

Census substitutes
HMR

Publications
Chris Maguire, *Bawnboy and Templeport: History Heritage Folklore* (1999)

TERMONAMONGAN PARISH, COUNTY TYRONE

Barony: Omagh West
Diocese: Derry
Places: Aghyaran, Killen, Killeter
Graveyards: Magherakeel, Termonamongan CI

Estate papers
Castle Stewart estate; Derry bishopric estate; Huntingdon estate

Census substitutes
HMR, FL

Other records
List of suspected United Irishmen to be apprehended, 1798: over 40 names mainly from Termonamongan parish – printed in Brendan McEvoy, *The United Irishmen in County Tyrone* (1998), pp 37–8

TERMONEENY PARISH, COUNTY LONDONDERRY

Barony: Loughinsholin
Diocese: Derry
Place: Knockcloughrim
Graveyard: Mullagh

Church records
For CI records see **Maghera**

Estate papers
Conolly estate; Derry bishopric estate; Vintners' Company estate

Census substitutes
HMR, DE, CPH, FL

TERMONMAGUIRK PARISH, COUNTY TYRONE

Barony: Strabane Upper
Diocese: Armagh
Places: Carrickmore, Creggan, Drumnakilly, Loughmacrory, Sixmilecross
Graveyard: Termonamaguirk (Carrickmore) Old

Church records
CI Termonmaguirk
Vestry book, 1786–   MIC1/340D/1; CR1/46/1

The vestry minutes include petitions from parishioners, one with *c*. 25 names, the other with *c*. 30 names, 1786; lists of the poor, 1791, 1794.

Estate papers
Armagh archbishopric estate; Belmore estate; Mervyn estate; Stewart estate, Termonmaguirk

Census substitutes
PB, HMR, FP, VAA, FL

Other records
Volume containing a list of the names of 'housekeepers' in 'Termont' (Termonmagurk), 1780: this lists 524 householders in all by townland (414 Roman Catholic, 58 Presbyterian and 52 Church of Ireland) – DIO/4/32/T/4/4/1

Publications
Glimpses of Carrickmore (2000)

TICKMACREVAN PARISH, COUNTY ANTRIM

Barony: Glenarm Lower
Diocese: Connor
Places: Carnalbanagh, Glenarm
Graveyards: Glore, Tickmacrevan CI

Church records
CI Tickmacrevan or Glenarm
Baptisms, 1719–23, 1727, 1788– ; indexes to   MIC1/72/1; T3054
baptisms, 1788– ; marriages, 1719, 1723, 1727–8,
1789– ; index to marriages, 1719–28 and 1788– ;
vestry minutes, 1718– ; transcript of vestry minutes,
1718– ; with marriages, 1719, 1723, 1727–8,
and baptisms, 1719–23

The vestry minutes include a list of the poor divided into first class and second class, 1788/9 (over 30 names); affidavit by parishioners which begins, 'We do voluntarily swear that we do not hold any lands or tenements to the yearly value of five pounds …', 1793 (*c.* 60 names organised by townland); list of the poor, 1799.

P Glenarm
Names of some members of the congregation in 1772 in connection with the liquidation of debts due to the minister and the perfecting of bonds to the minister – printed in S. Alex Blair, 'Presbyterianism in Glenarm', *The Glynns*, 9 (1981), pp 37–51

Estate papers
Agnew estate; Antrim estate; McNaghten estate; Stewart estate, Glenarm

Census substitutes
HMR, DP (Larne, Raloo, Carncastle, Kilwaughter, Glenarm and Ballyeaston)

Other records
Volumes of notes on the history of the Glenarm area – T3054/C

Publications
Jimmy Irvine, 'A map of Glenarm – 1779', *The Glynns*, 9 (1981), pp 52–61 (names tenants in Glenarm)
Felix McKillop, *Glenarm: A Local History* (1987)

TOMREGAN PARISH, COUNTIES CAVAN AND FERMANAGH

Baronies: Loughtee Lower, Tullyhaw (Cavan portion), Knockninny (Fermanagh portion)
Diocese: Kilmore
Place: Ballyconnell
Graveyard: Tomregan CI

Church records
CI Tomregan
Baptisms, 1797–   MIC1/218A/1

Estate papers
Annesley estate; Armagh archbishopric estate

Census substitutes
HMR

Publications
Beneath Slieve Rushen's Slopes: Kildallan-Tomregan ... (2000)

TRORY PARISH, COUNTY FERMANAGH
This parish was created out of **Devenish** *c.* 1779.

Barony: Tirkennedy
Diocese: Clogher
Places: Ballycassidy, Killadeas
Graveyards: Killadeas CI, Trory CI

Church records
CI Trory
Baptisms, 1779, 1784, 1796– ; marriages,   MIC1/94/1; CR1/19D/1
1779, 1799; vestry minutes, 1778–

Estate papers
Archdale estate; Clogher bishopric estate; Huntingdon estate

Census substitutes
FL

Other records
Names of male Protestants aged 17 and over, 1785 – T808/15259

Publications
J. A. M. McNutt, *The Story of Trory* (1978)

TULLAGHOBEGLEY PARISH, COUNTY DONEGAL

Barony: Kilmacrenan
Diocese: Raphoe
Places: Bloody Foreland, Bunbeg, Crolly, Dunlewey, Falcarragh, Gola Island,
    Gweedore, Tory Island
Graveyard: Tullaghobegly Old

Estate papers
Raphoe bishopric estate

Census substitutes
HMR

Publications
Gerry McLaughlin, *Cloughaneely: Myth and Fact* (2002)
Cathal Ó Searcaigh, *Tulach Beaglaoich Inne agus Inniu (Tullaghobegley Past and Present)* [*c*. 1993]

TULLYAUGHNISH see AUGHNISH

TULLYCORBET PARISH, COUNTY MONAGHAN
The parish of **Ballybay** was created partly out of Tullycorbet in 1798.

Barony: Cremorne, Monaghan
Diocese: Clogher
Place: Cahans
Graveyard: Cahans P, Tullycorbet Old

Church records
CI Tullycorbet
Baptisms, 1796–   MIC1/44

Index to baptisms, 1796–   CR1/44

P Cahans (originally Secession)
Baptisms, 1751–9, 1767– ; session minutes   CR3/25A/1, 2, 4
with discipline cases, 1751– ; indexes to
baptisms, and session minutes, 1751–

Marriages, 1770–1802   PHSI

Estate papers
Barton estate; Clogher bishopric estate; Dawson estate; Massereene estate

Census substitutes
HMR (included with Aghnamullen), FL

Publications
David Nesbitt, *Full Circle: A Story of Ballybay Presbyterians* (1999): includes the
subscribers to the call from Cahans to Rev. Thomas Clark, 1751; adult male
members of Clark's congregation who moved to Salem, New York, in 1764

TULLYFERN PARISH, COUNTY DONEGAL

Barony: Kilmacrenan
Diocese: Raphoe
Places: Kerrykeel, Milford
Graveyard: Tully

Estate papers
Clements estate; Grove estate; Raphoe bishopric estate; Trinity College Dublin estate;
Wray estate

Census substitutes
HMR, LP (Fannet), FL

Publications
Sheila Friel, *Milford: Towards the Millennium* (1997): reproduces a petition from the
inhabitants of the Trinity College lands regarding the reinstatement of John Breading
as tenant, 1698

TULLYLISH PARISH, COUNTY DOWN

Barony: Iveagh Lower (Upper Half)
Diocese: Dromore
Places: Bleary, Gilford, Lawrencetown, Tullylish
Graveyards: Lawrencetown RC, Moyallon Quaker, Tullylish Old, Tullylish P

Church records
CI Tullylish
Vestry minutes and accounts, 1792–   MIC1/71/1

Estate papers
Clanwilliam estate; Downshire estate; Hall estate, Strangford and Lower Iveagh;
Johnston estate; Lawrence estate

Census substitutes
DP (Seapatrick, Tullylish and Donochclony), FL

Other records
Names of 90 persons excommunicated by Church of Ireland diocese of Dromore
    between 1725 and 1740 – T426/1, pp 47–8
Marriage licences (28 entries), 1734–56, providing names and addresses – T426/1,
    pp 95–7
Resolution of linen drapers, freeholders and inhabitants of the Gilford area, 1772 –
    Belfast Newsletter, 29 May 1772
Copy of case for the Crown relating to certain indictments at Downpatrick assizes,
    April 1772, which concerned the murder of Rev. Samuel Morrell (Presbyterian
    minister of Tullylish), the destruction of Richard Johnston's house at Gilford, and
    the tendering of 'oaths and solemn engagements and other felonys against the late
    Acts', February 1773 – D207/1/12

Publications
M. P. Campbell, *A History of Tullylish* [1983]
R. S. J. Clarke (ed.), *The Heart of Downe. Old Banbridge Families from Gravestone
    Inscriptions, Wills and Biographical Notes* (1989)

Marilyn Cohen, *Linen, Family and Community in Tullylish, County Down 1690–1914* (1997)

R. I. Knight, *Tullylish Presbyterian Church, 1670–1970* (1970)

Joseph Nimmons, *Newmills Congregation, 1796–1947: Historical Sketch* (1948)

TULLYNAKILL PARISH, COUNTY DOWN

Barony: Castlereagh Lower
Diocese: Down
Place: Ardmillan
Graveyard: Tullynakill

Estate papers
Hamilton (Claneboye and Clanbrassil) estate; Downshire estate

TULLYNISKAN PARISH, COUNTY TYRONE
The name of this parish is also spelled Tullanisken.

Barony: Dungannon Middle
Diocese: Armagh
Place: Newmills
Graveyard: Tullaniskan CI

Church records
CI Tullaniskan
Baptisms, 1794– ; marriages, 1794– ;   MIC1/10A, 11
vestry minutes, 1791–

Estate papers
Armagh archbishopric estate; Castle Stewart estate

Census substitutes
HMR, VAA, RelC (Protestants and Catholics; includes townlands), FL

Freemasonry records
Minutes of Masonic lodge no. 182/774, New Mills, 1796–1836 – GLI

Publications
Eileen Elizabeth Donnelly, *A History of the Parish of Tullynisken, New Mills, Co. Tyrone, 1793–1993* (1993)

TULLYRUSK PARISH, COUNTY ANTRIM

Barony: Massereene Upper
Diocese: Connor
Places: Dundrod
Graveyard: Tullyrusk

Church records
For CI records see **Glenavy**

Estate papers
Conway estate

Census substitutes
HMR (included under Glenavy parish)

Publications
Charles Watson, *The Story of the United Parishes of Glenavy, Camlin and Tullyrusk* (1892)

TYNAN PARISH, COUNTY ARMAGH

Barony: Tiranny
Diocese: Armagh
Places: Killylea, Middletown, Tynan
Graveyard: Lislooney P, Tynan CI

Church records
CI Tynan

Baptisms, 1686–1723; marriages, 1683–1723; burials, 1683–1723; vestry minutes, 1699–	MIC1/12, 13, 18
Baptisms, 1686–95; marriages, 1683–1723; burials, 1683–1723	T808/15294

Transcriptions of baptisms, marriages and burials, 1683–1723, published in *Duiche Neill*, 15 (2006)

The vestry minutes include a list of names and addresses *c.* 1727 (possibly a poor list); details of the disposal of seats in the church, 1746; in general, much detail about the maintenance of roads in the parish and those responsible for this (see the article by Batchelor noted below).

Estate papers
Armagh archbishopric estate; Caledon estate; Houston estate; Johnston estate, Eglish; Maxwell estate; Stearne's Charity estate

Census substitutes
HMR, FP, VAA, CPH, FL

Freemasonry records
Minutes, 1787–1808, and accounts, 1787, of Masonic lodge no. 437, Middleton – GLI

Publications
John Batchelor, 'Tynan Church, County Armagh, and the people of the parish',
    Duiche Neill, 16 (2007), pp 149-77: extensive extracts from the vestry book
Thomas Hughes, *The History of Tynan Parish, County Armagh* (1910)
Seamus Mallon, *Historical Sketches of the Parish of Tynan and Middletown* (1995)
F. X. McCorry, *Parish Registers: Historical Treasures in Manuscript* (2004): includes
    information from the Tynan CI registers
J. J. Marshall, *History of the Parish of Tynan in the County of Armagh* (1932)

TYRELLA PARISH, COUNTY DOWN

Barony: Lecale Upper
Diocese: Down

Estate papers
Banks estate; Downshire estate; Ward estate

Census substitutes
FL, AC

Other records
View book of the great tithes of the deanery of Down, 1732 – D1145/D/1

URNEY PARISH, COUNTY CAVAN

Baronies: Loughtee Lower, Loughtee Upper
Diocese: Kilmore
Place: Cavan
Graveyards: Cavan Abbey, Urney Old

Church records
CI Urney (including the parish of Annageliffe)
Vestry minutes, 1737, 1741, 1753–99   MIC1/239

The vestry minutes include a list (purpose unknown) of *c.* 100 names, n.d. [*c.* 1753],
as well as poor lists, 1760–84 (that for 1775 has nearly 100 names)

Estate papers
Annesley estate; Farnham estate; Lanesborough estate; Pole estate; Saunderson estate

Census substitutes
HMR, FL

Corporation records: Cavan
Minutes of meetings of the town council, together with lists of conformist freemen,
    1697–1824, 1838–40 – NLI, MSS 5832–3
Corporation minute book, 1771–97 – Johnston Central Library, Cavan Town
    (microfilm)

Freemen of the borough of Cavan, 1697–1838 – printed in *Breifne*, 1:2 (1959), pp 87–112

Other records
Index from Registry of Deeds for Cavan Town, 1708–38 – T808/14142

Publications
Brendan Scott (ed.), *Cavan Town, 1610–2010: A Brief History* (2012)

URNEY PARISH, COUNTIES DONEGAL AND TYRONE

Baronies: Raphoe South (Donegal portion), Strabane Lower (Tyrone portion)
Diocese: Derry
Places: Castlederg, Clady, Sion Mills
Graveyards: Derg CI, Urney Old

Estate papers
Abercorn estate; Castle Stewart estate; Derry bishopric estate; Gage estate; Huntingdon estate

Census substitutes
HMR, LP (Urney), FL

Publications
T. P. Donnelly, *A History of the Parish of Ardstraw West and Castlederg* (1978)
William Haire, Craig Maxwell, *The Life and Times of Urney Presbyterian Church: 320 Years: 1654–2004* (2005)
Daniel McMenamin (ed.), *Urney: History, People, Place* (2011)
R. S. K. Neill, *A Short History of First Castlederg Presbyterian Church* (1993)
S. W. Thompson, *A Short History of Second Castlederg Presbyterian Church* (1953)

WARRENPOINT PARISH, COUNTY DOWN
This parish was formed *c.* 1840 out of **Clonallan**.

WITTER PARISH, COUNTY DOWN

Barony: Ards Upper
Diocese: Down

Church records:
For CI records see **Ballyphilip**

Estate papers
Savage-Nugent estate

Census substitutes
FL, AC

APPENDIX 2

Estate collections

This appendix lists by county some 350 estate collections with records from the seventeenth and eighteenth centuries. A detailed introduction to estate records is found in Chapter 6, which also includes suggestions for identifying the relevant estate collection. Each parish source guide in Appendix 1 lists relevant estate collections. While many of the estates listed below were held directly from the Crown by virtue of a royal patent, others were in the possession of middlemen, i.e. individuals who leased property from the owner of the estate and then sublet it to others. The latter scenario applied in particular to the estates of the London companies in County Londonderry and the bishopric lands in each diocese, though it pertained to many other situations as well.

While it has not been possible to list in detail every available pre-1800 estate record for Ulster, considerable efforts have been made to present the surviving material in as comprehensive and accessible a format as possible. Particular attention has been given to rentals (or rent rolls, rent books, etc), as generally these provide the easiest way of identifying a tenant farmer by townland. Collections of leases, particularly if these have been expertly catalogued by staff at PRONI, are also listed. Occasionally, records from just beyond 1800 have been included if these happen to be the earliest documents for a particular estate or contain material of particular value. It must be emphasised that there is great variability with regard to the quantity of material available for each estate. The larger collections run to thousands of individual items. On the other hand, for some estates there may be a solitary item from the pre-1800 period. It is important to note that even if records for a particular estate have suvived that is no guarantee that material exists for every townland in that estate.

Estates are listed under the name of the owner. This can be either the family surname or the aristocratic title held by the head of the family. The aristocratic title may have changed on a number of occasions during the seventeenth and eighteenth centuries. For example, the head of the landed Hill family rose through the ranks of the peerage on several occasions and was successively Viscount Hillsborough, earl of Hillsborough and marquess of Downshire. Cross-referencing is used to assist the researcher in identifying the relevant landed family. The location following the name of the landowner will usually be the main geographical focus of the estate or the name of the landowner's residence.

In a number of instances an individual landowner held lands in more than one county. If the nature of the estate collection allows it the records will be listed under the appropriate county. For example, the Belmore estate collection has been organised in such a way that it is possible to list separately the records pertaining to County Fermanagh and County Tyrone. On the other hand, the organisation of the Donegall estate collection means that it is not possible to divide the records properly between counties Antrim and Donegal. In this instance all Donegall estate material for the pre-1800 period has been grouped together under County Antrim. Cross-referencing is used to indicate if an estate archive with relevance to one county is listed under another county.

Depending on the volume and nature of the material in a particular collection, the available documentation may be listed by category or by the subdivisions of the estate (e.g. the manor). For instance, the Abercorn estate in counties Donegal and Tyrone was divided into five manors in the eighteenth century and the available records have been identified under each manor. Occasionally, the townlands covered by a particular document have been listed. Curly brackets – { } – have been used to indicate the pre-1800 parish in which these townlands are found. Brief introductions are given for a number of the collections listed below, though the researcher should also refer to the 'Introductions to significant privately deposited archives' that are available on the PRONI website, and also to the Collection Lists prepared by the National Library of Ireland and available on its website. Books and articles relating to particular estates are also noted.

COUNTY ANTRIM

Adair estate, Ballymena
Map of the estate of William Robert Adair, 1747: lands of Town & Parks of Ballymena, Drumfin, Dongall, Belley, Monaghan, Cabragh, Durniveagh, Clinty, Clogher, Craigywaren, Kirkinrela, Ballygarvey, Killyflugh, Drumfane, Dunclug, Bottam, Brucklymor {all Kirkinriola}, Loughmagary, Laymore, Ballyloghen, Corniny {all Ahoghill} – T1333/3
Map of estate, 1789 – T1310/1–3
Leases for Ballymena estate, 17th–18th century: catalogued in full, particularly good for 1680–1750 – D929 *passim*
Rent roll of the Ballymena estate, 1794 – D929/HA12/F3/2
Documentation relating to the Ballymena estate, 17th and 18th centuries – Suffolk Record Office (Lowestoft), 741/HA12

Adair estate, Loughanore
For more information on this estate, see the 'Introduction to the Adair of Loughanmore Papers' prepared by PRONI.

Ahoghill/Portglenone property
These lands, originally owned by the Stafford family, were purchased by Bishop Francis Hutchinson in 1728 and after his death in 1739 passed through a succession of owners (Hamilton, Crymble and Adair). The property comprised Ballybeg, Ballynafie, Carnearney, Craignageeragh and Limnaharry.
Leases, 1735–61, and an abstract of the leases subsisting in [1761?] – D3860/A/3
Leases issued by representative of the Crymble and Adair families, 1785–1846 – D3860/A/4

Straid property
Bundle of 25 leases of lands in Straid, parish of Ballynure, granted by Francis Clements of Straid, Edward Crymble of Clements Hill (Straid), Henry Clements Ellis of Prospect (Carrickfergus), etc, 1720–1830 – D3860/B/4

Carrickfergus property
Leases of Clements/Crymble/Ellis property in the town and liberties of Carrickfergus, 1652–1799 – D3860/B/5

Map of the estate of the late Francis Clements in Carrickfergus and County Antrim by William Hoy, 1751 – D3860/B/9

Loughanore property, etc
Account book containing rentals, accounts and valuations of the different estates of Thomas Benjamin Adair of Loughanmore, including Loughanmore itself, the Ahoghill property and Ballygowan and Edenderry, etc in County Down, 1802–06 – D3860/E/7

Adams estate, Ballyweaney
Miscellaneous documents, including leases, relating to the Adams family, 1776 onwards – D1518/2
See Chapter 15 for more documentation relating to this family

Agnew estate, Kilwaughter
Records relating to the management of the estate, 1636–1712 – NRS, GD154/505–534
List of tenants and their stock, *c.* 1645 – NRS, GD/154/514 (printed in Raymond Gillespie, *Colonial Ulster: The Settlement of East Ulster, 1600–1641* (1985), p. 228)
Leases, etc, 18th century onwards – T502 *passim*
Volume of maps, 1788, naming tenants: 18 townlands in Kilwaughter parish, 10 in Kilraghts, 9 in Carncastle, 2 in Larne and one each in the parishes of Kilbride, Tickmacrevan and the Grange of Doagh – T2309/1

Allen estate, Killead, Loughguile, etc
Maps of farms in Ballysculty {Killead}, naming tenants, 1786 – D3590/E
Map and survey of Ballanagashan [Ballynagashel] {Loughguile}, belonging to Robert Allen of Ballybreckan, naming tenants, 1766 – D3590/E

Antrim (MacDonnell family) estate, Ballycastle, Ballymoney, Clough, Glenarm, Larne, etc
Established by the Scottish MacDonnells, this was the largest estate in seventeenth-century Ulster, extending to some 330,000 acres, or 500 square miles, and covering almost all of north County Antrim. It also included lands in that part of County Londonderry on the east side of the River Bann. A wealth of information on the family is included in George Hill's book, *An Historical Account of the Macdonnells of Antrim* (1873). See also Jane H. Ohlmeyer, *Civil War and Restoration in the Three Stuart Kingdoms: The Career of Randall MacDonnell, Marquis of Antrim, 1609–1683* (1993; reprinted 2001). The 'Introduction to the Earl of Antrim Estate Papers' prepared by PRONI provides a detailed overview of the scope of the collection.

Leases
A vast collection of leases from the early 1600s onwards, arranged alphabetically by townland within barony (leases covering more than one townland and those covering more than one barony are listed separately) – D2977/3A
See also 'Tenants on the estates of the Earls of Antrim in the seventeenth century' in *DIFHR*, 23 (2000), pp 80–92, and 'Tenants on the estates of the Earls of Antrim in the eighteenth century' in *DIFHR*, 36 (2013), pp 19–40, both by Ian Montgomery

Lease books

Lease book of Glenarm barony, 1736 – D2977/3B/1

General return of leases and tenures, 1737–1821 – D2977/3B/2

Details of leases for Glenarm, Ballymoney and Larne, *c.* 1743 – D2977/3B/3

Counterpart lease register for Dunluce barony, Ballymoney and Coleraine Liberties, 1783, also used as a rent roll for Glenarm barony, 1795 – D2977/3B/4

Notebook containing lease extracts relating to Glenarm town, *c.* 1736–*c.* 1881 – D2977/3B/10

Notebook containing lease extracts relating to Larne town, 1736–1892 – D2977/3B/11

Notebook and copy containing extracts from rent ledger, *c.* 1685, 1720–58 – D2977/3B/12–13

Notebook and copy containing details of fee farm and renewable leases for lives, *c.* 1637–1781 – D2977/3B/17–18

Notebooks and copies providing details of how land was held and rent and fees payable for the following baronies: Cary, Upper and Lower Dunluce, Upper and Lower Glenarm, Kilconway and the North East Liberties of Coleraine, *c.* 1623–1785 – D2977/3B/19–27

Extracts of early grants, 1637–1737 – D2977/3B/29

Rentals

Rent roll, 1641 – T694/1

Old rental (*c.* 1690) of estates of earl of Antrim from the original in Glenarm Castle – TCD, MS 1059

Rent ledgers of the 'North' estate beginning in 1751 – D2977/9/1–4

Rent ledger of the 'South' estate beginning in 1791 – D2977/9/5

Maps and surveys

Survey and valuation of Antrim estate, 1734 – D2977/25/1A

Reference to map of the barony of Glenarm, 1734 – D2977/25/1B

Volumes of maps of the estate, 1734 – D2977/35/1–4 (originals returned to depositor; see T1703/1 (Cary), T2325/1 (Dunluce), T2325/3 (Glenarm), T2325/4 (Kilconway))

Volumes of maps of the estate, 1782 – D2977/35/5–7 (originals returned to depositor; see T1703/2 (Cary), T2325/2 (Dunluce), T2325/5 (Glenarm), T2325/7 (Kilconway))

Map of 'Old Town of Lairn alias Gardenmore', 1735, naming tenants – D2977/36/2/1

Map of Glenarm with a list of tenants, 1779 – D2977/36/3/1–2

Manor court records

COURT LEET

J. B. Hamilton (ed.), *Records of the Court Leet for the Manor of Dunluce in the County of Antrim Held in the Town of Ballymoney, 1798–1847* (1934) (originals destroyed)

Court leet book, manor of Glenarm, 1765–1812 – D2977/23/2/1

Bundle of loose papers relating to the court leet of Glenarm, 1786–1845 – D2977/23/2/3

Court leet book for the manor of Oldstone or Kilconway, 1773–1819 – D2977/23/4/1

Several pages of an account and receipts book concerning the treasurers of the manor of Oldstone, 1776–80 – D2977/23/4/2

MANOR COURT/COURT OF RECORD

Unbound section of a court book, manor of Dunluce, 1742–3 – D2977/23/3/1

Court book, manor of Glenarm, 1755–96 – D2977/23/1/1

Court book, manor of Glenarm, 1797–1814 – D2977/23/1/2

Unbound section of a court book, including records of courts for the manor of Oldstone, held in Ballymoney, 1742–3 – D2977/23/3/1

See also Ian Montgomery, 'The manorial courts of the earls of Antrim', *Familia*, 16 (2000), pp 1–23

Miscellaneous

Correspondence and other papers relating to the family, late 16th century onwards – D2977/5/1

Names of owners of lands on the estate in 1660 (not necessarily resident) – printed in George Hill, *An Historical Account of the Macdonnells of Antrim* (1873), pp 466–7

Report of a disturbance at Dunluce fair, 1663 – D2977/5/1/2/43

List of duties collected, *c.* 1720 (e.g. bushels of oats, hens, days of work) – printed in George Hill, *The Stewarts of Ballintoy* (1865, reprinted 1976), pp 55–7

Bundle of documents, including wages accounts of Antrim's servants, *c.* 1763; list of tenants of Duneykiltar [Dunmakelter], *c.* 1760 – D2977/25/2

See also **McGildowney estate** for additional records relating to the Antrim estate.

Banks estate, near Belfast

Rent rolls of property in Shankill parish leased by the Banks family from the marquess of Donegall, 1793–1812 (Ballymoney), 1800–09 (Ballygammon and Ballydownfine) – D3649/3/1, /2

Bateson (Bateson-Harvey from 1788) estate, Killoquin

Various deeds, etc relating to the Killoquin estate, 1753–1802, including an attornment by the tenants to the trustees of the late Richard Bateson, 1766: over 200 signatures or marks – Centre for Buckinghamshire Studies, D 140/95

Killoquin rent accounts, 1776–7 and 1777–8 – Centre for Buckinghamshire Studies, D 140/102

Killoquin rent roll and accounts, 1787–88, and rent account, 1789 – Centre for Buckinghamshire Studies, D 140/104

Rent roll, 1790, including statement of arrears, 1788–9: lands of Tamlaght, Fernagh, Tehorny, Drumcon, Gortereghy, Culmore, Ballydonnelly, Ballymaconnelly, Lisnagaver, Magheraboy, Gortahar, Moneyleck and Granagh {all Rasharkin}, and Desertderrin {Finvoy} – D3209/1

Letters relating to the estate, 1792 – D3209/2–9

Account book, 1786–7, offered for sale by Richard Ford Manuscripts (www.richardfordmanuscripts.co.uk/catalogue/15700); names include: Archibald McKendry, Samuel Strear, James Carson, David Smith, Wm Wallace, McConnel and McKinlay, Thos Ray

Boyd estate, Ballycastle

Rent roll of Boyd property in and around Ballycastle, 1799 – D1375/7/12

Boyd estate, Loughguile
Map of the estate of William Boyd of Ballynabantry, giving names of tenants, 1794: lands of Drumrankin, Carnamenagh and Carnagall {all Loughguile} – D1296/129

Brice estate, Kilroot
Book of maps of estate of Edward Brice in counties Antrim and Down, 1750–56: lands of Ballybreakach {Ballynure}, Ballybuttler {Donaghadee}, Ballygowan-more {Ballynure}, Ballywilliam {Donaghadee}, Carrickfergus, Granach {Ballyphilip} and Killroot – NLI, MS 19,848
See also **Brice estate** under **County Down**

Brytt estate, Carrickfergus
Map of William Brytt's estate in the Liberties of Carrickfergus, 1780, naming tenants – D2121/5/3

Caldwell estate, Ballymoney
Rent roll of the estate of John Caldwell, merchant, Ballymoney, 1797 – T3541/6/6

Caledon (Alexander family) estate, Ballycastle
Letters, rentals and accounts, 1788–96 – D2433/A/2/6/1–57 (/1 is a rent roll of 1788)
Letters and accounts, 1795–1800 – D2433/A/2/7/1–18
Rent roll of Lord Caledon's estate, 1793 – D1375/3/59/3
See also **Caledon estate** under **County Tyrone** for more records relating to this estate and background information on the landowning family.

Clements estate, Carrickfergus see **Adair estate, Loughanore**

Conway estate, Lisburn
The origins of this estate can be traced to the early seventeenth century. The landowning family's surname was originally Conway and later Seymour-Conway; the head of the family was created earl of Hertford in 1750 and marquess of Hertford in 1793. The *Calendar of the State Papers relating to Ireland* (see Chapter 4) includes much information on this estate in the 1650s and 1660s. For background reading, see Brenda Collins, 'Sources for a seventeenth-century Ulster estate: the Hastings (Irish) Papers in the Huntington Library, California', *Familia*, 24 (2008), pp 145–54, and by the same author, 'The Conway estate as an example of seventeenth-century "English" building styles in Ulster' in Olivia Horsfall Turner (ed.), *The Mirror of Great Britain: National Identity in Seventeenth-century British Architecture* (2012), pp 165–86.

Leases for Aghacarnon, Aghnedara, Ballydonaghy, Ballyvorally, Glenavy, Killough and Tullyrusk, 1741–53 – D491 *passim*
Leases for Aghadavy, Largymore and Lisburn (including an assignment of a lease of 1669), 1701–51 – D577 *passim*
Rental of the manor of Killultagh: Lisburn, Lambeg, Derryaghy, Magheragall, Magheramesk, Aghalee, Aghagallon, Ballinderry and Glenavy, 1719–23 – D427/1 (MIC664/1)

Rent roll, 1728–30 – D427/2 (MIC664/1)

Maps of the estate in the parishes of Blaris, Derryaghy, Lambeg and Magheragall, 1726, naming tenants – D427/3

Maps of the estate in the parishes of Tullyrusk, Camlin, Glenavy, Ballinderry, Aghagallon, Aghalee and Magheramesk, 1729, naming tenants – D427/4

Crymble estate, Carrickfergus see **Adair estate, Loughanore**

Dalway estate, Bellahill

Names of tenants in Slimcrow [Slimero], Duffshill and Edengreny, part of the estate of Marriott Dalway, 1791 – *Belfast Newsletter*, 15–19 July 1791

Davy estate, Cullybackey

Map of Charles Davy's estate at Cullybackey, 1760: Car[n]donaghy, Corbally, Dreen and Lisnafillan {all Ahoghill} – D2121/5/1

Dobbs estate, Castle Dobbs

Leases, 1776–92: lands of Dunturky and Lismenary {both Ballynure} – D162/110

The Registry of Deeds includes a number of transcripts of early 18th-century leases issued by Richard Dobbs (e.g. vol. 14, pp 288–90).

Donegall (Chichester family) estate, Belfast, Carrickfergus, Inishowen, etc

This massive estate, focused on south-east County Antrim (including Belfast) and the Inishowen peninsula in County Donegal, was founded by Sir Arthur Chichester in the early seventeeth century. For an account of its early development, see Peter Roebuck, 'The making of an Ulster great estate: the Chichesters, Barons of Belfast and Viscounts of Carrickfergus, 1599–1648', *PRIA*, 79C (1979), pp 1–25. The Chichesters rose through the ranks of the peerage becoming earls of Donegall in 1647 and marquesses of Donegall in 1791. Large swathes of their estate were let to middlemen. W. A. Maguire's extensive research notes on this estate are in PRONI (D4512).

Leases

Leases, early 17th century onwards, covering Belfast, Carnmoney, Carrickfergus, Donegore, Inishowen, etc – D509 *passim*

Leases, 1671 onwards (over 500 items prior to 1800) – D652 *passim*

Maps

Maps of the estate in Inishowen, County Donegal, and in County Antrim, 1767–70, naming tenants – D835/1/1–3

Rentals

Rental for Belfast, Moylinny, Ballylinny, Island Magee and Carrickfergus, 1719 – D2249/61

Rent ledgers, Antrim estate, 1783–6, 1787–97, 1798–1806 – D835/2/1–3

Rentals, 1775–82, 1798 (including a rental for Inishowen, County Donegal for 1741) – D835/3/1–2

Cash rent book, Antrim estate, 1796–1800 – D835/4/1

Other

Typescript volume of Donegall estate material, including accounts of payments and receipts, 1706–15 – T455/1 (see also D4512/4/4)

Vouchers, in the form of receipts to agents, received from, *inter alia*, employees, workmen, tradesmen, 1737 – T3425/3/12

Donegall estate letter book, 1771–4 – T1893/1

See also **Ellis estate**

Dungannon (Hill-Trevor family) estate, Island Magee, Raloo

Collection of leases, especially from 1750 onwards: lands include Ballycronan, Ballygowan, Ballykeel, Ballymoney, Ballypriorbeg, Ballyvolagh, Ballyvriland, Beltoy, Drumgurland, Dundressan, Killcovan, Portmuck – D778 *passim*

Collection of leases, many from 18th century: lands include Altyvallagh, Ballyryland, Ballyrickard, Ballywillin, Carneal, Altilevelly, Ballygowan and Tureagh – D1954/4 *passim*

Tenants in Raloo parish, property of the Hon. Arthur Trevor, 1765 – *Belfast Newsletter*, 23 Aug. 1765

Lands for letting on Lord Dungannon's estate, 1769 – *Belfast Newsletter*, 7 Feb. 1769

List of lands and tenants of Lord Dungannon on Island Magee, 1770 – *Belfast Newsletter*, 13 Feb. 1770

'Plan of the parish of Rallow [Raloo]', 1770, naming tenants – D1954/6/1

Dunlop estate, Chatham Hall

Advertisement for the letting of lands, naming tenants for the townlands of Carrycloghan {Grange of Drumtullagh?}, Coldugh, Lower and Upper Ballywindland, Ballywatick {all Ballymoney}, Castlecatt and Ballyloughbeg {both Billy}, 1775 – *Belfast Newsletter*, 27–30 June 1775

Edmonstone estate, Red Hall

Rent roll for the half year, 1777 – D233/7

Ledger of Sir Archibald Edmonstone's estate (purchased by the Ker family *c.* 1780), 1780–83 – MIC261

Edwards estate, Glendun

Rentals and agents' accounts of the Edwards estate, including Glendun, 1777, 1792 – MIC343/1 (the rental of 1777 identifies the tenants of Glendun as Hugh Boyd and Samuel Dunlop)

Rent rolls and accounts of Robert Harrison for the estates in Ireland of Mrs Mary Edwards, deceased, and of Gerard Anne Edwards, 1751–63 – Leicestershire Record Office, DE3214/9906

Ellis estate, Ballylinny

Map of Brooslee [Bruslee] and part of Ballygallogh {both Ballylinny} owned by Henry Ellis, naming tenants, 1793 – D1349/7/6

Rental of Bruslee and part of Ballygaloch, formerly owned by Henry Ellis, now owned by marquess of Donegall, 1800 – D2966/122/1

Forsythe, Ballyeaston
Leases issued by John Forsythe of Ballynure for lands at Ballyeaston, mainly 1788–96 – D1080/5 *passim*

Fullerton estate, Ballintoy
Four leases relating to lands at Ballintoy and Lemnaghmore, 1795–1803 – D2007/2/1

Gage estate, Rathlin Island
Estate book, *c.* 1789–1821 – D463/1

Haliday estate, near Belfast
Names of tenants in the townlands of Ballywenet, Ballyvaster and Ballysillen {all Shankill} held by Dr Haliday from the earl of Donegall, 1776 – *Belfast Newsletter*, 11–15 Oct. 1776

Hamilton estate, Cloughmills
Bound survey of lands of William Hamilton, 1738: very detailed, but limited
  information on tenants – D342/12
Rent roll of the estate of William Hamilton, 1744 – T2408/16
Rent roll of part of same to be sold, *c.* 1760 – T2408/20

Henry estate, Killead
Names of tenants in Se[a]cash and Brittish {both Killead}, property of Hugh Henry, 1754–5 – *Belfast Newsletter*, 20 Aug. 1754, 12 Sept. 1755

Hunter estate, Ballymena
Various 18th-century documents, including leases issued by members of the Hunter family, for property in and around Ballymena, including Todd's Hill, Leymore, Brocklamont, Ballyloughan {all Ahoghill} – D1364/A *passim*

Hutchinson estate, Portglenone
Account and notebooks of Bishop Francis Hutchinson, 1721–39 – DIO/1/22/1–3
An additional volume, including rentals of the Portglenone estate from the 1730s, has
  been accessioned by PRONI, but has not yet been catalogued.
See also **Adair estate, Loughanore**

Hutchinson estate, Stranocum
Miscellaneous papers, 1630–1736 – D2171 *passim*
Maps of the Stranocum estate, 1805: lands of Killyraver, Calheme, Dunaghy,
  Greenshields, Stranocum, Gladhill, Ballyrobin, Roseyards, Kirkhills {all
  Ballymoney}, Livery Lower {Derrykeighan}, Dungorbery {Kilraghts} – D408/1

Ker estate, Red Hall see **Edmonstone estate**

Kirk estate, Ballyclare and Carrickfergus
Correspondence, *c.* 1718–35 – T2524

Leases, 1629 onwards: 53 pre-1800, though not all relating to the Kirk family –
D2121/4 *passim*
Map of William Kirk's estate in Carrickfergus, 1786, naming tenants – D2121/5/4

Langford and Langford-Rowley estate, Crumlin, Templepatrick
Miscellaneous leases, including many from 17th and 18th centuries – D971/1/E
Vouchers, 1686–94 – MIC537/3
Rentals, surveys and valuations of the manor of 'Killelaugh', 1699–1700 – MIC537/3
Rent roll of estate of Sir Arthur Langford in Templepatrick and Carnmoney areas, 1700
– D2624/2
Rental of Killelagh and Ederowen, 1727 – MIC537/3
Rent rolls of Langford estate in Templepatrick and Crumlin areas, 1743, 1774, 1777,
1778, 1780 – D2634/4A–B, 6, 7, 8, 9
Accounts and arrears, 1750–52 – MIC537/3
Rental, survey and lease book, 1750–76 – MIC537/3

Legg(e) estate, Malone, etc
Maps of the estate of Alexander Legg in the barony of Dunluce and in Shankill parish,
1774, 1782, 1796, and Lacken near Ballyroney in the parish of Drumballyroney,
1781, 1791 – D915/18/1
Leases, 1777 onwards – D915/7/3
Map of Legg estate in the parish of Derrykeighan, 1790 – D915/18/3

Leslie estate, Leslie Hill
Four leases from James and Sarah Leslie for farms in Anticur {Rasharkin}, 1791 –
D2977/3A/5/2/4, /5, /7, /8
A few other pre-1800 leases are in PRONI – see eCatalogue for more details

McAulay estate
'A map of part of the estate of Alexander McAulay Esq., in the county of Antrim and
barony of Dunluce', 1763: Brackogh Upper, Brackogh Lower and Ballyboyland {all
Ballymoney} – D2433/A/13/2

McCollum estate, Cushendun
Maps of the estate of the heirs of Hugh McCollum, 1789: limited information on
tenants – D543/3

McGildowney estate, Ballycastle
Some material in this collection concerns the **Antrim estate**.
Rental of Glenarm, 1742 – D1375/5/2
Memorandum book of Edmund McGildowney recording receipts and expenditure in
connection with estate and business concerns (other than the earl of Antrim's estate),
1790–94 – D1375/7/1
Volume containing accounts of rents received by Edmund McGildowney in payment
of marchioness of Antrim's jointure, 1800–01 – D1375/5/3/1

McNaghten estate, Beardiville and Glenarm

Map of Francis McNaghten's estate in the parishes of Dunluce, Ballywillin and Ballyrashane, 1713: lands of Berdyville, Tuberdornan, Revalach, Reske, Islandcaragh, Tinearle, Ballyhunsly, Ballyclogh – T2292/1

Names of tenants in the townlands of Carnalbanagh, Tavanabrack, Upper and Lower Munny, Knockstakan {all Tickmacrevan}, Ballynamuntre, Culnane and Ballygown, part of the estate of Francis McNaghten, 1786 – *Belfast Newsletter*, 17–20 Jan. 1786

Macartney estate, Carrickfergus, Loughguile, etc

For more on the estate collection, see the 'Introduction to the Macartney Papers' prepared by PRONI. Background reading on this estate can be found in Peter Roebuck (ed.), *Public Service and Private Fortune: The Life of Lord Macartney, 1737–1806* (1983).

Leases

Abstracts of leases for lands near Carrickfergus, 1607–83, compiled *c.* 1770 – T2408/8A

17th- and 18th-century deeds and leases – D1062/2/1

Maps

Volume of estate maps, *c.* 1760–*c.* 1800, naming tenants – T1064/7/1–24

Volume of estate maps, *c.* 1760–*c.* 1800, naming tenants – D1062/2/4/1

Map of 'Loughgeel', *c.* 1770 – T1064/2/1

Map of lands in Dunluce and Kilconway baronies, 1790 – D588/1

Map of Loughguile estate, 1790 – T1064/6/1

Map of Dervock, 1802, naming tenants – D662/1

Miscellaneous

Memorandum books, 1790 – D557/1

Survey and valuation of estate, 1767 – D572/21/96 (MIC438/7)

Rentals

Printed rental of the Loughguile estate, 1759 – D1375/5/2

Rent rolls of Loughguile estate, 1768, 1789 – D426/3, 5

Rent roll of Loughguile, Dervock, Carrickfergus and Killinchy estates, 1790 – D2225/7/47 (MIC530/2)

Variations in rent rolls, 1793–6 – D2225/7/55 (MIC530/2)

Rent roll, 1796 – D572/21/98 (MIC438/7)

Rent roll of estates in counties Antrim and Down, 1801 – D572/21/101 (MIC438/7)

Magenis estate, Derrykeighan, etc see Magenis estate, Dromara, etc under County Down

Massereene estate (Clotworthy and Skeffington families), Antrim, Muckamore

The origins of this estate can be traced to the early 1600s and the acquisition of an estate focused on Antrim Town by an officer in the English army in Ireland, Hugh Clotworthy. His son John was created Viscount Massereene in 1660. He died without male heir in 1665 and his estate was inherited by his daughter Mary, wife of Sir John Skeffington of Fisherwick, Staffordshire, to whom passed the Massereene viscountcy.

In 1756, the earldom of Massereene was created for the fifth viscount. For more on the estate collection, see the 'Introduction to the Foster/Massereene Papers' prepared by PRONI. See also A. P. W. Malcomson, *The Extraordinary Career of the 2nd Earl of Massereene* (1972).

Rental of '16 Townes of Antrim', 1668, tenants listed alphabetically – D207/16/6

Rental of the manor of Muckamore, 1685: lands of Ballough, Bally Arnett, Rigg, Oldstone, Terragracia, Muckamore, Ballyharvey, Ballyneheeland, Isleland Bawne, Bally Shaneoge – D4084/1/4/1

Rent roll of Killylough estate, 1700–2 (125 tenants) – D562/216

Rent roll of Connor parish, 1705 (*c.* 50 tenants) – D562/210

Roster of duty days for Muckamore, 1709 (30 tenants) – D562/58

Rent roll and statements of debt for Muckamore, Ardmore, Ballynageeragh and The Grange, 1712–13 – D562/834

Rent roll of Muckamore, etc, 1715 (88 tenants) – D562/57

Duty book for Antrim, etc, 1733–4 – D562/99

Leases for Antrim parish and town, 1698 onwards – D4084/1/3/1

Leases for lands in other parts of County Antrim, 1670 onwards – D4084/1/3/2

Account of wages paid to 38 labourers, 1754 – D4084/1/5/2/1

Mitchell estate, Farranacushog

Rent roll of Fernagussog [Farranacushog] {Dunaghy}, Craigywarren and Ballymena {both Kirkinriola}, 1796 – D1364/E/1

Montgomery estate, Benvarden

Volume of maps of estate, 1788, naming tenants – T1638/31/1

Moore and Stewart Moore estate, Ballydivity and Clogh

Over 110 unsorted leases relating to the Ballydivity estate of James Moore, 1725–1848, and a volume containing a schedule of leases for the estate, *c.* 1764–*c.* 1839 – D915/7/1

Map of part of the estate of James Stewart Moore, 1793, naming tenants – D915/18/4A (townlands of Drumnagroagh, Glenleslie and Tullykittochs)

Miscellaneous 18th-century documents relating to Ballydivity, etc – D1835/31

Moore estate, Ballynacree

Various 17th- and 18th-century deeds relating principally to the property of the Moore family of Ballynacree in Finvoy, Killagan and Ahoghill parishes – D1066 *passim*

Moore estate, Cloverhill

Various 18th-century papers, including leases issued by Moore family – D2171 *passim*

Names of tenants, plus acres held, for Ballyquillen, Stredhavren, Dundesart and Ballinadrentah {all Killead}, 1770 – *Belfast Newsletter*, 2 Jan. 1770

Mount Stafford estate, Portglenone

Names of tenants on part of the Mount Stafford estate, 1782 – *Belfast Newsletter*, 26–30 July 1782

Mount Cashell (Moore family) estate, Galgorm, Glenwhirry, Racavan, Skerry
This vast estate was acquired by the Moore family, Lords Mount Cashell, in 1764. It comprised the Galgorm or Glenagherty estate (in Ahoghill, Connor and Kirkinriola parishes), the Kells estate (in Connor parish), the Braid estate (in Racavan and Skerry parishes), and the Glenwhirry estate (in the parish or territory of Glenwhirry), in all over 47,000 acres.

Printed rental and particulars of sale relating to the entire estate, 1847, with details of
    leases (many pre-1800, though names of original tenants not usually given) –
    D1911/6/4/2 (for the Braid estate, see also an Encumbered Estates Court rental and
    sale, 1850 – D3851/1)
Papers relating to the Galgorm estate, comprising leases and conveyances 1724–1868,
    some from Lord Mount Cashell to various tenants including members of the
    Raphael family, 1773–1846 – D3751/1A
Leases for lives, Racavan parish, 1788 – D1835/15
Money received from Glenwhirry for Mr Harrison, n.d. [pre-1775], naming tenants –
    D1494/3/6 (MIC506/1)
Copy rent account, 1777–93, naming tenants, but not townlands – D1494/3/44
    (MIC506/1)
Copy receiver's account for rents received to 1791 in Glenwhirry – D1494/3/42
    (MIC506/1)
Accounts of rents received from Glenwhirry, 1795–1804, naming tenants by townland
    – D1494/4/16 (MIC506/1)

Mussenden estate, Carnmoney
Rent roll, *c.* 1750: lands of Whitehouse, Jordanstown, Carnmoney, Ballycraigy, Ballyhenry, Cloughfern, Dunany and Ballyveally {all Carnmoney} – D354/285A (MIC510/2)

Neale estate, Magheramorne
Map of the manor of Magheramorne, property of John Neale, 1747: lands of Altilevelly, Ballyrickardmore, Ballyrickardbeg, Ballygowan, Beltoy, Carneal, Ballyvallagh, Ballyfore, Ballyryland and Tureagh {all Raloo} – D1602/1
See also **Dungannon estate**

O'Hara estate, Crebilly
Leases, *c.* 1740–*c.* 1800 – D1911/2
Maps of the estate in the parishes of Ballyclug, Connor and Dunaghy, 1783–4, naming
    tenants – T2971/1 (see also NLI, 14 A 24)
Names of tenants, plus date of commencement of leases and terms, in Leminary, Byers'
    Farm, Big and Little Tully and Stone Ditch, 1766 – *Belfast Newsletter*, 6 June 1766

O'Hara estate, O'Hara Brook, Ballymoney
Miscellaneous 18th-century documents relating to the O'Haras of O'Hara Brook –
    D1835/38
Names of tenants in the townlands of Bendorogue, Drumnahesky, Cross Upper and
    Lower, Drumreagh, Cabrogh, Eden (otherwise Mounthuely), Eden (otherwise

Cloint), Coltyseechan and Eden, part of the estate of Charles O'Hara of O'Hara Brook, 1777 – *Belfast Newsletter*, 9–12 Dec. 1777

O'Neill estate, Shane's Castle
The O'Neills of Shane's Castle (or Edenduffcarrick), on the northern shore of Lough Neagh, were the most important of the landowning families of Gaelic background in Ulster in the 1700s, owning an estate extending to some 60,000 or so acres. The various parts of the estate were:

> Edenduffcarrick (also known as Monterevedy) – mainly to be found in the parishes of Antrim and Drummaul and the Grange of Shilvodan
> Cashell (also known as Largy) – mainly to be found in the parish of Ahoghill (now Portglenone)
> Mulloghgane (also known as Feevagh) – mainly to be found in the parishes of Drummaul and Duneane
> Buckna (also known as Braid) – mainly to be found in the parishes of Racavan and Skerry

Unfortunately, pre-1800 records relating to the management of this estate are almost non-existent. A fire at Shane's Castle in 1816 is said to have destroyed almost all the family's documents, papers and records.

17th-century copy of a mortgage relating to the estate of Henry O'Neill of 'Edenduffcaricke' (Shane's Castle) naming tenants, 1638 – T1289/1
Tenants on the estate extracted from advertisements in the *Belfast Newsletter*, 1750–68 – printed in *DIFHR*, 39 (2016), pp 16–20 (*Belfast Newsletter*, 9 Nov. 1750, 16 Nov. 1756, 16 Aug. 1757, 3 Feb. 1758, 13 Feb. 1759, 26 March 1761, 17 Dec. 1762, 4 Jan. 1763, 31 May 1768)
Extracts from the manor court book of the manor of Cashel (Portglenone area), 1770–1825, printed in R. M. Sibbett, *On the Shining Bann: Records of an Ulster Manor* (1928), pp 78–143
Letters concerning the O'Neill family, 1689–1774 – NLI, MS 21,293

Owens estate, Holestone and Killead
The Owens family inherited the Holestone estate through the marriage of Henry Owens and Jane Gillilan[d] in 1724.

Survey of farms in Lisnataylor {Killead}, naming tenants, 1762 – D1824/B/1/1/6/12
Survey and plan of Holestone {Kilbride}, 1768 – D1824/B/1/1/5/1

Reford estate, Antrim
Miscellaneous documents relating to property held by the Reford family in and around the town of Antrim, including a map of Spring Farm of 1745 – T3029

Richardson estate, Carncastle
Map and survey of Sallagh, Lochdoe and part of Ballywillin {all Carncastle}, 1777 – D300/M/1
A few leases from 1760 onwards for 'Ballywoolen', Sallagh, Killyglen – D300/2/1 *passim*

Rowan estate, Ballymoney
Names of tenants in Upper and Lower Stroan, Upper Garry, Drumart and Glenyloagh {Ballymoney}, property of John Rowan, 1756 – *Belfast Newsletter*, 18 June 1756

Rowan estate, Mullans
Document, seemingly a recovery of debts, relating to the estate of the late Rev. Robert Rowan of Mullans, 1761, naming over 140 tenants – D1835/15B
Leases, 1784 – D1835/15

Saunders estate, Belfast, Carrickfergus, Newtownards and Comber
Rent roll, 1771–8 – D1759/3B/7 (MIC637/10)

Stewart estate, Ballintoy
34 expired leases for Ballintoy, etc, 1788–90 – D2007/1
List of deeds and papers relative to the sale of the Ballintoy estate, 1793 – D971/42/A/8/4
See also **Fullerton estate**

Stewart estate, Finvoy
Printed rent roll (incorporating a survey and valuation) of the 13 quarters near Ballymoney, part of the unsettled estate of Alexander Stewart, late of Acton (County Armagh), *c.* 1750: lands of Enogh, Unshenogh, Drumskea, Ballynamonie, Claghie, Knockan, Derra, Upper Derra otherwise Drumock, Lower Derra, Long Mullans, Broad Mullans, Cultifaghan otherwise Craigs called Slavebey, Scotch Craigs, Irish Craigs, Tulloghans – D642/G/7 (MIC593/9)

Stewart estate, Glenarm
Leases, etc for lands of Nicholas Stewart in and near Glenarm beginning in 1755 – D1080/5 *passim*
Rent roll of the property of Nicholas Stewart, in Glenarm, Libbert, Ballytober and Drumnacole, *c.* 1800 – D1080/5/91

Stewart/Traill, Ballylough
Originally a Stewart property, this estate was purchased by the Traill family in 1789–92. The documentation in D4081 relates to both periods of ownership.

Leases from 1762 onwards: lands of Ballylough, Ballyloughmore, Carnhill, Cavan, Cavanmore, Castlecatt, Drumcrottagh, Drumnagee, Drumnagessan, Lemnagh Beg – D4081/1/2

Stewart Moore estate see Moore and Stewart Moore estate

Traill estate see Stewart estate, Ballylough

Upton estate, Templepatrick
The head of the family was ennobled as Baron Templetown in 1776.

Deed of feoffment, 1625, naming tenants on estate – T712/1
Lands to be let with names of sitting tenants – *Belfast Newsletter*, 26 July 1768, 15 Nov.
   1768, 28 March 1769, 2–6 May 1777

Vesey estate, Carrickfergus
Map of part of the Vesey estate in Carrickfergus, 1722, naming a few tenants –
T2524/26

Wilson estate, Ballyclare
Names of tenants on the property of the late Nathaniel Wilson in Ballyclare, 1788–9
   – *Belfast Newsletter*, 28 Nov.–2 Dec. 1788, 12–16 Dec. 1788, 9–13 Jan. 1789

Wray estate, Dunseverick
23 leases for lives from Jackson Wray, 1766–72 – D915/7/2

COUNTY ARMAGH

For a detailed account of the division of this county into estates in the early 1600s, see
R. J. Hunter, *The Ulster Plantation in the Counties of Armagh and Cavan, 1608–1641*
(2012). This includes maps showing land ownership in the 1610s and 1641, which are
especially helpful in identifying the extensive lands that belonged to the Anglican
archbishop of Armagh.

Armagh archbishopric estate
This was an enormous estate and comprised lands mainly in the Ulster counties of
Armagh, Londonderry and Tyrone as well as Antrim, Cavan, Down and Monaghan
(in other words, there was archbishopric property beyond the Armagh diocesan
boundaries). Much of the estate was leased to middlemen. The 'Introduction to the
Armagh Diocesan Registry Archive' prepared by PRONI provides an overview of the
collection. The material relating to this estate is extensive and may be summarised as
follows.

Leases
Small folio volume providing details about leases to lands in the archbishopric, 1628–
   1722 – DIO/4/34/1/1
Abstracts from the Primate's leases: includes a folio volume entitled 'Of the Primacy or
   Archbishopric of Armagh, a rent roll from the 1st of May 1703, per Thomas Ashe,
   containing details of leases', 1685–1703; also an alphabetical list of tenants holding
   leases under the see with dates of granting, 1749 – DIO/4/34/2/2/1–8
Leases granted by the dean and chapter: includes a volume of lease abstracts, 1768–
   1802 – DIO/4/34/3/1–15
Leases granted by the Vicars Choral, 1703–64 – DIO/4/34/4/1
Abstracts of leases granted by the governors and guardians of Primate Robinson's library,
   1790–94 – DIO/4/34/5/1

Rentals

Volume of bound-in documents, 1524–1628 – DIO/4/5/2A–B. Includes: no. 10, rent roll of 1615; no. 11, survey of holdings in Armagh city; no. 12, rent roll of all lands and houses owned by the Primate, *c.* 1620; no. 16, rent roll of the see of Armagh, n.d. [early 17th century]; no. 17, rent roll of the rents payable quarterly to the Primate, n.d. [early 17th century]; no. 18, names of tenants bound by their leases to provide light horses to the Primate during time of war, n.d. [early 17th century]; no. 19, rent roll of lands and houses of the Primate, 1628; no. 20, arrears of rent in Counties Armagh and Tyrone, 1628.

'A Rent-Roll of All the Houses and Lands Belonging to the See of Armagh: With a Description of the Same Drawn up in the Time of Primate Hampton (circa 1620)' edited by L. P. Murray, *Archivium Hibernicum*, 8 (1941), pp 99–120

Volume of bound-in rentals for the lands of the archbishopric and houses in Armagh, 1628–1726 – DIO/4/35/1. Includes rentals, etc for 1628, 1629, 1631, 1636, 1639, 1640, 1660, 1661, 1663, 1664, 1686, 1709, 1726.

Extracts from rent rolls of see of Armagh, 1615–24 – T625/1

Rent rolls of archbishopric, n.d. [1676], 1724, 1742 – DIO/4/35/2, 6, 8

Rent roll of the estate of the archbishop of Armagh, 1678 – NLI, n.6071, p.6797

'A view or an account taken by Thomas Ashe Esq. in anno 1703 … of the archbishopric of Armagh' – DIO/4/35/3. Photostat copy available at T848/1 (see Chapter 5 for more on this source).

'Walter Dawson's rental', 1713 – DIO/4/35/4

Rental of Lord Primate's mensals at Armagh, 1743 – DIO/4/22/3/3

Rent rolls of the 'Cavan estate', 1779, 1782 – DIO/4/35/13

An old rent roll called 'Captain Chambers' rent roll', n.d. [?17th century] – DIO/4/22/1/1

Rent rolls of the Primate's mensal lands near Armagh, 1725, 1728, 1743 – DIO/22/3/1–2

Rent rolls of the see of Armagh, 1615–1746, including a list of the names of tenants returned at a manor court held by the archbishop of Armagh, 1714 – T729/1A–3B

Maps and surveys

A large collection of maps and surveys relating to lands in the archbishopric have been catalogued under DIO/4/22. What follows is a selection of these.

Map of Drumargue and Down for Lord Primate's new demesne, 1706 – DIO/4/22/4/4

Map of the town and homesteads of Kilmore, endorsed 'Hampton's holdings', 1707 – DIO/4/22/4/5

Map and survey of the townlands of Annagh, Tullynebre, Drumbeam, and Donaghmor[e] {Donaghmore, County Tyrone}, 1710 – DIO/4/22/4/6

'The old demesnes lately in lease to Capt. Walter Dawson, Richard Hall, James Ogle, Widow Willop and James McDonnell', [*c.* 1710] – DIO/4/22/4/7

'Demesnes of Armagh', 1714 – DIO/4/22/4/8

Map of Mr Fitzherbert's, Mr Tisdall's, Capt. Di[?x]ey's and Mr Dowdall's holdings in County Monaghan, [*c.* 1714] – DIO/4/22/4/12

Map of lands in the parish of Armagh held by Nicholas Averell of Coleraine: lands of Ballymoklmurry, 1716 – DIO/4/22/4/14

Map of the lands of Mr Gervais Walker in the parish of Armagh', endorsed 'Map of Ballynahown', 1717 – DIO/4/22/4/20

Survey of the Vicars Chorals' houses and tenements in the town and corporation of Armagh, 1720 – DIO/4/22/4/21

Map and survey of the townland of Lislea and part of the townlands of Lisbeno [sic], Enagh and Magheryarvell {Armagh}, 1730 – DIO/4/22/4/30

'A survey of part of the demesnes lately held by the under-named tenants of his Grace, the Lord Primate of All Ireland', 1730 – DIO/4/22/2/6

'Copy of a survey of that part of his Grace, Richard, Lord Archbishop of Armagh's estate, now held by the Rev. Dean Averell or his under-tenants, situated in the county of Armagh, 1765–6 – DIO/4/22/2/10

Map endorsed 'Dr Avard's [Averell's?] lands near Armagh', 1766 – DIO/4/22/4/36

'A survey of part of the lands within the corporation of Armagh, held by Thomas Townley Dawson Esq., under his Grace, the Lord Primate, and now in possession of the under-named persons', 1769 – DIO/4/22/2/12

'Survey of the lands adjoining the common', [c. 1775] – DIO/4/22/2/13

'Lands situated in the corporation of Armagh, lately surrendered to his Grace, the Lord Primate, and now in possession of the under-named persons, tenants-at-will', 1777 – DIO/4/22/2/14

'A map and survey of Killeeshill, held by Widow O'Neil and her under-tenants', 1767 – DIO/4/22/4/37

Map of the townland of Legmurran [Legmurn] in the barony of Dungannon, County Tyrone, 1768 – DIO/4/22/4/39

'Map of the parks situated near Armagh', endorsed 'Survey of Lisanally, Knockarnell, and other fields near Armagh', 1775 – DIO/4/22/4/45A-B

'Part of English Street in Armagh', 1774 – DIO/4/22/5/25

'Map of the townland of Ballyhanwood and quarterland of Gortgrib, alias Portgrib, and also part of the townland of Ballylissbredin, situated in the barony of Castlereagh and county of Down', 1795 – DIO/4/22/4/46

Manor court records

T. G. F. Paterson, 'The Armagh manor court rolls "Period 1625–1627": and incidental notes on 17th century sources for Irish surnames in Co. Armagh', *Seanchas Ardmhacha*, 2:2 (1957), pp 295–322

Volume of bound documents, of which no. 2 is a return of tenants' names of Armagh returned to a manor court held by the archbishop of Armagh in 1714, and a list of the chief undertenants in the manor of Armagh – DIO/4/22/1/1 (see also T729 and NLI, MS 3922 and MS 7371)

List of the manors annexed to the archdiocese of Armagh with the names of seneschals, c. 1775 – DIO/4/22/2/17

Case papers, mandates, etc, concerning Armagh manor court, 1751–1848 – DIO/4/40/2

Atkinson and Hoop(e) estate, Tartaraghan

Cash book for rents, 1778–85 [Atkinson family?] – D1815/2/1

Map of the 'lower half townland of Toigy [Teagy]' {Tartaraghan}, naming tenants, 1731 – D1815/4/1

Map of Drumanphy {Tartaraghan}, naming tenants, 1732 – D1815/4/2
Map of Clonakle {Tartaraghan}, naming tenants, 1780 – D1815/4/3

Ball estate, Cullyhanna
Box of expired leases, including some from late 18th century – D3012/2/1/1
(MIC566/2)

Barton estate see Jackson estate

Blacker estate, Carrick
Miscellaneous documents from the 17th century inwards, including leases for
    Ballyhannon, Breagh and Drummanconway – D959/10 *passim*
Map of the estate of Stewart Blacker in the parish of Seagoe, 1734 – D959/M/56

Brownlow estate, Lurgan
For background information on this estate, see the 'Introduction to the Brownlow
Papers' prepared by PRONI. See also Desmond McCourt, 'The maps of the Brownlow
estate and the study of the rural landscape in north Armagh', *UJA*, 3rd series, 20 (1957),
pp 114–22; W. H. Crawford, 'Tenants' occupations on the manor of Brownlow's-Derry,
Lurgan estate, County Armagh, *c.* 1670–1799', *Familia*, 16 (2000), pp 51–60; Kieran
Clendinning, 'The Brownlow family and the development of the town of Lurgan
in the 17th century', *Seanchas Ardmhacha*, 20:1 (2004), pp 100–23 and 20:2 (2005),
pp 106–32.

Leases and lease books
Lease books, 18th century – D1928/L/1
Leases for townlands in the estate and tenements in Lurgan, arranged alphabetically,
    17th and 18th centuries – D1928/L/2–177
A lease book of 1667–1711 was printed in full in Raymond Gillespie (ed.), *Settlement
    and Survival on an Ulster Estate* (1988)

Rentals
Rent rolls for the 17th and 18th centuries, including a rental of Sir William Brownlow's
    estate, 1636–77 [listed as missing] – D1928/R/5
Day book of rents paid to Henry McVeagh from Brownlowsderry and Richmount
    estates, 1709–1800 – D1928/A/1/1
Rent books, 1755–1804 – D1928/R/1/1–65
Large rent day book for Lord Lurgan's estate, 1796–9 – D1928/R/3/1

Maps
Volume of maps for manor of Brownlowsderry, 1751 – D1928/P/1A–B
Maps, 1751–94 – T2485/2
Map of Lurgan, 1794 – D1928/P/2

Miscellaneous
Names of William Brownlow's tenants in or near Lurgan, 1622 – MIC171/1
Accounts, some relating to the estate, 18th century – D1928/A/1

Estate court book for manor of Brownlowsderry, 1776–1847 – D1928/J/1

Wages books, 1748–83 – D1928/W/1–4

Estate and household account book of William Brownlow, 1752–4, which includes rent accounts for the estates in north Armagh and in counties Louth and Monaghan, and details of Brownlow's election expenses incurred in the 1753 by-election for County Armagh, 1752–4 – D1928/A/2/2

Burges estate see under **County Tyrone**

Caledon estate see under **County Tyrone**

Charlemont estate (Caulfeild family), Charlemont

Leases and lease books

Schedule of leases, *c.* 1750–1817 – T1176/1–6

Expired leases, 1782–1904, arranged in bundles by townland – D1644/1–30

Leases, 1788–1804 – D2394/1

Lease book of Charlemont estate, 1818–30, including a schedule of leases, some of which date back to the 18th century – D266/260A

Maps

Map of Moy and part of Drumgranon, 1771, naming tenants – D291/3

Map of Blackwatertown, 1782, naming tenants – T1208/1

Map of Cladybeg and Cladymore, 1786, naming tenants – D266/378/2

Rentals

Rental, mainly in the Charlemont, Blackwatertown and Loughgall areas, 1752–65 – T1175/2

Rent roll, 1774 – T387/1

Rental of Charlemont estates in counties Armagh and Tyrone for the years 1798–1800 – NLI, MS 2702

Miscellaneous

Copy statement of account, 1759–61 – D2644/1

Correspondence of James Caulfeild, first earl of Charlemont: 1,300 letters covering the period 1745–99 – Royal Irish Academy, MSS 12 R 9–21

Cope estate, Drumilly and Loughgall

Leases from 18th century: lands include Annaghmore, Ballytyrone, Drumilly, Drumnasoo, Lissheffield {all Loughgall}, Creenagh {Kilmore} – D1345 *passim*

Dawson estate, Armagh, Blackwatertown

For more on this estate, which also included extensive lands in County Monaghan, see the 'Introduction to the Dartrey Papers' prepared by PRONI. In 1770, Thomas Dawson was created Baron Dartry of Dawson Grove and in 1785 he was made Viscount Cremorne.

Collection of 18th-century leases: includes 85 leases dated 9 January 1794 from Viscount Cremorne for farms in Anacleary, Blackwatertown, Crockenrow, Drumcullen, Englishtown, Killmore, Mullinary and Mullylegan – D266 *passim*

Collection of leases, 1757 onwards – D526/2E *passim*

Rent roll of the estates of Lord Dartrey in counties Armagh and Louth, 1777, 1779 – NLI, MS 3283

List of tenements in Armagh city owned by Thomas Dawson, 1779 – D526/2E/22

List of leases in Blackwatertown delivered to Richard Olpherts, 1781 – D526/2E/23

Survey and valuation of estate of Thomas Dawson, 1st Baron Cremorne, *c.* 1800 – D526/2F/2

Rent roll of Lord Dartrey's church lands in County Armagh, 1781: lands (in addition to those listed above) of Drumash & Drumarm and Tullyhevin, plus Armagh city – D2394/3/2

Rent agreement, 1751, naming tenants: 67 names – D2394/3/1

Rent rolls, 1787, 1797 – NLI, MSS 3183, 3283, 3185

Survey of tenancies on Lord Cremorne's estate, Armagh city and county, 1793 – NLI, MS 10,264

De Salis estate, Tanderagee

List of tenants holding leases from the earl of Sandwich and Peter De Salis with observations on the state of lives in the manor of Clare 1733–87: lands of Brakagh, Unchinagh, Ballylisk, Ballyknock, Cordrain, Mullavilly, Lissaveague, Tonyvalton, Tonnaghmore, Cabragh, Coolyhill, Mullintur, Lisnabee, Modoge, Druminure, Clare, Ballyshielbeg, Cloghoge, Maymacullan, all in the manor of Clare – D763/2

List of tenants in possession of farms without leases, n.d. – D763/3

Leases for lives, 1764 onwards – D1393/1

List of tenants holding farms in jointure whose leases expired on death of Rt Hon. Lady Viscountess Fane, 1792 – D763/4

Observations and extracts of leases of part of northern estate, 1793 – D763/5

Memorandum on rentals, 1794 – D763/6

See also **Sandwich estate**

Dillon estate see Molyneux estate

Dungannon estate (Hill-Trevor family)

Leases from the 17th and 18th centuries (mainly 1750 onwards): lands include Aghanargen and Corglass {Drumcree}, Clondrutt [Clonroot] {Kilmore}, Dromart {Loughgall}, Drumgask and Moraverty [Moyraverty] {Seagoe} – D778 *passim*

Further records for this estate are listed under **County Antrim** and **County Down**.

Ensor estate, Ardress

18th-century leases issued by George Ensor of Ardress – D1134/1 *passim*; D1252/17/1A-C

Erne estate, Portadown

List of Lord Erne's fee farm rents received by Dean Cope in County Armagh, 1770–71 – NLI, MS 15,783 (1–3)

Account book of Lady Erne's property in counties Armagh and Tyrone and executors' journal of her estate kept by Rev. W. Digby and John King, 1786–1800 – NLI, MS 3209

Accounts of Lady Erne with, *inter alia*, her agent Robert Peebles for the Portadown estate, 1790s – NLI, MS 15,360

Fane estate see **De Salis estate**

Gosford (Acheson family) estate, Markethill
The origins of this estate can be traced to the early 1600s and further information on it can be found in the 'Introduction to the Gosford Papers' prepared by PRONI. The family owned additional lands in County Cavan, which are dealt with in that county section. In 1776, Sir Archibald Acheson was created Baron Gosford of Markethill and in 1785 he was made a viscount. The earldom of Gosford was created in 1806.

Affidavit of James Galbraith about the state of Sir Patrick Acheson's proportions of Clancarny and Coolmalish, 1639 – D2002/C/1

Map of the manor of Lower Coolmillish, 1693, naming tenants – D384/2

Map of manor of Clancairney, estate of Sir Archibald Acheson, 1754 – D385/1 (copy T2125/10/2)

Survey and rent roll of Hamilton's Bawn demesne, 1739 – D1606/6B/3

Map of Hamiltonsbawn estate, 1785 – D1606/6B/8

Rent rolls of the original Armagh estate, including notes on leases, 1787–99 – D1606/7A/1–5

Leases arranged by townland, including many from the 18th century – D1606/3

Volume containing an abstract of leases for the manors of Baleek and Coolmalish, 1801 – D1606/3/48/1

Hall estate, Mullaghglass see **Hall estate, Narrow Water** under **County Down**

Hall estate, Fews
Leases of parts of the Hall estate in Fews, 1737–72: Lassera, Coolderry, Anaghgadd, Cleranagh, Drumbally and Mounthill {all Creggan} – D4160/C/6

Valuation of Mr Hall's lands in Fews, 1756 – D4160/15/7

Rent rolls, 1792, 1800: lands of Mounthill, Cornconagh, Lower Drumbally, Clarinagh, Drumhook, Moybane (including Island Reagh & Parks), Annaghgadd, Drumbee, Clonalig, Cappy, Coolderry, Lissara – D4160/C/16/3

See also **Tipping estate, Newtownhamilton** in this county section and **Hall estate, Strangford and Lower Iveagh** under **County Down**

Hamilton estate, Ballynaleck
Rent roll of estate of James Hamilton of Ballynaleck, 1790 – D476/37

Hamilton estate, Hamiltonsbawn
Tenants on the estate of John Hamilton, 1617 – printed in *Familia*, 11 (1995), p. 92

Hoop(e) estate see **Atkinson and Hoop(e) estate**

Houston estate, Tynan
Map of Turry {Tynan} and Lower Ballymacully {Eglish} 1777, naming tenants – D2433/A/13/3

Report of commissioners appointed to value and prepare a scheme for the partition of the Houston estate, 1801: lands of Delay, Anagharap, Drumgolva, Clonticarty {all Tynan}, Ballymacullow Lower and Upper {Eglish}, Killylin {Grange} – D2433/A/1/21/11

Irwin estate, Keady

Maps
Map of part of the estate of Arthur Irwin in Derrynoose parish, naming tenants, 1758 – D2523/M/1
Map of Carnagh, naming tenants, 1766 – D2523/M/2
Map of Carrickduff owned by William Irwin, naming tenants, 1799 – D2523/M/3
Map of Kilcarn owned by William Irwin, naming tenants, 1799 – D2523/M/4

Rentals
Rental of Tievenamara, Kilcarn, Carrickduff and Crossnenagh {all Keady}, *c.* 1750–1800, including a list of writs and judgements, *c.* 1749–50 – D2523/1/1
Rental of same area, 1768–86 – D2523/1/2
Rental of Tievenamara, 1785–1834 – D2523/1/3

Jackson estate, Forkhill
Leases for the Forkhill estate, 17th and 18th centuries (70 from 1789–96): lands include Corkinagallia, Mullaghbane, Shanrow, Mullaghbawn, Cloughchunoe, Clarchill, Lissavanny, Carrickasticken, Shean, Doctor's Quarter, Latbirgid, Longfield, Corrickildreen, Ballykeel, Tullymachrive, Tievecrom, Aughadanove, Corrickildreen, Levallymore – D294 *passim*

Return of lands set on 1 Nov. 1788 by Mrs Susanna Barton, Forkhill estate, lately in possession of her brother Richard Jackson deceased – D294/10

Jenny estate, Derryanvil
Map of Derryanvil {Drumcree} belonging to Henry Jenny, 1757, naming tenants – D243/5

Johnston estate, Drumbanagher
Map of estate, 1784, naming tenants – T1175/3/1

Johnston estate, Eglish, Tynan
Rent rolls, 1785–1805: lands in 1785 rent roll are Artasooley, Anhoghananny, Ballybrocky, Culkeeran, Drumrush, Drumsallon, Derrydorragh, Dernasigh, Edenderry, Eglish, Garvaghy, Foyarr, Knockareagh, Kilcarn, Kilmetroy, Killyquin, Lisbanoe, Lisnafeedy, Lisdown, Mullantur, Mullyloughen, Pollnagh, Tullymore – T933/1–5

Rentals annually for the period 1791–1802 – NAI, M 3502

Ker estate, Navan

Leases in bundles arranged by townland of the estate of Mrs Hannah Ker of Dublin, 1791: lands include Creighan {Clonfeacle}, Drumbee, Navan {both Eglish}, Tullygarran {Grange} – D1747/1/1–4

Kilmorey estate, Newry see under County Down

Lenox-Conyngham estate see under County Londonderry

McCombe estate, Altamoyan

Large collection of 18th-century leases, many of them for lives – D462 *passim*

MacGeough-Bond estate, Drumsill

For more on this estate see the 'Introduction to the MacGeough Bond Papers' prepared by PRONI.

Leases, 1759 onwards – D288 *passim*
Box of miscellaneous 18th- and 19th-century rent material – D288/G/1
    Cash book, *c.* 1767–1817: index of names at start of book; includes an account of the grazing of the cattle on Cullcarn naming graziers, 1791
    'Interest book' begun by William MacGeough and continued by Joshua MacGeough *c.* 1767–1817: index of names at start of book
    'Mr Pooler's rent book', which appears to relate to the Bondville estate, 1770–82
    Volume combining a rent book with a cash book, *c.* 1766–1803: lands include Corran, Drummondmore, Culcairn, Ballymcowen, Ballycrumy
    Rentals of Eglish and Glengavelin {Tartaraghan}, 1779–81 and undated
    Accounts of rents, etc received from that part of the lands of Glenall leased by Joshua MacGeough from the see of Armagh, 1788–9: lands of Artasooley, Cullcarn, Mullenturr, Edenderry, Tullymore
    List of fines due to Joshua MacGeough, 1797–1804, from tenants in Lislea, Farnamucla, Corran, Lisnadill, Tullybrone(?), Ballymartrim, Terfeckan, Alistra
    Rent roll, 1787: lands of Derrycaw, Derrycorr, Derrycavra, Glengavlin – D288/97
    Account of work done at the house of Joshua MacGeough, Drumsill, 1788 – D288/101
    Rent roll for year ending November 1803 – D3012/2/2/13 (MIC566/10)
    Valuation of Umrecam with information on tenants, houses, etc, 1804 – D3012/2/2/12 (MIC566/10)

Manchester estate, Portadown and Tandragee

The manor of Ballymore was owned successively by the St John, Sparrow and Manchester families and comprised the lands of Ballymore, Cargans, Cornegat, Corrernagh, Crankey, Crewbeg, Derryallen, Knock, Lisbane, Mullahead, Mullaghglass, Tullyhappy and Tullyhue.

The manor of Kernan was owned successively by the Obins, Sparrow and Manchester families and comprised the lands of Ballincor, Balteagh, Bocomra, Clanrole,

Crossmaglen, Drumgor[e], Drumnagoon, Karn, Knockmena, Lisnaminty, Lisniskey, Lylo, Moyraverty, Seago, Tamnificarbit and Tarson.

The manor of Ballyoran was owned successively by the Powell, Obins, Sparrow and Manchester families and comprised the lands of Annagh, Clownagh, Corcrane, Corcullentrabeg, Corcullentramore, Garvaghy, Kilmarty, Mullentine and Selshon.

Leases, 1669 onwards: listed individually, *c.* 1,000 pre-1800 – D1248/L
Rentals, etc of Kernan and Ballymore, 1715–92 (mainly for the 1760s and 1780s) – D1248/R/79–105

See also **Obins estate** and **St John estate**

Maxwell estate, Fellows Hall
Rental of the manor of Balteagh, 1770–71 – T1307/1 (printed in *Duiche Neill*, 6 (1991))

Molyneux (formerly Dillon) estate, Castledillon
Names and freeholders and leaseholders on the estate of Sir John Dillon, 1622 – MIC171/1
Survey of the estate, 1696 – MIC215
Lease book of the manor of Castledillon with observations by William Molyneux and details on tenants' dwellings and land usage, *c.* 1700 – MIC80/3
Lists of tenants on the estate, 1617, 1696 – T636/1, pp 247–52
Rentals of the estate, 1721–2, 1722–3, 1723–4 – T636/1, pp 252–4
Rental of 1828 giving details from 18th-century leases – T636/1, pp 157–87

Nicholson estate, Tartaraghan
Maps of Killdaraghin, 1753, and Cranagill, 1768 {Tartaraghan} – T2167/1–2
Tenants in Cranagill and Derrylileagh, 1795–1843, endorsed 'No. 2 Rental 1800 1838' – T2289/9

Obins estate, Portadown
The Obins family owned the manors of Ballyoran and Kernan, which later became part of the Manchester estate. See **Manchester estate** for details of what survives for these properties in PRONI. The following items relating to the Obins estate are in the National Library of Ireland.

Rent receipt book of Mary Obins, 1753–63, and rental of the estate of Michael Obins, 1770–71 (includes some household accounts, 1804–06) – NLI, MS 4736
Accounts of Robert Jones, a blacksmith in account with Mary Obins, 1757–62 (includes domestic account book of a gentleman apparently resident in County Armagh, 1749–50) – NLI, MS 3514
Timber book for Obins estate, possibly late 1700s – NLI, MS 4737
Names of tenants and particulars of leases on the Obins (?) estate in Portadown and elsewhere in the parish of Drumcree, 1796 – NLI, MS 4741

Obre estate, Clantilew

18th-century leases (mainly from 1799) for lands of Eglish, Glanavelin {both Tartaraghan}, Foybeg and Drumenagh {both Drumcree} – D266 *passim*

Receipts for rent from Francis Obre, of the lands of Derrylee and Derryane {both Tartaraghan}, 1734–8 – D2538/A/42

Richardson estate, Bocombra

Rental of Bocombra {Seagoe}, 1756, and two surveys of same, 1757, 1775 – D1252/7/1

Richardson estate, Richhill

Four leases issued by William Richardson for Annaboe, Ballynahinch, Drumard {all Kilmore}, 1789–1812 – D2153 *passim*

Roe estate, Clonmakate

Survey of Clonmakate {Tartaraghan}, estate of Thomas Roe, 1782 – T2289/5

Rentals giving names of tenants in Clonmakate, 1782, 1783 – T2289/6, /8

Sachervell estate, Richhill

Map of part of the manor of Mullalellish owned by Henry 'Schacheverle', 1695, naming tenants – D384/3

St John estate, Tanderagee

Map and survey of Ballymore (1750), map of Tanderagee demesne (1791) and map of the manor of Clare (copied in 1806 from a survey of 1795) – D720/1–2 (see also NLI, 15 B 4 (12))

Maps of the manor of Ballymore and manor of Kernan, 1701 onwards – D727 *passim*

See also **Manchester estate**

Sandwich estate, Clare

Printed sale particulars of the estate of the earl of Sandwich, n.d. [pre-16 February 1807], giving details of tenancies from 18th century – T3059/1

See also **De Salis estate**

Simpson estate, Drumsavage

Leases from Thomas Simpson of Ballyards for farms in Drumsavage {Mullaghbrack}, 1778–92 – D522

Sparrow estate see **Manchester estate**

Stearne's Charity estate, Middletown

Stearne's Charity was founded under the will (1744) of John Stearne, Anglican bishop of Clogher, and was based on his estate at Middletown.

Rent roll of the Middletown estate, 1771–97, including receipts and other documents – DIO/4/9/5/5/13

Petitions from aggrieved tenants, 1776–c. 1795 – DIO/4/9/5/2/1–3

Arrears, 1788, 1793, naming tenants – DIO/4/9/5/5/36

Account, 1794, naming tenants: lands include Anacally, Anagola, Anareagh, Belneman, Cavandoogan, Feduff, Hanslough, Middletown, Ratrillick, Shantully, Tullybrick – DIO/4/9/5/5/1

Leases from the Trustees of Stearne's Charity, 1796–7 – DIO/4/9/5/6/1–11

Rental of the Middletown estate, 1798 – DIO/4/9/5/5/11

Rent roll of lands under lease, n.d. – DIO/4/9/5/5/38

Rent roll of lands not under lease, n.d. – DIO/4/9/5/5/39

Stewart estate, Acton

A map of the manor of Acton owned by Rev. Archibald Stewart, 'lying in the parishes of Killeavey, Loughgilly and Tanderogee', 1713: does not name tenants – NLI, 15 B. 4 (13)

Leases and maps, 1786 onwards – D1166 *passim*

Tipping estate, Newtownhamilton

Various documents, including leases, 1740–94 – D4160/C/8

Rent roll of the disputed lands possessed by Mr Tipping and those possessed by Mr Montgomery and withheld by him from Tipping, 1782: lands include Altnamechan, Curtamlett, Mullaghduff, Ballynarea, Tullyvallan {all Newtownhamilton} – D4160/C/8/9

Leases, 1692 onwards – D288 *passim*

See also **Hall estate, Fews**

Trinity College Dublin estate see under County Donegal

Verner estate see under County Tyrone

Whaley estate, Armagh

Survey of estate of Thomas Whaley (a minor), 1769 – T636/1, pp 143–51

Leases, 1773–91, mainly issued by the executors of Richard Chapple Whaley: lands include Ballynagall, Broughan, Farmacaff[l]y {all Lisnadill}, Munlurg [Mullurg] {Mullaghbrack}, Armagh – T1617/1 *passim*

Minor expenses book of Samuel Faulkner which includes mention of business transacted, leasing of land and business as agent for Thomas Whaley, 1783–5 – MIC21/1

Various documents arising from the agency of the Whaley estate by Samuel Faulkner, including accounts for rents, arrears, bad debts, etc, 1772–5; rental, 1776–8; arrears of rents, 1779–80; rent ledger, 1780–90; rent book, 1787–90; notes of rent agreements, 1789; rent receipt book, 1790–91; two copies of a survey of holdings in the city of Armagh, 1792 (copy of an original of 1769) – MIC21/2

Workman estate, Portadown

Miscellaneous documents from the 18th century including leases for Ballyoran, Corcreen, Portadown {all Drumcree} – D959/14/1 *passim*

COUNTY CAVAN

For a detailed account of the division of this county into estates into the early 1600s, see R. J. Hunter, *The Ulster Plantation in the Counties of Armagh and Cavan, 1608–1641* (2012). This includes maps showing land ownership in the 1610s and 1641. For a general background to landed estates in County Cavan, see P. J. Duffy, 'The evolution of estate properties in south Ulster' in W. J. Smyth and K. Whelan (eds), *Common Ground: Essays on the Historical Geography of Ireland* (1998), pp 84–109, which includes maps showing the network of estates in the county in the seventeenth and nineteenth centuries.

Annesley estate, Cavan, etc
The Annesley estate in County Cavan was divided into three portions: Ballyconnell, Cavan and Clonervy. For more on this estate collection, see the 'Introduction to the Annesley Papers' prepared by PRONI, which lists the townlands owned by the family in Cavan. See also **Annesley estate** under **County Down**.

Expired leases for the Cavan estate, late 18th century onwards – D1503/3 *passim*
Rough rent roll of the Cavan estate, *c.* 1802, but referring to 18th-century leases – D1503/4/2

Armagh archbishopric estate
Included among the archive of the Armagh diocesan registry in PRONI are two rent rolls of the 'Cavan estate', 1779, 1782 (DIO/4/35/13). These lands seem to have been scattered through a number of parishes including Castlerahan, Kilbride, Templeport and Tomregan.

Borrowes estate, Scrabby
Map of the lands of Corfree and Cornegran {Scrabby}, the estate of R. Borrowes, 1807–10 – NLI, MS 15 B. 8(13)

Brady estate, Clonervy see Richardson estate

Butler estate see Lanesborough estate

Carmichael estate see Farnham estate

Clements estate, Ashfield
For more on this estate, see Collection Lists Nos 49 and 81 prepared by the National Library of Ireland and also A. P. W. Malcomson (ed.), *The Clements Archive* (2010), published by the Irish Manuscripts Commission.

Leases from 1757 onwards – NLI, MS 33,833
Ledger, 1782–97 – NLI, MS 9624
House account book, 1791–1800 – NLI, MS 9818
Volume of maps of the manor of Ashfield, barony of Tullygarvey, 1775–1844 – NLI, MS 15.B.24; the maps include Carrigalway and Killicreeny (1775); Corabea (1800); Barragh (1801); Cortober (1799); Doharrick (1799); Largyn (1800)

Coote estate (earls of Bellomont), Cootehill

Seventy-three leases and renewals, mostly for three lives or 40 years, of premises in Cootehill, granted by Charles Coote, earl of Bellomont, and other members of the Coote family, 1766–1830 – NLI, D 6791–6863

Coyne estate, Drumlumman, etc

Volume of maps of the estate in counties Cavan and Westmeath, *c.* 1760: limited information on tenants; the lands in Cavan comprised Big Clonuse, Callanagh, Drumcorr, Garrysallagh Beresford, Kilgola, Killeboy, Killekeen, Knockanore, Lisnafea, Lisnatinne, Little Clonuse, Loghdovan, Muckram, Mullaghoran and Tideeghan – D2784/2/1

Craige estate, Kildallan and Killeshandra

Names of tenants on the estate, 1703–04, printed in *The Irish Ancestor*, 8:2 (1976), pp 86–7

Crofton estate, Kinawley

Rentals and accounts, 1769, 1783–1814 – NLI, MS 20,783
Rent roll of the estate of Hugh Crofton, 1792 – NLI, MS 4530

Culme estate see Farnham estate

Davenport estate, Tullygarvey

Survey of the estate of Simon Davenport Esq. in the barony of Tullygarvey, 1791: lands of Curravoy, Cullentragh, Upper and Lower Cornegall, Lisslea, Lisscloane – NLI, MS 21.F.37(028)

Farnham (Maxwell family) estate

The estate owned by the Maxwells, Lords Farnham, was, by the end of the 1700s, the largest in County Cavan. It was built up over many years through the acquisition of lands in various parts of the county. A detailed catalogue of the estate papers, prepared by Jonathan Cherry, can be found in the National Library of Ireland's Collection List No. 95. See also Jonathan Cherry, 'The Maxwell family of Farnham: an introduction', *Breifne*, 11:42 (2006), pp 125–47. The main portions of the estate are summarised below along with the parishes concerned.

Waldron estate

One of the original Plantation properties, this estate was purchased by Bishop Robert Maxwell in 1664; lands in the parishes of Kilmore, Urney and Annageliff.

Culme/Lisnamaine estate

Another of the original Plantation properties, this estate was purchased by Rev. Robert Maxwell from Jane Culme in 1715; lands in the parishes of Drumlane, Kildallan, Denn and Kilmore.

Massereene estate

A highly fragmented property created as a result of the Cromwellian land settlement, this estate was purchased by Rev. Robert Maxwell from the Massereene family in 1716;

lands in the parishes of Killinkere, Mullagh, Lurgan, Denn, Crosserlough, Ballymachugh, Drumlumman, Ballintemple, Kildallan and Templeport.

Hampson estate
Another estate created as a result of the Cromwellian settlement, this estate was purchased by the 1st Baron Farnham from Major Charles Hampson *c.* 1719; lands in the parishes of Castlerahan, Ballymachugh and Drumlumman.

Plunkett/Dunsany/Fortland estate
This property was purchased by the 1st Baron Farnham from Edward Plunkett, Lord Dunsany, in 1740; it later became the core of the Fortland estate; lands in the parishes of Ballymachugh, Kilbride and Lurgan.

Carmichael/Castle Craig estate
The manor of Castle Craig was purchased by the 1st Baron Farnham from John Carmichael in 1758; a further acquisition was made by the 2nd Baron in 1765; lands mainly in the parishes of Killashandra and Kildallan.

Cavan Town
The Farnham estate also included property in the town of Cavan, acquired in 1720, 1746 and 1764.

For a more detailed listing of the many items in this estate collection, see the abovementioned NLI Collection List No. 95. The documents set out below have been listed in order of manuscript reference number.

Rentals and valuations
Rent roll of the Carmichael estate, noting tenant names, the extent of holdings and the terms of the lease, 1759 – NLI, MS 41,114/19

Rent rolls of James Somerville's estate in Cavan Town, *c.* 1718, 1718 – NLI, MS 41,118/5, /7

Rent roll of Pladwell's part of Lisnamaine, 1699 – NLI, MS 11,491/1

Rent roll of the Lisnamaine estate, 1715 – NLI, MS 11,491/4

Rent roll of the Farnham and Munally estates, 1717 – NLI, MS 11,491/5

Rent roll of the Massereene estate, 1718 – NLI, MS 11,491/6

Rent roll of the Lisnamaine estate, 1718 – NLI, MS 11,491/7

Rent roll of the Massereene estate, 1720 – NLI, MS 11,491/9

Valuation of Massereene estate lands, *c.* 1720 – NLI, MS 11,491/10

Valuation and rent roll of the Lisnamaine estate, *c.* 1720 – NLI, MS 11,491/11

Rent roll of the Massereene estate with survey and valuation, *c.* 1720 – NLI, MS 11,491/12

Rent roll of the Massereene estate, 1728 – NLI, MS 11,491/14

Rent roll of the Farnham and Massereene estates, 1734 – NLI, MS 11,491/15

Rent roll of part of the estate to be sold pursuant to the will of the late earl of Farnham, *c.* 1799 – NLI, MS 11,491/19

Rent roll of some of Culme lands, including names of tenant, 1688 – NLI, MS 41,123/2

Rent roll of the estate of Jane Culme, including names of tenants, details of tenure and observations on leases, 1714 – NLI, MS 41,123/8

Rental of James Smyth's estate, Lavagh and Knockmore in Ballymachugh parish, c. 1779 – NLI, MS 41,145/2

Printed rent roll of part of the earl of Farnham's estates, c. 1799 – MS 41,154/1

Abstracts of rental income, including names of tenants owing arrears, 1800 – NLI, MS 41,154/2

Leases and lists of tenants

A large number of leases from the seventeenth century onwards exist within the Farnham estate collection. See Collection List No. 95 for more details, including townlands for the abstracts of leases listed below.

List of tenants on the Massereene estate giving the extent of their landholding with observations concerning the clauses in the leases, 1719–86 – NLI, MS 11,491/8

List of tenants on the Abbey Lands estate, giving the extent of their landholding with observations concerning the clauses in the leases, 1737–86 – NLI, MS 11,491/16

List of leases on various rural landholdings and in Cavan town, 1737–1814 – NLI, MS 11,491/17

Abstracts of leases for the Dunsany estate, 1736–90 – NLI, MS 41,134/1

Abstract of leases for the Hampson estate, 1714–88 – NLI, MS 41,137/1

Maps and surveys

Surveys of Corriroe, 1764, 1785, and Lisduff, 1764, 1769, 1794 – NLI, MS 41,155/2

Maps of lands in the estate from 1723 onwards – NLI, 21.F. 115–120 and MS Maps 278 M, 279 S, 280 S

Fingall (Plunkett family) estate, Virginia

Leases, conveyances, rentals, maps, surveys, plans, etc, 16th–19th centuries – NLI, MSS 8024–8028, 8030

Rent roll, 1750 – NLI, MS 8024

Fitzherbert estate, Shercock

Deeds, etc relating to Shercock, etc, 1656–1754 – NLI, D 6956–62

Lease for lands at Barnagrow, Killycleare, Cullis, 1739 – D645/37

Names of a few tenants on the estate of Andrew Fitzherbert, 1770 – *Belfast Newsletter*, 19 Oct. 1770

Gaven estate, Kilbride see **Nugent estate**

Gosford (Acheson family) estate, Arvagh

For more on this estate, which also included lands in County Armagh, see the 'Introduction to the Gosford Papers' prepared by PRONI, which includes a list of the townlands in the manor of Carrowdownan owned by the family in Cavan.

Leases from 1703 – D1606/3/44–5

Volumes of maps and surveys of estate, c. 1800 and 1801 – D1606/6/D/2–3

Haig estate, Clankee
Map of Robert Haig's estate in the barony of 'Clinkee' [Clankee], n.d. [late 1700s/early 1800s]: lands of Aughnahee, Tonyfole and Tullywaltra – NLI, MS 21.F.32 (015)

Headfort (Taylour family) estate, Virginia
Rentals (including property in Meath and Dublin), 1797–1800 – NLI, MS 48,587–48,591

Kilmore bishopric estate
Rental of the see estate, undated [late 1600s] – NLI, MS 41,575/6
Rent ledger of Joseph Storey, bishop of Kilmore, 1738–57; household account book of same, 1742–50 – NLI, n.3624, p.3242

Lanesborough (Butler family) estate, Belturbet
Deeds, 17th–19th centuries – NLI, D 8896–8926
Correspondence relating to estate management, 1780–82 – D1908/2/1

Massereene (Clotworthy and Skeffington families) estate, Castlerahan
For more on this family, see the entry for the estate under **County Antrim.**

Rent roll and statement of debts of Lord Massereene, 1712–13 – D562/834
Rent roll of the estate in Castlerahan parish, 1716 – D562/217
See also **Farnham estate**

Nesbitt estate, Lismore
Rental, 1784 – NAI, CAV 18/1/49

Nugent estate, Farren Connell
Miscellaneous Nugent of Farren Connell estate papers including: envelope of maps, valuations and drawings from 1765 onwards; outsize rent and account book, 1783–9; rentals and agent's accounts, 1794–1809 – D3835/C
Rentals, 1793, 1797: the Cavan townlands are Barcony, Raclahy Upper and Lower, Enagh Rock, Lismacannigan, Clintoduffy and Croppagh – D3835/C/6/19, /21
Rental of the estate of the late Luke Gawen, 1800: the solitary Cavan townland is Dungummin – D3835/C/6/23

Pleydell estate, Killinagh and Drumlane
Names of tenants in Aughavilly and Drummany {Drumlane}, owned by Jonathan Morton Pleydell, 1784 – *Dublin Evening Post*, 20 July 1784
Box of 46 leases (mainly for 3 lives), 1787–90 – D3480/25/1
Documentation, comprising correspondence and receipts, relating to the Pleydell estate, from the late 18th century; it includes:
  Rentals and accounts, 1798–1810 – T3530/2/5
  Tenants' petitions, proposals and memorials, 1796–1828 – T3530/2/16

Pole estate, Urney, etc
Valuations, rentals and surveys of the Pole estate in the parishes of Urney, Ballintemple and Ballymachugh, 1740–74 – NLI, MS 41,145/3

Pratt estate, Kingscourt and Cabra

Surveys, accounts, etc, 18th–19th centuries – NLI, MSS 13,314–13,327
Unsorted material, 17th–20th centuries – NLI, D 22,134–22,403
Map of property in Enniskeen parish, 1735 – NAI, M 5746

Richardson estate, Clonervy

The Richardsons of Drum, County Tyrone, owned lands in Cavan and also inherited part of the Clonervy estate, mainly to be found in the parish of Castleterra, following intermarriage with the Brady family.

Box of leases of the 18th and 19th centuries – D2002/L/3
Map of Banacho and Killitean {Denn}, 1801 – D2002/M/2

Sa(u)nderson estates, Castle Saunderson and Clover Hill

The origins of these estates can be traced to the land settlements of the mid seventeenth century. The family's surname was originally Sanderson, but in the 1700s the main branch changed the name to Saunderson in the unsuccessful pursuit of an extinct peerage. Another branch based at Cloverhill retained the original spelling. Most of the estate documentation that has been identified relates to the properties of the Sandersons of Cloverhill. For records relating to a Sanderson property at Manorcunningham, see under **County Donegal**.

Documentation relating to the Sanderson properties, beginning in 1695 – D3480/13
  A few items relate to the Castle Saunderson branch, but for the most part the material concerns the Cloverhill Sandersons; this collection has not been catalogued in detail. It includes:
    Rental, n.d. (early 19th century), giving details on when leases were issued (many from pre-1800) and observations on the status on the lives in the leases: lands of Belturbet, Clarebawn, Clonarna, Corlasallee, Corlat, Cormeen, Corravety, Crossroads, Curlogan, Drenan, Grahanagee, Lanavara, Latigholon, Lissenanana, Nockeasty, Pulluleam, Rahelston, Ranrina, Shanore, Thomas Court, Tulleycoe
Estate papers of the Sanderson family of Cloverhill from the mid 18th-century onwards, including a rental of lands in Lavey and Mullagh parishes, 1787 – NLI, MS 9492
Survey and map of Cloverhill demesne and other lands of Alexander Sanderson, c. 1771 – Cavan County Archives Service: Johnston Central Library, P017/0018
Rent roll of lands in Cavan settled on Mrs Anne Saunderson [of Castle Saunderson], 1779 – NLI, MS 13,340
Late 18th-century account book relating to the Castle Saunderson estate: includes accounts with various tradesmen, labourers, etc, and a rent roll of the estate of 1768 – Cavan County Library Service: Johnston Central Library, call no. 929.20941698 [digitised resource]

See also
[Henry Saunderson], *The Saundersons of Castle Saunderson* (1936)
Jonathan Cherry, 'The Sanderson family of Cloverhill and their County Cavan estate, c. 1780–1912', *Breifne* 10:40 (2004), pp 196–218 (includes names from the 1787 rental)

Smyth estate, Ballymachugh see **Farnham estate**

Somerville estate, Cavan Town see **Farnham estate**

Stanford estate, Kildallan
Deeds, leases, wills, etc, 1641–1823, including a map of the estate of Daniel Stanford in Kildallan parish, 1787 – NLI, n.526, p.799

Stewart Corry estate, Bailieborough
Tenants on the manor of Bailieborough, 1805 – listed in the Appendix to Thomas Hall, 'The history of Presbyterianism in East Cavan and a small portion of Meath and Monaghan' (1912); a copy of this unpublished study is held by Cavan County Library Service and is on the library's website

Storey estate see **Kilmore bishopric estate**

COUNTY DONEGAL

Abercorn estate see under **County Tyrone**

Abraham estate, Raphoe
Box of documents including: map and survey of the Commons of Raphoe, 1750 (no tenants' names); offer from prospective tenants with signatures and seals, 1753; rent roll of property at Raphoe with detailed observations on tenants, *c.* 1757; rental of Raphoe property held by the heirs of Mrs Rebecca Abraham, 1793–9; accounts, 1794–9; late 18th century leases – D1550/103/1

Alexander estate, Moville
Collection of 18th-century leases of the churchlands in the parish of Moville leased from the bishop of Derry, 1737, 1784–9 – D2433/A/1/24

Basil estate see **Lifford estate**

Boyne estate see **Clements estate**

Chambers estate, Conwal
Map of Meenatinny, Meenirroy and Meenaboll {all Conwal}, the property of William Chambers, 1795 – D2298/H/13/1

Clements estate, Kilmacrenan and Mevagh
For more on this estate, see the NLI Collection Lists No. 49 and No. 81 and A. P. W. Malcomson (ed.), *The Clements Archive* (2010).

Lord Boyne's rent roll, 1743 [the year in which estate was purchased by Nathaniel Clements] – printed in L. W. Lucas, *Mevagh Down the Years* (1972), pp 81–3
Maps of the estate, Kilmacrenan barony, 1779 – NLI, 14 A 17 (viewable on the NLI website; names of tenants printed in Lucas, *Mevagh*, pp 91–2)

Conolly estate, Ballyshannon and Castlefinn

A detailed overview of this large and somewhat scattered estate collection is provided by Patrick Walsh and A. P. W. Malcomson (eds), *The Conolly Archive* (2010), published by the Irish Manuscripts Commission. See also the 'Introduction to the Conolly Papers' prepared by PRONI. Patrick Walsh is the author of a biography of the founder of the dynasty, *The Making of the Irish Protestant Ascendancy: The Life of William Conolly, 1662–1729* (2010). Records relating to the properties owned by the family in Fermanagh and Londonderry are covered under the respective county section. See also J. B. Cunningham, 'William Conolly's Ballyshannon estate', *Donegal Annual*, 33 (1981), pp 27–44. With regard to the manor of Castlefinn, see also **Hamilton estate, Castlefinn** and **McCausland/Gage estate** for additional records.

Rentals

Rentals for the Donegal estate, 1680–87, 1726, 1728, 1774, 1782–6, 1800 – NLI, n.6212, p.6951

Rent roll of the manor of Ballyshannon, n.d. [early 18th century] and a survey and valuation of same, 1718, with details on tenants – D2094/24A–C

Rentals of the manor of Tirhugh (leased from Trinity College Dublin), 1686, 1692–4, 1706, 1709 – T2825/C/24

Rental of Castlefinn, 1707 – T2825/C/44/1

Rentals of the manor of Ballyshannon, including the College lands of Tirhugh and Bundrews, 1718, 1722, 1724–6 – T2825/C/26

Rental for part of the estate in the Ballyshannon area, 1728 – NLI, MS 17,302

Rent accounts for the manor of Ballyshannon, 1729 – D2094/33, 34

Rent roll of the Castlefinn estate, 1721–4 – D2094/23

Rent rolls, 1724–1831 – NLI, MS 17,302

Rent rolls, 1772–93 – NAI, M 6917/1–19

Rentals of the Ballyshannon estate, 1774, 1782–6, 1800 – T2825/C/36

Rentals of the Ballyshannon estate, including 1774, 1782–6, and rent accounts, 1777, 1785, 1789, 1790 – T3254/3 (see also NLI, n.5953, p.6486)

Other records

Miscellaneous 18th-century papers, including accounts and correspondence, relating to the Conolly estate at Ballyshannon – NLI, n.6212, p.6951

Correspondence relating to estate matters, 1718–29, 1731 – T2825/C/27

A list of the lives in each lease on the Ballyshannon estate, 1748 – NLI, MS 5751

Survey of property in Drumhome, 1770, naming tenants – MIC435/20

Delap estate, Ballyshannon

Leases relating to the Delap family concerning property in Ballyshannon, 1750–1801 – D2214/3/2

Legal, estate and correspondence papers relating to the Delap family, 1786–1830 – T1336/2

Various papers, including 18th-century leases, for property in Ballyshannon – T2295 *passim*

Donegall estate, Inishowen see under **County Antrim**

Erne (Creighton/Crichton family) estate, Lifford
This estate was owned in the early 1600s by Sir Richard Hansard and by the early eighteenth century it had come into the possession of the Creightons. The family moved swiftly through the ranks of the peerage in the latter part of the 1700s: Barons Erne in 1768; Viscounts Erne in 1781; and Earls Erne in 1789. For more on this collection, see the 'Introduction to the Erne Papers' prepared by PRONI. See also **Erne estate** under **County Fermanagh.**

Leases for the manor of Lifford, 17th and 18th centuries – D1939/18 *passim*
Fragment of memo concerning leases for Lifford and Dublin estates, *c.* 1750–70 – D1939/18/15/10
Survey of the estate, 1768–9 – D1939/19/2/14
'A list of lands in the map of Lifford Estate which Lord Erne wants to be inform'd of', *c.* 1770 – D1939/18/15/19
Rental of the corporation lands of Lifford and the length of the tenures, 1796 – D1939/18/14/6

Ferguson estate, Carndonagh
A book of maps of the farms in Carrickafodan and Tullenaree {both Donagh}, 1790 – NLI, MS 5023

Folliott estate, Ballyshannon
Rent book of the manor of Ballyshannon, 1680–87 – T2825/23/1
This estate was purchased by William Conolly in 1718; see also **Conolly estate.**

Forward estate, Newtowncunningham
This estate comprised lands that had been granted originally to two Cunninghams and William Stewart of Dunduff in the early 1600s. These lands were later acquired by the Forward family (Barons Clonmore, Viscounts Wicklow and earls of Wicklow). See NLI Wicklow Papers, Collection List No. 69.

Valuation of the Castle Forward estate by Archibald Stewart, 1727 – NLI, MS 4247
Volume of maps of the manor of Portlough: 12 from 1727; one each from 1780 and 1810 – NLI, MS 5585
Building accounts, *c.* 1735–9 – NLI, MS 10,470
Rent list for Church lands at Taughboyne, 1758 – MS 38,560(2)
Rent list of Castle Forward estate, 1785 – MS 38,561(2)
List of tenants and holdings on Castle Forward estate, 1785 – MS 38,561(3)
List of towns and tenants' names of the Burt estate, Dunduff estate, Church lands and Castle Forward estate; includes half yearly rent paid to William Forward [1800] – MS 38,561(1)
Rental, *c.* 1790 – NLI, MS 9582

Gage estate, Castlefinn see **McCausland/Gage estate**

Gleadowes estate, Raphoe
'Rent roll of Mr Gleadowes Concerns in the Town of Raphoe', n.d. [c. 1750], plus accounts from 1758 – D1550/103/1

Gore estate, Kilmacrenan
Miscellaneous estate documents relating to Gore lands in counties Donegal, Mayo, Sligo and Wexford, 1795–c. 1811 – T3200/5

Encumbered Estates Court rental for Manor Gore, otherwise Glenswilly, in Kilmacrenan barony, 1857: includes details of 18th-century leases – D1201/24A

The Registry of Deeds includes a number of transcripts of early 18th-century leases issued by Sir Ralph Gore for lands in County Donegal (see especially vol. 21, pp 550–51).

Grove estate, Grove Hall
Rent roll of the Grove Hall estate, 1790: lands of Grove Hall, Newtown-Grove, Aughawinny, Ray {all Kilmacrenan}, Mullagh-Heep {Tullyfern} – *Dublin Evening Post*, 9 Jan. 1790

Gutherie estate
Correspondence addressed to Francis Gutherie of Gagie, Scotland, largely from John and Robert Leslie, bishops of Raphoe, relating to the Gutherie estate in Raphoe diocese, 1637–63 – T1547

Hamilton estate, Brownhall
Various documents, including deeds from 1672, maps from 1777 and papers from 1702, relating to the Hamilton of Brownhall estate – TCD, 'Brownhall Papers'

Leases from 1796 – D3451/1/1

Surveys and maps of various townlands and farms from c. 1750 – D3451/1/7

Map of Ballintra, 1773 – D3451/1/7/16 (see article on this map by Sam Hanna in *Donegal Annual*, 70 (2018), pp 103–06)

See also Dermot James, *John Hamilton of Donegal, 1800–1884: This Recklessly Generous Landlord* (1998)

Hamilton estate, Castlefinn
Volume containing an 'Inventory of leases made by the late Councellor Hamilton' in the manor of Castlefinn, 1763–77 – D1449/7/1

For other records relating to the manor see **Conolly estate** and **McCausland/Gage estate**.

Hamilton estate, Castle Cunningham/Conyngham
Leases, 1734–85 – D2249 *passim*

Encumbered Estates Court rentals for the Castle Cunningham estate, 1857, 1858: include details of 18th-century leases – D1201/24A

Hamilton estate, Cavan
Rental of the 'Cavan estate', comprising the lands of Carnone, Upper Cavan {both Donaghmore}, Macherihee, Ruskie {both Raphoe}, Carrickbrack, Fendrum, Killenure {all Convoy}, Milltown, c. 1720 – MIC616/2

Hart estate, Kilderry, Muff
Rent roll of Major Hart's lands, n.d. [c. 1760], gives dates of leases issued – D3077/A/8/1
Valuation of quarterland of Sladeron {Fahan}, 1772 – D3077/A/8/6
Rent and cash accounts (including payments to labourers and accounts of livestock and 'shellen' sold), 1757–67, 1796–1803: lands mentioned include Ardmalin (Clonca}, Ardmore {Muff}, Ballyarnet, Ballynagard {both Templemore}, Craig {Muff}, Derryreel {Clondahorky/Raymunterdoney}, Erryrooymore {Raymunterdoney}, Muff {Muff}, Mullenbane; includes index of names (loose within volume) – NLI, MS 7885
See also **Vaughan estate**

Hayes estate, Ballybofey
Encumbered Estates Court rentals for the manors of Orwell and Burleigh, 1857: include details of late 18th-century leases issued by the Hayes family – D1201/24A

Keys estate, Gartan
Leases issued by George Keys, 1785: lands of Lower Stramore, Drumnasharragh, Inniskil Mountain, Newtown Drumsallagh {all Gartan} – D3608/2/50–53

Leslie estate, Pettigo see **Leslie estate, Glaslough** under **County Monaghan**

Lifford (Hewitt family) estate, Meenglass
Rentals for County Donegal estate, c. 1770 – Coventry History Centre, PA 1484/49/1–3
Leases for the townlands of Capry, Carrickmagra(th), Golan(d) and Meenbog, 1730–89 – Coventry History Centre, PA 1484/50–54; the early leases were issued by the Basil family, owners of the manor of Orwell in which the property was located

McCausland estate, Stranorlar
Rent roll of part of the manor of Stranorlar, 1740–71 – D669/22

McCausland/Gage estate, Castlefinn
In the early seventeenth century the manor of Castlefinn was owned by the Kingsmill family. In 1698, it was sold to William Hamilton, William Conolly, Oliver McCausland and Kingsmill Evans Mansfield. The complex history of this manor is discussed in two articles by Terry Dolan: 'Surveys and rentals: manor of Castlefinn, 1631–1835', *Donegal Annual*, 67 (2014), pp 73–8; and 'Ulster Plantation leases: the manor of Castlefinn, 1680–1827', *Donegal Annual*, 70 (2018), pp 122–31. For other records relating to the manor, see also **Conolly estate** and **Hamilton estate, Castlefinn.**

Survey of part of the Castlefinn estate, April 1780, naming tenants – D673/61

McClintock estate, Glenmaquin
Map of Lower Glenmaqueen {Raphoe} property of William McClintock, 1782, naming tenants – D642/G/9

Mansfield estate, Killygordon
Leases, 1706–15, 1737–96, 1766–1822 – D1550/78/1–3

Murray of Broughton estate, Boylagh and Banagh

For more on this estate collection, see the 'Introduction to the Murray of Broughton Papers' prepared by PRONI. See also Graeme Kirkham, '"No more to be got off the cat but the skin": Management, landholding and economic change on the Murray of Broughton estate, 1670–1755' in William Nolan, Liam Ronayne and Mairead Dunlevy (eds), *Donegal: History and Society* (1995), pp 357–80.

Rentals

'A Rentall of Rentts of the landes newely lett at this August 1638 …' – Muniment Room, Scone Palace, Perth (transcribed by Simon Elliott and printed in *Donegal Annual*, 54 (2002), pp 61–5)

Rent roll of proportions of Balliweell, Duncanally, Killkar and Monorgan in possession of Richard Murray, 1673 – D2860/24/1

Rental, n.d. [late 17th century] – D2860/25/11

Rent roll of Alexander Murray's estate, 1719 – D2860/4/25

'Rent roll of the estate … as the several tenants now propose', 1727 – D2860/25/10

Remarks on arrears in the manors of Castlemurray and Ballyboyle for the year ending 1 May 1732 – D2860/12/28

Rent arrears, 1749 – D2860/24/11

Rent arrears, 1751 – D2860/12/54–6

Rent roll of Killybegs estate, n.d. [*c.* 1755] – D2860/16/2

Leases

'A particular of the leases of the Manor of [Castle Murray deleted] Ballyweele that are out and were out', 1638 – Muniment Room, Scone Palace, Perth (transcribed by Simon Elliott and printed in *Donegal Annual*, 54 (2002), pp 61–5

Counterpart and expired leases, 1680–1728, 1751, 1789 – D2860/36/1–64

Accounts of rents and duties fixed on for leases, n.d. [*c.* 1730] – D2860/25/2

List of the leases signed by the trustees of Alexander Murray since 24 May 1731 – NRS, GD/10/944

Surveys

Surveys of the estate, one by Thomas Addi of Donaghadee from 1730, the other by John Hood of Moyle, County Donegal, from 1755, plus associated papers – D2860/25/1–11 (the original PRONI calendar contains a full transcript of this survey)

Survey and book of maps of Alexander Murray's estate in the baronies of Boylagh and Bannagh, 1749 – NLI, 21 F 66 (see also NLI, n.1929, p.1461)

Miscellaneous

Correspondence relating to the Murray of Broughton estate in County Donegal, 1694–1796 – NLI, MS 48,530/1–9

Memoranda about estate matters, *c.* 1740–80, including one of 1780 listing undertenants – D2860/26/1–13

Detailed letter by Thomas Addi about the Donegal estate, 1745/6 – T3250/1 (copied from NRS, GD 10/T291/946)

Raphoe bishopric of estate
Cash book of Bishop William Smyth, 1674–86 – NLI, MS 41,572/1 [missing]
A survey of the lands of 'Termond Magraagh' [Termon Magrath], 1682: does not name
   tenants, but includes much topographical detail as well as a preface dealing with the
   art of surveying – NLI, MS 19,786
Map of Ballymydonnel belonging to the bishop of Raphoe, 1795 – NLI, 15 B 16 (14)

Sanderson estate, Manorcunningham
Documentation relating to a property in Raymoghy parish owned by the Sandersons
of Cloverhill, County Cavan, including a map of the estate of Alexander Sanderson
of 1770 naming the tenants, and rentals beginning in 1801 – D3480/13. The lands
shown on the 1770 map comprise Ballyboe, Big and Little Gracky (Grawky), Great
(Big) Isle, Magherabeg and Magheramore; the village of Manorcunningham is shown
in some pictorial detail. For more on this family, see **Sa(u)nderson estate** under
County Cavan.

Stewart estate, Ards, etc
Account book, 1781–90, relating to the estate and personal affairs of Alexander Stewart
   of Ards, which records expenses and rent accounts in connection with the Mercers'
   proportion at Kilrea, County Londonderry, Ards and Killygordon, County Donegal,
   and 'Drummatticonnor', County Down – D2784/19
Letters to Alexander Stewart, 1771–1814 – D4137/A/1, /2

Stewart estate, Ballylawn
Acquired in the early seventeenth century, this was the original Irish property of the
Stewarts (Lords Londonderry) of Mount Stewart, County Down. See **Londonderry
estate** under **County Down.**

Leases, 1715–48 – D654/L/RE/76/1–5
Leases, 1710–26: lands include Big and Little Veagh, Tirkeeran, Ballylane [Ballylawn]
   – D2092/5 *passim* (also T1878)

Stewart estate, Fortstewart, Ramelton
Leases, 1699 onwards – D2358/2
Rent roll of Country Farm on Ramelton and Fanet estate, 1714 – D2358/3/1
Valuation of Ramelton estate, including a rental of 1727 – D2358/5/1
Account book, 1758–74, including a rent roll of Ramelton and Fannet from 1769, and
   a rental of Aughnish from 1767 – D2358/4/1
Surveys and valuations, 1770–*c.* 1800 – D2358/5/3–11
Rental of Ramelton estate, 1785–90 – D2358/3/2
Rent and fees for 'new leting' of part of estate, 1787 – D2358/3/3
Rental, 1789 – D2358/3/4
Current account book including list of rents for Fortstewart – *c.* 1783–*c.* 1798 –
   D2147/1/1

Stewart estate, Mount Stewart

This estate, also known as Cooleaghy or Dunduffsfort, was granted originally to William Stewart of Dunduff in the early 1600s. It was later acquired by the Forward family that rose to become the earls of Wicklow. There is an extensive set of early records relating to this estate among the Wicklow Papers in the National Library of Ireland (see **Forward estate** above). A detailed listing of these records was published in *DIFHR*, 34 (2011), pp 9–15.

Survey of part of the manor of Mount Stewart, Raphoe barony, belonging to Mrs Alice
    Stewart, 1717, including a terrier of 1726 – NLI, 15 B 16 (8)

Styles estate, Kilteevogue

Survey and valuation of the manor of Corlacky owned by Sir Charles Styles Bt and
    Colonel William Styles, 1773 – NLI, MS 402
Leases for Ballymalone [Ballynatone?], 1800 – D3480/58, 60, 61

Trinity College Dublin estate

As part of the scheme for Ulster Plantation, Trinity College Dublin was granted extensive lands in three Ulster counties – Armagh, Donegal and Fermanagh. The College's lands in County Donegal were to be found in the baronies of Kilmacrenan and Tirhugh, those in County Armagh in the barony of Armagh, and those in County Fermanagh in the barony of Clankelly. A large collection of documents, including rentals, leases, maps and petitions is available in the Manuscripts & Archives Research Library of TCD under reference MUN/P/24. Generally, the College's lands were leased to a series of middlemen, but the names of subtenants can be found in the records. What follows is a summary of the main items in this collection, listed in the order in which they appear in the catalogue.

Rental of lands in counties Armagh, Fermanagh & Donegal, n.d. [*c.* 1638–40] –
    MUN/P/24/123a
Rental of lands in County Donegal, n.d. [1630s?] – MUN/P/24/125
Petition of the English sub-tenants on the College's County Armagh lands seeking help
    in their dispute with Lady Caulfield, *c.* 1643(?) – MUN/P/24/135
Rent account for lands in the barony of Kilmacrenan, 1653–4 – MUN/P/24/137
Rental of Kilmacrenan for 3 years from All Saints, 1656 – MUN/P/24/138
Rental of College lands in the barony of Tirhugh, 1658 – MUN/P/24/141
List of rents in County Donegal, 1662 – MUN/P/24/159
Notes on rents due & received for Northern estates, 1668 – MUN/P/24/176
Receipt signed Jer. Moore for a year's valuation money for lands in County Donegal
    (tenants' names & holdings stated), 1672 – MUN/P/24/181
Account of the state of the College lands in Ulster presented by Dr Styles
    (denominations, tenants, rents and miscellaneous notes, especially on houses and
    timber), 1673 – MUN/P/24/184
Rental of lands in Colure, County Armagh, in lease to John Parnell, n.d. [*c.* 1680] –
    MUN/P/24/216
Arrears list for College's Ulster lands, 1681 – MUN/P/24/221
List of lands in Toaghy, County Armagh, with names of the immediate tenants under
    College, 1683 – MUN/P/24/231

List of lands in County Armagh, with sub-tenants and rent per acre, apparently drawn up by Henry Maxwell of College Hall, County Armagh, n.d. [1687 or later] – MUN/P/24/234

Rent roll for lands in County Fermanagh (tenants' names and rents only), 1683 – MUN/P/24/244

Petitions of the inhabitants of the College land in the barony of Kilmacrenan, for the restoration of John Braiding to the seneschalcy of the manor, one unsigned, the other with signatures, n.d. [1698?] – MUN/P/24/253–254

Descriptive survey of Ulster lands including tenants, denominations, acreages, valuation, and remarks on land type and use (pp 5–8 apparently an earlier version in a different order, of part of no. 259), n.d. [late 17th century] – MUN/P/24/258

Valuation of Ulster lands (tenants, denominations, acreages & valuations), n.d. [mid 17th century] – MUN/P/24/259

Note of the the College lands in Tirhugh held by the bishop of Ardagh (undertenants, denominations and rents), n.d. [mid 17th century] – MUN/P/24/260

Rough list of lands and tenants in counties Armagh, Donegal and Fermanagh, n.d. [mid 17th century?] – MUN/P/24/261

List of rents from lands in Tirhugh, n.d. [mid 17th century] – MUN/P/24/262

Rough list of tenants & holdings (County Armagh?), n.d. [mid or late 17th century) – MUN/P/24/268

Letter from Nath. Cooper to Rev. Benjamin Span, Letterkenny (rector 1694–1716), forwarding a rent roll of Capt. Hamilton's land (no. 273) & discussing the condition of the land., n.d. [late 17th/early 18th century] – MUN/P/24/272

Rental of lands in Donegal, n.d. [early or mid 17th century] – MUN/P/24/274

List of lands & tenants in County Donegal, n.d. [mid 17th century] – MUN/P/24/285

Journal of a tour of inspection of the northern estates by the Provost, Dr Gilbert & Dr Elwood, in pursuance of a decision of the Board, 1712 – MUN/P/24/347a

Certificate signed by 11 persons that it would be for the public good to have a fair at Ballanagolloglach, being the most suitable spot in the manor of Kilmacrenan, 1713 – MUN/P/24/348

Rough rent account for lands in County Fermanagh, 1770s – MUN/P/24/368

Vaughan estate, Buncrana, Porthall and Castledoe

This collection includes letters, accounts and other papers from the early 1700s onwards relating to the estate of George Vaughan (d. 1763), which was inherited by Gustavus Brooke, Henry Vaughan Brooke, and Henry Hart. The Doe estate (comprising Doe, Castledoe, South and North Maherabled, East, West and South Killoghcarrow, Ruskey, Derryfad, Umphryfad, Upper and Lower Cashell, Upper and Lower Scarvey, Drimcason, Drumnakelly and Kilhill) was acquired by George Vaughan Hart in 1797 – D3077/A/4

See also **Hart estate**

Wray estate, Dunfanaghy

Leases, correspondence, receipts, accounts and other documents, 1740 onwards: lands include Ballanascadan {Kilmacrenan}, Upper Ranny {Tullyfern}, Woodland {Aghanunshin}, Ardigary, Knockabreen – D2147/2/1, /4, /5

Miscellaneous 18th-century papers relating to the Wray estate – John Rylands Library, Manchester, RYCH/2467–2477 (includes a rent roll of the lands sold by Mr Wray of Ards, n.d. [*c.* 1764] – RYCH/2472)

See also Charlotte Violet Trench, *The Wrays of Donegal, Londonderry and Antrim* (1945), which includes numerous extracts from original documents.

COUNTY DOWN

Adair estate, Kilmood
Resolution of the tenantry of James Adair, 1783 – *Belfast Newsletter*, 4–7 Nov. 1783 (names only)

Allen estate, Ballywalter
Names of tenants in the townlands of Ballywalter, Ballyobigan {Inishargy}, Ballyfrench {Ballyhalbert}, Tullykevin {Greyabbey} and Cotton {Bangor}, part of the estate of Alexander Allen, a minor, 1776 – *Belfast Newsletter*, 6–9 Feb. 1776

Annesley estate, Castlewellan
The Annesley property in County Down was divided into four main portions: Castlewellan (around the town of that name), Bannfield (near Rathfriland and Hilltown; previously owned by the Close family), Newcastle (around the town of that name) and Dunlady (more scattered, but mainly around Dundonald). For more on this estate collection, see the 'Introduction to the Annesley Papers' prepared by PRONI, which lists the townlands owned by the family. See also **Annesley estate** under **County Cavan.**

Leases
Leases beginning in the 18th century relating to the County Down estate, arranged by townland – D1503/1
Leases beginning in the 18th century relating to the Annesley estate at Ballynahinch, including 30 leases issued on 30 November 1782 by Arthur Annesley for Cargacreevy {Annahilt}, Burren {Dromara/Magherahamlet} and Ballycreen {Magheradrool} – D500 *passim*

Maps
Map of the manor of Castlewellan owned by William Annesley Esq., 1742, naming tenants: lands of Backaderry, Ballymaginaghy, Ballymegrechan, Benra[w], Legananny, Leitrim, Maghrymayo and Sleavenaboley {all Drumgooland}, Castlewillian, Clarkhill {both Kilmegan}, Lurgan – T1025/1
Map and survey of part of Ballycreen, part of the estate of Arthur Annesley Esq., 1776 – D1167/3/1

Other
Rentals, 1788–9 – D1503/6/1A–B
Annotated almanac including payments to labourers and rent accounts for Slevenaboley {Drumgooland} and part of the Bannfield estate, 1765 – D1854/8/2

Annotated almanac including payments to labourers, 1768–9 – D1854/8/3
Copy out-letter books relating to estate administration, 1774–85 – D2309/4/3, /4 (see
    W. H. Crawford (ed.), *Letters of an Ulster Land Agent 1774–85 (The Letter-Books of
    John Moore of Clough, County Doom)* (1976))
Cash account book, 1775–93, 1825–35 – D1503/8/37
Timber account book, including notes on wages paid, 1792–1802 – D1503/8/38

Ardglass (Cromwell family) estate, Downpatrick

Rental of estate of Thomas, earl of Ardglass, 1669 – T724/2 (Cambridge,
University Library, Add. MS 3822), printed in *Lecale Miscellany*, 3 (1985), pp 54–6
Letters, copies of letters and accounts relating to the estates in Lecale barony, 1617–
    1725 – TCD, MS 11,353
Letters, receipts, affidavits of tenants and other papers relating to litigation concerning
    the estate of the earl of Ardglass, *c.* 1680–1686 – NLI, 10,985–6
See also **Southwell estate.**

Bagenal/Bayly estate, Newry, Mourne

The origins of the Bagenal estate and its successors can be traced to the acquisition of
the lordships of Newry and Mourne by Nicholas Bagenal in the middle of the sixteenth
century. In 1715, following the death of a subsequent Nicholas Bagenal, the estate was
divided between two of his cousins. Edward Bayly received four townlands in the Newry
area (as well as the County Louth lands and property in Wales), while Robert Needham
(or Nedham) acquired the main part of the Newry estate as well as the Mourne (Kilkeel)
estate. The Baylys, following a name change to Paget, rose to the titles of earl of
Uxbridge (1784) and marquess of Anglesey (1815). For more on this estate, see the
'Introduction to the Anglesey Papers' prepared by PRONI. Listed here are records
relating to the Bagenal and Bayly estates. Records relating to the **Needham estate** are
listed separately.

Rent roll of the town and lordship of Newry, 1575 – MIC322/1 (Harold O'Sullivan,
    'A 1575 rent-roll, with contemporaneous maps, of the Bagenal estate in the
    Carlingford Lough district', *Journal of the County Louth Archaeological and Historical
    Society*, 21:1 (1985), pp 31–47)
Rent roll of Nicholas Bagenal's estate, including the Lordship of Morne (Mourne),
    Newry town and the Lordship of Newry, 1688 – D619/7/1/1
Rent roll of the Bagenal estate, including the Lordship of Morne (Mourne) and
    Killowen, Newry town and the Lordship of Newry, 1714 – D619/7/1/2
Rent roll recording the chief tenants in possession of townlands in the Bagenal estate
    including a summary of the chief tenancy agreements, *c.* 1730 – D619/7/1/3
Rent roll of Sir Nicholas Bayly's estate: lands of Crobane, Derrylacka, Sheeptown and
    Dyserts, 1756 – D619/7/1/8
Surveyor's notebook naming chief tenants and undertenants in the townlands of
    Desarts, Sheeptown, Crobane and Derrilacka and the extent of their holdings, 1784
    – D619/3/6
Rent roll of the earl of Uxbridge's estate, 1792–3: townlands as above – D619/3/19

Bailie estate, Inishargy and Loughinisland

Rental of the late James Bailie's estate at Clough, 1786 – D4160/25/7

Rental of all the lands held by James Bailie at his decease, n.d. [c. 1786]: lands of Ballyhalbert, Ballywalter, Knocksticken, Ardilea {last two in Loughinisland} – D4160/25/11

Banks estate, Lecale

Printed advertisement for the sale of Thomas Banks's estate in Lecale, which is in the form of a rental and sales particulars, n.d. [1750]: lands of Ballyplunt {Rathmullan}, Carrignab {Tyrella}, Clontabeg, Corbally, Islemuck (Upper and Lower) {Tyrella}, Munycarragh {Kilmegan?}, Torela {Tyrella} – D2092/1/3, p. 41 (MIC596/1) (see also *Belfast Newsletter*, 14 Dec. 1750)

Bayly estate, Newry see Bagenal/Bayly estate

Blackwood estate, Clandeboye and Killyleagh

The origins of this estate can be traced to the seventeenth century. In 1800, the head of the family was ennobled as Baron Dufferin. In 1871 and 1888, respectively, the earldom of Dufferin and marquessate of Dufferin and Ava were created. For more on this estate and family, see the 'Introduction to the Dufferin Papers' prepared by PRONI.

Map and survey of the estate of Sir John Blackwood, *c.* 1720, naming tenants – T3666/1

Transcript of an Exchequer Bill of 28 April 1741 involving Robert Blackwood, naming 274 tenants: lands of Cherryvalley, Ringrevy, Littleballyhenry, Barnymackry, Troopersfield, Raffrey, Maghernycrosse alias Magherycoyle, Ballykile, Lislee, Monerea, Monlough, Ballybeen, Tullyhubbert, Adnislate, Tullygirvan, Ballycloghan and Ballygowan – T808/15009

Rent account books, 1739–82 – D1071/A/B/1/1–4

Cash books, 1720–39 (includes rent accounts, 1735–9) and 1752–74 – D1071/A/B/2/1–2

Vouchers, 1708–18, *c.* 1720–*c.* 1770 – D1071/A/C/1/39, /40

Survey of Ballygrott and Ballyskelly, 1743 – D1071/A/F/1

Leases, pre-1800 – D1071/A/J/1 (for other 18th-century leases see D1071/A/H *passim*)

Blundell estate, Dundrum see Downshire estate

Brice estate, Ballysallagh Major

Leases for 'Ballysalough' Major {Bangor}, 1760 – D500/17–19

Names of tenants in Ballysallagh Major, 1786 – *Belfast Newsletter*, 1–4 Aug. 1786

Correspondence relating to Edward Brice's property at Ballywilliam {Donaghadee}, *c.* 1800 – NLI, MS 13,537

See also **Brice estate** under **County Antrim** for a volume of mid 18th-century maps, which includes some townlands in County Down.

Camac estate see Mount Ross estate

Claneboye/Clanbrassil estate see **Hamilton (Claneboye and Clanbrassil) estate**

Clanwilliam (Meade family) estate, Gill Hall and Rathfriland
The origins of this estate are rather complex. An estate focused on Gill Hall, near Dromore, was established by the Magills in the mid to late seventeenth century. In 1701, this estate passed to the Hawkins family, owners of the Rathfriland estate. In 1765, the heiress of these properties, Theodosia Hawkins Magill, married Sir John Meade (created Viscount Clanwilliam and Baron Gilford in 1766, and earl of Clanwilliam in 1776). See the 'Introduction to the Clanwilliam/Meade Papers' prepared by PRONI and also A. P. W. Malcomson: '"A woman scorned?" Theodosia, Countess of Clanwilliam (1743–1817)', *Familia*, 15 (1999), pp 1–25.

Leases for the Gill Hall estate arranged by townland and catalogued individually, 1684 onwards: including lands of Ballintaggart, Ballymacarattybeg, Ballynagarrick, Drumcro and Drumo, Edenordinary, Greenan, Kilmore, Kilsorrel, Kinallen, Lisnagirrell, Lisnaward and Skeagh – D3044/A/4
Rent account book for Rathfriland estate, 1740–41 – D1629/1
Renewable lease book for Rathfriland estate, 1677–1831 – D875/4
Day book of renewable fines on leases for Rathfriland estate, 1771–1841 – D875/3
Maps of the Rathfriland estate, 1776, naming tenants – T855/1

Clewlow estate, Killinchy in the Woods
Leases for Killinchy in the Woods {Killyleagh}, 1738–88 – D1167/1/251–263

Close estate, Upper Iveagh
Map of part of the estate of Samuel Close in Upper Iveagh, 1723: lands of Teerigory, Munigor, Lisenisk, Anaghinshenah {all Drumballyroney}, Ballydough {Drumgath}, Ballygorienmore, Ballygorienbeg, Lisnamulligan, Tamery {all Clonduff} – D670/1
See also **Annesley estate**

Colvill(e) estate, Newtownards and Comber see **Londonderry estate**

Crawford estate, Florida see **Gordon estate**

De Clifford estate, Downpatrick see **Southwell estate**

Delacherois estate, Donaghadee see **Montgomery estate**

Dickson estate, Ballyclander
Map of Ballyclander {Ballee}, property of the co-heirs of the late William Dickson, including names of tenants and acreage held, 1759 – T2969

Downshire (Hill family) estate, Hillsborough
The founder of this vast estate was Moses Hill, an officer in the Elizabethan army in Ireland, who purchased extensive tracts of land from the O'Neills of Castlereagh and Magennises of Kilwarlin in the early 1600s. The estate was extended further by his successors through the acquisition, either by purchase or intermarriage, of lands at

Loughbrickland, Banbridge, Newry, Hilltown and Dundrum. The family also owned lands in other parts of Ireland, notably at Edenderry, County Offaly. In the eighteenth century the Hills advanced through the ranks of the Irish peerage, from Baron Hill of Kilwarlin and Viscount Hillsborough (1717), to earl of Hillsborough (1771) and finally marquess of Downshire (1789).

The PRONI 'Introduction to the Downshire Papers' is a good starting point to the vast estate collection. The creation of this estate is dealt with in W. A. Maguire, *The Downshire Estate in Ireland: The Management of Irish Landed Estates in the Early Nineteenth Century* (1972), which includes a map of the properties owned in County Down (p. 273). The author's extensive research notes on this estate are in PRONI (D4512). See also A. P. W. Malcomson, 'The Gentle Leviathan: Arthur Hill, 2nd Marquess of Downshire [1753–1801] …' in P. Roebuck (ed.), *Plantation to Partition: Essays in Ulster History in Honour of J. L. McCracken* (1981).

Correspondence
Eighteenth-century correspondence is listed under D607 and extends to several thousand letters and associated papers, most of them relating to the second marquess of Downshire. The material includes correspondence relating to the Blundell lands at Dundrum, acquired by the Hills in the late 1700s, including a volume of *c*. 100 pages containing copies of correspondence between Henry Hatch, Lord Blundell and William Trumbull, 1746–58 (D607/A/23, see also MIC17/1). Correspondence relating to the Hills themselves has been catalogued as follows:

Letters and papers of Wills Hill, second Viscount Hillsborough, first earl of Hillsborough, and first marquess of Downshire, 1746–93 – D607/B
Letters and papers of Arthur Hill, second marquess of Downshire, 1793–5 – D607/C
Letters and papers of the second marquess of Downshire, 1796 – D607/D
Letters and papers of the second marquess of Downshire, 1797 – D607/E
Correspondence of the second marquess of Downshire, mainly about the rebellion, 1798 – D607/F
Correspondence of the second marquess of Downshire, mainly about the Union, 1799 – D607/G
Correspondence of the second marquess of Downshire, 1800–01 – D607/H

Rentals
Rentals, rent rolls, rent ledgers and arrears relating to the disparate parts of the estate, some pre-dating the acquisition of the lands by the Hills, are listed chronologically below:

Rent roll of lands in Kilwarlin, Castlereagh, Slatnailes, and Upper Iveagh, 1698 – Berkshire Record Office, DED/E29
Rent roll of 'Killwarling', 1698 – T201/1
Rent roll of Banbridge estate, 1725 – D671/R1/1A
Rental of the Kilwarlin estate, 1732–4 – D4442/1
Dundrum rental, 1734 – D607/A/13
Rent rolls of Kilwarlin and Carrickfergus estates, 1744–5, 1745–6 – D2784/23/1/1–2

List of rents and arrears, Dundrum estate, 1747 – D607/A/41

An account of rents of the Dundrum estate, 1755 – D607/A/139–140

Rent roll of Lurganville and Ballygowan (Kilwarlin estate), 1763–4 – D671/R8/161

Statement of arrears of rent, Dundrum estate, 1796 – D607/A/517

Dundrum rent roll, 1801 – D671/V939

Rentals for Banbridge, Castlereagh, Hilltown, Kilwarlin and Newry starting in 1801 which provide details of leases issued in the 18th century – D671/R1/2, /R4/1, /R7/1, /R8/1, /R9/1

Large collection of 18th-century ledgers: these contain information on leases, lives in leases, etc – D671/A1

Leases and lease books

There is a vast collection of 18th-century leases. Pre-1750 leases have been catalogued under D671/LE, with those after 1750 under D671/L. These are arranged mainly in bundles by townland within the relevant portion of the estate. For the Kilwarlin estate alone there are over 250 pre-1750 leases. Lease books, beginning in 1794, but recording details of leases from *c.* 1700, are available under D671/A4. There are also lease agreements for the Dundrum estate, 1795–7 (D671/A40/1).

Miscellaneous

18th-century cash books, recording rent payments – D671/A2

18th-century specie books, recording rent payments – D671/A3

Alphabetical list of tenants in the Kilwarlin estate, *c.* 1800 – D671/A26/1

Moss book (for Kilwarlin estate?), 1757–77, recording names of tenants permitted to cut turf in the mosses – D671/A14/1

Dromore bishopric estate

See Chapter 2 for a discussion of the records relating to the estate of the bishop of Dromore.

Dufferin estate see Blackwood estate

Dunbar estate, Millisle

Map of the estate of George Dunbar: Drumfad and Ballyrolly {Donaghadee}, 1797 – T1242/1

Dungannon (Hill-Trevor family) estate, Breda

Collection of leases, mainly from 1750 onwards: lands include Ballyknockan, Ballylenny, Ballylesson, Ballymacena, Ballymaconaghy, Ballynahatty, Ballynavally, Cloghskelt, Crossgar, Deehommed, Dree, Drin, Dromiller, Edenderry, Gransha, Island Moyle and Bally Island Moyle, Lisnasure, Moneyrea, Monlough – D778 *passim*

Collection of leases, many from 18th century, for townlands including Ballynahatty, Moneyreagh, Ballynavally, Galwally, Crossgar and Deehommed – D1954/4 *passim*

See also Ben Simon, *A Treasured Landscape: The Heritage of Belvoir Park* (2005).

Echlin estate, Echlinville
Leases for Ballygraffin, Ballyhalbert {both Ballyhalbert}, Tullycross {Castleboy}, late
    18th century – T1009 *passim*
Map of Echlinville demesne {Ballyhalbert}, n.d. [*c.* 1790], naming tenants in adjoining
    farms – T1847/28

Fitzgerald estate see Kildare estate

Forde estate, Seaforde
Leases starting in 1714 (158 pre-1800) – D566 *passim*
Names of tenants in Drumnaquily {Kilmegan}, Muronclogher {Kilmore}, Drumgoland,
    Ardtanagh, Dunanew, Drumnakelly and Seaforde {all Loughinisland}, 1766 – *Belfast
    Newsletter*, 25 July 1766
Rental commencing in 1801 – D566/B/1/1

Fortescue estate, Mullafernaghan
This estate, mainly in the parish of Magherally, was acquired by the Downshires in the
early 1800s (hence the survival of the 1725 rental in the Downshire estate collection).

Rental, 1725: lands of Mullafernaghan, Drumnavaddy, Ballykelly, Ballycross,
    Ballygunaghan, Tonaghmore, Mill Lands – D671/R/1/1A
Leases, 1747–69, 1791–1806 – D4074/3/1, /2
Rent roll and cash account, 1804 – D4074/3/4

Gibbons estate, Ballykinler
Rent roll of part of the estate of Samuel Gibbons in County Down: lands of Ballyveston,
the 'Sea Wreck in the Shore', Lissoyd, Crawley's Quarter, Lismohan, Quoystown,
Cartown, The Warren and Kilners; very detailed information, including date of lease,
term unexpired, acres and rent, 1766 – *Belfast Newsletter*, 18 Nov. 1766

Gordon estate, Florida
The Florida manor estate was acquired by the Crawford family from the Montgomerys
of Rosemount in 1691 and passed to the Gordons in 1755.

Leases from 1764 onwards: lands of Ballybunden {Kilmood}, Ballymacashen,
    Drumreagh {both Killinchy}, Kilmood – D4204/C/1
Rent rolls beginning in 1790 – D4204/D/1
Correspondence of Robert Gordon concerning estate and other matters (including
    maps), 1758–1800 – D4204/E/1
Papers relating to the divisions of bog boundaries and mosses, 1762–79 – D4204/J/1
Surveys, maps and valuations from 1764 onwards – D4204/J/2
Envelope containing list of names of those who held the office of seneschal in the
    Lordship of the Manor of Florida, County Down since the year 1784 [*c.* 1965] –
    D2229/2

Hall estate, Ballyhornan

Map and survey of the estate of Rowley Hall, n.d. [*c.* 1730–40] – D424/89

Leases, 1731 onwards: lands include Ballybeg, Ballyhornan, Seahornan, Tollumgrange {all Dunsfort} – D424 *passim*

Hall estate, Narrow Water

Survey of the manor of Mullaghglass, County Armagh, 1730, naming tenants – D1540/1/8

Servants account book, 1783–1802, providing information on servants' wages, their character and length of service – D1540/1/48 [currently listed as missing]

Volume of maps of the manor of Mullaghglass and the Narrow Water estate, 1800, naming tenants – T2821/1A

Hall estate, Strangford and Lower Iveagh

Leases, principally issued by Francis Hall of Strangford, 1683–1759: lands of Karcasack {Magheralin}, Ballyvarl(e)y, Kernan, Coose, Dromore, Lisnefiffee and Gragerlogh (all Lower Iveagh barony), Strangford, Lignagapock (otherwise Moss Park), Lower and Upper Rossglass and Black Causey – D4160/C/2

Rental of lands in Lower Iveagh, 1707–08 – D4160/C/15/1

Survey of Kirnon [Kernan], naming tenants, 1737 – D4160/15/3

Arrrears for lands in Lower Iveagh, 1755 – D4160/15/5

Arrears out of the bishop's lease near Dromore, 1755: lands of Ballysallagh and Dromaghodoan {both Dromore} – D4160/15/6

Rent roll of that part of the Strangford estate lately possessed by Mrs Rebecca Hall, *c.* 1802 – D4160/15/10A–B

See also **Hall estate, Fews** under **County Armagh**

Hamilton (Claneboye and Clanbrassil) estate

The origins of this estate can be traced to the acquisition of vast tracts of land in north-east County Down in the early 1600s by Sir James Hamilton, the son of the vicar of Dunlop in Ayrshire. He was created Viscount Claneboye in 1622, while his son was created earl of Clanbrassil in 1647. On the death of the second earl without heir in 1675 this title became extinct (though was revived for another branch of the Hamiltons in the eighteenth century), after which the estate was divided among a number of claimants. See T. K. Lowry (ed.), *The Hamilton Manuscripts* (1867) for more information on this estate in the seventeenth century.

Maps of the estate by Thomas Raven, 1625, naming tenants – T870 (original volume in North Down Museum)

Entry book of tenancies, 1615–78 – T761/3

Letter book relating to estate, 1632–1715 – T761/7

Leases issued by the earl of Clanbrassil, 1671–5 – D4216/2/2

Rent roll, *c.* 1670, with early 18th-century annotations – T2253/1

Rental of 1681 of the lands of the Ards, Holywood and Bangor – printed in Lowry, *Hamilton Manuscripts*, pp 108–11

Rent roll of the jointure lands of Ann, late countess of Clanbrassil, 1688–92, parishes of Killyleagh, Killinchy and Tonochneive (Saintfield) – printed in Lowry, *Hamilton Manuscripts*, pp 125–32

Typed copy of a rent roll of the earl of Clanbrassil's estates in the County Down, 1623–75, NLI, n.82, p.279

Typescript copy of a rental of the estates of Henry, earl of Clanbrassil, listing terms of leases, with indexes of townlands (by barony) and names of tenants, *c*. 1675 – NLI, MS 1714

Photostat of a rent roll of the estates of Henry, earl of Clanbrassil, in County Down, 1670–80 – NLI, MS 784

A volume of typescript copies of correspondence largely between Hans Stevenson and William Hamilton, relating to lands in County Down and financial transactions relating thereto, 1694–1710, with earlier (from 1621) and later (to 1715) correspondence of various other persons – NLI, MS 1702

Hamilton estate, Tollymore

This estate was acquired by William Hamilton through his marriage to Ellen Magennis *c*. 1650. His grandson was created Viscount Limerick in 1719 and earl of Clanbrassil in 1756. The title died out with the death of the second earl in 1798 after which the estates passed to his sister, who had married the earl of Roden. See Robert Jocelyn (Earl of Roden), *Tollymore: The Story of an Irish Demesne* (2005).

Rent rolls of Tollymore, 1743, 1768–9 – MIC147/2
Letters, including correspondence about estate matters, 1679–96 – MIC147/8
Abstracts of accounts, Tollymore, *c*. 1790 – MIC147/9

Hawkins estate, Rathfriland see Clanwilliam estate

Holmes estate, Glastry

Leases issued by John Holmes of Belfast for farms in Glastry {Ballyhalbert/Inishargy}, 1779–93 – D332 *passim*

Hutcheson estate, Drumalig

Account of lives in leases of Mr Hans Hutcheson of Drumalig {Saintfield}, 1768 – D971/34/B/8

Innis estate, Manor of Glen Drumantine

Leases from the 18th century – T1514 *passim*
Rent roll, 1750–51: lands of Ballyblough, Ballylough, Carrickrovaddy, Corgory, Dromanitine, Dromiller, Lurganare {all Donaghmore}, Lisnaterny {Aghaderg} – T1514/58

See also **Magenis estate, Castlewellan and Dromantine**

Ker estate, Ballynahinch, etc

Leases for Ballymisert {Holywood}, 1796 – D500/93–95
Valuation of Ballynahinch, n.d. [*c*. 1802] – D500/96

Map of the town and lands of Clough {Loughinisland}, part of the estate of David Ker
Esq., 1787 – D1167/3/3

Private out-letter book of David Ker, including material concerning estate matters,
1791–1811 – D2651/2/85

Kildare (Fitzgerald family) estate, Ardglass and Strangford
Lecale estate title deeds and leases, 1514–1715 – D3078/1/29/1–8

Small folio volume containing copies of letters to the earl of Kildare, 1628–37,
including material on the Lecale estate – D3078/3/1/5

Transcripts of deeds, etc some of which are leases for the Lecale estate from the early
17th century – D3078/1/1/1–3

Leases by the earl and countess of Kildare, 1716–54 – MIC573/22

Map of the manor of Ardglass, 1734, naming tenants – D642/G/2 (MIC593/9)

Map of the Strangford estate, 1734, naming tenants – D642/G/3 (MIC593/9)

Survey of the manor of Ardglass, 1768: Rossglass, Kingfad, Crenkildare, Ballynaglogh,
Bright, Killdresser, Ballyvigoes, Ballygilbert, Ballyedock, Artole Irish, Artole English,
and Ardglass – D2223/M/1; T456/8

Names of 82 tenants of the Rt Hon. Charles Fitzgerald offering to assist HM service
with cars and horses, c. 1798: lands of Ballygilbert, Ringfad, Ballidock, Crew,
Ardtowel English, Ardtowel Irish, Ballyirgis, Ballinagalagh, Bright, Carabane,
Whigamstown, Tullycarnon and Ardglass – D272/18

Leases by the Rt Hon. Henry Fitzgerald, 1783–1823 – MIC573/22

Johnston estate, Gilford, etc
Rental of estate, 1725 – T1054/1

Rent roll of Richard Johnston's estate, 1731: lands of Loughans, Drumaran, Emdall,
Glaskermore, Glaskerbeg, Moybrick, Finnis, Derryneill, Garvegery, Clunmaghery,
Clanvaraghan, Slievenisky, County Down; Carricklais and Sheetrim, County
Armagh; and Cloughnart, Dunmadigan, Kingory, Carrachan, Mullaghboy, Killyleg,
Clossdaur and Kinnkelly, County Monaghan – T1007/38 (another copy at
T1175/1; see also NLI, n.809, p.1014)

Rent roll of lands to be sold in counties Armagh, Down and Monaghan, c. 1748 –
D1835/34

Map and survey of Drumaran and Loughans {both Tullylish}, 1769 – T1007/90

Rental, 1795 – T1007/194

Kilmorey estate, Newry and Mourne see Needham estate

Lambert estate, Dromore
Names of tenants in Ballymacormick and Quilly {both Dromore}, property of Ralph
Lambert, 1757 – *Belfast Newsletter*, 15 July 1757

Lascelles estate, Killough
Volume including rent accounts, 1796–7 – D1944/8/1

Lawrence estate, Lawrencetown, Tullylish
Lease of Lissnafiffy, which has an attached map showing tenants in adjoining farms, 1782 – D639/11

Rental of estate of Thomas Dawson Lawrence, covering townlands of Knocknagor, Coose, Lisnafiffy and Kiernon {all Tullylish}, 1796 – T426/1, pp 25–30

Leslie estate, Lecale
These were the Leslies of Ballybay, County Monaghan.

Leases arranged by townland of the estate in the barony of Lecale, 1793 onwards: lands include Ardmeen {Down}, Ballynaries [Ballynarry] {Saul}, Jordans's Crew {Ardglass/Ballee}, Rathmullan {Rathmullan}, Stone Island {Ballee} – D3406/D/8

Londonderry (Stewart family) estate, Mount Stewart
The basis of this estate was the acquisition of extensive lands in north-east County Down in the opening years of the seventeenth century by Sir Hugh Montgomery (see **Montgomery estate, Donaghadee, etc**). The Comber and Newtownards portion of the estate was sold to Robert Colvill(e) in 1675. In 1744, Alexander Stewart bought these lands from the Colvilles. His own ancestor had acquired the Ballylawn estate in County Donegal in the early 1600s. Alexander's son Robert advanced four steps through the ranks of the Irish peerage: Baron Londonderry (1789), Viscount Castlereagh (1795), earl of Londonderry (1796) and finally marquess of Londonderry (1816). See the 'Introduction to the Londonderry Estate Office Archive' prepared by PRONI. The story of the family is told in H. Montgomery Hyde, *The Londonderrys: A Family Portrait* (1979).

Leases and lease books
Pre-1750 leases arranged by townland and catalogued in full (including *c.* 150 issued by the Colvills) – D654/LE

Post-1750 leases arranged in bundles by townland – D654/L

Lease book for the town of Newtownards, 1726–1825 – D654/LB/1

Lease book for the towns of Newtownards and Comber, 17th century–1859 – D654/LB/2

Lease book of Newtown and Comber estates, 17th century–1802 – D654/LB/3

Lease reciting names of tenants in manor of Newtown, 1744 – D859/83

Rent rolls and rent ledgers
Rent rolls for the Comber estate, 1684, 1767, 1768, 1769 – D654/R2/1–6

Rent rolls of the Newtown and Greyabbey estates, 1740, 1744, 1767, 1768, 1769 – D654/R1/1A–7

Rent rolls of the Newtown, Greyabbey and Comber estates, virtually every year from 1769 – D654/R3/1

Rent ledgers for Newtown and Comber, 1791–8, 1797–1800 – D654/H3/1–3

Rent roll of the manor of Newtone, 1712–17 – Cambridge University Library, MS Add. 4349 (copy in NLI, n.5328, p.5437)

Maps
18th-century maps catalogued in full – D654/M

Macartney estate, Killinchy see **Macartney estate** under **County Antrim**

Magenis estate, Castlewellan and Dromantine
Volume of maps of Arthur Magenis's estates at Castlewellan and Dromantine, 1727 –
   T2215/1
See also **Innis estate**

Magenis estate, Dromara, etc
This estate included lands in counties Antrim, Armagh and Down and a summary of
the entire collection is presented below.

Rent rolls of the estate of Richard Magenis in counties Antrim, Armagh and Down,
   1754 (Antrim lands only), 1765, 1770 – D1835/34
Rental, 1761–89: Finnis, Sheeplandmore, etc – D1835/34
Account of lands out of leases, Finnis and Moybrick, *c.* 1762 – D1834/34
Leases for Sheeplandmore, etc, *c.* 1789–1799 – D1835/34
Surveys and maps of various farms, late 18th century – D1835/34
Names of tenants in Tullaghans, Lanahead, Carnany, Drumskea, Ballymoney,
   Drumock, Polemtamy, County Antrim, 1755 – *Belfast Newsletter*, 2 Jan. 1756
Names of tenants in Finnis and Moybrick {Dromara}, 1762 – *Belfast Newsletter*, 7 May
   1762

Magill estate, Ards
Accounts and receipts of the rents received out of the estate of Lucy Magill, alias
Johnson, in County Down, 1694–1708: lands include Kirkistowne, Ratalla,
Ballycranmore – NLI, MS 10,263

Magill estate, Gill Hall see **Clanwilliam estate**

Mathews estate, Newcastle and Mourne
Volume of maps, incorporating a survey and valuation of the Newcastle estate of
   Edward Mathews, 1737 – T2215/2
Printed rent roll of estates of Newcastle, Lisneward and Fennis, 1748, naming tenants
   and lives named in leases (together with current ages and annotated to indicate if
   an individual had died), with interesting observations – D562/889 (also D1835/34)
Rental of Edward Mathews's property in Ballinran and Ballaghanery, Lordship of
   Mourne, *c.* 1752 – D207/19/104

Maxwell estate, Saintfield etc
Assignment with rental attached, Robert Maxwell to James Maxwell of Drum
[?Drumbeg], 1674–5: lands of Drumcha, Criviargan, Glumteneglare, Lisdalgan,
Oughly, Lisdawnen, Killmure, Bresagh, Killinchie, Ballimullen, Ballialligan, Tolleveery,
Ballimillin – T640/120

McNeill, estate, Drumbo
Names of tenants of Roger Hamilton McNeill in Knockbracken, Melough, Bellykairn, Bellyesson and Bellyocklis, 1777 – *Belfast Newsletter*, 12–15 Aug. 1777

Meade estate, Rathfriland see Clanwilliam estate

Moira estate see Rawdon estate

Montgomery estate, Donaghadee, Newtownards, Comber, Kilmore
The origins of this estate can be traced to the acquisition in the early seventeenth-century of a huge acreage in north-east County Down by Sir Hugh Montgomery of Braidstane in Ayrshire, Scotland, later created Viscount Montgomery of the Ards. For more on the story of this family in the seventeenth century, see George Hill, *The Montgomery Manuscripts* (1869). In 1661, Sir Hugh Montgomery's grandson was created earl of Mount Alexander; the title died out with the death of the fifth earl in 1757. He had been married to Marie Angélique De La Cherois (Delacherois) and on her death in 1771, the estate passed to her relatives. The estate records listed below are found principally in PRONI collection D4389, though this has not yet been fully catalogued. Still to be listed are manor court records (/G), rentals and accounts (/J), maps, plans and surveys (/K), and correspondence (/L).

Leases
Leases issued by the representatives of the Montgomery family, 1618–77 (mainly 1671–77) – D4389/E/1
Leases issued by the earl of Mount Alexander and others, 1678–1752 (mainly 1678–97) – D4389/E/2
Leases relating to Cherryvalley and Comber, 1639 onwards – D4389/E/3
Leases relating to High Street, Donaghadee, 1730 onwards – D4389/E/14
Leases relating to Main Street, Donaghadee, 1728 onwards – D4389/E/15
Leases relating to Great Street/Millisle Road, Donaghadee, 1770 onwards – D4389/E/16
Leases relating to Dirty Vennal, Donaghadee, 1760–70 – D4389/E/17
Leases relating to Bow Lane, Donaghadee, 1782 onwards – D4389/E/18

Other records
Rent roll of Donaghadee parish and 'Killmore' (the churchlands in Kilmore parish), 1729 – D2223/9/6
Court leet books of the manor of Donaghadee, *c.* 1770–91, 1792–9; volume recording the business done at the Three Weeks Court of Record in and for the manor of Donaghadee, 1771–83 – MIC321/1–3
Volume recording the business done at the Three Weeks Court of Record in and for the manor of Donaghadee, 1800–10 – MIC321/4

Montgomery estate, Rosemount, Greyabbey
This estate originated in the early seventeenth century with a son of Sir Hugh Montgomery – Sir James Montgomery – and in the early 1700s it passed to another branch of the Montgomery family. See George Hill, *The Montgomery Manuscripts* (1869).

A schedule of the debts to be discharged by James Montgomery Esq., 1685–91 – T1030/9A (printed in Hill, *Montgomery Manuscripts*, p. 383)

Rent roll of Rosemount estate, 1725, including the townlands of Ballynester/Ballymurphy, Bogleboe, Grangee/Flushinhill, Gordenall and Greyabbey – T1030/21

Map of part of Ballynester and Ballymurphy, 1789, naming tenants – T1030/1

Map of Kirkistown and Ratallagh {both Ardkeen}, 1791, naming tenants (owned by Robert Johnston, but leased by Montgomery family) – T1031/2

Moor estate, Bangor

Rent roll of Rathgill and Ballow {both Bangor}, part of the estate of John Moor Esq., 1773 – D1494/3/25 (MIC506/1)

Mount Ross estate, Portaferry

Printed rental of the Mount Ross estate near Portaferry, *c.* 1780: lands of Ballyhendry, Ballyhairly, Corrog, Ballybranigan, Derry, Ballycalm, Ballyfuneragh and Ballygavigan – D2092/1/3, p. 31 (typescript copy at T656/1, no. 74)

Map and survey of part of the estate of Turner Camac Esq., 1775 (on reverse 'Old map of Mountross') – D552/B/3/3/65

See also D552/B/3/2/189 and D552/B/3/2191–3.

Needham (or Nedham) estate, Newry and Mourne

The background to this estate is discussed in the above introduction to the **Bagenal/Bayly estate**. In 1822, the owner of this estate was created earl of Kilmorey. See also the PRONI 'Introduction to the Kilmorey Papers'.

Leases, including many from the 18th century, catalogued by townland or street in Newry – D2638/B *passim*

Two addresses and a letter to William Nedham from his tenants in Newry with over 400 signatures, 1768 – NLI, MS 8163

Rent ledgers covering estates in counties Armagh, Down and Louth, 1810–11, providing details of leases, 1731–1811 – D2638/G/3/1–2

Nicholson estate, Bangor

Leases from William Nicholson of Balloo for lands in Balloo, Ballyholme and Ballymagee {all Bangor} beginning in 1785 – D447 *passim*

Patterson estate, Magheralin

Names of tenants in Lismain, Tullynacross and Drumelin {all Magheralin}, property of the Patterson family (held under the bishopric of Dromore), 1762, 1770 – *Belfast Newsletter*, 18 May 1762, 7 Sept. 1770

Perceval-Maxwell estate, Finnebrogue and Groomsport

The estate comprised two principal portions: Finnebrogue, near Downpatrick; and Groomsport, near Bangor. For more on this family and estate collection, see the 'Introduction to the Perceval-Maxwell Papers' prepared by PRONI, which includes a list of the townlands in the estate.

Estate accounts, *c.* 1700, naming tenants but not townlands, and a rent roll of 1702–3
  for the Bangor estate – D1494/3/4 (MIC506/1)
Leases, 17th century onwards – D2480/2
Map of Groomsport, 1763, naming tenants – D3244/J/2
Survey of Groomsport, 1763, naming tenants – D3244/J/2 (copy at T1023/70)
Rent rolls for estates in the barony of Lecale and in the parish of Bangor, 1743–1800
  – T1023 *passim*
Rent roll, 1742–3 – T518/1
List of arrears of rent, Lecale and Bangor estates, 1745 – T1023/32

Pollock estate, Killinchy
Rent roll, accounts, etc, 1792–1803, relating to Ballymacreely and Carrickruskey,
acquired, via a mortgage, by John Pollock in trust for Lord Downshire – MIC619/1

Pottinger estate, Mount Pottinger, Ballymacarrett
Letters and other documents concerning Thomas Pottinger's estate at Mount Pottinger,
Ballymacarrett, County Down, 1744–81 – Cumbria Archive and Local Studies Centre,
Whitehaven, DCU/Comp. 15/5

Price (later Perceval Price), estate, Saintfield
Miscellaneous deeds, including 18th-century leases – D650 *passim*
Rent rolls, Saintfield estate, 1751 – D240/1
Rental, Saintfield estate, 1776: lands of Aghandarragh, Ballyagharty, Carricknasessnah,
  Carsons, Creevytennent, Drumaconall, Glassdrumon, Killynure, Lessons, Lisdalgon,
  Lisdoonan, Lisowen, Saintfield – D536/1
Rent book, Saintfield estate, 1767 – D650/62A
Rental for the manor of Saintfield, 1788–1802 – T2101/3–4
Rent arrears, 1751–2 – D993
Names of tenants in Drumaconnell, Tullywestnacunagh, Lessons, Carsons, Killynure,
  Lisdoonan, Ballyagharty, Aghandarragh and Lisowen, 1773 – *Belfast Newsletter*,
  9–13 July 1773

Rawdon estate, Moira and Ballynahinch
This estate was founded by Sir George Rawdon in the seventeenth century. In 1750,
Sir John Rawdon was created Baron Rawdon of Moira and in 1761 he was made earl
of Moira. His son, a veteran of the American War of Independence, became the
marquess of Hastings in 1816. Voluminous 17th- and 18th-century material relating
to the Rawdon estates at Brookhill, County Antrim, and Moira (the Clare estate) and
Ballynahinch (the Kinelarty estate), County Down, is available in PRONI (T3765/L).

Rentals
Arrears of the Kinelarty estate, 1703 – T3765/L/2/14/1
May rental for Moira estate with a list of lives dropped, 1704 – T3765/L/2/15/1–2
Rentals of all the Rawdon estates in Ireland and England, 1717, 1723–5 –
  T3765/L/2/19/1–6
Rent rolls of Brookhill, Kinelarty and Clare estates, 1717 – T3765/L/2/14/7

Rent roll of Kinelarty estate, 1791–7: lands of Ballynahinch, Ballykine, Ballymaglave, Ballylone, Loughinisland, Crevytenant, Drumsnad, Glasdrummond, Ballymacarn, Dunmore, Edendarve, Drumgavelin, Drumkeeragh, Douglen and Guiness – D3044/A/5/1

Surveys

Survey of Madam Dorety Rawdon's part of the manor of Kinelarty, n.d. (early 18th century) – T3765/L/2/14/9

Survey of Sir John Rawdon's lands in the manor of Kinelarty, n.d. (early 18th century) – T3765/L/2/14/10

Survey by Sir John Rawdon to determine how many Protestants and Catholics lived in each townland in his estate, 1716 – Huntington Library, California, Hastings MSS, Box 75

Maps

Maps of the earl of Moira's estate in Kinelarty, 1782: lands of Upper and Lower Ballykine, North and South Ballylone, North and South Ballymacarn, North and South Ballymaglave, Ballynahinch, Crevitenant, Douglen, Drumgavelin, Drumkeeragh, Drumsnad, Dunmore, Edendarve, Glassdrummond, Guiness – T1451/4

Other

Leases beginning in 1712 for estate at Ballynahinch: lands of Ballymacarn, Ballymaglave, Glassdrummond – D500 *passim*

Lease book containing extracts of leases for the Rawdon estate at Ballynahinch and also the Townparks of Downpatrick, 1760–1847 – D1167/1/391

Articles of agreement for farms in Dunmore, 1763 – D500/21

Letters, tenants' petitions, etc for Ballynahinch, 1681–1704 – T3765/L/2/12/1–8

Leet rolls for the manor of Kinelarty, 1705, 1706, 1707, 1708 – T3765/L/2/14/2, /3, /4, /5

See also **Ker estate** and **Southwell estate**

Reid (Read/Reed) estate, Ballycopeland

Rentals of the Ballycopeland {Donaghadee} estate, 1797–1800 and 1855 – NLI, MS 8901

Map of Ballycopeland, 1800 – NLI, 21 F. 103(1)

Ross estate, Portavo, Holywood, Dundonald

Maps of estate of Captain James Ross, 1732, naming tenants: lands of Ballyfoaderlie, Ballyhemnly, Ballymenanitra, Ballymisca, Ballyrogan, Balow juxta Mare, Carrowbousty, Church Quarter, Copeland Island, Dunover, Gillinahirk, Knocknagoney, Moore Park, Nuns Quarter, Orlog, Portavoe – T1451/1

Rent roll of part of the estate of Captain Ross of Portavoe, 1750 – *Belfast Newsletter*, 2 Jan. 1749 [1750]

Ross estate, Rostrevor
Bundle of 18th-century documents, including a rental of Rostrevor, *c.* 1770 –
 D2223/15/32
Leases for Rostrevor, etc, 1764 onwards – D2223/5/122

Saunders estate, Newtownards, Comber see under County Antrim

Savage estate, Ardkeen
c. 100 leases for lives issued by Francis Savage, relating to Ballycran, Lisbane, etc;
miscellaneous bundle of documents including writs to appear at the manor of Ardkeen,
18th century; small volume comprising the grand jury book for the manor of Ardkeen,
c. 1779–84, including two lists of inhabitants of the manor arranged by townland,
1779 and 1783 – D2223/15/10

Savage estate, Portaferry
This old Anglo-Norman family was in possession of the southern end of the Ards
peninsula prior to the 1600s. In 1812, Andrew Savage changed his name to Nugent
on inheriting the estate of a Nugent kinsman in County Westmeath. Books on the
family include:

> George Francis Savage-Armstrong, *The Ancient and Noble Family of the Savages
> of the Ards, with Sketches of English and American Branches of the House of
> Savage: Comp. from Historical Documents and Family Papers* (1888)
> George Francis Savage-Armstrong, *A Genealogical History of the Savage Family in
> Ulster: Being a Revision and Enlargement of Certain Chapters of "The Savages
> of the Ards"* (1906)

See also the 'Introduction to the Nugent of Portaferry Papers' prepared by PRONI.

Title deeds and leases to the Savages from 1568 onwards – D552/B/1/1
Leases from the Savages from 1615 onwards (277 pre-1800) – D552/B/1/2
Accounts, receipts from 1630 onwards – D552/B/3/1
Rentals, 1641, 1644–6, 1718 and then fairly regularly for the rest of the 18th century
 – D552/B/3/2
Correspondence, including letters on 18th-century estate business – D552/A/2, /4
Printed rent roll of part of the estate, 1746 – D552/B/2/1/157
Rent rolls of lands to be sold, n.d. [post-1746] – D552/B/2/1/159–60, /162
Household expenses, 1751–66 – D552/B/3/1/156
Wages ledgers for Portaferry estate, giving particulars of employee, gross wages,
 deductions, etc, 1788–9 – D552/B/3/1/89
Tradesmen's accounts, etc, 1797–1841 – D552/B/3/1/48

Sharman estate, Banbridge
Maps of Levallyreagh {Dromara} (1730, 1771), Cappagh {Annaclone}, Lisnacreevy
 {Drumballyroney} and Creevy {Aghaderg} (*c.* 1803) – D856/B/4/1–3
Miscellaneous documents including: a list of 40-shilling freeholders and £10 leaseholders
 on the Banbridge estate, 1765; arrears of rent and warrant from William Sharman to

Patrick Lavery (bailiff) 'to seize the cattle and other goods and chattels' on offenders' farms, 1787; summary of the leases on the estate, *c.* 1770 – D856/B/6/1

Southwell estate, Downpatrick

In 1703, Edward Southwell married Elizabeth, daughter of Vere Essex Cromwell, fourth earl of Ardglass. In 1776, the grandson and namesake of this Edward Southwell became Baron de Clifford. In addition to the items listed below, there is some material in the Bristol Archives under references 42725 and 45317 (see Bristol Archives catalogue). For earlier material, see **Ardglass estate.**

Leases

Leases issued for the following townlands: Conlig Quarter, Annacloy (1792–), Ran Quarter, Annacloy (1792–), Sufficial Quarter, Annacloy (1770–), Ballynoe (1790–), Ballyvange (1792), Carnagrane [Cargebane] (1790–), Downpatrick (1790–), Erenagh (1790–), Legamaddy (1790–), part of Lisboy and Island of Lisbane (1790–), Listooder (1749–), Marshallstown (1790–), Saul (1790–), Castle Quarter, Quoile (1790–), Ferry Quarter, Quoile (1792–), Quarter Cormick (1777), Old Sound (1790) – D1167/1 *passim*

18th-century leases for Ballydargan, Carabawn {Bright} – D2223/10/1–2

Lease book containing extracts of leases for the Moira (Rawdon) estate at Ballynahinch and also the Townparks of Downpatrick, 1760–1847 – D1167/1/391

Rentals

Rent roll, 1700 – T518/1

Rental of the manor of Down, *c.* 1705 (typed version) – T793/1

Rent roll, 1742–3 – T518/1

Rent roll, 1742–4 – D3300/19/1

Rent roll, 1743–4 – D1759/3B/2 (MIC637/9)

Rent roll, with rent arrears, 1751–2 – D2961, see also T943/1

Rental of Downpatrick and surrounding townlands, 1789–92 – D3696/C/6

Maps and surveys

Survey of estate, *c.* 1700, mainly concerned with infrastructure, but naming some tenants – D477B

Survey of Downpatrick, 1708, including an index of tenants and comments on houses – D477/A

Map of the manor of Downpatrick, 1710 – NLI, 15 B. 19(26)

Map of Downpatrick, 1729, naming tenants – D3300/19/1

Maps of Ballycreen (1776), Ballykine (1786) and Clough (1787), naming tenants – D1167/3/1–3

Stevenson estate, Killyleagh see Blackwood estate

Vaughan estate, Donaghmore

Leases and lease memorials for the Donaghmore estate (owned by the archbishop of Armagh and leased to the Vaughan family), 1732 onwards: lands of Ardkeeragh,

Anaghbane, Aughnacavan, Bushkill, Cargaghbane, Ringbane, Ringclare, Ringolish and Tullymurry – D2666/3

Wallace estate, Tonaghmore
Tenants in Tonaghmore {Saintfield}, part of the estate of Robert Wallace, 1754 – *Belfast Newsletter*, 20 Sept. 1754

Ward estate, Castleward and Bangor
It was in the late sixteenth century that the first of the Wards acquired the property near Strangford subsequently named Castle Ward. Part of the Bangor lands came into the family's possession following the marriage, in 1709, of Michael Ward and Anne, daughter and co-heiress of James Hamilton of Bangor. Michael's son Bernard was created Baron Bangor in 1770 and Viscount Bangor in 1781. Lord Bangor extended the family's property through the purchase, among other lands, of the rest of the Bangor estate in 1779. In 1786, his son Robert bought lands in and around Kircubbin from the Bailies of Inishargy. See the 'Introduction to the Ward Papers' prepared by PRONI for more on this family and estate, including the townlands that formed part of it.

Leases
Five boxes of expired leases, including many from 18th century, arranged in bundles
   by townland – D2092/4
Leases from the 17th and 18th centuries, catalogued in full – D2092/5
Leases issued by the Hon. Edward Ward for properties in and around Bangor, 1786–
   90 – D4216/2/4

Rentals
Rent rolls of Ward estate at Bangor, 1746–7 – D5, D6
Rent rolls 'in and near Killough', 1748, 1750 – D2092/1/7, pp 92, 110
Rentals of the Ward estate, 1752, 1756 – D2092/6/1–2
Rental of Edward Ward's portion of the estate in Lecale, 1799 – printed in *Lecale
   Review*, 1 (2003), pp 44–7

Correspondence
Exceptionally detailed 18th-century estate correspondence – D2092/1

Other records
Accounts beginning in 1743, including lists of arrears, 1743 and 1753 – D2092/6/10
Estate maps, 1778 onwards – D2092/3

Waring estate, Ballynafern
Rent roll of Ballynafern, {Annaclone}, property of Richard Waring, *c.* 1750 – T1023/40

Waring estate, Garvaghy
Maps, surveys and leases, etc, 1662–1731 – T3425/1/1–35
Map and survey of the estate of John Waring of London, 1725, naming tenants in the
   townlands of Garvaghie, Feddeny and Carnew {all Garvaghy} – T1922/2

Waring estate, Waringstown
157 original and copy letters mainly relating to Clanconnell lands, 1641–*c*. 1700; letters and accounts, *c*. 1667–*c*. 1700 – D695
Valuation of Waringstown, 1696 – printed in E. D. Atkinson, *An Ulster Parish: Being a History of Donaghcloney (Waringstown)* (1898), pp 156–8
A large collection of records relating to this estate remains in private custody.

Whyte estate, Loughbrickland
Leases, 1738 onwards – D2918/1/1
Rentals, 1738, 1740, 1746–7, 1749–50, 1762, 1765–80, 1783, 1788 – D2918/2/1–21
Rent accounts, 1792–1803 – D2918/2/22–43
Correspondence, 1773–1801 – D2918/3/1
Maps, some from the 18th century – D2918/6

COUNTY FERMANAGH

Archdale estate, Castle Archdale, Devenish
Map of the estate in the barony of Lurg, 1733 – T1174/1
Map of Aghinver, 1734 – T1174/2
Rent roll of estate in Devenish parish, 1753 – printed in W. B. Steele, *The Parish of Devenish, County Fermanagh: Materials for Its History* (1937), p. 108
Rent roll of estate in Devenish parish, 1799 – printed in Steele, *The Parish of Devenish*, p. 108
See also Henry Blackwood Archdale, *Memoirs of the Archdales: With the Descents of Some Allied Families* (1925)

Balfour estate, Lisnaskea
This estate was founded by the Balfours in the early seventeenth century. In the early nineteenth century it was acquired by the Erne family. See **Erne estate** for additional records relating to this property.

Interrogatories and other papers in cases involving Charles Balfour and property in Fermanagh, various dates, 1666–*c*. 1699 – NLI, MSS 10,285–10,287
Eighty rentals of Balfour (and other?) properties in counties Fermanagh, Louth and Meath, various dates, 1685 and 18th–19th centuries, NLI, MSS 10,259–10,262
Account book of domestic and estate expenses (of Charles Balfour of Castle Balfour?), 1697–1710 – NLI, MS 9536
Documents in a case involving William Balfour and lands in Fermanagh, 1713–14 – NLI, MS 10,288
Maps of the Balfour estate in Fermanagh, 1726–1810 – NLI, 16 H 1(5–10, 18)
Miscellaneous 18th-century Balfour letters, including: 16 letters to or by William T. Balfour, 1756–7; six letters concerning the purchase of lands in Fermanagh by Blayney Balfour from Denis Doran, 1772–1775; 29 letters from Blayney Balfour and Anne Marie Balfour while abroad *c*. 1786–1791 – NLI, MS 10,376

Memoranda on the state of tenure of various parts of the Balfour estates, mostly
    1761–7, with some notes on rents due – NLI, MS 9590
Miscellaneous accounts, including notes of rental returns, 1776–86 – NLI, MS 11,908
Rent rolls of the estates of the Balfour family in counties Louth, Meath and Fermanagh,
    1767–1778 and 1782–5 – NLI, MSS 9543–9544
Draft pleas in a case concerning the heirs and tenants of William Balfour, giving lists
    of lands and tenants in Fermanagh, *c.* 1780 – NLI, MS 10,305

Barton estate, Clonelly
Map of Kilmore {Drumkeeran}, 1769 – D1016/4

Belmore estate (Lowry Corry family), Castle Coole
The origins of this estate can be traced to the seventeenth century. In 1656, the property
was purchased by John Corry, a Belfast merchant. His great-granddaughter Sarah
married Galbraith Lowry of Aghenis, County Tyrone, and their son, Armar Lowry
Corry, was created Baron Belmore in 1781, Viscount Belmore in 1789 and earl of
Belmore in 1797. For more on this family and estate collection, see the 'Introduction
to the Belmore Papers' prepared by PRONI. The fourth earl of Belmore was a noted
antiquarian whose best known work is *The History of Two Ulster Manors* (1903). A
detailed study of the family is Peter Marson, *Belmore: The Lowry Corrys of Castle Coole,
1646–1913* (2007). Further records relating to this estate are listed under **County
Tyrone.**

Leases, arranged by townland, 1708 onwards – D3007/A/23
Rentals of the County Fermanagh estate, beginning in 1759 – D3007/B/4
Maps, surveys and valuations, beginning in 1718 – D3007/D/1
Vouchers of the County Fermanagh estate, beginning in 1780 – D3007/C/3
Workmen's account books, 1794–6 – D3007/B/5

Brooke estate, Colebrooke
The first of the Brookes in Ireland was an Elizabethan soldier who arrived at the end
of the sixteenth century. He was subsequently granted an estate focused on Donegal
Town, County Donegal. The Fermanagh estate was a product of the Cromwellian and
Restoration land settlements. For more on this family and estate collection, see the
'Introduction to the Brookeborough Papers' prepared by PRONI. The first chapter in
Brian Barton, *Brookeborough: The Making of a Prime Minister* (1988) includes useful
background information.

Maps and surveys of townlands in the estate, many from 18th century – D998/1 *passim*
Leases beginning in 1713, catalogued in full (186 pre-1800) – D998/26 *passim*
Lease book recording leases from *c.* 1735, but mainly 1750–1818, information on lives
    given in detail; 'Observations' column includes many references to emigration to
    America – D998/19/1
Leases for various townlands, beginning in the 18th century – D3004/A/3–4
Leases in the manor of Brookeborough, beginning in the 18th century, listed
    alphabetically by townland, but not catalogued individually – D3004/B/2/1
Rent receipt book, 1799–1815 – D3004/B/2/1

Caldwell estate, Castle Caldwell

This estate and landowning family has been the focus of investigation by J. B. Cunningham; see especially his book, *Castle Caldwell and Its Families* (n.d.), and his article 'The Castle Caldwell estate in 1780 and the recent arrest of the highwayman Francis McHugh (Prionsias Dubh)', *Clogher Record*, 12:3 (1987), pp 261–4. See also Mervyn Busteed, *Castle Caldwell, County Fermanagh: Life on a West Ulster Estate, 1750–1850* (2006), and by the same author, 'The practice of improvement in the Irish context: the Castle Caldwell estate in County Fermanagh in the second half of the eighteenth century', *Irish Geography*, 33 (2000), pp 15–36.

Rental of the estate, 1770 – John Rylands Library, Manchester, B 3/28/5
Account and receipt books, etc, 1744–83 – John Rylands Library, Manchester, B 3/28 *passim*
Estate accounts, 1784–5, 1789–91 – John Rylands Library, Manchester, B 3/44/1, 3
Rental, 1786 – John Rylands Library, Manchester, B 3/44/2
Day accounts of work at Castle Caldwell, 1796–7 – John Rylands Library, Manchester, B 3/44/6–7
See also 'Leases and miscellania' in Cunningham, *Castle Caldwell and its Families*, pp 181–92

Clogher bishopric estate see under County Tyrone

Conolly estate, Ballinamallard

Letters and accounts relating to the manor of Newporten, 1718–19, 1726–9 – T2825/C/20
Survey and valuation of the manor of Newporten, 1718, with information on tenants – D2094/24A–C
Rent account for Newporten estate, 1774 – D2094/47
For more on this estate, see under **County Donegal.**

Cooper estate, Rossfad, Boho, etc

For more on this estate collection, see the 'Introduction to the Coopershill Papers' prepared by PRONI. D4031 is closed on preservation grounds; use MIC603.

'Rent roll … for arrears due November 1757, and three years rent due and ending November, 1760', including observations – D4031/C/6/1
Rental rolls, 1770, 1774, 1796 – D4031/C/6/2, /3, /9
Rents received, Rossfad and Tyrone lands, *c.* 1783 – D4031/C/6/10
Survey of Tyrone and Rossfad lands, 1793 – D4031/C/6/7
Rentals, including a rental of the Boho churchlands, 1803 – D4031/C/19/1–20
Bundle of miscellaneous documents, including rentals, 1769–1805 – D4031/C/14/1–82
Lease and renewal of premises in Enniskillen, 1769, 1800, with receipts for rent paid for same, 1785–9 – D4031/C/11/1–13
Lists and abstracts of deeds and leases, 1771–92 – D4031/12/1–5
Surveys of Drumshane (1779) and Rossfad, Drumconny and Drumshane (1791) – D4031/C/15/1–2

Dawson estate, Clones
This estate was purchased from Hugh Willoughby Montgomery by the Dawsons of Dartrey, County Monaghan, and sold by them before the end of the 18th century.

Rent roll, *c.* 1745 – D3053/4/6/1 [currently listed as missing]

Eccles estate, Shannock
Documents relating to William Eccles of Shannock and to his Fermanagh lands, 1731–76 – D4105 *passim*

Various 18th-century papers, including leases: lands include Dristernan, Annagheele, Cornamucklagh, Gortnedarragh, Lisroone, Annaghilly, Knopoghin – T962 *passim*

Ely estate, Castle Hume
This estate was originally founded by the Hume family in the early seventeenth century. In 1736, the Hume heiress married Nicholas Loftus, later to be created earl of Ely. For more on the Hume and Loftus families and the estate collection, see the 'Introduction to the Ely Papers' prepared by PRONI, which includes a list of the townlands in the estate. See also A. P. W. Malcomson, 'A house divided: The Loftus Family, earls and marquesses of Ely, *c.* 1600–*c.* 1900' in David Dickson and Cormac O Gráda (eds), *Refiguring Ireland: Essays in Honour of L. M. Cullen* (2003), pp 184–224.

Rent roll, 1742 – D535/1

Over 300 expired leases and *c.* 60 maps of townlands and tenements in the manors of Ardgart, Drumcose, Tully and Moyglass, 1724 onwards (mainly 1769–78) – D580 *passim*

Map of part of the manors of Tully and Ardgart, part of the estate of the marquess of Ely, with names of tenants, 1787 – NLI, 16 H 1(12)

Rental of part of the estate, 1793 – printed in W. B. Steele, *The Parish of Devenish, County Fermanagh: Materials for Its History* (1937), p. 109

Enniskillen (Cole family) estate, Florence Court
This estate was founded in the early 1600s by Captain (later Sir) William Cole. The family rose through the ranks of the peerage as Barons Mount Florence (1760), Viscounts Enniskillen (1776) and earls of Enniskillen (1789). For more on this family and estate collection, see the 'Introduction to the Enniskillen Papers' prepared by PRONI, which includes a list of the townlands in the estate. See also A. P. W. Malcomson, 'The Enniskillen Family, estate and archive', *Clogher Record*, 16:2 (1998), pp 81–122. Despite the extent and antiquity of the estate, the quantity of surviving material for the period 1600–1800 is disappointing.

Map of Enniskillen and adjoining townlands, 1772 – D53/1

Lease book, 1613–1879, including notes on leases for the Glenawley, Knockninny, Magheraboy, Montagh, Tirkennedy and Enniskillen estates – D1702/5/1

Miscellaneous leases, etc from the 17th and 18th centuries – D1702/1 *passim*

Erne estate (Creighton/Crichton family), Crom
The origins of this estate can be traced to the early seventeenth century. Additional lands were acquired and by the early nineteenth century the Fermanagh estate included lands at Crom, Callowhill, Derrylin Killynick, Lisnaskea, Knockballymore and Enniskillen, in addition to properties in other counties. The Creightons (the spelling was changed to Crichton in the late nineteenth century) moved swiftly through the ranks of the peerage in the latter part of the 1700s: Barons Erne in 1768; Viscounts Erne in 1781; and Earls Erne in 1789. For more on this estate and its complex history, see the 'Introduction to the Erne Papers' prepared by PRONI and A. P. W. Malcomson, 'The Erne estate, family and archive' in Eileen Murphy and William Roulston (eds), *Fermanagh: History and Society* (2004), pp 203–39. See also **Balfour estate** in this county section and **Erne estate** under **County Donegal**.

Leases
Leases relating to the Crom, Aghalane and other estates, from 1616 – D1939/11
Leases relating to the Callowhill and Eyles Irwin estates, from 1725 – D1939/13
Leases relating to the Cole-Hamilton estate in and north of Enniskillen and the
    Crawford estate at Drumgamph, etc, from 1746 – D1939/14
Leases relating to the Balfour estate at Lisnaskea, from 1616 – D1939/15
Leases relating to the Knockballymore estate, from 1735 – D1939/22

Rentals
Rental of Dresternan, *c.* 1630 – D1939/21/3
Rent rolls of the Balfour estate, Lisnaskea, 1632, 1636 – D1939/15/2/1–2 (see John
    Johnston, 'Settlement on a plantation estate: the Balfour rentals of 1632 and 1636',
    Clogher Record, 12:1 (1985), pp 92–109)
Rentals and other papers relating to the Lisnaskea estate, 1695–1770 – D1939/17/J
Rent roll of the manors of Liggin and Dresternan, 1714–15 – D1939/21/2
Rentals of the Balfour estate, 1735–89 – NLI, MS 10259
Rental of Mr Montgomery's estate in counties Monaghan and Fermanagh, 1739 –
    D1939/19/6/2
Rentals of the Crom estate and manor of Highgate, 1747, 1749 – D1939/19/6/3
Rental and survey of the bishop's lease held under the see of Clogher, *c.* 1800 –
    D1939/22/3/4

Maps
Volume of maps of part of the manor of Aghalane, 1775 – D1939/2/4

Hassard estate, Skea
Collection of 18th-century leases – D2469 *passim*
Rent roll of estate, 1732 – D2469/16

Hume estate see **Ely estate**

Irvine estate, Castle Irvine
A few deeds, including leases, late 17th/early 18th centuries – T1118 *passim*

See also 'The Original of the Family of the Irvines or Erinvines Written by Doctor Christopher Irvine of Edenburg, Physician General and [Historiographer] of Scotland, and sent to his Brother Sir Gerrard Irvine of Castle Irvine in Ireland, Anno Domini 1678': endorsed, 'The old Manuscript Copy made by Dr. Christopher Irvine Jn. of Castle Irvine of his father's Dr. Christopher Irvine's Senior tract of the Original of the Irvine Family' – T1118/3

Lanesborough estate see under County Cavan

Lendrum estate, Ballinamallard
Leases, 1773 onwards – D1834/1 *passim*
Maps of the estate, 1788 – T2735/1

Lennox estate, Boa Island
Printed sale particulars of the estate of William Lennox, including lands in County Fermanagh, 1778 – T3161/1/26

Madden estate see under County Monaghan

Maguire estate, Tempo
The writings of W. A. Maguire are particularly instructive on this estate. See 'The lands of the Maguires of Tempo in the seventeenth century', *Clogher Record*, 12:3 (1987), pp 305–19; 'The estate of Cu Chonnacht Maguire of Tempo: a case history from the Williamite land settlement', *Irish Historical Studies*, 27:106 (Nov. 1990), pp 130–44; and 'The Maguires of Tempo: vicissitudes of a County Fermanagh family' in Eileen Murphy and William Roulston (eds), *Fermanagh: History and Society* (2004).

Leases, 1737–8, 1773, 1785, 1790, 1793, 1795 – D2922/E–H *passim*
Survey of the estate, 1799 – D2922/H/2

McClintock estate, Clones
Deeds, leases, etc from 1723 onwards: lands include Rathmoran and Cleenagh – D4132/D/2, D3
Some of these lands were previously held by the Eccles family: see **Eccles estate.**

Montgomery estate, Derrygonnelly see under County Tyrone

O'Brien estate, Monea
Abstracts of leases for the manor of Castletown beginning in 1790 – printed in W. B. Steele, *The Parish of Devenish, County Fermanagh: Materials for Its History* (1937), p. 108

Trinity College Dublin estate see under County Donegal

Vaughan estate, Manor Hassett
Survey of the western end of Mr Vaughan's estate in County Fermanagh, n.d. (mid 18th century): names tenants for Clareview {Magheraculmoney}, Fartagh, Feddans and Letterkeen {all Drumkeeran} – DIO/4/9/7/3

Various documents concerning problems with tenants, 18th century – DIO/4/9/7 *passim*

Weir estate, Devenish
Documents including leases for lives relating to Monaghan and Shankill {both Devenish}, 1786–94 – D1096/11/1A

COUNTY LONDONDERRY

Two major works by James Stevens Curl – *The Londonderry Plantation, 1609–1914* (1986) and *The Honourable the Irish Society and the Plantation of Ulster, 1608–2000* (2000) – examine in some detail the activities of the London companies and the Irish Society in this county. Curl's *Londonderry Plantation* includes chapters on each of the principal London livery companies. This volume is particularly useful in determining the succession of middlemen on the estates of the companies. An earlier volume of immense value is T. W. Moody, *The Londonderry Plantation, 1609–41: The City of London and the Plantation in Ulster* (1939). See also the section on the Great Parchment Book in Chapter 4.

Antrim estate see under **County Antrim**

Bacon estate, Magilligan, Knockantern and Ballywillin
Lease of 1735 naming 6 tenants in Glenmanus {Ballywillin} – D660/1
A few 18th-century leases – D1550/149/1
Rent roll of William Bacon's estate in Ballymaclary {Magilligan} and Glenmanus with a list of his debts, 1740 – D1550/149/1/4
Survey with map of Knockantern {Coleraine}, 1741 – D1550/149/1/5
Rental of the late William Bacon's lands in Magilligan, 1785 – D1514/1/3/2
Map and survey of Knockantern and Loughan {Kildollagh} with tenants' names, 1792, copied 1807 – D1550/149/1/23

Beresford estate
This widely scattered estate was built up over the course of the seventeenth century. The Beresford family was also the lessee of the estate of the Fishmongers' Company from 1747 onwards. The family was ennobled as Viscount Tyrone (1720), earl of Tyrone (1746) and marquess of Waterford (1799). Very few records relating to the family's extensive properties in County Londonderry are in the public domain. A few additional items may be discovered using the PRONI eCatalogue and there may be a large collection of records in private custody.

Volume of maps of Sir Marcus Beresford's estate in County Londonderry, 1717: much topographical detail, but only the map of the South Liberties of Coleraine includes names of tenants; for reference purposes the other townlands featured are: Mayoghill, Bovagh and Caheny {all Aghadowey}; Drumsaragh {Tamlaght O'Crilly}; Mayboy {Aghadowey}, Boleran, Crockindollagh, Glenkeen {all Errigal}; Cullyramer, Culnaman, Movenis and Moneydig {all Desertoghill}; Coolnasillagh and Ballyrogan {both Errigal}; Grannagh, Clooney, Artikelly, Gortnamoney, Magheraskeagh and

Tullyarmon {all Aghanloo}; Ballycarton, Ballymaglin, Ballymoney, Drumaderry and Tircorran {all Aghanloo}; Edenmore, Ballyleagry, Drumagosker {all Balteagh}; Ballyhanna, Lisnagrib, Largantea and Stradreagh {all Aghanloo}; Ballyrisk Beg, Largyreagh, Gortgarn, Glenkeen, Tirmaquin, Ballyavelin and Ballynahery {all Drumachose}; Killybready {Aghanloo}, Bolea, Carrydoo, Gortcorbies {all Drumachose}; Derry Beg, Terrydoo, Carnet, Aghansillagh and Gortnarney {all Balteagh}; Drumgavenny, Drumsurn {both Balteagh}; Drumadreen, Mulkeeragh, Drumneechy {Bovevagh}; Moneyguiggy, Kilhoyle {both Balteagh}; Drumramer, Ballycrum, Leck {all Drumachose}; Formil {Bovevagh}, Moneysharvan and Lenamore {Dungiven}; Ballyness, Ballymacallion and Smulgedon;   Derryork, Gortgarn and Gortnagross {all Dungiven}; Camnish, Inishconagher and Gorticlare {all Bovevagh} – NLI, MS L 405

Leases beginning in 1799 – D1118/12 [closed for conservation]

Canning estate, Garvagh
Box of deeds including some 18th-century leases – Garvagh Museum

Clothworkers' Company estate, Dunboe, Killowen
Map of the estate by Thomas Raven, 1622, with information on tenants, printed in
    Londonderry and the London Companies, edited by D. A. Chart (1928)
Current accounts, 1620–1852; selected estate extracts, 1683–1712 – MIC146/1–15
Rental of the manor of 'Killowen', n.d. [*c.* 1640?] – T724/1
Rent receipts of tenants on Clothworkers' proportion, 1662 – T640/92
Chancery bill listing 34 tenants, 1664 – T808/11342
See also **McClelland/Maxwell estate**

Conolly estate, Bellaghy, Eglinton and Limavady
William Conolly purchased the Limavady estate from the Phillips family in 1697 and in the eighteenth century his family leased the estates of the Grocers' and Vintners' companies, focused, respectively, on Eglinton (then called Muff) and Bellaghy. Further background information on the Conolly properties is found in the entry on the estate under **County Donegal**. See also E. A. Currie, 'Fining down the rents: the management of the Conolly estates in Ireland, 1734–1800', *The Journal of the Derry Diocesan Historical Society* (1979), pp 25–38.

Limavady estate and Grocers' estate
Leases issued by the Conolly family beginning in 1700 – D1118/3 *passim*
Abstracts of leases on the Limavady estate, *c.* 1700–*c.* 1780 – D2094/58
Rentals and accounts for the manor of Newtownlimavady, the church-lands of
    Drumachose and the Grocers' proportion, 1718, 1721, 1724–9, including a list of
    names of tenants who had left their farms for New England in 1718 – T2825/C/11
    (see Richard MacMaster, 'Emigrants to New England from the Conolly estates,
    1718', *Journal of Scotch-Irish Studies*, 1 (Spring 2000), pp 18–23)
Correspondence relating to the Limavady estate, 1718–31 – T2825/C/27
Rent rolls of the Limavady estate, 1729 – D2094/26, 27
Rent rolls of the Grocers' proportion, 1729 – D2094/31, 32

Rentals and surveys of individual farms, etc in the Limavady estate, 1781–4 – T2825/C/15

Book of maps of Limavady estate, 1698 – T820/1 (original in Limavady Museum)

Map of the manor of Limavady, 1782, naming tenants in some townlands (includes typescript list of named tenants) – T821/1

Rent roll of the Limavady estate, *c.* 1800 – D2094/79

Rental of Limavady estate, 1802 – T2825/C/16/1

Vintners' estate

Rent roll of the Vintners' proportion, 1718 – D2094/21 (printed in *DIFHR*, 38 (2015), pp 13–14)

Rent rolls of the Vintners' proportion, 1729 – D2094/29, 30

Rentals of the Vintners' proportion, 1775, 1776 – D2094/50, 51

Rent accounts of the Vintners' proportion, 1775, 1776 – D2094/53, 54

Correspondence relating to the Vintners' estate, 1777–1802 – T2825/C/18

Rentals of the Vintners' estate, 1778, 1781–2, 1786, 1795–1801 – T2825/C/19

Rentals of the Vintners' proportion, 1788, 1788–90, 1791–3 – D2094/76, 77, 78

Conyngham estate see **Lenox-Conyngham estate**

Curtis estate, Coleraine

Names of tenants in houses and farms in and near Coleraine, part of the estate of Griffin Curtis, 1769 – *Belfast Newsletter*, 6 Oct. 1769

Dawson estate, Castledawson

Two estate accounts of Moyola, 1682–99 – D1470/3/2A–B

Estate account of Moyola, *c.* 1709 – D1470/3/3

Rent roll of Moyola, 1706, including townlands of Anaghmoar, Shanmolagh {both Magherafelt} Ballymaguigan, Derrygarave {both Artrea}, Leitram and Tamniaran {both Ballyscullion} – D1470/6/7

Extracts from manor of Castledawson rental, 1707–45 – T865/1

See also **Graves estate**

Derry bishopric estate, all parishes in the diocese of Derry

Rentals, 1617, 1688, 1708, 1719 – D683/31, 275, 278, 287

Lesses of the see of Derry, *c.* 1696 – D683/240

Lease rents of the see of Derry, 1718 – D683/286

Many of the documents in the D683 collection have been transcribed in T. W. Moody and J. G. Simms (eds), *The Bishopric of Derry and the Irish Society of London, 1602–1705*, 2 vols (1968–83).

Numerous petitions from tenants of the lands of the bishopric, 1768–1803 – D2798/3 *passim*

Rental of lands belonging to the bishopric to be let in Clonleigh parish, 1790 – D2798/3/59

Drapers' Company estate, Moneymore, Ballynascreen, Desertmartin
For more information on this estate, see the PRONI 'Introduction to the Drapers'
Company Estate Archive', which includes a list of the townlands in the estate. The
collection D3632 is now closed and researchers should access it on microfilm
(MIC617).

Rentals
Bound typescript volume containing various documents, mainly from the early 17th
   century, though also rentals for 1728 and 1749 – T635/1–15
Rental, 1614–15 – D3632/A/30
Rent roll, 1622 – D3632/A/180
Rental and account, 1622–4 – D3632/A/184
Rental, 1623 – D3632/A/190
Rent roll, 1728 (when the estate was leased by William Rowley) – D3632/K/1
Ledgers, 1750–96 – D3632/F/2
Rent roll, 1790 – D3632/K/2
Rent roll, 1793 – D3632/K/3

Maps
Map of the estate by Thomas Raven, 1622, with information on tenants, printed in
   Londonderry and the London Companies, edited by D. A. Chart (1928)
Map and survey of the tenements and parks in Moneymore, 1730 – D3632/P/5
Maps of the Kilcronaghan and Desertmartin, Ballynascreen, and Moneymore divisions
   of the estate, 1792–3 – D3632/P/6–8

Other
Petitions from British inhabitants of the estate for their leases, 1611 – D3632/A/22
An account of William Conyngham's management of Moneymore proportion, 1690–
   95, naming tenants by townland – D1470/3/16
Letters about tenures of leases and rent arrears, 1728–56 – D3632/A/356
Notes on the holdings of the company's tenants for making out their leases, n.d.
   [pre-1800] – D3632/A/340

See also **Rowley (including Langford Rowley) estate**

Du Pré estate, Aghadowey
This estate was leased from the Ironmongers' Company of London.
Fifty leases issued by Rebecca du Pré and others, including Lord Caledon, 1791–8:
   lands of Carnamucklagh, Clarehill, Clontagh, Collans, Droghead, Dunstaple {all
   Aghadowey}, Colebane, Edenbane {both Desertoghill}, Lissamore, Cul(l)row (both
   Agivey), Culdrum {Aghadowey/Macosquin}, Drumcroon {Macosquin}, Crossaudley
   – D668/R/33–46

Fishmongers' Company estate, Ballykelly and Banagher
Map of the estate by Thomas Raven, 1622, with information on tenants, printed in
   Londonderry and the London Companies, edited by D. A. Chart (1928)

Expired leases, etc relating to the manor of Walworth, 1613–1880 – LMA, CLC/L/FE/G/154/MS07270

Chancery bill naming 43 tenants in the manor of Walworth, 1701 – T808/11309

Survey of the manor of Walworth, 1717 – T2499/1 (LMA, CLC/L/FE/H/005)

Map of the manor of Walworth, 1732: only a few names – D519/1

Account book, 1775–6, possibly relating to the Fishmongers' Company estate: details payments to labourers, fishermen, etc – T3990/1

See also R. J. Hunter, 'The Fishmongers' Company of London and the Londonderry Plantation, 1609–41' in Gerard O'Brien (ed.), *Derry & Londonderry: History and Society* (1999) pp 205–58.

Gage estate, Magilligan

Leases issued by the Gage family, 1714 onwards – D673 *passim*

Rent book of the southern half of Magilligan parish, 1718–65: lands of North and South Ballyleighery, Duncrun, Tamlaghtard, Clagan, Tamlaghtbeg, Ballymargy, Erny, Ballinlig, Carrowreagh, Minearny, The Warren, Drumnahay, Oughtymoyle, Ballymultimber, Ballyscullion, Drumavally, Lenamore, Margymonaghan, Ballymulholland, Clooney; the volume also includes the names of those (from the parish or estate?) who served on the assizes, sessions, and courts leet 1725–57; also the names of constables of Magilligan parish, 1724–46 – D673/4A

Survey of part of Magilligan parish belonging to Hodgson Gage, 1768, naming tenants – D673/56

Survey of part of Magilligan parish belonging to Marcus Gage, 1800, naming tenants – D673/95A

See also Graeme Kirkham, 'Economic diversification in a marginal economy: a case study' in Peter Roebuck (ed.), *Plantation to Partition: Essays in Ulster History in Honour of J. L. McCracken* (1981), pp 64–81.

Goldsmiths' Company estate, New Buildings

Map of the estate by Thomas Raven, 1622, with information on tenants, printed in *Londonderry and the London Companies*, edited by D. A. Chart (1928)

Certificate relating to 1622 Plantation survey listing freeholders, leaseholders and undertenants, over 50 names – MIC9B/12A

'The severall inhabitants in the Mannor of Goldsmiths which was summoned to appear at a Court Leet held at New Buildings for the said mannor the 19th day of April 1716': over 200 names arranged by townland – MIC9B/12A

See also **Ponsonby estate**

Graves estate, Castledawson

18th-century deeds and leases for Castledawson, etc – D1062/4/B

A list of the leases granted by Admiral Graves to his tenants in the manor of Castledawson, 1768 – D1062/4/B/15

A list of the tenants and rent payments made for the townlands of Mullaghboy {Ballyscullion}, Aughrim {Artrea} and Drumlamph {Maghera}, 1772–1809 – D1062/4/C/3

Letters to Admiral Graves concerning Castledawson, 1775–9 – D1062/4/C/4

See also **Dawson estate**

Grocers' Company estate, Eglinton

Map of the estate by Thomas Raven, 1622, with information on tenants, printed in *Londonderry and the London Companies*, edited by D. A. Chart (1928)

See also **Conolly estate**

Haberdashers' Company estate, Aghanloo, Dunboe

Rent roll, n.d. [17th century] – T640/1

Papers relating to the Haberdashers' proportion, *c.* 1614–1616, including names of tenants, freeholders from Scotland, and payments to craftsmen – T520/1

Rent roll, 1623 – T640/22

Map of the estate by Thomas Raven, 1622, with information on tenants, printed in *Londonderry and the London Companies*, edited by D. A. Chart (1928)

See also **McClelland/Maxwell estate**

Hart estate see under County Donegal

Hervey/Bruce estate, Downhill

This was the personal estate of George Augustus Hervey, earl of Bristol and bishop of Derry (1768–1803).

Rentals of the earl of Bristol's lands in Magilligan, *c.* 1780 and 1795 – D1514/1/3/1, /5

Rental and valuation of the earl of Bristol's lands in Dunboe, *c.* 1780s and *c.* 1790s – D1514/1/3/3–4

List of workmen, 1780s – D1514/1/1/41/1

Manuscript valuation book for Magilligan (Tamlaghtard) parish, *c.* 1800 – D1514/2/4/16

Survey of land taken from undernamed tenants and enclosed with Circular Road and demesne wall, n.d. [late 18th century]: lands of B'Madakin, Miltown, Ballywoodock, Glebe and Drimagully {all Dunboe} – D2798/3/88

Heyland estate, Coleraine, etc

Names of tenants in Gortfadd {Errigal}, Lisnamuck, Gorran, Balnakelly and Ballybrittan {all Aghadowey}, 1764 – *Belfast Newsletter*, 9 Oct. 1764

Tenants in Castlerace, Cashell, Keltess, Kilmacurnel {Macosquin}, 1779 – *Belfast Newsletter*, 29 Jan.–2 Feb. 1779

Rent roll relating to Coleraine, 1792–5, with names of tenants, dates of leases, observations – D668/R/49/1

Roll relating to Killowen, 1802, with observations on leases, etc – D668/R/49/3

Irish Society estate, Coleraine and Londonderry

The Honourable the Irish Society, as it became known, was the body established by the City of London to oversee the scheme of plantation involving the London livery companies in the newly created county of Londonderry. See James Stevens Curl, *The Honourable the Irish Society and the Plantation of Ulster, 1608–2000* (2000). The Irish Society was a landowner in its own right and had specific responsibility for promoting the development of Coleraine and the city of Londonderry. The large collection of records relating to the Irish Society is now in the London Metropolitan Archives (LMA) under reference CLA/049 and a PDF of the catalogue is available. The records at LMA include court minute books beginning in 1664 (CLA/049/AD/01), letter books from 1664 onwards (CLA/049/AD/07), general ledgers from 1688 onwards (CLA/049/FN/03), and receipt books starting in 1663 (CLA/049/FN/04). Many, though not all, of these items have been microfilmed by PRONI (MIC9A). Among the items of particular interest is a list of the names of bidders for leases in 1733 (LMA, CLA/049/AD/01/010; PRONI, MIC9A/6). The LMA collection also includes leases from the Irish Society to its tenants, some of which pre-date 1800.

Rentals

Rental of Coleraine, n.d. [*c.* 1640?] – T724/1

Rental of Coleraine and Londonderry, 1679, listing tenants to whom 30-year leases were issued in 1662 – LMA, CLA/049/EM/03/001

Rental of Coleraine and Londonderry, 1700, headed 'According to the Rent Roll settled by the Irish Society's Commissioners 1692'; names in alphabetical order – LMA, CLA/049/EM/03/002

Rental of Coleraine, *c.* 1746, names in alphabetical order – T656/1, no. 60

Rental of Londonderry, 1746, names in alphabetical order – T656/1, no. 61

Rental of tenements in Waterside, Coleraine, 1756 – T656/1, no. 62

Rental of Coleraine and Londonderry, 1756 – D573/1

Rental of Coleraine and Londonderry, 1777 – LMA, CLA/049/EM/03/003

Rental of Irish Society's property in Londonderry and Coleraine, 1782 – D668/A/13–16

Rental of Londonderry and Coleraine, 1794 – D573/2

Surveys

Description of lands in the city of Londonderry, 1695 – LMA, CLA/049/EM/02/001 (PRONI, T3380/2)

Book of reference to maps of Coleraine and Londonderry, 1734 – LMA, CLA/049/EM/02/002

Book of reference to map of the city of Londonderry, 1738 – LMA, CLA/049/EM/02/004 (PRONI T3380/3)

Book of reference to map of the town of Coleraine, 1738 – LMA, CLA/049/EM/02/003 (PRONI, T3380/4)

Book of reference to map of Coleraine, 1758 – LMA, CLA/049/EM/02/005

Book of reference to map of Londonderry, 1758 – LMA, CLA/049/EM/02/006

Review of houses in Coleraine and Londonderry, 1765, including remarks on their condition, etc – CLA/049/EM/02/007

See also Andrew Kane, *The Town Book of Coleraine* (2016), which includes 'Acre' tenants in Coleraine in 1738 extracted from a map in the possession of the Irish Society, Coleraine (p. 89); a list of town tenants, 1738–58, naming the leaseholder in 1738, with supplementary information from 1756 and 1758 (pp 90–93); and the rental of 1777 with additional information from the 1794 rental (pp 94–6).

Ironmongers' Company estate, Aghadowey

Printed extracts from the Company committee minute books, 1609–16; maps, *c.* 1610, 1724, 1725 (tenants not named) – T2161

Map of the estate by Thomas Raven, 1622, with information on tenants, printed in *Londonderry and the London Companies*, edited by D. A. Chart (1928)

Rental of the manor of Agivey, n.d. [*c.* 1640?] – T724/1

Survey of estate by Isaac Pyke, 1725, containing detailed descriptions of townlands and naming tenants – MIC145/9

Valuation of estate by John Hood, 1765, naming tenants and with occasional observations on them – MIC145/8

Rent rolls for, respectively, Mrs Sarah Bryan's part of the estate, John Macky's part and Mr Lecky's part, all *c.* 1765 – MIC145/8

See also **Du Pré estate** and J. W. Kernohan, *The County of Londonderry in Three Centuries: With Notices of the Ironmongers' Estate* (1921)

Jackson estate, Killowen, Aghadowey and Articlave

Large collection of 18th-century leases, many of them relating to Aghadowey parish – D668

Rent roll, 1782, with arrears for 1781 – D668/A/3

Rent book, 1788: lands of Ballyhern [Ballycairn?], Castletoothery, Kilcranny and Waterside {all Killowen}: over 130 names – D668/A/7

Rent rolls of part of George Jackson's estate, 1792, 1793, 1794, 1797 – D668/A/4, /4A, /4B, /4C

Rent roll, 1798–9 – D668/A/5

Rent book, 1799–1801 – D668/A/10

Lists of arrears on estate, 1798, 1799 – D668/A/9A–B

Rent roll of Joseph Weir's part of the estate, 1796: lands of Ballyhern, Castletoothery, Kilcranny and Waterside – D668/A/16

Rentals, 1768–74 (rather tattered), 1794 – D668/A/16

Rental, 1800 – D4164/A/24 (published in *Bann Disc*, 9 (2003))

Langford estate see Rowley (including Langford Rowley) estate

Lenox-Conyngham estate, Springhill

Rental of William Conyngham's estate, 1683–4 – printed in *Analecta Hibernica*, 15 (1944), pp 357–8

Rental of Springhill estate, 1786 – D1449/3/1

Volume of maps of estate, 1722, naming tenants – D1449/5/1

18th-century correspondence, some of which relates to estate management – D1449/12 *passim*

Leases from the 18th century – D847/6

See also Mina Lenox-Conyngham, *An Old Ulster House: Springhill and the People who Lived in it* (2005; new edition of 1946 original)

McCausland estate, Tobermore

Map of Monishinair [Moneyshanere] and Gortree, part of the estate of Dominick McCausland, 1792 – T1932/2

Various 18th-century documents including leases for Cloughfin, Gortree and Moneyshanere {all Kilcronaghan} – D1550/149/2

McClelland/Maxwell estate, Aghanloo and Dunboe

Rental, 1630 – T640/31

Leases for farms in Dunboe/Killowen, 1655–6 – T640/59–60, 62–82

Statements of rents and leases, 1666 – T640/105

Rent rolls, 1669, 1684 – T640/108, 138

(The originals of the records listed T640 in PRONI are in the National Records of Scotland under RH15/91).

See also **Clothworkers' Company estate** and **Haberdashers' Company estate**

McNeal estate, Magilligan

Tenants in Cloney and Upper Oughleymore {both Magilligan}, property of Mrs Elizabeth McNeal of Woodtown, 1771 – *Belfast Newsletter*, 22 Nov. 1771

Massereene estate see **Vintners' Company estate**

Maxwell estate see **McClelland/Maxwell estate**

Mercers' Company estate, Kilrea

Map of the estate by Thomas Raven, 1622, with information on tenants, printed in *Londonderry and the London Companies*, edited by D. A. Chart (1928)

Printed volume of Mercers' Company Irish estate minutes, 1609–63 – D2436/1

Rentals and accounts, 1628–33 – LMA, CLC/L/CH/G/006/MS03115

Rental of the manor of 'Killreagh', n.d. [*c*. 1640?] – T724/1

Rental of estate, 1714 – MIC225/2

Rent roll of estate then held by Alexander Stewart, 1768 – D654/R/4/1

Account book of Alexander Stewart including rent accounts for Mercer's estate, 1781–90 – D2784/19

The Registry of Deeds includes transcripts of leases issued in 1714–16 by John McMullan, tenant of the Mercers' Company estate

Merchant Taylors' Company estate, Macosquin

Map of the estate by Thomas Raven, 1622, with information on tenants, printed in *Londonderry and the London Companies*, edited by D. A. Chart (1928)

Rental of the Merchant Taylors' estate, 1694–5 – T656/1, no. 40

Rental of Merchant Taylors' estates, post-1729 (prepared for court case in 1735) – T656/1, no. 52

See also **Richardson estate**

Phillips estate, Limavady

A 70-page account book, 1684–93 – T2825/C/5/1

Leases issued by George Phillips, 1674/5–96 – D1118/3/1

Bundle of documents mainly relating to the Phillips estate at Limavady, 1662–99 including leases, 1682–94 – D1550/147/1–21

See also **Conolly estate**

Ponsonby estate, New Buildings

Survey of the manor of Goldsmiths, naming tenants, 1771 – D3482/1

Leases issued by Richard Ponsonby for Craigstown, Curryfree, Drumconan, Tirkeeveny, Warbleshinney {all Clondermot}, 1788–96 – D1170/1

See also **Goldsmiths' Company estate**

Richardson estate, Somerset

The Richardsons acquired a lease of the Merchant Taylors' Company estate – known as the manor of St John the Baptist – in the late 1720s, taking up resident at Somerset by the River Bann.

Rental of the manor of St John the Baptist, the estate of John Richardson, under the agency of Samuel Faulkner, 1772–6 – MIC21/2

Account of the arrears of rent, 1748 – T1617/4/1A–B (does not name tenants)

Minor expenses book of Samuel Faulkner which includes mention of business transacted, leasing of land and business as agent for John Richardson, 1783–5 – MIC21/1

See also **Merchant Taylors' Company estate**

Rowley (including Langford Rowley) estate, Castleroe and Tobermore

Miscellaneous 17th- and 18th-century papers, including leases – MIC537/1–3

Leases, 1660 onwards – D1118/3/4

Rentals, valuations and accounts, 1683–1705 – MIC537/3

Vouchers, 1686–94 – MIC537/3

Tenants on the church lands that had been leased from the bishop of Derry by Sir John Rowley, 1692/3: lands in the parishes of Aghadowey, Desertoghill, Errigal, Killowen, Macosquin (Camus-juxta-Bann) and Tamlaght O'Crilly – TCD, MS 1995–2008/271

Rentals of estate in and around Tobermore with details of building clauses in leases, 1725, 1727 – D642/H/1–2 (MIC593/9)

Map of the Tobermore estate, 1724, naming tenants – D642/G/4 (MIC593/9)

Map of Derrynoid {Ballynascreen}, 1734, naming tenants – D642/G/6 (MIC593/9)

Rental and account, 1744–50 – MIC537/3

Names of tenants in Ballyness, Cammus {both Macosquin}, Ballybrittan, Drumacrae, Mullanabrone (all Aghadowey}, Ballynameen, Mulletra (both Desertoghill} and Kearn, part of the estate of Hercules Langford Rowley, 1780 – *Belfast Newsletter*, 25–29 Feb. 1780

See also **Derry bishopric estate** and **Drapers' Company estate**

Salters' Company estate, Magherafelt

For more information on this estate see the 'Introduction to the Salters' Papers' prepared by PRONI. Many of the items in D4108 have now been microfilmed (MIC631).

Map of the estate by Thomas Raven, 1622, with information on tenants, printed in *Londonderry and the London Companies*, edited by D. A. Chart (1928)

Rental of the manor of Magherafelt, n.d. [*c.* 1640?] – T724/1

Petition from the inhabitants of the manor of Sal, *c.* 1720: 23 names – D4108/14G

Rentals of the Salters' estate, 1752, 1766, 1772, 1774, 1783, 1790 – D4108/15G/1, 16O, 16R, 16Y, 16Z/8, 17B (the rental of 1752 was printed in W. H. Maitland, *History of Magherafelt* (1916, reprinted 1988 and 1991), pp 17–19)

Rentals, 1778–1800 – D654/R/4/2A–5

List of the inhabitants of the Salters' estate who ought to attend courts leet and baron, 1752, names arranged by townland – D4108/15F

Skinners' Company estate

Map of the estate by Thomas Raven, 1622, with information on tenants, printed in *Londonderry and the London Companies*, edited by D. A. Chart (1928)

Map of the estate with names of tenants in Dungiven, 1740 – D3067/1

A survey, rental and plans of the manor of Pellipar, 1792 – LMA, CLC/L/BA/G/018/MS05202/001

Staples estate, Lissan see under County Tyrone

Stewart estate see Mercers' Company estate and Salters' Company estate

Strafford estate, Bellaghy

The Byng family, earls of Strafford, acquired an interest in the Vintners' Company estate at Bellaghy through intermarriage with the Conollys.

Several hundred 18th-century leases relating to lands in County Londonderry – D1062/1/8A–12

Composition volume of 29 maps and surveys, 1743–*c*. 1847 – D1062/1/14

See also **Conolly estate** and **Vintners' Company estate**

Tyrone estate see Beresford estate

Vintners' Company estate, Bellaghy

Map of the estate by Thomas Raven, 1622, with information on tenants, printed in *Londonderry and the London Companies*, edited by D. A. Chart (1928)

Rental of the manor of 'Lisneycourt', n.d. [*c*. 1640?] – T724/1

Counterparts of leases issued by Viscount Massereene for the Vintners' estate in 1698 – D1550/148/1–18

See also **Conolly estate** and **Strafford estate**

Waterford estate see Beresford estate

COUNTY MONAGHAN

For a general background to landed estates in County Monaghan, see P. J. Duffy, 'The evolution of estate properties in south Ulster' in W. J. Smyth and K. Whelan (eds), *Common Ground: Essays on the Historical Geography of Ireland* (1998), pp 84–109, which includes maps showing the network of estates in the county in the seventeenth and nineteenth centuries. See also Peter Collins, *County Monaghan Sources in the Public Record Office of Northern Ireland* (1998), published by PRONI, which includes introductions to many of the important estate collections.

Anketell estate, Trough barony
Rental, 1784–7 – MIC309/1, printed in *Clogher Record*, 11 (1984), pp 403–20

Barrett Lennard estate, Clones
For more on this estate, see the 'Introduction to the Barrett Lennard Papers' prepared by PRONI. The originals of the records microfilmed by PRONI are in the Essex Record Office. Copies of these items are also available in PRONI under T2529. Many of the letters in the collection have been transcribed and these are available in a PRONI calendar.

Bundles of 245 leases, 1581–1808 – MIC170/1
About 400 letters and reports of agents, 1684–1859 – MIC170/1, /2, /3
Bundles of 247 documents consisting of rentals, accounts and vouchers – MIC170/3, /4
Map of Clones, 1768, naming tenants – MIC170/4
Clones rent rolls of the 1630s, 1638, 1640 – printed in *Clogher Record*, 16 (1997), pp 95–100
Clones rent rolls, 1679, 1681 – printed in *Clogher Record*, 13 (1988), pp 126–8
Lease abstracts for the Clones estate: over 200 items from the 17th and 18th centuries – printed in *Clogher Record*, 18 (2003), pp 53–84

Barton estate, Lough Bawn
Information on tenants in the 18th century – printed in *Clogher Record*, 15:2 (1995), pp 137–45

Bath estate (Thynne family), Farney
This estate approximated to the eastern half of the barony of Farney in south County Monaghan and came into the possession of the Thynne family (viscounts Weymouth from 1682 and marquesses of Bath from 1789) in the late seventeenth century. Estate records at Longleat, Wiltshire, were microfilmed for the National Library of Ireland in 1964. Other records relating to the property are in the Shirley Papers in PRONI. For more information, see the 'Introduction to the Bath and Brownlow Estate Papers' prepared by PRONI. See also E. P. Shirley, *Some Account of the Territory or Dominion of Farney* (1845) and the following articles by Lorcán Ó Mearáin: 'The Bath estate 1700–1777', *Clogher Record*, 6 (1967), pp 333–60; and 'The Bath estate, 1777–1800', *Clogher Record*, 6 (1968), pp 555–73.

Rent roll, 1732; schedule of leases, *c.* 1735; rentals, 1756, 1776, 1778–1810; agents' accounts, 1777–1808 – NLI, p.5894
Survey and abstract of leases granted in the Weymouth estate, post-1719 – D3531/S/3/1
Survey of Weymouth estate in Farney, *c.* 1730 – D3531/S/4/1
See also **Essex estate** and **Shirley estate**

Blayney estate, Castleblayney
For more on this estate, see the 'Introduction to the Blayney of Castleblayney Papers' prepared by PRONI. This estate was acquired by the Hope family in the mid 1800s.

Survey of that part of the Aghnamallow estate belonging to Lord Blayney, 1762: lands
of Aughnamallow, Ballagh, Cabragh, Creagh, Rusky {all Drumsnat}, Cavangarvin,
Lisnashanagh {both Kilmore}, Cloghernaught, Coughin {both Killeevan} –
D1421/3/4

Castleblayney rent book, 1772 – Monaghan County Museum; printed in *Clogher
Record*, 10 (1981), pp 414–18

Box of miscellaneous estate papers including rentals of 1783 and 1791, and an account
book of 1786 containing details of wages paid to gardeners, labourers, etc –
D1421/1/68

Bundles of leases, *c*. 1790 onwards – D1421/2

Blayney estate, Monaghan

Rent roll of Lady Blayney's lands in the parishes of Tedavnet and Monaghan, 1790,
including details of leases, 1713–99 – T3729/1

See also **Rossmore estate**

Brownlow estate, Farney

This estate seems to have been acquired by the Brownlows of Lurgan, County Armagh,
in the late seventeenth century. For more information, see the 'Introduction to the Bath
and Brownlow Estate Papers' prepared by PRONI.

Unbound sheets of rent roll for the estate, including lands in County Monaghan,
c. 1742–52 – D1928/R/5/4

Estate and household account book of William Brownlow, 1752–4, which includes
rent accounts for his estate, including his lands in County Monaghan –
D1928/A/2/2

Rentals of the estate in Farney, 1755–94 – D1928/R/1 *passim*

Rent roll of the estate in Farney, 1758 – D1928/A/1/7

Cairnes estate see **Rossmore estate**

Clermont (Fortescue family) estate, Monaghan

Volume of maps of the estate of the earl of Clermont, 1791 – MIC624/1

See also **Rossmore estate** and A. P. W. Malcomson, 'The earl of Clermont: a forgotten
Co. Monaghan magnate of the late eighteenth century', *Clogher Record*, 8 (1973),
pp 19–72.

Clogher bishopric estate see under **County Tyrone**

Cremorne estate see **Dawson estate**

Crofton estate, Errigal Truagh, etc

Surveys and valuations of the estate, 1719–84 – NLI, MS 20,798

Maps of the estate, 1754–1802 – NLI, 26 I 2 (1–8)

Rentals and accounts, 1769, 1783–1814 – NLI, MS 20,783

Rental, 1792 – NLI, MS 8150

Leases mainly for 'Errigle' parish beginning in 1785 – NLI, D 26,931–26,956

Dawson estate, Dartrey
For more on this estate, which also included extensive lands in County Armagh, see the 'Introduction to the Dartrey Papers' prepared by PRONI. See also June Brown, 'Dartrey: the rise and fall of an Irish estate', *Clogher Record*, 18:2 (2004), pp 269–78. In 1770, Thomas Dawson was created Baron Dartrey of Dawson Grove and in 1785 he was made Viscount Cremorne.

Maps
Maps of townlands and farms, 1710 onwards – D3053/2
Photostat copy of volume of maps, 1768, naming tenants – T3170/1
Volume of 20 maps, 1779, naming tenants' estate – NLI, MS 3181

Rentals
Rental, *c.* 1780 – NLI, MS 3282
Rental, 1790 – NLI, MS 3184
Rental, 1796–7 – NLI, MS 3674
Rentals, 1800–1 – NLI, MSS 3186–7
Survey and rental, n.d. [1802] – D3053/8/12/1
A list of tenants giving rents and terms of leases, *c.* 1800 – NLI, MS 1696

Dartrey estate see **Dawson estate**

Essex estate, Farney
This estate originated with a grant of the barony of Farney to the first earl of Essex in 1575. Following the death of the third earl in 1646, the estate was divided with the western half going to the Shirleys and the eastern half eventually coming into the possession of the Thynne family (viscounts Weymouth and marquesses of Bath). See **Bath estate** and **Shirley estate** for additional records and also E. P. Shirley, *Some Account of the Territory or Dominion of Farney* (1845) for further background information.

Lease from the Essex estate, 1624, naming some tenants – printed in *Clogher Record*, 13 (1990), pp 100–14
See also Patrick J. Duffy, 'Farney in 1634: An examination of John [*recte* Thomas] Raven's survey of the Essex estate', *Clogher Record*, 11 (1983), pp 245–56.

Evatt estate, Tedavnet
Maps of Corrinshigoe, Aughnacalcuile and Mullytigorrie owned by Humphrey Evatt, 1730: tenants not named – NLI, MS 2794

Forster estate, Killeevan
Volume of maps of Forster estate in counties Monaghan and Tyrone, 1795–1805 – D1105/2
Rent book of Killeevan estate, 1802–05 – MIC661/A/1
Typescript rent book of Killeevan estate, 1802–03 – MIC661/A/6

Johnston estate, Aghabog etc
Printed rentals and associated papers, 1750–51 – D3053/6/10/1–6

See also **Johnston estate, Gilford** under **County Down** for more County Monaghan estate material.

Kane estate, Donaghmoyne
Deeds, lease, etc from 1761 onwards: lands include Drumsnaught {Donamoyne} – D4132/C/6

Kane estate, Errigal Truagh
Rentals of the Kane estate, 1764 and 1801, and some 18th-century accounts – Monaghan County Museum; printed in *Clogher Record*, 13 (1990), pp 72–91, with a map of the estate

Ker estate, Newbliss
Information on tenants from estate records, 1790–*c*. 1830 – printed in *Clogher Record*, 12 (1985), pp 110–26

Leslie estate, Ballybay
Leases arranged by townland, 1780 onwards – D3406/D/5
Survey of Ballybay estate owned by Rev. Dr Henry Leslie, including maps, 1786 –
    Monaghan County Museum; over 150 names extracted from it printed in *Clogher Record*, 11 (1982), pp 71–6
Various deeds, etc, 1657–79 and 1750 onwards – NLI, p.8403

Leslie estate, Glaslough
In 1665, the Glaslough estate was purchased by John Leslie, the nonagenarian Anglican bishop of Clogher. His descendants still reside there today. In addition to extensive lands in County Monaghan, the family was the long-term lessee of the Pettigo estate, part of the bishopric lands of Clogher, which straddled the boundary between counties Donegal and Fermanagh, and was in possession of a number of townlands in County Tyrone. For more information, see the 'Introduction to the Leslie Papers' by PRONI, which includes a list of the townlands attached to the estate. This introduction was prepared prior to the transfer of the bulk of the archive from Castle Leslie to the National Library of Ireland where it has been catalogued under reference MS 49,495 (some oversized items are listed separately). See also Anthony Doyle, *Charles Powell Leslie (II)'s Estates at Glaslough, County Monaghan, 1800–41: Portrait of a Landed Estate Business and its Community in Changing Times* (2001).

Leases
Leases for the estate in County Monaghan, 1736 onwards – NLI, MS 49,495/1/9–14
Leases for the estate in County Donegal, 1764 onwards – NLI, MS 49,495/1/15–19
Leases for the estate in County Tyrone, 1785–95 – NLI, MS 49,495/20
Leases for the estate in County Fermanagh, 1786–95 – NLI, MS 49,495/21
Tenancy agreements, 1659 onwards – NLI, MS 49,495/23
Other lease-related documentation, 1732 onwards – NLI, MS 49,495/26–37

Rentals and accounts
Rental of Glaslough estate, 1751–66 – NLI, MS 5783
Rentals of Glaslough and Emy estates, 1765–80, 1802 – NLI, MS 5809

Acounts for Glaslough and Emy, 1781–99 – NLI, MS 49,495/1/42
Rentals and accounts for Glaslough and Emy, 1800–20 – NLI, MS 49,495/1/43
Rentals and accounts for Pettigo, 1777–1824 – NLI, MS 49,495/1/48

Maps and surveys
Maps and surveys for the Monaghan estate, 1765 onwards – NLI, MS 49,495/1/131
Maps and surveys for the Tyrone estate, 1770–79 – NLI, MS 49,495/1/133

Other
List of tenants on the Glaslough estate, 1763 – NLI, MS 49,495/34
Tenant wills and related documentation, 1784–1814 – NLI, MS 49,495/1/119
Estate correspondence, 1776–96, 1799–1820 – NLI, MS 49,495/1/75–76
Accounts, expenditure, bills receipts, 1779 onwards – NLI, MS 49,495/1/110–111
Bills and receipts for goods and services provided to the Leslie family, 1758–65, 1766–
    69, 1770–76, 1777–1812 – NLI, MS 49,495/1/122–125

Madden estate, Hilton Park
The family also owned the Manor Waterhouse estate in County Fermanagh. For more
information, see the 'Introduction to the Madden Papers' prepared by PRONI.

Deeds and leases from the early 17th-century onwards – D3465/A *passim*
Small octavo volume containing notes on plants and trees, garden layout, etc, including
    a 'list of good gardeners' giving the specialities and characteristics of each named
    individual, *c.* 1730–1798 – D3465/G/3 (MIC594/7)
Volume of maps of estate in Galloon parish, 1766, naming tenants: due to changes in
    parish boundaries the area covered by these maps is now in Currin parish –
    D3465/G/2/2 (MIC594/7)
Three maps of parts of the Manor Waterhouse estate, including one of Cady and
    Rooskey, part of the demesne lands, 1774–9 – D3465/G/8/1 (MIC594/7)

Massereene estate, Clones, etc
Rent roll and statement of debts of Lord Massereene, 1712–13 – D562/834
Rentals of the estate in County Monaghan from the early 19th century, but providing
    details of leases from the mid-18th century – D1739/3/9, 10
Leases, 1693 onwards – D4084/1/3/3

Moore estate, Ematris
Rent rolls, 1702–16 – printed in *Clogher Record*, 15 (1995), pp 135–6

Murray estate see **Rossmore estate**

Rossmore estate, Monaghan
Though the Rossmore Papers in PRONI have the prefix 'T', which usually indicates
copies, they are in fact originals. The documents had been transferred to PRONI for
conservation and copying not long before Lord Rossmore's house was destroyed by
terrorists. Subsequently, it was agreed that the original records would remain in PRONI.

The history of this estate and the families associated with it is particularly complex and researchers should refer to the 'Introduction to the Rossmore Papers' prepared by PRONI for more information.

Correspondence, 1705–33, from the time the estate was owned by the Cairnes family – T2929/2
Leases arranged in bundles by townland starting in the 18th century – T2929/36
See also **Blayney estate, Monaghan** and **Clermont estate**

Shirley estate, Farney

This property approximated to the western half of the barony of Farney and came into the possession of the Shirley family in the mid seventeenth century. For more on this estate, see the 'Introduction to the Shirley Papers' prepared by PRONI. Some of the records in this collection relate to the **Essex estate** in the late sixteenth and early early seventeenth centuries and others relate to the **Bath estate** which occupied the eastern half of the barony of Farney. See also E. P. Shirley, *Some Account of the Territory or Dominion of Farney* (1845) for additional background information.

Calf-bound album containing 119 pages of various leases, rentals, surveys and maps from the early 17th century onwards, including a rent roll of lands in the barony of Farney, 1695 (p. 21), arrears of rent from tenants in the Farney estate, 1708–17 (pp 23–31), list of *c.* 160 tenants in the Farney estate, 1729 (p. 107) – D3531/A/4
Calf-bound album containing 137 letters written to members of the Shirley family by their agents, 1729–1816: 11 are pre-1760 with 20 post 1800 – D3531/A/5
Rentals, 1726, 1771 – D3531/R/1/1–2
Other 18th-century maps and surveys – D3531/S *passim*
Leases, 1738 onwards, including runs of leases from major re-lettings in 1777 and 1799 – D3531/T *passim*

The following Shirley estate material is in Warwickshire County Record Office:

Bundles of leases, 1770, 1777; three small boxes of loose leases, 1799; two bundles of leases, 1792–1825, 1729–1829 – CR 229/223
Map of the west part of the barony of Farney, surveyed in 1734 and mapped in 1735, with an inset plan of the west side of the town of Carrickmacross accompanied by a key giving tenants' names – CR 229/123/1
'A Map of the West Moiety of the Barony of Farney ... surveyed in the years 1789, 1790' with a sketch of Carrickmacross in pencil – CR 229/123/2
Rentals of the Farney estate, 1777, 1800–1802 & n.d – CR 229/Box 2/1
Bundle of Farney rentals, beginning in 1735 – CR 229/Box 2/2

Singleton estate, Fort Singleton

Leases, 1759 onwards: lands of Bragan, Crossnacalouf [Crossnacaldoo], Derrykinnagh Beg, Derrykinnagh More {all Errigal Trough}, Derrilla, Mullyjordan, Tonyfinnigan {all Donagh} – D988 *passim*

Templetown (Upton family) estate, Muckno
Maps of Lord Templetown's estate, 1797, 1800 and undated: lands of Aghnadamph, Alsmeed, Creaghanroe, Curratantha, Drumcrib, Grig, Irrerow [Erryroe], Liseenan, Lissdony, Longfield, Lurganearly, Tavanaskea, Tomogrow, Tullycaghey {all Muckno}, Annayalla, Corlieghdharragan, Corracloghan, Fassan [Tassan], Moneyvolan {all Clontibret}, Drumgarra {Ballybay} – NLI, MS 21 F. 41 (023–036)

Verner estate see under **County Tyrone**

Westenra estate see **Rossmore estate**

Weymouth estate see **Bath estate**

COUNTY TYRONE

Abercorn (Hamilton family) estate, Strabane
The Abercorn estate was the largest in County Tyrone and one of the most important in Ulster. It owed its origins to James Hamilton, first earl of Abercorn, who was granted two manors – Donelong and Strabane – in Strabane barony in 1610. The subsequent history of the estate is complex, but through purchase and inheritance by the beginning of the eighteenth century it comprised four manors in Tyrone – Cloghogall, Derrywoon, Donelong and Strabane – and the manor of Magavelin and Lismochery in County Donegal. In 1790, the ninth earl of Abercorn was created marquess of Abercorn and in 1868 his grandson was made duke of Abercorn. For more on this family and estate, see William J. Roulston, *Abercorn: The Hamiltons of Barons Court* (2014) and W. H. Crawford, *The Management of a Major Ulster Estate in the Late Eighteenth Century: The Eighth Earl of Abercorn and his Irish Agents* (2001). See also the 'Introduction to the Abercorn Papers' prepared by PRONI.

Correspondence
The real strength of this estate collection is the voluminous correspondence that has survived for the 18th century, most of which comprises letters to and from the eighth earl of Abercorn and his Irish agents (D623/A). Transcripts or summaries of these letters can be read via the PRONI eCatalogue. Extracts from the Abercorn correspondence were published as *The Abercorn Letters*, edited by John Gebbie (1972).

Manor of Cloghogall (lands in the parishes of Donaghedy and Leckpatrick)
Rent roll of Ballymagorry, n.d. (*c.* 1720) – D623/C/2/1
Rental, 1794–1809, with details of the November 1787 letting of the entire manor – D623/C/4/2
Maps of the manor of Cloghogall naming tenants, 1777 – D623/D/1/16/13–33
Valuation of the manor of Cloghogall, 1777 – D623/D/1/18/1

Manor of Derrywoon (lands in the parish of Ardstraw)
Rental, 1794–1809, with details of the November 1787 letting of the entire manor – D623/C/4/7

Maps of the manor of Derrywoon naming tenants, 1777 – D623/D/1/16/61–72
Valuation of the manor of Derrywoon, 1777 – D623/D/1/19/1

Manor of Donelong (lands in the parish of Donaghedy)
Rental, 1794–1809, with details of the November 1787 letting of the entire manor –
    D623/C/4/3
Maps of the manor of Donelong naming tenants, 1777 – D623/D/1/16/1–12

Manor of Magavelin and Lismochery (lands in the parishes of Taughboyne and Raymoghy)
Survey of the manor of 'Magavelin' by Archibald Stewart, 1718 – D623/D/1/3/1
Rental, 1794–1809, with details of the November 1787 letting of the entire manor –
    D623/C/4/8
Maps of the manor of Magavelin and Lismochery naming tenants, 1781 –
    D623/D/1/16/73–91
Lease book of the Donegal estate from 1782 – D623/B/11/1

Manor of Strabane (lands in the parishes of Ardstraw, Camus-juxta-Mourne and Urney)
Claims concerning the manor of Strabane, 1700–01, printed in *DIFHR*, 24 (2001),
    pp 85–6
Printed rental of the manor of Strabane, *c.* 1702, printed in *DIFHR*, 24 (2001), p. 86
Rental, 1794–1809, with details of the November 1787 letting of the entire manor –
    D623/C/4/1
Maps of the manor of Strabane naming tenants, 1777 – D623/D/1/16/34–60
Valuation of the manor of Strabane, 1777 – D623/D/1/17/1

Miscellaneous
Leases, 1614–1734 (surprisingly few pre-1800 leases to tenants survive) – D623/B/13
Letter of 1755 giving details of tenants at Stragolane *c.* 1704–14 – D623/A/31/65
Petition from the tenants of the jointure lands to Hon. James Lord Viscount Paisley,
    c. 1736 – D623/A/6/37
A muster roll of the Abercorn estate, naming over 200 tenants in possession of firearms,
    1745 – printed in *DIFHR*, 21 (1998), pp 71–3
Volume recording tenant right sales in Tyrone and Donegal, *c.* 1800 – D623/B/4

Anglesey (Annesley family) estate, Orritor see **Castle Stewart estate**

Annesley estate, Clonoe
Leases, 1798 onwards: lands of Lower Menagh, Dernagh, Annaghmore, Lower
Shanless, Magheramulkenny {all Clonoe} – D474 *passim*

Belmore (Lowry Corry family) estate, Beragh and Sixmilecross
Further records relating to this estate and background information on the family are
provided in the estate entry under **County Fermanagh**. The records listed here concern
the manor of Finagh and other Tyrone property. See also Earl of Belmore, *The History
of Two Ulster Manors* (1903).

Leases arranged by townland, 1740 onwards – D3007/A/24
Leases, 1787–96 – D674 *passim*
Rental of County Tyrone estate, 1777–86 – D624/1
Rentals of the County Tyrone estate, beginning in 1777 – D3007/B/3
Vouchers of the County Tyrone estate, beginning in 1777 – D3007/C/2
Survey and valuation of part of the Belmore estate in County Tyrone, *c.* 1800, including
    comments on the standard of the tenants – D3007/D/1/6/1

Blessington estate see **Mountjoy estate**

Boyle estate, Drumquin
Several 18th-century deeds relating to the property of the Boyle family of Kirlish in
    the Drumquin area – D580 *passim*
Abstract of incumbrances affecting lands of Carony, 1788–1816 – D4494/2

Burges estate, Parkanaur

Rentals
Rental, 1794–5: lands of Stakernagh, Edenacrannon, Terrenew, Tullyallen and
    Kill[y]moyle {all Donaghmore}, County Tyrone; Annaloist {Seagoe}, Derryneskan
    {Drumcree}, Ballyscandal {Eglish}, and the city of Armagh, County Armagh –
    T1007/193
Rental of Tyrone estate, 1797 – T1007/207
Rental of Armagh and Tyrone estate, 1798–1809 – T1007/216

Maps
Volume of maps with observation on the tenancies, *c.* 1798 – T2256
Map of Edenacrannon, 1750, naming tenants, with observations of 1799 – T1007/61
Map of Tullyallen, 1769, naming tenants – T1007/93
Map of Terrenew, Stakernagh, Edenacrannon, Killmoyle and Tullyallen, 1774, naming
    tenants – T1007/108
Map of Tullyallen, 1799, naming tenants – T1007/224

Miscellaneous
Booklet of letters re estate and genealogical matters, 1722–1822 – T2494; MIC191
18th-century observations and leases – D1594
Notebook containing copies of leases and remarks on tenants, *c.* 1700–1902 – T1085/2
Lists of tenants, 1750–71 – T1054/2

Cairns estate, Killyfaddy
A list of the counterparts of the tenants' leases for the estate of James Cairns, *c.* 1738–
    1786: lands of Killyfaddy, Dromore, Mullans, Carntall Beg, Augher, Corboe, Fogart,
    Corrode, Laccaboy, Mossgrove – D2559/1/7
Rent roll and survey of estate, 1780 – D2559/3/3
Rent rolls of part of the estate to be sold, 1793, 1795 – D2559/3/3–5
Rent rolls, *c.* 1800 – D2559/3/8, 10–11

Tenants in Killyfaddy whose rents are raised, *c.* 1800 – D2559/3/9

Portion of rental: lands of Killyfaddy, Cantall, Dromore, Fogart, Killaney, Mullans, Aghindrumman, Tatnadaveny, Mallabeny, Corboe, *c.* 1800 – D2559/3/11

Caledon (Alexander family) estate, Caledon

James Alexander purchased this estate, comprising lands in counties Armagh and Tyrone, in 1776 from the earl of Cork and Orrery whose family had come into possession of it through intermarriage with a Hamilton family that had acquired the property in the 1660s. James Alexander was created Baron Caledon in 1790, Viscount Caledon in 1797 and earl of Caledon in 1800. The estate collection includes documents dating back to the Hamilton period of ownership. See the 'Introduction to the Caledon Papers' prepared by PRONI.

Large collection of leases from the second half of the 1600s onwards – D2433/A/1 *passim*

Rentals of the estate, 1766, 1796, 1799 – D2433/A/6/1–3

Draft valuation and rental of the estate, 1774 – D2433/A/5/1

Estate papers and correspondence re Caledon, 1750–1765 – D2433/A/2/1

Letterbooks, 1775–1802 – D2433/A/3/1–3

Ledgers, account and cash books, 1773 onwards – D2433/A/4/1

Lease book of the estate which provides a summary of leases from 1735 and a statement of the position of these leases in the 1770s – D2433/A/5/3

Names of tenants in the townlands of Aghasallagh, Ards, Cavanboy, Creivelaght, Cumber, Dyon, Derrygooley, Derrylappan, Knockguiny, Lismuldown, Tanagh {all Aghaloo}, Cor Tynan {Tynan}, 1781 – *Belfast Newsletter*, 13–17 July 1781

Four accounts of wages for servants at Caledon House, 1794–7 – D2433/A/9/1

Castle Stewart (Stewart/Stuart family) estate, Stewartstown and Castlederg

The origins of this estate can be traced to the early 1600s and the acquisition by the Stewart/Stuart family of lands forming the manors of Castle Stewart and Forward. The title Baron Castle Stewart was created in 1619, followed many years later by the viscountcy of Castle Stewart (1793) and earldom of Castle Stewart (1800). The manor of Orritor (Orator/Auraghter), alias Manor Annesley, was acquired in 1782. A fourth manor – the manor of Hastings or Castlegore – was inherited in 1820, though records relating to the time it was owned by the Edwards family are in the Castle Stewart collection. See the 'Introduction to the Castle Stewart Papers' prepared by PRONI and Andrew Godfrey Stuart, *A Genealogical & Historical Sketch of the Stuarts of the House of Castlestuart in Ireland* (1854).

Leases for the manor of Hastings, alias Castlegore, 18th century – D1618/5/1, /2

Leases for the manors of Castle Stewart and Forward, 17th–18th centuries – D1618/5/5–10

Leases for the manor of Orritor, 18th century – D1618/5/11, /12

Originals and typescript copies of 17th- and 18th-century correspondence and other related papers – D1618/15 *passim*

Rental of Castle Stewart estate, 1768 – D476/258A

See also **Staples estate**

Charlemont (Caulfeild family) estate, Castlecaulfeild see under **County Armagh**

Clogher bishopric estate
Map of 'the Demesne or Mensal lands belonging to the See of Clogher', 1745 –
    T2148/1 (map reproduced in Jack Johnston, *The Clogher Story* (2015), p. 30)
Leases of the see of Clogher, counties Fermanagh, Monaghan and Tyrone, 1746–79 –
    NLI, MS 5853
Accounts of Clogher leases, rents and fines, *c.* 1780–*c.* 1790 – DIO/2/10/29

Cooper estate see under **County Fermanagh**

Cork and Orrery estate see **Caledon estate**

Drelincourt Charity estate
Rental for Legmurran {Ballyclog} and Lisnaclare {Clonoe}, n.d. [18th century] –
    DIO/4/9/3/3, /5
Valuation of above townlands, naming tenants with observations, n.d. [18th century]
    – DIO/4/9/3/4

Eccles estate, Fintona
Leases, etc, 1671 onwards (over 150 pre-1800) – D526 *passim*
Notebook containing a copy lease book, including names of the lives in the leases and
    often their ages, 1751–1850 – D1368/1 (transcribed by Len Swindley and printed
    in *DIFHR*, 39 (2016), pp 3–10
Various 18th-century papers, including leases: lands include Liskey, Fintona,
    Tonaghmore, Tireenan {all Donacavey} – T962 *passim*

Edie estate, Coolaghy
Leases by Nathaniel Edie relating to Coolaghy {Ardstraw}, 1784–1805 – D847/24/36

Edwards estate, Castlegore see **Castle Stewart estate**

Erne estate, Strabane
Account book of Lady Erne's property in counties Armagh and Tyrone and executors'
    journal of her estate kept by Rev. W. Digby and John King, 1786–1800 – NLI, MS
    3209
List of Lady Erne's rents in Strabane, 1795 – NLI, MS 15,783
Accounts of Lady Erne with, *inter alia,* her agent James Hamilton for the Strabane
    estate, 1790s – NLI, MS 15,360

Foljambe estate, Newtownsaville
In 1722, Sir George Savile came into possession of the manor of Cecil; after 1784 it
passed to Francis Ferrand Foljambe. Papers relating to the management of this estate
are in the Nottinghamshire Archives and many have been copied by PRONI. See also
Jack Johnston, *Glenhoy: The First 200 Years* (1979), which includes names from the
rental of the Savile (Foljambe) estate of 1738 and leaseholders in the manor of Cecil in
1769. The Registry of Deeds includes many leases from Sir George Savile to his tenants
(mainly in volumes 91–93).

Rentals of the manor of Cecil with the churchlands of Errigal, 1732–3, 1735–8 (rental for 1737 has observations on tenants) – T3381/2/1–8

Rentals, accounts and letters, 1783–1811 – T3381/5/1–63

Leases of farms in the manor of Cecil, 1769: nearly 100 names in total – T3381/4/1–8

Vouchers for charges in John Speer's accounts for the rents of the manor of Cecil, 1787–94 – T3381/7

Survey of the manor of Cecil, 1796 – T3381/9/1

Survey and valuation of the manor of Cecil, 1800 – T3381/10/1–7

Drawings and plan of diamond and streets for Savilestown with description of site and suggested improvements, 1758 – Nottinghamshire Archives, DD/SR/202/4

Letters, petitions, etc from Irish tenantry covering a range of different issues, *c.* 1770–1820 – Nottinghamshire Archives, DD/FJ/11/1/7/289–339

Forbes estate, Aghintain
Volume of maps of the estate of the Hon. John Forbes at Mount Stewart or Aghintain, 1777, naming tenants – T1132/1

Forster estate, Pomeroy
Rent roll of Lisnagleer and Drumconor {both Pomeroy}, 1786 – D2469/36

Volume of maps of Forster estate in counties Monaghan and Tyrone, 1795–1805 – D1105/2

Gardiner estate see Mountjoy estate

Gervais estate, Augher
Household account book, 1767–78 – T1287/2

Gorges estate, Errigal Keerogue
Rental of part of the estate of Hamilton Gorges sold to John Doherty in trust for Thomas Verner, 1785: lands of Millix, Brackagh, Irish Shantavny {all Errigal Keerogue}, Eskermore {Clogherny?} (very poor condition) – D847/7/C/1

Hall estate, Collermoney
Rent roll of Collermoney {Leckpatrick}, 1775 – D2649/15/3/4

Hamill estate, Strabane
'Observations of H[ugh]. Hamill Esq.'s title and interest in the Lordship of Strabane', *c.* 1685 and other documents relating to properties in Strabane in the 1600s – D1939/18/10/2, /3

Hamilton estate, Caledon see Caledon estate

Hamilton estate, Dunnamanagh
This estate comprised lands in the parishes of Donaghedy and Badoney. There is no major archive for this estate, though a few scattered items, mainly leases, can be found in PRONI. However, a significant number of leases issued to tenants in the second half of the eighteenth century were registered in the Registry of Deeds, Dublin. Abstracts

from a dozen of these leases for lands in Donaghedy were published in William J. Roulston, *Three Centuries of Life in a Tyrone Parish: A History of Donagheady from 1600 to 1900* (2010), pp 181–3.

Hamilton estate, Manor Elieston
Rental of estate of Sir Claud Hamilton of Shawfield, 1613–19 – MIC285/1; T544

Hamilton Moore estate, Killyman
Leases from James Hamilton Moore for lands of Bogbane, Correny, Gortshalgan, Keenaghan, Kinnegoe {all Killyman}, Killycolp {Desertcreat} 1764–69 – D235/27–30; T877/75, 87

Hill estate, Desertcreat
Deeds concerning Aughnagreagh, Barradhasshan [Bardahessiagh], Derrygortinea, Mullinure {all Desertcreat}, 1660s–1670s – D1118/6/2

Huntingdon estate, Castlederg
These lands had originally been granted to Sir John Davies in the early 1600s and through marriage came into the possession of the Hastings family, earls of Huntingdon. Later the manor of Hastings, focused on Castlederg, was acquired by the Edwards family and eventually by the Castle Stewarts (see **Castle Stewart estate**).

Rent rolls of the estate in counties Fermanagh and Tyrone, 1633–66 – Huntington Library, California, Hastings MSS, Box 78
Survey of the Countess of Huntingdon's lands, n.d. [*c.* 1664] – Huntington Library, Hastings MSS, Box 76

Kane estate, Dromore and Omagh
Deeds, leases, etc, 1761 onwards: lands include Curley (otherwise Cranny), Mullancross, Kildrum, Drumconnis {all Dromore} and property in Omagh {Drumragh} – D4132/C/7

Knox estate, Dungannon
For most of the seventeenth century this estate was owned by the Chichesters. It was purchased by a Belfast merchant, Thomas Knox, in 1692. A subsequent Thomas Knox was created Baron Welles of Dungannon in 1781 and Viscount Northland in 1791. The second viscount was granted the earldom of Ranfurly in 1831. For more information on the family and estate, see the 'Introduction to the Ranfurly Papers' prepared by PRONI.

Rentals
Rent rolls of the town and manor of Dungannon, 1745, 1747 – D235/20, /22
Rent ledger, Dungannon estate, 1781–91 – D235/159
Rent roll of Dungannon estate, 1795 – D235/45

Leases
Leases, 1694 onwards – D4183/5, /6, /10, /14

Leases from the 18th century onwards – D235 *passim*

Leases, 1699 onwards – D1932/8 *passim*

List of tenants in the town and manor of Dungannon 'whose Minnitts are in Jon Jourdan's hands …', *c.* 1729 – D235/55

List of lessees and tenants in Dungannon area, 1750–1812, naming lives in leases – D235/158

Extracts of leases, 1757–1832 – T953/1

Maps

Map and survey of manor of Dungannon, 1710, naming tenants – D1018/A/1 (see T587/1 for another version)

Volume of maps of estate, 1770 – D1932/7/1

Leslie estate see under **County Monaghan**

Lindesay estate, Loughrey

Rental of estate, 1745–61 – NLI, MS 5204

Rent ledger, 1778–1817 – NLI, MS 5205

Survey of estate, *c.* 1800, naming tenants – NLI, MS 2584

Lowry estate, Drumragh

Collection of leases from second half of 18th century mainly issued by Rev. James Lowry and Rev. John Lowry: lands include Aughnamoyle, Tamlaght {both Drumragh}, Aghadulla (Harper) {Dromore}, Lisgarry {Drumragh?} – D474 *passim*

Lowry estate, Pomeroy

18th-century leases: Aghafad, Cavanacaw, Cavanakeeran, Corrycroar and Crockbrack, Gortnagarn, Killea and Bawn, Lurganeden, Pomeroy, Tanderagee {all Pomeroy}, Coraneny, Gortindarragh, Limehill, Memore {all Desertcreat}, Dernaseer {Donaghmore} – D1132/10

Envelope of loose pages of Pomeroy estate rentals, 1767–1803 – D1132/12/1

Pomeroy estate rental, 1791–4 – D1132/12/1A

Box of estate maps, 1759–1873 – D1132/19/1

Macghee estate, Strabane

Leases from the 17th and 18th centuries relating to property in Strabane issued by the Macghees and other families – D1062/4/A

McCausland estate, Ardstraw

List of tenants in the manor of Ardstraw, 1720s (leased by the McCauslands from the bishop of Derry) – extracted from the Registry of Deeds and printed in *DIFHR*, 24 (2001), p. 84

McCausland estate, Omagh

Advertisement for the sale of lands in and near Omagh belonging to Alexander McCausland, naming some of the occupiers, especially in the town of Omagh – *Londonderry Journal*, 4 March 1774

Maxwell estate, Ballyclog
18th-century leases for Curglasson and Killoon {Ballyclog} – D2223/9/10

Mervyn estate, Augher, Omagh and Trillick
Leases, 1694–1741 – D3007/A/13
Rental of the Mervyn estates, 1719: names tenants in Omagh and Trillick – T359/1, p. 169
Rent book of Colonel Mervyn's estate, 1769–70: covering Augher, Omagh and Trillick properties – D2023/3/1/2

Montgomery estate, Fivemiletown and Derrygonnelly
The Fivemiletown (Blessingbourne) portion of this estate was in County Tyrone, while the Derrygonnelly lands were in County Fermanagh.

Rentals
Rent roll of Derrygonelly, 1753 – T359/1, p. 23
Rent rolls, Derrygonnelly estate, 1759, 1767 – D464/26, /28
Rent rolls of estates in Fermanagh and Tyrone, 1792–4, 1793–1801, 1797 – D464/74, /75, /84
Rent roll of Blessingbourne, 1752: 35 tenants – D627/16
Rental and account books, Blessingbourne, 1769–1810 – D627/21
Rental of Fivemiletown, 1773 – D627/23
Receipt book of rents, Fivemiletown, 1783–6 – D627/37
Rental and survey naming tenants with observations, County Tyrone, 1787–9 – D627/46
Rentals of estate for most years, 1784–1800 – D627 *passim*
Rental of *c.* 1810 covering the period 1780–1840, manor of Blessingbourne, County Tyrone, and manor of Drumcrow, County Fermanagh – D627/80

Maps, surveys and valuations
Maps of holdings in estate, 1743, 1745, 1750, 1780 – D482 *passim*
Survey of the manor of Blessingbourne, 1726 – D627/4
Valuation of Blessingbourne, 1767 – D627/20
Maps of Timpany, County Tyrone, 1775, naming tenants – D627/24
Maps of Col. Hugh Montgomery estate in County Fermanagh, 1792–1813 – NLI, MS L 409

Miscellaneous
Account book, 1744–50 – D627/14
Lists of cattle grazed on Mulnaverl (Mulnavale), County Tyrone, 1777–8, *c.* 1780 – D627/25, /29
85 names and addresses of men 'ditching in Mulinavel' (Mulnavale), 1779 – D627/30
Returns of the lives in leases, Blessingbourne, *c.* 1783 – D627/33–36
Names of 95 freeholders in the manor of Blessingbourne, *c.* 1795 – D627/56

Mountjoy (Stewart family) estate, Newtownstewart

The origins of this estate can be traced to the early seventeenth century and the acquisition of extensive lands by Sir William Stewart. A subsequent William Stewart was created Viscount Mountjoy in 1683 and yet another William Stewart was created earl of Blessington in 1745. Following the earl's death without issue in 1769, the estate passed to the Gardiners, for whom the viscountcy and earldom were later revived. See NLI Collection List no. 67.

List of tenants in the Mountjoy estate, Newtownstewart, 1734 – published in *DIFHR*, 24 (2001), p. 84

Collection of counterpart leases issued by William Stewart, first earl of Blessington, 1763–6 – NLI, MS 36,585

Names of occupiers of farms in Mullaghmain, Crockawidall and Ednasavellagh, held by Samuel Moore of Bell Hill from the representatives of the earl of Blessington, 1779 – *Belfast Newsletter*, 15–19 Jan. 1779

Case papers, depositions, etc, mainly in connection with a lawsuit, 1769–77 – T3765/J/2

Letters and legal case papers including petitions from tenants of the Mountjoy estate, 1787–98 – T3765/J/3

Moutray estate, Favour Royal, Augher

Leases, 1714 onwards – D2023/1

Rental and miscellaneous account books, 1757–63, 1795–1825 – D2023/3/1/1, /3

Rent account books, 1762–5, 1771–3 – D1716/16

Notebook listing Favour Royal leases, 1765–1862 – D2023/1/13

Servants' account book, 1795–1859 – D2023/4/2/1

Northland estate see Knox estate

Orrery estate see Caledon estate

Perry estate, Perrymount

Leases, 1785–97: lands include Mullaghmore, Renelly [Ranelly], Seskinore, Tullyrush {all Clogherny} – D526/1

Powerscourt (Wingfield family) estate, Benburb

The origins of this estate can be traced to the acquisition of a sizeable estate in the parish of Clonfeacle by Sir Richard Wingfield, first Viscount Powerscourt, in the early 1600s. See NLI Collection List no. 124.

Leases arranged in bundles alphabetically by townland, 1700 onwards – D1957/2

Index book of leases, 1740–1804 – D1957/2/46

Letting of lands of Benburb extracted from the counterparts of the tenants' leases, 1739–56 – D1957/2/48

Lands to be land on the Powerscourt estate, naming tenants by townland, 1770–71 – *Belfast Newsletter*, 5 June 1770, 10 May 1771

Survey of the manor of Benburb, 1771 – MIC280/1; NLI, n.6235, p.6978 (see *Duiche Neill*, 20 (2012))
Register of leases for Powerscourt estate (not just Tyrone) beginning in 1775 – NLI, MS 16,384
Book entitled 'Old leases on Benburb estate', *c.* 1779–*c.* 1801 – D2634/1

Ranfurly estate see **Knox estate**

Richardson estate, Drum, Kildress

Correspondence
Letters and associated receipts and legal case papers to Alexander Richardson of Drum, 1697–1729, and William Richardson of Drum, 1729–48 – D2002/C/3, /5
Miscellaneous business letters to David Richardson of Drum, 1758–92 – D2002/C/6
Letters and papers of William Richardson of Drum, including a few of his younger brother, Benjamin, concerning estate and business affairs, and local politics and administration, 1768–1808 – D2002/C/8

Other records
Rough Drum rental, 1791–2 – D2002/C/6
Boxes of leases, starting 1636 – D2002/L/1–2
Maps of a number of townlands from *c.* 1780 onwards, including Knockaleery and 'Domain of Drum' – D2002/M

Richardson estate, Tullyreavy
17th- and 18th-century deeds relating to the Tullyreavy {Desertcreat} estate – D1118/6/2

Sanderson estate, Tullylagan
Leases for Cady {Desertcreat}, 1730–39 – D645/29–30, /36
Leases to Greer family, 1770–75 – T1173/1

Singleton estate, Fort Singleton
Leases, 1774 onwards: lands of Carricklongfield {Aghaloo}, Annaghmore – D988 *passim*

Speer estate, Rahoran
Map and survey of Rahoran {Clogher}, naming tenants, 1796 – D847/20/C/1

Staples estate, Lissan
The origins of this estate can be found in the early seventeenth century. From around the middle of the eighteenth century members of the Caulfeild family were involved heavily in the management of this estate. For more information, see the 'Introduction to the Staples Papers' prepared by PRONI.

18th-century maps and surveys, catalogued in full – D1567/C *passim*
Envelope containing accounts with Thomas Caulfeild and a rental of the Castle Stewart and Lissan estates, 1767, 1776–8 – D1567/D/1/1/1–3

Rental of part of W. J. Stephenson's estate in County Tyrone to be sold, 1772 – D1567/D/1/2/1

Envelope containing rentals of Castle Stewart and Lissan estates, 1786–9 – D1567/D/1/4/1–3 (that for 1786 has been transcribed by Colin Kennedy and printed in *DIFHR*, 29 (2006), pp 83–6)

Bills, receipts and vouchers to the Rt Hon. John Staples, Thomas Caulfeild of Moy, and James Caulfeild, including some relating to building work, 1784–6 – D1567/E/1/1

Stewart estate, Killymoon

This is another estate that originated in the early seventeenth century. For more information on the family and collection, see the 'Introduction to the Stewart of Killymoon Papers' prepared by PRONI.

Leases

Three leases for farms in Gortatray {Donaghenry}, 1758–61 – D32

Rentals

Rental of estate, 1767 (only a few townlands) – NLI, MS 9627

Rentals, 1786–8 – NLI, MS 766

Rent roll, 1786–8, published in Henry L. Glasgow, *History of Cookstown* (2008), pp 82–97

Rent and account book kept by David Richardson of Drum, apparently as agent for the Drumshambo, Clohog and Grange property of James Stewart of Killymoon, and his younger brother, Henry, 1788–90 – D2002/R/1/1

Maps and surveys

'The survey and estaemation of the sixteen towns or Mannor of Clananise', n.d. but 18th-century – NLI, MS 8734/1

Map of estate at Cookstown, 1736, naming tenants (very faint) – D3/1

Survey of estate, 1767 – NLI, MS 9627

Map of the estate of James Stewart, 1798, naming tenants: lands of Sherrigrim, Tullaghmore, Ross, Lurgie – D647/32/1

Map of the estate of James Stewart, *c.* 1798, naming tenants: lands of Allen, Murree, Little Muree, Gortavale, Crossdernot, Mulnagore, Drummond, Carlonen, Moynagh, Annaghquin, Drumballyhugh – D647/32/2

Map of Mulnagore, *c.* 1800, naming tenants – D647/32/4

The following maps of the Stewart estate are in the National Library of Ireland and are 1798 or undated:

Drummond, Crossdermot, Mulnagore, Curlonan, Moree, Drumballyhugh … and Moynagh – NLI, 21.F.47 (012)

Kilcronagh, Ballyreagh, Knockacunny, Annaghmore, Annaghananam and Annaghteigh – NLI, 21.F.47 (013)

Tullaghmore, Ross, Lurgy and Sherrigrin, 1798 – NLI, 21.F.47 (014)

Cloonawadda and Aughakinduff – NLI, 21.F.47 (015)

Glenburrisk, Gortnagola and Kilmore – NLI, 21.F.47 (016)

Congo, Gortnaglusk and Ballymenagh, 1798 – NLI, 21.F.47 (017)

Mulnahunch, Coolhill, Lisfearty, Eskragh, Cranslough, Clontyfallow, Dernaborey, Castletown, Knocknarney, Carranteel and Lisconduff – NLI, 21.F.47 (018)

A map of part of the estate of James Stewart situated in the parish of Arboe, 1803: lands of Anneeter Beg, Anneeter More, Ardean, Cluntoe [Richardson], Lurgyroe, Kinrush ... and Killycanavan – NLI, MS 21.F.47 (011)

Miscellaneous
Late 18th-century household miscellany manuscript book from Killymoon Castle – D4524/1

Stewart estate, Omagh and Killyman
Valuation of estate of Alexander Stewart near Omagh and in Killyman parish, *c.* 1747, naming tenants – D3698/2

Survey of Hamilton Stewart's estate in Drumragh parish, 1776: covers the townlands of Creevan, Firreagh, Loughmuck and Gaumy and names names tenants, with an undated list of changes to tenancies at the end of the volume – D847/21/C/4

Rentals of the Omagh estate, 1788, 1797 – D847/21/C/6

Stewart estate, Termonmaguirk
Tenants' land reference sheet, estate of Sir John Stewart, *c.* 1800 – D1021/2

Story estate, Corick
Servants and labourers' account book, 1790–1826; rent book of the Corick estate, 1791–1813 – MIC42/1

Typescript 'The Economics of Country Life in Co. Tyrone at the end of the 18th Century from Contemporary Records', 1790–1811, compiled from records kept by Rev. Dr Story of Corick – T2854/2

Verner estate, Churchill
Leases etc relating to lands in counties Armagh and Tyrone beginning in 1641 – D2538/A *passim*

Large collection of 18th-century leases for counties Armagh, Monaghan and Tyrone – D236 *passim*

Rental and valuation of Ballygawley, 1785 – D236/539

Rental of Tyrone estate, 1788–92 – D236/487A

Welles estate see Knox estate

APPENDIX 3

Archives and libraries

Listed below are repositories with seventeenth- and eighteenth century material relating to the province of Ulster. This listing is not exhaustive, but it covers places identified in this book as having documentation of relevance. Information on access arrangements and opening hours will be found on the website of each institution.

ARMAGH ROBINSON LIBRARY
(formerly Armagh Public Library)
43 Abbey Street, Armagh, BT61 7DY
Northern Ireland
Website: http://armaghrobinsonlibrary.co.uk/wp

ARMAGH COUNTY MUSEUM
The Mall East, Armagh, BT61 9BE
Northern Ireland
Website: https://visitarmagh.com/places-to-explore/armagh-county-museum

BERKSHIRE RECORD OFFICE
9 Coley Avenue, Reading
Berkshire, RG1 6AF
England
Website: www.berkshirerecordoffice.org.uk

BODLEIAN LIBRARY
Broad Street
Oxford, OX1 3BG
England
Website: www.bodley.ox.ac.uk

BRISTOL ARCHIVES
B Bond Warehouse, Smeaton Road
Bristol, BS1 6XN
England
Website: www.bristolmuseums.org.uk/bristol-archives

CAMBRIDGE UNIVERSITY LIBRARY
West Road
Cambridge, CB3 9DR
England
Website: www.lib.cam.ac.uk

CARDINAL TOMÁS Ó FIAICH LIBRARY & ARCHIVE
15 Moy Road
Armagh, BT61 7LY
Northern Ireland
Website: www.ofiaich.ie

CAVAN COUNTY LIBRARY SERVICE:
JOHNSTON CENTRAL LIBRARY
(Local Studies and Archives)
Farnham Street, Cavan Town
Ireland
Website: www.cavanlibrary.ie

CENTRE FOR BUCKINGHAMSHIRE STUDIES
County Hall, Walton Street
Aylesbury, HP20 1UU
England
Website: www.buckscc.gov.uk/services/culture-and-leisure/centre-for-buckinghamshire-studies

COVENTRY HISTORY CENTRE
(now the Coventry Archives & Research Centre)
Herbert Art Gallery and Museum, Jordan Well
Coventry, CV1 5QP
England
Website: www.theherbert.org/history_centre/default.aspx

DONEGAL COUNTY ARCHIVES SERVICE
Three Rivers Centre, Lifford
Ireland
Website: www.donegalcoco.ie/culture/archives

DONEGAL COUNTY LIBRARY
Central Library, Oliver Plunkett Road
Letterkenny
Ireland
Website: www.donegallibrary.ie

FRIENDS HISTORICAL LIBRARY
Quaker House, Stocking Lane
Dublin 16
Ireland
Website: https://quakers-in-ireland.ie/historical-library

GENEALOGICAL OFFICE see NATIONAL LIBRARY OF IRELAND

GRAND LODGE OF FREEMASONS OF IRELAND: MUSEUM, LIBRARY & ARCHIVE
17–19 Molesworth Street
Dublin 2
Ireland
Website: http://freemason.ie/museum-library-archive

HUNTINGTON LIBRARY
1151 Oxford Road
San Marino, CA 91108
United States of America
Website: www.huntington.org

JOHN RYLANDS LIBRARY
150 Deansgate
Manchester, M3 3EH
England
Website: www.library.manchester.ac.uk/rylands

LEICESTERSHIRE RECORD OFFICE
(Record Office for Leicestershire, Leicester and Rutland)
Long Street, Wigston Magna
Leicester, LE18 2AH
England
Website: www.leicestershire.gov.uk/leisure-and-community/history-and-heritage/visit-the-record-office

LIBRARIES NI
Branches across Northern Ireland
Website: www.librariesni.org.uk

LINEN HALL LIBRARY
17 Donegall Square North
Belfast, BT1 5GB
Northern Ireland
Website: www.linenhall.com

LONDON METROPOLITAN ARCHIVES
40 Northampton Road
London, EC1R 0HB
England
Website: www.cityoflondon.gov.uk/things-to-do/london-metropolitan-archives/Pages/default.aspx

MELLON CENTRE FOR MIGRATION STUDIES
Ulster American Folk Park, 2 Mellon Road
Omagh, BT78 5QU
Northern Ireland
Website: www.qub.ac.uk/cms

METHODIST HISTORICAL SOCIETY OF IRELAND
Edgehill College
9 Lennoxvale
Belfast, BT9 5BY
Northern Ireland
Website: http://methodisthistoryireland.org

MONAGHAN COUNTY LIBRARY
(Local Studies Collection)
98 Avenue, Clones
Ireland
Website: https://monaghan.ie/library

MONAGHAN COUNTY MUSEUM
1–2 Hill Street
Monaghan Town
Ireland
Website: https://monaghan.ie/museum

MUSEUM OF ORANGE HERITAGE
Schomberg House
368 Cregagh Road
Belfast, BT6 9EY
Northern Ireland
Website: www.orangeheritage.co.uk/archives

NATIONAL ARCHIVES OF IRELAND
Bishop Street
Dublin 8
Ireland
Website: www.nationalarchives.ie

NATIONAL LIBRARY OF IRELAND
(including the Genealogical Office)
Kildare Street
Dublin 2
Ireland
Website: www.nli.ie

NATIONAL RECORDS OF SCOTLAND
General Register House, 2 Princes Street
Edinburgh, EH1 3YY
Scotland
Website: www.nrscotland.gov.uk

NEWRY AND MOURNE MUSEUM
Bagenal's Castle, Castle Street
Newry, BT34 2BY
Northern Ireland
Website: www.bagenalscastle.com/museum

NORTH OF IRELAND FAMILY HISTORY SOCIETY: RESEARCH CENTRE/RANDAL GILL LIBRARY
Unit C4, Valley Business Centre
Newtownabbey, BT36 7LS
Northern Ireland
Website: www.nifhs.org/research-centre

NOTTINGHAMSHIRE ARCHIVES
County House, Castle Meadow Road
Nottingham, NG2 1AG
England
Website: www.nottinghamshire.gov.uk/culture-leisure/archives

PRESBYTERIAN HISTORICAL SOCIETY OF IRELAND
Assembly Buildings, Fisherwick Place
Belfast, BT1 6DW
Northern Ireland
Website: www.presbyterianhistoryireland.com

PUBLIC RECORD OFFICE OF NORTHERN IRELAND
2 Titanic Boulevard
Belfast, BT3 9HQ
Northern Ireland
Website: www.nidirect.gov.uk/proni

REGISTRY OF DEEDS
Henrietta Street
Dublin 1, Ireland
Website: www.prai.ie

REPRESENTATIVE CHURCH BODY LIBRARY
Braemor Park
Dublin 14, Ireland
Website: www.ireland.anglican.org/about/rcb-library

ROYAL IRISH ACADEMY
19 Dawson Street
Dublin 2, Ireland
Website: www.ria.ie

SUFFOLK RECORD OFFICE
Lowestoft Library, Clapham Road South
Lowestoft, NR32 1DR
England
Website: www.suffolkarchives.co.uk

THE NATIONAL ARCHIVES
Kew, Richmond
Surrey, TW9 4DU
England
Website: www.nationalarchives.gov.uk

TRINITY COLLEGE DUBLIN:
MANUSCRIPTS & ARCHIVES RESEARCH LIBRARY
Dublin 2, Ireland
Website: www.tcd.ie/library/manuscripts

ULSTER HISTORICAL FOUNDATION
44D Belfast Road
Newtownards, BT23 4TJ
Northern Ireland
Website: www.ancestryireland.com

ULSTER MUSEUM
Botanic Gardens,
Belfast, BT9 5AB
Northern Ireland
Website: www.nmni.com

UNION THEOLOGICAL COLLEGE:
GAMBLE LIBRARY
108 Botanic Avenue
Belfast, BT7 1JT
Northern Ireland
Website: www.union.ac.uk/About-Union/Gamble-Library.aspx

WARWICKSHIRE COUNTY RECORD OFFICE
Priory Park, Cape Road
Warwick, CV34 4JS
England
Website: http://heritage.warwickshire.gov.uk/warwickshire-county-record-office

APPENDIX 4

Locations in Ulster

The following listing includes some 600 locations in Ulster, giving the civil parish and county in which each one is found. The places range from towns and villages to districts and topographical features.

Location	Civil parish	County
Acton	Ballymore	Armagh
Aghadowey	Aghadowey	Londonderry
Aghadrumsee	Clones	Monaghan
Aghagallon	Aghagallon	Antrim
Aghalane	Kinawley	Fermanagh
Aghalee	Aghalee	Antrim
Aghnamullen	Aghnamullen	Monaghan
Aghyaran	Termonamongan	Tyrone
Ahoghill	Ahoghill	Antrim
Ahorey	Kilmore	Armagh
Aldergrove	Killead	Antrim
Altmore	Pomeroy	Tyrone
Annaclone	Annaclone	Down
Annacloy	Inch	Down
Annadorn	Loughinisland	Down
Annag(a)ry	Templecrone	Donegal
Annaghmore	Loughgall	Armagh
Annahilt	Annahilt	Down
Annalong	Kilkeel	Down
Annsborough	Kilmegan	Down
Antrim	Antrim	Antrim
Arboe	Arboe	Tyrone
Ardara	Killybegs Lower	Donegal
Ardglass	Ardglass	Down
Ardmillan	Tullynakill	Down
Ardmore	Clondermot	Londonderry
Ardress	Loughgall	Armagh
Ardstraw	Ardstraw	Tyrone
Armagh	Armagh	Armagh
Armoy	Armoy	Antrim
Arney	Cleenish	Fermanagh
Arranmore Island	Templecrone	Donegal
Articlave	Dunboe	Londonderry
Artigarvan	Leckpatrick	Tyrone
Artikelly	Aghanloo	Londonderry
Arva(gh)	Killeshandra	Cavan
Attical	Kilkeel	Down
Aughafatten	Skerry	Antrim
Augher	Clogher	Tyrone
Aughnacloy	Carnteel	Tyrone

Location	Civil parish	County
Baileysmills	Drumbo	Down
Bailieborough	Bailieborough	Cavan
Ballerin	Errigal	Londonderry
Ballinagh	Kilmore	Cavan
Ballinamallard	Magheracross	Fermanagh
Ballindrait	Clonleigh	Donegal
Ballinode	Tedavnet	Monaghan
Ballintoy	Ballintoy	Antrim
Ballintra	Drumhome	Donegal
Balloo	Killinchy	Down
Ballooly	Garvaghy	Down
Ballsmill	Creggan	Armagh
Ballyalbany	Tedavnet	Monaghan
Ballybay	Ballybay	Monaghan
Ballybofey	Stranorlar	Donegal
Ballybogy	Dunluce	Antrim
Ballycarry	Templecorran	Antrim
Ballycassidy	Trory	Fermanagh
Ballycastle	Ramoan	Antrim
Ballyclare	Grange of Doagh	Antrim
Ballyconnell	Tomregan	Cavan
Ballycopeland	Donaghadee	Down
Ballyeaston	Ballycor	Antrim
Ballygall(e)y	Carncastle	Antrim
Ballygawley	Errigal Keerogue	Tyrone
Ballygorman	Clonca	Donegal
Ballygowan	Comber/Killinchy	Down
Ballyhagen	Kilmore	Armagh
Ballyhaise	Castleterra	Cavan
Ballyhalbert	Ballyhalbert	Down
Ballyheelan	Ballymachugh	Cavan
Ballyholme	Bangor	Down
Ballyhornan	Dunsfort	Down
Ballyjamesduff	Castlerahan	Cavan
Ballykelly	Tamlaght Finlagan	Londonderry
Ballykinler	Ballykinler	Down
Ballylesson	Drumbo	Down
Ballyliffin	Clonmany	Donegal
Ballymac(a)nab	Lisnadill	Armagh
Ballymagauran	Templeport	Cavan
Ballymagorry	Leckpatrick	Tyrone
Ballymartin	Kilkeel	Down
Ballymena	Kirkinriola	Antrim
Ballymoney	Ballymoney	Antrim
Ballynahinch	Magheradrool	Down
Ballynure	Ballynure	Antrim
Ballyrashane	Ballyrashane	Londonderry

Location	Civil parish	County
Ballyreagh	Carnteel	Tyrone
Ballyrobert	Grange of Ballyrobert	Antrim
Ballyronan	Artrea	Londonderry
Ballyroney	Drumballyroney	Down
Ballyshannon	Kilbarron	Donegal
Ballyskeagh	Lambeg	Down
Ballyvoy	Culfeightrin	Antrim
Ballywalter	Ballywalter	Down
Balnamore	Ballymoney	Antrim
Banbridge	Seapatrick	Down
Bangor	Bangor	Down
Bannfoot	Montiaghs	Armagh
Baronscourt	Ardstraw	Tyrone
Bawnboy	Templeport	Cavan
Belcoo	Cleenish	Fermanagh
Belfast	Shankill/Knockbreda	Antrim/Down
Bellaghy	Ballyscullion	Londonderry
Bellanaleck	Cleenish	Fermanagh
Bellananagh	*see* Ballinagh	
Bellanode	*see* Ballinode	
Bellarena	Magilligan	Londonderry
Belleek	Belleek	Fermanagh
Belleek(s)	Loughgilly	Armagh
Belturbet	Annagh	Cavan
Benburb	Clonfeacle	Tyrone
Bendooragh	Ballymoney	Antrim
Beragh	Clogherny	Tyrone
Bessbrook	Killevy	Armagh
Birches, The	Tartaraghan	Armagh
Blacklion	Killinagh	Cavan
Blackskull	Donaghcloney	Down
Blackwatertown	Clonfeacle	Armagh
Bleary	Tullylish	Down
Bloody Foreland	Tullaghobegly	Donegal
Boardmills	Killaney/Saintfield	Down
Boho	Boho	Fermanagh
Bolea	Drumachose	Londonderry
Boleran	*see* Ballerin	
Boneybefore	Carrickfergus	Antrim
Bottlehill	Kilmore	Armagh
Bovedy	Tamlaght O'Crilly	Londonderry
Brantry	Aghaloo	Tyrone
Bready	Donaghedy	Tyrone
Brookeborough	Aghavea	Fermanagh
Broughderg	Lissan	Tyrone
Broughshane	Racavan	Antrim
Bruckless	Killaghtee	Donegal

Location	Civil parish	County
Bryansford	Kilcoo	Down
Buckna	Racavan	Antrim
Bunbeg	Tullaghobegly	Donegal
Buncrana	Fahan Lower	Donegal
Bundoran	Inishmacsaint	Donegal
Burnfoot	Burt	Donegal
Burren	Clonallan	Down
Burt	Burt	Donegal
Burtonport	Templecrone	Donegal
Bushmills	Billy/Dunluce	Antrim
Butlersbridge	Castleterra	Cavan
Cabragh	Killeeshil	Tyrone
Caddy	Drummaul	Antrim
Cahans	Tullycorbet	Monaghan
Caledon	Aghaloo	Tyrone
Camlough	Killevy	Antrim
Campsie	Cappagh	Tyrone
Cappagh	Pomeroy	Tyrone
Cargan	Dunaghy	Antrim
Carland	Donaghmore	Tyrone
Carnalbanagh	Tickmacrevan	Antrim
Carncastle	Carncastle	Antrim
Carndonagh	Donagh	Donegal
Carnlough	Ardclinis	Antrim
Carnmoney	Carnmoney	Antrim
Carnteel	Carnteel	Tyrone
Carrick	Glencolumbkille	Donegal
Carrickaboy	Denn	Cavan
Carrickaness	Eglish	Armagh
Carrickfergus	Carrickfergus	Antrim
Carrickmacross	Magheross	Monaghan
Carrickmore	Termonmaguirk	Tyrone
Carrigans	Killea	Donegal
Carrigart	Mevagh	Donegal
Carrowdore	Donaghadee	Down
Carryduff	Drumbo	Down
Castleblayney	Muckno	Monaghan
Castlecaulfield	Donaghmore	Tyrone
Castledawson	Magherafelt	Londonderry
Castlederg	Urney	Tyrone
Castlefin(n)	Donaghmore	Donegal
Castlereagh	Knockbreda	Down
Castlerock	Dunboe	Londonderry
Castleshane	Monaghan	Monaghan
Castlewellan	Kilmegan	Down
Cavan	Urney	Cavan
Chapeltown	Dunsfort	Down

Location	Civil parish	County
Charlemont	Loughgall	Armagh
Charlestown	Montiaghs	Armagh
Church Hill	Gartan	Donegal
Church Hill	Inishmacsaint	Fermanagh
Churchtown	Lissan	Londonderry
Churchtown	Tamlaght O'Crilly	Londonderry
Clabby	Enniskillen	Fermanagh
Clady	Tamlaght O'Crilly	Londonderry
Clady	Urney	Tyrone
Cladymore	Kilclooney	Armagh
Clare	Ballymore	Armagh
Claudy	Cumber Lower	Londonderry
Clo(u)gh	Dunaghy	Antrim
Cloghan	Kilteevoge	Donegal
Cloghcor	Leckpatrick	Tyrone
Clogher	Clogher	Tyrone
Clones	Clones	Monaghan
Clonmany	Clonmany	Donegal
Clonoe	Clonoe	Tyrone
Clontibret	Clontibret	Monaghan
Clough	Loughinisland	Down
Cloughey	Castleboy	Down
Cloughmills	Killagan	Antrim
Cloverhill	Annagh	Cavan
Coagh	Tamlaght	Tyrone
Coalisland	Clonoe	Tyrone
Cogry	Grange of Doagh	Antrim
Coleraine	Coleraine/Killowen	Londonderry
Comber	Comber	Down
Conlig	Bangor	Down
Connor	Connor	Antrim
Convoy	Convoy	Donegal
Cookstown	Derryloran	Tyrone
Cooneen	Aghalurcher	Fermanagh
Cootehill	Drumgoon	Cavan
Corkey	Loughguile	Antrim
Craigantlet	Newtownards	Down
Craigs	Craigs	Antrim
Cranagh	Bodoney Upper	Tyrone
Cranford	Kilmacrenan	Donegal
Cranny	Desertmartin	Londonderry
Crawfordsburn	Bangor	Down
Creeslough	Clondahorky	Donegal
Creggan	Creggan	Armagh
Creggan	Termonmaguirk	Tyrone
Creggan	Templemore	Londonderry
Crolly	Tullaghobegly	Donegal

Location	Civil parish	County
Cross Roads	Donaghmore	Donegal
Crossgar	Kilmore	Down
Crossmaglen	Creggan	Armagh
Crumlin	Camlin	Antrim
Culcavey	Blaris	Down
Culdaff	Culdaff	Donegal
Cullaville	Creggan	Armagh
Cullybackey	Craigs	Antrim
Cullyhanna	Creggan	Armagh
Culmore	Templemore	Londonderry
Culnady	Maghera	Londonderry
Cultra	Holywood	Down
Curran	Maghera	Londonderry
Cushendall	Layd	Antrim
Cushendun	Culfeightrin	Antrim
Darkley	Keady	Armagh
Derriaghy	Derryaghy	Armagh
Derry	Templemore	Londonderry
Derryboy	Killyleagh	Down
Derrygonnelly	Inishmacsaint	Fermanagh
Derrykeighan	Derrykeighan	Antrim
Derrylin	Kinawley	Fermanagh
Derrynoose	Derrynoose	Armagh
Derrytrasna	Montiaghs	Armagh
Dervock	Derrykeighan	Antrim
Desertmartin	Desertmartin	Londonderry
Doagh	Grange of Doagh	Antrim
Dollingstown	Magheralin	Down
Donagh	Galloon	Fermanagh
Donaghadee	Donaghadee	Down
Donaghcloney	Donaghcloney	Down
Donagheady	Donaghedy	Tyrone
Donaghmore	Donaghmore	Tyrone
Donegal	Donegal	Donegal
Donemana	*see* Dunnamanagh	
Doochary	Inishkeel/Lettermacaward	Donegal
Douglas Bridge	Ardstraw	Tyrone
Downhill	Dunboe	Londonderry
Downings	Mevagh	Donegal
Downpatrick	Down	Down
Dowra	Killinagh	Cavan
Draperstown	Ballynascreen	Londonderry
Dromara	Dromara	Down
Dromore	Dromore	Down
Dromore	Dromore	Tyrone
Drum	Currin	Monaghan
Drumaness	Magheradrool	Down

Location	Civil parish	County
Drumaroad	Loughinisland	Down
Drumbeg	Drumbeg	Down
Drumbo	Drumbo	Down
Drumintee	Killevy	Armagh
Drumlee	Drumgooland	Down
Drumnakilly	Termonmaguirk	Tyrone
Drumquin	Longfield West	Tyrone
Drumraighland	Tamlaght Finlagan	Londonderry
Drumsurn	Balteagh	Londonderry
Dunadry	Grange of Nilteen	Antrim
Dundonald	Dundonald	Down
Dundrod	Tullyrusk	Antrim
Dundrum	Kilmegan	Down
Dunfanaghy	Clondahorky	Donegal
Dungannon	Drumglass	Tyrone
Dungiven	Dungiven	Londonderry
Dungloe	Templecrone	Donegal
Dunkineely	Killaghtee	Donegal
Dunlewey	Tullaghobegly	Donegal
Dunloy	Finvoy	Antrim
Dunmurry	Drumbeg	Antrim
Dunnalong	Donaghedy	Tyrone
Dunnamanagh	Donaghedy	Tyrone
Dunnamore	Kildress	Tyrone
Dunseverick	Billy	Antrim
Dyan	Aghaloo	Tyrone
Eden	Carrickfergus	Antrim
Edenderry	Drumbo	Down
Ederney	Magheraculmoney	Fermanagh
Eglinton (formerly Muff)	Faughanvale	Londonderry
Eglish	Clonfeacle	Tyrone
Emyvale	Donagh	Monaghan
Enniskillen	Enniskillen	Fermanagh
Erganagh	Cappagh	Tyrone
Eskra(gh)	Clogher	Tyrone
Fahan	Fahan Upper	Donegal
Falcarragh	Tullaghobegly/Raymunterdoney	Donegal
Fallagloon	Maghera	Londonderry
Feeny	Banagher	Londonderry
Finaghy	Drumbeg	Antrim
Finnis	Dromara	Down
Fintona	Donacavey	Tyrone
Fintown	Inishkeel	Donegal
Fivemiletown	Clogher	Tyrone
Florencecourt	Killesher	Fermanagh
Flurrybridge	Jonesborough	Armagh
Forkill	Forkill	Armagh

Location	Civil parish	County
Frosses	Inver	Donegal
Galbally	Pomeroy	Tyrone
Galgorm	Ahoghill	Antrim
Garrison	Devenish	Fermanagh
Garryduff	Ballymoney	Antrim
Garvagh	Errigal	Londonderry
Garvaghey	Errigal Keerogue	Tyrone
Garvary	Enniskillen	Fermanagh
Garvetagh	Ardstraw	Tyrone
Gilford	Tullylish	Down
Gillygooly	Drumragh	Tyrone
Gilnahirk	Knockbreda	Down
Glack	Tamlaght Finlagan	Londonderry
Glangevlin	Templeport	Cavan
Glascar	Aghaderg	Down
Glasleck	Shercock	Cavan
Glaslough	Donagh	Monaghan
Glastry	Ballyhalbert	Down
Glen	Mevagh	Donegal
Glenanne	Loughgilly	Armagh
Glenariff	Layd	Antrim
Glenarm	Tickmacrevan	Antrim
Glenavy	Glenavy	Antrim
Glencolumbkille	Glencolumbkille	Donegal
Gleneely	Culdaff	Donegal
Glenelly	Bodoney Upper	Tyrone
Glengormley	Carnmoney	Antrim
Glenhull	Bodoney Lower	Tyrone
Glenmornan	Leckpatrick	Tyrone
Glenoe	Raloo	Antrim
Glenone	Tamlaght O'Crilly	Londonderry
Glenravel	Dunaghy/Skerry	Antrim
Glenshane	Dungiven	Londonderry
Glenties	Inishkeel	Donegal
Glenullin	Errigal	Londonderry
Glenveagh	Gartan	Donegal
Glynn	Glynn	Antrim
Gola Island	Tullaghobegly	Donegal
Gortaclare	Clogherny	Tyrone
Gortin	Bodoney Lower	Tyrone
Gortnahey	Bovevagh	Londonderry
Gowna	Scrabby	Cavan
Gracefield	Artrea	Londonderry
Gracehill	Ahoghill	Antrim
Grange	Grange of Ballyscullion	Antrim
Greencastle	Bodoney Lower	Tyrone
Greencastle	Kilkeel	Down

Location	Civil parish	County
Greencastle	Moville Lower	Donegal
Greenisland	Carrickfergus	Antrim
Greyabbey	Greyabbey	Down
Greysteel	Faughanvale	Londonderry
Groggan	Drummaul	Antrim
Groomsport	Bangor	Down
Gulladuff	Maghera	Londonderry
Gweedore	Tullaghobegly	Donegal
Hamiltonsbawn	Mullaghbrack	Armagh
Hillhall	Drumbeg	Down
Hillsborough	Hillsborough	Down
Hilltown	Clonduff	Down
Holywell	Cleenish	Fermanagh
Holywood	Holywood	Down
Inch Island	Inch	Donegal
Inishrush	Tamlaght O'Crilly	Londonderry
Inniskeen	Inniskeen	Monaghan
Inver	Inver	Donegal
Irvinestown	Derryvullan	Fermanagh
Jerrettspass	Killevy	Armagh
Jonesborough	Jonesborough	Armagh
Katesbridge	Drumballyroney/Newry	Down
Keady	Keady	Armagh
Kells	Connor	Antrim
Kellswater	Connor	Antrim
Kerrykeel	Tullyfern	Donegal
Kesh	Magheraculmoney	Fermanagh
Kilcar	Kilcar	Donegal
Kilcogy	Drumlumman	Cavan
Kilcoo	Kilcoo	Down
Kilkeel	Kilkeel	Down
Kill	Kildrumsherdan	Cavan
Killadeas	Trory	Fermanagh
Killaloo	Cumber Lower	Londonderry
Killeen	Clonoe	Tyrone
Killen	Termonamongan	Tyrone
Killeshandra	Killeshandra	Cavan
Killeter	Termonamongan	Tyrone
Killinchy	Killinchy	Down
Killough	Rathmullan	Down
Killowen	Kilbroney	Down
Killybegs	Killybegs Upper	Donegal
Killygordon	Donaghmore	Donegal
Killylea	Tynan	Armagh
Killyleagh	Killyleagh	Down
Killyman	Killyman	Tyrone
Kilmacrenan	Kilmacrenan	Donegal

Location	Civil parish	County
Kilmore	Kilmore	Armagh
Kilmore	Kilmore	Cavan
Kilmore	Kilmore	Down
Kilnaleck	Crosserlough	Cavan
Kilrea	Kilrea	Londonderry
Kilskeery	Kilskeery	Tyrone
Kinallen	Dromore	Down
Kinawley	Kinawley	Fermanagh
Kincasslagh	Templecrone	Donegal
Kingscourt	Enniskeen	Cavan
Kingsmills	Loughgilly	Armagh
Kircubbin	Inishargy	Down
Kirkistown	Ardkeen	Down
Knockcloghrim	Termoneeny	Londonderry
Knocknacarry	Layd	Antrim
Knocknamuckly	Seagoe	Armagh
Lack	Magheraculmoney	Fermanagh
Laghey	Killyman	Tyrone
Laghy	Drumhome	Donegal
Lambeg	Lambeg	Antrim
Larne	Inver/Larne	Antrim
Laurelvale	Kilmore	Armagh
Lawrencetown	Tullylish	Down
Leitrim	Drumgooland	Down
Letterbreen	Cleenish	Fermanagh
Letterkenny	Conwal	Donegal
Lifford	Clonleigh	Donegal
Ligoniel	Shankill	Antrim
Limavady	Drumachose	Londonderry
Lisbellaw	Cleenish	Fermanagh
Lisburn	Blaris	Antrim
Liscolman	Billy	Antrim
Lisnadill	Lisnadill	Armagh
Lisnarick	Derryvullan	Fermanagh
Lisnaskea	Aghalurcher	Fermanagh
Listooder	Kilmore	Down
Loanends	Killead	Antrim
Londonderry	Clondermot/Templemore	Londonderry
Loughanure	Templecrone	Donegal
Loughbrickland	Aghaderg	Down
Loughgall	Loughgall	Armagh
Loughgilly	Loughgilly	Armagh
Loughguile	Loughguile	Antrim
Loughinisland	Loughinisland	Down
Loughmacrory	Termonmaguirk	Tyrone
Loup, The	Artrea	Londonderry
Lower Ballinderry	Ballinderry	Antrim

Location	Civil parish	County
Lurgan	Shankill	Armagh
Lyle's Hill	Templepatrick	Antrim
Mackan (-en)	Killesher	Fermanagh
Macosquin	Macosquin	Londonderry
Maddan (-en)	Derrynoose	Armagh
Maghaberry	Magheramesk	Antrim
Maghera	Maghera	Londonderry
Magherafelt	Magherafelt	Londonderry
Magheralin	Magheralin	Down
Magheramorne	Glynn	Antrim
Magheraveely	Clones	Fermanagh
Maghery	Tartaraghan	Armagh
Magilligan	Magilligan	Londonderry
Maguiresbridge	Aghalurcher	Fermanagh
Malin	Clonca	Donegal
Mallusk	Grange of Mallusk	Antrim
Manorcunningham	Raymoghy	Donegal
Markethill	Mullaghbrack	Armagh
Martinstown	Skerry	Antrim
Mayobridge	Clonallan	Down
Meigh	Killevy	Armagh
Middletown	Tynan	Armagh
Milford	Lisnadill	Armagh
Milford	Tullyfern	Donegal
Millisle	Donaghadee	Down
Milltown	Antrim	Antrim
Milltown	Drumlane	Cavan
Minerstown	Rathmullan	Down
Moira	Moira	Down
Monaghan	Monaghan	Monaghan
Monea	Devenish	Fermanagh
Moneydig	Desertoghill	Londonderry
Moneyglass	Duneane	Antrim
Moneymore	Artrea/Desertlyn	Londonderry
Moneyneany	Ballynascreen	Londonderry
Moneyrea(gh)	Comber	Down
Moneyslane	Drumgooland	Down
Moorfields	Ballyclug	Antrim
Moortown	Arboe	Tyrone
Moss-side	Grange of Drumtullagh	Antrim
Mount Hill	Raloo	Antrim
Mount Stewart	Greyabbey	Down
Mountcharles	Inver	Donegal
Mountfield	Cappagh	Tyrone
Mountjoy	Cappagh	Tyrone
Mountjoy	Clonoe	Tyrone
Mountnorris	Loughgilly	Armagh

Location	Civil parish	County
Mountnugent	Kilbride	Cavan
Movanagher	Kilrea	Londonderry
Moville	Moville Lower	Donegal
Mowhan	Loughgilly	Armagh
Moy	Clonfeacle	Tyrone
Moygashel	Clonfeacle	Tyrone
Muckamore	Grange of Muckamore	Antrim
Muff	Muff	Donegal
Muff (now Eglinton)	Faughanvale	Londonderry
Mullagh	Castlerahan	Cavan
Mullaghbawn	Forkill	Armagh
Mullaghglass	Killevy	Armagh
Myroe	Tamlaght Finlagan	Londonderry
Narin (-an)	Inishkeel	Donegal
Narrow Water	Warrenpoint	Down
Navan	Eglish	Armagh
New Buildings	Clondermot	Londonderry
Newbliss	Killeevan	Monaghan
Newcastle	Kilcoo	Down
Newmills	Tullyniskan	Tyrone
Newtown Crommelin	Newtown Crommelin	Antrim
Newtownards	Newtownards	Down
Newtownbreda	Knockbreda	Down
Newtownbutler	Galloon	Fermanagh
Newtowncunningham	All Saints	Donegal
Newtownhamilton	Newtownhamilton	Armagh
Newtownstewart	Ardstraw	Tyrone
Omagh	Cappagh/Drumragh	Tyrone
Orritor	Kildress	Tyrone
Park	Learmount	Londonderry
Parkgate	Donegore	Antrim
Pettigo	Templecarn	Donegal
Plumbridge	Bodoney Upper	Tyrone
Pomeroy	Pomeroy	Tyrone
Portadown	Drumcree/Seagoe	Armagh
Portaferry	Ballyphilip	Down
Portavogie	Ballyhalbert	Down
Portballintrae	Dunluce	Antrim
Portbraddan	Ballintoy	Antrim
Portglenone	Portglenone	Antrim
Portnablagh	Clondahorky	Donegal
Portnoo	Inishkeel	Donegal
Portrush	Ballywillin	Antrim
Portsalon	Clondavaddog	Donegal
Portstewart	Ballyaghran	Londonderry
Poyntzpass	Ballymore	Armagh
Raholp	Ballyculter	Down
Ramelton	Aughnish	Donegal

Location	Civil parish	County
Randalstown	Drummaul	Antrim
Rannafast	Templecrone	Donegal
Raphoe	Raphoe	Donegal
Rasharkin	Rasharkin	Antrim
Rathfriland	Drumgath	Down
Rathmullan	Killygarvan	Donegal
Ravernet	Blaris	Down
Red Bay	Layd	Antrim
Red Hall	Templecorran	Antrim
Redhills	Annagh	Cavan
Richhill	Kilmore	Armagh
Ringsend	Aghadowey	Londonderry
Rock	Desertcreat	Tyrone
Rockcorry	Ematris	Monaghan
Ros(s)lea	Clones	Fermanagh
Rosnakill	Clondavaddog	Donegal
Rosses, The	Lettermacaward/Templecrone	Donegal
Rossglass	Rathmullan	Down
Rossnowlagh	Drumhome	Donegal
Rostrevor	Kilbroney	Down
Rousky	Bodoney Lower	Tyrone
St Johnsto(w)n	Taughboyne	Donegal
Saintfield	Saintfield	Down
Sandholes	Desertcreat	Tyrone
Scarva	Aghaderg	Down
Scotch Street	Drumcree	Armagh
Scotshouse	Currin	Monaghan
Scotstown	Tedavnet	Monaghan
Scrabo	Newtownards	Down
Scriggan	Dungiven	Londonderry
Seaforde	Loughinisland	Down
Seskinore	Clogherny	Tyrone
Shane's Castle	Drummaul	Antrim
Shercock	Shercock	Cavan
Shrigley	Killyleagh	Down
Silverbridge	Creggan/Forkill	Armagh
Sion Mills	Urney	Tyrone
Sixmilecross	Termonmaguirk	Tyrone
Sixtowns	Ballynascreen	Londonderry
Slemish	Racavan	Antrim
Smithborough	Clones	Monaghan
Soldierstown	Aghalee	Antrim
Somerset	Macosquin	Londonderry
Spa	Magheradrool	Down
Staffordstown	Duneane	Antrim
Stewartstown	Donaghenry	Tyrone
Ston(e)yford	Derryaghy	Antrim
Strabane	Camus-juxta-Mourne	Tyrone

Location	Civil parish	County
Stradone	Larah	Cavan
Straid	Ballynure	Antrim
Straid	Learmount	Londonderry
Strangford	Ballyculter	Down
Stranocum	Ballymoney	Antrim
Stranorlar	Stranorlar	Donegal
Straw	Ballynascreen	Londonderry
Swanlinbar	Kinawley	Cavan
Swatragh	Killelagh	Londonderry
Tamlaght	Derryvullan	Fermanagh
Tandragee	Ballymore	Armagh
Tartaraghan	Tartaraghan	Armagh
Tassagh	Keady	Armagh
Teelin	Glencolumbkille	Donegal
Teemore	Kinawley	Fermanagh
Templepatrick	Templepatrick	Antrim
Tempo	Enniskillen	Fermanagh
Termon	Kilmacrenan	Donegal
Threemilehouse	Drumsnat/Kilmore	Monaghan
Tobermore	Kilcronaghan	Londonderry
Tollymore	Maghera	Down
Toome (-bridge)	Duneane	Antrim
Tory Island	Tullaghobegly	Donegal
Trillick	Kilskeery	Tyrone
Tullintrain	Cumber Upper	Londonderry
Tullyherron	Loughgilly	Armagh
Tullyhogue	Desertcreat	Tyrone
Tullylish	Tullylish	Down
Tydavnet	Tedavnet	Monaghan
Tynan	Tynan	Armagh
Tyrone's Ditches	Ballymore	Armagh
Upper Ballinderry	Ballinderry	Antrim
Upperlands	Maghera	Londonderry
Vinecash	Kilmore	Armagh
Virginia	Lurgan	Cavan
Vow, The	Finvoy	Antrim
Waringsford	Garvaghy	Down
Waringstown	Donaghcloney	Down
Warrenpoint	Warrenpoint	Down
Washing Bay	Clonoe	Tyrone
Waterfoot	Layd	Antrim
Wattlebridge	Drummully	Fermanagh
Whiteabbey	Carnmoney	Antrim
Whitecross	Ballymyre	Armagh
Whitehead	Templecorran	Antrim
Whitehouse	Carnmoney	Antrim
Woodburn	Carrickfergus	Antrim

MAPS

Counties in the province of Ulster

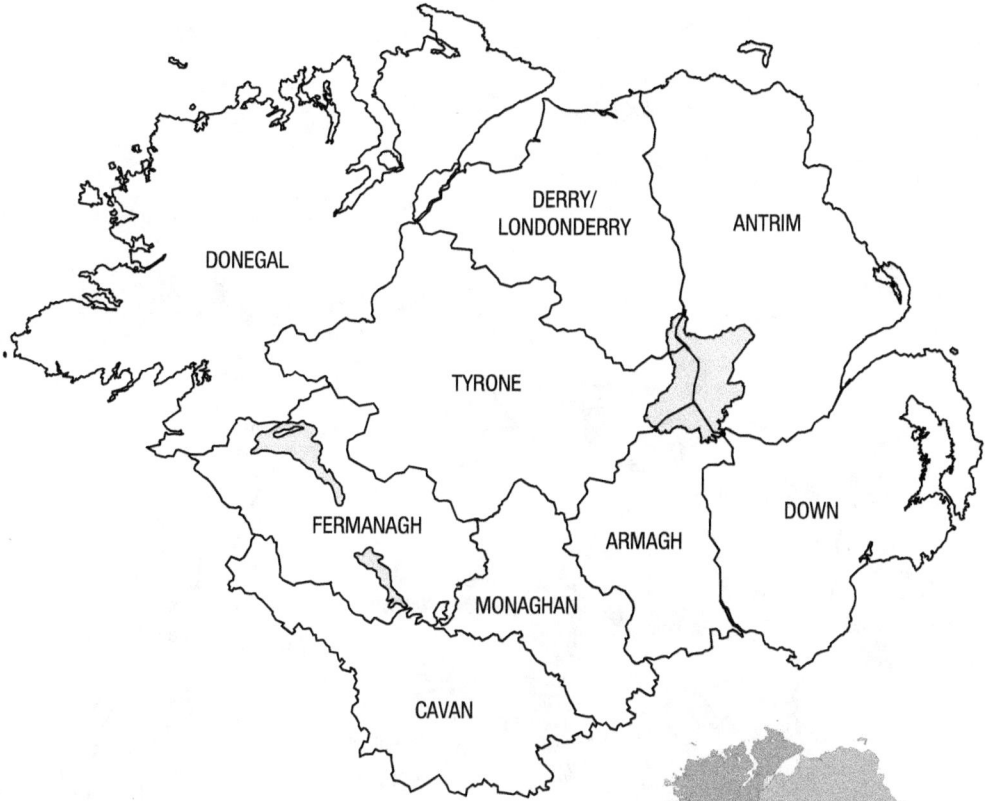

Map of the island of Ireland with the province of Ulster highlighted. The area in mid-grey shading is modern Northern Ireland.

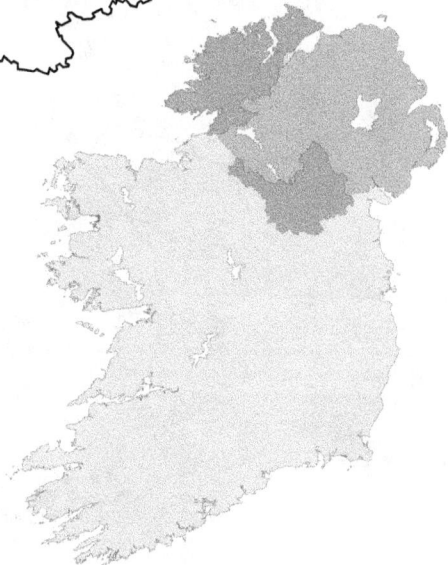

Civil Parishes of County Antrim

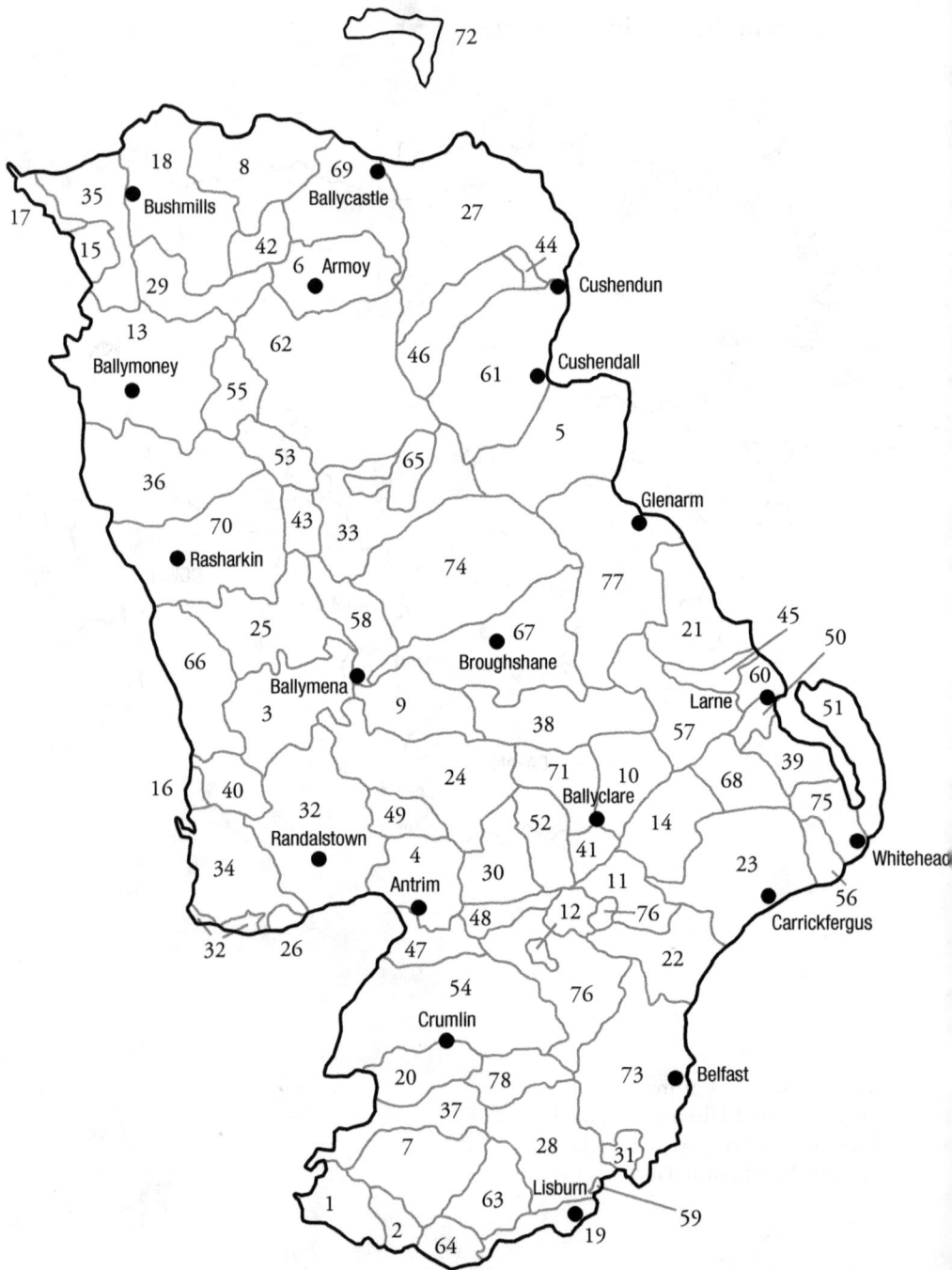

PARISHES

1	Aghagallon	40	Grange of Ballyscullion
2	Aghalee	41	Grange of Doagh
3	Ahoghill	42	Grange of Drumtullagh
4	Antrim	43	Grange of Dundermot
5	Ardclinis	44	Grange of Inispollan
6	Armoy	45	Grange of Killyglen
7	Ballinderry	46	Grange of Layd
8	Ballintoy	47	Grange of Muckamore
9	Ballyclug	48	Grange of Nilteen
10	Ballycor	49	Grange of Shilvodan
11	Ballylinny	50	Inver
12	Ballymartin	51	Island Magee
13	Ballymoney	52	Kilbride
14	Ballynure	53	Killagan
15	Ballyrashane	54	Killead
16	Ballyscullion	55	Kilraghts
17	Ballywillin	56	Kilroot
18	Billy	57	Kilwaughter
19	Blaris	58	Kirkinriola
20	Camlin	59	Lambeg
21	Carncastle	60	Larne
22	Carnmoney	61	Layd
23	Carrickfergus	62	Loughguile
24	Connor	63	Magheragall
25	Craigs	64	Magheramesk
26	Cranfield	65	Newtown Crommelin
27	Culfeightrin	66	Portglenone
28	Derryaghy	67	Racavan
29	Derrykeighan	68	Raloo
30	Donegore	69	Ramoan
31	Drumbeg	70	Rasharkin
32	Drummaul	71	Rashee
33	Dunaghy	72	Rathlin
34	Duneane	73	Shankill
35	Dunluce	74	Skerry
36	Finvoy	75	Templecorran
37	Glenavy	76	Templepatrick
38	Glenwhirry	77	Tickmacrevan
39	Glynn	78	Tullyrusk

Civil Parishes of County Armagh

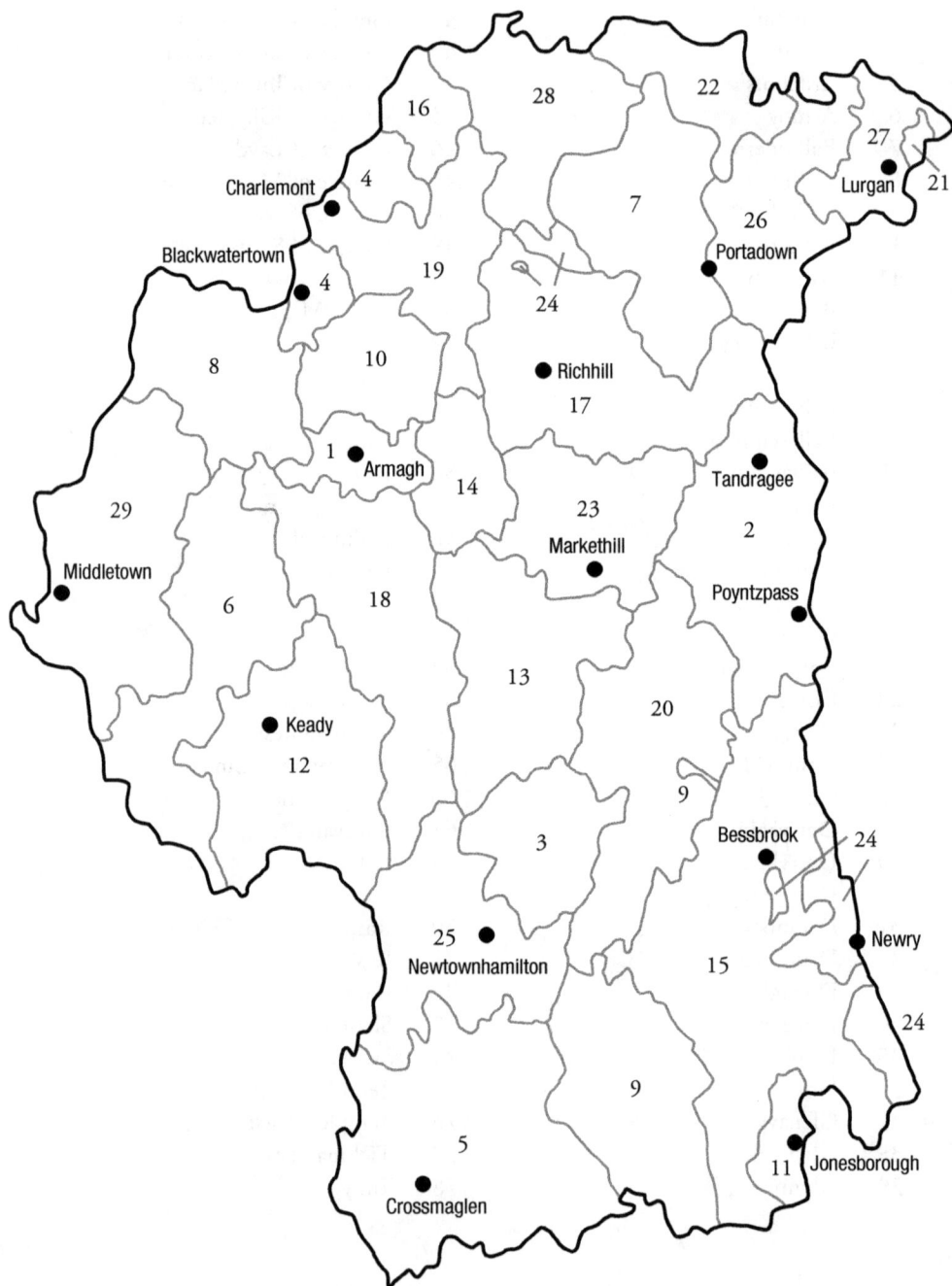

PARISHES

1	Armagh	16	Killyman
2	Ballymore	17	Kilmore
3	Ballymyre	18	Lisnadill
4	Clonfeacle	19	Loughgall
5	Creggan	20	Loughgilly
6	Derrynoose	21	Magheralin
7	Drumcree	22	Montiaghs
8	Eglish	23	Mullaghbrack
9	Forkill	24	Newry
10	Grange	25	Newtownhamilton
11	Jonesborough	26	Seagoe
12	Keady	27	Shankill
13	Kilclooney	28	Tartaraghan
14	Kildarton	29	Tynan
15	Killevy		

Civil Parishes of County Cavan

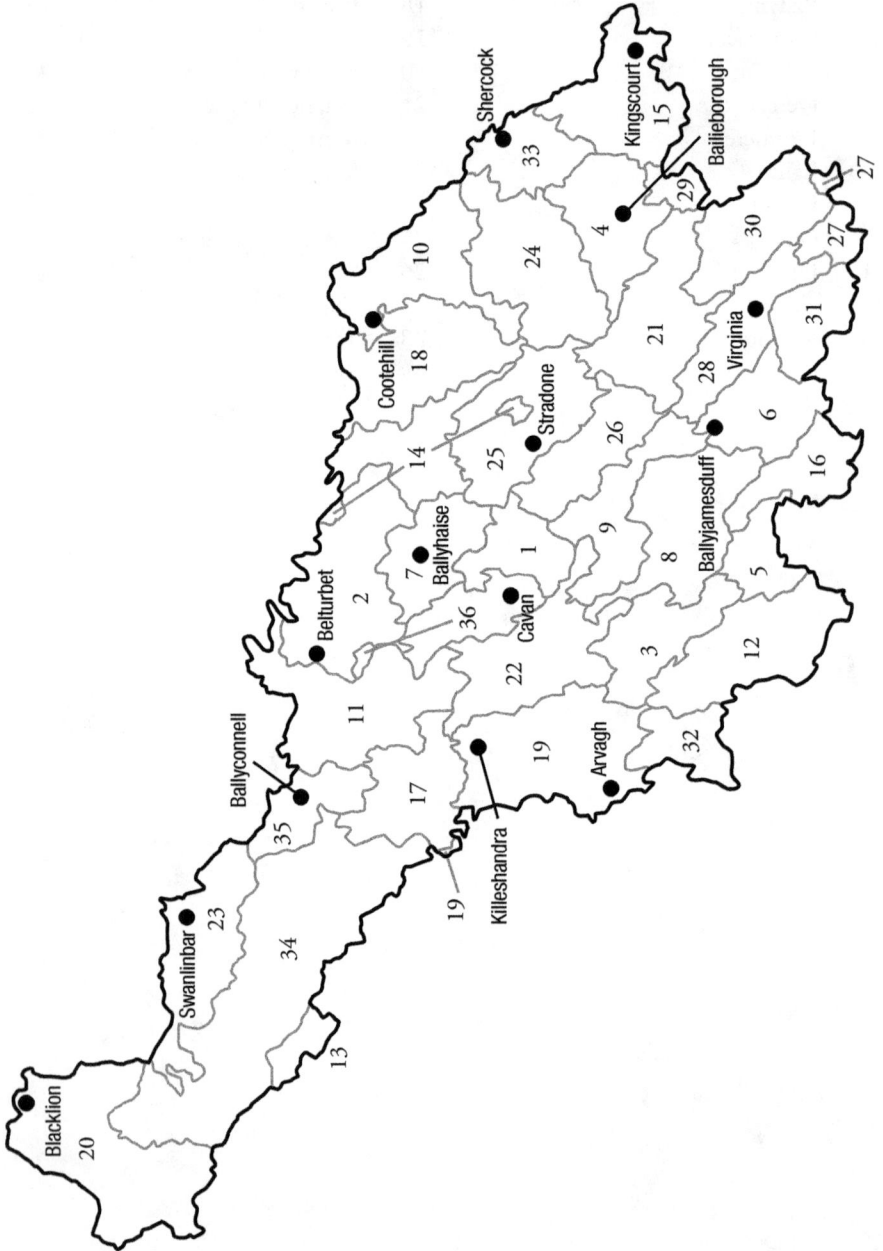

PARISHES

1	Annagelliff	19	Killashandra
2	Annagh	20	Killinagh
3	Ballintemple	21	Killinkere
4	Bailieborough	22	Kilmore
5	Ballymachugh	23	Kinawley
6	Castlerahan	24	Knockbride
7	Castleterra	25	Larah
8	Crosserlough	26	Lavey
9	Denn	27	Loughan or Castlekeeran
10	Drumgoon	28	Lurgan
11	Drumlane	29	Moybolgue
12	Drumlumman	30	Mullagh
13	Drumreilly	31	Munterconnaught
14	Drung	32	Scrabby
15	Enniskeen	33	Shercock
16	Kilbride	34	Templeport
17	Kildallan	35	Tomregan
18	Kildrumsherdan	36	Urney

Civil Parishes of County Donegal

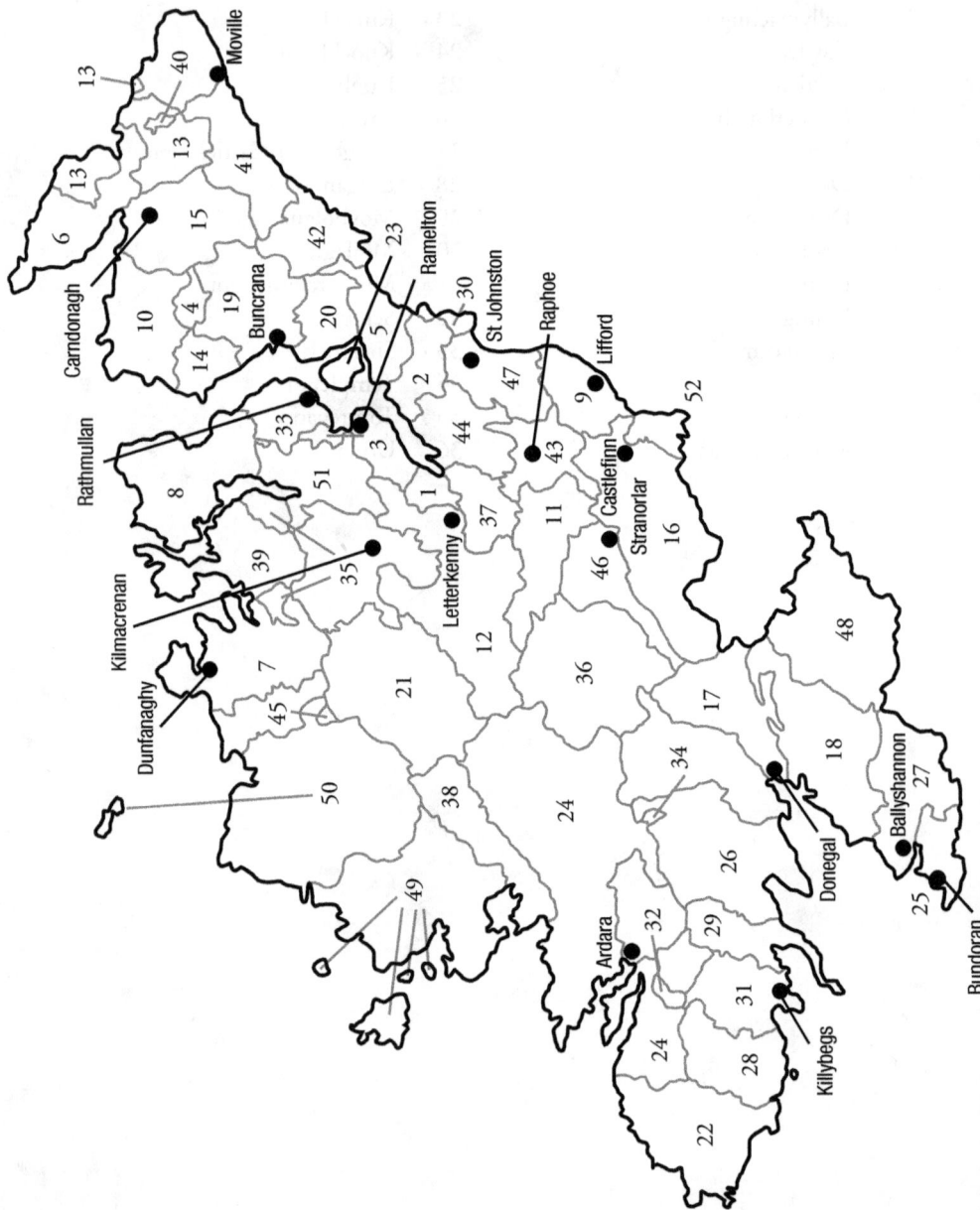

PARISHES

1	Aghanunshin	27	Kilbarron
2	All Saints	28	Kilcar
3	Aughnish	29	Killaghtee
4	Barr of Inch or Mintiaghs	30	Killea
5	Burt	31	Killybegs Upper
6	Clonca	32	Killybegs Lower
7	Clondahorky	33	Killygarvan
8	Clondavaddog	34	Killymard
9	Clonleigh	35	Kilmacrenan
10	Clonmany	36	Kilteevoge
11	Convoy	37	Leck
12	Conwal	38	Lettermacaward
13	Culdaff	39	Mevagh
14	Desertegny	40	Moville Lower
15	Donagh	41	Moville Upper
16	Donaghmore	42	Muff
17	Donegal	43	Raphoe
18	Drumhome	44	Raymoghy
19	Fahan Lower	45	Raymunterdoney
20	Fahan Upper	46	Stranorlar
21	Gartan	47	Taughboyne
22	Glencolumbkille	48	Templecarn
23	Inch	49	Templecrone
24	Inishkeel	50	Tullaghobegley
25	Inishmacsaint	51	Tullyfern
26	Inver	52	Urney

Civil Parishes of County Down

PARISHES

1	Aghaderg	36	Hillsborough
2	Annaclone	37	Holywood
3	Annahilt	38	Inch
4	Ardglass	39	Inishargy
5	Ardkeen	40	Kilbroney
6	Ardquin	41	Kilclief
7	Ballee	42	Kilcoo
8	Ballyculter	43	Kilkeel
9	Ballyhalbert	44	Killaney
10	Ballykinler	45	Killinchy
11	Ballyphilip	46	Killyleagh
12	Ballytrustan	47	Kilmegan
13	Ballywalter	48	Kilmood
14	Bangor	49	Kilmore
15	Blaris	50	Knockbreda
16	Bright	51	Lambeg
17	Castleboy	52	Loughinisland
18	Clonallan	53	Maghera
19	Clonduff	54	Magheradrool
20	Comber	55	Magherahamlet
21	Donaghadee	56	Magheralin
22	Donaghcloney	57	Magherally
23	Donaghmore	58	Moira
24	Down	59	Newry
25	Dromara	60	Newtownards
26	Dromore	61	Rathmullan
27	Drumballyroney	62	Saintfield
28	Drumbeg	63	Saul
29	Drumbo	64	Seapatrick
30	Drumgath	65	Shankill
31	Drumgooland	66	Slanes
32	Dundonald	67	Tullylish
33	Dunsfort	68	Tullynakill
34	Garvaghy	69	Tyrella
35	Grey Abbey	70	Warrenpoint

Civil Parishes of County Fermanagh

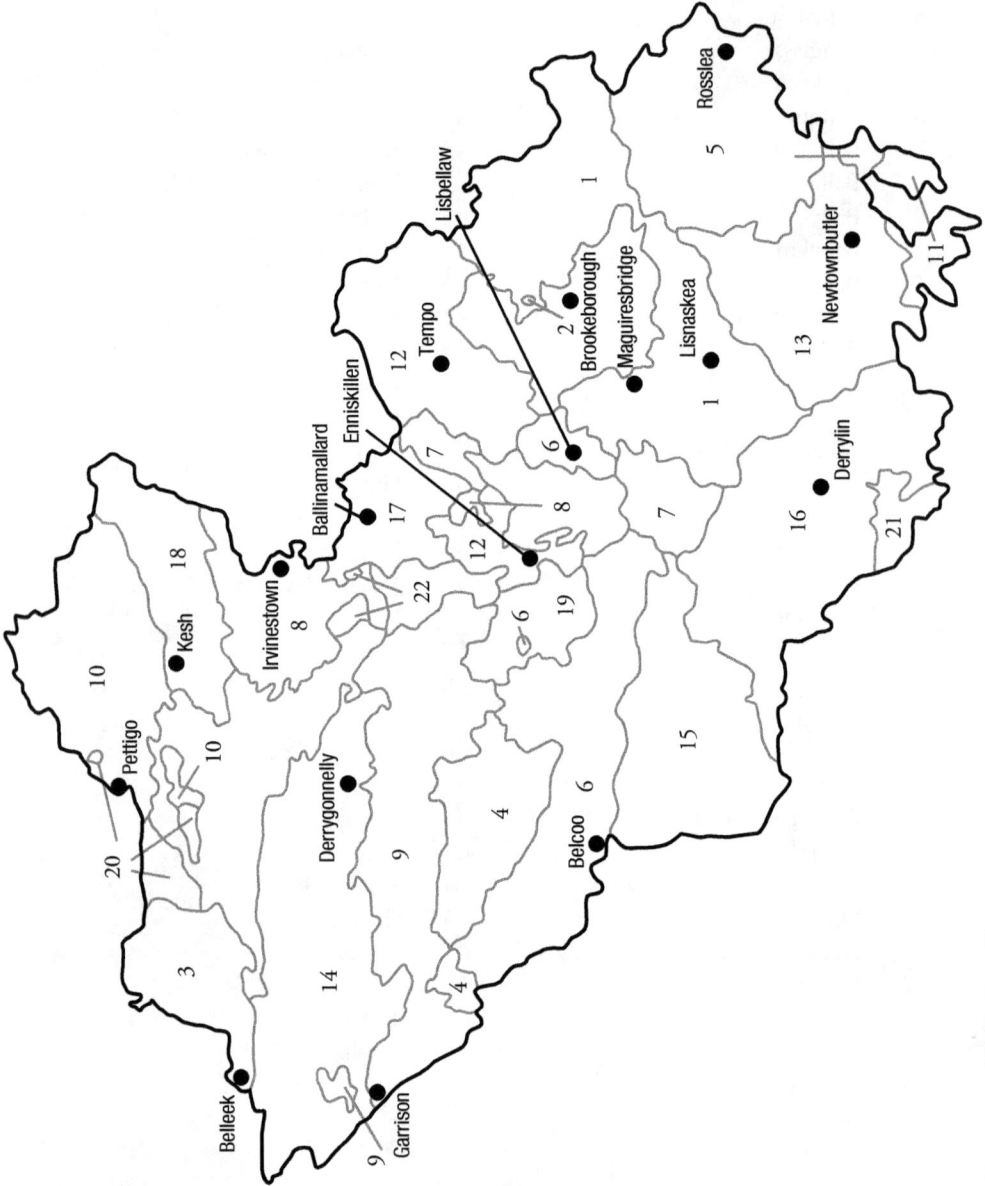

PARISHES

1	Aghalurcher	12	Enniskillen
2	Aghavea	13	Galloon
3	Belleek	14	Inishmacsaint
4	Boho	15	Killesher
5	Clones	16	Kinawley
6	Cleenish	17	Magheracross
7	Derrybrusk	18	Magheraculmoney
8	Derryvullan	19	Rossorry
9	Devenish	20	Templecarn
10	Drumkeeran	21	Tomregan
11	Drummully	22	Trory

Civil Parishes of County Londonderry

PARISHES

1	Aghadowey	24	Desertoghill
2	Aghanloo	25	Drumachose
3	Agivey	26	Dunboe
4	Arboe	27	Dungiven
5	Artrea	28	Errigal
6	Ballinderry	29	Faughanvale
7	Ballyaghran	30	Formoyle
8	Ballymoney	31	Kilcronaghan
9	Ballynascreen	32	Kildollagh
10	Ballyrashane	33	Killelagh
11	Ballyscullion	34	Killowen
12	Ballywillin	35	Kilrea
13	Balteagh	36	Learmount
14	Banagher	37	Lissan
15	Bovevagh	38	Macosquin
16	Carrick	39	Maghera
17	Clondermot	40	Magherafelt
18	Coleraine	41	Tamlaght
19	Cumber Lower	42	Tamlaght Finlagan
20	Cumber Upper	43	Tamlaght O'Crilly
21	Derryloran	44	Tamlaghtard
22	Desertlyn	45	Templemore
23	Desertmartin	46	Termoneeny

Civil Parishes of County Monaghan

PARISHES

1	Aghabog	13	Inishkeen
2	Aghnamullen	14	Killanny
3	Ballybay	15	Killeevan
4	Clones	16	Kilmore
5	Clontibret	17	Magheracloone
6	Currin	18	Magheross
7	Donagh	19	Monaghan
8	Donaghmoyne	20	Muckno
9	Drummully	21	Tedavnet
10	Drumsnat	22	Tehallan
11	Ematris	23	Tullycorbet
12	Errigal Trough		

Civil Parishes of County Tyrone

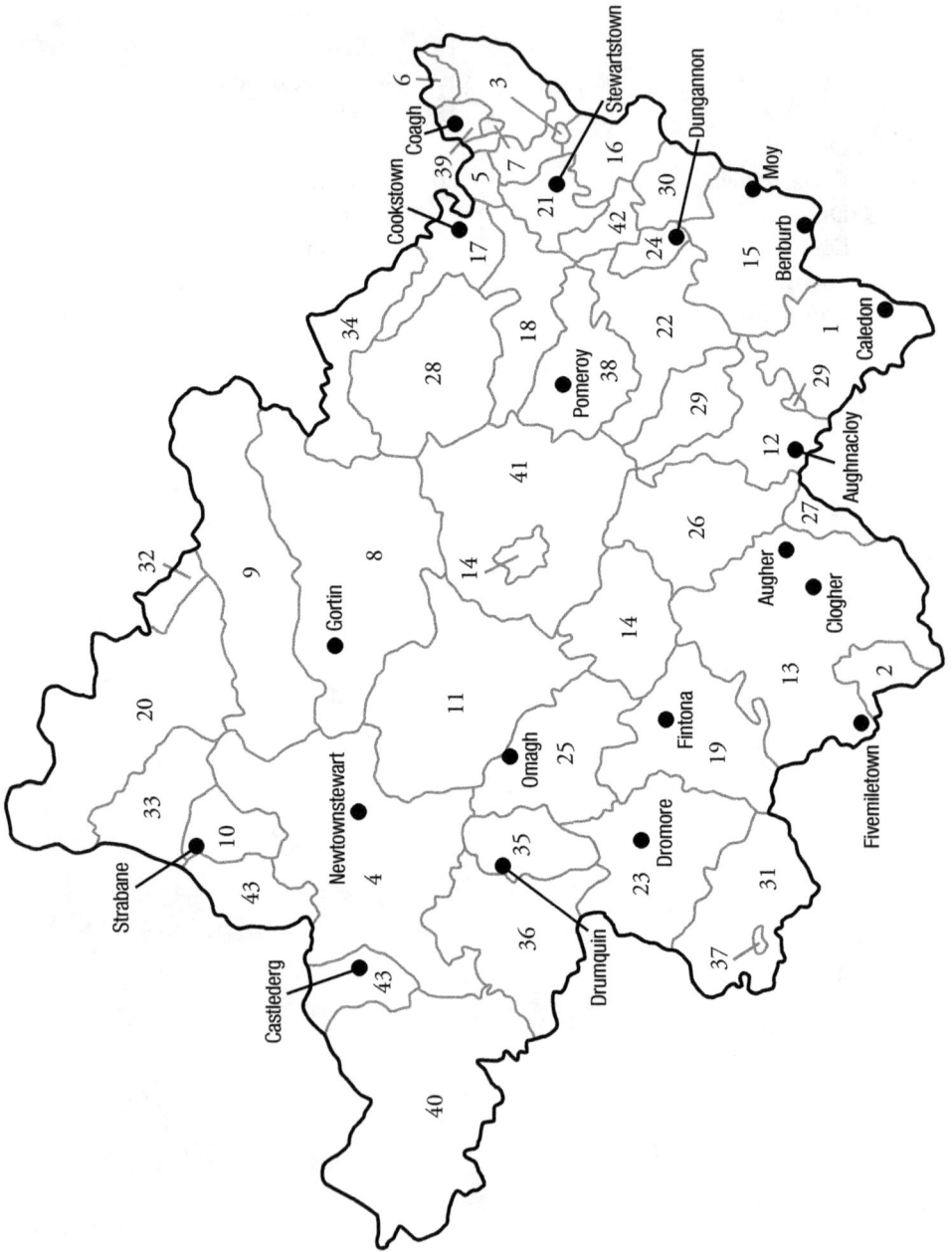

PARISHES

1	Aghaloo		23	Dromore
2	Aghalurcher		24	Drumglass
3	Arboe		25	Drumragh
4	Ardstraw		26	Errigal Keerogue
5	Artrea		27	Errigal Trough
6	Ballinderry		28	Kildress
7	Ballyclog		29	Killeeshil
8	Bodoney Lower		30	Killyman
9	Bodoney Upper		31	Kilskeery
10	Camus-juxta-Mourne		32	Learmount
11	Cappagh		33	Leckpatrick
12	Carnteel		34	Lissan
13	Clogher		35	Longfield East
14	Clogherny		36	Longfield West
15	Clonfeacle		37	Magheracross
16	Clonoe		38	Pomeroy
17	Derryloran		39	Tamlaght
18	Desertcreat		40	Termonamongan
19	Donacavey		41	Termonmaguirk
20	Donaghedy		42	Tullyniskan
21	Donaghenry		43	Urney
22	Donaghmore			

SUBSCRIBERS

Roger Blaney (Ruairí Ó Bléine), Ard Mhic Nasca, Contae an Dúin
Nicola Cousen, Victoria, Australia
Melanie McLennan, Ontario, Canada
Prof. F. J. Smith, Belfast
Dr Brian Trainor (in memory of)

Greg Aasen
Amy Abbott
Patricia Adams
Rick Adams
Stuart Adams
Terence Adams
Iris Dempsey Adamson
Atua Ake
Cory Alderfer
Dr John Alexander
R. H. (Harry) Allen
Trasey F. Allen
Carolyn Ruth Anderson
Debby Warner Anderson
Fred Anderson
Nancy Anderson
Ronald George Anderson
William Joseph Anderson
Anna Angell
Paul Anthony
Doug Arbuckle
Mike Armstrong
Robert Arthur
Arnold Arthurs
Linda Asberry
Wilma Ashbridge
Sharie Woods Aspden
Samuel Wm Aylesworth
Steve Bailey
Carol Baillie
Peter Baillie
Prof. Sir George Bain
Hilda Baker
Stanley Baker
Christine Ball
Janet Banks
Charles Barber
James Patrick Robert
    Barbour
Geoff Barker
Murray Barkley
Margaret F. Barnes
Jennie Barrera

Sylvia Barrett
Kate Barron
Shirley Bartlett
Richard Barton
Lorraine Bartoni
Phineas Baugher
Leverne Baxter
Stanley Baxter
David Ian Beattie
Catherine Beck
Brian Beeley
Gary V. Bell
Colin Bendall
Frances Benson
Robert Berg
Timothy Beringer
Anna Bianchi
James Birney
Henry John Black
Elizabeth Blakley
Peter Blatchford
Devon Blean
Andy Bloomer
Anne M. Bobigian
Pamela Bocci
Olive M. Boden
Michael Bogues
Jacqueline Bonar
Terri Borden
Valerie Bowden
Alan G. Boyd
Terry Boyd
Samantha Boyle
Terence Boyle
Peter Bradish
Adrian Brett
Diane Brewer
Clive Broadbent
Vincent Brogan
Colin Brooks
Judith Brooks
Joyce Brown
Kristy Brown

Jeanette McLean Brown
Anne Maharay Bryant
Doris Bryant
Evelyn Buck
Shirley Bulley
Ernest Bullock
James S. Bunting
Maggie Burch
Donna Burden
Cela Burge
Jerry Burke
John Burnett
Barrie Burns
John Burns
John Burt
George Busby
Janice Butner
David Byers
Steven Byess
Kristen Bylan
Audrey Byrne
Elizabeth Douthitt Byrne
Colin Caldwell
Erin Caldwell
Charles Calhoun
Frank Cameron
Wendy Cameron
Alan Campbell
Carol B. Campbell
Cheryl Campbell
Paul Campbell
Michele Cantley
William Capper
Carl Cardey
Terry Cardwell
David Carey
Mardi Carlson
Rosemary Carnahan
Norah Reynolds Carothers
Barry Watson Carpenter
Cynthia Hylton Carpenter
Elizabeth A. Carrey
Ann Carroll

Joseph Carroll

Ron Carson

Sandra Carter-Duff

James Caruth

Emily Cary

Robyn Casillas

Nicole Cebuliak

Don Chambers

Rosemary Chambers

Mildred Chase

Greg Chatham

Brian Cherry

Betsy Gray Chervenak

Sharon McKelvey Cianciola

Alice Ciccarelli

Debbie Cipolletti

Patricia Cirone

Brendan Clarke

Raymond Clarke

Sean Clarke

Virginia Clarke

Susan Lee Clasen

Bob Clay

Wayne Coates

Tedd Cocker

Stuart Cockerill

Helen Cockle (née Dermit)

Brenda Collins

Jenny Collins

Judi Collison

Edward Conner

Helen Connor

Thomas Connor

Anne M. Convery

Gayle Coogan

Ross Cook

Maureen Cooke

Merlyn Don Cooper

James Cooros

Peter Copes

Sonia Cornelius

Robert Corrins

Richard Corson

Sandra Coulter

Bernard J. Couming

Anne Coury

Chris Cowan

Ray Cowan

Ray Cowan

Yvonne Cowieson

Alan Craig

Mitzi Crane

Margaret Cranfield

David C. Cranston

Neil Craven

Gerard Crawford

James Crawford

Jim Crawford

Lynn Crawford

Miranda Crotsley

Jack Walter Cullin

Lyle Cumberland

Jennifer Cunningham

Prof. James Stevens Curl

Todd Curran

Dennis C. Currey

Jennie Currie

Donald Dale

Merv Dale

Robert Dale

Ann Dalton

Jan Daly

Brian Dane

Victoria Daniel

Chris Dart

Karen Daubert

Robert Davidson

Dr Walter F. Davidson

David Davies

Edward Davis

Rosemary Dawson

Linda Dean

Thomas Deas

L. Judith Decrisci

Janice DeGroot

John Delve

Jeannine Demicco

Barbara Dempsey

Margie Dempsey

John Dennett

Denis Desmond

Karla Diamond

Christopher Dick

Doris Dickenson

Watson Disoza

Brian Dixon

Martha Donagrandi

Susan A. Donegan

Thomas Doran

David Dowell

Michael Downerd

Lawrence Downing

Rosemary Doyle

Gerald Dudek

Deanna Riley Duet

John Dugan

Bill T. Dunbar

Norine Duncan

Frances M. Dunlop

Margaret P. Dunne

Dr Bruce Durie

Brenda Dutertre

Margot Dwyer

Robert Eager

Terry Eakin

Ann Eccles

Ann Eddington

Jane Edgar

Maggie Edmonston

Helen Edwards

Linda Ellard

Elinor Elliott

Robert Elliott

Simon Elliott

Elizabeth Elsasser

David Engan

Robert Epperson

Fred Erskine

Warren Ervin

Ann Esslinger

Marlene Evans

Steven Ewing

Lillie McKeen Fairchild

Jennie Fairs

FamilySearch International

H. Jean Farquharson

Carole Faux

Dr David Faux

Semmes Favrot

James Ferguson

Thomas Ferguson

Rixanne Fergusson

Richard Ferman

Stephen Duncan Ferris

William I. Ferris

Gary Fettis

Valerie Fielding

Thomas Finley

Fiona Fitzsimons

Edward Fleet

Caroline Fleetwood

Rob Fleming

Clyde Fletcher

Deborah Flint

Maura Flood

Kathleen Flynn-O'Sullivan

Dale Fogarty

Fred Forde

Dennis Forsythe

John G. Forsythe
Lynda Fort
Linda Forward
Sally Forwood
Biddy Foster
Desmond Foster
Julia Foster Blatchford
Jerri Fowler
Karen Fraiser-Scott
Robin Fraser
Michael Fraser-Allen
Deborah Frazier
Lynn Freeman
George Fulton
Maryellen Galbally
Alice Gallagher
Jesse A. Galt
Maureen Gamble
Terry Gardiner
Paul Gardner
Kathie Garnham
Betty Garrad
Patricia Garvin
Adrian Gault
Rob Gay
Thomas Gayner
Genealogical Society
    of Queensland
Genealogical Society
    of Victoria
Paul Gettys
Dave Gibson
David Gibson
Don Gibson
Frederica W. Gibson
Roy Gibson
Susan Gilbert
Alastair Gillies
John Girvan
Jan Gladden
Kathryn Gleason
Darlene Glum
Lynn Godwin
Theresa W. Goldhammer
Carolyn Golowka
Carolyn Goodfellow
Graham Goodfellow
Judy Goodman
James Gordon
John G. Gordon
Terence Gordon
Margaret S. Gowdy
Marjie Gowdy

William C. Gracey
J. Grady
Erin Graham
Rebecca Graham
Sheelagh Duffin Graham
Karen Miller Grant
Barry Gray
Clare Gray
Gary Gray
John Gray
Wilson Gray
Harriet Greaney
Marie-Therese Green
Rob Green
Sally Early Guiney
David Guy
R. M. Hadden
Jenna Hahn
Gillian Häkli
Douglas Hall
Marion Hall
Timothy McClelland
    Halligan
Brenda Joan Hamilton
C. A. Hamilton
Claire Shannon Hamilton
Robert Hamilton
Robert Edward Hamilton
Robert Guy Hamilton
Roderick J. Hamilton
Harold Hanham
Katelyn Hanna
Thomas Hanna
Thomas B. Hanna
Patrick Hannan
Patricia Hannum
Yvonne Hanvey
Barbara Harding
Alice Hardy
David B. Harkness
Thomas Harkness
Maureen Harmon
David Harrison
Frank Harrison
Terence Hart
Arlene Hartin
Elizabeth Hartnett
Eric F. Hartney
Richard Hassell
Leonard Hatrick
Vivienne Hawthorne
Kristine Hayes
Frances Heales

Ann Heatherington
David Hefferman
Judy Hellstrom
James K. Helsby
Keith Hemsley
Marc Henderson
Gib Henry
Louise (Martin) Henson
Sandra Hewlett
Anne Higham
Peter Hill
Jean Hillan
C. J. Hillis
Ken Hodson
Matt Hoggarth
Linda Waddell Holcomb
Scott Holl
Lynda Hooper
Mrs Elizabeth Hornett
Joan Hosford
Linda Houston
Richard Hudson
James Huey
Margaret Huff
Jim Hughes
Mrs Maria Hunt
David Hunter
Terri Hunter
Bill Hurford
Barbara M. Hurley
Brian Hutchison
Brad Hyndman
Richard Ifft
Terry Ingles
Kenneth Irvine
Anne Irwin
David Irwin
Robert Irwin
Roy A. Jack
Jane Jackson
Norman Jackson
Seamus Jackson
Vikki Jacobsen
Delene Jamieson
Sherry Jarvis
Ian Jenkins
John Johnston
Lynn Johnston
Niall Johnston
Peter Johnston
Christina Johnston née
    Glendinning
Alice Jones

David Jones
Donna Jones
Edward M. Jones
Gareth Jones
E. A. Jorgensen
Virginia Justice
Lisa Kallioniemi
Erik Kamermans
Dr Daniel Ross Kane
Karalee Kane
Catherine Karayanis
Lynn Karcich
Laura B. Keane
Richard P. Keating
Linda Keller
Charles Kelly
Edward Kelly
Gerard Kelly
Ian Kelly
Sherry Kemery
Cllr Colin G. D. Kennedy
Jane Kennedy
Robert Kenney
Ronald Kernaghan
Rosemary Kerr
Tom Kerr
Clare Lawler Kilgallen
Kelley Kilgannon
Kathryn Kimball
Betty King
Roger King
Rob Kirk
Douglas Kirkpatrick
Jane Hyndman Klein
Mike Knowles
Nancy Koester
Victoria Kolakowski
Ginny Koulopoulos
Paul and Nedra Kristensen
Mary Jane Kuffner Hirt
George B. Laban
Becky LaBlanc-Willis
Jim Lamb
Mandi Lamb
Marjorie Lang
Brendan Langan
Patricia Laubscher
Jane Laughlin
Desmond Lavery
Joe Lavery
Dennis Lawrence
Patricia Leaden
Cynthia J. Lear

Liz Horrell LeCour
John Lee
Jon Lee
Jeanne LeFever
Carolyn Leinweber
Wade Lennox
Sally Ann Lentz
Pam Lessiter
Adam J. Levin
Ciaran Lewis
Linda Lindsay
David Little
Kay Lobegeiger
Faye Logue
David Lonczak
Julie Lonczak
Bruce Long
Mike Long
Ian Love
Nancy Low Choy
   (née Johnston)
Donna Lowe
Annie Lowe (née Wilson)
Linde Lunney
Terry Lyle
Sharon Lynne Martin
John Lyons
Mrs Leone Lyons
Rod Mac Conaill
George Macallister
George Alexander
   MacAllister
Margaret Macaulay
William MacCallum
Annie Murdock
   McAleese MacIntyre
Jane Campbell MacIntyre
David Mackenzie
Ronan Mackey
Mary-Jan Mackisack
Brian C. Maclachlan
Virginia MacLatchy
Richard Maclean
Liisa Macnaughton
Robert J. Macoubrie
Marilyn MacPherson
Graeme Madden
Marie Maddocks
H. A. Maginnis
William L. Maher
Doug Maltman
Diane Mann
Claudia March

Lewis Marquardt
Collette Marquess
Bryan Marshall
Helen Marshall
Trevor Marshall
Ann Martin
Jenny Martin
Lyn R. Martin
Nancy Maryboy PhD
Stuart Mason
Tom W. Matchett
Karen J. Mathewson
Gerry Matthews
Mrs Uladh Brontë
   Matthews
Graham Mawhinney
William Mawhinney
Todd Maxwell
Sandra May
Elisabeth Maynard
Enid Mayrs
Diane McAlister
Deborah McAninch
   Hobson
William McAnlis
Michael McAteer
Jay McBride
Matthew Allen McBride
Elaine McCabe
Darcy McCandless
Pat McCarrick
Michael McCartney
Dave McCausland
Robert Ivan McCausland
Martin M'Caw
Ian McCay
Pat McClain
Michael McClary
Douglas McClean
Susan McClean
Martin Wilson McClelland
Wayne McClelland
Lawrence McClimon
Ian McClumpha
Mark McClure
Robert McClure
Patricia McColm
Lee McConaghy
William R. I. McConnell
Gerald McConniffe
Paul McConville
Elizabeth L. McCormick
Michael Warren McCormick

Don McCortney
Carol P. McCoy
Mary McCoy
Joshua McCrary
Elizabeth McCullough
Grace McCullough
William McCullough
Brian McDermott
Stephen McDermott
David McDonald
Linda McDonald
Phyllis McDonald
Michael McDowell
Stewart McElhannon
James McElherne
Paul McElroy
Drew McEwan
Patricia McFadden
Catherine Patricia
    McFetridge
Mark McGaughey
Frederick C. McGee
William McGee
Margaret Mary McGhee
Louise McGowan
Jack McGrail
Bridget McGrath
Richard McGreary
Malcolm Donald McGrice
Tom McGrogan
Gary McGuigan
Denise McGuire
Carol McHardy
Douglas McIldoon
Alan McIlravie
Matthew J. McIlvenna
Margaret H. McIntyre
David McKamey
Colin McKay
Karen McKee
Laura McKee
Michael McKee
Willie McKee
Rodney Mckelroy
Derek McKelvey
Charles McKenna
Barbra McKenzie
Laurie McKeown
Michael McKillip
Carole McKillop-Mash
Alicia McKinley
Mark McKinney

Mark McLaren
David McLaughlin
Judith McLaughlin
Lorraine McLaughlin
George McLean
Margaret McLean
Wilfrid McLean
Terry A. McMaster
Doreen McMaster-LeBlanc
Dr John McMillan
Patrick McMillan
Abbie McMillen
William McMillen
Richard McMurray
Robert McNaughton
J. Duncan McNeill
Larry McNutt
Margaret McPherson
Allister J. McSparron
M. McSparron
Malcolm McSparron
William J. Mc Sparron III
Malcolm McVittie
Peter McWilliam
Kevin Meade
Julie Mealy
Anne Meringolo
Barry Merrill
Mary Mertz
Rolls Mervyn
Caitriona Miles
David Miller
Hugh T. H. Miller
Karen Kane Miller
Rebecca Miller
Thomas Miller
Linda Miller Wilson
Adrienne Z. Milligan
William Alan Milliken
Patricia Mills
Ted Mills
Dr Sandra Millsopp
Melinda Millwee-Britten
Gerald Milner
Paul Milwright
David Mitchell
Lewis Mitten
Michael Mizenko
Peter Monahan
Mike Mondloch
June (Devlin) Monteith
Erick Montgomery

Ian Montgomery
Patricia Mooney Smith
Andy Moore
Bob Moore
John Moore
Robert Moore
Terry Moore
David Moorhead
Terri Morace
Tony Morgan
Robin Josephine Morgan
    née Dinley
Susan Morris
Rayna Morris née Dickson
Elizabeth Morrison
Francine Morrison
Gary Morrison
Mike Morrow
Alan Muise-Benner
Pamela Mulholland
Chris Mullen
Deborah Mullins
Ian Mulroy
Patricia Murchie
Francis Murray
Ian Murray
Marie Murray
Sean Murray
Susan Murray
Joe Murray Senior
Alison Mutter
Gerald Myers
Harriet Myers
Steven W. Myers
Glenn Neal
Diana Neal-Lafranchi
David Neelands
Prof. Gareth Neighbour
Patrick Neill
Ian Neilson
Deborah Dorrian Nelson
Keith Nelson
Pearl Nesbitt
Jo Ellen Neumayr
William Neville
Neil Newman
Jim Nibbelink
Peter L. Nicholas
Wilson Nicholl
Carol Nichols
John T. Nichols
Margaret Nicholson

Allie Nickell
Lynn Nickell
Todd Ninman
Irving Nixon
Irving Nixon
John M. Noble
Margaret Norcross
David Norton
NUI Galway: James
    Hardiman Library
Michael Ó Doibhilin
Kevin O'Barr
Jennifer O'Connor
Pat O'Fallon
James Michael Ogden
William Oltmanns
Christine Wallace Ondish
David O'Neill
Tracey O'Neill
Sietse Oostra
Jill A. Orcutt
David Orr
Robert & Gail Orr
Seán Osborne
Neil Otto
Kathleen Denison
    Overbaugh
Margaret Beattie Page
Chuck Palmer
Robert Park
Marie Parker
Liz Riley Parks
Elizabeth McKay Passuello
Wendy Patterson
Nick Patton
Joyce E. Pavelko
Sorcha Peirce
E. Anne Perkins
Lawrence Perry
Nicholas Perry
Sue B. Peters
Ann Petrauskas
Ross D. Petty
Liz Phillips
Michelle Pintar
Marla Pisarek
Alan Platt
Charlotte Powell
Penelope Power
Christopher Preston
Mary Purchase
Rosemary Purdue

Queen's University Belfast:
    Special Collections &
    Archives
Andrew Quinn
Cliff Radcliffe
Brian Radford
Alan Rainey
Renee Ralston
Joseph Ramsay
Rudy Ramsey
Bill Randall
Annie Rappeport
Sarah Rawlings
Christine Rawls
Dave Ray
Bayard Rea
Kevin P. Reagan
Maureen K. Reed
Wendy Reid
Carolyn Reimel
Lorrie Renker
Douglas Renton
Don Revels
Sandy Reynolds
Raymond Rice
Michelle Rice Roberts
Thomas G. Richards
Mark John Richardson
Racheal Therese Richardson
Elizabeth Richmond
Wally Riddle
Neil Ritchie
Robert Rival
Harold Roberson
Dodo Roberts
Ann Kathleen Robinson
Ben Robinson
Carole F. Robinson
Chris Robinson
Sarah Robinson
Dave Robison
Glenda Rode-Bramanis
Anita Romaniuk
Alexander Romanov-Hughes
Laura Rosquist
Elizabeth Ross
Lea Rosser
Craig Rouse
Bruce Roy
Carol Russell
Mary A. Russell
Valerie Russell (née Wilson)

Cori Russon
Michael Rutledge
Jacquelyn Ruttinger
Gregory R. Sahlen
Ted Salthouse
Joan Sampieri
Daniel Sandoval
Roy Satterthwaite
Claire Saul
Bill Savage
Richard George Sayre
Barbara Scanlon
Gwen Scheffer
Elizabeth Schulmeister
Brendan Scott
Margaret Scott
Peter G. W. Scott
Norlayne Lee Scott-Gaare
Jennifer Seale
Jean Sebesta
Helen Seeney
Nancy Culley Sellar
David Serviss
Bill Shand
James Shannaham
Alice Shannon
Steve Sharpe
Gary Shaw
George Shaw
Sydney Shaw
Joseph Sherk
Richard Morey Sherman
Cathie Sherwood
John Shiels
Helen P. Shimek
Suzanne Shimek
Stephany Shinpock
Robert Shippobobtham
Michael Sienkiewicz
Zygmunt Sikorski-Mazur
Jane Simmons
Nancy Simmons
Paul Simpson
Brian Singleton
Brian Singleton
Joseph Skelly
Larry Slavens
Dr Veronica Sloan
Donde Hart Smith
Jennifer Smith
John Edward Dudley Smith
Mary Anne Smith

Murdock Smith
Ruth Smith
Eamonn Smyth
Greig Sneddon
Kathryn Snodgrass-Schultz
Rodney Solenberger
Ida K. Somers
Cheri Gibson Sorensen
Elizabeth Speck
Samuel Renwick Speer
Debra Spindle PhD, MLIS
Kevin Stamber
Laurie Stanbrook
George R. Stanculescu
Candice Baldridge Stanelle
June Staughton
Sandra Steed
John Steel
Jill Steer
William Sterett
Anne Stevenson
Gerald Stevenson
Edward Stewart
George Stewart
Julie-Ann Stewart
Dr Keith Stewart
Sharon Stewart
Stephen Stewart
John Stirrat
Martin Stockdale
Karin Stocking
Collette Stone
M. Stoneman
Jim Stothers
Helen Stowell (Hamilton)
William Stranney
Theresa Strasser
Donald Sturgeon
Ruth Sullivan
Alan Sutton
Brenda Sutton
Patricia Swan
Margaret Wadham Swan
Drew Swenson
Lennard Swindley
Laura Sykes
Brian Symonds
Tessa Szczepanik
Rita Taggart
Ken Tarbox
Ann Tatangelo
Dennis Tate

John Tate
Allan Taylor
Sandy Taylor
Marcia McElhinny Thayer
Gary Thew
Margaret Thiffault
Ian Thirlwell
Carol Thomas
Margaret Thomas
Teresa Thomas
Robert Thompson
Elizabeth Thomson
Elizabeth Thomson
Margaret Thomson
Lynette Thorne
Kevin Thur
Brian Todd
Eugene Torbert
Donald Tornberg
Eve Traill
Santa Algeo Traugott
Susan Triangle
Hilary Tulloch
David Tumilty
Brian S. Turner
James Turner
Jeremy Turner
Kathleen Turner
James Turtle
Elizabeth Tussey
Alicia Tyler
Jane Van Nort
Jillian van Turnhout
Sherry Vaughan
Joscelyn Vereker
Jennifer Verner
Bob Verner-Jeffreys
Bonita Voigt
Mary Wack
Nigel Wadsworth
Clarence Waldon
Jeffery C. Walker
Nancy Wallace
Neil Wallace
Esther Walter
Beatrice Walters
Barry F. Ward
Paula Kelley Ward
Janelle W. Warden
Laura Watkins
John Watson
S. Weames

Graham Webster
Ann Weir
John Weir
Michael Weir
Beata Welsh
Maurice West
Suzanne West
Herb Westman
Denise Weston
Neil Wheatley
Howard Wheeldon
Christopher White
Lesley White
Lorrie White
Jody Whited
John Whitmarsh-Knight
Karen Whittaker
Dr E. H. Timothy Whitten
Alan Whittle
Elma Wickens
Richard (Dick) Wilkin
Gordon Wilkinson
Linda Wilkinson
Byron Williams
    (McCaughan)
Neville Williamson
Barbara Wilson
Bryan Wilson
Isla Argue Wilson
Janice Wilson
Linda Wilson
Rosemary Winkler
Cynthia Cook Winterhalter
Teddy Witbeck
Michele Witowski
John Wladis
Rebecca Malone Wojewoda
Brian Woods
Gerard Woods
Kelly Woynarowich
Brian Wright
Bruce Wright
F. A. Wright
Pamela Wright
Val Wylie
Sheree Wyllie
Linda Wyman
Daniel Edward Yarrow
Wendy Perry Yasaki
Charles Young
January Zeh

INDEX

www.ingramcontent.com/pod-product-compliance
Lightning Source LLC
Chambersburg PA
CBHW051706020426
42333CB00014B/874